WORFIELD IN THE FIFTEENTH CENTURY

A TRANSLATION OF THE MANOR COURT ROLLS OF WORFIELD

PART 3 1399-1431

Jane Smith

ISBN: 978-0-9573505-8-8

JS Books WV6 7UE

Acknowledgments

These translations are the result of collaboration between Ralph Collingwood, Paul Walshe, the late Cicely Taylor and myself. The aims of the project were to understand the development of Worfield Manor from the earliest surviving court rolls and to make the history available in an English translation. For a number of years we have been working on this, initially face to face, and since Covid on Zoom. Our modus operandi takes the form of Paul sight reading the document, Ralph fine tuning and translating the most difficult passages, and me typing the translation. Both Ralph and Paul bring with them wider experience in Medieval Latin than mine. I bring my knowledge of Worfield, and together we make a good team. It is important to say that this was my idea and I take full responsibility for any errors.

It goes without saying that I cannot thank Ralph Collingwood and Paul Walshe for the work they have put into these translations over many years, and there are others I must thank. Firstly, the late Sylvia Watts allowed me to join a Medieval Latin group, Ordericus Vitalis, and fantastic teacher that she was, gave me the belief that I would one day get the hang of this mysterious language. I would have struggled even more than I did but Paul and Cicely took me under their wings and gave me invaluable help in the early days. Shropshire Archives have provided us with digital images and particular thanks are due to Nat Stevenson and others who have frequently put themselves out to help us.

Finally, the medieval craftsmen who made the elaborately decorated doors which hang in St Peter's Church, have provided the image of the two cockerels on the back cover of the book. The doors date from the twelfth century and were found in the late nineteenth century in an out-house at the vicarage. (Cranage, D. H. S., Churches of Shropshire, Volume 10, Hobson & Co)

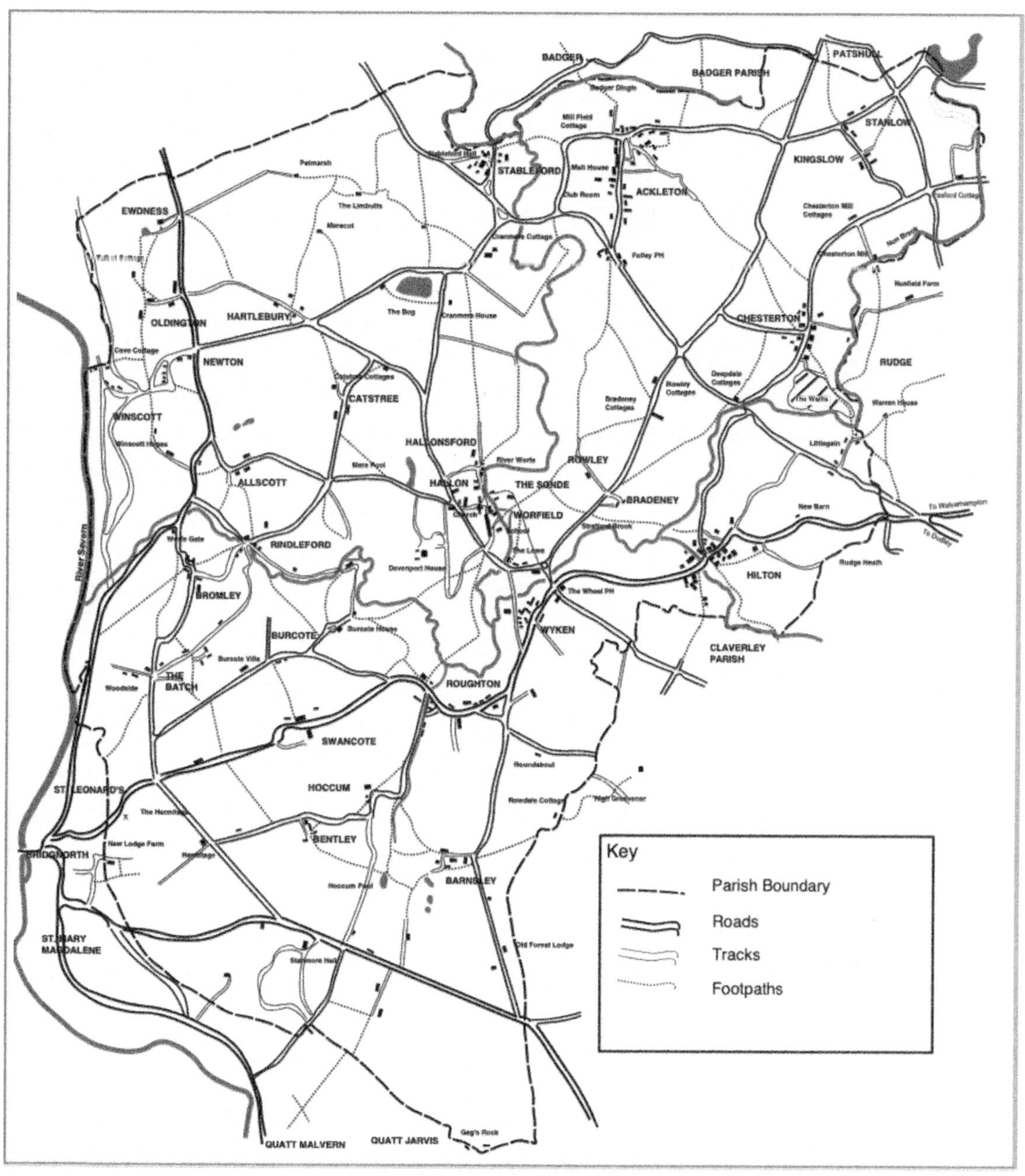

The Parish of Worfield in 1933, taken from a map drawn by Joy Wigram who took a double first at Cambridge and taught at Worfield school 1932-3. The map was a silver wedding gift to the Revd. & Mrs Lunt who gave it to the Parochial Church Council. For many years the map hung in the Old Club Room and at the time of writing is in the Church.

Introduction

Worfield is fortunate in having an almost complete run of manor court rolls from 1327 until at least the latter part of the eighteenth century. Held at Shropshire Archives, they offer an opportunity to follow the development of an English manor in a number of ways, such as its local governance, economy and social structure. Family historians looking at court rolls for the first time may find that they are able to trace a line in surprising detail , such as the names of spouses, next of kin, and dates of death. Many of the families mentioned have descendants in the locality today or at least within memory, such as the Brays, Rowleys, Golds, Childes, Doveys, Lees, Parlours, Canns, Bradeneys, and Hoccoms. House names inevitably change over time but Brook House in Roughton is one which has endured from the fourteenth century, and probable longer had we had the evidence to prove it. Thanks to Mr Foxall who added the field names to the tithe map of 1840 (Shropshire Archives series 7305), we can easily compare the nineteenth century names with those of the fourteenth and fifteenth. Inevitably some of the old names, such as the River Churle, now known as the Nun Brook, Stratford Brook, and Hilton Brook, have been lost but many others survive, such as the field names of Nedge in Newton, Ewdness Meadow, and Hitchcock's Yard and Wightwick's Innage in Chesterton. Some are still recognisable with a little imagination.The hamlet of Ewyke is now lost but field names such as York Bank, and Yoke Field give us a clue to its location.

Given the richness of the data within court rolls it is surprising that so many languish in archives untranslated. Perhaps it is not just the highly abbreviated Medieval Latin with a smattering of equally obscure Middle English, which are the only obstacles but in some cases, as with Worfield, the sheer volume of documents is daunting.

We have tried to be as faithful as we can to the original text - to use the same formatting and phraseology, except for the amercements which in the rolls are written over a person's name. Here they are given in brackets alongside the name to make for easier reading. Words written above the line appear as superscripts in this translation unless there is an omission mark and it is obvious they were an omission in the text. Inevitably there are words we can't read, for one reason or another. If we really have no idea I have left a blank. If the document is damaged and the word is illegible then this is noted, and if we are uncertain of the translation the word is in italics often followed by the Latin word in () with * showing the location of extension marks. Unfortunately extension marks do not always clarify which letters are missing. For example, I have taken the (usually curled) macron which appears at the end of Oldyngton, Chesturton and Hulton to be an extra 'e' but sometimes the macron is straight suggesting that the extension should be Hultoun and Chesturtoun.'k' endings have an extension which we initially took to be an 'es' ending but which we then thought was simply an 'e', or perhaps no addition at all! For those who are particularly interested in the palaeography, please refer to the original documents which are held at the Shropshire Record Office.My comments are written within square brackets. You will note that the amounts of amercements often don't tally with those in the body text. I may have made an error but often they are not the same in the original.

The Manor of Worfield covered an area of about 12,000 acres in which around 30 townships were (and still are) scattered across the landscape with Worfield village roughly in the centre. The parish is reputed to be the second largest in the country, stretching to the Severn on the west and bounded by the parishes of Stockton, Badger, and Pattingham to the north, Rudge to the east, Claverley to the east and south, and Quatt and Quatford to the south. Apart from following the Nun Brook on the east and the Severn on the west, there are no clearly defined topographical landmarks, so how it became a unit is something of a mystery. With minor changes, the parish today is roughly the same in extent as it was in medieval times.

Worfield is an odd name and there are various suggested derivations. Margaret Gelling (The Place Names of Shropshire, Volume 1, published by the English Place Name Society 1990) suggests 'open land on the R. Worfe', while Ekwall proposed a derivation from the Old English wōrig meaning wandering, as in meandering. Gelling further suggests a derivative of Wyrgan, to strangle, from the twists and turns of the river as it wends its way to the River Severn. The meandering of the Worfe as it traverses the parish makes both 'wandering' and 'contorted,' accurate descriptions of the River, but there is a town in Germany called Worfelden and I wonder if the Saxon settlers simply named Worfield after their home in Germany. There may well have been similarities in topography. Worfelden comes from 'ur' meaning moist and 'feld' meaning a plain or open land which describes Worfield's situation perfectly.

So why Worfield and not Urfield, or Wurfield, which is how it is pronounced, you may ask? That I can't answer, except that 'o' is often pronounced 'u' as in 'work'. By the fifteenth century Burcote has the spelling we see today, but in the fourteenth century rolls it was often written as Borcote. A 'w' preceding a vowel is not unusual and in the sixteenth century court rolls Oldington is sometimes written Woldington[1].

The light sandy soil of the parish made for easy cultivation by our ancestors after they had cleared away the natural vegetation of woodland. The flat or gently undulating land made it easy to work, and the many metal detected finds[2] indicate settlement from the neolithic era. The Worfe and other streams provided several gifts to its medieval inhabitants; power to run both fulling and corn mills, fish, and irrigation to enrich water meadows. Glaciers cut through the otherwise flat terrain creating valleys with steep sides of sandstone and natural caves which could be lived in. Within the manor of Worfield (now within Bridgnorth) was the Saxon Hermitage of Athelardestan who is believed to be the brother of King Athelstan. The sandstone rock was also quarried and used for building. Mason's marks can be seen in many places, such as Rindleford, and Worfield village near St Peter's Well on the road to Hallonsford. The church itself is built of sandstone and is easily the largest stone structure in the parish. Even this is dwarfed by the earliest settlement identifiable today, the Iron Age hill fort at Chesterton, a 9.5 hectare site which was once home to the Cornovii, and later used by the Romans.

Worfield village sits as close to the Worfe as it can without being in danger of flooding and one can see the attraction of the site. It has all the advantages of the manor in one small area; a fertile plain stretching along the Worfe, a river full of fish, and sandstone rock for shelter from the elements. Once Earl Leofric built the church in Worfield there was no doubt that this would be the administrative centre of the Manor.

Before the Conquest, the church administered both the religious and secular life of its people but afterwards these functions were split. The authority of the church was restricted to taking care of the souls of its parishioners while their secular lives were subject to a different authority, the lord of the manor. The church's area of authority was called the parish and the lord of the manor's area, the manor. In the court rolls we have but brief glimpses of how the church impacted people's lives but when they appear they are important because our knowledge is so scant. Thomas Manlove, the vicar, went fishing in the waters of the lady without a licence in 1421, and William Aleyn formerly the vicar of Worfield, was brought to court on a plea of deception in 1420. In 1422, there was a clash of economic interests between the Lady of the Manor and the Dean and Chapter of Lichfield concerning 3 shops (workshops) built on the waste of the lady from which Lichfield had been profiting. The lady took them into her own hands which is an interesting reflection on the relative power of the church and the lady of the manor. The Dean and Chapter of Lichfield also had a fulling mill and land at Wyken for which they were obliged to maintain Wyken Bridge. This ecclesiastical presence in Wyken may have predated the Norman Conquest but exactly what form it took we have yet to discover.

Prior to the Conquest, Earl Aelfgar (son of Earl Leofric and Lady Godiva) held Worfield but in 1086 at the time of Domesday, Hugh Montgomery became Lord of the Manor of Worfield which was then in the Hundred of Seisdon in Staffordshire[3]. When Hugh de Montgomery died, the Lordship of Worfield was inherited by his brother Robert de Belleme whose attempt to depose Henry I led to Worfield Manor being taken into the King's hands[4]. In 1238, Worfield passed out of the hands of the monarchy to the Hastings family, and so it remained until the beginning of the fifteenth century when it was acquired by Reginald Lord Grey of Ruthyn who sold it to Sir William Beauchamp, Lord Bergavenny[5]. In 1403, William Beauchamp re-stated the customs of the manor[6] which are summarised below.

- The villeins must attend court every 3 weeks.
- Villeins can dispose of their land as long as it goes through the courts so that the lord of the manor has possession and the villein has livery.
- Villeins cannot be evicted because of default of appearance in court & personal service.
- Villeins must grind within the manor unless the mills are being repaired.

- The miller must take only the authorised tolls or he will be punished.
- Every year the villeins must elect a provost to serve the law and he will 'associate to himself' a bailiff to serve the lord. The provost is to have 6s 8d for his service and the bailiff 3s 4d taking no other fees or perquisites.
- The tenants must mow, rake and windrow all the meadows of the lord within the Barony aforesaid at their own proper costs and charges, receiving only from the lord as an allowance for the same a sheep of the value of 16d.
- The Provost and Bailiff may not take any part of the hay made from the said meadows to their own use however the custom in this particular may have heretofore been to the contrary.
- The tenants must pay heriots and escheats as accustomed.
- Under-age tenants who have inherited or bought lands either by themselves or a friend must, on reaching full age come to court to take possession of any alienation made during their infancy.
- Land alienated by a widow which was for her own use during her life in a way detrimental to the heirs of her husband may be reclaimed by the heirs of the husband although this was not previously the case.
- The lord of the manor may meet his council to determine his rights in the manor.
- The lord of the manor will uphold other good customs and practices in use.
- The rights of every person should be saved and no-one injured or affected.

The fact that Worfield had been held by the King gave its inhabitants freedoms from tolls, serving on assize juries, and the expense of sending knights to parliament[7]. Worfield tenants had the right to bring pleas to its courts, indeed they had to first implead in the Worfield court and only if there was no satisfaction could they then take the case to another court[8]. The lord/ lady of the manor was also free to manage law and order within the manor without interference from the King's representatives. In 1398, the extent of the authority of the lord within the liberty of Worfield was evident when a royal bailiff entered Wyken without permission. This offence was not only described as in disinheritance of the lord, in contempt of the king but also against the law and custom of the liberty from ancient times[9]. Worfield's status as a liberty gave it the right to hold the View of Frankpledge every six months, to enforce the assize of bread and ale, to take the proceeds of strays and, as has been mentioned, to maintain law and order. It was John of Hastings who, in 1292, had claimed the right of infangthief, and a survey of the manor in 1391 noted that in addition the lord had the right of outfangthief ie not only could the lord punish an offender within the manor but could pursue him outside the manor if necessary, and bring him back within the domain to be dealt with[10]. It would appear that even hanging took place. For example, Thomas Gille in 1420 may well have been hanged within the manor [11].

Ackleton had a unique position amongst Worfield's townships in that for the purposes of land holding it was part of Badger Manor[12], but for the purposes of law and order was in Worfield Manor. Part of the Forest of Morfe covered an area south of the River Worfe making it subject to special forest laws in addition to those of the manor.

The Parish & Manor of Worfield, its townships, and the extent of the Forest of Morfe.

How Worfield's court rolls have survived is an interesting story, and down to a few people who recognised their significance and made an effort to safeguard them. The P314 collection of

Worfield manor court rolls begins in 1327, the first year of the reign of King Edward III. Held before the lord of the manor's steward, the court proceedings were copied into Latin by the steward's clerk. Where in the manor the court rolls were then held isn't known at the time of writing but in 1724, "Mr Thomas Beech of Hilton gave twenty pounds for the bringing in of the Court Rolls into the Chest in the Church. He also gave thirteen shillings and fourpence annually for ever to be paid out of the rent of highmore meadow now in the possession of Mr Thomas Smythe of Hilton for the yearly bringing in of the said Rolls; and upon the same account there is since added the yearly sum of six shillings and eight pence yearly for ever, to be paid out of the rent of a piece of ground (called Browns round-hill) now in the possession of Mr Bradburne of Chesterton [13]."

It was in the church chests that the Court Rolls were found in the late nineteenth century by John Randall, the author of the book, 'Worfield and its Townships'. Randall was curious about the contents of the chests and the local blacksmith was recruited to free the locks. The chests were found to be crammed with old Worfield documents which Randall handed over to another antiquarian, the Revd. T. Mayo, who lived in Bromley, to dry out and put in order. I imagine they were then returned to the church. The vicar at the time, the Revd. E. P. Nicholas had every intention of doing something with the material but never got round to it, and it was left to the Revd. Cyril Lee to deposit them in the Public Record Office in the 1930s. Cyril Lee wrote as follows in Worfield Parish Magazine in January 1937[14]. "For I don't know how many years, certainly over a hundred, there have lain in an untidy heap in the old coffer in Worfield Church, a miscellaneous collection of old parchment rolls and smaller parchment scraps. No-one seems to know how they got there nor where they came from. About two years ago Mrs Cunliffe obtained the services of Miss Auden, who is an expert in such matters, to go through this collection and try to put them in some order. This preliminary work she did very well indeed. On December 15th and 16th last, with the consent of the Church Council, I packed all these rolls and papers into 3 boxes and took them up to the Public Record Office in London. There I spent two days going through them all with expert officials. We have dated, and tied into bundles, and temporarily labelled the great bulk of them. They form a very interesting collection going back almost consecutively to Richard II in 1370, that is two hundred years earlier than our Church registers begin. As a basis for a history of Worfield they are invaluable, giving as they do all the old place names and family names and proceedings of the manorial courts held in the middle ages. It seems to me a crime (and the Public Record Office heartily agree with me) to let these interesting documents lie there and gradually decay, unread and untranslated, and with them to suffer for ever the loss of such unique material for a local history. It is my earnest hope in 1937 to seriously undertake this work of translation."

In 1938, Cyril Lee moved from Worfield to a new parish without beginning the translation but without his diligence Worfield's court rolls may well have been destroyed. There is still another more modern mystery: How and when did the rolls get from the Public Record Office to the Shropshire Archives?

General References

Gelling, M., *The Place Names of Shropshire, Volume 1,* (The English Place Name Society, 1990)
Gelling, M., *The Place Names of Shropshire, Volume 6. The Hundreds of Brimstree and Bradford South,* (The English Place Name Society, 1990)
Gibbs, Spike, *Lordship, State Formation and Local Authority in Late Medieval and early Modern Studies* (Cambridge University Press 2023)
Gibbs, Spike, *Felony Forfeiture at the Manor of Worfield, C.1370–C.1600,* in The Journal of Legal History, Volume 39, 2018, pages 253-277
Randall, J., *Worfield and its Townships* (Madeley, 1887)
Smith, J., *Worfield. The History of a Shropshire Parish from Earliest Times* (Share our Past 2017)
Smith, J., *Margery the Mustard Maker. Tales from in and Around Worfield* (JS Books 2021)

References

1. Shropshire Archives. 5586/1/237, November 1579
2. https://finds.org.uk/
3. The Domesday Book
4. Randall, J., *Worfield and its Townships,* page 7 (Madeley, 1887)
5. R. I. Jack, 'Hastings, John, thirteenth earl of Pembroke (1347–1375)', *ODNB*; Christine Carpenter, 'Beauchamp, William (V), first Baron Bergavenny (*c.*1343–1411)', *ODNB*; R.I. Jack, 'Grey, Reynold, third Baron Grey of Ruthin (*c.*1362–1440), *ODNB*.
6. William Salt Library, SMS 352
7. D. M. Stenton, ed., *The Great Roll of the Pipe for the Sixth Year of the Reign of King John: Michaelmas 1204 (Pipe Roll 50),* London, 1940, 158; Randall, *Worfield and its Townships,* pp. 9-10
8. Shropshire Archives P314/W/1/1/135, 25 Nov. 1382; P314/W/1/1/212, Richard II, undated; P314/W/1/1/637, 30 Jun 1530; P314/W/1/1/642, 21 Nov. 1532; P314/W/1/1/646, 23 Sep. 1533; P314/W/1/1/698, 22 Oct. 1554; P314/W/1/1/794, 19 Feb 1579
9. Shropshire Archives P314/W/1/1/208, 4 Dec. 1398.
10. The National Archives JUST 1/741 rot. 23 d; DL, 43/14/3/fo71
11. Shropshire Archives P314/W/1/1/255, 23 April 1420
12. Shropshire Archives Ackleton Manor collection 513/2 which are held within the Badger Hall collection 513
13. Bequest Board St Peter's Church, Worfield. At the time of writing these hang in the vestry
14. Recently deposited in Shropshire Archives

Glossary

Acre	Area of land which could be ploughed by a team of oxen in a day
Admittance	When a person was admitted to a copyhold or customary tenancy
Affeerors	Officers appointed by the court, one for the lord and one for the tenants, to determine the amercement to be taken from an offender
Amercement	Fine for a breach of a bylaw or order
Assize of Bread & Ale	Law which regulated the measure, price, and quality of bread & ale
Bailiff	Overseer of the manor
Baulk	An uncultivated strip between other strips and possibly also a pathway to the field or boundary
Bushel	8 gallons of dry matter eg corn
Butt	A small piece of land at the end or the edge of a ploughed strip
Court Baron	Held by the lord for free and unfree tenants
Customs of the Manor	Customs and services by which tenants held their land
Deforce	To unlawfully deprive someone of their rightful property
Demesne	Land reserved for the lord's own use
Dredge	Mixture of corn, often oats and barley
Edysshe	Aftermath after a crop has ben taken
Ell	Measure of cloth, usually about 45 inches
Escheat	Right of lord for the return of land and/or property on the death of a tenant or the commitment of a serious crime
Essoin	Excuse for attending court eg because of sickness or absence from the manor.Three essoins were allowed before attendance was required
Estreat	Extracts from court rolls of fines to be collected
Fealty	Allegiance to the lord
Feoffment	Grant of land in fee simple
Fine	A payment
Forestalling	Obstructing someone's path
Forland	Part of the headland in the common fields
Frith & Grith	Saxon system of keeping the peace within a community (in roll after 1467)
Furlong	Length of a furrow which could be ploughed before turning the oxen
Hatch	Hurdle for a gateway
Hayward	Overseer of the hay harvest
Heriot	Death duty. Usually the best beast to be paid to the lord
Homsoken	House breaking
Hue & cry	Raising the alarm if a crime was committed
Leet Court	Dealt with minor criminal offences, appointed ale tasters & managed the assize of bread & ale
Leyrwite	Fornication
Mainpernor	A person who stands surety for another
Mark	13s 4d or two thirds of a pound
Messuage	Dwelling house with outbuildings & land associated with it
Multure	Corn toll paid to the miller for milling corn
Nook	39 acres equalled 3 nooks in a Barnsley title deed 1787, a third of a virgate, but the actual area depended on the quality of the ground. This was the first reference we found to a specified area and then, in 1402, (P314/W/1/1/221) there is a reference to someone taking half a virgate which is defined as a nook.
Pannage	Grazing for pigs
Parrock	Small paddock close to farmstead
Quarter	28lbs of grain or 8 bushels
Recovery	Livestock taken eg from the pound without authorisation

Glossary

Reeve	Official elected annually by the tenants to receive payments for the lord
Regrate	Retail sellers who had bought ale to retail
Selion	Strip in common field
Staking	Stakes set in river to trap fish
Stanking	Pond for keeping fish
Steward	Officer of lord. Either he, or the sub steward, presided over the court
Strike	Measure of grain - varied between half a bushel and four bushels
Surrender	Part of the mechanism for transferring customary land. Firstly it was put in the hands of the lord and then taken out of their hands to the use of a new tenant who was admitted & paid a fine at ingoing
Suit of court	Service requiring attendance at court
Tallet	Upper part of barn where hay was stored
Tenant at will	Held land at the will of the lord
Thrave	24 sheaves
Toft	The meaning seems variable, sometimes it seems to be a messuage, at other times there is a clear distinction & messuage and toft are mentioned together. Often the toft is named simply as a yard eg Prestes Yard. In 1400 it is a place for a building to be erected
Villein	A tenant who had to provide services to the lord
Virgate	About 30 acres
Waste	Uncultivated land
Yardland	Same as a virgate

1399 P314/W/1/1/213 &/214

P314/W/1/1/213

Worfeld	Great court held there on the 24th day of October in the first year of the reign of King Henry IV [1399]
the 12	John Eudenas, John Hethe, John Tumpkyns, Roger Cattestre, Roger Richardes, Robert Hogge, William Ewyk, Stephen Bradeney, Roger Bromleye junior, Roger Waltone, Roger Broke, Thomas Wyntur } all sworn
Kyngeslowe & Stanlowe	Townships there present nothing
Chesturtone	Township there presents nothing
Hultone	Township there presents nothing
Rowlowe, Bradeneye, Asturhul, Ewyke, Soonde	Townships there present nothing
Rougtone, Barndeley, Hokkombe, Swancote amerced 2s	Townships there present that Thomas Barbour (4d) chaplain who should appear at this court to make his tenure made default so he is in mercy. And that Richard Westone (6d) forestalled Alice the wife of Thomas Jankys. And that the same Alice raised the hue and cry by mouth on the said Richard Westone (6d) justly. And that the same Richard (6d) forestalled John the son of Thomas Jankyns and hit (2d) the same John
Burcote, Burcote, Ryndelforde, Bromley amerced 3s 4d	Townships there present that a certain piece of land called Yoremoor lying in Bromleye within the manor of Worfeld is enclosed & separated from the said manor of Worfeld & joined to the domain of Brugge by the bailiffs (40d …) & the community of the town of Brugge therefore [blank]
Newtone, Cattestre, Awescote, Wynnescote amerced 4d	Townships there present that John Munsterleye (4d) who should have appeared at this court to make his tenure made default so he is in mercy.
Eudenas, Oldyntone amerced 16d	Townships there present that John (4d) the son of William Oldyngtone forestalled Thomas the son of Roger Richardes. And that William the brother of the same Thomas raised the hue and cry by mouth on the said John (6d) justly. And that Thomas (6d) the son of Roger Richardes hit William the son of William Oldyngtone so he is in mercy
Stapelforde strays 1 steer to respond	Township there presents one black steer aged 2 years came as a stray now in this week price 4s
Aklyntone amerced 18d	Township there presents that Roger Dalleye (6d) forestalled Agnes the daughter of Thomas Hethe and drew blood (6d) from the same Agnes. And that the same Agnes raised the hue and cry by mouth on the said Roger (6d) justly.

1399 P314/W/1/1/213 &/214

Halen amerced 8d	Township there presents that John Haukys (4d) chaplain & William Broke (4d) who should appear at this court to make their tenure made default so each of them is in mercy.
Worfeld amerced 8d	Township there presents that John Henene (4d) who should appear at this court to make his tenure made default so he is in mercy. And that William (4d) Dorre is a regrater of bread and ale so he is in mercy
Wyke amerced 3s 8d	Township there presents that Robert Smyth (4d) who should appear at this court to make his tenure made default so he is in mercy. And that William (6d) Kyngessone made an assault on Richard Walkar so he, William, is in mercy. And that the same William (6d) drew the blood of the said Richard. And that Richard (6d) the son of Richard Walkar forestalled William Kyngessone and drew blood (6d) from the same William so the said Richard the son of Richard is in mercy. And they say that Alice Baret (6d) raised the hue and cry by mouth on Thomas Heyne unjustly so the said Alice is in mercy. And that John Billyngesley (6d) broke into the pound of Thomas Heyne. And that William Webbe (4d) of Rougtone made an assault on William Gerbod so the said William Webbe is in mercy
The ale tasters amerced 14s 8d	present that Richard Bulveys (2s) ~~(4s)~~ (2s) brewed 12, John Eudenas (6d) (6d) 3, John Bewmes (8d) ~~(8d)~~ nil because did not break the assize 4, William Hustar (8d) (8d) 4, William Baret (12d) (12d) 6, Stephen Bradeneye (2d) (2d) 1, Peter Hultone (2d) (2d) 1, Margery Tournour (2d) (2d) 1, William Ewyk (2d) (2d) 1, Robert Smyth (2d) (2d) 1, Thomas atte Soonde (2d) (2d) 1, John Aleyn (2d) (2d) 1, Roger Broke (2d) (2d) 1, William Bruggende (4d) (4d) 2, John Billyngesle (2d) (2d) 1, Roger Smyth (2d) (2d) 1, Thomas Huggen (2d) (2d) 1, William Gerbod (2d) (2d) 1, William Dorre (2d) (2d) 1, Thomas Tresel of Aclyntone (2d) (2d) 1 & John Smyth (2d) (2d) 1 and that all these sold against the assize & they were using illegal measures so each of them is in mercy except that Elena Bewmes did not use nor sell ale with illegal measures
The 12 jurors	present that the townships aforesaid and the tasters of ale have well and faithfully presented. And they say on their oath that Hawiscea the wife of Thomas Coliar on the day of the Finding of the Holy Cross [May 3] in the 22nd year of the reign of King Richard II feloniously broke [?into] the house of Thomas Swancote in Stapelforde and there feloniously was stolen six shillings and eight pence in silver of the goods of Thomas Swancote
Amerced 6d	William Barkar (6d) the beadle of the lord is in mercy because he made an uproar in the court against an order by the steward
pain for keeping the peace	The sureties of Roger Waltone of Swancote concerning the keeping of the peace against Richard Bromley of Swancote and the lord King's people under a pain of twenty pounds namely William Webbe, William Gerbod, Robert Smyth, Roger Gerbod The sureties of Richard Bromleye concerning the keeping of the peace against Roger Waltone of Swancote and the lord King's people namely William Gold, Richard Bulveis, William Barkar, Richard Bradeneye under a pain of twenty pounds
grant of mills for the term of seven years at fixed rent	It is granted by the lord to William Skyrmor of Worfeld the mills of the lord there to hold to himself and his [heirs] from the feast of St Michael the Archangel last past until to the feast of St Michael the Archangel seven years thereafter next following fully completed rendering thence annually to the lord £8 of legal money at the usual

times in equal portions. And the aforesaid William Skirmor, his heirs and assigns for the whole time to maintain and repair the mill aforesaid in everything at his own expense and to have built and repaired it at the end of his term aforesaid in everything well and competently will build and repair without default of the lease by the bail and pledge of William Webbe of Rougtone, Hamond Humeleye, John Billyngesleye, William Bruggende, William Newe, John Bewmes, Elcok Mustardmon, John Tumpkys, William Gold, Thomas Hoggemonessone, William Wylot & Robert Haukys. It is granted to the aforesaid William to take large timber to maintain and to repair the said mills as often as will have been necessary by the view and delivery of the supervisor who will have been for the time

Election of the reeve

John Barndeleye retired from his office of reeve to which office William Newe entered upon by the election of the homage to serve the lord in the said office from the feast of St Michael the Archangel last past until the feast of St Michael the Archangel thereafter next following and is sworn

Affeerors: Roger Cattestre, John Hethe
Sum of this court 28s 8d

P214/W/1/1/214

Worfeld

Small court held there on Wednesday next after the feast of St Katherine the Virgin in the first year of the reign of King Henry IV after the conquest [26 November 1399]

the 12 jurors

amerced 12d

the next

The inquest held for the lord by the oath of Roger Kyngeslowe, William Ewyke, Thomas Rugge, John Hethe, Roger Richardes, Robert Hogge, William Towart, William Newe, Nicholas Stanlowe, William Coletes, Thomas Hugge, Roger Broke who sworn say on their oath that William Stapelforde (2d) & Thomas Barbour (2d), chaplains, William Boon (2d), Richard Hethe (2d), Richard Whitebrok (2d) & John Munsterleye (2d) who owe suit at this court to make their tenure made default so each of them is in mercy. And they say that Thomas Jones who held of the lord by the custom of the manor 1 cottage in Haalen on the day he died and for which the lord will have heriot and escheat from him they seek a day for the truth thence at the next and it is granted by the prayer of the aforesaid inquest

fine 10s

Joan Rowlowe came and surrendered into the hands of the lord one messuage with 3 nooks of land adjacent in Hultone called Heynes Place to the use of Thomas the son of John Rowlowe the which Thomas came and took from the lord the aforesaid tenements to hold to himself and his heirs according to the custom of the manor by services and customs which are thence due. And he gives to the lord for a fine for ingress thence to hold 10s, made fealty and is seized pledge for the fine John Nielde

fine 14d

Symon Taillour and Alice his wife came and surrendered into the hands of the lord two acres of arable land lying in hultonefeld at Edithscross of which one acre lies from one side of the road and the other acre lies on the other side of the road to the use of Elcok Mustardmon who came and took from the lord the said two acres of land with their appurtenances to hold to himself and his heirs according to the custom of the manor for services and customs thence due. And he gives to the lord for a fine 14d and made fealty and he has seisin

William Hounesworth & Margery his wife came and surrendered into the hands of the lord one cottage with curtilage adjacent in Soonde called Houndeslowe to the use of Agnes their daughter after their deaths. The which Agnes came and took from the lord the aforesaid cottage with curtilage to hold to the said Agnes and her heirs after the death of the said William and Margery according to the custom of the manor by services and customs thence due. And she gives to the lord for a fine 16d & made fealty pledge for the fine William Baret

fine 16d

Richard Bromleye came and surrendered into the hands of the lord one toft with one nook of land adjacent in Bromleye within the manor of Worfeld to the use of John his son. The which John came and took from the lord the aforesaid tenements to hold to himself and his heirs after the death of the aforesaid Richard & Alice his wife according to the custom of the manor by services and customs thence due. And he gives to the lord for a fine 4s made fealty and has seisin

fine 4s

Dawkyn of Okene and Amiscer his wife came and surrendered into the hands of the lord two cottages in Haalen next to the castle to the use of Roger Jones and Edith his wife who came and took from the lord the aforesaid cottages to hold to the said Roger & Edith and their heirs according to the custom of the manor by services and customs which are thence due. And they give to the lord for a fine 12d, made fealty and are seized

fine 12d

the next concerning damages of the mill not affeered

Still the 12 jurors present and say on their oath that the use of the land of new made next to the water mill of the lord at Worfeld has deteriorated next to the Wrongegate from the default of Thomas Knotte the supervisor of the work. And that the stone work on both sides of the said gates has damaged and flattened the floodgates in default of the aforesaid Thomas's supervision

And they say that all the defective works of the aforesaid mill are from the default and negligence of the aforesaid supervisor to what damages to the lord they have a day to present the truth of the matter at the coming of the council of the lord at whose coming it was affeered by their oath at 6s 8d

John Bewmes (2d) is in mercy because he is not prosecuting against William Baret in a plea of debt

amerced 4d

Robert Taillour (2d) plaintiff & Agnes Ody defendant in a plea of trespass are for a licence to agree and the said Robert put himself in mercy

Affeerors: Roger Richardes, Thomas Rugge

Sum of this court 18s 10d price of damages for the lord's mill as yet not affeered [above they are affeered at 6s 8d]

P314/W/1/1/214

Small court held at Worfeld on Thursday next before the feast of St Thomas the Apostle in the first year of King Henry IV after the conquest [18 December 1399]

the 12

Roger Waltone	Thomas Rugge	Robert Hoggen
Roger Richardes	William Bruggende	Nicholas Rowlowe
Stephen Bradeney	Roger Swancote	Roger Kyngeslowe
Mathew Bullok	Roger Mathew	William Billynesleye

amerced 8d

sworn say on their oath that Richard (2d) S… [illegible], William Stapelford (2d) , Thomas Barbour (2d) & Richard (2d)…[illegible] who owed suit at this court to make their tenancy made default so each of them is in mercy

the next

Still the plea between Thomas Wyntur plaintiff & John Robynes defendant in a plea of trespass adjourned by the prayer of the parties

1399 P314/W/1/1/213 &/214

the 12 jurors present that William Rugge who held of the lord one cottage with curtilage in Soonde has died after whose death the lord has nothing for heriot nor escheat because nothing was found but they have a day better to enquire for the lord in what way he held on the day he died adjourned to the next. On this came Alice Rugge the closest heir of the same William and took from the lord the aforesaid cottage with curtilage to hold to herself and her heirs according to the custom of the manor by services and customs which are thence due. And she gives to the lord for a fine 16d made fealty and is seized

fine 4s

John Holigreve came and took from the lord one messuage with one nook of land adjacent in Halon within the manor of Worfeld being in hand from the surrender of Roger Gille as is clear in the court held on Thursday next after the feast of the Nativity of St John the Baptist last past to hold from the said John & his heirs according to the custom of the manor by services and customs thence due & he gives to the lord for a fine 4s made fealty & has seisin

fine 2s 6d

William Hugynes of Bekkeburye came and took from the lord one nook of land called Oldefeldes in Kyngeslowe within the manor of Worfeld being in the hands of the lord from a surrender of John Hethe as clear in the court held on Monday next after the feast of St Margaret the Virgin in the 23rd year of the reign of King Richard II to hold from the said William and his heirs according to the custom of the manor by services and customs which are thence due and he gives to the lord for a fine 2s 6d made fealty and is seized

fine 2s 6d

William Huggynes above-named & surrendered into the hands of the lord the aforesaid nook of land to the use of Nicholas Stanlowe the son of Stephen Robart the which Nicholas came and took from the lord the said nook of land with its appurtenances to hold to the said Nicholas and his heirs according to the custom of the manor by services and customs thence due and he gives for a fine 2s 6d made fealty and is seized

Concerning the heriot of William Hulle and Thomas Jones it is to enquire in the next. And that the plea between Thomas Wyntur plaintiff and John Robyns defendant in a plea of trespass adjourned until the next by the prayer of the parties

Affeerors: Roger Swancote, William Gerbod

Sum of this court 11s price of heriot & escheat of William Hulle and Thomas Jones still to be decided

1400 P314/W/1/1/215

Worfeld

Small court held there on Monday next after the feast of St Benedict the Abbot in the first year of the reign of King Henry IV after the conquest [22 March 1400]

the 12 jurors

Inquest held for the lord by the oath of Roger Richardes, Roger Walton, William Ewyk, Stephen Bradeney, Thomas Rugge, John Hethe , Roger Mathewe, Nicholas Rowlowe, Robert Hogge, Thomas Wyntur, Mathew Bullok & Roger Swancote of Bromley who say on their oath that Thomas Barbour (2d) chaplain & William Boon (2d) who are bound to make suit in this court made default made so each of them is in mercy

heriot 1 ox
the next

And that Thomas Knotte of Alvescote who held of the lord by the custom of the manor one messuage with three nooks of land in lower tenure has died whereof there falls to the lord 1 red ox for heriot which is not sold nor appraised until the coming of the council of the lord and concerning other escheats and heriots falling to the lord from the death of the same tenant they seek a day better to enquire until the next and it is granted to them and the tenement remains in the hands of the wife of the same deceased by their custom

Distrain

Philip Dawe plaintiff appeared against William the son of Roger Gold in a plea of debt pledge for the prosecution William Gerbod the which William is summoned and did not come so distrain

amerced 2d

John Robyns (2d) put himself in mercy for a licence to agree with Thomas Wyntur in a plea of trespass

Fine 8s

William Stapelforde chaplain came and surrendered into the hands of the lord one messuage with half of one virgate of land at Hokkombe within the manor of Worfeld to the use of Thomas Harleye the which Thomas came and took from the lord the aforesaid tenements with appurtenances to hold to himself and his heirs from the lord by services and customs which are thence due according to the custom of the manor. And he gives to the lord for a fine 8s, made fealty and has seisin pledge for the fine John Barndele & Thomas Heyne

Fine 16d

Alice Rugge came and surrendered into the hands of the lord one cottage with curtilage adjacent in Sonde within the manor of Worfeld the which William Rugge held to the use of William Newtone chaplain who came and took from the lord the said cottage with curtilage with appurtenances to hold from the lord to himself and his heirs according to the custom of the manor by services and customs which are thence due. And he gives to the lord for a fine 16d, made fealty and has seisin

took
Fine 3s 4d

Richard Bulveis came and surrendered into the hands of the lord one toft with half of one virgate of land in Chesturtone within the manor of Worfeld the which William Stevenes & Margaret his wife held to the use of William the son of Nicholas Rowlowe who came and took from the lord the said tenements with appurtenances to hold from the lord to the said William and his heirs according to the custom of the manor by services and customs which are thence due. And he gives to the lord for a fine 3s 4d and no more because it has no appurtenances nor building He made fealty and is seised

John Hulle of Roughtone & Joan his wife came there, she confessed and examined according to the custom of the manor there, and surrendered into the hands of the lord an eighth part of one toft with half of one nook of land in Roughtone called

Brokhousplace and a sixth part of one messuage with half of one nook of land of Hullehousplace in Roughtone aforesaid to the use to the use of John their son who came and took from the lord the aforesaid tenements with appurtenances to hold to
Fine 3s 4d himself and his heirs from the lord according to the custom of the manor by services and customs thence due. And he gives to the lord for a fine 3s 4d and made fealty and is seized in the manner aforesaid

Thomas Coliar and Hawiscia his wife came and surrendered into the hands of the lord one messuage with half of one virgate of land in Stapelforde which land is called Galianesplace of the right and inheritance of the aforesaid Hawistia to the use of Thomas Merwalle and Margery his wife who came and took from the lord the
Fine 5s aforesaid tenements to hold to the said Thomas and Margery and their heirs from the lord according to the custom of the manor by services and customs thence due. And they give to the lord for a fine 5s, made fealty and are seized

Concerning the heriots and escheats of William Hulle deceased who held from the lord settled in the next small court to be held after the feast of Easter next following on the day on which he died one land called Horscroft in lower tenure in Roughtone and Thomas Jones deceased settled in the next small court held after the feast of Easter next following who died seized of one cottage in Haale adjourned until the coming of the council of the lord

Sum of this court 21s 6d price of the aforesaid ox concerning a heriot which will be sold in the next court to be held after the feast of Easter next following

1400 P314/W/1/1/216

Worfeld	Great court held on Thursday next after the Feast of St Mark the Evangelist in the first year of the reign of King Henry IV after the conquest [29 April 1400]
the 12 jurors	John Eudenas, John Hethe, Robert Hoggen, Roger Cattestre, Roger Waltone, Thomas Wyntur, William Euwyke, John Barndeley, Roger Broke, Roger Richards, Stephen Bradeney, Roger Swancote of Bromley
Kyngeslowe & Stanlowe amerced 6d	townships there present that Thomas Glover (6d) of Patyngham fished in the severalty water of the lord without licence within the manor of Worefeld so the said Thomas is in mercy
Chesturtone amerced 10d Next inquiry	township there presents that Thomas Collier (4d) who should have appeared at this court to make the tenure made default so he is in mercy. And that John Grene (6d) of Patyngham drew the blood of a certain stranger whose name is not known. And concerning other diverse offences there made against the peace of the lord King and the freedom of the manor there they have a day to present the truth of the matter until the next great court
Hultone amerced 8d	township there presents that Alice of Hullehous (6d) forestalled William Goold and she hit the same William so the same Alice is in mercy (2d)
Rowlowe, Bradeney, Asturhull, Ewykes, Sonde amerced 3s 4d	townships there present that Robert Taillour (6d) forestalled Agnes Bernard and drew blood (8d) from the same and that the same Agnes raised the hue and cry (8d) by mouth on the said Robert justly. And that Alice (4d) the daughter of Roger Mathewes forestalled William Gerbod and drew blood (6d) from him. And that the said William (6d) forestalled the said Alice and threw (2d) her in the water so he is in mercy
Roughtone, Barndeley, Hokkombe, Swancote amerced 8d	townships there present that Thomas Barbour (4d) chaplain and Richard Saldynges (4d) who should have appeared at this court to make the tenure made default so each of them is in mercy.
Burcote, Burcote, Ryndelford & Bromley amerced 3s 8d	townships there present that Richard Hethe (4d) who should have appeared at this court to make the tenure made default so he is in mercy. And that the Bailiff (3s 4d) and community of the township of Bruggenorth enclosed a certain parcel of land called Yoremore in Bromley in the manor of Worfield to the nuisance and damage of the lord & tenants of the same manor so the the said bailiff & community are in mercy
Newtone, Cattestre, Alvescote, Wynnescote amerced 4d strays 18d	townships there present that John Munsterley (4d) who should have appeared at this court to make the tenure made default so he is in mercy. And they present that one hive came as a stray & concerning one swarm of bees coming out of the same hive which are in the custody of John Robyns and appraised in full court at 18d thence the bailiff is answerable to the more profit of the lord
Eudenas & Oldyngtone amerced 10s	townships there present that the bailiff and community of Bruggenorth obstructed the King's way within the liberty of the manor of Worefeld near to the gate of the mill of Penstone to the damage of the lord of the same manor and his tenants there and to the nuisance of the King's people so the said Bailiff (10s) and the community are in mercy. So it is ordered etc.
Stapulford	township there presents nothing

Aclyntone amerced 20d

township there presents that John Underhull obstructed and enclosed a common footpath leading to the common well called Penkewalle in Aclyntone within the liberty of the manor of Worefeld to the nuisance of the neighbours there so the said John (12d) is in mercy and it is ordered to the same to open the said footpath and break the enclosure of the same under pain and peril which will be incumbent. And that Simone atte Broke (6d) forestalled David Walshe and hit the same David so the said Symone (2d) is in mercy

Halen amerced 12d

township there presents that John Haukys (4d) chaplain, William atte Broke (4d) and Warynges Bereward (4d) who should have appeared at this court to make their tenure made default so each of them is in mercy.

Wyke amerced 2s 2d

township there presents that Henry Barber (6d) made an assault on John Mustarder and drew blood (6d) from him. And that Richard (12d) the son of Richard Walker made an assault on Thomas Heyne so the said Richard son of Richard so in mercy. And that Joan Baret (2d) is a regratrix of bread so she is in mercy

Worefeld amerced 2s 4d

township there presents that Robert Taillour (6d) forestalled Alice Herdemon & made an assault on the same Alice so the said Robert (8d) is in mercy. And that the same Alice (6d) forestalled the aforesaid Robert Taillour and made an assault on the same Robert so the said Alice (8d) is in mercy

The ale tasters amerced 12s

present that John Eudenas (4d) brewed 1, Robert Eudenas (4d) 1, Peter of Hulton (4d) 1, William Baret (12d) 3, Robert Smyth (12d) 3, John Billyngsley (8d) 2, William Dorre (16d) 4, John Stanlowe (4d) 1, Matilda the daughter of Roger Cattestree (4d) 1, John Smyth (4d) 1 Thomas atte Sonde (4d) 1, John the son of John Rowlowe (4d) 1, William Bruggende (4d) 1, John Beumes (16d) 4, Thomas Merwall (4d) 1, Richard Aldith (4d) 1, John atte Walle (4d) 1, Roger Smyth (4d) 1, Margery Newe (4d) 1, Alice the daughter of Roger of Cattestree (4d) 1, John, the son of Richard of Bradeney (4d) 1, Agnes Polehouse (4d) 1, William Cartere (4d) 1, John Walkere (4d) 1, William Skyrmour (4d) 1, Richard Bulveys pardoned 6. They sold against the assize and used illegal measures so each of them is in mercy

[Stitched to the side] Memorandum that in accordance with the presentation and oath of the 12 jurors at this court to remain in the hands of William Ewik and William Cartere the goods and chattels of Richard Westone which were withheld for felony as were judged which goods and chattels are appraised by the oath of the same inquiry to the value of 20s which were not enrolled for him and from because William Banastre escheator of the lord King in the County of Salop demanded the goods to the use of the lord King for escheat. So they remain as above until the right is determined between the council of the lord and the said escheator

the 12 jurors

present that the townships aforesaid and the ale tasters have presented well and faithfully and with nothing concealed except those which are adjourned until the next great court

Affeerors: William Ewikes, John Hethe
Sum of this court 40s 8d
Thence in the expenses of the steward being there for 1 day and 1 night 5s

1400 P314/W/1/1/216

Worefeld	Small court held there on Thursday next after the Feast of St Augustine in the first year of the reign of King Henry IV after the conquest [2 Sept 1400]

the jury for the lord	William Ewikes	Nicholas Rowlowe	Robert Hoggen
	John Hethe	Stephen Bradeney	Roger atte Broke
	Roger Swancote	Thomas Rugge	John Barndeley
	Roger Richardes	Mathewe Bulloces	Thomas Wyntur

amerced 16d adjourned not affeered until the coming of the council	who say on their oath that Thomas Collier (4d), John Morfeld chaplain (4d), William Boon (4d) and Thomas Barbour chaplain, (4d) who should have made suit at this court to make the tenure made default so each of them is in mercy
heriot 3s 11d escheat 20d heriot 3s 11d	And that Henry Done who held of the lord of one nook of land by the custom of the manor in Halen within the manor of Worfeld has died after whose death there falls to the lord for heriot half of one cow which was sold by the bailiff for 3s 11d. Also there falls to the lord from the death of the same, 1 piglet for escheat which was sold for 20d. And they say that Thomas Jones who held of the lord one cottage as is clear in the penultimate court preceding has died & whence there falls to the lord half of one cow which half was sold by the bailiff of the lord price 3s 11d and for escheat nothing because there was nothing
fine for heriot and escheat 3s 6d	Thomas Lekhull made a fine with the lord for the heriot and escheat of Walter Hull deceased with the council of the lord and he gives for a fine 3s 6d and thus is granted by the said council by the pledge of Roger Mathewes
heriot 9s	The Bailiff presents 9s received for one ox sold and coming from the heriot of Thomas Knotte
fine 6d	John Munsterley made a fine with the lord for relief from suit of court from the feast of Easter last past until the Feast of St Michael. And he gives to the lord for a fine 6d
fine 6d	Roger Batemon made a fine with the lord for relief from suit of court from the feast of Easter last past to the Feast of St Michael. And he gives for a fine 6d
	[Sum of the court is obscured at the bottom of the page] Expenses of the steward being there for 1 day and 1 night 18d

More on the dorse

Worefeld	Small court held there on Thursday next after the Feast of Raising of the Holy Cross in the first year of the reign of King Henry IV after the conquest [16 September 1400]

the 12 jurors	William Ewikes	John Hethe	Roger atte Broke
	Roger Richardes	John Barndeley	Thomas Wyntour
	Stephen Bradeney	Robert Hoggen	Nicholas Rowlowe
	Roger Waltone	Roger Swancote	Thomas Rugge

Amercements not affeered until the coming of the council of the lord. Heriot 6s escheats nothing	Who say on their oath that Thomas Collier, (4d), Thomas Barbour, chaplain, (4d) Richard Saladyng (4d) & Richard Hethe (4d) who should have made suit at this court to make the tenure made default so each of them is in mercy. And they say that Roger Aldith who held of the lord 2 messuages with one virgate of land in lessure tenure in Stapulford within the Manor of Worefeld has died after whose death there falls to the lord 6s in the name of heriot and for other escheats nothing because nothing was

found as accounted by the oath of the homage. And half the land and tenements aforesaid remain in the hands of the lord and the other half of the said tenements remain by the custom of the manor with Thomas Swancote and Margery his wife as of the right of the same Margery. On which came the same Thomas and Margery and took from the lord all the land and tenements which were taken into the hands of the lord after the death of the aforesaid Roger Aldith in Stapulford aforesaid within the manor aforesaid as the closest heirs of the same Roger deceased as of the right of the same Margery to hold to the said Thomas and Margery and their [heirs] from the lord according to the custom of the manor by services and customs which were thence formerly owed. And they give for a fine 6s 8d made fealty to the lord and were seised

fine 6s 8d

Matilda the daughter of Alice Rugge came and took from the lord two cottages in Worefeld being in the hands of the lord by the death of Alice Rugge to hold from the lord the said two cottages to herself and her [heirs] according to the custom of the manor by services & customs thence owed and she gives to the lord for a fine 2s, made fealty and is seised

fine 2s

Philip Dawe came in court and surrendered into the hands of the lord half of one messuage with one nook of land in Hokkombe within the manor of Worefeld to the use of John his son who came and took the said land and tenement with appurtenances to hold to himself and his [heirs] from the lord after the death of the said Philip his father and Joan his wife according to the custom of the manor by services and customs which are thence owed. And he gives to the lord for a fine 3s, made fealty and is seised

fine 3s

John Rys made a fine with the lord for an inquiry of the 12 men to enquire whether the same John of right and by their custom paid to the lord 6s 8d which Thomas Stones in the time he was steward of the manor there ordered to raise from the same John unjustly as he believes by the summoning of Thomas Knotte who being the reeve of the manor there then raised or Thomas Knotte who for the sake of the same issue raised and he gives to the lord for a fine 12d. On which the inquiry was held by the oath of John Barndeley, Roger Richardes, Roger Waltone, Roger atte Broke, Roger Matheu, Robert Hoggen, Thomas Rugge, Roger Gerbod, John atte Walle, Thomas Jankyns, Roger Swancote and Roger Hichcoces who sworn and thence charged said on oath that Thomas Knotte and his heirs and executors paid the lord aforesaid 6s 8d of right and by their custom because John Rys in the time which was of the same steward was thence charged unjustly by the said Thomas Stones who was not a tenant in the Manor of Worefeld

fine 12d

Alice Newe surrendered into the hands of the lord all the land and tenements which she holds in Chesturtone within the manor of Worfeld called Bishoppeslond to the use of William Newe her son who came and took from the lord the land and tenements with appurtenances to hold to himself and his [heirs] after the death of the said Alice from the lord by the custom of the manor by services thence due and accustomed and he gives for a fine 4s made fealty and is seized

fine 4s

increased rent 6d

When Richard Bradeney formerly held a certain fishery in Cherle which was taken into the hands of the lord etc. because it was accounted that his right to the title of the said fishery was held and for the trespass he was amerced etc. Afterwards in this court came the same Richard and took from the lord the said fishery of new demise to hold to himself for the term of his life rendering thence annually to the lord 6d at the usual times. And he gives for a fine nothing because of a free pardon, made fealty and has seisin

fine 12d

Fine 10d

Isabell Mulleward made a fine with the lord to have an inquiry by the 12 to be held to enquire whether the same Isabell might settle with the lord for one cottage with curtilage in Halen or Roger Gille who claims the title of right in the same. And she gives for a fine 12d. On which the inquest was held on the oath of William Ewikes, Roger Cattestre, Robert Huggen, Roger Richardes, Thomas Rugge, William Gerbot, Roger Broke, John Barndeley, William Coletes, John Hethe, Stephen Bradeney and Roger Swancote who say on their oath that the aforesaid Isabell has a better right to make a fine for the said tenements because Roger Gille to whose use the said tenements were surrendered broke the agreement between the same etc. On which came the said Isabell and took from the lord the aforesaid tenements to hold from the lord to herself and her [heirs] according to the custom of the manor by services thence due and she gave to the lord for a fine 10d and made fealty and was seized

Fine 10d

Isabell Mulleward above-named came and surrendered into the hands of the lord one cottage with curtilage in Halen which John Hely formerly held to the use of Wariner Bray who came and took from the lord the said cottage with curtilage with appurtenances to hold from the lord to the said Wariner and his [heirs] according to the custom of the manor and he gives 10d for a fine, made fealty, and is seized

Sum 25s 4d Price of amercements not affeered as ordered
Expenses of the steward being there for holding the court there 20d

1400 P314/W/1/1/217

Worfeld	Great court held there on Monday next before the Feast of the Apostles Simon & Jude in the second year of the reign of King Henry IV [25 October 1400]
Essoins	Roger Gille himself for appearance at the great court by Richard Aldith & William Englys for the same by William Barker
the 12 jurors	John Eudenas, John Thomkys, Robert Hoggen, Roger Cattestre, Stephen Bradeney, Roger atte Broke, William Ewykes, Roger Walton, John Barndeley, John Hethe, Roger Richardes, Mathew Bulloces
Kyngeslowe & Stanlowe	townships there present nothing
Chesturtone amerced 18d	township there presents that Thomas Colier (4d) who should have appeared at this court to make the tenure made default so he is in mercy. And that William Banastre (8d) formerly servant of John Wrottesley drew the blood of Thomas Sewall and the same Thomas was forestalled so the said William (6d) is in mercy
Hultone	township there presents nothing
Roulowe, Bradeney, Asturhull, Ewykes & Sonde	townships there present nothing
Roughtone, Barndeley, Hockombe & Swancote amerced 4d	townships there present that Thomas Barbour (4d) chaplain who should have appeared at this court to make the tenure made default so he is in mercy
Burcote, Burcote, Rendelford & Bromley amerced 4d	townships there present that Richard Hethe (4d) who should have appeared at this court to make the tenure made default so he is in mercy
Newtone, Cattestre, Alvescote, Wynnescote	townships there present nothing
Eudenas & Oldyngtone	townships there present nothing
Stapulford amerced 16d	township there presents that Roger Gille (6d) made homesoken on Thomas Merewalle. And they say that the same Roger Gille (6d) forestalled Margery the wife of the said Thomas and hit her so the same Roger (4d) is in mercy.
Aclyntone	township there presents nothing
Halen amerced 2s 4d	township there presents that William atte Broke (4d) who should have appeared at this court to make the tenure made default so he is in mercy. And that John Walker (12d) forestalled John the son of William of Oldyngtone and that William son of the said William Oldyngtone raised the hue and cry by mouth on the said John justly so the said John (12d) is in mercy

1400 P314/W/1/1/217

Wyke
amerced 2s

township there presents that Richard son of Richard Walker drew the blood of Margery Pipere so the same Richard (12d) the son is in mercy. And that Margery Heyne unjustly raised the hue and cry by mouth on Richard the son of Richard Walker so the said Margery is in mercy (8d). And that Thomas Heyne obstructed a certain common footpath at the end of the village of Wyke to the nuisance of the neighbours so Thomas (4d) is in mercy. And nevertheless he is ordered to amend the default of the same footpath before the next court under pain and peril which will be imposed

Worefeld

township there presents nothing

The ale tasters
amerced 6s 6d

present that William Dorre (18d) brewed 3, John Smyth (12d) 2, Sibill the servant of Sibill Swancote (6d) 1, Richard Bulveys (18d) 3, William Bruggende (6d) 1, John Beumes (6d) 1, John Elcokes (6d) 1 & Roger Matheue (6d) 1 and that all sold against the assize and used illegal measures so each of them is in mercy.

the 12 jurors
amerced 12d
pain

present that the township of Worefeld concealed a certain King's way in the township of Worefeld has deteriorated by the encroachment of water so the said township (12d) is in mercy and nevertheless it is ordered the said township to fittingly repair the said way before the next court under a pain of half a mark

fine 12d
the next

Thomas Swancote of Stapulford made a fine for a council of 12jurors to be held to enquire of the correct discharge of a certain water course flowing from the enclosure of the same Thomas by the orchard of William Toward in Stapulford. on which 12 jurors present thence are charged and have a day fully to render the truth until the next [court]. And he gives for a fine 12d

amerced 12d

Thomas Heyne plaintiff against the township of Wike in a plea of unjust presentation etc. And he says that the said township unjustly presented when they said that the same Thomas unjustly blocked a certain common footpath at the end of the village of Wike etc. And the aforesaid township presented in court that it was a just presentation not an unjust and so they put themselves on the judgment of 12 jurors and the said Thomas similarly on which the aforesaid 12 jurors thence charged say on their oath that the township aforesaid well and faithfully presented so the said Thomas is in mercy for his unjust plea

election of ale tasters

William Gerbode and Richard Bradeney junior are elected to the office of ale taster and are sworn

Affeerors: Thomas Rugge, John Hethe. Sum of this court 17s 4d

The dorse

[Only the following sureties are written on the back]

pain

Sureties of Robert Taillour to keep the peace towards Henry Barker and Roger Hattone and the people of the lord King by the pledges of Robert Wermone, clerk, Roger Cattestre, John the son of Nicholas Roulowe and John atte Walles. Under a pain £10

Sureties of Henry Barker and Roger Hattone to keep the peace towards Robert Taillour and the people of the lord King by the pledges of Thomas Tresull, William Newe, William Barker and Robert Barker under a pain £10

1400 P314/W/1/1/217

Sureties of Thomas Rugge to keep the peace towards John Eudenas and the people of the lord King namely William Billingsley, Nicholas Roulowe, William Newe and William Wilot under a pain £10

pain Sureties of Thomas Rugge to keep the peace towards Richard Bulveys and the people of the lord King namely Roger Richards, Roger Walton, Roger of Bromleye and John of Bromleye under a pain £10

Sureties of Thomas Huggen to keep the peace towards the said Richard Bulveys and the people of the lord King namely John Hethe, William Newe, John Coletes and Walter Rugge under a pain £10

1400 P314/W/1/1/218

Worefeld

Small court held there on Thursday next after the Feast of St Andrew the Apostle in the second year of the reign of King Henry IV [2 December 1400]

the 12

William Ewikes	Stephen Bradeney	William Gerbod
Thomas Rugge	Roger atte Broke	Thomas Wyntur
Roger Waltone	Robert Hoggen	Roger Matheu
John Barndeley	Thomas Swancote	William Billyngesley

amerced 10d
heriot 1 cow
7s 6d
fine 20s

Who say on their oath that Thomas Colier (2d), John Moudveld (?Morveld) chaplain (2d), Richard Saladyn (2d), Thomas Barbour, chaplain (2d) and Richard Hethe (2d) who should have made suit at this court to make the tenure made default so each of them is in mercy. And they say that William Colettes who held of the lord by custom of the manor one messuage with one virgate of land with appurtenances in Hultone has died after whose death there falls to the lord one cow in the name of heriot price 7s 6d and they have nothing for escheat. And the tenements remain in the hands of the lord until etc.. And afterwards came John Colettes son and heir of the said William and took from the lord the messuage and virgate of land aforesaid with appurtenances to hold to himself & his [heirs] according to the custom of the manor. And he gives to the lord 20s for a fine to be paid before the Feast of St Michael the Archangel next in the future by the pledge of Thomas Hugen and John Bradeney and made fealty to the lord and thence has seisin

amerced 8s 4d

And they say that Agnes (40d) the daughter of William Robyns was married to Roger the son of Roger Wille a licence from the lord thence not obtained so etc.. And that Margery Don (5s) widow of the lord was married to John Holigreve without a licence of the lord.

Held in the hands of the lord

And that Margery Don surrendered into the hands of the lord one messuage and one nook of land with appurtenances in Halen to the use of John Holigreve

distrain

Walter Rugge plaintiff against Stephen Bradeney in a plea of trespass pledge for the prosecution Richard Bulveys so it is ordered the bailiff distrain the said Stephen that he is at the next [court] to respond to the aforesaid Walter
The same Walter plaintiff against the same Stephen in a plea of trespass pledge for the prosecution the said Richard Bulveys and it is ordered to distrain the said Stephen that he is at the next court to respond to the aforesaid Walter

a day

William Skirmour plaintiff against John Rogeres in a plea of trespass pledge for the prosecution Richard Bulveys who have for a licence to agree until the next [court]

amerced 6d
the next

Simon atte Broke plaintiff against Agnes Dorre in a plea of debt pledge for the prosecution William Newe the reeve. And because the same reeve (6d) did not summon the said Agnes to this court so he is in mercy. And it is ordered the same to attach her to respond to the aforesaid Simon in the next [court]

amerced 6d

William Briane is in mercy for not prosecuting against John Payne of Norton in a plea of debt

amerced 6d

William Goold of Hulton put himself in mercy for a licence to agree with William atte Bruggende in a plea of debt

distrain

Thomas Swancote plaintiff against William Toward in a plea of trespass pledge for the prosecution Richard Bulveys and it is ordered to attach William to respond to the plaintiff before the next [court]

Roger Batemon made a fine with the lord for suit of court to be commuted from the ine 12d — feast of St Michael last past until the Feast of St Michael then next in the future. And he gives for a fine 12d

Emma Hoore plaintiff against Stephen Bradeney and Thomas Huggen in a plea of land pledge for the prosecution Nicholas Stanlowe so it is ordered the bailiff summon the said Stephen and Thomas before the next court to respond to the aforesaid Emma in the plea aforesaid

the next

Nicholas Stanlowe, plaintiff against John Rys and Isabell his wife in a plea of land pledge for the prosecution Roger Roulowe who were not summoned so it is ordered the said John and Isabell are summoned before the next[court] to respond to the aforesaid plaintiff in the plea aforesaid

Robert Rendlelord plaintiff against Richard Hethe in a plea of land pledge for the prosecution Matthew Bulloces so it is ordered to the bailiff to summon the aforesaid Richard that he is at the next [court] to answer the plaintiff aforesaid

Robert Inggemon and Margary his wife plaintiffs against Rose formerly wife of Thomas Knotte in a plea of land pledge for the prosecution John Eudenas. so it is ordered to the bailiff to summon the said Rose before the next [court] to answer the aforesaid Robert and Margary in the plea aforesaid

Election of the reeve

William Dorre and Agnes his wife plaintiffs against Thomas Neeld in a plea of land pledge for the prosecution William Gerbot so it is ordered to summon the said Thomas before the next to respond to the aforesaid William and Agnes in the plea aforesaid

William Newe withdrew from the office of reeve to which office entered Nicholas Roulowe by the election of the homage of the lord and is sworn

fine 40s

Stephen Bradeney came here in court and took from the lord one messuage and one half virgate of land with appurtenances in Worefeld which were formerly Walter Harries' to hold to himself and his [heirs] according to the custom of the manor. And he gives for a fine 40s paid within the accounts by the pledge of Roger Walton and thence has seisin and made fealty and afterwards they were granted to John Rys to hold to himself and his [heirs] according to the custom of the manor under the same fine and thence has seisin and made fealty to the lord

fine 26s 8d

John Rys made a fine with the lord because he was married to Isabell widow of the lord without a licence and because he occupied the messuage and half a virgate of land aforesaid unjustly and without a licence from the lord and he gives for a fine 26s 8d paid within the accounts by the pledge of Stephen Bradeney

fine £13 6s 8d

John Eudenas is by agreement with the council of the lord to hold from a grant of the lord one messuage and one virgate of land with appurtenances in the village of Asturhull which Robert his uncle had formerly held. To have & to hold to the said John, his heirs and assigns under free tenure from the lord and his heirs by rent and services within the ancient extent of Worefeld satisfied under sufficient security to hold to the same John, his heirs, and his assigns by the lord by the costs of the said John to be made at a future time. For which agreement and grant the aforesaid John is to pay £13 6s 8d within two years next in the future at the feast of the Sacred Annunciation of the Blessed Mary and Michael the Archangel in equal portions by the pledge of Thomas of Swancote and Richard Bulveys

pannage for pigs 3s

The bailiff is charged regarding pannage in the woods of Southeley for this year 3s

Affeerors Thomas Rugge, John Hethe
Sum of this court £18 15s 6d

Worfeld	Small court held there on Thursday next after the Feast of the Purification of the Blessed Virgin Mary in the 2nd year of the reign of King Henry IV [3 February 1401]
the 12 amerced 6d	Inquiry held for the lord by the oath of Robert Hogge, Roger Waltoun, William Ewyk, Roger Richardes, John Hethe, John Barndeleye, Stephen Bradeneye, Matthew Bullok, Thomas Hugge, Roger Broke, Thomas Wyntur and Roger Bromleye who say on their oath that Thomas Barbour, chaplain (2d), Richard Hethe (2d), Thomas Harley (2d) who should make suit at this court to make the tenure made default. So each of them is in mercy
tenements in the hands of the lord the next	And that Joan Stanlowe, widow, formerly the wife of Nicholas Stanlowe who held of the lord by custom of the manor 2 messuages with one virgate of land with appurtenances on the day he died and concerning heriot and escheat they have a day to present the truth of the matter until the next [court]. And the tenements remain in the hands of the lord until.
Heriot 1 sheep 17d	And they say that Robert the son of Thomas Wermod has died and the lord has from his death one sheep in the name of heriot price 17d
Tenement in the hand of the lord	Thomas Lekhull surrendered into the hands of the lord one toft with half a virgate of land within the manor of Worfeld in Rougtone called Horscroft to the use of John Huwessone and thus the tenement to remain in the hand of the lord until
a day	Henry Barker plaintiff appeared against Thomas Wermod in a plea of trespass pledge for the prosecution William Barkar. And he says that the same Thomas unjustly with his dogs killed four of Henry's sheep in the township of Haalen at the feast of Easter last past to the damage of Henry of 6s 8d who thence have a day to agree until the next [court]
distrain	William Skyrmour plaintiff of Elcock Mustardmon pledge Robert Barkar in a plea of trespass pledge for the prosecution John Smyth who summoned did not come so distrain
the next	Plea between Walter Rugge, plaintiff and Stephen Bradeney defendant twice in a plea of trespass } And between William Skyrmour plaintiff and John Rogers defendant in a plea of trespass } as is clear in the last court preceding by the prayer of the parties And between Symon atte Broke not prosecuting and Agnes Dorre defendant in a plea of debt } And between Thomas Swancote plaintiff and William Towart defendant in a plea of trespass }
	Emma Hoore plaintiff against Stephen Bradeneye & Thomas Hugge in a plea of land as is clear in the last court who summoned did not come so distrain
distrain	Nicholas Stanlowe plaintiff against John Rys and Isabell his wife in a plea of land as is clear at the last court who summoned did not come so distrain
	Robert Ryndelford plaintiff against Richard Hethe in a plea of land as was clear at the last court who summoned did not come so distrain
	Robert Inggemon and Margaret his wife plaintiffs against Rose the widow of Thomas Knotte in a plea of land who summoned did not come so distrain
	William Dorre and Agnes his wife plaintiffs against Thomas Nelde in a plea of land who summoned did not come so distrain

1400 P314/W/1/1/219

William atte Broke plaintiff against Thomas Hugge in a plea of land pledge for the prosecution William Cartar & Richard Bulveys who is not summoned so let it be done
William Meger and Margery his wife plaintiffs against Roger Cattestre of Wode and Alice his daughter in a plea of land. Pledge for the prosecution Richard Bulveys who is not summoned so let it be done
Richard Bruggende plaintiff against Margery Stevenes in a plea of land pledge for the prosecution Richard Bulveys who is not summoned so let it be done

Sum of this court 23d
Expenses of clerks of the court & others coming to hold this court 16d

Worfeld	Great Court held there on Thursday next after the Feast of St Mark the Evangelist in the 2nd year of the reign of King Henry IV [28 April 1401]
Kyngeslowe & Stanlowe	townships there present nothing
Chesturtone amerced 6d	township there presents that Symon Taillour (3d) and Thomas Coliar (3d) who should make suit at this court to make the tenure made default so each of them is in mercy
Hultone amerced 6d	township there presents that Roger Haludaye made homsoken on William Gold so the same Roger (6d) is in mercy
Rowlowe, Bradene, Asterhul, Ewyk, Soonde amerced 7d waif 1d	townships there present that Thomas Nicols (3d) made default of appearance so he is in mercy. And that Margery Caye unjustly took one hen of Thomas atte Soonde price of the hen 1d so the said Margery (4d) is in mercy
Roughtone, Hokcoumbe, Barndeley, Swancote amerced 9d	townships there present that Thomas Barbour (3d) made default of appearance and they say that a certain piece of land called Stony Rudyng a common is enclosed at the open time to the nuisance of the neighbours in default of Philip Dawe (6d) and John his son so each of them is in mercy
Burcote, Burcot, Ryndelford & Bromleye amerced 7d Inquiry for strays	townships there present that Richard Hethe (3d) who should have appeared at this court to make his tenure made default so he is in mercy. And they say that the King's way in Ryndelford has deteriorated from the default of Richard Hethe so the same Richard (4d) is in mercy and it is ordered the same repair the same defect of the way before the next great court under pain and peril which will be incumbent And they say said in the custody of Roger Swancote is one mother ewe with one lamb etc. which came as strays at the Feast of the Nativity of the lord last past
Alvescote, Wynnescot, Newtone, Cattestre amerced 3d strays 6d remaining strays inquiry	townships there present that John Foular (3d) made a default of appearance so he is in mercy. And they say that in a certain tree of John Fouler is 1 swarm of bees etc. And they say that in the custody of Richard Witebrok is a swarm of strays price 6d
Ewdenas, Oldyntone amerced 9d	townships there present that William Oldyntone (3d) who should have appeared at this court to make the tenancy made default so he is in mercy. And they say that John the son of William Oldyntone forestalled William Freman so the said John (6d) is in mercy

1400 P314/W/1/1/219

Akeltone	township there presents nothing
Stapelford	township there presents nothing
Worfeld	township there presents nothing
Haalen amerced 6d	township there presents that John Haukes (3d), chaplain and William atte Broke (3d) who should have appeared at this court to make the tenure so each is in mercy
Wyken amerced 6d strays	township there presents that Thomas Heyne has in a certain tree 1 swarm as a stray etc. And they say that John Bewmes (6d) is a tanner of hides (corei) so he is in mercy

[The dorse]

The tasters amerced 6s 8d	of ale present that John Bewmes (14d) brewed 7 [times], John Smyth (8d) 4, Thomas Sonde (4d) 2, John Aleyn (2d) 1, William Dorre (2d) 1, Walter Rugge (2d) 1,William Hustar (2d) 1, John Billingesle (6d) 3, William Baret (6d) 3, Stephen Bradeney (2d) 1, Roger Smyth (2d) 1, John Coletes (2d) 1, John son of John Rowlowe (2d) 1, Robert Galyan (2d) 1, Mathew Bullok (2d) 1, Roger Knotte (2d) 1, John Eudenas (2d) 1, Robert Eudenas (2d) 1, William Bruggende (2d) 1, Richard Bulveys (14d) 7. And all sold against the assize so each of them is in mercy
The 12 jurors	present that the townships aforesaid and the tasters of ale well and faithfully presented and concealed nothing of whom the names are written below
The Bailiff stray cow 5s 4d	presents one cow coming as a stray at the Feast of St Peter which is said in chains in the first year of the reign of King Henry IV price 5s 4d
amerced 4d	Memorandum that here the bailiff is charged regarding 4d for the amercements of William Tresel, chaplain, still not affeered for a certain trespass presented by the township of Haalen as is clear in the great court held on Wednesday in the feast of St George in the 22nd year of the reign of King Richard II.

Affeerors John Hethe, Thomas Rugge.
Sum of this court: 17s 10d
Expenses of the steward and others coming to hold this court 3s 4d

Inquiry	of the great court by the oath of William Ewyk, John Tumpkys, Roger Cattestre, Roger Richardes, Roger Waltoun, Stephen Bradeneye, John Barndeleye, Robert Hogge, Thomas Rugge, Roger Broke, Roger Swancote and Thomas Wyntur
Court	Small held at Worfeld on Tuesday on the eve of St Mathew the Apostle and Evangelist in the second year of the reign of King Henry IV [20 September 1401]
Inquiry	held for the lord by the oath of William Newe, William Bruggende, William Gerbod, Thomas Hugge, William Towart, Robert atte Yate, Roger Hichecockes, Thomas Rugge, John Jannes, Roger Kyngeslowe, Thomas Jankys & Roger Smyth who say on oath that Thomas Coliar (2d), Richard Hethe (2d), John Fouler (2d) & Thomas Barbour chaplain (2d) who should make suit at this court to make the tenure made default so each of them is in mercy. And they say that William Boon has died and that

he was a tenant of the lord and concerning heriot and escheat of the same they seek a day to present at the next [court] and it is granted for this reason etc.

heriot 7s

And they say that Richard Bradeneye who held from the lord by the custom of the manor one message with one virgate of land in Bradeney on the day he died and the lord has for heriot 1 steer sold by the bailiff for 7s. And the tenements remain with Margery his wife by their custom

7s 6d

And that William the son of John atte Walle has died and the lord has in the name of heriot one heifer price 7s 6d

heriot 1 sheep 8d

And they say that William the son of Adam Robynes has died and the lord has for heriot 1 sheep price 8d

amerced 6s 6d

And they say that Margery Newe (2s) is married within the manor so she is in mercy
And that Joan the daughter of Stephen Bradene is married within the manor and she gives to the lord for contempt 2s
And that Margery daughter of Richard Aldith was married outside without a licence so the same Margery (2s 6d) is in mercy

amerced 2d

And that Roger Knyt (2d) made a trespass in the lord's wood for greenery so he is in mercy

tenement in the hands of the lord

And that Joan Stanlowe who held of the lord by custom of the manor one message with half a message with 3 nooks of land and half a nook in Stanlowe has died and concerning heriot and escheat the lord has nothing because they say she had no goods nor chattels. And the tenement remains in the hands of the lord

amerced 4d

Thomas Wermod (4d) puts himself in the mercy of the lord for a licence to agree with Henry Barker in a plea of trespass

a day

Still the plea between Walter Rugge plaintiff and Stephen Bradneye defendant in a plea of trespass is adjourned to the next [court] by the prayer of the parties

amerced 2d

William Skirmour (2d) put himself in the mercy of the lord for a licence to agree with John Rogers in a plea of trespass

amerced 2d

Simon atte Broke (2d) is in mercy because he is not prosecuting against Agnes Dorre in a plea of debt

the next

Thomas Swancote plaintiff and William Towart defendant in a plea of trespass have a day to agree until the next [court] by the prayer of the parties

amerced 2d

Elcok Mustardmon (2d) is in mercy for default against William Skirmour in a plea of trespass by the pledge of Robert ~~Barbour~~ Barkar and it is ordered to distrain the aforesaid Elcok to respond to the aforesaid William at the next [court] in the plea of trespass

8 pleas concerning land as shown in the last small court to be heard at the next

At this court the bailiff is charged concerning 16d of amercements not affeered at the time of the last accounts namely concerning a certain small court held on Thursday next after the Feast of St Augustine in the first year of the reign of King Henry IV. And concerning 16d of amercements not affeered in the time of the last accounts as is clear in the court held on Thursday next after the Feast of the Raising of the Holy Cross held in the first year of the reign of the King aforesaid

1400 P314/W/1/1/219

Affeerors: Thomas Rugge & John Hethe

Sum of this court 26s

In the expenses of the clerk of the court and others being there to hold this court 2s 4d

Sum of 5 courts held for this year £21 18s 7d

1401 P314/W/1/1/220

	Great Court held at Worfeld on Tuesday the eleventh day of October in the 3rd year of the reign of King Henry IV [11 October 1401]
Kyngeslowe Stanlowe	townships there present nothing
Hulton amerced 4d	township there presents that William Gold forestalled Roger Halydaye so the said William (4d) is in mercy
Chesturton	township there presents nothing
Asterhul, Ewyk, Rowlowe, Bradeney, Soonde amerced 4d strays 1 swarm	townships there present that John Hethe forestalled Richard Hethe so the said John (4d) is in mercy. And they say that in the village of Asturhul in a certain tree there is a swarm of bees coming as a stray in the summer time last past
Rougton, Barndele, Hokkombe, Swancote amerced 3s 3d strays 1 swarm	townships there present that Thomas Barbour (3d) chaplain made default of appearance at this court to make the tenancy so the said Thomas is in mercy. Also they present one swarm coming as a stray in the summer time last past which is in the custody of Robert Yate . And they say on their oath that Thomas the son of Thomas Jankys unjustly made a recovery on William Webbe so the said Thomas (4d) the son of Thomas is in mercy. And they say that the same Thomas the son of Thomas unjustly made a recovery on Stephen the son of William Webbe so the same Thomas (4d) the son of Thomas is in mercy. And they say that the same Stephen forestalled (4d) Thomas Jankys and drew blood (4d) from him the said Thomas so the said Stephen is in mercy. And they say that William Webbe forestalled (4d) Thomas Jankys and drew blood (4d) from him. And they say that Thomas the son of Thomas Jankys forestalled (4d) William Webbe & drew blood (4d) from the same William so the said Thomas the son of Thomas is in mercy. And they say that Stephen Webbe forestalled John the son of Thomas Jankys so the said Stephen (4d) is in mercy
Burcote, Burcote & Bromleye amerced 3d	townships there present that Richard Hethe made a default of appearance at this court to make the tenancy so the same Richard (3d) is in mercy
Cattestre, Alvescote, Wynnescote, Ryndelford, Newtone amerced 3d	townships there present that John Munsturleye made a default of appearance so the said John (3d) is in mercy
Ewdenas & Oldyntone	townships there present nothing
Stapelford	township there presents nothing
Akeltone	township there presents nothing
Haalen	township there presents that John Haukes (3d) chaplain, William Hattone (3d),

Haalen amerced 2s	William Jones (3d) & Warynges Bereward (3d) who made [default] of appearance at this court to make the tenancy so each of them is in mercy. And they say that Robert Galian is a regrater of bread and ale so the same Robert (12d) is in mercy
Worfeld the next	township there presents that in the village of Worfeld is a certain way unfit, deteriorated in what way and by what or by whom they have a day to present the truth of the matter in the next [court]
Wyke amerced 18d strays 1 swarm Inquiry	township there presents that Isabell the daughter of William Cartar raised the hue and cry by mouth on Joan the daughter of William Baret justly so the said Joan (4d) is in mercy. And they say that there is in the custody of Thomas Heyne 1 swarm of bees coming as a stray in the summer time last past. Also concerning 1 other swarm coming as a stray they now doubt so thence they have a day to present at the next [court]. Also they say on their oath that William Yngemon unjustly & against the peace of the lord King made an assault twice on Thomas Heyne in Wyke on Wednesday next after the feast of St Gregory the Pope in the third year of the reign of King Henry IV so the said William (6d) is in mercy. And they say that William Webbe made an assault on Thomas the son of Thomas Jankys so the said William (4d) is in mercy. Also they present that William Yngemon forestalled Thomas Coupar so the said William (4d) is in mercy
The tasters amerced 3s 6d	of ale present that John Bewmes (9d) brewed 3, Richard Bulveys (3d) 1, John Smyth (9d) brewed 3, Thomas atte Sond (3d) brewed 1, William Ewyk (3d) brewed 1, William Hustar (3d) 1,John Billyngesley (3d) brewed 1, William Baret (3d) brewed 1, Robert Smyth (3d) brewed 1. And they all sold against the assize so each of them is in mercy. And they say that William Skyrmour is a regrater of ale and did not show the seal so the same William (3d) is in mercy
The 12 jurors	namely John Eudenas, Roger Cattestre, William Ewyk, John Tumkys, Roger Waltone, Stephen Bradeneye, Roger Richardes, Robert Hoggen, Nicholas Rowlowe, John Barndeleye, Thomas Rugge & Thomas Wyntur jurors say on their oath that the townships aforesaid and the tasters of ale have well and faithfully presented and concealed nothing

[Next page]

Affeerors	Roger Richardes } Stephen Bradeneye } Sum of this court· 11s 5d Thence in the expenses of the steward 3s 9d	The price of strays aforesaid and the price of strays in the last great court preceding not yet determined for this reason… not complete etc.

Worfeld	Small court held there on Tuesday overleaf said namely the eleventh day of October in the year of the reign of King Henry IV [11 October 1401]
Inquest amerced 8d held in the hands of the lord inquest	held for the lord by the oath of William Ewyk, Roger Waltone, Stephen Bradeneye, Roger Richardes, Roger atte Broke, Thomas Rugge, Robert Hogge, Thomas Wyntur, John Hethe, John Barndeleye, Mathew Bullok & Roger Bromleye who say on their oath that Thomas Barbour chaplain (2d) made a fine, Richard Hethe (2d), Thomas Tresel (2d), John Munsterleye (2d) & Roger Hattone (2d) who made default of suit of court at this court to make the tenancy so each of them is in mercy. And they say that by the death of Amister Barndeleye there falls into the hands of the lord one nook of land at Barndeleye which land is held by custom. And thus it remains in the hands of the lord and concerning heriot and escheat of the same Amister and William Boon formerly her husband they have a day to enquire until the coming of the council of the lord

1401 P314/W/1/1/220

fine 12d

to be paid in the last court this year

Lucy Mullwart made a fine with the lord for having an inquest of the 12 of the office (ex officio) to enquire of the way of evidence concerning her right of one acre lying on the Egge within the manor of Worfeld and one Stakyng in the Severn next to a place called Waschyng place. And she gives for a fine 12d. On which the inquest was held by the oath of Roger Hychecokes, Mathew Bullok, Roger Swancote, William Palhok, William Ewyk, Richard Aldith, Robert Hogge, Thomas Wyntur, William Barkar, Thomas Rowlowe, Richard Whitebrok & John Robyns which jurors seek a day concerning the full verdict to render thence at the next and it is granted by the steward with the agreement of the parties

Verdict

Which at the inquest is pending at the suit of Thomas Swancote of the 12 now it is presented by the oath of the inquest thence previously charged that the water course in the enclosure of Thomas Swancote in Stapelford is out of its natural course by the orchard of William Towarte from the time of which memory does not exist on which they say that now the land in the said orchard is increased by which the said water is not able to go out as it was accustomed to depart etc. On which it is ordered that the said land thus in the aforesaid enlarged orchard be set aside & removed by the view of the township there before the feast of the birth of the lord next in the future under pain and peril which will be incumbent

fine 12d

Thomas Barbor chaplain made a fine with the lord for suit of court to be commuted from the date of this court until the feast of St Michael now next in the future and he gives for a fine 12d

pannage of Soudeleye 12d

The pasture of the wood of Soudleye from the feast of St Michael last past until the feast of St Martin now next in the future namely for 6 weeks to be sold to the townships of Cattestre by the bailiff of the lord for 12d

distraint

John the son of Nicholas Rowlowe plaintiff against Thomas Heyne in a plea of debt who summoned did not come so distrain

a day

William Euleys chaplain plaintiff appeared himself against William Oldyntone in a plea of broken agreement pledge for the prosecution Nicholas Rowlowe who have a day to agree until the next court

distraint

William Webbe plaintiff appeared himself against Thomas Jankys in a plea of trespass so it is ordered to the bailiff that he distrain the aforesaid Thomas that he be at the next [court] to respond to the aforesaid William in the plea aforesaid

distraint

Thomas Toward plaintiff appeared himself against John Oldyntone in a plea of debt pledge for the prosecution William Gerbod who is summoned did not come so distrain

the next

The plea between Walter Rugge plaintiff & Stephen Bradeneye defendant in a plea of trespass And between William Skyrmour plaintiff and Elcok Mustardmon defendant in a plea of trespass } adjourned to the coming of the council of the lord

amerced 2d

William Toward (2d) put himself in mercy for a licence to agree with Thomas Swancote in a plea of trespass

1401 P314/W/1/1/220

Election of the reeve	Nicholas Rowlowe withdrew from the office of reeve which office John Janne enters by the election of the homage of the lord and he is sworn
the next	Still 8 pleas of land as is clear in the penultimate small court preceding adjourned until the coming of the council of the lord
Affeerors	named within Sum of this court 3s 10d

1402 P314/W/1/1/221

Worfeld — Small Court held there on Tuesday the seventh day of March in the 3rd year of the reign of King Henry IV [7 March 1402]

Inquest — held for the lord by the oath of William Ewyk, Roger Richardes, Roger Waltonn, John Barndeleye, Nicholas Rowlowe, Roger Broke, Stephen Bradeneye, Thomas Rugge, Thomas Wyntur, Mathew Bullok, John Hethe & Robert Hogge who say on their oath

amerced 4d — that Richard Hethe (2d) & John Munsterleye (2d) who should have made suit at this court to make the tenancy defaulted so each of them is in mercy

And they say that Richard Hethe surrendered into the hands of the lord half of one virgate of land with all its appurtenances in Bromley called the Howelond totally & wholly just as previously held by the aforesaid Richard to the use of John Janne & John the son of Elie Bromley. And thus it remains in the hands of the lord etc. On which came John Janne, above-named & took from the lord half the aforesaid land

fine 4s — namely one nook with its appurtenances to hold from the lord to the same John Janne, Alice his wife & their [heirs] according to the custom of the manor for rent, services & customs thence due. And they give to the lord for a fine 4s, made fealty & are seised

Afterwards came John the son of Elie Bromley and took from the lord the other half of the aforesaid land namely one nook with its appurtenances to hold from the lord to the said John the son of Elie & Christine his wife and their [heirs] according to the

fine 4s — custom of the manor for services and customs which are thence due. And they give to the lord for a fine 4s, made fealty and are seised

Richard Saladyn, son and heir of Amister Saladyn came and took from the lord half of one messuage with one nook of land adjacent with appurtenances in Barndeleye which were taken into the hands of the lord by the death of the aforesaid Amister as is

fine 5s — clear in the last court preceding to hold from the lord to the same Richard and his [heirs] according to the custom of the manor for rent, services and customs which are thence due. And he gives to the lord for a fine 5s made fealty and has seisin

Matilda Stanlowe daughter of Nicholas Stanlowe took from the lord two messuages with one virgate of land adjacent at Stanlowe which tenements were taken into the hands of the lord by the death of Joan Stanlowe the mother of the aforesaid Matilda and concerning which tenements the same Joan died seized to hold from the lord the aforesaid tenement to the aforesaid Matilda and her [heirs] for rent, services, and

fine 16s — customs thence due according to the custom of the manor. And she gives to the lord for a fine 16s and has seisin not making fealty because it is covered by Thomas Muychehale by what title to enquire. Further it is ordered to the bailiff that he distrain the aforesaid Thomas that he is at the next court to make fealty to the lord

John Huwessone took from the lord one toft with half of one virgate of land called Horscroft in Rougtone which was taken into the hands of the lord from the surrender

fine 8s — of Thomas Lekhul to the use of the aforesaid John as is clear in the small court held on Thursday next after the feast of the Purification of the Blessed Mary the Virgin in the second year of the reign of King Henry IV to hold from the lord the said tenements to the said John and his [heirs] by services and customs which are thence due according to the custom of the manor. And he gives to the lord for a fine 8s made fealty and is seised

fine 12d

John Huwessone above-named surrendered into the hands of the lord two parcels lying separately of which one parcel lies in the field of Swancote on Depedale with a hedge adjacent, the other parcel lies in the field of Swancote called Wodendale with one parcel of a certain hedge adjacent which parcels of land were of half a virgate of land called Horscroft to the use of John Janne and Alice his wife who came and took from the lord the said parcels of land with the parcels of hedges to hold to the same John and Alice and their [heirs] according to the custom of the manor. And they give to the lord for a fine 12d and made fealty and are seised

fine 12d
increased rent 1d

John Walkar of Ryndelford took from the lord one parcel of land lying on the soil of the lord at Ryndelford on the hill called Teyntrehull the which parcel of land contains in length 140 feet and in width 120 feet according to certain metes and bounds marked to hold from the lord the aforesaid parcel of land to the aforesaid John and his [heirs] in an enclosure according to the custom of the manor rendering thence annually to the lord one penny of silver at the feast of St Michael. And he gives to the lord for a fine 12d, made fealty and is seised

fine 12d

next to be settled in the next court following

William Gold gives to the lord 12d for an inquest by 12 to be had by the 12 to enquire if he should have the better right in a certain parcel of meadow called Lynotesparrok in Hultonn which parcel of meadow Roger Gold of Hultonn sold to him in his tenure or William Gold in his demand. On which the inquest was held by the oath of Roger Richardes, Roger Waltone, Stephen Bradeneye, William Bruggende, John atte Walle, Roger Smyth, John Barndeley, John Hethe, Thomas Hugge, Nicholas Roulowe, Thomas Rugge & Thomas Wyntur who sworn and charged seek a day thence to render the truth at the next [court] and it is granted to them by the consent of the parties

The law

Roger Richardes plaintiff appeared against John Reignald in a plea of trespass and he says that with the new and old ordinances it should be that no-one who holds by the custom of the manor within the manor of Worfeld ought to pursue against another tenant of the same tenure of the same manor in no places except in the court of the lord of the aforesaid manor without the licence of the lord etc. Against which arrangement the same John made the said Roger come to the Hundred of Brimestre unjustly etc. to the damage of the said Roger 3s 4d. And the same John present denied this. And he has a day thence for the law in the next with 6 hands by the pledge of John Tumpkys

The law

Roger Waltone plaintiff against John Reignald in a plea of trespass and he says that with the arrangement that no-one who holds by the custom of the manor within the manor of Worfeld should have made any suit against another tenant of the same tenure of the same manor except in the lord's court of the aforesaid manor without licence from the lord etc. against which ordinance notwithstanding the same John made the said Roger come to the Hundred of Brimestre unjustly etc. to the damage of the same Roger 3s 4d. And the same John present denied this. And thence he has a day for the law in the next [court] with 6 hands by the pledge of John Tumpkys

The law

Stephen Bradeneye plaintiff against John Reignald in a plea of trespass. And he says that when no tenant of the manor of Worfeld of lesser tenure should have made no suit against another tenant of the same manor except in the lord's court held within the manor aforesaid without a licence from the lord etc. the same Stephen at the suit of the said John took to the hundred court of Brimestre unjustly etc. to the damage of the said Stephen 3s 4d. And the same John present denies all this and thence has a day for the law in the next [court] with 6 hands by the pledge of John Tumpkys

Robert Barkar plaintiff against John Reignald in a plea of trespass and he says that when no tenant of the manor of Worfeld of lesser tenure should have made any suit against another tenant of the same manor except in the court of the lord held within the manor aforesaid without licence from the lord etc. the same Robert at the suit of the said John travelled to the hundred court of Brimestre unjustly etc. And the said John present denies this and thence has a day for the law in the next [court] with 6 hands by the pledge of John Tumpkys

the law

Richard Hethe (2d) put himself in mercy for a licence to agree with William Skyrmour in a plea of trespass

amerced 2d

Still of the court
[Dorse]

Roger Hichecokes plaintiff against Richard Hethe in a plea of trespass who is not yet attached so let it be done

distrain

Roger Cattestre plaintiff against Richard Hethe in a plea of trespass etc. so it is ordered to the bailiff that he distrain the aforesaid Richard that he is at the next [court] to respond to the aforesaid Roger in the plea aforesaid

distrain

distrain

Roger Broke plaintiff against Richard Hethe in a plea of trespass who is not distrained so let it be done

distrain

Nicholas Rowlowe plaintiff against Richard Hethe in a plea of debt who was summoned did not come so to distrain

distrain

William Kynvastone plaintiff against Richard Hethe in a plea of debt pledge for the prosecution Richard Bulveys who was summoned did not come so distrain

distrain

William Toward plaintiff against Richard Hethe in a plea of debt pledge who was summoned did not come so distrain

Emmota Hoore plaintiff against Thomas Huggem of Hultoun in a plea of land pledge for the prosecution Thomas Wyntur etc. who seeks from the same Thomas one messuage with one virgate of land adjacent in Hultoun which tenement is called Roger's place Upyntoun as of her right and heredity of which no more now because adjourned to the coming of the council of the lord by the prayer of the parties

The next

John the son of Nicholas Rowlowe plaintiff against Thomas Heyne in a plea of debt who have a day to agree at the next [court] by the prayer of the parties

a day

Thomas Toward plaintiff against John Oldyntoun in a plea of debt pledge for the prosecution William Towarte. And he says that the same John was owing to him [and] should have paid certain items of silver at terms between the same defined which items of silver the same John borrowed to recover the said items of silver at terms wholly passed by at which terms the said silver items were not paid although it was very often requested, and nor yet, but detained to the damage of the said Thomas. And the said John present in court wholly denies this and thence has a day for the law in the next [court] with 6 hands pledge for the prosecution William Oldyntone

The law

1402 P314/W/1/1/221

Plea between	William Heuley chaplain plaintiff & William Oldyntonn defendant in a plea of broken agreement
	And between William Webbe plaintiff & Thomas Jankys defendant in a plea of trespass
the next	And between Walter Rugge plaintiff & Stephen Bradeneye defendant in a plea of trespass
	And between William Skyrmor plaintiff & Elcok Mustardmon defendant in a plea of trespass
still	8 pleas concerning plea of land adjourned until the coming of the council of the lord etc.

Affeerors: Roger Richardes, Stephen Bradeneye

Sum of this court	40s 6d
Thence in expenses	3s 4d
And in increased rent	1d

1402 P314/W/1/1/222

Worfeld — Small Court held there on Tuesday the 28th day of March in the 3rd year of the reign of King Henry IV after the conquest [28 March 1402]

fine 6d — John Munsterleye made a fine with the lord for suit of court to be commuted from the date of this court until the Feast of St Michael next in the future. And he gives for a fine 6d

fine 16d
fine 16d — William Hattone surrendered into the hands of the lord one cottage with curtilage adjacent in Haalen on the castle to the use of Roger Hattonn the which Roger came and took from the lord the aforesaid cottage with curtilage adjacent with its appurtenances to hold to himself and his [heirs] from the lord according to the custom of the manor. And he gives to the lord for a fine 16d, made fealty to the lord, and thus is seised. On which came the same Roger Hattonn and surrendered into the hands of the lord the aforesaid cottage with the adjacent curtilage to the use of Robert the son of Robert Yngemon the which Robert the son of Robert came and took from the lord the whole of the aforesaid cottage with the curtilage with its appurtenances to hold from the lord to himself and his [heirs] according to the custom of the manor. And he gives to the lord for a fine 16d, made fealty, and is seised

the 12 jurors
amerced 2d — Inquest held by the oath of Roger Richardes, Roger Waltone, William Ewyk, Stephen Bradeneye, William Bruggende, Roger Broke, Thomas Wyntur, Mathew Bullok, Roger Hichecokes, Thomas Hugge, William Gerbod & Roger Smyth who say on their oath that John Wottone (2d) who [owed] suit at this court to make tenure made default so the said John is in mercy

amerced 4d — Robert Barkar the beadle of the lord presents that Richard Bulveys (2d), Roger Cattestre (2d) & Nicholas Rowlowe have animals depasturing in the meadow of the lord who thence put themselves in the mercy of the lord

verdict — By which at the inquest pending at the suit of William Gold of Aklyntone concerning the right of a certain parcel of meadow as is clear in the last court preceding now it is presented by the oath of the 12 whose names are written in the said last court preceding namely that the same William Gold of Aklyntone has the better right in the said parcel of meadow in his tenure than William Gold of Hultone in his claim. On which it is judged that the same William Gold of Aklyntone should hold the same parcel of meadow just as he previously held until etc.

amerced 2d — Thomas Heyne (2d) put himself in mercy for a licence to agree with John the son of Nicholas Rowlowe in a plea of debt etc.

amerced 2d
distrain — Roger Hichecokes plaintiff appeared against Richard Hethe in a plea of trespass the which Richard attached and charged did not come so the same Richard (2d) is in mercy

amerced 2d
distrain — Roger Cattestre plaintiff against the said Richard Hethe in a plea of trespass which Richard attached and charged did not come so Richard (2d) is in mercy

amerced 2d
distrain — Roger Broke plaintiff appeared against the said Richard Hethe in a plea of trespass who attached and charged did not come so the said Richard (2d) is in mercy

amerced 2d
distrain — Nicholas Rowlowe plaintiff against Richard Hethe above-named in a plea of debt as is clear in the last court preceding who summoned and attached did not come so the same Richard (2d) is in mercy

1402 P314/W/1/1/222

amerced 2d distrain	William Kynvastone agreed plaintiff against Richard Hethe in a plea of debt who attached and charged did not come so Richard (2d) is in mercy
amerced 2d distrain	William Toward plaintiff appeared against Richard Hethe in a plea of debt who attached and charged did not come so the said Richard (2d) is in mercy
amerced 8d distrain	John Regnald who had a day for the law at this court against Roger Richardes, Roger Waltone, Stephen Bradeneye & Robert Barker separately in a plea of trespass as in the last court preceding now [are] for a licence to agree. And the said John put himself (8d) in mercy
amerced 2d	John Oldyntone (2d) and his pledge are in mercy because of a default of law at this court against Thomas Toward in a plea of debt as is clear in the last court preceding
amerced 2d	William Oldyntone (2d) put himself in mercy for a licence to agree with William Henley/Heuley chaplain in a plea of broken agreement

pleas the next	Between William Webbe plaintiff & Thomas Jankys defendant in a plea of trespass And between William Rugge plaintiff & Stephen Bradeneye defendant in a plea of trespass And between William Skyrmour plaintiff & Elcok Mustardmon defendant in a plea of trespass	} Adjourned until the next by the prayer of the parties

the next	William Gold of Aklyntone plaintiff appeared against William Gold of Hultone in a plea of trespass. Pledge for the prosecution Robert Barkar who have a day
the next	Still 9 pleas of land adjourned until the coming of the council of the lord

Affeerors: William Newe, Stephen Bradeneye
Sum of this court 5s 10d
Thence in expenses of the steward 2s

1402 P314/W/1/1/223

Worefeld	Great Court held there on Tuesday 18th April in the 3rd year of the reign of King Henry IV after the conquest [18 April 1402]
Kyngeslowe & Stanlowe	townships there present nothing
Chesturtone amerced 2d	township there presents that Thomas Coliar (2d) who should have appeared at this court to make the tenure made default so the said Thomas is in mercy
Hultone	township there presents nothing
Rowlowe, Bradeneye, Asturhul, Ewyk, Soonde amerced 8d	townships there present that William Skyrmour forestalled Richard Knokyn so the said William (4d) is in mercy. And they say that the King's way in Soonde has deteriorated in default of Thomas Nicols so the said Thomas (4d) is in mercy. And it is ordered the same Thomas properly repair the defect of the same way before the next [court] under pain and peril which will be incumbent
Rougtone, Barndele, Hoccombe, Swancot	townships there have nothing to present
Burcote, Burcote, Ryndelford & Bromle	townships there present nothing
Alvescote, Wynnescote,, Cattestre, Newtone Inquiry at the next	The townships there present one sheep coming as a stray at the feast of the Purification of the Blessed Mary the Virgin last past appraised at 12d
Ewdenas, Oldyntone	townships there present nothing
Stapelford	township there presents nothing
Akeltone amerced 4d	township there presents that Thomas the son of John Tumpkys forestalled Thomas Tresel so the said Thomas (4d) the son of John is in mercy
Haalen amerced 2d remaining not affeered	township there presents that John Haukys (2d) chaplain who should have appeared at this court to make the tenure made default so the said John is in mercy. And they say that William Skirmour (4d) forestalled Emma Hoore and drew blood (6d) from the same Emma so the said William is in mercy. And they say that the same Emma raised the hue and cry by mouth on the said William justly so the same William (6d) is in mercy
Worfeld amerced 4d	township there presents that the King's way extending by the middle of the village the same is deteriorated in default of Matilda Rugge so the said Matilda (4d) is in mercy. And it is ordered to the said Matilda that she properly repairs the defect of the same road before the next under pain and peril which will be incumbent

Wyke
amerced 16d
Waif 1d

township there presents that William Yngemon made homsoken on William Baret so the said William Yngemon (6d) is in mercy. And they say that Alice Baret wife of the aforesaid William Baret raised the hue and cry by mouth on the said William Yngemon (4d) justly so the same William Yngemon is in mercy. Also they present that a certain foreign beggar woman whose name is not known unjustly took against the peace one parcel of linen price 1d from the house of William Baret so the said foreign woman is in mercy (2d). And they say that Richard Walkar broke the pound of Thomas Heyne so the said Richard (4d) is in mercy

The ale tasters
amerced 3s 6d

present that John Bewmes (6d) (3d) brewed 3, Richard Bulveys (6d) (3d) 3, John Smyth (6d) (3d) 3, Thomas Sonde (4d) (2d) 2, John son of John Rowlowe (2d) (1d) 1, John Billyngsley (4d) (2d) 2, William Baret (2d) (1d) 1, Robert Ewdenas (2d) (1d) 1, Robert Taillour (2d) (1d) 1 & Walter Rugge (2d) (1d) 1 And that all the said brewers sold against the assize so each of them is in mercy

The 12 jurors
abandoned goods 2d
amerced 18d remaining not affeered until the coming of the council of the lord

Inquiry held by the oath of Roger Cattestre, John Tumpkys, Roger Waltone, Roger Richardes, Thomas Rugge, Stephen Bradeneye, John Barndeleye, Roger Broke, Thomas Wyntur, Robert Hogge, Nicholas Rowlowe & Mathew Bullokes who say on their oath that Alice the wife of John Coliar unjustly took 1 pint of beans from Roger Hethe price of the beans 2d so the said Alice (6d) is in mercy. And they say that this presentment was concealed by the township of Akeltonn so the said township (12d) is in mercy. Also they say that William Ewyk (4d) forestalled Richard Bulveys and drew blood (6d) from him so the said William is in mercy. And they say that Eleanor the wife of William Ewykes forestalled Thomas Madeleye (2d) and hit him (2d) so the said Eleanor is in mercy. And that this was concealed by the township of Rowlowe, Bradeneye, Ewyk & Sonde so the said township (8d) is in mercy. They say that the aforesaid 12 jurors on their oath that all other townships aforesaid and the ale tasters have well and faithfully presented and concealed nothing

Affeerors : Nicholas Roulowe, Stephen Bradeney
Sum of this court 9s 3d price that is not affeered and the price of 1 swarm from a stray being in a certain tree at Asturhull as is clear by the presentment of the townships there in the last great court aforesaid
Thence in the expenses of the steward 2s 6d

William Carter appropriated one swarm being strays in the village of Wikes in the last great court aforesaid being in the custody of Thomas Heyne

Worefeld

Small court held there on Thursday the 7th day of the month of September in the third year of the reign of King Henry IV [7 September 1402]

The law

Roger Cattestre plaintiff presented himself against Richard Hethe in a plea of broken agreement and he says that the same Richard did not keep certain agreements in the same namely when he agreed to deliver a certain house to John Smyth in Worefeld for a certain term between them arranged which house despite being frequently requested he was not willing to free to the same John just as agreed and still not to the damage of Roger 20s and the said Richard being present in court denies this and has a day for the law in the next with 6 hands pledge for the law John Hethe

The law

Roger Broke plaintiff presented himself against Richard Hethe in a plea of broken agreement and he says that the same Richard agreed to hand over to John Smyth two houses in Worefeld on a day and in a year between them assigned which houses he was not willing to free to the said John as agreed nor still to the damage of Roger himself of 26s 8d and the said Richard being present in court denies this and he has a day for the law in the next with 6 hands pledge John Hethe — The law

Roger Hichecokes plaintiff presented himself against the said Richard Hethe in a plea of broken agreement and he says that the same Richard made certain agreements with him namely that he had certain pasture in Bromley at a certain time which agreements he was not willing to observe to the damage of Roger himself 30s and the said Richard being present in court denies this and he has thence a day for the law in the next with 6 hands pledge for the law Nicholas Newtone

The law — Nicholas Roulowe executor of a witness of Stephen atte Lee plaintiff presented against the said Richard Hethe in a plea of debt and he says that the same Richard and his witness aforesaid owed payment of 15s 6d for the goods of the aforesaid Stephen deceased at a certain day, place and year past the which debt despite frequent requests by the said executor he is not willing to pay nor still but detains to the damage of the said Nicholas 3s 4d and the said Richard being present denies this and he has thence a day for the law in the next with 6 hands pledge for the law John Hethe

The law — William Webbe plaintiff presented himself against Thomas Jankys in a plea of trespass. And he said that the same Thomas by himself and his servant unjustly took and with his animals destroyed the herbage of William himself in Roughton in summer time last past to the damage of William himself 3s 4d. And the said Thomas present denies this and he thence has a day for the law with 6 hands. Pledge for the law Stephen Bradeney

amerced 2d — Richard Hethe put himself in mercy for a licence to agree with William Kynvartone plaintiff in a plea of debt

amerced 2d — William Toward is in mercy because he is not prosecuting his plea against Richard Hethe in a plea of debt

The next — The plea touching Walter Rugge plaintiff and Stephen Bradeney defendant in a plea of trespass
And between William Skirmour plaintiff and Elcoces Mustardmon defendant in a plea of trespass

amerced 2d — William Goold of Hulton is in mercy for a licence to agree with William Goold of Akelton in a plea of trespass

The next — Still 9 pleas of land adjourned until the coming of the council of the lord

Sum total of the court 6d

1402 P314/W/1/1/224

Worefeld	Small Court held there on Thursday 28th September in the 3rd year of the reign of King Henry IV after the conquest [28 September 1402]
Essoins	Roger Batemon & John Rys themselves from common suit by Stephen Bradeney & John Reynaldes
[Essoined] by John Hethe whence the law	{Richard Hethe defending himself against Roger Cattestre in a plea of broken agreement {The same Richard defending himself against Roger Hichecokes in a plea of broken agreement {The same Richard defending himself against Roger Broke in a plea of broken agreement {The same Richard defending himself against Nicholas Roulowe in a plea of debt
The next	A day is given between William Webbe plaintiff and Thomas Jankyns defendants under the law in a plea of trespass until the next by the prayer of the parties
	Nicholas Roulowe plaintiff of Richard Hichecokes in a plea of debt pledge for the prosecution John Janyn

Roger Richardes	Stephen Bradeney	Thomas Rugge	Thomas Wyntur
Roger Waltone	Roger atte Broke	John Hethe	William Gerbot
Nicholas Roulowe	John Barndeley	Robert Hoggen	Mathew Bulloces

Amerced 4d Heriot 1 cow with calf 10s Escheat 1 horse 3s, 2 sows & 5 piglets 7s Fine 10s	who say on their oath that Richard Hethe (2d) and William Billingesley (2d) who are suitors at this court made default to make their tenure so each of them is in mercy. And they say that Roger Swancote of Swancote who held from the lord one messuage with half a virgate of land adjacent by the custom of the manor in Bromley on the day he died after whose death the lord will have in the name of heriot one black cow *taget* with one calf suckling price 10s and thus sold in full court by the reeve Thomas Swancote. And that the lord has from the same death for escheat one black horse price 3s and two sows and five piglets price 7s and thus sold in full court by the aforesaid reeve the said Thomas Swancote. And the tenements remain in the hands of the lord. On which came William the son and heir of the aforesaid Roger and took from the lord the aforesaid messuage and land with appurtenances to hold to himself and his [heirs] from the lord according to the custom of the manor. And he gives for a fine 10s, made fealty & is seised. Pledge for the fine Thomas of ~~fine~~ Swancote & Richard Bromley
Heriot 1 ox & 1 cow 16s Escheat 1 horse with 1 colt 5s 10d, 5 piglets 7s 6d Tenements in the hands of the lord	And they say that Robert Wermot chaplain who held from the lord by custom of the manor one messuage with one toft and five nooks of land in Halen has died at whose death the lord will have in the name of heriot one ox and one cow price 16s and thus sold by the reeve. And that there falls to the lord concerning escheat from the death of the same deceased one horse with one colt price 5s 10d and five piglets price 7s 6d and thus the said escheat is sold by the reeve. And the tenements remain in the hands of the lord
Inquest	Still the aforesaid jury seeks evidence from the court rolls of the lord for a view of the said rolls if Roger Swancote deceased above-named was seised on the day of his death of one messuage and half of one virgate of land with a third part of one nook of land in Bromley for the greater profit of the lord for the reason of heriot and escheat still not presented and because the said rolls are in the custody of Richard

Bulveys who is not in…(p*uu) they seek a day until they have had an inspection of the said rolls

Fine 10d — Hamo Humeley and Matilda his wife came and surrendered into the hands of the lord two acres of land in the field of Hulton of which one lies at Walleford between the land of Stephen Bradeney & William Bruggende. The other acre lies in the Yatehousfeld & is called the Piketacre to the use of Roger Smyth and Alice his wife to hold from the lord to the said Roger and Alice and their [heirs] according to the custom of the manor. And he gives for a fine 10d, made fealty, and they are seised. And the aforesaid Matilda confessed and examined before the steward said that she voluntarily of her own will made herself the coheir of her husband

Fine 16d — John Smyth came and surrendered into the hands of the lord one cottage with curtilage adjacent in Sonde to the use of Richard Hichecockes to hold from the lord according to the custom of the manor to himself and his [heirs]. And he gives for a fine 16d, made fealty, and is seised

Tenement in the hands of the lord — The Bailiff presents that Edith Collier surrendered into the hands of the lord one toft with half a virgate of land in Chesturton which was formerly Richard Colier's to hold to the use of Margery & Emma his daughters and thus the tenements remain in the hands of the lord until etc.

Fine 2s — Robert Barker & Roger Hatton made a fine with for an inquest of 24 to be held of the office to enquire of their right of a certain old rent of their land and tenements owed in Halen from the time of which the memory of man does not exist & which rent of their predecessors was taken by custom from the land and tenements formerly Henry atte Yate's and Thomas Wyntur's. And they give for a fine 2s. On which the inquest was held by the oath of Roger Richardes, Roger Waltone, Nicholas Roulowe, Stephen Bradeney, Roger atte Broke, John Barndeley, Thomas Rugge, John Hethe, Robert Hoggen, Thomas Wyntur, William Gerbot, Mathew Bulloce, Roger

the next — Hichecockes, William Bruggende, William Palhokes, Richard Aldith, William Barker, Thomas Roulowe, Richard Whitebroces, John Robyns, William Holygreve, Robert atte Yatte, Roger Mathewe & Thomas Tresull who seek a day for the verdict until the next

Verdict — Who at the ex officio inquiry pending at the suit of Lucy Mullewart hereupon it is presented by the oath of the inquest thence held as is clear in the small court held on Tuesday the 11th day of October last past that the same Lucy in a certain acre of land lying on the Egge thus has the right. And that the fishing place called Stakynges in the Severn at Washyngplace lying from the right of assart there that the same Lucy should hold

Remaining — Still 9 pleas of land adjourned until the coming of the council of the lord

Election of reeve — John Jannesson who is elected reeve to serve the lord in the office of reeve for the whole of this year past and to carry everything of the same year in the same office withdrew. To which office came Thomas Jankyns by the election of the homage of the lord for the present year in the future and is sworn

Affeerers Nicholas Roulowe, Stephen Bradeney
Sum of this court 43s 10d
Thence in expenses of the steward 5s

1402 P314/W/1/1/225

Worefeld	Great Court held there on Wednesday the 11th day of October in the 4th year of the reign of King Henry IV after the conquest [11 October 1402]
Kyngeslowe & Stanlowe	townships there present nothing. Chestertone township there presents nothing. Hultone township there presents nothing
Rowlowe, Bradeney, Asturhul, Ewyk, Soonde amerced 4d strays 6d	townships there present that William Ewyk who should have appeared at this court to make the tenure made default so the said William (4d) is in mercy. And they say that in the custody of Thomas Soonde is a certain sheep coming as a stray before the feast of St Michael last past. Price of the sheep 6d
Roughtone, Barndeley, Hoccombe, Swancote amerced 2d	townships there present that Thomas Barbour chaplain who should have appeared at this court to make the tenancy made default so the said Thomas (2d) is in mercy.
Burcote, Burcote, Ryndelford & Bromle	townships there present nothing
Alvescote, Wynescote, Cattestre, Newtone amerced 2s	townships there present that Nicholas Thacchar (2d) made a default of appearance so etc.. And they say that John Oldyntone forestalled (4d) John Richardes and hit him so the said John (6d) is in mercy. And that Thomas Richardes forestalled (4d) John Oldyntone & drew blood (6d) from him so the said Thomas is in mercy. And that John Richardes hit John Oldyntone so the said John (2d) is in mercy
Stapelford	township there presents nothing
Akeltone amerced 4d	township there presents that William Wilot broke … of John …so the said William (2d) is in mercy and that Isabell the wife of Roger Hethe forestalled William Wilot so the said Isabell (2d) is in mercy
Haalen amerced 14d Waifs 2d	township there presents that John Haukys (2d) chaplain & William Billyngesle (2d) who should have appeared at this court to make the tenure made default so each of them is in mercy. And they say that William Billyngesle raised the hue and cry by mouth on Henry Barkar unjustly so the said William (6d) is in mercy. And they say that Alice Wyntur unjustly took one hen of John Sewstar price 2d so the said Alice (4d) is in mercy
Ewdenas, Oldyntone amerced 18d	townships there present that John (4d) the son of William Oldyntone forestalled Thomas Yngemon and made a recovery on him so the said John (2d) is in mercy. And that the same John made an assault (2d) on Thomas the son of Roger Richardes and forestalled (4d) him so the said John is in mercy. And they say that the same John forestalled (4d) Thomas Richardes and made an assault on him so the said John (2d) is in mercy
Wyke	township there presents nothing

Worfeld amerced 8d	township there presents that John Joneson (2d) who should have appeared at this court to make the tenure made default so the said John is in mercy. And they say that the King's way in Worfeld is deteriorated in default of Matilda Rugge so the said Matilda (2d) is in mercy. And they say that Richard Lyones chaplain forestalled William Lowe so the said Richard (4d) is in mercy
The tasters of ale amerced 3s 4d	present that John Bewmes (6d) brewed 3, William Ewyk (4d) 2, William Wermod (8d) 4, Richard Bulveis (6d) 3, John Aleyn (2d) 1, Robert Taillour (12d) 6 & William Hustar (2d) 1 And that all sold against the assize so each of them is in mercy
The 12 jurors	Inquest held by the oath of John Ewdenas, Roger Cattestre, Roger Richardes, Roger Walton, Stephen Bradeneye, John Barndeleye, Robert Hogge, John Tumpkys, Roger atte Broke, Nicholas Rowlowe, William Barkar & William Newe who say on their oath that the townships aforesaid and the tasters of ale have well and faithfully presented and concealed nothing

Sum 10s 2d

[The Dorse]

Worefeld	Small court held there on ....[illegible] in the fourth year of the reign of King Henry IV
Fine 6d	John Munsterleye made a fine for suit of court to be commuted from the feast of St Michael last past until the said feast of St Michael next in the future & he gives for a fine 6d
Fine 4s	Isabell the wife of Thomas of Kynggesseslowe came in court & surrendered into the hands of the lord one messuage & 1 nook of land with appurtenances which were Roger of Kynggeslowe's in the same to the usc of Thomas Jankyns & Matilda his wife according to the custom of the manor by services thence due. And the said Thomas gives to the lord for a fine 4s and made fealty
Heriot	Roger Swancote junior has died whereof there follows one ox price 8s & they seek an adjournment until at the next [court]
heriot 1 ox 7s 6d, escheat 4 piglets 4s 6d & 1 horse 4d	The homage presents that John Dawe who held from the lord by custom of the manor one messuage with half a virgate of land at Hoccombe has died after whose death the lord will have one ox for heriot price 7s 6d. And 4 piglets for escheat price 4s 6d and 1 horse in the custody of the bailiff not yet appraised. On which the bailiff is charged on behalf of the lord that the aforesaid heriot and escheat … are sold …for the greater profit of the lord. And the tenements remain in the hands of his wife
Heriot 1 sheep 12d	And they say that Thomas Wyntur who held from the lord by custom of the manor one messuage and half a virgate of land in Haale on the day he died and the lord has for heriot 1 sheep price 12d. And they say that he has nothing for escheat. And the tenements remain in the hands of his wife until etc.
The next	Inquest ex officio at the suit of Robert Barker adjourned until the next [court]

amerced 2d — William Webbe (2d) put himself in mercy for a licence to agree with Thomas Jankys in a plea of trespass

the next — Still a day is given between Roger Hichecokes plaintiff and Richard Hethe defendant in a plea of broken agreement under the law

amerced 2d — John Hethe is in mercy for contempt because he withdrew from the court without licence

amerced 2d — Nicholas Rowlowe is in mercy for his unjust plea against Richard Hethe in a plea of debt

Fine 8s — Edith Coliar who previously surrendered into the hands of the lord one toft with half a virgate of land with appurtenances in Chesturtone called Waltones place etc. now came & took from the lord the aforesaid toft and land to hold from the lord for the term of her life and after her death that half of the said tenements should remain to Margery the daughter of the same Edith to hold to the said Margery and her [heirs] from the lord according to the custom of the manor. And the other half of the said tenements should remain to Emma daughter of the aforesaid Edith to hold from the lord to the same Emma and her [heirs] according to the custom of the manor. And thus it is said the tenements *should be held* for the steward to hold from the lord in the manner aforesaid. And she gives to the lord for a fine 8s and made fealty

12d — Emma Hoore made a fine with the lord for an inquiry of 12 ex officio to be held to enquire who is the closest heir of Roger Upintone and whether one messuage and one virgate of land the which was Adam Upintone's in Hultone was in the hands of the lord or not. And she gives for a fine 12d. On which the inquiry was held by the oath of Roger Richardes, Stephen Bradeneye, Nicholas Rowlowe, Roger Walton, Thomas Rugge, William Bruggende, John Barndeleye, Robert Hogge, Roger Kyngeslowe, Mathew Bullok, Roger Broke & William Gerbod etc. who seek a day until the next [court] thence to render the verdict

Still the plea between Walter Rugge plaintiff and Stephen Bradeney defendant in a plea of trespass adjourned

And between William Skirmour plaintiff and Elcok Mustardmon in a plea of … adjourned

And between Nicholas Rowlowe plaintiff and Richard Hichecokes defendant in a plea of debt adjourned by the prayer of the parties

Sum of this court 26s …
Also of the inquiry … …[Note: This may be crossed through]

1403 P314/W/1/1/226

Worefeld	Great court held there on Wednesday on the feast of St Mark the Evangelist in the fourth year of the reign of King Henry IV after the Conquest [25 April 1403]
Kyngeslowe & Stanlowe	townships there present nothing
Chesturtone amerced 10d	township there presents that Margaret Stevenes raised the hue and cry justly on William Rugge (6d) so the said William is in mercy. And that the same Margaret blocked one footpath in Chesturtoun unjustly so the said Margaret (4d) is in mercy
Hultone amerced 4d	township there presents that Margery the wife of William Gold broke into the pound of the lord so the said Margery (4d) is in mercy
Rowlowe, Bradeney, Asturhull, Ewyk & Soonde	townships there present nothing
Roughtone, Barndele, Hokkombe, Swancote	townships there present nothing
Burcote, Burcote, Ryndelford & Bromle	townships there present nothing
Alvescote, Wynescote,, Cattestre, Newtone	townships there present nothing
Stapelford	township there presents nothing
Akeltone amerced 10d	township there presents nothing but that Thomas Tresel (4d) forestalled Thomas Tumpkys & drew blood from him so the said Thomas (6d) is in mercy
Haalen	township there presents nothing
Ewdenas, Oldyntone	townships there present nothing
Wyke amerced 4s 2d strays 8d	township there presents that Richard Dureyate formerly the servant of Hamond Humele forestalled (4d) Thomas Heynes and drew blood (6d) from him so the said Richard is in mercy. And that Margery the wife of the aforesaid Thomas raised the hue and cry justly on the said Richard so the said Richard (6d) is in mercy. And they say that Joan Malcher (2d) hit Richard Hethe unjustly and drew blood (4d) from him so the said Joan is in mercy. And they say that Robert Taillour made homsoken (4d) on Matilda Ody. And that the same raised the hue and cry justly on the said Robert so the said Robert (4d) is in mercy. And they say that Robert Ryndelford (2d) hit Richard

1403 P314/W/1/1/226

Wyke [Contd.] amerced 4s 2d	Hethe & drew blood from him so the said Robert (6d) is in mercy. And they say that Richard the son of Richard Walkar broke into the pound of Thomas Heyne so the said Richard (4d) is in mercy. And they say that Agnes Heyne raised the hue and cry justly on Richard Dureyate so the said Richard (4d) is in mercy. And that Alice Baret (4d) raised the hue and cry unjustly on William Yngemon so the said Alice is in mercy.
strays 8d	And they say that in the hands of Thomas Heyne is 1 sheep coming as a stray at the feast of All Saints last past. Price for the sheep 8d
	[Note: there is no presentation from Worfield. Perhaps it was included in Wyke or Haalen]
The tasters of ale amerced 3s 2d	present that John Billyngesle (6d) brewed 3 , William Nore (2d) 1, William Yngemon (2d) 1, John Yate (4d) 2, Robert Smyth (2d) 1, John Smyth (8d) 4, Walter Rugge (2d) 1, William Lowe (2d) 1, Thomas Soonde (4d) 2, John atte Walle (2d) 1, Robert Ewdenas (2d) 1 & Thomas Merwalle (2d) 1,.And that all sold against [the assize] so each of them is in mercy
The 12 jurors amerced 10d	Inquest held by the oath of John Ewdenas, Roger Cattestre, Roger Richardes, Roger Waltone, Stephen Bradeneye, John Barndele, Robert Hogge, John Tumpkys, Roger atte Broke, Nicholas Rowlowe, William Barkar & William Newe who say on their oath that the townships aforesaid and the tasters of ale had well and faithfully presented and concealed nothing except that Thomas Hugges forestalled (4d) Richard Bulveis and drew blood from him which was adjourned until at this court so the said Thomas (6d) is in mercy
Appointment of the tasters of ale	William Gerbod and Richard Turbevyle tasters of ale withdrew from their office to which office John Robyns and Thomas atte Soonde entered
	Sum of this court 10s 10d
~~Fine 20d~~	~~Waryng Braye & Isabell his wife surrendered into the hands of thelord one cottage with curtilage in Haalen which John Huly formerly held to the use of Robert Tayllour and Alice his wife who came and took from the lord the said cottage and curtilage with appurtenances to hold from the lord to the same Robert and Alice and their [heirs] according to the custom of the manor by services thence due. And they give to the lord for a fine 20d and made fealty~~
Concerning	the proceedings of the small court at the place, day, and year above-stated etc.
The 12 jurors amerced 10d	Inquiry held for the lord by the oath of Roger Hichecokes, William Bruggende, Roger Gerbod, Roger Kyngeslowe, John Janne, Thomas Hugge, Thomas Rugge, Nicholas Stanlowe, John Hethe, Mathew Bullok, William Gerbod, Roger Matheus who say on their oath that William Ewyk (2d), Thomas Barbour (2d) chaplain, John Joneson (2d), John Haukys chaplain (2d), & William Billyngesle (2d) which suitors made default at this court to make their tenure so each of them is in mercy
held in the hand of the lord Heriot 1 ox price 8s 4d	And they say that at the death of Roger Bromley is held in the hand of the lord one message with half a virgate of land with a third part of one nook of land in lesser tenure in Bromle whereof the lord has 1 ox in the name of heriot being in the custody of the bailiff etc. price 8s 4d
	And they say that Isabell Swancote who held of the lord by custom of the manor 1

2 heriots, 1 ~~ox~~ cow & 1 steer price 11s. Escheats 4s 1 colt price 6d To enquire	messuage with one virgate of land in Swancote and one toft with one virgate of land in Bradeneye on the day she died at whose death the lord has 2 heriots namely one black cow with a white head price 7s and 1 young red steer price 4s and for escheat 1 pig with 4 piglets price 4s and 1male colt colour fallow in the custody of the bailiff not yet appraised but afterwards appraised at 6d and the tenements remain in the hand of the lord until. So it is ordered to the bailiff to make thence profit for the lord. On which came Thomas Swancote and claimed 1 messuage with 1 virgate of land in Swancote by virtue of a certain fine thence previously made whereof to enquire etc.
{	Richard Hethe is in mercy because he is not prosecuting against Roger Hichecokes in a plea of debt
amerced 4d {	The same Richard is in mercy because he is not prosecuting against the said Roger in a plea of trespass
The law	Nicholas Rowlowe still a plaintiff against Richard Hichecokes in a plea of debt etc. who seeks from the said Richard 6d which he unjustly detains etc. to his damage 6d. And the said Richard present here denies entirely and he has a day for the law with 6 hands in the next [court] by the pledge of Roger Hichecokes
amerced 2d	Walter Rugge is in mercy for his unjust plea against Stephen Bradene in a plea of trespass
amerced 4d to recover	William Skirmour plaintiff still the plaintiff against Elcok Mustardmon in a plea of trespass etc. And he says that the same Elcok unjustly at night fished in his weir to the damage of the said William 7s. And the same Elcok present recognised the trespass to the value of 20d etc. and the other part of the said trespass he sufficiently acknowledged and each of them is in mercy
amerced … [illegible] to recover	Emma Hoore plaintiff against William Skyrmour in a plea of trespass pledge for the prosecution Richard Bulveis. And she says that the same William unjustly against the peace beat and badly treated her to the damage of Emma herself 30s. The which William present seeks assessment etc. 2s 6d whereof he pays 2s. And the said William 2d is in mercy
pain	Sureties of William Skyrmour to keep the peace towards Emma Hoore and the people of the lord King under pain of 100s namely Thomas Hugges and Thomas Muychale
Fine 12d	John Huwessone made a fine with the lord for an inquiry of 12 ex officio to be desired to enquire of the right and manner of tenure of one land in Roughtoun called Horscroft is held. And he gives for a fine 12d. On which the inquiry was held by the oath of the inquisitors above charged for the lord etc.
Amerced 6d	Richard Hethe who had a day regarding the law against Roger Cattestre in a plea of broken agreement defaulted of the law. So it is judged that the same Roger should have his damages. And the said ~~William~~ Richard and his pledge are in mercy
to recover amerced 4d	The same Richard who had a day regarding the law against Roger Broke in a plea of broken agreement defaulted of the law. So it is judged that the same Roger should have his damages. And the same-Richard and his pledge are in mercy

amerced 2d

The same Richard who had a day at this court regarding the law against Roger Hichecokes in a plea of broken agreement defaulted of the law. So etc. And the said Richard is in mercy

[The Dorse. Several lines illegible at the top of the page]

Verdict

Which at the inquest pending… Robert Barkar and Robert Hatton now present … … bythe oath of the 24 that the same Robert…………….cottage formerly John … that Roger …. …whereof the cottage formerly Nicholas Webbe ……….

Increased rent 20s

To this court came Richard … and took from the lord full licence to fish …… waters of the lord within the manor of Worefeld to make weirs wherever he may be permitted in the name of the lord except from ponds and gates and the fisheries of the mills and … the lord and his ancestors… the tenants had in times past weirs… and fisheries in the said water to hold to the said Richard and his [heirs] from the date of this court until the end of six years next following and fully completed and rendering thence annually to the lord twenty shillings of good money at the feast of St Michael and the Annunciation of the Blessed Mary the Virgin divided into equal portions. And if it should happen the aforesaid rent in part or in full at any time aforesaid is to be in arrears that then the bailiff of the manor is well able to … the aforesaid rent and if there were arrears to be satisfied in full

~~Sum of the small court 27s 8d~~
~~…………….20s whereof charged 60s~~ for trespass …in this year

Fine 5s

Afterwards came William Towart & surrendered into the hand of the lord one messuage with one nook of land in Stapelford called Towardesplace to rehold the said messuage and land for the term of his life and Agnes his wife. And after the death of the said William and Agnes that the said messuage and land should remain with Thomas Richardes of Stapelford & Agnes his wife to hold to the same Thomas and Agnes his wife and their [heirs] from the lord according to the custom of the manor. And thus the said tenements are granted by the steward to hold from the lord in the manner aforesaid. And they give to the lord for a fine 5s and made fealty

Fine 6s 8d

William the son of Roger Swancote came and took from the lord one messuage and half a virgate of land with a third part of one nook of land in Bromleye being in the hand of the lord by the death of Roger Swancote to hold to the said William and his [heirs] according to the custom of the manor from the lord by services thence due. And he gives to the lord for a fine 6s 8d and made fealty

Fine 5s

John Holygreve came and took from the lord one messuage & one nook of land in Haalen the which Henry Doon held and which lie in the hand of the lord from the surrender of Margery the wife of the same John to hold from the lord to the said John and Margery and their [heirs] according to the custom of the manor by services and customs thence due. And they give to the lord for a fine 5s and made fealty

Increased rent 2s

To this court came Elcok Mustardmon and took from the lord one place in the water of the lord called Worw under the Hongynge Rocke of Soudeleye to make one weir for fishing to hold the said weir to the said Elcok and his [heirs] from the lord according to the custom of the manor rendering thence annually to the lord two shillings at the usual terms

1403 P314/W/1/1/226

At this court the bailiff is charged on behalf of the lord that he faithfully does his diligence to sell all heriots and escheats and strays in whatever way falling to the lord this year and by the 12 to appraise dearer for the greater profit of the lord under pain and peril which will be incumbent

Inquiry for the lord

~~…small court~~
~~44s~~
4d

Afterwards to this court came William Wermod son of Thomas Wermod and took from the lord one messuage, one toft, and five nooks of land with appurtenances in Haalen within the manor of Worfeld which formerly Robert Wermod chaplain held as a whole just as the aforesaid Robert held and which the aforesaid Robert sold to the aforesaid William for a certain sum of money and before his death surrendered into the hand of the lord to the use of the aforesaid William to hold from the lord this … to the said William and Joan his wife and their heirs according to the custom of the manor by services and customs which are thence due. And they give to the lord for a fine 26s 8d and for a certain promise for the said tenements formerly made to the lord by the aforesaid Robert, chaplain, the executors of the same Robert deceased owe to the lord for the reason of the same permission arising from the lands and tenements aforesaid and before the steward and the council of the lord in full court …(mot*) 40s. They made fealty to the lord and thus they are seized by the steward etc.

Fine £3 6s 8d

At this court all tenants of lesser tenure within the manor of Worfeld together willingly and of their own accord gave and yielded to the lord William de Bello Campo [William Beauchamp] to have his good lordship £6 13s 4d sterling to be paid in this form which follows - namely on the feast of St Michael the Archangel next in the future after the date of this court £22 4s 5d. And on the feast of St Michael the Archangel thence next following £22 4s 5d. And on the feast of St Michael the Archangel thence next following £22 4s 6d. And for these gifts the lord granted all his tenants aforesaid that they should have & hold all their lands and tenements which they now hold in peace from the beginning (origine)… [one word indistinct] until at this court without disturbance or expulsion by the lord and his council saving the rights … [one word indistinct] he permits. And that all the tenants mentioned should have and hold all their lands and tenements under the form of certain customs of the same tenancies made by the lord and his council and signed by the seal of the arms of the lord. And at the aforesaid payment well and faithfully at the feast aforesaid faithfully made the aforesaid tenants bind themselves and each of them in fealty to the lord, his heirs and executors for their lands and tenements and all their goods

Sum total of this court 111s
And for increased payment for fishing in Worff 22s whereof for trespass in the waters for the fifth year 11s
And of the fine for tenants etc. £66 13s 4d

Affeerors: Roger Cattestre, Roger Kyngeslowe

……………………

1404 P314/W/1/1/227

Worefeld	Small court held there on Thursday on 20th day of March in the fifth year of the reign of King Henry IV after the Conquest [20 March 1404]
The 12 jurors Heriot 1 ox and 2 cows 24s Escheat 1 sow 4 piglets and 3 small pigs 7s 6d	Inquiry held for the lord by the oath of Roger Richardes, William Ewyke, Stephen Bradeneye, Roger Waltone, Robert Hogge, William Bruggende, Thomas Rugge, Nicholas Roulowe, Mathew Bullok, Robert Barkar, Roger Kyngeslowe & Roger Broke who say on their oath that William Towart who held from the lord by the custom of the manor three messuages and three half virgates of land with appurtenances in Stapelford within the manor of Worfeld has died at whose death the lord has 3 heriots namely one ox and 2 cows price 24s. And for escheat 1 sow with 4 piglets & 3 small pigs price 7s 6d
Heriot 1 ox and 2 cows 21s Tenements in the hand of the lord	And they say that Agnes who was the wife of the aforesaid William Towart within a short time after the death of the same William her husband died seised of all lands and tenements aforesaid at whose death the lord will have3 heriots namely 1 ox & 2 cows appraised by the aforesaid inquiry at the value of 21s. Concerning which all heriots and escheats the reeve is charged to respond to the lord to the greater profit. And that concerning the aforesaid lands and tenements three nooks of land remain in the hand of the lord until
Heriot 1 cow, 1 year old calf & 2 sheep 12s. Escheat 20d. Tenements in the hand of the lord	And they say that Thomas Wermod who held of the lord by the custom of the manor one virgate of land in Haalen & one nook of land in Cattestre within the manor aforesaid on the day he died whereof the lord will have 3 heriots namely one cow price 6s 8d, one year old calf price 3s 4d and one sheep price 12d. And for escheat one horse price 20d concerning which heriots and escheats the bailiff is charged to respond to the greater profit to the lord. And concerning the aforesaid tenements there remains in the hand of the lord three nooks of land
Heriot 1 ox 10s Escheat 1 small pig 12d	And they say that Roger Hattone who held from the lord by the custom of the manor one message with one nook of land adjacent with appurtenances in Haalen within the manor aforesaid has died concerning whose death the lord will have one ox in the name of heriot price 9s. And for escheat one small pig price12d and of which heriot and escheat the bailiff is charged to respond to the greater profit to the lord. And the tenements remain in the hand of Agnes his wife until
Heriot & escheat nothing for the reason shown. Tenements in the hand of the lord	And they say that Roger Rowlowe of Burcote who held from the lord by the custom of the manor two messuages with one virgate of land adjacent in Burcote within the manor aforesaid has died whereof the lord will have nothing for heriot and escheat because the same Roger was a pauper and had nothing. And concerning the tenements aforesaid there remains in the hand of the lord 1 messuage and half a virgate of land
Heriots and escheats nothing Tenements in the hand of the lord	And they say that John Kyngessone who held of the lord by custom of the manor 2 messuages and six nooks of land with appurtenances in Roughtone within the manor aforesaid has died who had no goods nor chattels concerning whose death the lord has no heriot nor escheat. And the tenements remain in the hand of the lord

1404 P314/W/1/1/227

Heriot 1 cow 5s
Escheat 4 piglets 12d
Next Inquiry

And that Richard Turbeville of Hultone who held of the lord by the custom of the manor one messuage and three nooks of land with appurtenances in Hultone within the manor aforesaid has died whereof the lord will have in the name of heriot one cow price 5s and for escheat 4 piglets price 12d concerning which heriot and escheat the bailiff is charged to respond to the greater profit to the lord. And they say that there are bees the number of hives not known but thence they have a day to present the truth of the matter in the next [court]. And the tenement remains in the hand of Agnes his wife. And the said escheat of the bee hives is to be settled in the last court this year

Held in the hand of the lord
…

And they say that John Hethe surrendered into the hand of the lord one messuage with half a virgate of land in Kyngeslowe within the manor aforesaid to the use of John Guldene and Matilda the daughter of the same John Hethe. And thus the tenements remain in the hand of the lord

Held in the hand of the lord

And that Matilda the daughter of William Ewyk surrendered into the hand of the lord one messuage with half a virgate of land adjacent in Haalen within the manor aforesaid to the use of John Billyngesleye and Matilda his wife. And the tenements remain in the hand of the lord

Held for a fine to be made

And that Nicholas Stanlowe surrendered into the hand of the lord a quarter part of one nook of land in Stanlowe within the manor aforesaid to the use of John his eldest son after the death of the same Nicholas. And thus remains for a fine to be made until

Held in the hand of the lord

Still remaining in the hand of the lord one messuage with one virgate of land adjacent in Bradeneye within the aforesaid manor as is clear in the last court preceding

Fine 2s

To this court came Richard Bromleye and he made a fine with the lord for an inquiry to be held to enquire concerning his right which he has in one messuage with half a virgate of land adjacent in Bromle within the manor of Worfeld namely whether he has the better right for the term of his life in the said messuage and land now in his claim or William the son of Roger Swancote in his tenure etc. And he gives for a fine 2s. On which the inquiry was held by the oath of Roger Hichecokes, William Ewyk, Stephen Bradeney, Roger Waltone, Robert Hogge, William Bruggende, Thomas Rugge, Nicholas Rowlowe, Mathew Bullok, Robert Barker, Roger Kyngeslowe, Roger Broke, John Barndeley, Roger Hichecokes, John Janne, William Gerbod, Roger Matheus, Nicholas Stanlowe, Thomas Hugge, Roger Smyth, John atte Walle, Roger Gerbod, William Newe & William Billyngesleye who are judge and jury between the petitioner and tenant seek a day concerning the truth until the next. And it is granted to them

Recovered
Amerced 6d

Richard Hichecokes who has a day at this court concerning the law with 6 hands against Nicholas Rowlowe plaintiff in a plea of debt defaulted of the same law on which it is judged that the said Richard recompense the said complainant the debt ~~with damages~~ according which he demanded in the last court preceding. And nevertheless the said Richard (6d) and his pledge are in mercy

Fine 12d

Richard Hichecokes made a fine with the lord for an inquiry by 12 to be held to enquire whether he has the better right in one acre of land in Bromleyelyre within the manor of Worfeld in his claim or John Janne which said acre of land he holds in his tenure. And he gives for a fine ~~2s~~ 12d. On which the inquiry was held by the oath of Roger Richardes, William Ewyk, Roger Broke, John Barndeleye, Thomas Hugge, Mathew Bullok, Roger Gerbode, Robert Hogge, William Gerbod, William Barkar,

1404 P314/W/1/1/227

William Bruggende & Thomas Swancote who are sworn and tried between the parties aforesaid have a day to render thence concerning the verdict until the next [court].

Inquiry of the office at the suit of Emma Hoore adjourned to the next [court]

The next

Still 9 pleas of land adjourned until the coming of the council of the lord

Adjourned

Fine 12d — Robert Haukys made a fine for an overview of old court rolls of the lord. And he gives for a fine 12d

Affeerors: Roger Richardes, William Ewyk
Sum of this court £4 5s 8d

~~Thence with respect to 12d for a fine of Robert Haukys~~ paid for auditor ~~because he alleged that the said …[illegible] received profit concerning this payment for the scrutiny of the rolls~~

Expenses of the clerk of the court of the lord being there with 1 horse for one day 12d

Held in the hand of the lord — The bailiff presents that John Oldyntone surrendered into the hand of the lord four acres of arable land in the field of Hultone within the manor of Worfeld to the use of Roger Smyth and Alice his wife. And thus remains in the hand of the lord

1404 P314/W/1/1/228

Worefeld	Great court held there on Tuesday on 15th day of April in the fifth year of the reign of King Henry IV after the Conquest [15 April 1404]
The 12 jurors	John Ewdenas John Tumpkys Roger Broke Roger Cattestre John Hethe William Bruggende William Ewyk John Barndeleye Thomas Rugge Roger Waltoun Robert Hogge William Barker
Kyngeslowe Stanlowe stray still remaining	townships there present 1 black heifer coming as a stray at the Feast of the Purification of the Blessed Mary last past which remains in the custody of the reeve
Chestertone amerced 22d Waifs 1 horse 2s	township there presents that Thomas Coliar who should have appeared at this court to make the tenancy did not appear so the said Thomas (4d) is in mercy. And they say that there is there 1 horse coming as a waif price of the horse 2s whereof the reeve is charged to respond to the lord to the greater profit. And they say that Margaret Tresele broke into the pound of John Regnald three [times] so the same Margaret (18d) is in mercy
Hultone amerced 2s 6d stray remains	township there presents that Margaret Tresele broke into the pound of William Bruggende so the said Margaret (6d) is in mercy. And they say that Alice the wife of William Gold forestalled Agnes Polhous so the said Alice (12d) is in mercy. And that the same Agnes raised the hue and cry by mouth on the said Alice justly so the same Alice (12d) is in mercy. And they say that there is there 1 black heifer coming as a stray now in the last week past which remains in the custody of the reeve
Rowlowe, Bradeney, ASterhull, Ewyk, Soonde amerced 4d	townships there present that Thomas Nicoles who should have appeared at this court to make the tenancy did not appear so the said Thomas (4d) is in mercy
Roughtone, Barndele, Hokkombe, Swancote amerced 2s 8d	townships there present that Thomas Barbour chaplain (4d) & Thomas Forster (4d) who should have appeared at this court to make the tenancy did not appear so each of them is in mercy. And they say that William Broke forestalled William Kyngessone so the said William (12d) is in mercy. And that Edith the wife of the same William Kyngesson raised the hue and cry by mouth on the same William Broke justly so the said William (12d) is in mercy
Burcote, Burcote, Rundelford, Bromley amerced 2s 8d	townships there present that Richard Hethe (4d) & Thomas Brynketoun (4d) who should have appeared at this court to make the tenancy did not appear so each of them is in mercy. And they say that William Kyngesson forestalled (12d) Roger Broke and drew blood from him the said Roger so the said William (12d) is in mercy. And that Robert Galian forestalled John Rogers so the said Robert (12d) is in mercy
Alvescote, Wynescote, Cattestre, Newtone amerced 4d	townships there present that Richard Hethe who should have appeared at this court to make the tenancy did not appear so the said Richard (4d) is in mercy.

Stapelford	township there presents nothing
Ewdenas & Oldyntone townships amerced 4d	townships there present that Thomas Yngemon who should have appeared at this court to make the tenancy did not appear so the same Thomas (4d) is in mercy
Akeltone amerced 9s 8d strays 1 sow with 4 piglets 1s & 1 swarm 18d	township there presents that Roger Dalyleye forestalled Agnes the daughter of Nicholas Newtoun so the said Roger (4d) is in mercy. And that the same Agnes raised the hue and cry by mouth on the said Roger justly so the said Roger (6d) is in mercy. And that the same Roger forestalled Thomas the son of John Tumpkys so the said Roger (12d) is in mercy. And they say that the same Thomas drew the blood of the said Roger Dalyley so the said Thomas (12d) is in mercy. And that Alice the wife of John Tumpkys raised the hue and cry by mouth on the said Roger justly so the said Roger (12d) is in mercy. And that William Cooke broke the pound of John Tumkys so the said William (6d) is in mercy. And that the same William Cooke made homsoken on the said John Tumkys so the same William (8d) is in mercy. And that John Nycoles broke the pound of Roger Dalileye so the said John (8d) is in mercy. And they present that 1 young sow came as a stray now at the feast of Easter last past with 4 piglets of the issue of the same sow which and which remain in the custody of the reeve etc. And they say that Roger Dalileye forestalled Nicholas Newtoun so the said Roger (12d) is in mercy. And that John Dalileye forestalled (12d) Thomas Tumpkys and they say that John Dalileye (12d) forestalled Thomas Tumpkys and drew (12d) blood from the same Thomas so the said John is in mercy. And that Thomas Tumpkys forestalled Roger Dalileye so the said Thomas (12d) is in mercy. And they say that there is in the custody of Roger Dalileye 1 swarm of bees coming as a stray price 6d. And the aforesaid sow with piglets is appraised by the township at 12d
Wyke amerced 12s 10d	township there presents that William Cartar who should have appeared at this court to make the tenancy did not appear so the said William (4d) is in mercy. And they say that William Yngemon forestalled (12d) John Smyth & drew blood (12d) from the same John so the said William is in mercy. And they say that William Cartar made homesoken on Thomas Cowpar so the said William (8d) is in mercy. And they say that Alice Baret (12d) raised the hue and cry by mouth twice on William Yngemon (12d) whereof once justly and the other unjustly so both of them are in mercy. And that John Henene (12d) forestalled John Smythesson and drew blood (12d) so the said John Henene is in mercy. And that Thomas Smythesson drew the blood of the aforesaid John Henene so the said Thomas (12d) is in mercy. And they say that William Yngemon broke the pound of John the son of Robert Smyth so the said William (6d) is in mercy. And they say that Agnes the wife of John Smyth forestalled (8d) Alice the servant of the vicar of the church of Worfield and drew blood (8d) from the same Alice so the said Agnes is in mercy. And they say that the same Alice justly raised the hue and cry by mouth on the same Agnes so the same Agnes (12d) is in mercy
Haalen anerced 4d	township there presents that William Noore forestalled Robert Taillour so the said William (4d) is in mercy
Worefeld amerced 7s 8d	township there presents that John Ryes (4d) & William Mulwart (4d) who should have appeared at this court to make the tenancy did not appear so each of them are in mercy. And they present that John Henene (12d) forestalled John Smyth and drew blood (12d) from him and also unjustly raised the hue and cry on the same John Smyth so the said John Henene (12d) is in mercy. And they say that William Henene

(12d) forestalled Alice the wife of William Skyrmour and from her drew blood so the said William Henene (12d) is in mercy. Also they present that William Skyrmour (12d) forestalled William Henene and drew blood from him (12d) so the said William Skyrmour is in mercy

The tasters of ale present that Thomas Rowlowe brewed 1 (6d), Robert Taillour 8 (4s), William Lowe 1 (6d), Richard Bulveise 11 (5s 6d), William Hustar 2 (12d), John Ewdenas (12d) 2, William Bruggende 4 (2s), John Rowlowe 2 (12d), William Wermod 7 (3s 6d), Roger Dalleye 2 (12d), John Wilot 1 (6d), the son of Roger Gold 1 (6d), Robert Smyth 2 (12d), Alice Baret 1 (6d),, John Billyngesleye 8 (4s), Elena Taillour 2 (12d), William Skyrmour 2 (12d), John Smyth 4 (2s), Thomas Gold 4 (2s), Thomas Burcote 1 (6d), William Ewyke 2 (12d), William Mullwart 3 (18d), Edith Coliar 1 (6d), William Wilot 1 (6d), John Yate 1 (6d), John Aleyne 1 (6d), Alice Ferour 1 (6d), Henry Barkar 1 (6d), Nicholas Herdemon 1 (6d), William Cartar 1 (6d), Symon Taillour 1 (6d), John Bradeneye 1 (6d), John Baret 1 (6d), Thomas Hugge 1 (6d), Thomas Hugge 1 (6d), Walter Rugge 1 (6d), Robert Barkar 1 (6d), John Bromleye 1 (6d) & Robert Ewdenas 1 (6d), and that all sold against the assize and used illegal measures so each of them is in mercy

amerced 63s 6d

amerced 12d

Roger Dalileye plaintiff appeared against the township of Akeltoun concerning an unjust presentation. And he says they when they presented that Thomas Tumpkys drew blood from Roger himself etc. and that the same Roger forestalled Thomas himself which is unjust to the damage of Roger himself etc. and the aforesaid township present say that the presentation there was just and not unjust and here puts itself on a great inquiry and also the same Roger plaintiff similarly etc. On which the 12 jurors thence charged say on their oath that the township aforesaid of Akeltone well and truthfully presented so the said Roger (12d) is in mercy for his unjust plea

The 12 jurors present that the townships aforesaid and the tasters of ale have well and faithfully presented except that they say that John Englich forestalled (12d) Thomas Jankys and drew blood (12d) from him so the said John is in mercy. And that the township of Wyke concealed this so the said township (12d) is in mercy. And they say that John Nicoles broke into the pound of Roger Dalileye not affeered here because affeered above so the said township (12d) is in mercy. And they say that the said John Englich raised the hue and cry unjustly on Thomas Jankyis so the said John (12d) is in mercy

amerced 4s

Recovery amerced 6d

John Smyth plaintiff appeared against William Yngemon in a plea of debt pledge for the prosecution William Bruggende etc. who seeks from the said William 5s he owes him for various trespasses on him there by William himself etc. And the said William present recognises the said debt of 5s to him. On which it is ordered the bailiff raise the said debt from the goods and chattels from the same William to the use of the aforesaid John to pay before the next [court] and the said William is in mercy

distrain

William Skyrmour plaintiff against William Henene in a plea of trespass pledge for the prosecution John Yate who is not attached nor summoned so let it be done

a day the next

Margaret Dodemastoun plaintiff against Robert Yngemon in a plea of debt pledge for the prosecution the reeve who have a day until the next

distrain

Robert Yngemon plaintiff against Thomas Heyne in a plea of debt pledge for the prosecutionThomas Jankys so it is ordered to the bailiff to distrain the same Thomas that he is at the next to respond to the aforesaid Robert in the plea aforesaid amerced 4d — Richard Knokyn is in mercy because he is not prosecuting against Emmoter Hore in a plea of debt

distrain — John Darras plaintiff against Richard Lyones chaplain in a plea of debt pledge for the prosecution Richard Bulveys who is summoned did not come so distrain

amerced 4d

distrain — William Huggeford chivaler [knight] plaintiff against William Mulwart in a plea of debt pledge for the prosecution Richard Bulveys who is attached by 1 horse did not come. So the said William Mulwart (4d) is in mercy. And it is ordered to the bailiff that he is better distrained for the next [court]

Concerning the proceedings of the small court held on the place, day, and year above stated

Fine 13s 4d — Thomas Richardes and Agnes his wife daughter and heir of William Towartes deceased, came and took from the lord one messuage with half of one messuage and three nooks of land with appurtenances in Stapelford within the manor of Worfeld which fell into the hands of the lord after the death of the aforesaid William Towartes and Agnes his wife deceased as is clear in the last small court preceding to hold to the said Thomas and Agnes and their heirs from the said heir from the lord according to the custom of the manor by services and customs thence due and accustomed. And they give to the lord for ingress thence to have 13s 4d. And made fealty. And thus they are seized

Fine 20s — William Kyngessone son and heir of John Kyngessone deceased came and took from the lord 2 messuages and 6 nooks of land with appurtenances in Roughtone within the manor aforesaid which fell into the hands of the lord after the death of the aforesaid John Kyngessone deceased to hold to the same William and his [heirs] from the lord according to the custom of the manor by services and customs thence due and accustomed. And he gives to the lord for ingress thence to have 20s. And he made fealty to the lord and is seized

Look behind on the back
King Henry IV 5th [year]
[The Dorse]
[Top of the document is very faint and difficult to read]

Fine 20s — John Billyngesleye & Matilda his wife came and took from the lord one messuage with half a virgate of land adjacent in Haalen within the manor of Worefeld with appurtenances which Matilda the daughter of William Ewyke surrendered into the hands of the lord to the use of John & Matilda his wife as is clear in the last court preceding to hold to the said John & Matilda … … from the lord according to the custom of the manor by services and customs thence due and …they give to the lord for a fine …[20s] And made fealty to the lord

Fine 14s — William Wermod son and heir of Thomas Wermod deceased came and took from the lord one toft & three nooks of land with appurtenances in Haalen within the manor aforesaid which tenement is called Cattestrelond and fell into the hands of the lord after the death of the aforesaid Thomas Wermod as is clear in the last court preceding to hold to the said William and his heirs from the lord according to the custom of the manor by services and customs thence due. And he gives to the lord for ingress thence to have 14 shillings. And he made fealty to the lord and thence had seisin etc. On this it was found by examination and inspection of the court rolls & … …the said William

Tenement in the hands of the lord

that …[after] the death of the aforesaid Thomas his father there should have fallen into the hands of the lord half of one nook of land within the manor aforesaid for which half nook of land for which it is still not possible to find that a fine was thence made and … … and he does not wish to make. So the said half nook of land still remains in the hands of the lord afterwards thence to make a fine … …

Fine 20s

John Rowlowe came and took from the lord one messuage with half a virgate of land adjacent with appurtenances in Haalen within the manor aforesaid which John Haukys chaplain and John his son surrendered into the hands of the lord to the use of the aforesaid John Rowlowe as is clear in the last small court preceding to hold to the said John Rowlowe and Joan his wife and to their heirs from the lord according to the custom of the manor by services and customs thence due and accustomed. And he gives to the lord for ingress thence to have 20s. And he made fealty to the lord. Furthermore it is granted to the same John Rowlowe by the council of the lord that when John the son of John Haukys clerk aforesaid reaches to his full age, he will make to the said John Rowlowe full title of the aforesaid lands and tenements under the same fine

Fine 13s 4d

Thomas Swancote came and took from the lord one messuage with one virgate of land adjacent with appurtenances in Bradeneye within the manor aforesaid which tenements remain in the hands of the lord as is clear in the last small court preceding to hold to the said Thomas, Margery his wife and their heirs from the lord according to the custom of the manor by services and customs thence due and accustomed. And they give to the lord for a fine 13s 4d. And they made fealty to the lord and are seized

Fine 5s

Roger Smyth came and took from the lord four acres of land lying in the fields of Hultone within the manor aforesaid which acres of land John Oldyntoun surrendered into the hands of the lord to the use of the said Roger as is clear in the last small court preceding. Of which acres indeed aforesaid one lies at Lynlond in Stretfordfeld, the second acre lies in Dadymersch in Middelfeld the third acre lies in Fulfordesfeld on Whetforlonges and the fourth acre contains in itself 2 seliones of which one lies extending from Steveneshorles until Endemeredale & the other selion of land by itself lies at the Slo in Middelfeld to hold the said land to himself and Alice his wife and their heirs from the lord according to the custom of the manor by services and customs thence due. And he gives to the lord for a fine 5s and made fealty to the lord

Fine 13s 4d

William Wermod & Joan his wife confessed & examined according to the custom of the manor surrendered into the hands of the lord one toft with land called Chaumburleyneslond in Haalen within the manor aforesaid & half a virgate of land called Massieslond in the same Haalen at the end of the toft of the same land and all the meadow of the same half virgate of land wholly excepted. And also surrendered into the hands of the lord three parcels of meadow of which one parcel lies at the end of the meadow called Hememedewe, a second parcel of meadow lies in Hamondesmedewe & a third parcel of meadow lies at the end of the meadow called Bromleysemedewe to the use of Henry Barker & Margery his wife the which Henry and Margery came and took from the lord the aforesaid toft & half a virgate of land & three parcels of meadow except for the exceptions to hold to the said Henry and Margery and their heirs from the lord according to the custom of the manor by services and customs thence due and accustomed. And they give to the lord of a fine for ingress thence to have 13s 4d. And they made fealty to the lord

John Stanlowe came and took from the lord a quarter part of one messuage with a quarter part of one nook of land with appurtenances in Stanlowe within the manor

1404 P314/W/1/1/228

aforesaid which tenements Nicholas Stanlowe father of the same John surrendered into the hands of the lord as is clear in the last small court preceding etc. under such form that the same Nicholas will hold the said tenements for the whole term of his life
Fine 3s 4d from the lord according to the custom of the manor. And after the decease of the same Nicholas that the aforesaid quarter part of the messuage and nook of land remains with the aforesaid John to hold to himself and his heirs from the lord according to the
amerced 6d custom of the manor by services and customs thence due. And thus the said tenements are granted by the steward. And to the lord for a fine 3s 4d. And he made fealty to the lord

William Walker (6d) put himself in mercy for a licence to agree with a certain stranger
pain woman whose name is not known in a plea of debt by the pledge of the reeve

Sureties of Roger Dalileye for the keeping of the peace towards John Tumpkys & the
pain people of the lord King under a pain of £10 namely John Hethe, William Bruggende, William Gerbod, Henry Barker

pain Sureties of William Yngemon for the keeping of the peace towards Thomas Heyne & the people of the lord King under a pain of £10 namely Robert Ewdenas, Robert Yngmon, Robert Dalleye & John atte Walle

Sureties of Thomas Heyne for the keeping of the peace towards William Yngemon each under £10 namely Roger Matheus, Roger Smyth, William Webbe & Richard Bulveys

Thomas the son and heir of Roger Rowlowe came & took from the lord one messuage with half of one virgate of land with appurtenances in Burcote which fell into the hands of the lord after the death of the aforesaid Roger as is clear in the last court preceding thus held on Thurdsay 20th March last past to hold the said messuage and
Fine 13s 4d land to the said Thomas and his heirs from the lord according to the custom of the manor by services and customs thence due. And they give to the lord for a fine 13s 4d

Sum of this court £11 11s 6d price of 2 strays above named and the price of 13s 4d for a fine of John Gilden until it was tried in the court of the lord etc.

Concerning the expenses of the steward nothing here because in one bill under the seal of Sir John Prat and because in the same ?suit?

1404 P314/W/1/1/229

Worefeld — Small court held there on Monday on the last day of June in the fifth year of the reign of King Henry IV after the Conquest [30 June 1404]

Essoins — Thomas Rowlowe, Richard Bromle, John Ryes, Roger Batemon & William Jones essoined of common [suit] by the reeve

Amerced 4d, distrain — William Skyrmor plaintiff against William Henene in a plea of trespass who attached & charged did not come. So the said William Henene (4d) is in mercy. And it is ordered to the bailiff to distrain him better that he is at the next [court] to respond to the aforesaid William Skyrmour in the plea aforesaid

Amerced 3d — Robert Yngemon (3d) put himself in mercy for a licence to agree with Margaret Dodemostone in a plea of debt

Amerced 4d, distrain — Robert Yngemon plaintiff against Thomas Heyne in a plea of debt the which Thomas attached & charged did not come. So the same Thomas (4d) is in mercy. And it is ordered to the bailiff to distrain him better that he is at the next [court] to respond to the aforesaid Robert in the plea aforesaid

Amerced 3d — Richard Liones clerk(3d) put himself in mercy for a licence to agree with John Darras plaintiff in a plea of debt

Amerced 3d — William Huggeford chivaler plaintiff & William Mulwart defendant in a plea of debt for a licence to agree. And the said William Mulwart (3d) put himself in mercy

A day the next — John Regnald plaintiff appeared against Margaret Tresele in a plea of trespass pledge for the prosecution Thomas Jankys who have a day to agree until the next [court] by the prayer of the parties

Amerced 3d — William Mulwart (3d) put himself in mercy for a licence to agree with William Skyrmor in a plea of debt etc.

Amerced 2d — William Hustar (2d) is in mercy because he is not prosecuting against John Smyth and John his son in a plea of trespass etc.

Amerced 2d

Amerced 2d — William Lowe (2d) is in mercy because he is not prosecuting against Richard Liones clerk and Joan his servant in a plea of trespass

Recovery, Amerced 2d — William Skyrmor plaintiff against Emmota Hoore in a plea of debt. Pledge for the prosecution John Bromle the which William seeks from the said Emmota 1 bushel of malt he handed over out of a loan etc. And the said Emmota present acknowledges the said debt. So the same Emmota (2d) is in mercy

Amerced 6d — Alice (6d) the daughter of Robert Stevenes is in mercy because she is not prosecuting against Margery Stevenes in a plea of land

the 12 jurors, Amerced 12d — Inquiry held for the lord by the oath of William Ewyk, Roger Kyngeslowe, Roger Richardes, Stephen Bradeneye, Roger Broke, John atte Walle, Roger Waltone, John Rowlowe, William Gerbod, William Bruggende, Thomas Swancote & Robert Hogge who say on their oath that John Hethe (2d), John Morfeld (2d) clerk, John Huwessone (2d), Thomas Barbour (2d) clerk, Thomas Forster (2d) & Thomas Brynketone (2d), who made default of suit at this court to make the tenure so each of them is in mercy

1404 P314/W/1/1/229

remaining not affeered	And they say that Roger Matheus married Alice his daughter } to John Smyth within the manor a licence from the court of the }continuing until lord not obtained }the will of the And that Robert Barkar married Matilda his daughter } council of the lord within the manor a licence from the court of the lord not obtained } is thence known
The Verdict	Which at the inquiry of the 12 ex officio pending at the suit of Emmote Hoore now it is presented by the oath of the inquiry thence previously held that Agnes Upyntone was the closest heir of Roger Upyntone. And that there are no tenements remaining in the hands of the lord
Fine 12d The next	Margaret Tresele made a fine with the lord for an inquiry by 12 ex officio to be held to enquire if he has a common way with horse and cart in the meadow called Goosemedewe under the castle in Chestertone or not. And he gives to the lord for a fine 12d. On which the inquiry was held by the oath of William Ewyk, Roger Kyngeslowe, Roger Richardes, Roger Waltone, John Rowlowe, William Gerbod, William Bruggende, Stephen Bradeneye, Roger Broke, Thomas Swancote, William Barkar, & Robert Hogge
Fine 12d The next	Roger Cattestre & William Barkar made a fine with the lord for an inquiry by 12 ex officio to be held to enquire if Richard Hethe justly by custom was able to sell to John Smyth two cottages in Worefeld or not which cottages Alice Rugge formerly held. And if the sale of the said cottages was made to John Smyth as demised in default of the said Richard Hethe or the said John Smyth which suit was made by the name of John Bradeneye by the oath of Roger Richardes, Nicholas Rowlowe, Stephen Bradeneye, John Barndeleye, Thomas Rugge, John Janne, Thomas Swancote, Roger Gerbod, Roger Kyngeslowe, William Gerbod, Mathew Bullok & John Rowlowe who seek a day to render their verdict thence until the next [court]
Fine 12d The next	Emmota Hore plaintiff against Thomas Hugge in a plea of land. Pledge for the prosecution Richard Bulveys. The which Emmoter seeks from the said Thomas one messuage with one virgate of land adjacent in Hultone as his right and she says that the same Thomas unjustly holds the said messuage and land and withheld it from her. And the aforesaid Thomas present in court says that the aforesaid Emmoter does not have the right in the land and tenements aforesaid and that the holds he same tenements & land as of his right and that he has full right in the same and thence he puts himself on an inquiry. And the aforesaid Emmoter similarly who made a fine for an inquiry of 12. And they give for a fine 12d. On which the inquiry was held by the oath of Henry Barkar, John Rowlowe, Roger Waltone, John Barndeleye, Stephen Bradeneye, William Bruggende, William Gerbod, Roger Kyngeslowe, Roger Broke, Roger Matheus, John Janne, & William Newe who are to judge and try between the parties aforesaid seek a day for the verdict thence to render until the next [court] and by the will of the parties it is granted to them
Amerced 4d	John atte Walle (4d) is in mercy because he withdrew from court without licence
Fine 2s	The bailiff is charged here concerning 2s of a certain fine John Rowlowe made for the inspection of old court rolls of the lord namely to see and know how John Haukes chaplain was seised of a certain tenement in Haalen for which end the said rolls were scrutinised at the request of the said John Rowlowe on Monday in the week of Pentecost last past

1404 P314/W/1/1/229

Is not prosecuting
Is not affeered because a fine to be paid

Who at the inquiry by 12 pending between Richard Hichecokes petitioner and John Janne tenant in a plea of land to be settled until another fine will thence have been made and that the said Richard seeking against the said John, tenant, is not prosecuting in the plea aforesaid

Affeered Roger Waltone, William Ewykes
Sum of this court 9s ~~Thence adjourned 2s~~ settlement about to be heard ~~for the fine of John Rowlowe because he alleges that the lord received the profit of this fine nevertheless~~
In expenses of the clerk of the court being there with one horse for one day for the reason of holding this court 6d

1404 P314/W/1/1/230

Court	Small held at Worefeld on Friday on the feast of St James the Apostle in the fifth year of the reign of King Henry IV after the conquest [25 July1404]
Amerced 9d	Richard Bromley (3d), John Ryes (3d), Roger Batemon (3d) did not come to warrant their essoins so each of them is in mercy
The 12 jurors Amerced 8d	Inquiry held for the lord by the oath of William Ewyk, Roger Kyngeslowe, Roger Richardes, Roger Waltone, John Rowlowe, William Gerbod, Stephen Bradeneye, Roger Broke, John atte Walle, Thomas Swancote, William Barkar, & Robert Hogge who say on their oath that Thomas Barbour (2d) clerk, Thomas Forster (2d), Richard Bromle (2d) & Richard Hethe (2d), who are bound to make suit at this court made default so each of them is in mercy
 Heriot 1 cow 6s 8d tenements in the hand of the lord The next. Inquiry	And they say that John Hulle surrendered into the hand of the lord two messuages and six nooks of land with appurtenances in Roghtone within the manor of Worfeld to re-hold the said tenements for the term of his life and for the term of the life of Joan his wife according to custom. And after their deaths that the said tenements remain to Roger the son of the aforesaid John and his [heirs]. And thus the aforesaid tenements remain in the hand of the lord for a fine to be made. On which they say that the said John Hulle died from whose death the lord has one cow in the name of heriot price 6s 8d of which cow the reeve is charged to respond to the greater profit of the lord. And of escheat they seek a day to enquire what there was until the next. And they have a day in the hope of greater profit. And the tenements still remain in the hand of the lord as above
   Heriot 1 ox 9s Escheat 5s	And they say that Thomas Nelde who held of the lord by the custom of the manor one messuage & half a virgate of land with half of one nook of land with appurtenances in Haalen within the manor aforesaid on the day he died after whose death the lord has in the name of heriot one black ox price 9s. And for escheat 1 sow with 7 piglets suckling of the issue of the same with 1 small sow which escheat is appraised by the oath of the inquiry aforesaid at 5s concerning which heriot and escheat the reeve is charged to respond to the greater profit of the lord. And the tenements still remain in the hand of Petronilla who was his wife by their custom
Inquiry	And concerning the death of Richard Walker they have a day until the next [court] to enquire if any profits fall due to the lord or not etc.
  Fine 12d Verdict	12d is given to the lord for a fine for an inquiry by the 12 ex officio to be held for William Nore to enquire if that cottage which Thomas Nelde surrendered at Waltone in Worfeld was rightly surrendered or not by their custom etc. On which the inquiry was held by the oath of William Ewyk, Roger Kyngeslowe, Roger Richardes, Roger Waltone, John Rowlowe, William Gerbod, Stephen Bradeneye, Roger Broke, John atte Walle, Thomas Swancote, William Barkar, & Robert Hogge who say on their oath that Thomas Nelde above-named justly surrendered the aforesaid cottage by their custom
	Richard Hichecokes who is not prosecuting against John Janne in a plea of land as is clear in the last small court came here again & the plaintiff appeared against the said John in a plea of land and made a fine with the lord for an inquiry of the 12 to be held. And he gives for a fine 12d. On which on behalf of the lord it is ordered to the bailiff that he makes to come before the next [court] the inquiry of 12 thence previously held under oath and between the parties to judge as is clear in the last but one court

preceding to do that on behalf of the lord to them (eis) … [the word has 6 minims followed by getur with an extension over the middle part] between the parties aforesaid

Held in the hand of the lord

Richard Hichecokes came here and surrendered into the hand of the lord one cottage with curtilage adjacent with appurtenances in Soonde within the manor of Worfeld to the use of William Newtone chaplain. And thus it remains in the hand of the lord until

Held in the hand of the lord

William Gold came here and surrendered into the hand of the lord one cottage with curtilage adjacent called Lakehous and one small parcel of meadow also lying in Hultone within the manor of Worfeld & nine selions of land lying in the three common fields of Hultone and also one parcel of meadow called Bylade in Hultone the same parcel of meadow John atte Walle formerly held all of which tenements the same William Gold as it is said above surrendered into the hand of the lord to the use of John Coletes and Isabell his wife and the heirs of their bodies legitimately issuing. And if it should happen that the said John and Isabell die without legitimate heirs of their bodies then all the same tenements with their appurtenances to the aforesaid William and his rightful heirs they are fully reverted etc. And thus the aforesaid tenements remain in the hand of the lord

Held in the hand of the lord

William Gold above-named surrendered into the hand of the lord one meadow called Waturlade in the field of Hultone next to Pailbrok to re-hold the said meadow for the term of his life according to the custom of the manor from the lord. And after the death of the said William that the said meadow remains to John Coletes and Isabell his wife and the heirs of their bodies legitimately issuing etc. And if it should happen that the said John and Isabell die without legitimate heirs of their bodies issuing then the whole of the aforesaid meadow should remain to the rightful heirs of the aforesaid William. And thus the said meadow remains in the hand of the lord

Land in the hand of the lord

John Bradeneye surrendered there into the hand of the lord three acres of land lying in the common field of Hultone to the use of John Coletes and Isabell his wife. And thus they remain in the hand of the lord until

Fine 4d

Thomas Brynketone gives to the lord 4d concerning a fine for suit of court to be commuted from the date of this court until the feast of St Michael next in the future. Pledge for the fine John Robynes

Amerced 6d {

William Skyrmor (2d) is in mercy because he is not prosecuting against William Henene in a plea of trespass etc.

Robert Yngemon (2d) put himself in mercy for a licence to agree with Thomas Heyne plaintiff in a plea of debt

Emmota Hore (2d) is in mercy because she is not prosecuting against Thomas Hugge in a plea of trespass by the pledge of Thomas Jankys

Amerced 4d
Distrain

John Regnald still plaintiff against Margaret Tresele in a plea of trespass who is attached by the pledge of Thomas Jankys did not come so the said Margaret is in mercy. Further it is ordered to the bailiff to better distrain her before the next [court]

Is not prosecuting
Not affeered because fine paid

Where at the inquiry by 12 ex officio pending at the suit of Margaret Tresele now the same Margaret is not prosecuting etc. which inquiry of the matters was adjourned in the last small court preceding

1404 P314/W/1/1/230

The next	Where at the inquiry by 12 pending at the suit of Roger Cattestre & William Barkar adjourned until the next [court]
Distrain	William Holygreve plaintiff appeared against Emmota Hore in a plea of trespass pledge for the prosecution Thomas Jankys who is not attached nor charged so let it be done
Amerced 2d Distrain	Thomas Jankys plaintiff against William Baret & Alice his wife in a plea of debt who are attached by one bowl and 1 plate did not come so the said William & Alice are in mercy & it is ordered to the bailiff to better distrain the said William and Alice to the next [court]
Recovery Amerced 2d	William Newtone chaplain plaintiff against Thomas Jankys in a plea of debt pledge for the prosecution John Nelde who seeks from the said Thomas 13s 4d in money which he received from the same William from a loan etc. And the said Thomas present recognises the said debt etc. So the same Thomas (2d) is in mercy
Recovery Amerced 2d	The same William Newtone chaplain plaintiff appeared against Roger Cattestre in a plea of debt. And he says that he lent the same Roger 13s 4d in money to be repaid to him at a certain place and day between them fixed this present year at which place and day although it was very frequently requested the said debt was not paid to him nor still but he detains to the damage of William. And the aforesaid Roger present in court recognises the said debt so the said Roger (2d) is in mercy
Recovery Amerced 2d	William Newtone chaplain plaintiff against Thomas Swancote in a plea of debt. And he says that the same Thomas received from him 13s 4d in money in a loan to be repaid by him at a certain place and day in the past this year at which place and day the said debt was not paid although frequently requested nor still but he detains to the damage of the said William. And the aforesaid Thomas present in court recognises the said debt etc. On which it is judged that the said debt to the aforesaid plaintiff is paid. And the said Thomas (2d) is in mercy

Afeerors: Nicholas Rowlowe, William Ewykes

Sum of this small court 25s 11d

In expenses of the clerk of the court being at the house of the reeve there with one horse to eat 4d

1404 P314/W/1/1/231

Court Small held at Worefeld on Tuesday next after the feast of St Mathew the Apostle in the fifth year of the reign of King Henry IV after the conquest [23 September 1404]

Essoins Richard Bromley, Thomas Merwalle, Roger Batemon, William Palhogges, William Wermod & John Munsterleye essoined themselves from common [suit] by the reeve Thomas Jankys

John Regnald (2d) is in mercy because he is not prosecuting against Margaret Tresel in a plea of trespass

Amerced 4d Emmota Hoore (2d) attached and charged is in mercy for a default against William Holygreve in a plea of trespass. And it is ordered to the bailiff that he better distrain

distrain the aforesaid Emmota that she is at the next [court] to respond to the aforesaid William in the plea aforesaid

William Baret & Alice his wife who are attached by one kitchen (culina) to respond to

Amerced 2d Thomas Jankys in a plea of debt in mercy because they did not come. And it is ordered to the bailiff that he better distrain before the next [court] to respond to the

distrain aforesaid Thomas in the plea aforesaid

William Holygreve not prosecuting plaintiff appeared against William Jones in a plea of

distrain trespass pledge for the prosecution William Barker who is not attached so let it be done

Roger the son of John Hulle deceased came here and took from the lord two messuages and six nooks of land with appurtenances in Roughtone within the manor

Fine 20s of Worefeld which formerly the said John Hulle surrendered into the hands of the lord to the use of the aforesaid Roger as is clear in the last court preceding to hold to the same Roger and his heirs from the lord after the death of Joan his mother according to the custom of the manor by services thence due and accustomed. And the said Roger gives to the lord of a fine 20s to pay thence 10s within the next accounts and 10s before the feast of the Annunciation of the Blessed Mary thereafter next following

Roger Mathewes is charged here of 2s 6d because he married Alice his daughter

Contempt 6s 8d without a licence from the lord and no more because she was married within the manor

And that Robert Barkar by the council of the lord is charged of 4s because he married Matilda his daughter within the manor a licence from the lord thence not obtained

William Newtone clerk came and took from the lord one cottage with curtilage

Fine 16d adjacent with appurtenances in Soonde within the manor of Worefeld which Richard Hichecokes surrendered into the hands of the lord to the use of the same William as is clear in the last court preceding to hold to the said William and his heirs from the lord according to the custom of the manor by services and customs thence owed. And he

Pannage for Sowdeleye 10s gives to the lord for a fine 16d and thus has seisin

The reeve is charged here on account of 10 shillings of pannage for pigs in the wood of Sowdeleye for the present year past and for the last year preceding

Joan Sewstar surrendered into the hands of the lord one cottage with curtilage adjacent with appurtenances in Haale within the manor aforesaid to re-hold the said cottage with curtilage for the term of her life from the lord according to the custom of the manor. And after her death that the said cottage with curtilage remains to Thomas the son of William Gold who came and took from the lord the said cottage with curtilage to hold to himself and his [heirs] from the lord after the death of the aforesaid Joan according to the custom of the manor by services thence due and accustomed. And the said Thomas gives to the lord for a fine 12d. And thence has seisin

Fine 12d

Richard Hethe surrendered into the hands of the lord one toft and one nook of land with appurtenances in Awescote to the use of Roger the son of Nicholas Rowlowe to hold for a term of seven years next following from the lord according to the custom of the manor. And the said Roger gives to the lord for a fine 3s 4d. And made fealty to the lord

Fine 3s 4d

William Wermod took from the lord half of one nook of land of those lands and tenements of which Thomas Wermod the father of the same William died seised as is fully clear in the court held on Tuesday the 15th day of April last past to hold from the lord the said half nook of land to the said William and his heirs according to the custom of the manor by services and customs thence due. And he gives to the lord for a fine 2s 6d. And thus has seisin. Until they inspect the old court rolls on behalf of the lord for the lands and tenements of which Thomas Wermod died seised they still don't know if any part of the same lands and tenements remain still in the hand of the lord for to make a fine etc.

Fine 2s 6d

Inquiry

Escheat 23½d

Thomas Jankys the reeve is still charged of 23½d received for honey coming from escheat at the death of Richard Turbevyle

Inquiry

held for the lord by the oath of the 12 jurors

Roger Richardes	John Janne	Robert Hogge
Thomas Rugge	John Hethe	Robert Barker
Roger Waltone	Nicholas Rowlowe	William Gerbode
Stephen Bradeneye	Roger Broke	Mathew Bullokes

Amerced 14d

The which jury say on their oath that Thomas Muychale (2d), Thomas Gold (2d), Thomas Barbour clerk (2d), Richard Hethe (2d), Thomas Tresel (2d), William Billyngesle (2d) & John Holygreve (2d) who should have made suit at this court to make the tenure made default so each of them is in mercy

Heriot and escheat nothing as shown Held in the hand of the lord

And they say that Margaret Saladyn who held from the lord by custom of the manor one messuage and half a virgate of land with appurtenances in Barndeleye has died whereof for heriot & escheat the lord has nothing because she was a pauper & had no chattels. And they say that John the son of Richard Saladyn is the same Margaret's closest heir and aged 2 years. And the tenements remain in the hand of the lord to the use of the same heir for a fine to be made

Heriot 2 sheep 2s 6d escheat nothing tenements in the hand of the lord

And they say that Roger Wylle of Burcote who held from the lord by custom of the manor one messuage and three nooks of land with appurtenances in Burcote has died whereof the lord will have 2 heriots namely 2 sheep appraised by the aforesaid inquiry at 2s 4d. And of escheat nothing because there was nothing. And they say that Roger his son is his heir and aged 20 years and more. And the tenements remain in the hand of the lord for a fine to be made to the use of the same heir

And they say that Joan Sewstar who held one cottage with curtilage in Haalen has died whereof the lord will have in the name of heriot half of one cow appraised at 3s

Heriot 2 sheep 3s 3d escheat 4s 8d	3d. And for escheat 3 piglets appraised at 4s Afterwards the said three piglets are sold by the inspection of the clerk of the court by the lord and bailiff for dearer for 8d under condition if it pleased the council of the lord. And the cottage with curtilage remains with Thomas the son of William Gold by virtue of a fine thence previously made as is clear above
The next	Inquiry of the office pending at the suit of Roger Cattestre adjourned until the next [court] by the prayer of the parties

Look at the back

[The dorse]

Still of the court

heriot 2 cows 13s 4d	Still the 12 jurors say on their oath that William Ewyk who held of the lord by the custom of the manor one messuage and one virgate of land at Ewyk and one messuage and half a virgate of land with appurtenances in Haale on the day he died whereof the lord will have 2 heriots namely 2 cows price 13s 4d. And for escheat they say that he had nothing etc. And the tenements remain by the custom of the manor with Elianor the widow of the same William
No fine because it was made in the last court preceding	Richard Hichecokes plaintiff appeared against John Janne in a plea of land . The which Richard seeks from the said John one acre of land lying in Bromleylyre which acre of land is a parcel of land of his tenement of Bromleye and was from the time of which the memory of man does not exist and which acre of land the same John withheld from him and unjustly holds to the damage of the said Richard. And the aforesaid John present says that the same acre of land he holds justly as a parcel of his tenement and on this he puts himself on the inquiry. And the aforesaid Richard similarly. On which at the suit of the same Richard by virtue of a fine made in the last court preceding, the inquiry was held by the oath of Roger Richardes, Nicholas Rowlowe, Roger Broke, John Barndeleye, Thomas Hugge, Mathew Bullok, Roger Gerbod, Robert Hogge, William Gerbod, William Barkar, William Bruggende & Thomas Swancote who are sworn and to judge between the parties aforesaid have a day to render thence the verdict until the next [court]
Fine respited	On Friday last past old court rolls of the lord were searched & surveyed at the request of Thomas Rowlowe who thence made a fine with the lord. And he gives for a fine
Increases of heriots sold by the bailiff 3s 1d	The bailiff presents that he received to the profit of the lord from an increase in the selling of 3 heriots of William Towart beyond which were appraised by the inquiry 2s. And from the increase sale of the escheat of the same William beyond the price appraised by the inquiry 8d. And of 1d from the increase of the sale of the escheat of Thomas Wermod. And from 4d received from the increase on the sale of 1 ox coming from the heriot of Roger Hattone
Tenement remains in the hand of the lord	Still the land and tenements which were surrendered into the hands of the lord to the use of John Coletes in Hultone as is clear in the last court preceding remain in the hand of the lord until etc.

Sum of this court 74s 11½d

Expenses of John Boerley the steward being there for one night for the sake of holding this court with 8 horses with all accounted 5s 7d

1404-1405 P314/W/1/1/232

Worefeld

Small court held there on Wednesday next after the feast of St Katherine the Virgin in the sixth year of the reign of King Henry IV after the conquest [26 November 1404]

Essoins

John Billyngesleye, John Fowler, William Newe, John Rowlowe, John Huewssone & John Morefeld clerk from common [suit] by the clerk

William Holygreve (2d) is in mercy because he is not prosecuting against William Jones in a plea of trespass

Amerced 6d

Emmota Hore (2d) is in mercy because she is not prosecuting against William Holygreve in a plea of trespass

William Baret (2d) & Alice his wife put themselves in mercy for a licence to agree with Thomas Jankys in a plea of debt

distraint

John the son of Roger Taillour of Bekkebury plaintiff against William Oldyntoun in a plea of debt pledge for the prosecution Thomas Jankys who is summoned did not come so distrained and the said Thomas is admitted attorney for the plaintiff to win or to lose whatsoever

The 12 jurors
Amerced 10d

The inquiry held for the lord by the oath of Roger Richardes, Nicholas Rowlowe, Roger Waltone, Stephen Bradeneye, Robert Hogge, Roger Broke, Thomas Rugge, John Barndeleye, Roger Kyngeslowe, William Barker, William Gerbod and Mathew Bullok who say on their oath that Thomas Muychhale (2d), Thomas Barbour clerk (4d), Thomas Brynketone (2d) & William Byllyngesleye (2d) who are bound to make suit at this court made default so each of them is in mercy

Heriot half a cow 3s 8d
Tenement in the hand of the lord

And they say that Thomas the son of William Gold who held from the lord by the custom of the manor one cottage with curtilage adjacent with appurtenances in Haale within the manor of Worfeld on the day he died whereof the lord will have in the name of heriot half of one cow price 3s 8d. And of escheats they say that there was nothing. And the tenement remains in the hand of the lord to the use of John Cattestre and Rose his wife *for him and from him* (pro eo ex eo) because the same Thomas before his death surrendered the said tenement into the hand of the lord to the use of the aforesaid John and Rose. And thus as above-said it remains in the hand of the lord until the fine thence will have been made etc. It is being paid in the court held on the 1st day of July next after the date of this court

Tenement in the hand of the lord

And they say that Roger Walker surrendered into the hand of the lord one cottage with curtilage adjacent in Worfeld to the use of Margery his wife. And thus it remains in the hand of the lord until the fine thence will have been paid in the court to be held on the 1st day of July next after the date of this court

John Hethe made a fine with the lord for an inquiry of 24 ex officio to be held for consideration and determination on the form of a certain presentation in the first court of the last year preceding held on the 20th day of March in the fifth year of the above-said King. Of which presentation is in tone such. And they say that John Hethe surrendered into the hand of the lord one messuage with half a virgate of land adjacent in Kyngeslowe to the use of John Gildene & Matilda his wife the daughter of the same John Hethe for which tenements she was charged by the council of the lord at 13s 4d as is clear in the memorandum of the same last year which fine was not enrolled in the rolls of the lord's court nor as yet but postponed until it was determined justly and faithfully in the court of the lord for him and from him that the same John Hethe says that in the manner aforesaid no tenements were surrendered but he says in this court being personally present he acknowledged a personal interest and publicly confessed before the steward being in the hearing of the homage of the lord he published that he surrendered into the hands of the lord one messuage and 3 nooks of land with appurtenances in Kyngeslowe to have back the said tenements to himself and Alice his wife for the term of the lives of both of them from the lord according to the custom of the manor. And after their decease that the aforesaid tenements will remain with John Gildene and Matilda his wife and their heirs and in this manner he surrendered and still newly surrendered. And the aforesaid tenements remain in the hand of the lord for a fine to be made and also the aforesaid John Gildene present in court publicly and openly in part and in whole agreed the confession of the aforesaid John Hethe. And he gives to the lord for a fine 2s. On which the inquiry was held by the oath of John Barndeleye, Roger Hichecokes, Thomas Swancot, William Gerbod, John atte Walle, Roger Mathew, Roger Gerbod, Henry Barker, John Janne, Nicholas Stanlowe, Roger Smyth, Thomas Hugge, William Wermod, Richard Aldith, Thomas Merwalle, Thomas Tresel, Richard Hichecokes, Thomas Rowlowe, Richard Whitebrok, John Robyns, Thomas Rowlowe, Robert atte Yate, Roger Batemon & Thomas Soonde which jurors have a day to render thence the verdict until the next [court] etc. Afterwards it is being settled in the small court held on the 6th day of April next after the date of this court

Fine 2s

Mathew Bullok & Agnes his wife confessed & examined according to the custom of the manor there surrendered into the hands of the lord two messuages and one virgate of land with appurtenances in Alvescote within the manor of Worfeld to have back from the lord the said tenements for the term of the life of each of them according to the custom of the manor. And after their deaths that the aforesaid tenements with their appurtenances should remain with John their son and Amistie the wife of the same John and their heirs and assigns to hold from the lord according to the custom of the manor by services and customs thence due. And thus the aforesaid tenements are granted by the steward. And they give to the lord for a fine 13s 4d, made fealty to the lord. And thus they are seized

Fine 13s 4d

Which is presented at the inquiry pending between Richard Hichecokes plaintiff and John Janne defendant in a plea of land concerning 1 acre of land lying in Bromleylyre as is clear in the last court preceding namely the last court of the last year preceding it is presented by the inquiry thence held thus by the oath of Roger Richardes, Nicholas Rowlowe, Roger Broke, John Barndeleye, Thomas Hugge, Mathew Bullok, Roger Gerbod, Robert Hogge, William Gerbod, William Barker, William Bruggende & Thomas Swancot who say on their oath that the aforesaid John, John Janne has full right in the aforesaid acre of land. So it is judged that the same John Janne henceforth should hold the aforesaid acre of land just as he formerly held. And the said Richard (2d) for his unjust plea is in mercy

Verdict amerced 2d

There still remains in the hand of the lord one cottage with curtilage, 1 parcel of meadow and 9 selions of land in Hultone which William Gold surrendered into the hands of the lord with 1 parcel of meadow called Bylade to the use of John Coletes and Isabel his wife in the manner and form as is clear in the court held on Friday on the feast of St James the Apostle in the 5th year of the King aforesaid until a fine thence made. It is being settled in the small court held on the 1st day of July next following the date of this court

Tenements remaining in the hand of the lord

Also remaining in the hand of the lord 1 meadow called Waterlade in Hultone aforesaid which the same William Gold surrendered to the use of the aforesaid John & Isabell until the fine thence made as is clear in the same court held on Friday on the feast of St James in the 5th year of the reign of the King aforesaid in the manner which is shown in the same court. It is being settled in the small court held on the first day of July next after the date of this court

Tenement remaining in the hand of the lord

Also there remains in the hand of the lord 3 acres which John Bradeneye surrendered into the hands of the lord to the use of the aforesaid John Coletes and Isabel according to the manner which is clear in the same court held on Friday on the feast of St James the Apostle in the 5th year of the reign of the King aforesaid. It is being settled in the small court to be held on the 1st day of July next following the date of this court

Tenement in the hand of the lord

Also there remains in the hand of the lord 1 messuage and half a virgate of land at Barndeleye to the use of John the son and heir of Richard Saladyn deceased as is clear in the court held on Friday on Tuesday next after the feast of St Mathew the Apostle in the 5th year of the reign of the King aforesaid. It is being settled in the small court to be held on the 1st day of July next following the date of this court

Concerning the herbage and profit of Sowdeleye adjourned for the present year until the coming of the council of the lord afterwards it is settled in their presence in the small court held on the first day of July after the date of this court

Ordination of the reeve

Thomas Jankys withdrew here from his office of reeve which office Thomas Towart entered by the election of the homage. And is sworn

Sum of this small court 20s 6d

Expenses of the clerks of the court being there with 1 horse. Richard Bulveys the reeve and the beadle 12d

Court

small held at Worfeld on the 20th day of January in the sixth year of the reign of King Henry IV after the conquest [20 January 1405]

Essoins

Henry Barker himself from common suit by Robert Barker

amerced 6d

John Billyngesleye (2d), John Fowler (2d), & John Huwessone (2d) are in mercy because they did not come to warrant their essoins

The 12 jurors

Inquiry held for the lord by the oath of Nicholas Rowlowe, John Barndeleye, Roger Richardes, Roger Waltone, John Hethe, Thomas Rugge, Stephen Bradeneye, William Gerbod, Thomas Swancot, Thomas Jankys, William Barker & Mathew Bullokes who say on their oath that Thomas Muychhale (2d), Roger Batemon (4d), John Huwessone (2d), Thomas Barbour clerk (4d), Thomas Forster (2d), Thomas Brynketone (2d), Roger atte Touneshende (2d), John Fowler (2d), Thomas Tresel (2d) & John Billyngesleye (2d) who are bound to make suit at this court made default so each of them is in mercy

amerced 2s

Fine 6d

Thomas Brynketone gives to the lord 6d for his suit of court to be commuted from the date of this court until the feast of the Nativity of St John the Baptist next in the future after the date of this court. Pledge for the fine Roger Waltone

This is an agreement made in full court between Richard Bromleye on the one part & William the son of Roger Swancot on the other part in full court in this form which follows namely that the same Richard has annually for the term of his life 7 bushels of corn namely 4 bushels of rye and 3 bushels of barley to receive annually for the said

Fine 6d — term on the feast of St Michael the Archangel from 1 messuage and half a virgate of land in Bromleye which Thomas Yonge formerly held within the manor of Worefeld etc. and they give to the lord for this enrolment 6d

Adjourned until the next { A day is given between John the son of Roger Taillour plaintiff and William Oldyntoun defendant in a plea of debt by the prayer of the parties

{ And between William Hustar plaintiff and Robert Taillour defendant in a plea of debt

{ Which at the inquiry by the 24 ex officio pending at the suit of John Hethe as is clear in the last court preceding adjourned until the next [court] etc.

Fine 3s — Margery Newe surrendered into the hands of the lord one toft and one nook of land with appurtenances in Chestertone within the manor of Worfeld to rehold them to the said Margery and Robert the son of William atte Bruggende their heirs and assigns according to the custom of the manor the which Robert afterwards the husband of the said Margery and the said Margery his wife took the said tenement from the lord to hold to themselves, their heirs and assigns according to the custom of the manor. And they give to the lord for a fine 3s and made fealty to the lord. And thus are seized

Fine 5s — Robert atte Bruggehende and Margery his wife surrendered into the hand of the lord one toft and one nook of land with appurtenances in Chestertone within the aforesaid manor of Worfeld to the use of William Newe and Christian his wife, their heirs and assigns. The which William and Christian took from the lord the said tenement to hold from the lord to themselves, their heirs and assigns according to the custom of the manor. And they give to the lord for a fine 5s, made fealty. And thus are seized

Sum of this court 11s 6d

Worefeld — Expenses of the clerk of the court for one day there, of Richard Bulveys, the reeve & the beadle 12d
Small court held there on Monday the 6th day of April in the sixth year of the reign of King Henry IV after the conquest

The 12 jurors amerced 6d — Inquiry held for the lord by the oath of Nicholas Rowlowe, Roger Richardes, Stephen Bradeneye, Roger Waltone, John Hethe, Thomas Rugge, Roger Broke, John Barndeleye, Robert Hogge, William Barker, Mathew Bullok & Roger Gerbod who say on their oath that Thomas Barbour clerk (4d), & Roger Batemon (2d) who are bound to make suit at this court made default. So each of them is in mercy

Contempt { And they say that Margery Newe widow of the lord married herself to Robert Bruggende within the manor a licence from the lord not obtained afterwards. It is being settled in the small court held on the first day of July after the date of this court

{ And that Richard Aldith married Christian his daughter within the manor to William the son of Roger Bromley without a licence from the lord. It is being settled in the small court held on the first day of July after the date of this court

Tenement in the hand of the lord — Reginald of Roughtoun surrendered into the hands of the lord one cottage with curtilage adjacent in Roughtoun within the manor of Worfeld to the use of Thomas Jankys junior. Thus it remains in the hand of the lord for a fine to be made. It is being settled in the court to be held on the 1st July next after the date of this court

1404-1405 P314/W/1/1/232

Symon Taillour surrendered into the hands of the lord one one parcel of meadow called Parrok at Stretford in Chesturtone within the manor of Worfeld to the use of John the son of John of Rowlowe. Thus it remains in the hand of the lord for a fine to be made, it is being settled in the court to be held on the 1st July next after the date of this court

William Bruggehende surrendered into the hand of the lord one messuage and one virgate of land with appurtenances in Hultone within the manor of Worfeld to rehold the said tenement for the term of his life to hold from the lord according to the custom of the manor. And after the death of the said William that the aforesaid tenement with its appurtenances to remain with Robert the son of the said William and Margery the wife of the same Robert to hold from the lord to the same Robert and Margery and the heirs of their bodies legitimately issuing according to the custom of the manor. And if it should happen the said Robert and Margery should die without heirs of their bodies legitimately issued then the aforesaid tenement should remain with the closest heirs of the aforesaid William Bruggende etc. Thus the tenement remains in the hand of the lord until the fine thence made is settled in the court held on the first day of July next following the date of this court etc.

Sum of this court 14d

In expenses of the clerk of the court,
Richard Bulveys the reeve and the beadle
at table 10d

1405 P314/W/1/1/233

Worefeld	Great court held there on Tuesday the fifth day of May in the sixth year of the reign of King Henry IV after the conquest [5 May 1405]
Essoins	John Hethe, Robert Yngemon, Robert Taillour & Richard Hethe from appearance by the clerk of the court
The 12	John Ewdenas, Roger Richardes, Stephen Bradeney, Roger Cattestre, Roger Waltone, John Barndeleye, John Tumpkys, Roger Kyngeslowe, William Gerbod, Robert Hugge, Roger Broke, William Barker } Sworn
Kyngeslowe, Stanlowe amerced 8d	townships there present that John Nelde (4d) & Thomas Muychhale (4d) whose appearance to make the tenure at this court could not be found
Chesturtone	township there presents nothing
Hultone strays 6d	township there presents one swarm of bees coming as a stray remaining in the custody of Stephen Bradeney price 6d
Asturhull, Ewyk, Rowlowe, Bradeney, Soond waifs 10d amerced 3s	townships there present that William Henene (4d) whose appearance to make the tenure at this court could not be found so the said William is in mercy. And they say that a certain unknown unjustly took from the fulling mill of Hamon Humele a small parcel of cloth price 10d. And they present that Henry Barker forestalled William Hustar and drew blood from the same William so the said Henry both for forestalling (8d) and for the flowing of blood (12d) is in mercy. And they say that Agnes the wife of the same William raised the hue and cry by mouth (12d) justly on the said Henry so the same Henry is in mercy
Roughton, Barndele, Hoccombe, Swancote amerced 12d 3 strays 18d	townships there present that Thomas Barbour clerk whose appearance to make the tenure at this court could not be found so the said Thomas (4d) is in mercy. And they say that William the son of Roger Broke forestalled John the son of Thomas Jankys so the said William (8d) in mercy. And they say that in the custody of William Kyngessone is one swarm of bees coming forth as a stray price 6d. In the custody of John Janne is 1 swarm of bees price 8d. And in the custody of Roger Broke is one swarm of stray bees price 4d
Burcote, Burcote, Bromleye amerced 4d	townships there present that Robert Beechhay who should have appeared at this court to make the tenure did not appear so the said Roger (4d) is in mercy
Ryndelford,	Alwescote, Wynnescote, Cattestre, Newton townships there present nothing
Ewdneas, Oldynton amerced 4s	townships there present that William Oldynton blocked a certain footpath in Oldynton to the nuisance of the neighbours so the said William (12d) is in mercy. And they say that John the son of William Oldynton made an assault on John Jenkys unjustly so the said John (12d) the son of William is in mercy. And they say that Alice the wife of the said John the son of William raised the hue and cry by mouth on the said John Jenkys unjustly so the said Alice (12d) is in mercy. Also they say that John the son of William broke the pound of John Ewdenas so the said John (12d) the son of William is in mercy

Stapelford strays 4d amerced 3s 4d	township there presents 1 swarm of bees coming as strays in the custody of Roger Hogge price 4d. Also they present that Thomas Merwall forestalled (8d) John Merwalle & drew blood (12d) from the same John. So the said Thomas both for the forestalling and for the flowing of blood is in mercy. And they say that the same John Merwalle forestalled the said Thomas again & drew blood from the same Thomas. So the said John both for the forestalling (8d) and for the flowing of blood (12d) is in mercy.
Aclyntone strays 4d amerced 5s 4d	township there presents that Roger Hethe (12d) made homesoken on Alice the wife of William Gold so the said Roger is in mercy. Also they say that the same Alice forestalled the said Roger and drew blood from him. So the said Alice both for the forestalling (8d) and for the flowing of blood (12d) is in mercy. Also they say that Robert Hawkys broke the arrest made by the bailiff. So the said Robert (12d) is in mercy. Also they say that in the custody of Richard Underhull is 1 swarm of bees coming as a stray price 4d. And that John the bailiff of Baggesore unjustly distrained Elias Mustardmon within the liberty & took the distraint thence outside the liberty. So the said John (20d) is in mercy
Haalen amerced 7s 4d	township there presents that Robert Taillour forestalled (8d) John Walshe and drew blood (12d) from the same John so the said Robert both for forestalling and for the flowing of blood is in mercy. And that the same John forestalled (8d) the said Robert again and drew blood (12d) from him so the said John both for forestalling and for the flowing of blood is in mercy. And they say that John Henene (8d) forestalled Robert Taillour & drew blood (12d) from him so the said John both for forestalling and for the flowing of blood is in mercy. And that the same Robert forestalled (8d) again the said John and drew blood (12d) from him so the said Robert both for the forestalling and for the flowing of blood is in mercy. Also they say that Thomas Merwalle junior forestalled (8d) the servant of Robert Hogge so the said Thomas is in mercy
Worfeld amerced 3s	township there presents that Robert Taillour with force and arms and against the peace of the lord King broke (12d) [into] the house of John Henene in Worfeld at night and assaulted (12d) and made homsoken on the said John. And hit (12d) and badly dragged Agnes the wife of the said John so the said Robert is in mercy
Wyke strays 6d amerced 5s 4d	township there presents that William Yngemon made a recovery (2s) on Thomas Jankys the reeve of the lord done in his office so the said William is in mercy. And they say that William Duddeleye (2s) made an assault on a certain unknown him who he forestalled and hit so the said William is in mercy. And they say that William Newtoun chaplain forestalled (8d) Sir Philip chaplain so the said William is in mercy. Also they say that in the custody of William Rowlowe is 1 swarm of stray bees price 6d. And they say that William the son of Roger Broke forestalled (8d) John Jankys so the said William is in mercy
The ale tasters amerced 35s 6d	present that Thomas Muychhale (6d) brewed 1, John Stanlowe (6d) 1, William Gold (6d) 1, Stephen Bradeney (6d) 1, William Bruggend (6d) 1, Robert Smyth (12d) 2, William Yngmon (12d) 2, Margery Newe (6d) 1, John Billiyngesle (4s) 8, JohnYate (18d) 3, Robert Taillour (3s 6d) 7, Walter Rugge (12d) 2, Richard Bulveys (3s 6d) 7, Robert Barber (12d) 2, Henry Barker (6d) 1, Agnes Hattone (6d) 1, John Cattestre (6d) 1, John Smyth senior (18d) 3, John Smyth junior (6d) 1, William Skyrmour (6d) 1, John Oldyntone (6d) 1,Eleanor Ewyk (12d) 2, John Ewdenas (6d) 1, Thomas Soonde (18d) 3, Symon Broke (6d) 1, Robert Bruggende (6d) 1, John Baret (6d) 1, William Nore (6d) 1, Roger Dalleye (6d) 1, Stephen Humele (6d) 1, John Elcok (6d) 1, Robert Ewdenas (6d) 1, William Gold (6d) 1, John Jonesson of Roulowe (6d) 1,

Hamo Humele (6d) 1, William Carter (6d) 1, Robert Galian (6d) 1, Thomas Richardes (6d) 1, Roger Knyght (6d) 1, Roger Cattestre (6d) 1, John Fischer (6d) 1 and all sold against the assize so each of them is in mercy

The 12 jurors waifs 12d amerced 20s & fine 8d strays 6d	present that the township of Stapelford in their presentation concealed that Margery the servant of Thomas Towart entered the home of Thomas Swancot in Stapelford and from there took and took away silver and shoes price 12d of the goods of Agnes the daughter of the said Thomas Swancot and Margery the wife of the said Thomas so both the said township (12d) in mercy for the concealment of the aforesaid and the said Margery (6s 8d) the servant are to make a fine with the lord. Also they say that the township of Haale concealed a certain forestalling that William the son of Roger Swancot made on Nicholas the servant of Robert Hogge so both the said township (12d) and the said William (8d) in mercy. And that the same Nicholas (8d) reforestalled the aforesaid William so both the said Nicholas and the township (12d) in mercy. Also they say that the township of Roughton concealed a certain forestalling which William Broke made there on John the son of Roger Mathew so both the said township (12d) and the aforesaid William (8d) in mercy. And that the township of Worfeld concealed that the Canons (12d) of Lichfeld obstructed the king's highway there to the nuisance of the people of the lord King so both the said township (12d) and the Canons are in mercy. And they say that the ale tasters concealed in their presentation about this, that Robert Smyth (6d), John Yate (6d), John Billyngesleye (6d), , Robert Taillour (6d), Thomas Soonde (6d), John Smyth (6d), Richard Bulveys (6d) & John Fischer (6d), sold ale illegally without sealed measures so both the said tasters (12d) and the said brewers are in mercy. And that the township of Kyngeslowe concealed in their presentation 1 swarm of bees price 6d in the custody of John Hethe so the said township is in mercy
The election of ale tasters	Thomas Hugge & John Bromleye are elected tasters of ale and are sworn
Strays from the preceding year	Concerning 2 heifers from strays remaining etc. and presented in the great court in the preceding year namely the 5th year of the reign of King Henry IV appraised and settled in the small court held on Tuesday next after the feast of St James the Apostle next after the date of this court

Affeerors: Roger Cattestre, Roger Richardes
Sum of this court £4 15s

Worefeld	Small court held there on Wednesday the first day of July in the sixth year of the reign of King Henry IV after the conquest [1 July 1405]
Essoins	Thomas the son of John Rowlowe himself from common suit by the clerk
The 12 jurors amerced 13d Contempt 20s Increased escheat 2s	Inquiry held for the lord by the oath of Nicholas Rowlowe, Roger Waltone, Stephen Bradeneye, William Gerbod, Thomas Swancote, William Barker, Thomas Rugge, Nicholas Stanlowe, Mathew Bullok, Roger Broke, John Janne & Thomas Hugge who say on their oath that John Huwessone (3d), Thomas Barbour clerk (4d), Thomas Forster (3d) & Richard Bromley (3d) who made a default of suit at this court to make the tenure so each of them is in mercy. Also they present that Eleanor Ewyk (6s 8d), Agnes Hattone widow of the domain (6s 8d) & Emmota (6s 8d) the daughter of Thomas Muychhale married not obtaining a licence from the lord so each of them is in mercy for contempt. And they say that Thomas Jankys formerly the reeve of the lord was able to sell pigs of the eacheat of William Towart for 2s at a higher price than that at which they were appraised in the rolls of the lord in the last year preceding etc.

concerning which the same Thomas is charged

Fine 2s

John Cattestre and Rose his wife came and took from the lord one cottage with curtilage adjoining in Haalen with appurtenances in the manor of Worefeld which Thomas the son of William Gold surrendered into the hands of the lord to the use of the aforesaid John and Rose just as is clear in the small court held at Worefeld on Wednesday next after the feast of the Blessed Katherine the Virgin last past to hold the aforesaid cottage with curtilage with appurtenances from the lord to the said John and Rose their heirs and assigns according to the custom of the manor by services and customs thence due. And they give to the lord for a fine 2s. Thus they have seisin. And they made fealty to the lord

Heriot 9s 6d

The executors of the will of Richard Walker deceased of Wyke made a fine with the lord of 1 heriot from the death of the same Richard who held 1 cottage with curtilage in Worefeld. And they give for a fine 9s 6d pledge for the fine Roger Cattestre

Fine 2s

To this court came Margery who was the wife of Richard Walker deceased & took from the lord one cottage & curtilage with appurtenances in Worfeld remaining in the hand of the lord from the surrender of the aforesaid Richard deceased to the use of the aforesaid Margery as is clear in the small court of Worfeld held on Wednesday next after the feast of the Blessed Katherine the Virgin last past to hold the aforesaid cottage & curtilage with appurtenances to the said Margery & her heirs from the lord according to the custom of the manor by services and customs thence due. And she gives to the lord for a fine 2s. Thus she has seisin. And she made fealty to the lord

Fine 20s

When lately John Hethe surrendered into the hands of the lord one messuage and three nooks of land with appurtenances in Kyngeslowe within the manor of Worfeld in the form which is clear in the small court held on Wednesday next after the feast of the Blessed Katherine the Virgin last past and afterwards it was ended by an inquiry of 24 in the small court held on Monday the 6th day of April last past. Now comes the aforesaid John Hethe and took from the lord the aforesaid messuage and three nooks of land aforesaid with appurtenances to hold to the same John and Alice his wife for the whole of the life of both of them from the lord according to the custom of the manor by services and customs thence due. And after the death of the aforesaid John Hethe and Alice that the aforesaid messuage and three nooks of land aforesaid with its appurtenances should remain with John Gildene and Matilda his wife and their heirs or assigns to hold from the lord according to the custom of the manor by services and customs thence due.And they give to the lord for a fine 20s by which fine thus the tenement aforesaid is granted by the steward. Thus they are seised. And they made fealty to the lord

Fine 6s 8d

To this court came John Coletes & Isabell his wife and took from the lord one cottage, one curtilage, two parcels of meadow and nine selions of land with appurtenances in Hultone within the manor of Worfeld which tenement William Gold surrendered into the hands of the lord to the use of the said John & Isabell as is clear in the court held on Friday on the feast of St James the Apostle in the 5th year of the reign of the king aforesaid to hold from the lord the aforesaid tenement to the aforesaid John and Isabell and the heirs of their bodies legitimately issuing according to the customs of the manor by services and customs thence due. And if it should happen the aforesaid John & Isabell die without heirs of their bodies legitimately issuing then the aforesaid tenements with their appurtenances should revert and remain with the aforesaid William Gold and his heirs according to the form of the surrender of the tenements aforesaid. And they give to the lord for a fine 6s 8d. Thus they are seised. And they made fealty to the lord

To this court came William Gold & took from the lord one meadow called Waturlade in the field of Hultone next to Pailbrok within the manor of Worfeld the which meadow remains in the hand of the lord from a surrender by the same William as is clear in the court held on Friday on the feast of St James the Apostle in the year last past namely in the 5th year of the reign of King Henry IV after the conquest to hold the said meadow from the lord to the aforesaid William for the whole of his life according to the custom of the manor by services and customs thence due and after the death of the aforesaid William that the aforesaid meadow with appurtenances should remain with John Coletes and Isabell his wife and the heirs of their bodies

Fine 5s

legitimately issuing to hold from the lord according to the customs of the manor. And if it should happen the aforesaid John & Isabell should die without heirs of their bodies legitimately issuing then the aforesaid meadow with appurtenances should remain with the rightful heirs of the aforesaid William. And thus the aforesaid meadow is granted by the steward. And they give to the lord for a fine 5s thus they are seised. And made fealty to the lord

John Coletes & Isabell his wife took from the lord three acres of land lying in the common field of Hultone within the manor of Worfeld the which acres of land John Bradeneye lately surrendered into the hands of the lord to the use of John & Isabell as

Fine 20d

is clear in the court held on Friday on the feast of St James the Apostle in the 5th year of the reign of the aforesaid King Henry IV to hold from the lord the said three acres of land to the aforesaid John Colettes and Isabell his wife and their heirs from the lord according to the customs of the manor by services and customs thence due. And they give to the lord for a fine 20d thus they are seised. And they made fealty to the lord

John Saldyn son of Richard Saldyn and heir of Margaret Saladyn took from the lord one messuage and half a virgate of land with appurtenances in Barndeleye within the manor of Worfeld which tenement remains in the hand of the lord after the death of Margaret Saldyn as is clear in the court held on Tuesday next after the feast of St

Fine 6s 8d

Mathew the Apostle in the 5th year of the reign of King Henry IV to hold from the lord the aforesaid tenement with its appurtenances to the aforesaid John and his heirs according to the customs of the manor by services and customs thence due. And he gives to the lord for a fine 6s 8d thus he is seised. And he made fealty to the lord

The bailiff is charged here to raise from Margery Newe 6s 8d because the same Margery married herself to Robert the son of William Bruggehende within the manor not obtaining thence a licence from the lord

Contempt 13s 4d

Also he is charged concerning 6s 8d to raise from Richard Aldith because he married Christiana his daughter to William the son of Roger Bromeleye within the manor not without a licence from the lord

Thomas Jankys junior comes and took from the lord one cottage with curtilage adjacent in Roughtone within the manor of Worfeld remaining in the hand of the lord

Fine 3s 4d

from a surrender by Reginald Roughtone to the use of the same Thomas as is clear in the small court held of Monday the 6th day of April last past to hold the aforesaid cottage with curtilage to the aforesaid Thomas and his heirs from the lord according to the custom of the manor by services and customs thence due. And he gives to the lord for a fine 3s 4d. He is seised. And he made fealty to the lord

1405 P314/W/1/1/233

When William Bruggehende lately surrendered into the hands of the lord one messuage and one virgate of land with appurtenances in Hultone within the manor of Worfeld according to the form which is clear in the small court held on Monday the 6th April last past etc. now comes the said William and took from the lord the aforesaid messuage and virgate of land with appurtenances to hold to the same William for the whole of his life from the lord according to the custom of the manor by services and customs thence due. And after the death of the said William the aforesaid messuage & virgate of land should remain with Robert the son of William and Margery the wife of the same Robert according to the form of the aforesaid surrender to hold from the lord the aforesaid tenement to the same Robert and Margery and the heirs of their bodies legitimately issuing according to the custom of the manor. And if it should happen the said Robert and Margery should die without heirs of their bodies legitimately issuing then the aforesaid tenement with its appurtenances should remain with the closest heirs of the aforesaid William Bruggende. And they give to the lord for a fine 20s for which fine the aforesaid tenements are thus granted by the steward. They are seised. And they made fealty to the lord

Fine 20s

To this court comes John the son of John Rowlowe and took from the lord one parcel of meadow called Parrokes at Stretford in Chesturtone within the manor aforesaid which parcel of meadow Symon Taillour surrendered into the hands of the lord to the use of the aforesaid John the son of John as is clear in the small court held on Monday the 6th day of April last past to hold the said parcel of meadow to the said John the son of John and his heirs from the lord according to the custom of the manor by services and customs thence due. And he gives to the lord for a fine 20d, is seised. And he made fealty to the lord

Fine 20d

Sowdeleye herbage 3s 4d

The bailiff is charged in 3s 4d for herbage and profit of the wood of Sowdeley from the feast of St Michael last past until the feast of St Martin thereafter following namely for 6 weeks this year etc.

To this court came William Gerbod and took from the lord half of one messuage and 1 nook of land called Yngelbrondeslond in Haalen within the manor aforesaid which half tenement Thomas Gerbod clerk formerly held and thence died seised as it is said just as is clear in the small court held on Monday the 6th April last past to hold from the lord the tenement aforesaid to the aforesaid William and his heirs according to the custom of the manor by services and customs thence due. And he gives to the lord for a fine 3s 4d. He is seised. And he made fealty to the lord

Fine 3s 4d

Thomas Nicols surrendered into the hands of the lord one cottage with curtilage adjacent in Soonde within the manor of Worfeld to the use of Nicholas Stanlowe and his heirs the which Nicholas came and took from the lord the aforesaid cottage with curtilage to hold to himself and his heirs from the lord according to the custom of the manor by services and customs thence due. And he gives to the lord for a fine 3s 4d. He is seised. And he made fealty to the lord

Fine 3s 4d

Thomas Brynketone surrendered into the hands of the lord one toft and half a virgate of land with appurtenances in Boorcote within the manor aforesaid to the use of John the son of Roger Waltone, his heirs & assigns. The which John took from the lord the aforesaid tenement with appurtenances to hold to himself and his heirs from the lord according to the custom of the manor by services and customs thence due. And he gives to the lord for a fine 8. He is seised. And he made fealty to the lord

Fine 8s

1405 P314/W/1/1/233

It is presented by the oath of Richard Bulveys that William Bryan surrendered into the hands of the lord one parcel of meadow in Stapelford within the manor aforesaid in the long meadow to the use of William Newtone the chaplain. The which William the chaplain took from the lord the aforesaid small parcel of meadow to hold to himself and his heirs from the lord according to the custom of the manor by services and customs thence due. And he gives to the lord for a fine 5s. He is seised. And he made fealty to the lord

Fine 5s

To this court came Roger the son and heir of Roger Willes of Burcote deceased and took from the lord one messuage, half of one messuage, and three nooks of land with appurtenances in Boorcote within the aforesaid manor which tenements were taken into the hand of the lord to the use of the aforesaid heir after the death of the aforesaid Roger Willes as is clear in the court held at Worfeld on Tuesday next after the feast of St Mathew the Apostle in the 5th year of the reign of King Henry IV to hold the aforesaid tenements to the said Roger the heir and his heirs from the lord according to the custom of the manor by services and customs thence due. And he gives to the lord for a fine 10s. He is seised. And he made fealty to the lord

Fine 10s

Inquiry — Still it is to be enquired on behalf of the lord concerning the heriot and escheat of Thomas Gerbod clerk, deceased and what they were

adjourned — Still Thomas Jankys plaintiff against Thomas Yngmon in a plea of detention of goods who have a day adjourned until the next [court] by the prayer of the parties

Distraint — Margaret Tresel plaintiff against William Abbot who is not yet attached so let it be done in a plea of trespass

amerced 4d — Margaret Tresel (4d) is in mercy for an unjust plea against William Bruggehende

Adjourned — Henry Whitebrok plaintiff appeared against Thomas Soonde in a plea of trespass twice. Pledge for the prosecution John Rowlowe who have a day adjourned until the next [court] by the prayer of the parties

recovery amerced 4d — Thomas Hugge plaintiff against Margaret Tresel in a plea of trespass pledge for the prosecution Stephen Bradeney whereof he complains that the same Margaret has hedges and enclosures unfit, broken and open to his damage 2s etc. And the said Margaret present thence put herself on an inquiry of 12 by whom the damage was assessed at 11½d

recovery amerced 4d — William Bruggehende plaintiff against Margaret Tresel in a plea of trespass etc. And he says that the hedges and enclosures of the same Margaret [are] useless, broken and open to the nuisance and damage of the said William 2s etc. which Margaret present thence put herself on an inquiry of 12. Affeered at 11½d

recovery amerced 4d — Stephen Bradeney plaintiff against Margaret Tresel in a plea of trespass etc. And he says that the enclosures of Margaret herself [are] unfit to his nuisance and damage 3s etc. the which Margaret present thence put herself on the said inquiry of 12. Assessed at 11d

recovery amerced 4d — William Gold plaintiff against Margaret Tresel in a plea of trespass . Pledge for the prosecution William Hugge. And he says that the hedges & enclosures of Margaret herself are broken and open to his nuisance and damage 2s. And the said Margaret

1405 P314/W/1/1/233

recovery
amerced 4d

present thence put herself on the judgment of the 12. Assessed at 11½d

recovery
amerced 4d

John atte Walle plaintiff against Margaret Tresel in a plea of trespass etc. And he says that the enclosures of Margaret herself are broken and open to his nuisance and damage 2s. And the said Margaret present thence put herself on the 12. Assessed at 11½d

recovery
amerced 4d

John Coletes plaintiff against Margaret Tresel in a plea of trespass etc. And he says that the same Margaret has hedges and enclosures broken and open which she is not willing to repair and enclose but expressly refuses to the damage of the said John 3s. And the said Margaret present thence put herself on the 12. Assessed at 11½d

recovery
amerced 4d

Roger Smyth plaintiff against Margaret Tresel in a plea of trespass . Pledge for the prosecution John Coletes whereof he complains that the enclosures of the said Margaret are useless, fallen, and open to his nuisance and damage 2s. And the said Margaret present thence put herself on the 12. Assessed at 11½d

The verdict of the 12 jurors

On which the inquiry was held for the trial thence to be held between the parties aforesaid namely 7 tenants of Hultone above-named plaintiffs and the said Margaret Tresel by the oath of John Hethe, Roger Kyngeslowe, Richard Hichecokes, John Nelde, John Jonessone, William Newe, Robert Yate, William Cattestre, John Barndeleye, John Bromleye, Henry Barker & Thomas Rowlowe who sworn say on their oath that the enclosures of the aforesaid Margaret are useless, fallen down, and open and harmful to the grave damage of all the tenants aforesaid of Hultone which damages to the above parcels are assessed. And the said Margaret is in mercy

Fine for 12 ex officio 12d

Verdict

John Tumkys, William Newe and their kinsmen, sureties of William Skymour lessee of the mill of the lord made a fine with the lord for an inquiry of 12 ex officio to be held to enquire on this that when lately the aforesaid William Skymour lessee withdrew and suddenly fled from the country whither they do not know to the great damage of their pledges etc. if Thomas Jankys who was the reeve in the time of the departure of the said lessee would have in any way by force, council or procurement the departure of the same William Skymour or not. And they give to the lord for a fine 12d. On which the inquiry was held by the oath of John Janne, Mathew Bullok, William Billyngesley, William Gerbod, William Barker, Roger Mathew, Roger Kyngeslowe, Thomas Merwalle, Thomas Soonde, Robert atte Yate, Henry Barker & Roger Gerbod who say on their oath that they were not able to find that the said Thomas Jankys had notice of the departure of William Skymour nor that it was from his advice on his part

Distraint

Thomas Jankys plaintiff appeared against Richard Hethe in a plea of debt who summoned did not come so etc.

fine 2s

To this court comes Elena Jones and surrendered into the hands of the lord one cottage with curtilage adjacent in Haale within the manor aforesaid to recover the said tenement for the term of her life according to the custom of the manor. And after the death of the same Elena that the aforesaid tenement with its appurtenances should remain with Roger her son and Edith the wife of the same Roger to hold to the same Roger and Edith and their heirs from the lord according to the custom of the manor by services and customs thence due. And they give to the lord for a fine 2s. They are seised. And they made fealty to the lord. And so the tenement aforesaid is granted by the steward

1405 P314/W/1/1/233

fine 5s

Alice Wyntur surrendered into the hands of the lord one messuage and 1 nook of land with appurtenances in Haale within the manor aforesaid to the use of John her son. The which John came and took from the lord the said tenement to hold to himself and his [heirs] from the lord according to the custom of the manor by services and customs thence due . And he gives to the lord for a fine 5s. He is seised. And made fealty to the lord

Affeerors: Nicholas Rowlowe, Stephen Bradeney

Sum of this court £7 18s 7d

Worfeld

Small court held there on Tuesday next after the feast of St James the Apostle in the sixth year of the reign of King Henry IV after the conquest [28 July 1405]

Essoins

Roger Smyth, John Fowler, Thomas Swancot, Richard Bromleye, Thomas Tresel, William Cattestre, Nicholas Rowlowe, John Holigreve, Roger atte Towneshende & John Hethe themselves from common [suit] by the bailiff

The 12 jurors
amerced 20d

Inquiry taken for the lord by the oath of Roger Richardes, Roger Waltoun, Stephen Bradeneye, John Barndeleye, Thomas Rugge, Roger Broke, Robert Hogge, Mathew Bullok, Roger Kyngeslowe, Henry Barker, William Gerbod & John Rowlowe who say on their oath that Thomas Muychhale (2d), Thomas Coliar (2d), Roger Batemon (2d), John Huwessone (2d), Thomas Barbour clerk (4d), Thomas Forster (2d), John Munsterleye (2d), Andrew Fekkenham (2d) & John Ryes (2d) who made default of suit at this court to make the tenure so each of them is in mercy

Recovery
amerced 4d

Margaret Tresel plaintiff against William Abbot in a plea of trespass and she says that the same William unjustly with his animals destroyed the corn and grass of Margaret herself in Hultone to the damage of Margaret herself 10s. And the said William present thence put himself on the judgment of the aforesaid inquiry. Thus the same damages by the oath of the same inquiry agreed between the parties were assessed at 2s. And the said William (4d) is in mercy

amerced 8d

Thomas atte Soonde(8d) put himself in mercy for a licence to agree with Henry Whitebrok plaintiff in a plea of trespass twice

Strays
2 heifers
12s 2d

The bailiff is charged here in 5s 6d concerning the price of 1 heifer coming as a stray as is clear in the great court in the year preceding by the presentation of the townships of Kyngeslowe & Stanlowe and thus by the said townships appraised
And concerning 6s 8d for 1 heifer, a stray, presented in the same court by the township of Hultone thus appraised on the oath of the same township

The next

Plea between Thomas Jankys plaintiff and Thomas Yngmon defendant in a plea of trespass	} adjourned until
And between the said Thomas Jankys plaintiff & Richard Hethe defendant in a plea of debt	} the next

When Thomas Jankys was serving the lord in the office of reeve two and a half years last past for which years [were] in the time of the pestilence there fell to the lord diverse heriots, escheats, and strays appraised by the 12 as is clear by the record of the rolls of the court of the said years all of which the aforesaid Thomas had and received when it was ordered that thence he should answer to the greater profit of the lord for the faithful supervision and council. The which Thomas in his account concerning the increased sales of them did not answer to the lord except only concerning 3s 1d. On which it is certified by the council of the lord that he could have sold the said heriots, escheats & strays for a higher price than they were valued to the profit of the lord. And for the truth thence to be known an inquiry is held for the lord by the oath of Roger Kyngeslowe, John Barndeleye, William Gerbod, Robert Hogge, William Newe, John atte Walle, John Janne, John Byllyngesle, William Barker, John Nelde, Robert atte Yate & Thomas Rowlowe who seek a day for the full truth thence to render until the next [court] for the sake of this matter to be examined for the greater profit of the lord

The next Inquiry

Affeerors: Thomas Rugge, Roger Hychecokes

Sum of this court 14s 10d

Expenses of the clerks of the lord's court
with 1 horse for 1 day of
Richard Bulveys reeve and the beadle 16d

1405-1406 P314/W/1/1/234

	Great court held at Worfeld on Wednesday the 28th day of October in the 7th year of the reign of King Henry IV after the conquest [28 October 1405]
Essoins	William Newtone chaplain, John Wynter+, Thomas Coliar+, Roger Gille+ & Thomas Muychhale themselves from appearance by John Hethe reeve
amerced 4d	Richard Hethe (4d) is in mercy because he did not come to warrant his essoin
the 12	Richard Bulveys, Nicholas Rowlowe, John Tumpkys, Andrew Fekkenham, Stephen Bradeneye, Robert Hogge, Roger Cattestre, John Barndeleye, Roger atte Broke, Roger Richardes, Roger Waltone, Mathew Bullokes
Kyngeslowe, Stanlowe	townships there present nothing
Chesturtone amerced 2s	township there presents that Margaret Tresel & John her son made a recovery on the bailiff of the lord so the said Margaret (12d) & John (12d) are in mercy
Hultone	township there presents nothing
Rowlowe, Bradeney, Asturhull, Ewyk, Soonde amerced 4d strays 12d	townships there present that William Henene who is bound to make appearance at this court did not appear so the said William (4d) is in mercy. And they say that William atte Wode took at Ewyk honey and wax coming as a stray price 12d
Roughtone, Barndeley, Hokkombe, Swancot amerced 4d	townships there present that Thomas Barbour clerk who is bound to make appearance at this court did not appear so the said Thomas (4d) is in mercy
Burcote, Burcote, Ryndelford, Bromley amerced 8d strays 3s 4d	townships there present that Richard Hethe (4d) and Roger Beechhaye (4d) who are bound to make appearance at this court did not appear so each of them is in mercy. Also they present one black heifer coming as a stray at the feast of the Nativity of the Lord last past which is in the custody of John Walker. Price of the heifer 3s 4d. They present also one mare coming as a stray at the feast of the Annunciation of the Blessed Mary the Virgin which is in the custody of the township of Bromleye price of the mare 12d
Alvescote, Wynnescote, Cattestre, Newtone	townships there present nothing
Ewdenas & Oldyntone amerced 4d	townships there present that John Jonkys who are bound to make appearance at this court did not appear so the said John (4d) is in mercy.
Stapelford	township there presents nothing
Aklyntone amerced 4d	township there presents that Margaret the wife of Simon atte Broke forestalled John the servant of Roger Dalleye so the said Margaret (4d) is in mercy
Wyke amerced 18d	township there presents that Alice Baret raised the hue and cry by mouth on Robert Yngmon unjustly so the said Alice (6d) is in mercy. Also they present that William Yngmon (12d) broke the pound of John Ryes so the said William is in mercy

Haalen	township there presents nothing
Worfeld amerced 2s 8d waifs 1d	township there presents that Nicholas Herdemon (4d) & John Henene (4d) who are bound to make appearance at this court did not appear so each of them is in mercy. Also they present the King's road in Worfeld is blocked and damaged by marshy ground and water from the default of Matilda Rugge so the said Matilda (6d) is in mercy. Also they present the common way is damaged and partly blocked in Worfeld aforesaid by dung at the higher *part/glade* of the cemetery (ad superiorem saltum cimiterii) in default of William Wermod (6d) so the said William is in mercy. And they say that Richard Smyth (12d) unjustly took mill dust [fine floury grain thrown out by a grain mill] in the mill of Worfeld price 1d so the said Richard is in mercy
The tasters of ale amercements 17s 6d	present that John Smyth of Soonde brewed 4 [times] (2s), Thomas Soonde 4 (2s), Margery Wermod 1 (6d), Joan Bulveys 4 (2s), Robert Galian 5 (2s 6d), Henry Barker 1 (6d), William Gold of Hultone 1 (6d), John Billyngesleye 2 (12d), Thomas Rowlowe of Hultone 1 (6d), Thomas Muychhale 1 (6d), John Stanlowe 1 (6d), John Oldyntone 1 (6d), Richard Barewe 1 (6d), William Rowlowe 1 (6d), William Yngmon 2 (12d), John the son of Robert Smyth 1 (6d), John Yate 1 (6d), Hamund Humeley 1 (6d), Roger Dalleye 1 (6d), Thomas Taillour 1 (6d) and that all sold against the assize so each of them is in mercy
the 12	Jurors present and say on their oath that John Child on Monday the 26th day of October at Alvescote within the liberty of Worfeld feloniously stole together one cow and two heifers price 13s 4d of the goods and chattels of Thomas Tresel in the seventh year of the reign of King Henry IV. And they say that there falls to the lord as forfeit from the goods and chattels of the same felon the cow and heifers aforesaid and one horse with saddle and bridle price 17s, one small knife a dagger price 2d, one horn with one baldric with silver binding price 10s and one sword not appraised which were determined by the steward, the constables of the peace and the township of Haalen for taking and seizing. Also they present that the township of Aklyntone concealed here that Margaret the wife of Simon atte Broke made homesoken on John Wylot so both the said township (12d) and Margaret (6d) are in mercy. Also they present that the townships of Stapelford, Aklyntone, Kyngeslowe, Stanlowe and the tenants of seven nooks of land in Chesturtone ought and are accustomed from the time of which no memory exists to repair and maintain a certain bridge called Stapelfordbradebrugge. And that the townships of Wyke, Hultone, Bradeney, Asturhul, Ewyk, Soonde, Barndeley, Hokkombe and the tenants of the remainder of the township of Chesturtone ought and are accustomed from the time of which no memory exists to repair and maintain a certain bridge called Wykebradebrugge. And that the township of Roughtone ought and are accustomed from the time of which no memory exists to repair and maintain a certain bridge called Halfbrugge. And that the townships of Swancot, Burcot, Burcot, Bromley & Ryndelford ought and are accustomed to repair and maintain from the time of which no memory exists a bridge called Ryndelfordbrugge. And that the townships of Halen, Cattestre, Alvescot, Wynnescot, Newtone, Oldyntone & Ewdenas ought and are accustomed from the time of which no memory exists to repair and maintain a certain bridge called Worfbrugge the which bridges are in disrepair and not maintained being in default of the townships and hamlets aforesaid to the nuisance of the people. So it is ordered to the tenants of the townships and hamlets aforesaid to properly repair and build the bridges aforesaid before the feast of St Michael the Archangel next in the future under pain of 20s forfeit to the lord namely concerning the townships and hamlets aforesaid to repair just as they are charged to the repair and building of them
amerced 18d	
pain	

1405-1406 P314/W/1/1/234

Affeerors: Roger Cattestre, Roger Richardes
Sum of this court 73s 5d

Worfeld	Small court held there on Monday on the feast of St Thomas the Apostle in the seventh year of the reign of King Henry IV after the conquest [21 December 1405]
Essoins	Roger Kyngeslowe, Roger Batemon, Andrew Fekkenham & Thomas Muychhale from common [suit] by Richard Bulveys
amerced 4d	Thomas Tresel (4d) is in mercy because he did not come to warrant his essoin
the 12 jurors amerced 16d	Inquiry held for the lord by the oath of Nicholas Rowlowe, Roger Waltone, Roger Richardes, Stephen Bradeneye, Thomas Rugge, John Barndeleye, Roger atte Broke, Robert Hogge, Mathew Bullok, Henry Barker, William Gerbod & Nicholas Stanlowe who say on their oath that Thomas Barbour (4d) chaplain, Richard Bromleye (4d), John Munsterleye (4d) & Roger Towneshende (4d), who are bound to make suit at this court made [default] so each of them is in mercy
amerced 4d distraint	Thomas Jankys plaintiff against Richard Hethe in a plea of debt etc. the which Richard attached & charged did not come so the same Richard (4d) is in mercy. And it is ordered he is better distrained before the next [court] to respond in the plea aforesaid
adjourned to the next	A day is given between Thomas Jankys plaintiff & Robert Yngmon defendant in a plea of trespass until the next [court]
distraint	William Bruggende plaintiff against Margaret Tresel in a plea of trespass pledge for the prosecution Thomas Hugge
distraint	Henry Whitebrok plaintiff against Robert Taillour in a plea of debt pledge for the prosecution William Barker the which Robert summoned did not come so to distrain
Election of reeve	Thomas Towart withdrew from the office of reeve to which office approaches John Hethe by the election of the homage of the lord and is sworn

Sum of this court 2s

Court	Small [court] held at Worfeld on Wednesday the 10th day of March in the 7th year of the reign of King Henry IV after the conquest [10 March 1405/6]
amerced 4d distraint	Thomas Jankys plaintiff against Robert Yngmon in a plea of trespass the which Robert attached and charged did not come so the same Robert (4d) is in mercy. And it is ordered to better distrain Robert himself before the next [court]
amerced 4d distraint	William Bruggende plaintiff against Margaret Tresel in a plea of trespass who attached and charged did not come so the same Margaret (4d) is in mercy. And it is ordered to better distrain Margaret herself before the next [court]
amerced 6d	Robert Taillour put himself in mercy for a licence to agree with Henry Whitebrok in a plea of debt

amerced 4d distraint	Thomas Jankys plaintiff against Richard Hethe in a plea of debt the which Richard attached & charged did not come so Richard himself (4d) is in mercy. And to better distrain before the next [court]
amerced 4d distraint	Thomas Hugge plaintiff against William Newe in a plea of debt pledge for the prosecution Richard Bulveys the which William attached & charged did not come so the same William (4d) is in mercy. And it is ordered to better distrain before the next [court]
amerced 4d distraint	Mathew Bullok plaintiff against John Oldyntone in a plea of trespass pledge for the prosecution Richard Bulveys the which John distrained & charged did not come so the same John is in mercy. And to better distrain him before the next [court]
amerced 4d distraint	The same Mathew Bullok plaintiff against John Soonde in a plea of trespass pledge for the prosecution Richard Bulveys the which John attached & charged did not come so the he is in mercy. And to better distrain before the next [court]
amerced 4d distraint	John Hokkombe plaintiff against William Yngmon in a plea of debt pledge for the prosecution John Jonesone who attached & charged did not come so William (4d) himself is in mercy. And it is ordered to better distrain before the next [court]
amerced 6d	Roger Mathew is in mercy because he is not prosecuting against John Muttone in a plea of trespass
amerced 4d distraint	Richard Hichecokes plaintiff against Richard Hethe in a plea of broken agreement pledge for the prosecution William Newe which Richard attached & charged did not come so he is in mercy. And it is ordered to better distrain before the next [court]
the law	Agnes Turbevyle plaintiff against Thomas Jankys in a plea of debt pledge for the prosecution William Gold the which Agnes seeks from the said Thomas 2s of silver which he owes to the same Agnes and unjustly detains to the damage of the same Agnes 6d. And the same Thomas present denies all this and thence he has a day for the law in the next [court] with six [hands] pledge for the law etc.
amerced 4d distraint	Agnes Turbevyle plaintiff against Thomas Heyne in a plea of debt pledge for the prosecution John Bradeneye the which Thomas attached & charged did not come so the same Thomas is in mercy. And to better distrain before the next [court]
the law	Thomas Jankys plaintiff against Agnes Turbevyle in a plea of debt pledge for the prosecution Robert Ewdenas who seeks from the said Agnes 6d which the same Agnes owes him and unjustly detains etc. And the said Agnes present denies all this and thence she has a day for the law in the next with 6 hands
amerced 6d	Symon atte Brok & *his amercement* in mercy because he is not prosecuting against Thomas Heyne in a plea of debt
Deception and contempt	Thomas Jankys formerly reeve of the lord put himself in the grace of the lord because while the same Thomas was reeve and custodian of the bag and rolls of the courts in the same under the seal of Henry Dunfowe clerk of the domain of Worfeld was having sealed the same Thomas fraudulently & deceptively without notice of the steward, the clerks aforesaid or others of the council of the lord unsealed and opened the bag and withdrew the rolls and took and in the same, in the roll of the lord of one court held

there on the 11th day of October in the fourth year of the reign of King Henry IV after inspection (teriacionem) and audit of his accounts did enter and write that a certain Isabell the wife of Thomas Kyngeslowe surrendered into the hand of the lord one messuage and two nooks of land with appurtenances which were formerly Roger Kyngeslowe's in the same to the use of the same Thomas & Matilda his wife and that the same Thomas took the same tenements the lord to hold from to himself and Matilda his wife according to the custom of the manor for a fine of 4s & although the whole matter aforesaid being totally unknown both to the steward and the clerk and all others of the council of the lord. And although from the fine aforesaid nothing to be answered to the lord. And the same Thomas put himself in the grace of the lord because at the time aforesaid he did write and enrol fraudulently and deceptively without the notice of the lord or other of his ministers in the roll of the court of the lord held at Worfeld on the feast of St Mark the Evangelist in the fourth year of the aforesaid King's reign after inspection and audit of his accounts that a certain Warynis Braye and Isabell his wife surrendered into the hand [of the lord] 1 cottage with curtilage in Haalen that John Huly formerly held to the use of Robert Taillor and Alice his wife the which Robert & Alice took the cottage aforesaid with curtilage from the lord to hold to themselves & their heirs according to the custom of the manor under a fine of 20d although the matter aforesaid remained unknown to the lord and all his ministers and although from the fine aforesaid nothing is answered to the lord. And the same reeve put himself in the grace of the lord because he at the time aforesaid fraudulently and deceptively without notice of the lord or any of his ministers did write and enter into the roll of the court of the lord held at Worfeld on the 15th day of April in the 5th year of the King aforesaid the same reeve allowed a certain amercement of twelve pence on John Englys for a hue and cry unjustly by him raised without any such presentation being made by the homage at any time and although from the amercement aforesaid nothing is answered to the lord because all the aforesaid enrolments by him in the manner aforesaid were done after the inspection and audit of the accounts of the reeve aforesaid. Nevertheless the said Thomas's fines and amercements aforesaid in his extracts in a similar way did write and enrol them to make a raising to the use of his own profit the which deception and contempt remains to the damage for the overview of the council of the lord. And on this the said Thomas found sureties namely John Ewdenas, Robert atte Wode & Roger Cattestre to attend and await. And the messuage, cottage and land above-written remain in the hand of the lord until the parties pursue them under a fine made to the lord to have seisin

tenements in the hand of the lord

the next

It is granted by the steward of the lord to Roger son of Nicholas Rowlowe two assarts together lying in the field of Alvescote called Stony Rudyinges and Hockenhull, one small moor in the same township called Chellesmore to hold to himself, his heirs and assigns according to the custom of the manor. Rendering to the lord annually at the usual terms by equal portions 14d that is ancient rent as it is said. And thence he has seisin. And he gives nothing for a fine because the tenements aforesaid are leased at a high price (care). But the said Roger is charged for all his lands and tenements a distraint for the rent aforesaid in case sufficient distraint is not able to be found in the parcels aforesaid

fine nothing for the reason shown

Inquiry taken for the lord by the oath of Andrew Fekenham, Roger Richardes, Nicholas Rowlowe, Stephen Bradeney, Roger Waltone, Robert Hogge, Roger atte Broke, Mathew Bullok, William Bruggende, Roger Smyth & Thomas Merwalle who say on their oath that Thomas Muychhale (4d), Thomas Barbour clerk (4d) & Thomas Colyare (4d) who are bound to make suit of court at this court made default so each of them is in mercy

The 12 jurors

amerced 12d

Escheats concealed and found 20d amerced 10s

When lately an inquiry of 12 was charged on behalf of the lord to enquire if Thomas Jankys formerly the reeve during his time sold heriots and escheats falling to the lord faithfully to the greater profit of the lord as he was ordered by the steward as is clear in the last court in the last year preceding and thence was answering to the lord. Now it is presented and found by the oath of the same inquiry that the same Thomas the reeve sold the escheats of Thomas Wermod and Thomas Nelde for a higher price for 20d with he charged himself in his account for which sum the same Thomas is charged. And nevertheless for the deception the same Thomas in mercy (10s)

fine 5s

Warynges Bray and Isabell his wife surrendered into the hand of the lord one cottage with curtilage in Haalen which John Huly formerly held to the use of Robert Taillour and Alice his wife who came and took from the lord the said cottage and curtilage with appurtenances to hold from the lord by the same Robert and Alice and their [heirs] according to the custom of the manor by services thence due. And they give to the lord for a fine 5s. And they are seized

It is ordered

the next

It is ordered the reeve on behalf of the lord to seize into the hand of the lord one messuage and 1 nook of land in Chestertone which Robert the Haywart formerly held and which Thomas Rugge and Margery his wife surrendered into the hand of the lord to the use of Nicholas the Frenche formerly the servant of the said Thomas to hold to himself and his [heirs] according to the custom of the manor as is clear in the court of Worfeld held there on the feast of St Denis in the sixth year of the reign of King Richard II the which land and tenements fell to the lord as escheat because the said Nicholas died without an heir as it is said. And also it is ordered the same reeve to distrain the land holders in the township of Aklyntone that they are at the next court of Worfeld to be held after the feast of Easter next in the future without further delay to do homage to the lord and fealty and other services owed to the lord. And further to show how they are ingressed

Fine 4s

Robert Taillour made a fine as able to brew and sell ale by legal measure from the date of this small court until at the end of 1 year fully completed for which he gives to the lord for a fine 4s pledge for the fine Robert Barker. And thus it is granted by Richard Peper overseer of the lord

Licence

It is granted to Richard Parlour before the steward from the agreement of a great inquiry by the township of Haalen and the whole homage of the lord that the same Richard henceforth will be able to enclose lawfully a certain parcel of land or waste within the township of Haalen called Moderlashelde in severalty for the whole year at the will of the lord and the tenants aforesaid as long as he behaves well towards the same without disturbance

John Hawkys clerk and John his son the said John the son then being below age at the court held at Worfeld on the 20th day of March in the fifth year of the reign of King Henry IV surrendered into the hand of the lord one messuage and half a virgate of land with appurtenances in Haalen to the use of John Rowlowe and Joan the wife and afterwards the same John Rowlowe & Joan his wife came back before the steward and in the court held there on the 15th day of April in the 5th year of the King aforesaid took from the lord the messuage and half a virgate of land aforesaid with appurtenances to hold from the lord to themselves, their heirs and assigns according to the custom of the manor. And they give to the lord for a fine 20s. And thence have seisin the said John the son of John Hawkys still being under-age. And afterwards

Ratification

came the aforesaid John son of John Hawkys at his full age of 21 years & more in this court held on the place, day and year which [are] above and before the steward approved, confirmed, and ratified the rights and possession of the aforesaid John Rowlowe and Joan his wife of the messuage and half virgate of land aforesaid with its appurtenances and further remised and quitclaimed for himself and his heirs to the aforesaid John Rowlowe and Joan his wife, their heirs and assigns, the whole right and claim which he has in the messuage and half virgate of land aforesaid with its appurtenances forever

The next

It is ordered by the steward to the bailiff or the reeve of the domain of Worfeld on behalf of the lord that under pain and peril which will be incumbent to examine, to write & to enrol all the pigs and piglets wheresoever and whosoever of the tenants or residents being within the domain being within the feast of St Michael the Archangel last past and the feast of St Martin henceforth next following except the pigs and piglets within the townships of Haalen, Cattestre, Alvescot, Wynnescote & Ryndelford so that they have the number of them and the names of the owners before the steward or the council of the lord in the next court to stand and receive that which on behalf of the lord in this matter *will be bound* (iniungetur) to them by right

Pannage and agistement of Sowdeley amerced 18s 7d

It is presented that in the wood of the lord this year in the enclosure at that time Robert Barker had 5 pigs (10d), William Holygreve 4 pigs (8d) & 5 piglets (5d), Roger Cattestre of Haalen 2 pigs (4d) & 1 piglet (1d), William Billyngesleye 5 pigs (10d) & 6 piglets (6d), Petronilla Nelde 3 pigs (6d) & 4 piglets (4d), Roger Jones 1 pig (2d), John Holygreve 4 pigs (8d) & 6 piglets (6d), Roger Cattestre of Cattestre 5 pigs (10d) & 6 piglets (6d), Mathew Bullok 5 pigs (10d) & 4 piglets (4d), Richard Whitebrok 5 pigs (10d), John Robynes 6 pigs (12d), Thomas Tresel 6 pigs (12d), Thomas Yonge 4 pigs (8d), William Wermod 5 pigs (10d) & 6 piglets (6d), Henry Barker 3 pigs (6d) & 1 piglet (1d), William Barker 6 pigs (12d). And that John Rogers (8d) and John Walker (4d), Roger Knyght (2d) & Roger atte Touneshende (8d) had diverse animals grazing in the same wood at the aforesaid time for which they thence put themselves in the mercy of the lord

Held in the hand of the lord

John Walker came and claims 1 parcel of meadow lying in [blank] which parcel of meadow Richard Hethe surrendered into the hand of the lord to the use of the same John as it is said by the oath of the reeve. On which came Richard Hichecokes and claims the said parcel of meadow because he bought the same parcel of meadow from Richard Hethe as he says. Thus the same parcel of meadow remains in the hand of the lord with the profit from the same until the right has been judged between the parties aforesaid

Charging of the constables

Thomas Hugge and Robert Ewdenas are elected to the office of constable. And are sworn

Affeerors: Roger Cattestre, Roger Richardes
Sum of this court 42s 9d

In the expenses of John Boerley the steward and others coming for the sake of holding this court to hold and to judge the 2 courts preceding and to oversee the affairs of the lord and to remain there for 3 days and 3 nights all accounted before Richard Peper the receiver of the lord 40s 6½d

1405-1406 P314/W/1/1/234

Worfeld	Small court held there on Tuesday 20th day of April in the 7th year of the reign of King Henry IV after the conquest [20 April 1406]
Essoins	Roger Batemon, John Huwessone & Andrew Fekkenham themselves & each of them made essoin by John Hethe
Amerced 4d	John Wynter (4d) in mercy because he did not come to warrant his essoin
The 12 jurors Amerced 7d	An inquiry held for the lord by the oath of Roger Richardes, John Janne, Roger Waltone, Stephen Bradeney, John Barndeleye, Robert Hogge, William Barker, Nicholas Stanlowe, Nicholas Rowlowe, Mathew Bullok, Roger Broke & William Newe who say on their oath that Thomas Barbour (4d) clerk & John Wynter (3d) who are bound to make suit at this court defaulted so each of them is in mercy
Heriot & escheat nothing for the reasons shown Held in the hand of the lord	And they say that Margery Stevenes who held from the lord by custom of the manor one messuage and half a virgate of land called Huggelond in Chestertone and also one toft and half a virgate of land called Gosselond in Chestertone on the same day she died whereof for heriot and escheat nothing fell to the lord because she had nothing. And the tenements aforesaid remain in the hand of the lord, one nook of land excepted about which it is to be surveyed in the ancient rolls etc. It is said by the aforesaid jurors that John the son of William Stevenes is the closest heir of the aforesaid Margery and aged 17 years and more
Amerced 6d	Thomas Jankys (5d) plaintiff & Robert Yngemon (1d) defendant in a plea of trespass are for a licence to agree and both put themselves in mercy for the decision of arbiters
The next	The suit between bailiff in mercy William Bruggende plaintiff & Margaret Tresel defendant in a plea of trespass adjourned until the next [court]
Amerced 4d Distraint	Roger atte Towneshend (4d) fine pledge in mercy is in mercy because he did not have Richard Hethe to respond to Thomas Jankys in a plea of debt. And it is ordered to the bailiff to better distrain the said Richard Hethe that he is at the next [court] to respond to the said Thomas in the plea aforesaid
Amerced 6d	William Newe put himself in mercy for a licence to agree with Thomas Hugge in a plea of debt
Amerced 6d	John Oldyntone put himself in mercy for a licence to agree with Mathew Bullok in a plea of trespass
Amerced 6d	William Yngmon put himself in mercy for a licence to agree with John Hokkombe in a plea of debt
Amerced 4d Distraint	Roger Towneshende pledges in mercy & John Walker in mercy because they did not have Richard Hethe to respond to Richard Hichecokes in a plea of broken agreement. And adjourned to the next [court] to better distrain the same Richard
Amerced 6d	Agnes Turbevile in mercy for her unjust suit against Thomas Jankys in a plea of debt
Amerced 2d The next	Agnes Turbevile plaintiff is not prosecuting against Thomas Heyne in a plea of debt as is clear in the last court preceding in mercy for the lack of a statement of the complaint. And she has a day until the next [court] to amend etc.

1405-1406 P314/W/1/1/234

Amerced 6d	Agnes Turbevile & her amercement in mercy because she defaulted concerning her law against Thomas Jankys in a plea of debt
The next	Alice Dolemon plaintiff [not prosecuting] against William Dalicote in a plea of debt pledge for the prosecution John Hethe who is not summoned so let it be done
Amerced 12d	Robert Taillour put himself in mercy for a licence to agree with Thomas Jankys twice, 1 in a plea of trespass & 1 in a plea of debt
Amerced 12d	Thomas Jankys put himself in mercy for a licence to agree with Robert Taillour in a plea of trespass twice
Amerced 6d	Adam Spicer plaintiff against Agnes Gold in a plea of debt who are for a licence to agree. And the same Agnes puts herself in mercy
Amerced 6d	John Henene puts himself in mercy for a licence to agree with Robert Taillour in a plea of trespass
The law	Adam Spicer plaintiff against Alice Baret [default of law] in a plea of debt pledge for the prosecution William Gerbod who seeks from the said Alice 3s 4d in silver which she owes to him and unjustly detains despite frequently being requested to pay. And the said Alice present denies this and thence has a day for the law in the next [court] with 6 hands pledge for the law Roger Cattestre
The next	Adam Spicer plaintiff against Emoter Dalley [pledge Roger Dalley] in a plea of debt pledge for the prosecution Roger Richardes who is not summoned so let it be done
Amerced 6d	Adam Spicer is in mercy because he is not prosecuting against William Wermod in a plea of debt
The next	Thomas Richardes plaintiff against John Fischer [pledge T ...] in a plea of debt pledge for the prosecution Thomas Tresel who is not summoned so let it be done
Amerced 6d	John Soonde puts himself in mercy for a licence to agree with Mathew Bullokes in a plea of trespass
Fine for deception & contempt 66s 8d	When Thomas Jankys lately the reeve of the domain of Worefeld put himself in the grace of the lord for diverse deceptions and contempt remaining to be determined by inspection by the council of the lord as is clear in the last court preceding on which it being ordained and determined by the council of the lord at Bergavenny on the 25th day of March last past as the steward is told on behalf of the lord by Richard Peper Receiver there that the same Thomas the reeve for his deceptions and contempts aforesaid is at a fine with the lord of 66s 8d and that he has the freeing and seisin of lands and tenements whereof the deception by him arose under fines put by him entered in the rolls of the courts and under this fine above-said he *becomes* a pauper (causa paupertatis sue) [Note: I was trying to get the sense of the fines causing the impoverishment so the sense is right but not an exact translation]

Affeerors: Nicholas Stanlowe, Roger Smyth

Sum of this court with the fine of Thomas Jankys £3 15s 5d

Expenses of the clerk of the lord's court being there with 1 horse for 1 day. Richard Bulveys the reeve and the beadle for the reason of holding this court 2s

1405-1406 P314/W/1/1/234

Worefeld	Great court held there on Friday the last day of April in the seventh year of the reign of King Henry IV from the conquest [30 April 1406]
Essoin	William Rugge himself from appearance by John Hethe
amerced 12d	John Wynter (4d), Thomas Coliar (4d) & Roger Gille (4d) did not come to warrant their essoin. So each of them is in mercy
the 12	Richard Bulveis, Nicholas Rowlow, Thomas Swancote, Roger Cattestre, Stephen Bradene, Roger Kyngeslowe, Roger Richardes, John Barndele, William Wermod, Roger Waltone, Roger atte Broke, Mathew Bullok
Kyngeslowe, Stanlowe	Townships there present nothing
Chesturtone amerced 12d	Township there presents that Margaret Tresel raised the hue and cry by mouth on William the servant of Thomas Rugge deceased unjustly so the said Margaret (12d) is in mercy
Hultone amerced 6d	Township there presents that David Walschmon was forestalled by Peter Hultone so the said Peter (6d) is in mercy
Rowlow, Bradene, Asturhul, Ewyk, Soonde amerced 2s 10d	Townships there present that William Henene (4d) who is bound to make appearance at this court did not appear so the said William is in mercy. Also they say that John Englich clerk made homesoken on Thomas Taillour and forestalled the same Thomas. So the said John both for the homesoken (12d) and for the forestalling (6d) is in mercy. And they say that Robert Taillour made homesoken on John Jonesone Rowlowe so the said Robert (12d) is in mercy
Roughtone, Barndele, Hoccombe, Swancot amerced 4d	Townships there present that John Huwessone (4d) who is bound to make appearance at this court did not appear so the said John is in mercy.
Burcot, Burcot, Ryndelford, Bromle amerced 8d	Townships there present that Richard Hethe (4d) & Roger Beechhay (4d) who are bound to make appearance at this court did not appear so each of them is in mercy.
Alvescot, Wynnescot, Cattestre, Newtone	Townships there present nothing
Ewdenas, Oldyntone amerced 18d	Townships there present that William the son of William Oldyntone forestalled (6d) John his brother and from the same John drew blood (12d) so the said William the son of William both for the forestalling and for the bloodshed is in mercy
Stapelford	Township there presents nothing
Akeltone amerced 2s 2d	Township there presents that William Gold (4d), Richard Hethe (4d) & Roger Hethe (4d) who are bound to make appearance at this court did not appear so each of them is in mercy. And they say that Margaret the wife of Simon atte Broke forestalled Alice Undurhull so the said Margaret (6d) is in mercy. Also they say that Robert Pikersley

Akeltone [contd.]	made an assault on John the son of William Goold so the said Robert (8d) is in mercy
Wyke amerced 20d	Township there presents that William Bruggende made an assault on William Rowlowe so the said William (8d) is in mercy. Also they say that Alice Baret raised the hue and cry by mouth unjustly on William Yngmon so the said Alice (12d) is in mercy
Haalen amerced 3s 8d wait 4d	Township there presents that John Wynter (4d) who is bound to make appearance at this court did not appear so the said John is in mercy. Also they present that William the son of John Billyngesley entered the house of Roger Gille and from thence took and carried away unjustly 4 pence in silver. So the said William is in mercy assessed at 3s 4d
Worefeld amerced 7s	Township there presents that John Henene who is bound to make appearance at this court did not appear so the said John (4d) is in mercy. Also they present that John Englisch (3s 4d) clerk forestalled Henry Barker & hit the same Henry so the said William is in mercy. And they say that the King's highway there is damaged by the blocking of the water course there by Matilda Rugge (3s 4d) so the said Matilda is in mercy
The ale tasters 25s 4d	present that Richard Bulveis brewed 5 [times] (3s 4d), Thomas Soonde 3 (2s), Agnes Smyth 4 (2s 8d), Elena Taillour 2 (16d), Thomas Haselwode 1 (8d), John Billyngesley 3 (2s), Robert Bruggende 1 (8d), Robert Ewdenas 1 (8d), John Smyth junior 2 (16d), John Walle 1 (8d), Thomas Hugge 1 (8d), John Baret 1 (8d), Thomas Richardes 1 (8d), Walter Rugge 1 (8d), Hamund Humele 1 (8d), Roger Smyth 1 (8d), Peter Huchen 1 (8d), Roger Hethe 1 (8d), Mathew Bullok 1 (8d), John the son of John Rowlowe 1 (8d), William Yngmon 2 (16d), William Carter 1 (8d), John Walker 1 (8d), William Mulwart of Ryndelford 1 (8d) and that all sold against the assize so each of them is in mercy
the 12 jurors amerced 3s 10d	present that the township of Wyke in their presentation concealed namely that William Rowlowe made an assault on Margery the servant of Thomas Hultone so the said township (12d) is in mercy for the concealment and the same William (8d) is in mercy for the assault aforesaid. And they say that all the brewers presented by the tasters broke the assize and sold by illegal measures so they are all in the mercy assessed above. And they say that Richard Barewe (6d), Thomas Soonde (6d), William Gerbod (8d) and William Kyngessone (6d) butchers, sold meat at high prices so each of them is in mercy
pain supervised	It is ordained by the agreement of the steward and the whole domain that each of the brewers within the domain will in the future time brew good and fit beer and each should sell it by legal measures and should maintain in all assizes without default that if they fail they will pay and will give to the lord from each brewing 3s 4d
forfeit 1 horse 20s	The reeve is charged for one horse price 20s remaining in his custody which fell to the lord as chattels forfeit from the goods of William Mulwart a felon taken and arrested for diverse thefts

Affeerors: Nicholas Rowlowe, Thomas Rugge
Sum of this court £3 11s 10d

1405-1406 P314/W/1/1/234

Worefeld	Small court held there on Monday next after the feast of St Mathew the Apostle in the 7th year of the reign of King Henry IV from the conquest [27 September 1406]
The 12	Roger Richardes, John Barndeleye, William Wermod Roger Waltone, Roger atte Broke, Mathew Bullok Nicholas Rowlow, Thomas Swancote, John Janne Stephen Bradene, Roger Kyngeslowe, Nicholas Stanlowe
amerced 6d heriot 1 ox, 1 cow 14s 4d escheat 1 horse, 1 sow with 4 piglets & 4 pigs 12s	The jury for the lord say on their oath that John Wynter (3d) & Richard Hethe (3d) who are bound to make suit at this court made default so each of them is in mercy. And they say that Roger Hichecokes who held from the lord by custom one messuage, one toft & three nooks of land in Bromle has died after whose death there fell to the lord 1 ox price 8s, 1 cow price price 6s 4d in the name of heriot. And in the name of escheat 1 horse price 6s, 1 small sow with 4 piglets price 2s & 3 pigs price 4s which goods and chattels remain in the custody of the reeve until overseen by the Receiver of the lord if they are of a greater price or not. And the tenements aforesaid remain with Joan his wife for the term of her life by the custom of the manor
heriot 1 ox, 1 cow 15s escheat 1 horse, 2 sows & 6 pigs 9s 8d	And they say that Thomas Rugge named who held from the lord in Chesturtone by custom one messuage, 1 toft, one virgate & 3 nooks of land with appurtenances has died after whose death there will fall to the lord 1 ox price 8s, 1 cow price7s, in the name of heriot and in the name of escheat 1 horse price 4s, 2 small sows and 6 pigs price 5s 8d which goods and chattels remain in the custody of the reeve until overseen by the Receiver of the lord if they are of a greater price or not. And the tenements aforesaid remain to Margery his wife for the term of her life by their customs etc.
Supervised which fine is charged in the accounts aforesaid	It is ordered by the steward on behalf of the lord that he makes to raise without further delay to the use of the lord from John Ewdenas, Thomas Swancot & Richard Bulveys pledges of the same John £13 6s 8d to the lord from the same debt of a certain fine which the same John made with the council of the lord for 1 messuage and 1 virgate of land with its appurtenances in Asturhull which Robert his uncle formerly held as is clear in the great court held at Worefeld on Thursday next after the feast of St Andrew the Apostle in the second year of the reign of King Henry IV after the conquest
Escheat 4 horses 21s	And afterwards the same reeve is charged concerning 2 horses price 17s coming to the lord from the escheat of Thomas Rugge above named and concerning two horses price 4s coming as the escheat of Roger Hichecokes above deceased
Issue of the meadow 10s overseen	The same reeve is charged concerning 10s for the hay and herbage of 1 meadow in Ryndelford sold by him for two & a half years past which meadow remains in the hand of the lord from a surrender by Richard Hethe as is clear in the court rolls in the last year preceding
Issue 16d overseen	The same reeve is charged this year concerning 16d of the issue of 1 nook of land remaining in the hand of the lord by the death of Nicholas the Frenche as is clear in the rolls of the court for this year last of ancient rent
Increase 8d overseen	The same reeve freely is charged concerning 8d from the increase this year of a certain pasture called Wollemorelye demised by him beyond the ancient rent 12d to Thomas Muychhale

+ Thomas Richards

Fine 13s 4d

John Fowler and Margery his wife, the said Margery confessed and examined by the steward, surrendered into the hands of the lord one messuage and half a virgate of land with appurtenances in Newtone to the use of Thomas Richards and Margery his wife the which Thomas & Margery his wife came in court and took from the lord the messuage and half virgate of land aforesaid with its appurtenances to hold to themselves and the heirs of their bodies between them legitimately procreated from the lord according to the custom of the manor by services and customs thence due and accustomed. And if it should happen the said Thomas and Margery die without heirs of their bodies legitimately procreated then the aforesaid messuage and half virgate of land is to remain and revert to the closest heirs of the said Thomas according to the custom of the manor. And they give to the lord for a fine at ingress 13s 4d and made fealty and in the same manner they are seized etc.

Fine 10s

Thomas Barbour clerk and Katherine his sister surrendered into the hand of the lord one toft and half a virgate of land with appurtenances in Hoccombe to the use of Roger Gerbod and Agnes his wife the which Roger and Agnes his wife came in court and took from the lord the toft and half a virgate of land aforesaid with its appurtenances to hold to themselves and the heirs of their bodies legitimately procreated and for default of their issue to the heirs and assigns of the said Roger for ever from the lord in fee by services and customs thence due according to the custom of the manor. And they give to the lord for a fine 10s. And thence they have seisin and made fealty to the lord

Fine 13s 4d

John the son of William Stevenes kinsman and heir of John Stevenes and Margery his wife deceased came here in court and took from the lord 2 messuages and one virgate of land with appurtenances in Chesturtone,4 parts of one nook of land the same which Margaret relict of the said William Stevenes now holds for the term of her life excepted to hold to the same John the son of William and his heirs by the right of heredity from the lord by services and customs thence due according to the custom of the manor. And he gives to the lord for a fine 13s 4d. And he has seisin and made fealty to the lord

Fine 12d

William Holygreve surrendered into the hand of the lord 2 cottages in Haalen and afterwards he came here in court and took the said cottages to himself and Emmoter his wife to hold for the term of their lives. And after the death of the same to John the son of the same William and Margery his wife and the heirs of their bodies between them legitimately issued and for default of their issue to the heirs and assigns of the said John for ever from the lord in fee according to the custom of the manor by services thence due and accustomed. And they give to the lord for a fine 12d and no more because paupers

Fine 5s

Fine 3s 4d

Roger atte Towneshende surrendered into the hand of the lord one nook of land with appurtenances in Haalen, two acres of land in the same which Petronilla Nelde holds excepted to the use of Edith the daughter of Henry Barker. The which Edith took the said nook of land with appurtenances except the pre-exception to hold to herself and her heirs and assigns for ever from the lord according to the custom of the manor by services and customs thence due. And she gives to the lord for a fine 5s. And she made fealty and is seized. And afterwards the aforesaid Edith made a fine with the lord for herself to marry wherever and whosoever is pleasing to her. And she gives to the lord for a fine 3s 4d pledge for the fine Richard Bulveys

Fine and licence 20s

Roger Waltone surrendered into the hand of the lord one messuage and half a virgate of land with appurtenances in Swancote the which Roger in court took back the messuage and half a virgate of land with its appurtenances to hold to himself for the term of his life and after his death to John the son of the same Roger and Agnes his wife and the heirs of their bodies legitimately issued and for default of their issue to the rightful heirs and assigns of the same Roger for ever from the lord by services and customs thence due and accustomed. And they give to the lord for a fine at ingress and for a licence from the lord to marry Agnes namely 20s. And they made fealty and are thus seized

Fine 13s 4d

William Holygreve surrendered into the hand of the lord one toft and half a virgate of land with appurtenances in Haalen and afterwards took back in court the toft and half a virgate of land aforesaid with its appurtenances to hold to himself for the term of his life and after his death that it remains with John the son of the same William and Margery his wife and the heirs of their bodies between them legitimately procreated and for default of their issue to the heirs and assigns of the said John for ever from the lord according to the custom of the manor by services & customs thence due and accustomed. And they give to the lord for a fine 13s 4d and made fealty. And thus they are seized

stray or waif 1 ox 11s Fine for contempt and deception 3s 4d

Thomas Jankys in the time in which he was reeve seized one ox colour fallow (Falwe) price 11s coming as a stray or as a waif which ox he did not present in the court of the lord nor enrol but freed the said ox outside the liberty without a warrant from the steward or any of the council of the lord just as recognised before the steward in court. So the said Thomas is charged by the lord for the price of the ox aforesaid and furthermore to a fine with the lord for deception and contempt (3s 4d)

amerced 4d distraint

Thomas Tresel the beadle (4d) is in mercy because he did not distrain Margaret Tresel to respond to William Bruggende in a plea of trespass. And it is ordered to the bailiff to distrain the same Margaret before the next [court] to respond to the said William in the plea aforesaid

amerced 4d distraint

Roger atte Towneshend (4d) still is in mercy because he did not have Richard Hethe to respond to Thomas Jankys in a plea of debt. And it is ordered to the bailiff to distrain the same Richard before the next [court] to respond to the said Thomas in the same plea

amerced 4d distraint

Still Richard Hethe and his pledges namely John Walker & Roger Touneshende in mercy for default against Richard Hichecokes in a plea of broken agreement. And it is ordered to the bailiff to better distrain the said Richard to respond to the said Richard in the plea of broken agreement

amerced 6d

Agnes Turbeville in mercy because she is not prosecuting against Thomas Heyne in a plea of debt

amerced 6d

Alice Dolemon in mercy because she is not prosecuting against William Dalicote in a plea of debt

amerced 6d

Alice Baret & her pledge in mercy because of her failure in law against Adam Spicer in a plea of debt

amerced 4d distraint	Roger Dalley in mercy because he did not have Emmoter Dalley to respond to Adam Spicer in a plea of debt. And it is ordered to the bailiff to better distrain Emmoter that she is at the next [court] to respond to the said Adam in the plea aforesaid
amerced 4d distraint	Thomas Soonde in mercy because he did not have John Fischer to respond to Thomas Richardes in a plea of debt. And it is ordered to distrain John himself that he is at the next [court] to respond to the said Thomas in the plea aforesaid
amerced 6d	William Oldyntone junior put himself in mercy for a licence to agree with John his brother in a plea of trespass
amerced 6d	The same William Oldyntone put himself in mercy for a licence to agree with the said John his brother in a plea of debt
amerced 6d	John Fischer is in mercy for an unjust plea against Alice Wyntur in a plea of trespass
Recovery amerced 6d	The same John Fischer plaintiff against Alice Wyntur in a plea of debt pledge for the prosecution Richard Bulveys who seeks from the said Alice 11d in silver which she owes him etc. and unjustly detains etc. And the said Alice present recognised the said debt. And the said Alice is in mercy
Distraint	Henry Barker plaintiff against William Pallehogge in a plea of trespass
Distraint	William Oldyntone plaintiff offered himself against John his son in a plea of debt who summoned did not come so to distrain
The next	Katherine Rugge plaintiff against Richard Bocher in a plea of debt pledge for the prosecution John Hethe who is not summoned so let it be done
Supervision to the next	Still it is ordered to the reeve on behalf of the lord to distrain the land of the tenants of Akeltone that they are at the next court of Worefeld on Monday without delay to make homage to the lord and fealty and other services owed to the lord. And further to show how they are ingressed in the same etc.
Ordination of the reeve	Thomas Swancote is elected by the homage of the lord to serve the lord in the office of reeve for the year next in the future. And he is sworn
Overview	Concerning the inspection of the writing in the rolls of pigs as is clear above in the roll adjourned etc. until (£7 19s)

Affeerors: Nicholas Rowlow, Thomas Hugge
Sum of this court £9 3s 4d price of fine of Asturhull

In the expenses of John Boerley the steward being there with 6 horses for 3 days and 3 nights for the sake of holding two courts here and for other diverse negotiations of the lord to oversee and to try 27s 6d

1406-1407 P314/W/1/1/235

Worefeld	Great court held at Worfeld on Tuesday the 23rd day of October in the eighth year of the reign of King Henry IV after the conquest [23 October 1406]
amerced 6d	Walter R…[torn] is in mercy because he should have come to warrant his essoin
the 12	Robert Ewdenas Stephen Bradeney William Gerbode Roger Cattestre Roger Waltone Roger Kyngeslowe Roger Richardes Robert Hogge Mathew Bullok John Tumpkys William Wermod Roger Broke
Kyngeslowe, Stanlow strays 2d	townships there present one swarm of bees coming as a stray price 2d which is in the custody of Roger Kyngeslowe whereof the reeve is charged to respond to the greater profit to the lord
Chesturtone amerced 2s	township there presents that William Prestis made an assault on John Stevenes so the said William (12d) is in mercy. And they say that the same John Stevenes made an assault on the aforesaid William so the said John (12d) is in mercy
Hultone	township there presents nothing
Rowlowe, Bradeney, Asterhull, Ewyke, Soonde amerced 10d	townships there present that William Henene who is bound to make an appearance at this court did not appear so the said William (6d) is in mercy. Also they present that John Yate forestalled Robert Taillour so the said John (6d) is in mercy
Roughtone, Barndele, Hokkombe, Swancote amerced 6d	townships there present that Thomas Forster who is bound to make an appearance at this court did not appear so the said Thomas (6d) is in mercy
Burcote, Burcote, Ryndelford, Bromle strays 3 swarms 18d	townships there [present] 2 swarms of bees came as a stray price 12d which are in the custody of Roger Willen. Also they present 1 swarm of bees which is in the custody of Richard Hichecokes price 6d. Concerning which the reeve is charged to respond for the greater profit to the lord
Alvescote, Wynescot, Cattestre, Newtone strays 6d	townships there present 1 swarm of bees price 6d which is in the custody of Roger Cattestre concerning which the reeve is charged to respond to the greater profit to the lord
Ewdenas, Oldyntone amerced 13s 6d Waifs 3d	townships there present that Richard Baret (6d), John Colynes (6d), Richard Baret junior (6d) and Henry Pertone (6d) unjustly made paths illegally for the middle of the fields of Ewdenas to the damage and nuisance of the neighbours there so each of them is in mercy. And they said that John Oldyngtone forestalled Alice the wife of William Oldyntone so the said John (6d) is in mercy. And they said that John Oldyntone broke into the pound of John Jonkys so the said John Oldyntone (12d) is in mercy. Also they present that John Oldyntone is a regrater of bread and ale and sold ale by illegal measure so the same John (3s 4d) is in mercy. And they say that Agnes (3s 4d) the wife of William Oldyntone unjustly took from the house of John Oldyntone 1 pound of candles price 1½d so the said Agnes is in mercy. Also they say that John Oldyntone entered the house of William Oldyntone and from thence unjustly took one pound of

	candles price 1½d so the said John (3s 4d) is in mercy
Stapelford amerced 18d	township there presents a homsoken made by Henry Dalleye (6d), John Elys (6d) and John Skarlet (6d) so each of them is in mercy
Akeltone amerced 7s	township there presents that John Glover forestalled Roger Dalley so the said John (6d) is in mercy. And they say that that the same Roger Dalley (12d) drew the blood from the same John Glover, so the said Roger is in mercy. And they say that the same John Glover drew the blood (12d) of John Baret so the said John Glover is in mercy. And they say that the same John Glover drew the blood of John Dalley so the said John Glover (12d) is in mercy. And they say that John Dalley (6d) forestalled Thomas Tresel so the said John is in mercy. And they say that Richard Parlour made homesoken on Thomas Gold so the said Richard (6d) is in mercy. Also they say the same Thomas Goold raised the hue and cry by mouth on the said Richard Parlour justly so the said Richard (12d) is in mercy. And they say that John Dalley drew the blood of Thomas Tresel so the said John (12d) is in mercy. Also they say that Richard Parlour forestalled John Elcok so the said Richard (6d) is in mercy
Haalen amerced 2s 6d	township there presents that William Englich (6d) who is bound to make appearance at this court did not appear so the said William is in mercy. Also they say that John Cattestre forestalled (6d) Robert Taillour so the said John is in mercy. Also they say that John Bokenhale forestalled (6d) Robert Taillour so the said John is in mercy. And they say that Isabell Barker raised the hue and cry by mouth (12d) on William Barker justly so the said William is in mercy
Wyke	township there presents nothing
Worfeld amerced 12d	township there presents that Richard Parlour who is bound to make appearance at this court did not appear so the said Richard (6d) is in mercy. Also they present the King's highway there is deteriorated by a water blockage from a default by Matilda Rugge so the same Matilda (6d) is in mercy
The tasters of ale amerced 22s 2d	present that William Nore brewed 1 (6d), John Smyth (5 brewings 2s 6d), Robert Barker (3 18d), William Oldyntone 1 (6d), John Bewmes (3 18d), John Walle 1 (6d), John Smyt 1 (6d), John Billyngesleye 1 (6d), John Yate 1 (6d), William Gold 1 (6d), Thomas Soonde 1 (6d), William Robynes 1 (6d), Henry Barker 1 (6d), Roger Jones 1 (6d), Robert Galian (2 2s) whereof 1 measure illegal, William Webbe 1 (6d), Stephen Humele (2 2s), Walter Rugge 1 (6d), Thomas Muychhale 1 (6d), and Richard Bulveys 6 (6s 8d) and used illegal measures so etc.
The 12 jurors Forfeit 2s	say on their oath that the townships aforesaid and the tasters of ale have well and faithfully presented and concealed nothing. Further they say that Richard Durgate formerly the servant of Hamond Humeleye has 1 sword price 2s as of the forfeiture of John Fisher felon concerning which the reeve is charged to respond to the greater profit of the lord
Forfeit 13s 4d	Also the reeve is charged concerning 13s 4d to raise from Thomas Hugge and William Bruggende for 2 oxen falling to the lord as from the forfeiture of William Mulwart who was seized & arrested for several thefts

Forfeit 13s 4d

The reeve still is charged concerning the goods and chattels below written falling to the lord from the forfeiture of John Fischer from the thefts of the clerk committed for the felonies namely concerning 6 silver spoons price 10s, 1 horse price 4s 6d, 11d cash, 6 pigs with 4 piglets price 14s, 1 cow price 5s 6d, 1 young female pig price 4s, 1 old coffer price 8d, 1 box price 4d, 1 verjuice barrel price 4d, 1 wheel price 2d, 1 wooden water container with screen price 11d, 1 pipe price 12d, 1 stand price 12d, 1 pail price 1½d, 1 herring barrel price 6d, 1 chair price 2d, 2 tables price 6d, 2 benches price 3d, 1 trough (alveus) price 1d, 1 breadbasket price 4d, 1 shallow dish (tornel) price 2d, 1 brass cooking pot price 20d, 1 parcel of firewood, price 6d, half of 1 salted pig price 12d, 1 yard of white cloth price 12d, 1 old blanket price 8d, 1 old gown price 8d, 2 lees of yarn price 2d, 2 stones of wool price 2s, 2 daggers price 4d, 1 crushing hammer (crussyngmale) price 12d, 1 iron can with 1 tripod price 2s, 1 spit with 1 iron fork price 6d, 1 balance, 1 beam, 1 balance of metal with 1 avoirdupois weight price 4s 4d, 1 iron adze price 3d, 1 vetus for a horse, 44 bars (gaddes) of steel price 10d, 6 brasiers price 4d, 1 pound of lead price 1d, 1 old woolsack price 18d, 1 old rope price 6d, 1 bolster price 3d and 1 hatchet price 2d which good above were inspected by the supervisor of the lord

contempt 3s

Also the reeve is charged concerning 3s to raise to the use of the lord concerning Nicholas Stanlowe, Roger Kyngeslowe and Thomas namely from each of them 12d for contempt because at the time of the delivery of the aforesaid John Fischer felon before the steward they did not wish to account as they were charged by the bailiff of the lord

Affeerors: Robert Ewdenas, Roger Richardes
Sum £6 18s ½d

Worfeld

Small court held there on Thursday the 17th day of March in the eighth year of the reign of King Henry IV after the conquest [17 March 1407]

Inquiry held for the lord by the oath of

Roger Richardes	Stephen Bradeney	William Gerbod
John Barndeleye	Roger Waltone	Roger Kyngeslowe
Thomas Swancote	Robert Hogge	Mathew Bullok
Nicholas Rowlowe	William Wermod	Roger Broke

the 12

heriot 2 oxen 15s escheat 1 horse 4s

Tenements in the hand of the lord

jurors say on their oath that Thomas Forster (3d) who is bound to make suit at this court did not come so the said Thomas is in mercy. And they say that Margery Rugge who held of the lord one messuage, one toft, one cottage, seven nooks and three acres of land with appurtenances in Chesturtone has died whereof there falls to the lord 2 oxen in the name of heriot price 15s and for escheat 1 horse price 4s concerning which heriot and escheat the bailiff is charged to answer to the greater profit of the lord. And they say that Alice the wife of Richard Hichecokes is her closest heir. And the tenements remain in the hand of the lord

Fine 10s

John Walker comes in court and took from the lord one meadow at Ryndelford formerly Richard Hethe's and William his son to hold to himself and his heirs according to the custom of the manor. And he gives to the lord for a fine 10s and thence has seisin

Richard Hethe and William his son surrendered into the hand of the lord one messuage and one nook of land called Puttelond in Alvescote within the manor of Worfeld to the use of John Walker of Ryndelford the which John came here in court

Fine 5s — and took from the lord the aforesaid messuage and nook of land with appurtenances to hold to himself, his heirs and assigns from the lord according to the custom of the manor. And he gives for a fine 5s to be paid in the accounts and thence has seisin

Fine 20d — Richard Hethe above-named and William his son surrendered into the hand of the lord one cottage, one curtilage and one moor with appurtenances in Ryndelford the which William Ryndelford held to the use of the aforesaid John Walker the which John Walker came here in court and took from the lord the aforesaid cottage, curtilage, and moor with appurtenances to hold to himself, his heirs and assigns according to the custom of the manor. And he gives to the lord for a fine 20d and thence has seisin

Fine 10s — John Wyntur of Haalen and Margery his wife surrendered into the hand of the lord one messuage & half a virgate of land with appurtenances in Haalen the which Thomas Wyntur held called Smytheslond to the use of Robert Barker & Isabell his wife the which Robert & Isabell came here in court and took from the lord the aforesaid messuage & half a virgate of land with appurtenances to hold to themselves, their heirs and assigns from the lord according to the custom of the manor. And they give to the lord for a fine 10s to be paid in the accounts and thence have seisin

Fine 12d — John Aleyn and Alice his wife surrendered into the hands of the lord one cottage with appurtenances in Worfeld of the right of Alice and afterwards they received the said cottage from the lord to hold to themselves, their heirs and assigns according to the custom of the manor. And they give to the lord for a fine 12d and thence have seisin

Fine 2s — John of Severne surrendered into the hand of the lord two cottages, one croft called Forgecroft, with 1 selion in Roughtone to the use of John Skynner the which John came here in court and took from the lord the aforesaid cottages, croft and selion to hold to himself, his heirs and assigns from the lord according to the custom of the manor. And he gives to the lord for a fine 2s and thence has seisin

Increased rent 8d — It is granted by the lord to Andrew of Fekkenham & Elionor his wife, William Ewyke and Katherine his wife a certain pasture called Wolmorelyre within the domain of Worefeld to hold to themselves, their heirs and assigns from the lord according to the custom of the manor rendering thence annually to the lord 20d namely 12d from ancient rent and 8d from an increase. And for a fine they give nothing and thence have seisin etc.

amerced 6d — Margaret Tresel (6d) put herself in mercy for a licence to agree with William Bruggende in a plea of trespass

amerced 6d — Thomas Jankys (6d) is in mercy because he is not prosecuting against Richard Hethe in a plea of debt

amerced 6d — Richard Hichecokes (6d) is in mercy because he is not prosecuting against Richard Hethe in a plea of broken agreement

amerced 6d — Emmoter Dalley (6d) put herself in mercy for a licence to agree with Adam Spicer in a plea of debt

amerced 6d — Thomas Richardes (6d) is in mercy because he is not prosecuting against John Fisher in a plea of debt amerced 6d — William Palhok (6d) put himself in mercy for a licence to agree with Henry Barker in a plea of trespass

amerced 4d
distrain — William Oldyntone plaintiff against John his son in a plea of debt who is attached and charged did not come so the said John (4d) and his amercement are in mercy. And nevertheless it is ordered to the bailiff to better distrain John to the next [court] to respond to the aforesaid William in the plea aforesaid

amerced 6d — Katherine Rugge (6d) is in mercy because he is not prosecuting against Richard Bocher in a plea of debt

amerced 4d
distrain — Hamond Humeley (4d) is in mercy because he did not have John pledge Hamond Humeley the servant of Roger Baker of Brugge to respond to Roger Swancote in a plea of debt and nevertheless he is distrained. Adjourned to the next [court] to respond to the aforesaid Roger in the plea aforesaid

named
Fine 22s — Richard Hichecokes and Alice his wife the daughter and heir of Margery Rugge came here in court and took from the hands of the lord one messuage, one toft, one cottage, seven nooks of land and three acres of land with appurtenances in Chesturtone of the right and heredity of the aforesaid Alice to hold them from the lord according to the custom of the manor. And they give to the lord for a fine 22s and thence had seisin

Survey of heriots 7s 6d — The reeve is charged concerning 1 ox 7s 6d coming to the lord in the name of heriot from the death of William Gold who died seised of 1 cottage with 1 parcel of meadow in Hultone just as is found by the examination of the rolls. And for escheat of the same William still nothing falls to the lord because there was nothing. And the tenements remain to John Colet by custom. Concerning which heriot the reeve aforesaid is charged to respond to the greater profit of the lord

Affeerors: Robert Eudenas, Roger Richardes
Sum of this court £4 3s 3d

Expenses of John Borley steward being there for 2 days, 2 nights with 12 horses when arranging the 2 courts aforesaid 9s 3d as is clear in the schedule concerning the parcel thence settled

1407-1408 P314/W/1/1/236

Worfeld	Small court held there on Tuesday the 4th day of October at the beginning of the ninth year of the reign of King Henry IV [4 October 1407]
Essoins	Thomas Rowlowe of Hultone, John Holigreve, John Stevenes, John Bromleye & John Ries themselves from common [suit] by the reeve
Inquiry amerced 9d	Inquiry held for the lord by the oath of Roger Waltoun, Nicholas Rowlowe, Roger Richardes, Stephen Bradeneye, John Barndeleye, William Newe, John Hethe, Mathew Bullok, William Wermod, Robert Hogge, Andrew Fekkenham & Roger Broke who say on their oath that Thomas Forster (4d), Thomas Towart (4d) & John Morfeld clerk (4d) who are bound to make suit at this court did not come so each of them in mercy
heriot 1 ox 8s 6d Tenements in the hand of the lord the next	And they say that Roger Kyngeslowe who held of the lord by custom of the manor one toft, half a virgate and one parcel of land with appurtenances in Kyngeslowe has died whereof there fell to the lord in the name of heriot 1 brown ox price 8s 6d for which the reeve is charged to respond to the greater profit of the lord and they have a day to present in the next [court] who is his closest heir. And the tenements remains in the hand of the lord to be settled in the next small court following
heriot 1 steer 5s 6d Tenements in the hand of the lord	And they say that the aforesaid Roger Kyngeslowe sick before his death surrendered into the hand of the lord one messuage and half a virgate of land with appurtenances in Kyngeslowe aforesaid to the use of John Reignald etc. for which messuage and land the lord will have 1 ruby steer price 5s 6d as from the heriot of the same Roger.The said the surrender is not withstanding because it was too little before his death. And the tenement remains in the hands of the lord. To be settled in the next small court following
Escheat 6s 11½d supervise	And from escheat of the same Roger Kyngeslowe they say that the lord will have by their custom 1 horse price 2s 6d, 2 pigs, 1 young pig, 3 piglets price 3s 4d and half of two hives of bees price 13½d. And still there remains one hive of bees up to the next [court] as they believe as then it can be determined etc. for which escheat the reeve is charged to respond to the greater profit of the lord by the supervision of the supervisor of the lord
Supervision The next	And they say that John Reignald aforesaid immediately after the death of the aforesaid Roger Kyngeslowe died before a fine could be made with the lord for the tenement aforesaid. So concerning the heriot and escheat of the same John they seek a day for rendering the full verdict until the next [court]. And also who is the closest heir of the said John Reignald. And a day is granted to them until the coming of the council of the lord to be settled in the next small court following
Fine 5s	William Rowlowe came here in court and surrendered into the hands of the lord one toft and half a virgate of land with appurtenances in Chesturtone which William Ewyk formerly held to the use of John Rowlowe and Margery his wife the which John and Margery came and took from the lord the aforesaid tenements with appurtenances to hold to themselves and their [heirs] from the lord according to the custom of the manor for rent, services and customs thence due. And they give to the lord for a fine 5s thus granted by Richard Peper as is reported to the Steward by Richard Bulveys thus they are seized
Amerced 6d	William Oldyntone (6d) is in mercy because he is not prosecuting against John his son in a plea of debt

1407-1408 P314/W/1/1/236

Amerced 4d
Distrain

Hamund Humeleye (4d) is in mercy because he did not have John the servant of Roger Baker to respond to Roger Swancote in a plea of debt further on behalf of the lord it is ordered to the bailiff to better distrain the aforesaid John that he is at the next [court] to respond to the aforesaid Roger in the plea aforesaid

Election of the reeve

Thomas Swancote the reeve withdrew here from his office of reeve which office is entered into by Richard Aldith by the election of the homage of the lord. And he is sworn

Increase on sale 8d

The bailiff is charged here concerning 8d increase on the sale of pigs falling due to the lord from the escheat of Roger Kyngeslowe assessed by the inquiry aforesaid at 3s 4d as is clear above because above this they were sold by Richard Bulveis and the reeve on the other part by the said 8d namely to Joan the widow of John Reignald

Fine 2s

Richard Hethe surrendered into the hands of the lord one toft called Howeplace in Bromleye to the use of John Jannesone, Alice his wife and John Eliesone Bromleie and Christian his wife the which John, Jannesone, Alice his wife and John Eliesone Bromleie and Christian his wife came here in court and took from the lord the aforesaid toft to hold from the lord in this manner namely half the said toft aforesaid to John Jannesone, Alice his wife and their heirs according to the custom of the manor and the other half of the same toft to the said John Eliesone Bromleie and Christian his wife and their heirs according to the custom of the manor. And they give to the lord for a fine 2s. And in the manner aforesaid they are seized

Fine 8d

Thomas Rowlowe of Burcote & Roger Wille made a fine with the lord for a licence to have admittance between them in exchange to two parts of two curtilages in Burcote. And they give to the lord for a fine 8d

Sum of this court 30s ~~13d~~ 10½d

In expenses of the clerk of the court of the lord being there with 1 horse for 1 day, Richard Bulveis the reeve and the beadle accounted between the said Richard and the reeve 16d

Worfeld

Small court held there on Saturday next after the feast of St Gregory the Pope in the ninth year of the reign of King Henry IV after the conquest [17 March 1408]

Essoins

John Walker, John Huwessone, Andrew Fekkenham, Richard Bromle & William Kyngessone themselves from common [suit] by the reeve

The 12 sworn
amerced 6d

Inquiry held for the lord by the oath of Stephen Bradeneie, Nicholas Rowlowe, Roger Richardes, Roger Waltoun, John Barndeleie, John Hethe, William Newe, Robert Barker, Robert Hogge, Roger Broke, William Gerbode & Mathew Bullokes who say on their oath that Roger Batemon (3d) & Thomas Forster (3d) who are bound to do suit at this court made default. So each of them is in mercy

heriot 2 steers 13s 4d
escheat 2 horses, 1 boar, 1 hive & wax 4s 5d

And they say that Richard Hichecokes who held from the lord by the custom of the manor one messuage and one nook of land at Bromleye and one toft and half a virgate of land in Chestertoun on the day he died from whose death the lord will have in the name of heriot 2 oxen price 13s 4d. And for escheat 2 horses price 3s 4d, one boar price 6d, 1 hive of bees price 6d and wax in a certain old hive price 1d from which heriot and escheat the reeve is charged to respond to the greater profit of the lord. And the tenement aforesaid remains with Alice the widow of the same deceased by their custom

heriot 1 ox 7s 6d escheat 1 sow & 3 piglets 20d next supervision

And they say that John Munsterleye who held of the lord one messuage and half a virgate of land by the custom of the manor at Newtoun has died whereof the lord will have in the name of heriot one ox price 7s 6d. And for escheat 1 young sow with 4 piglets price 20d. And concerning 1 horse there they seek a day to render the full verdict until the next [court] and it is granted. For which heriots and escheats the reeve is charged to respond to the greater profit of the lord. And the tenements remain with Sibill the widow of the deceased. Until the aforesaid is settled as is clear below in the small court held on Tuesday the 7th day of August next following [settlement is added later]

Heriot and escheat nothing for the reason shown. Tenement remains in the hand of the lord

And they say that John Skynner who held of the lord by the custom of the manor one cottage with curtilage adjacent in Roughtoun has died whereof from heriot and excheat the lord will have nothing because there was nothing. Further they say on their oath that the same John Skynner before his death surrendered into the hand of the lord the aforesaid cottage with curtilage to the use of William his son. And thus it remains in the hand of the lord to be settled in the small court held there on Tuesday the 7th day of August next following this year [settlement is added later]

heriot 1 steer 7s escheat 2 horses, 1 sow with 8 piglets 5s 8d, 1 pig remaining

Fine 12s

The aforesaid jurors say that because Roger Kyngeslowe surrendered into the hand of the lord one messuage and half a virgate of land in lesser tenure with appurtenances in Kyngeslowe to the use of John Reignald, his heirs and assigns the which John immediately on this died before thence a fine with the lord could be made as is clear in the last small court preceding. On which they say that this does not hinder their custom, he died as if a tenant and that from his death the lord will have in the name of heriot 1 ox price 7s. And for escheat 2 horses price 8s, 1 young sow and 8 small pigs price 5s 8d and to be settled below in the court held on the 7th day of August next following [added later] 1 pig for which price a day is sought to render the verdict until the next [court]. And it is granted to them for better. On which comes Joan the widow of the aforesaid John Reignald and took from the lord the aforesaid messuage and half virgate of land with appurtenances as if in the name of the same John Reignald to hold from the lord for the term of the life of the same Joan according to the custom there required according to the custom of the manor. And after the death of the said Joan the aforesaid tenement with its appurtenances to remain to the rightful heirs of the aforesaid John Reignald. And she gives to the lord for a fine 12s. And made fealty to the lord

Fine 12s

John Hethe & Alice his wife, sister and heir of Roger Kyngeslowe came here in court and took from the hands of the lord one toft and half a virgate of land with appurtenances in Kyngeslowe of which Roger Kyngeslowe died seized as the right and inheritance of the aforesaid Alice to hold to the said John and Alice the heirs and assigns of Alice herself from the lord according to the custom of the manor. And they give to the lord for a fine 10s. And thence they have seisin

nothing (n[a])

Fine 5s

To this court comes Alice the daughter and heir of Thomas Rugge and Margery his wife and took from the hands of the lord one toft and one nook of land with appurtenances in Chesturtoun as the inheritance of the aforesaid Alice to hold to the said Alice and her [heirs] according to the custom of the manor. And she gives to the lord for a fine 5s. And she has seisin pledge for the fine John Hethe

Tenement in the hand of the lord	Robert Taillour and Alice his wife surrendered into the hand of the lord one cottage with curtilage adjacent in Haalen which John Huly formerly held to the use of John Bokenhale & Margery his wife. And thus it remains in the hand of the lord etc. settled below in the court held on the 7th day of August next following [settlement is added later]
Distrain	John Rogers [agreed (con)] plaintiff against Joan Malcher [recognised (r*)] in a plea of debt who summoned did not come so distrain
Distrain	Thomas Tumpkys [not prosecuting] plaintiff against John Hethe in a plea of debt pledge for the prosecution Richard Aldith who summoned did not come so distrain
Distrain	Roger Dalileie plaintiff against Stephen [+] Humeleye in a plea of debt pledge for the prosecution John Tumpkys who summoned did not come so distrain
Amerced 4d Distrain	Hamund Humeleie [agreed] (4d) is in mercy because he did not have here John [recognised] formerly the servant of Roger Baker of Brugge to respond to Roger Swancote in a plea of debt. And on behalf of the lord it is ordered to the bailiff to better distrain the aforesaid John that he be at the next [court] to respond to the aforesaid Roger, plaintiff, in the plea aforesaid
	Still concerning 1 hive of bees from the escheat of Roger Kyngeslowe as is clear in the last court preceding adjourned until the next [court]

Sum of this court £3 15s 5d
In expenses of the clerk of the court Richard Bulveis, the reeve and the beadle 15d between the said Richard and the reeve accounted

Worfeld	Great court held there on Monday 23rd April in the ninth year of the reign of King Henry IV after the conquest [23 April 1408]
Essoins	Robert Taillour & Thomas Muychhale themselves from appearance by the reeve

the 12

Roger Cattestre	Roger Richardes	Mathew Bullok
Richard Bulveys	Stephen Bradeneye	William Gerbod
Robert Ewdenas	Roger Waltone	Robert Hogge
John Tumpkys	William Newe	Henry Barker

Kyngeslowe & Stanlowe amerced 10d	Townships there nothing presented. Chesturtoun township there present that John Stevenes (6d) forestalled John Nelde. And that the same John Nelde (6d) forestalled the said John Stevenes so each of them is in mercy
Hultone stray 10d	township there presents one boar coming as a stray at the feast of St Martin last past which is in the custody of Thomas Hugge price 10d
Asturhull, Ewyk, Rowlowe, Bradeneye, Sonde amerced 16d	townships there present that William Henene who is bound to make appearance at this court did not appear so the said William (4d) is in mercy. And they say that Thomas the son of Richard Bradeneye made an assault (6d) on Thomas Knyght & also the same Thomas forestalled (6d). So the said Thomas son of Richard is in mercy

1407-1408 P314/W/1/1/236

Roughtone, Barndeleye, Hokkombe, Swancote amerced 3s 6d	townships there present that Thomas Forster pardoned by the steward who is bound to make appearance at this court did not appear. And they say that Richard Parlor forestalled (6d) Thomas Jankys & drew blood (12d) from him. So the said Richard is in mercy. Also they present that William Kyngesone drew the blood (12d) of Alice his maid so the said William is in mercy. And they say that the common way in Roughtone is damaged by the water course running there from the default of the township of Roughtone to the nuisance of the neighbours there. So the said township (12d) is in mercy
Burcote, Burcote, Ryndelford & Bromley strays 2s 8d amerced 18d	townships there present 2 sheep coming as strays which are now in the custody of the reeve price 2s 8d. Also they present that William Prestus forestalled (6d) Margery Lautoun the which Margery raised the hue and cry by mouth (12d) on the said William justly so the said William both for the forestalling and for the hue and cry is in mercy
Alvescote	Wynnescote, Cattestre, Newtoun townships there nothing presented.
Ewdenas, Oldyntoun amerced 9s	townships there present that John Jonkys forestalled John Oldyntoun and from him drew blood. So the said John Jonkys both for the forestalling (6d) and for the bloodshed (12d) is in mercy. Also they say that Alice the wife of John Oldyntoun raised the hue and cry (12d) on the said John Jonkys justly so the same John Jonkys is in mercy. Also they say that John (18d) the son of William Oldyntoun & William (18d) his brother forestalled John Jonkys & from him drew blood. so each of them both for the forestalling and for the flowing of blood is in mercy. Also they present that Roger the son of John Jonkys raised the hue and cry on John Oldyntoun & William his brother justly. So the said John (12d) & William (12d) are in mercy. And they say that John Oldyntoun forestalled Alice the wife of William his brother. So the said John (6d) is in mercy. Also they present that John Oldyntoun (12d) broke the pound of John Jonkys. So the said John Oldyntoun is in mercy
Stapelforde amerced 6s 8d	township there presents that John Elcok (6s 8d) unjustly blocked the course of the water of Worw to the nuisance of the neighbours there. So the said John is in mercy
Akeltone strays 4d amerced 5s	township there presents 1 infirm horse came as a stray at the feast of the Purification of the Blessed Virgin Mary last past which is in the custody of the reeve price 4d. And they say that Thomas Tresele forestalled John Elcok. So the said Thomas (6d) is in mercy. Also they present that the same John Elcok forestalled (6d) the said Thomas and from him drew blood (2s) so the said John is in mercy. And they say that John Hancokes made an assault on John Baret. So the said John Hancokes (12d) is in mercy. Also they say that the aforesaid John Elcok overstocked the pasture holding unjustly his animals so the same John (12d) is in mercy
Haalen amerced 8s	township there presents that Roger Gille made an assault on Henry Barker unjustly so the said Roger (6d) is in mercy. And they say that Robert Taillour (6d) forestalled John Cattestre and drew blood (12d) from him so the said Robert is in mercy. And they say that the same John Cattestre forestalled the said Robert so the said John (6d) is in mercy. Also they say that the same Robert Taillour forestalled Alice Cattestre so the said Robert (6d) is in mercy. Also they present that Roger Cattestre of Haalen forestalled John Bokenhale so the said Roger (6d) is in mercy. And they say that Edith Jones made homesoken (4d) on Elena Jones so the same Edith is in mercy. And that Elena Jones raised the hue and cry (8d) on Edith Jones justly so the said Edith is in mercy. Also they say that Thomas Tresle junior forestalled (6d) Robert Yngmon and

Haalen	drew blood (2s) from him. So the said Thomas is in mercy. And they say that John Stevenes forestalled (6d) Robert Yngmon & made homesoken (6d) on the said Robert Yngmon so the said John is in mercy
Wyke strays 10d amerced 3s 6d	township there presents that John the son of Robert Smyth forestalled (6d) William Dalicote & hit (12d) the same William so the said John is in mercy. And they say that Edith the wife of William Dalicote raised the hue and cry (12d) on the said John justly so the said John is in mercy. And they say that Matilda the wife of John Billyngesleye made an assault (4d) on Agnes the wife of Stephen Humeleye and from her drew blood (8d) so the said Matilda is in mercy. Also they present one swarm of bees coming as a stray which is in the custody of William Nore price 10d
Worfeld amerced 4s 10d	township there presents that John Henene (4d) who is bound to make appearance at this court did not appear so the said John is in mercy. And they say that William the son of Richard Barewe forestalled (6d) John the son of John Bradeneye & drew blood (12d) from him. So the said William is in mercy. And they say that William Piper of Hokkombe (12d) made homesoken on Richard Bocher and on the same Richard made an assault (2s). So the said William is in mercy
The ale tasters amerced 23s	present that Richard Bulveys brewed 4 (2s), Robert Taillour 6 (3s), John Oldyntoun 1 (6d), William Oldyntoun 1 (6d), William Huster 1 (6d), John Billyngesleye 1 (6d), John Pomell 1 (6d), Stephen Humeleie 1 (6d), John Yate 2 (12d), John Sonde 1 (6d), Thomas Sonde 4 (2s), John Smyth 5 (2s 6d), John Halle 1 (6d), John Bewmes 5 (2s 6d), Roger Dalley 1 (6d), John Aleyn 1 (6d), William Gold 1 (6d), John Bradeneye 1 (6d), Roger Knotte 1 (6d), John Kynwartoun 1 (6d), Roger Smyth 1 (6d), Hamond Humeleie 1 (6d), at Roughtoun 2 (12d) and that all sold against the assize and were using illegal measures. Also they present that John Oldyntoun in selling ale set aside the seal for the reason of malice while he had ale to sell. So the said John (12d) is in mercy and each of the brewers is in mercy
The 12 jurors amerced 3s	say on their oath that the townships aforesaid and the tasters of ale have well and faithfully presented and concealed nothing. Further they say on their oath that Richard (12d) the son of John Smyth, Thomas (12d) the son of Thomas Merwalle & Roger Gille (12d) fished in several waters of the lord without a licence from the lord. So each of them is in mercy
Fine for tanning hides 12d	John Bewmes made a fine with the lord for tanning hides for the present year to whom a licence is granted. And he gives 12d to the lord for a licence
amerced 6d	Joan Malcher (6d) put herself in mercy for a licence to agree with John Rogeres in a plea of debt
amerced 6d	Thomas Tumpkys (6d) plaintiff is in mercy because he is not prosecuting against John Hethe in a plea of debt
amerced 6d	John (6d) formerly the servant of Roger Baker put himself in mercy for a licence to agree with Roger Swancote in a plea of debt
Pannage & herbage of Sowdeleye for 2 years 20s	The bailiff has to respond concerning 20s as from herbage and pannage in the wood of Sowdeleye for 2 years last past namely to raise from the tenants of the township of Haalen

1407-1408 P314/W/1/1/236

Affeerors: Roger Cattestre, Nicholas Rowlowe

Sum of this court £4 17s 6d

Expenses of John Boerleie the steward are contained and written at the end of the small court next following

Worfeld	Small court held there on Tuesday the 7th day of August in the ninth year of the reign of King Henry IV after the conquest [7 August 1408]
The 12 for the lord	Roger Richardes, John Janne, Mathew Bullok, Stephen Bradeneye, Roger Broke, William Gerbod, Roger Waltoun, John Barndeleye, Robert Hogge, William Newe, Thomas Hugge, Henry Barker } all sworn
remains nothing here because settled below	Who say on their oath that 2 virgins and 1 widow were married for which the lord will have a fine. And that there remains in the hand of the lord for a fine to make 1 nook of land at Chesturtone, three cottages at the Sonde and 1 cottage at Haalen etc. for which the women are to make a fine for the land and cottages with the lord as is clear below
the next	Richard Thorne plaintiff against Thomas Hugge in a plea of land pledge for the prosecution William Newe
Amerced 4d distrain	The bailiff (4d) is in mercy because he did not distrain Stephen Humeleye to respond to Roger Dalileye in a plea of debt further on behalf of the lord it is ordered to the bailiff to distrain the said Stephen that he is at the next [court] to respond to the aforesaid Roger in the plea aforesaid
Fine 6s 8d	John Golde and Alice his wife made a fine with the lord because the said John was married to the aforesaid Alice without obtaining a licence from the lord. And they give to the lord for a fine 6s 8d to be paid within the accounts
Fine 2s	Robert Taillour and Alice his wife surrendered into the hands of the lord one cottage with curtilage adjacent in Haalen which John Huly formerly held to the use of John Bokenhale & Margery his wife the which John Bokenhale & Margery his wife came in court and took from the lord the said cottage & curtilage aforesaid with its appurtenances to hold to themselves and the heirs of their bodies legitimately procreated according to the custom of the manor. And in default of issue of them that it remains to the rightful heirs and assigns of the aforesaid Alice. And they give to the lord for a fine 2s to be paid within the accounts. And they made fealty to the lord and they thence have seisin. It is clear also concerning the said surrender in the court held on Saturday next after the feast of St Gregory last past this year
Fine 4s	John Skynnor surrendered into the hands of the lord two cottages, one croft with one selion in Roughtoun to the use of William his bastard son, his heirs and assigns the which William came in court and took from the lord the said cottages, croft and selions to hold from the lord to himself, his heirs & assigns according to the custom of the manor. And he gives to the lord for a fine 4s to be paid within the accounts. And thence he has seisin

1407-1408 P314/W/1/1/236

William Newtoun chaplain surrendered into the hands of the lord two cottages with curtilages adjacent in Sonde to the use of Joan the daughter of John Smyth, her heirs and assigns the which Joan came in court and took from the lord the two cottages and curtilages aforesaid with their appurtenances to hold to herself, her heirs and assigns from the lord according to the custom of the manor. And they [why they and not she?] give to the lord for a fine 4s to be paid within the accounts. And she is seized. And she made fealty to the lord

Fine 4s

Roger Yngmon surrendered into the hand of the lord two cottages with curtilages adjacent in the village of Haalen which was formerly Robert Yngmon's to the use of William Holigreve and Emmeline his wife, their heirs and assigns the which William and Emmeline his wife came in court and took from the lord the two cottages and curtilages aforesaid with their appurtenances to hold to themselves, their heirs and assigns from the lord according to the custom of the manor. And they give to the lord for a fine 4s and are seized

Fine 4s

Alice the Walker surrendered into the hand of the lord one cottage with curtilage adjacent in Sonde to the use of John Glover his heirs and assigns the which John came in court and took from the lord the said cottage with curtilage aforesaid with its appurtenances to hold to himself, his heirs and assigns from the lord according to the custom of the manor. And he gives to the lord for a fine 2s to be paid within the accounts. And he made fealty to the lord and is seized

Fine 2s

The bailiff here is charged by the steward to receive to the use of the lord one horse as of the escheat of John Munsterleie deceased price 6s and on behalf of the lord it is ordered that the same is supervised by the supervisor of the lord

Escheat 6s

William Prestes and Alice Rugge his wife, she confessed and examined according to the custom of the manor, surrendered into the hands of the lord one nook of land with appurtenances called Blencheslond in Chesturtoun to the use of Thomas Rugge the which Thomas came here in court & took from the lord the aforesaid nook of land with its appurtenances to hold to himself for the term of his life from the lord according to the custom of the manor. And after the death of the said Thomas the whole of the aforesaid land with its appurtenances should fully revert to Alice aforesaid and her heirs. And he gives to the lord for a fine 5s, made fealty to the lord. And thus he is seized

Fine 5s

William the son of Roger Swancote of Bromleie and Isabell [is it Alice or Isabell?] his wife made a fine with the lord because the same William was betrothed to the said Alice without obtaining a licence from the lord. And they give to the lord for a fine 6s 8d to be paid within the accounts

Fine 6s 8d

William Prestes and Alice his wife made a fine with the lord because the same William was married to the said Alice without obtaining a licence from the lord. And they give to the lord for a fine 13s 4d to be paid within the accounts

Fine 13s 4d

William Prestes and Alice his wife daughter and heir of Thomas Rugge and Margery his wife gave to the lord for 2 heriots falling due to the lord for one cottage and three acres of land in Chesturtoun after the death of the aforesaid Thomas and Margery to be held in severalty by them 10s 6d

Heriot 10s 6d

1407-1408 P314/W/1/1/236

Escheat 2s

The bailiff is charged for 2s for the killing of certain pigs of the lord as escheat from John Reignald stolen and hidden whereof the sheriff has to respond

Sum of this court £3 6s 6d

In expenses of John Boerleie the steward being there for 2 days and 2 nights for the reason of holding 2 courts 20s 3½d

Worfeld

Small court held there on Tuesday next after the feast of the Exaltation of the Holy Cross in the ninth year of the reign of King Henry IV after the conquest [18 Sept.1408]

Essoins

Henry Barker & John Holigreve themselves from common [suit] by the reeve

the 12 jurors

remaining not assessed

Inquiry held for the lord by the oath of Stephen Bradeneie, Roger Richardes, Roger Swancote, Nicholas Rowlowe, Robert Hogge, John Janne, John Walker, Roger Broke, Thomas Hugge, Mathew Bullokes, John Hethe, & Thomas Rowlowe who say on their oath that Thomas Muychhale, Nicholas Stanlowe, Roger Batemon, John Huwessone, John Morfeld chaplain, John Barndeleie, William Gerbod, Thomas Forster and Andrew Fekkenham who are bound to do suit at this court made default. So each of them is in mercy

Increases on the sale of heriots and escheats 6s 10d

The bailiff is charged concerning 14d of increase on the sale of 1 steer falling due to the lord in the name of the heriot of Roger Kyngeslowe assessed by an inquiry at 5s 6d because it was sold for a higher price by the said 14d by Richard Bulveis and the reeve as falling to the lord as is clear above in the first court of this year. The same bailiff has to respond concerning 2s 6d increase of the sale of 1 horse falling due to the lord as escheat of the same Roger as is clear in the same first court appraised by the inquiry at 2s 6d because it was sold by the said Richard and the reeve for 5s. The same bailiff is charged for 20d of the increase on the sale of 2 horses from the escheat of Richard Hichecokes assessed by the inquiry at 3s 4d as is clear above in the 2nd small court of this year because they were sold more dearly by the aforesaid Richard and the reeve by the said 20d. Also he is charged concerning 6d of the increase on the sale of 1 horse judged escheat of John Munsterleie as is clear above in the last small court preceding assessed before the steward at 6s because it was sold at a higher price by the said Richard and the reeve by the said 6d. And the same bailiff is charged of 2s increase on the sale of 2 horses of the escheat of John Reignald assessed by the inquiry at 8s as is clear above in the second small court this year because they were sold for a higher price by the aforesaid Richard and the reeve by the said 2s

Fine 3s

John Oldyntone, John Kynvartone and Margery his wife surrendered into the hands of the lord three acres of land lying divided in the field of Hultoun to the use of John the son of Stephen Bradeneye the which John son of Stephen came and took from the lord the aforesaid three acres of land with appurtenances to hold to himself and his [heirs] from the lord according to the custom of the manor. And he gives to the lord for a fine 3s. And he has seisin

Fine 2s

John Coletes & Isabell his wife surrendered into the hands of the lord two acres of land lying divided in the field of Hultone to the use of John & Roger the sons of Stephen Bradeneie the which John & Roger came and took from the lord the aforesaid two acres of land with appurtenances to hold to themselves and their [heirs] from the lord according to the custom of the manor. And they give to the lord for a fine 2s. And they have seisin

Fine 10d — John Coletes & Isabell his wife above-named surrendered into the hands of the lord one selion of land by itself lying in the field of Hultoun to the use of William the son of William Bruggende his [heirs] & assigns the which William the son of William came here in court and took from the lord the aforesaid selion of land with appurtenances to hold to himself and his [heirs] from the lord according to the custom of the manor. And he gives to the lord for a fine 10d because thence seisin is granted by Richard Bulveis

Remaining to supervise — Still remaining in the hand of the lord 1 hive of bees from the escheat of Roger Kyngeslowe except that a quarter part of the same hive is of the goods of St Peter's Church of Worfeld as is presented by the oath of the inquiry aforesaid with profit of the same if anyone settles, until it is supervised by the supervisor of the lord

Adjourned — Still the plea between Roger Dalileie plaintiff and Stephen Humeleie defendant in a plea of debt adjourned until the next [court]

Sum of this court 13s 8d prices not assessed

In expenses of the clerk of the court of the lord being there with 1 horse, Richard Bulveis the reeve and the beadle 9d

1408-1409 P314/W/1/1/237

Worfeld	Small court held there on Wednesday the 4th day of October at the beginning of the 10th year of the reign of King Henry IV after the conquest [4 October 1408] [not actually a Wedesday]
Essoins	John Huwessone & Thomas Richardes themselves for common [suit] by Richard Aldith still the reeve
Amerced 2s 3d	The reeve is charged to raise 2s 3d from Thomas Muychhale, Nicholas Stanlowe, Roger Batemon, John Huwessone, John Morfeld clerk, John Barndeleie, William Gerbod, Thomas Forster & Andrew Fekkenham for their amercements at the last court of the preceding year then not affeered namely from each of them 3d because they did not come to the said court
The 12 sworn Amerced 9d	Inquiry held for the lord on the oath of Stephen Bradeneie, Roger Richardes, Nicholas Rowlowe, Roger Waltone, John Barndeleie, Robert Hogge, William Newe, Henry Barker, John Walker, Roger Broke, John Janne & William Gerbod who say on their oath that Andrew Fekkenham, John Ries & Thomas Forster who are bound to make suit at this court made default so each of them is in mercy
Fine 12d Tenement in the hand of the lord oversee	Roger Cattestre made a fine with the lord for an inquiry by the aforesaid 12 ex officio to be held to enquire if one tenement namely 1 toft and half a virgate of land called Lovestikkelond in Haalen is in the hand of the lord for a fine thence to be made etc. And if it is in the hand of the lord whoever is the closest heir to take the said tenement from the hand of the lord by their custom. And he gives to the lord for a fine 12d. On which the 12 jurors whose names are above-named thence sworn and charged say on their oath that the tenement aforesaid remains in the hand of the lord by their custom until a fine was thence made with the lord. And who is the closest relative to take the said tenement out of the hands of the lord they seek a day thence to render the full truth until the next [court]
Fine 5s	Edith Colier, John Dalileie and Emmelina his wife the daughter of the same Edith surrendered into the hands of the lord half of one toft and one nook of land of the tenement called Waltoneslond in Chesturtone to the use of the same John Dalilieie. And the aforesaid Emelina confessed and examined before the steward says that this is done voluntarily of her own free will without coercion from her husband aforesaid. On which came here the aforesaid John Dalileie & took from the lord the aforesaid half of the toft and the nook of land to hold to himself, Emeline his wife and their heirs and assigns from the lord according to the custom of the manor by services and customs thence due. And they give to the lord for a fine 5s, made fealty to the lord and are seized
Tenement in the hand of the lord Oversee	Nicholas Stanlowe surrendered into the hand of the lord one cottage with curtilage adjacent in Sonde to the use of William Beore & Agnes his wife the which cottage Thomas Nicols formerly held. And so it remains in the hands of the lord until settled in the next court following
Escheat 2s	The bailiff presents that still remaining in the hands of William Prestes 1 boar from the escheat of Richard Hichecokes deceased price 2s of which the reeve is charged
Distrain	Thomas Towart plaintiff against John Rowlowe & William the brother of John himself in a plea of debt who summoned did not come so distrain

Distrain	The same Thomas Towart plaintiff against Thomas Yngemon in a plea of debt who summoned did not come so distrain
The next	John Bromleie plaintiff against Sibill Newtone in a plea of debt who is not summoned so let it be done
Election of the reeve	Richard Aldith withdrew here from the office of reeve to which office approached Thomas Hugge and Thomas Merwalle by the election of the homage. And it is by the agreement of the aforesaid inquiry Thomas Hugge is affirmed for the better. And he is sworn

Sum of this court 11s
In expenses of the clerk of the court Richard Bulveys the reeve and the beadle accounted between Richard Bulveis and the reeve for 1 day 15d

Worfeld	Small court held there on Tuesday next after the feast of the Conception of the Blessed Mary the Virgin in the 10th year of the reign of King Henry IV after the conquest [11 December 1408]
Essoins	Roger Batemon, John Waltone & Henry Barker themselves of common suit by Richard Bulveis
Amerced 4d	John Huwessone is in mercy because because he did not come to warrant his essoin
The 12	Stephen Bradeneie, John Walker, Roger Broke } John Hethe, Mathew Bullok, John Janne } Roger Richardes, William Wermod, William Newe } Roger Waltone, Thomas Hogge, Thomas Merwalle }
Amerced 6d	sworn who say on their oath that Andrew Fekkenham (3d) & John Huwessone (3d) who are bound to make suit at this court did not come so each of them is in mercy
Heriot & escheat remain still Oversee	And they say that Richard Bromleie who held of the lord by the custom of the manor one messuage and one nook of land with appurtenances in Bromleie has died outside the manor at Barewe. And concerning heriots and escheats of the same deceased they have a day to present until the next [court]. Furthermore John Bromleie the son and executor of the same deceased found a pledge namely Roger Smyth and John Hethe to satisfy the lord that it was just on their part. And the tenement remains in hand until the lord has what was then just concerning the heriot is settled in the small court to be held on the 9th day of July next after the date of this court
Tenement in the hand of the lord oversee	And they say that Robert Taillour surrendered into the hands of the lord one cottage with curtilage adjacent in Haalen to the use of John Hethe. And it remains in the hand of the lord to be settled in the small court to be held on the 9th day of July next after the date of this court
Fine 2s	William Beore & Agnes his wife came here in court and took from the hand of the lord one cottage with curtilage adjacent in Sonde which Nicholas Stanlowe surrendered into the hands of the lord to their use as is clear in the last court preceding to hold to the said William and Agnes, their heirs and assigns from the lord according to the custom of the manor by services and customs thence due. And they give to the lord for a fine 2s. And they have seisin

1408-1409 P314/W/1/1/237

	{	Thomas Towart plaintiff, John Rowlowe & William the brother of John himself, defendants in a plea of debt have a day to agree until the next [court] by their prayer
Adjourned Oversee	{	A day is given between Thomas Towart plaintiff and Thomas Yngemon defendant in a plea of debt until the next [court] by the prayer of the parties
	{	And between John Bromleie plaintiff & Sibill Newtone defendant in a plea

Sum of this small court 2s 10d

Expenses of the clerk of the court of the lord Richard Bulveys the reeve and the beadle accounted between Richard Bulveis and the reeve 15d

Worfeld	Small court held there on Tuesday the 22nd January in the 10th year of the reign of King Henry IV after the conquest [22 January 1409]
Essoins	John Morfeld clerk and Thomas Richardes themselves of common [suit] by the reeve
The 12 jurors amerced 12d	Inquiry held for the lord by the oath of Roger Richardes, Roger Waltone, John Barndeleie, Roger Broke, John Hethe, John Rowlowe, William Newe, William Cattestre, John Walker, John Janne, Stephen Bradeneie & Mathew Bullok who say on their oath that Andrew Fekkenham (3d), Roger Batemon (3d), John Ries (3d) & Thomas Forster (3d) who are bound to make suit at this court made default of the same suit so each of them is in mercy
Heriots 4 27s oversee	And they say that Thomas Swancote who held of the lord by the custom of the manor four tenements within the manor of Worfeld namely one messuage and one virgate of land in Swancote, one toft and one virgate of land in Bradeneie and 2 messuages and one virgate of land in Stapelford on the day he died from whose death the lord has four heriots for the 4 tenements aforesaid namely 3 oxen price 21s and 1 cow price 6s
Escheats 1 horse, 2 hives, 1 sow & 3 piglets 6s 8d Increase on sale 20d	And they say that concerning escheats of the same Thomas the lord will have one infirm horse and 2 hives of bees price 3s, 1 young sow price 16d & 3 piglets price 2s etc. which heriots and escheats are sold by the reeve for a higher price by 20d. Furthermore they seek a day until the next [court] to enquire on behalf of the lord if more escheats in any way could be found. And the tenements remain in the hand of Margery widow of the said deceased until by the council of the lord overseen
Tenement in the hand of the lord oversee	And they say that Agnes Turbevylle daughter of Thomas Turbevyle of Hultone surrendered into the hands of the lord one messuage and three nooks of land with appurtenances in Hultone to the use of Hugh Baker for the term of his life. And it remains in the hand of the lord until it is settled on the 9th day of July next following [Last sentence written later]
oversee	And they say that Agnes Turbevyle aforesaid married herself to Hugh Baker a licence from the lord thence not obtained to be settled on the 9th day of July after the date of this court [added later]
amerced 4d	Roger Batemon is in mercy because he did not come to warrant his essoin
amerced 6d	John Rowlowe & William his brother defendants put themselves in mercy for a licence to agree with Thomas Thowart plaintiff in a plea of debt

amerced 6d	Thomas Towart plaintiff and Thomas Yngemon defendant in a plea of debt for a licence to agree. And the same Thomas Yngemon put himself in mercy
amerced 6d	John Bromleie is in mercy because he is not prosecuting against Sibill Newtone in a plea of debt
adjourned	Still the suit between Richard Thorne plaintiff and Thomas Hugge defendant in a plea of land adjourned until the next

Sum of this court 37s 10d

In expenses of the clerk of the court being there with one horse the reeve and the beadle only at the lunch (prandium) 6d

Worfeld	Great court held there on Monday the 22nd day of April in the 10th year of the reign of King Henry IV after the conquest [22 April 1409]
Essoins	William Hugynes, Roger Batemon + & John Bokenhale themselves for appearance by Thomas Hugge the reeve

The 12			
	Roger Cattestre	Roger Richardes	Roger Broke }
	Richard Bulveis	Roger Waltone	John the son of Nicholas Rowlowe }
	Robert Ewdenas	Stephen Bradeneie	William Wermod } all sworn
	John Tumpkys	John Walker	Thomas Toward }

Kyngeslowe. Stanlowe amerced 6d	townships there present that Thomas Muychhale who is bound to appear at this court did not appear so the said Thomas (6d) is in mercy
Chesturtoun	township there presents nothing. Rowlowe, Bradeneie, Asturhull, Ewyk, Sonde townships there present nothing
Hultoun strays 12d	township there presents 1 infirm horse coming as a stray at the feast of the Purification of the Blessed Mary the Virgin last past price 12d
Roughtoun, Barndle, Hoccombe, Swancot amerced 6d	townships there present that William Skynner who is bound to appear at this court did not appear so the said William (6d) is in mercy. Also they present that Richard Parlour forestalled John the son of Thomas Jankys however he is pardoned by the steward
Burcote, Burcote, Ryndelford, Bromleie	townships there present nothing
Cattestre, Alwescote, Wynnescote, Newtone amerced 2s	townships there present that Roger Towneshende who is bound to appear at this court did not appear so the said Roger (6d) is in mercy. And they say that John Jonkys forestalled (6d) John Oldyntone and drew blood (12d) from him so the said John Jonkys both for the forestalling and for the bloodshed is in mercy

1408-1409 P314/W/1/1/237

Ewdenas, Oldyntone amerced 12d	townships there present that John the son of William Oldyntone made a boundary breach on John Jowkys in Oldyntone so the said John the son of William (12d) is in mercy
Stapelford	township there presents nothing.
Akeltoun amerced 3s waifs 4d	township there presents that Emelina the wife of Thomas Tresele broke the pound of Roger Dalileie so the said Emelina (12d) is in mercy. And they say that Roger Hethe unjustly diverted the common water course in the village of Akeltoun from its due course to the nuisance of the neighbours there. So the said Roger (12d) is in mercy. Also they present that Sibill atte Broke unjustly took 1 goose of Symon atte Broke price of the goose 4d. So the said Sibill (12d) is in mercy
Haalen amerced 4s 6d	township there presents that John Bokenhale forestalled (6d) Robert Taillour and drew blood (12d) from him. So the said John is in mercy. And they say that Robert Taillour made an assault (12d) on John Bokenhale and drew blood (12d) from him. So the said Robert is in mercy. Also they say that the same Robert Taillour justly raised the hue and cry by mouth on the said John Bokenhale so the said John (12d) is in mercy
Wyke amerced 18d stolen goods 11s 6d strays 6d	township there presents that Thomas Cowper (6d), William Rowlowe (6d & John Ries (6d) who are bound to appear at this court did not appear. So each of them is in mercy. And they say that John Brezenok is arrested for theft within the township of Wyke having in goods and chattels in the township aforesaid at the time of his arrest 5s 8d in money, 1 small sack of hemp price 12d. 1 cover (mappam) price 10d, 1 horse with a bridle price 4s sold by him to John Smyth. Also they present 1 swarm of bees as strays in the custody of William Carter price 6d concerning which the reeve is charged to respond to the greater profit to the lord
Worfeld amerced 18d	township there presents that John Bewmes (6d) forestalled Alice Gold. And that the same Alice raised the hue and cry (12d) by mouth on the said John justly. So the said John both for the forestalling and for the raising of the hue and cry is in mercy
the tasters of ale amerced 15s 2d	present that Thomas atte Sonde (18d) brewed 3, John Smyth of Sonde (18d) 3, John Bewmes (18d) 3, Robert Galian (12d) 2, William Nore (6d) 1, John Smyth of Wyke (12d) 1. John Rowlowe (12d) 1, John Baret (6d) 1, John atte Walle (6d) 1, Thomas Merwalle (6d) 1, William Newe (16d) 1, Hamund Humele (12d) 1 & that Joan Bulveis (3s 4d) is a common brewer and how much she has brewed they don't know. And they say that all the aforesaid brewers sold against the assize furthermore they say that John Smyth of Wyke, John Rowlowe, William Newe, Hamund Humele & Joan Bulveis used illegal measures so they are in mercy
	The 12 jurors present that the townships aforesaid and the tasters of ale have well and faithfully presented etc.
Pain	Sureties for Roger Dalileie to keep the peace towards Thomas the son of Thomas Jankys and the people of the lord King under a pain of £10 namely Robert Ewdenas. Nicholas Stanlow, Thomas Soonde & John Smyth

Affeerors: Robert Ewdenas, Stephen Bradeneie

Sum of this court 43s

The expenses of the steward are contained in the next small court following

1408-1409 P314/W/1/1/237

Worfeld Small court held there on Tuesday the 9th day of July in the 10th year of the reign of King Henry IV after the conquest [9 July 1409]

	John Janne	Mathew Bullok	Roger Mathew }	
the 12	John Bromleie	Roger Gerbod	John atte Walle}	
	William Barker	Roger Towneshende	John Waltone }	all sworn
	John Billyngesle	Roger Smyth	John Jonessone }	

Fine 20s

Thomas Hugges & Margery his wife surrendered into the hand of the lord one messuage and one virgate of land with appurtenances in Hultone called Adameslond Upyntone to the use of Richard Thorne his heirs and assigns the which Richard came in court and took from the lord the messuage and virgate of land aforesaid with appurtenances to hold to himself, his heirs and assigns from the lord according to the custom of the manor. And he gives to the lord for a fine 20s. And afterwards the same Richard surrendered in the same court the messuage and virgate of land aforesaid with appurtenances into the hands of the lord to the use of the aforesaid Margery so that the same Margery is able to hold and to possess so much for the term of her life from the lord according to the custom of the manor. And after her death the messuage and virgate of land aforesaid wholly reverts to the aforesaid Richard, his heirs and assigns for ever to hold from the lord according to the custom of the manor. To which Margery the messuage and virgate of land aforesaid with its appurtenances is granted by the lord in like manner to hold from the lord for the term of her life according to the custom of the manor. And after her death the messuage and virgate of land aforesaid with its appurtenances should remain to the aforesaid Richard, his heirs and assigns for ever to hold from the lord according to the custom of the manor. And he gives to the lord for a fine 13s 4d

Fine 13s 4d

Fine 15s

It is granted by the lord to Hugh Baker and Agnes his wife, the heirs and assigns of the said Agnes, one messuage and three nooks of land with appurtenances in Hultone which the same Agnes first surrendered into the hands of the lord to hold to their heirs and the assigns of the said Agnes from the lord according to the custom of the manor. And they give to the lord for a fine 15s. And they have seisin

Fine 6s 8d

John the son of Philip Dawes surrendered into the hands of the lord the reversion of one messuage and half a virgate of land with appurtenances in Hoccombe to the use of Thomas the son of Thomas Jankys, his heirs and assigns which ought to revert to the same John after the death of John Malcher who holds it for the term of his life. The which Thomas the son of Thomas the reversion of the messuage and the half a virgate of land aforesaid with its appurtenances is granted by the lord to hold to himself, his heirs and assigns from the lord after the death of the said John according to the custom of the manor. And he gives to the lord for a fine 6s 8d

Fine 2s

William Henene surrendered into the hand of the lord 2 cottages with 2 curtilages adjacent in Soonde to the use of John Henene his son and Agnes his wife, their heirs and assigns. The which John the son & Agnes came in court and took from the lord the cottages aforesaid with the curtilages to hold to themselves, his heirs and assigns from the lord according to the custom of the manor. And they give to the lord for a fine 2s. And they are seised

John Hethe came here in court and took from the lord one cottage with appurtenances in Haalen which Robert Taillor previously surrendered into the hands of the lord to the

Fine 2s	use of the same John to hold to the same John, his heirs and assigns from the lord according to the custom of the manor. And he gives to the lord for a fine 2s. And he is seised. And afterwards the same John surrendered into the hand of the lord in the same court the cottage aforesaid with curtilage to the use of Alice the wife of Robert Taillor, her heirs and assigns. The which Alice came in court and takes from the lord the said cottage with its appurtenances to hold to herself, her heirs and assigns from
Fine 2s	the lord according to the custom of the manor. And she gives to the lord for a fine 2s and is seised
Fine 20s	Robert atte Yate surrendered into the hands of the lord 2 messuages and one virgate of land with appurtenances in Roughtone to the use of William his son and Agnes his wife & the heirs of their bodies legitimately procreated and in default of the issue of them to the rightful heirs and assigns of the aforesaid William.The which William & Agnes came in court & took from the lord the aforesaid messuage and virgate of land with appurtenances to hold to themselves & the heirs of their bodies legitimately procreated & in default of none of them, to the rightful heirs of the aforesaid William for ever according to the custom of the manor. And they give to the lord for a fine 20s. And they are seised
Fine 10s	Hawisia Lewte & Richard her son surrendered into the hands of the lord one messuage and half a virgate of land with appurtenances in Stapelforde to the use of Thomas Merewalle junior his heirs and assigns. The which Thomas came here in court and takes from the lord the aforesaid messuage and half a virgate of land with appurtenances to hold to himself, his heirs and assigns from the lord according to the custom of the manor. And he gives to the lord for a fine 10s. And he is seised
Fine 3s 4d	It is granted by the lord that John the son of Hugh of Wottone will be able to lease from John Janne of Swancote 1 toft and half a virgate of land in Roughtone called Horscroftes for the term of 6 years next following meanwhile to be made for the said John as his attorney of the suit at the court of Worfeld. And he gives to the lord for a fine 3s 4d
Fine 5s	Agnes Turbvile widow made a fine with the lord because she married Hugh Baker a licence from the lord not obtained. And she gives for a fine 5s
Oversee	John Billyngesleie is granted by the lord 1 croft called Mulnecroftes in Worfeld to hold from the lord to himself, his heirs and assigns according to the custom of the manor rendering thence annually to the lord at the usual terms 5s. And he will have enclosure when it should be necessary to enclose the said croft from the handing over of the ministers of the lord
Heriot 10s	The bailiff is charged concerning 10s in the name of heriot from the death of Richard Bromleie by the pledge of John Hethe & Roger Smyth and there being nothing to the lord for escheats because there was nothing within the domain
+ Fine 10s	Alice Stevens surrendered into the hands of the lord one messuage and half a virgate of land in Haalen to the use of William Stevenes her brother, his heirs and assigns. The which William comes in court and takes from the lord the said messuage and half a virgate of land with appurtenances to hold to himself, his heirs and assigns from the lord according to the custom of the manor. And he gives to the lord for a fine 10s. And he has seisin
amerced 6d	John Hoccombe is in mercy because he is not prosecuting against William Yngman in a plea of debt by the pledge of the reeve

amerced 3d
distrain

William Bruggende plaintiff against Margaret Tresele in a plea of trespass etc. And because Richard Bulveis before this day did not summon nor distrain the said Margaret so he Richard (3d) is in mercy. And it is ordered to the bailiff to distrain her before the next court

the next

Joan Frаunceis plaintiff against Margaret Stevenes in a plea of debt pledge for the prosecution Richard Bulveis so it is ordered to summon the said Margaret before the next

amerced 6d

Roger Dalileie plaintiff against Thomas the son of Thomas Jankys in a plea of trespass pledge for the prosecution John Rowlowe. And he says that the same Thomas unjustly broke and opened at Akeltone the hedges and enclosures of Roger himself and destroyed his grass there to the damage of the said Roger of half a mark. And the said Thomas the son of Thomas then present said that he did not make damage of such a value and thence put himself on the judgment of the homage and the aforesaid Roger similarly. Thus because by the judgement of the homage thence charged they said the damage is assessed at 12d. And the said Thomas is in mercy

amerced 6d
To recover

Roger Wilileie plaintiff against Thomas Jankys in a plea of broken agreement pledge for the prosecution Thomas Tresele. And he says that the same Thomas agreed with the same Roger to hold his tenement in Roughtone and thence rent certain lands between them fixing to pay and also to repair, maintain and to support the roofing of the buildings of the tenement aforesaid. Which agreements the same Roger broke and did not keep to the damage of Roger himself 20s. And the aforesaid Thomas present thence put himself on an inquiry and the said Roger similarly. On which the 12 jurors whose names are named above thence charged say on their oath that the same Thomas broke diverse agreements on his part to the damage of Roger himself of 6s 8d which it is ordered to raise. And the said Thomas is in mercy

the next

Thomas Hugge plaintiff against Hugh Baker in a plea of trespass pledge for the prosecution John atte Walle

the law

Hugh Baker plaintiff against Thomas Hugge in a plea of trespass etc. pledge for the prosecution John atte Welle. And he says that the same Thomas unjustly with his animals destroyed the herbage of the same Hugh in Hultone on certain days and in the year to the damage of the same Hugh of 20s. And the aforesaid Thomas denied this and thence he has a day for the law in the next [court] with 6 hands by the pledge of John atte Walle

amerced 6d
To recover

Thomas Jankys plaintiff against Richard Parlor in a plea of trespass etc. And he says that the same Richard unjustly with force and arms assaulted him & brought beating and outrages to the same Thomas to the damage of Thomas himself of 10s. And the said Richard present thence put himself on the judgment of the homage etc. which damage on his part is agreed by both parties assessed by the oath of the homage at 5s 6d. And the said Richard is in mercy

the next

Thomas Hugges plaintiff against Hugh Baker & Agnes his wife in a plea of trespass who have a day to respond until the next [court]

the next

Richard Parlor plaintiff against Thomas Jankys in a plea of trespass pledge for the prosecution Thomas Tresele

1408-1409 P314/W/1/1/237

the next	Thomas Jankys plaintiff against Richard Parlor in a plea of trespass pledge for the prosecution Thomas the son of the aforesaid Thomas
amerced 6d	Richard Thorne plaintiff and Thomas Hugges defendant in a plea of land are agreed. And the said Richard put himself in mercy
	Affeerors: Stephen Bradeney, Robert Ewdenas Sum of this court £7 2s 1d Expenses of John Boerleie the steward being there for 2 days and 2 nights for the 3 courts aforesaid this year until here 26s 6d
Worfeld	Small court held there on Tuesday the 30th day of July in the tenth year of the reign of King Henry IV after the conquest [30 July 1409]
Essoins	William Yate, Andrew Fekkenham, John Hethe & Thomas Forster themselves of common [suit] by the reeve
the 12 jurors amerced 3d	Inquiry held for the lord by the oath of Roger Richardes, Roger Waltone, Nicholas Rowlowe, Stephen Bradeneie, John Walker, Roger Cattestre, William Wermod, John Barndeleie, Nicholas Stanlowe, Thomas Merwalle, Roger Broke & John Bromleie who say on their oath that William Prestes who is bound to make suit at this court did not appear so the said William (3d) is in mercy
Fine 6d	Roger Batemon made a fine for suit of court to be commuted from the date of this court until the feast of St Michael the Archangel next in the future. And he gives for a fine 6d
Fine 12d	Thomas Rugge son of William Rugge made a fine of 12d with the lord for an inquiry of 12 to be held ex officio to enquire concerning the metes and bounds and a parcel of land pertaining to the same nook of land called Blencheslond in Chesturtoun etc. pledge for the fine the reeve. On which the inquiry held by the oath of Stephen Bradeneie, Roger Richardes, John Rowlowe, John Bromleie, Roger Cattestre, Roger Waltone, William Gerbod, John Barndeleie, John Walker, Thomas Merwalle, Roger Broke, Nicholas Stanlowe, the which jurors seek a day for the verdict until the next [court] until it is inspected and so it remains
A day the next	The plea between William Bruggende plaintiff and Margaret Tresel defendant in a plea of trespass adjourned until the next [court] by the prayer of the parties
the next	A day is given between Joan Fraunceis plaintiff and Margaret Tresel defendant in a plea of trespass until the next [court]
the next	Thomas Hugge plaintiff and Hugh Baker defendant in a plea of trespass have a day to agree until the next [court] following as before
A day under the law	Hugh Baker plaintiff and Thomas Hugge defendant in a plea of trespass have a day as above under the law
the next	Thomas Hugge aforesaid plaintiff and Hugh Baker & Agnes his wife, defendants in a plea of trespass have a day by the prayer of both parties

amerced 6d — Richard Parlor plaintiff & Thomas Jankys defendant in a plea of trespass for a licence to agree. And the same Richard (6d) put himself in mercy

amerced 6d — Thomas Jankys plaintiff & Richard Parlor defendant in a plea of trespass for a licence to agree. And the said Thomas (6d) put himself in mercy

distrain — John Glover plaintiff against Richard Underhull in a plea of trespass pledge for the prosecution William Beore who summoned did not come so to distrain

distrain — John Hokkombe plaintiff against Robert Taillour in a plea of debt pledge for the prosecution Thomas Hugge who summoned did not come so to distrain

distrain — The same John Hokkombe plaintiff against William Gold in a plea of debt by the pledge aforesaid who summoned did not come so to distrain

amerced 6d — Robert Taillour is in mercy because he is not prosecuting against John Hokkombe in a plea of broken agreement by the pledge of John Glover

amerced 6d; To recover — Thomas Towart plaintiff against Robert atte Wode and John atte Walle in a plea of debt who seek from the same 6s in silver which they ought to have paid to him on the feast of the Finding of the Holy Cross last past in the church of Worfeld on which day and place the said debt was not paid although it was frequently requested nor still but they still detain. And the aforesaid Robert and John present in court recognise the said debt. So they are in mercy. Furthermore on behalf of the lord it is ordered to the bailiff to raise the said debt to the use of the aforesaid Thomas etc,

More on the back side

Still of the court

the law — Thomas Yngemon plaintiff against Robert Ewdenas in a plea of trespass. Pledge for the prosecution William Yngemon. And he says that the same with force and arms against the peace on certain days and in the year of the now King sought and took away the corn of the same Thomas in the field called Oldyntonesfeld in Oldyntone to the damage of the same Thomas 20s. And the aforesaid Robert denied all this and is thence to the law in the next [court] with 6 hands by the pledge of William Gerbod

the next — Thomas Yngemon above-named plaintiff against the aforesaid Robert Ewdenas in a plea of trespass etc. who have a day until the next [court] to agree

distrain — Thomas Sonde plaintiff against William Huster in a plea of trespass who is not summoned nor attached so let it be done

Affeerors: Roger Richardes, Stephen Bradeneie
Sum of this court 3s 9d
In expenses of the clerk of the court, Richard Bulveis the reeve and the beadle 12d

Worfeld — Small court held there on Tuesday next after the feast of the Raising of the Holy Cross in the 10th year of the reign of King Henry IV after the conquest [17 September 1409]

Essoins — Thomas Richardes, William Prestes, Jphn Stevenes, Thomas Tresle, John Dalleie & John Holigreve themselves of common [suit] by the reeve

amerced 8d	Andrew Fekkenham (4d) & Thomas Forster (4d) in mercy because they did not come here to warrant their essoin
the 12	Roger Cattestre, Roger Richardes, Stephen Bradeneie, Roger Waltone, Nicholas Rowlowe, John Barndeleie, Thomas Towart, Roger Broke, Mathew Bullok }, William Wermod }, John Hethe }, John Walker }
amerced 9d	sworn say on their oath that Andrew Fekkenham (3d), Thomas Merwelle (3d) & Thomas Forster (3d) who are bound to make suit at this court did not come so each of them is in mercy
heriot nothing as clear Escheat 2s tenement remains in the hand of the lord	And they say that Matilda Oldyntone who held of the lord by the custom of the manor one toft, one nook of land and one cottage with curtilage in Newtone on the day she died whereof concerning the heriot of the same deceased the lord has nothing because there was nothing. And concerning escheat of the same the lord will have by their custom 1 young sow and 1 piglet price 2s for which the reeve is charged to respond to the greater profit of the lord. And they say that Agnes the daughter of the aforesaid Matilda is her closest heir. And the tenement remains in the hand of the lord until
Fine 5s Fine 10s	And they say that Sibill atte Sonde surrendered into the hands of the lord one messuage and half a virgate of land with appurtenances in Newtone to retake the said messuage and half a virgate of land to herself only for the term of her life from the lord according to the custom of the manor so that after her death the aforesaid messuage and half virgate of land with appurtenances will remain with Richard the son of Robert Ewdenas and Emeline his wife the daughter of the aforesaid Sibill, her heirs and assigns to hold from the lord according to the custom of the manor. On which the aforesaid Sibill came back into court and took from the lord the aforesaid messuage and half a virgate of land with appurtenances to hold to herself only for the term of her life from the lord according to the custom of the manor. And she gives to the lord for a fine 5s. And after the death of the same Sibill the aforesaid messuage and half virgate of land with appurtenances are granted by the steward to the aforesaid Richard & Emmeline, her heirs and assigns to hold from the lord according to the custom of the manor. And they give to the lord for a fine 10s. And they are seised in the manner aforesaid
amerced 6d	Richard Underhull (6d) is in mercy for contempt of court for insulting John Glover
Adjourned	Still a day is given between William Brugghende plaintiff & Margaret Tresel defendant in a plea of trespass by the prayer of both parties
amerced 3d distrain	The bailiff is in mercy because he did distrain Margaret Tresel to respond to John Franceis in a plea of trespass. Further on behalf of the lord the bailiff is ordered to distrain the said Margaret to respond to John at the next [court] in a plea of trespass
amerced 18d	Hugh Baker put himself in mercy for a licence to agree with Thomas Hugge plaintiff & defendant in a plea of trespass three times as is clear in the preceding last court
amerced 6d	John Glover plaintiff put himself in mercy for a licence to agree with Richard Underhull defendant in a plea of trespass

the next — Still John Hoccombe plaintiff against Robert Taillour in a plea of debt who is still not summoned nor distrained because he lingers out of the country and has nothing whereof it is possible to distrain as is clear in the presentation by the oath of the bailiff

amerced 6d — John Hokkombe plaintiff & William Gold defendant in a plea of debt are for a licence to agree. And the said William put himself in mercy

amerced 6d — Thomas Yngemon is in mercy for his unjust plea against Robert Ewdenas in a plea of trespass

amerced 6d — The same Thomas Yngemon plaintiff & Robert Ewdenas defendant in a plea of trespass are for a licence to agree. And the same Robert put himself [in mercy]

amerced 3d distrain — The bailiff is in mercy because he did not distrain William Huster to respond to Thomas Sonde in a plea of debt as is clear it was ordered to him. Further on behalf of the lord it is ordered to the bailiff to distrain the aforesaid William this side of the next to respond to the aforesaid Thomas in the plea aforesaid

Tenement remains in the hand of the lord — Walter Rugge and Edith his wife surrendered into the hands of the lord 2 cottages in Worfeld of which 1 is called Popeplace and the other cottage is called Palmers to retake the said 2 cottages for the term of the lives of either/both of them from the lord according to the custom of the manor. And after the death of the said Walter and Edith the 2 cottages aforesaid with their appurtenances should remain with Adam Corior & Alice his wife, the daughter of the said Walter and Edith & the heirs of their bodies legitimately issuing. And if it should happen the said Adam and Alice die without heirs of their bodies legitimately issuing then the aforesaid 2 cottages with its appurtenances revert to the rightful heirs and assigns of the aforesaid Walter. And thus they remain in the hand of the lord until a fine is thence made with the lord

Survey — In the next it should be enquired concerning 4 oxen by Thomas Hugge received and freed etc. Also to be enquired concerning 6s 8d of the goods of John Fischer forfeit to the lord the which 6s 8d Adam Spicer of Bruggenorth owes to John Fischer a felon committed for felony just as was related to the clerk of the court by the said Adam etc. Also still remaining the profits of the wood and pasture of Sowdeleie for the present year still not assessed

sum 22s 11d

Fine 7s — John Nicols son of Thomas Nicols & Agnes his wife the daughter and heir of Matilda Oldyntone came here in court and took from the hand of the lord one toft, one nook of land and one cottage with appurtenances of which the aforesaid Matilda died seised in Newtone as is clear above as the right and heredity of the aforesaid Agnes to hold to the said John and Agnes from the lord according to the custom of the manor. And they give to the lord for a fine namely for the toft and nook of land 5s. And for the cottage 2s. And thus they have seisin

1408-1409 P314/W/1/1/237

Fine 4s

It is granted by the lord to Adam Corior and Alice his wife the reversion of 2 cottages which Walter Rugge and Edith his wife surrendered to the use of them as is clear above to hold the aforesaid 2 cottages with the reversion of the same when it should happen namely after the death of the aforesaid Walter and Edith to the aforesaid Adam and Alice and the heirs of their bodies legitimately procreated from the lord according to the custom of the manor. And if it should happen the said Adam and Alice die without heirs of their bodies legitimately issuing then the aforesaid 2 cottages with its appurtenances will be fully reverted to the aforesaid Walter Rugge and his heirs to hold from the lord according to the custom of the manor. And they give to the lord for a fine 4s. And in the manner aforesaid they are seised

Affeerors: Stephen Bradeney, John Hethe

Sum of this court 33s 11d

Afterwards to be charged concerning 4d of the increase on selling 1 horse from outside appraised by the 12 at 12d

Thence in expenses of the clerk of the court Richard Bulveis the reeve and the beadle 12d

1409-1410 P314/W/1/1/238

Worfeld	Small court held there on Tuesday next after the feast of the Saints the Apostles Simon & Jude in the 11th year of the reign of King Henry IV after the conquest [29 October 1409]
Essoins	John Morfeld clerk, John Barndeleie, John Waltone, William Yate & Roger Wille themselves from common [suit] by Thomas Hugge
amerced 4d	John Stevenes is in mercy because he did not come to warrant his essoin
The 12	Roger Cattestre, John Bromleie, Roger Gerbod, Roger Waltone, Roger Broke, William Wermod, Roger Richardes, Thomas Merwalle, John Janne, Stephen Bradeneie, William Newe, William Gerbode } sworn
Fine 12d	Roger Batemon made a fine with the lord for suit of court to be commuted from the date of this court until the feast of St Michael the Archangel next in the future. And he gives for a fine 12d pledge for the fine Roger Smyth
Fine 12d	Andrew Fekkenham gives to the lord 12d for a fine for suit of court to be commuted from the date of this court until the feast of St Michael next in the future. And it is granted by Richard Peper the supervisor there
Fine 4d	Thomas Forster gives to the lord 4d for a fine for suit of court to be commuted from the date of this court until the feast of St Michael next in the future. And it is granted by the aforesaid supervisor there because he is the forester
adjourned to supervise	Still a day is given between William Bruggehende plaintiff and Margaret Tresele defendant in a plea of trespass until the next etc. Furthermore the same Margaret submitted herself on the ordinance of the lord and his council towards all the tenants of the manor there concerning all offences towards the said tenants before this time caused by her by the surety of Thomas Hugge & John Hethe. And on this John Stevenes undertook to save and to serve the same pledge towards the lord and his tenants indemnified
the law	Still Joan Fraunceis plaintiff against Margaret Tresel in a plea of trespass pledge for the prosecution Richard Bulveis. And she says through Richard Bulveis her attorney that the same Margaret unjustly took away sheep and other goods of the same Joan to the damage of the said Joan 6s 8d. And the said Margaret present denies all this and is thence to the law in the next court with 6 hands pledge for the law Thomas Tresel
Distrain	Still on behalf of the lord it is ordered to the bailiff to distrain Robert Taillour that he is at the next court to respond to John Hoccombe in a plea of debt
Adjourned	Still a day is given until the next [court] between Thomas Sonde plaintiff & William Huster defendant in a plea of debt by the prayer of both parties
Supervise	On behalf of the lord it is ordered to the bailiff to seize into the hands of the lord 1 staking in the water of the lord called Worw near the well of St Peter
Fine 20d	Alice Gold made a fine with the lord to brew bread and ale to sell from the date of this court until the feast of St Michael the Archangel next in the future under the condition aforesaid namely that she sells by legal measure and weight & holds to the assize in all. And she gives for a fine 20d

1409-1410 P314/W/1/1/238

Fine 3s 4d

Richard Bulveis & Joan his wife made a fine to brew bread and ale to sell from the date of this court until the feast of St Michael next in the future under the condition aforesaid namely that they sell by legal measure and weight & hold to the assize. And they give for a fine 3s 4d

amerced 3d
sold 1 oak to burn 4d

The 12 jurors present that John Stevenes who is bound to make suit at this court did not come. So the said John is in mercy.
And they say that 1 oak in Sowdeleie is burnt by whom they don't know but the value for firewood is 4d concerning which the bailiff is charged to respond to the greater profit of the lord if it is possible

Pain

And they say that John Glover the miller holds in the mill 4 Setter (Recches) dogs, pigs & hens who destroy and damage the corn of the tenants of the lord to the grave damage of the said tenants. Which it is ordered he remove the said dogs, pigs, and hens from the entrance of the mill under pain of 6s 8d

Supervise

And they say that the same John the miller did not make his office in the mill aforesaid which it is ordered on behalf of the lord that in future he well and faithfully serves and holds his office in the said mill etc.

to be supervised

The 12 jurors are charged here by Richard Peper the supervisor of the lord to enquire concerning a certain fulling mill at Ryndelford in what manner it is held and from old was held. On which the aforesaid 12 namely Roger Cattestre, Roger Waltone, Roger Richardes, Stephen Bradeneie, John Bromleie, Roger Broke, Thomas Merwalle, William Newe, Roger Gerbod, William Wermod, John Janne, William Gerbode, who are sworn and charged say on their oath that at Ryndelford within the manor of Worfeld is one fulling mill of lower tenure and held from the lord according to the custom of the manor and in the same manner has been held from old as is clear by the record of the old rolls of the courts of the lord. Furthermore they say that Robert Ryndelford, son of William is the closest heir now to take from the lord and to pay for the same according to the custom of the manor

Fine 5s

Alice Stevenes surrendered into the hands of the lord one nook of land with appurtenances in Haalen which land Thomas Stevenes formerly held to the use of William Stevenes, his heirs and assigns. The which William came here in court and took from the lord the aforesaid nook of land with appurtenances to hold to himself and his [heirs] from the lord according to the custom of the manor. And he gives for a fine 5s. And is seised in the manner aforesaid

Election of reeve

Thomas Hugge withdrew here from the office of reeve to which office enters William Webbe of Roughtone by the election of the aforesaid inquiry. And he is sworn

Constables

John Janne & William Carter are elected constables by the aforesaid 12 jurors. And they are sworn

Ale tasters

John Billyngesleie & Thomas Rowlowe of Hultone are affirmed ale tasters by the election of the aforesaid 12 jurors. And they are sworn

Sum of this court 13s 3d
Expenses of ...[blank] Brugge, Richard Peper & other ministers of the lord being there for the supervision of diverse negotiations of the lord 5s 6d

1409-1410 P314/W/1/1/238

Worfeld	Small court held there on Tuesday next after the feast of the Conception of the Blessed Mary the virgin in the 11th year of the reign of King Henry IV [10 December 1409]
Essoins	John Nicoles & John Hethe themselves from common [suit] by William Webbe the reeve
The 12 jurors Heriot 1 ox 9s 4d Escheat 1 affram, 3 piglets 7s	Inquiry taken for the lord by the oath of Roger Cattestre, Roger Waltone, Roger Richardes, Stephen Bradeneie, John Bromle, Roger Broke, Thomas Merwalle, William Newe, Roger Gerbode, William Wermod, John Janne & William Gerbod who say on their oath that Alice Bullok who held from the lord by the custom of the manor one messuage and half a virgate of land with appurtenances at Alvescote within the manor of Worfeld on the day she died whereof the lord will have in the name of heriot 1 ruby ox price 9s 4d. And concerning escheat of the same deceased they say that the lord will have1 draught animal (affram) price 4s & 3 piglets price 3s. And concerning which heriots & escheats the reeve is charged to respond to the greater profit of the lord. And the tenement remains with John Robynes for the term of his life by their custom
Adjourned Supervise	Still a day is given between William Bruggehende plaintiff & Margaret Tresel defendant in a plea of trespass etc.
Essoin	Joan Franceis plaintiff against Margaret Tresele in a plea of trespass is essoined already by Richard Bulveis whence the law
Distrain	Still it is ordered to the bailiff that he distrains Robert Taillour that he is at the next [court] to respond to John Hoccombe in a plea of debt
Adjourned	And still a day is given between Thomas Sonde plaintiff & William Huster defendant in a plea of debt etc..
Distrain	{Richard agreed the son of Robert Ewdenas plaintiff against Sibill atte Sonde in a {plea {of broken agreement pledge for the prosecution Richard Bulveis {The same Richard agreed plaintiff against the said Sibill in a plea of trespass pledge {for the prosecution Richard Bulveis
Increase on the sale of heriots and escheats 22d	The reeve is charged here concerning 22d increase on the sale of the heriots and escheats of Alice Bullok above-named. The heriots of the same above were affeered by the inquiry at 9s 4d. By the reeve & Richard Bulveis they were sold at a higher price by 12d. 1 draught animal (affram) was affeered by the aforesaid inquiry at 4s by the same reeve and Richard it was sold at a higher price by 6d. And 3 piglets affeered at 3s were sold at a higher price by 4d Affeerors: Roger Waltone, Stephen Bradeneie Sum of this court 18s 2d
Worfeld	Small court held there on Tuesday next after the feast of the Beheading of St John the Baptist in the eleventh year of the reign of King Henry VI after the conquest [2 September 1410]
Essoins	Nicholas Stanlowe, John atte Welle, Thomas Tresele, Thomas Rowlow of Hiltone & Thomas Coliar themselves from common [suit] by William Webbe the reeve

1409-1410 P314/W/1/1/238

Margin	Entry
amerced 4d	John Nicols (4d) & John Hethe (4d are in mercy because they did not come here to warrant their essoin
the 12 jurors amerced 6d	Inquiry taken for the lord by the oath of Roger Cattestre, Stephen Bradeneie, Roger Richardes, Roger Waltone, William Newe, William Wermod, Thomas Merwalle, John Walker, John Barndeleie, John the son of Nicholas Rowlowe Roger Gerbod & Mathew Bullok who say on their oath that Andrew Fekkenham, John Hethe, Roger Batemon & John Nicols who are bound to make suit at this court did not come but because the aforesaid Andrew & Roger Batemon made a fine for their suit to be commuted for the present year as is clear above in the first court of this year so now they are released. And the aforesaid John (3d) & John (3d) are in mercy
Heriot 8s Escheat nothing Tenement remains in the hand of the lord	And they say that Alice Hullehous who held of the lord by custom one messuage and half a virgate of land in Hultone has died whereof the lord has one ruby cow in the name of heriot price 8s concerning which cow the reeve is charged to respond to the greater profit of the lord. And concerning escheat they said by their oaths that there was nothing. And the tenement remains in the hand of the lord [settled below]. Furthermore they say that John Hullehous, son of the aforesaid Alice, deceased, is her closest heir
Relief 3s 10d Supervise	Still the 12 jurors present that Robert Yngemon who held from the lord freely one toft and half a virgate of land with appurtenances in Oldyntone has died who had nothing for heriot to the lord. And they say that Thomas son of the said Robert legitimately procreated between the same Robert & Margaret formerly his wife is his closest heir & holds the tenement aforesaid which tenement is charged annually at 23d as of fixed rent. And he gives to the lord for relief 3s 10d. Furthermore it is ordered to the bailiff that he distrains the aforesaid Thomas that he is at the next to make fealty to the lord etc. to settle if he was
Fine 10s	John Hullehous son and heir of Alice Hullehous deceased above-named came here in court & took from the hands of the lord one messuage and half a virgate of land with appurtenances in Hultone as of his heredity after the death of the aforesaid Alice to hold to himself and his [heirs] from the lord according to the custom of the manor by services & customs thence due. And he gives to the lord for a fine 10s. And he is seized

Turn over

Still concerning the court

Margin	Entry
amerced 18d	Richard the son of Robert Ewdenas put himself in mercy for a licence to agree with Sibill atte Sonde in 3 pleas namely of trespass (6d), broken agreement (6d), & debt (6d)
distrain	Thomas Sonde plaintiff against John Henene in a plea of trespass who summoned did not come
distrain	John Glover plaintiff against William Yngemon in a plea of debt who summoned did not come
distrain	William Holigreve plaintiff against Thomas Yngemon & Edith his wife in a plea of trespass who summoned did not come
distrain	Henry Barker plaintiff against John Rogeres in a plea of trespass twice who is not summoned nor distrained so let it be done

amerced 6d — John Bromleie plaintiff & Margery Lawtone defendant in a plea of trespass for a licence to agree. And the said Margery (6d) put herself in mercy

amerced 6d — Margery Lawtone (6d) put herself in mercy for a licence to agree with John Robyns in a plea of trespass

amerced 6d — William Port (6d) chaplain plaintiff against Robert Port in a plea of debt pledge for the prosecution Richard Bulveis who is for a licence to agree. And the said William put himself in mercy

distrain — Thomas Jankys junior plaintiff against Richard Parlour in a plea of broken agreement who summoned did not come so distrain

Adjourned until the next — {Still a day is given to agree between William Bruggende plaintiff & Margaret Tresel defendant in a plea of trespass until the next

{And between John Hoccombe plaintiff & Robert Taillour defendant in a plea of debt

{And between Thomas Sonde plaintiff & William Huster defendant in a plea of debt

amerced 6d — Joan Fraunceis & Margaret Tresel defendant are agreed in a plea of trespass. And the said Joan (6d) put herself in mercy by the pledge of Richard Bulveis

Tenement in the hand of the lord — John Morfeld chaplain surrendered into the hands of the lord one toft and three nooks of land called Pirieplace in Roughtone & one messuage with one nook of land adjacent in Roughtone the same with appurtenances to the use of William Webbe & Margery his wife to hold to themselves for the term of both their lives from the lord according to the custom of the manor so that after their deaths all the aforesaid tenement with its appurtenances remains with Stephen the son of the said Stephen [Note: is this incorrect? Should it be William?] & Margery & Alice the wife of the same Stephen & the heirs of their bodies legitimately procreated between them. And in default of issue from them to the rightful heirs & assigns of the aforesaid Stephen & Margery etc. And thus it remains in the hand of the lord until etc. Afterwards it is settled in the next year following in the court held on Wednesday the first day of the month of April namely in the 12th year of the reign of King Henry IV

The right & claim remain in the hand of the lord — Thomas Colier & Hawisia his wife surrendered into the hands of the lord all right and claim which they have in one messuage & three nooks of land with appurtenances in Bradeneie as of the right of the same Hawisia to the use of Richard Bradeneie & Joan his wife & the heirs between them procreated. And in default of issue from them to the rightful heirs and assigns of the same Richard. And the aforesaid Hawisia confessed & examined before the steward says that she did this voluntarily by her will without coercion from her husband aforesaid. And the right & claim remains in the hand of the lord until a fine has thence been made with the lord etc. Settled in the next year following in the court held on Wednesday the first day of the month of April namely the 12th year of the reign of King Henry IV

Tenement in the hand of the lord — Margery Hounesworth formerly the wife of William Hondesworth surrendered into the hands of the lord one cottage with curtilage adjacent in Sonde to the use of William Huster & his heirs. And thus it remains in the hand of the lord until a fine has thence been made with the lord. Afterwards settled in the next year following in the court held on Wednesday the first day of the month of April namely the 12th year of the reign of King Henry IV

1409-1410 P314/W/1/1/238

Tenement in the hand of the lord

Thomas Muychhale & Matilda his wife surrendered into the hands of the lord 2 messuages, one virgate of land & half a nook of land in Stanlowe as of the right of the same Matilda to the use of Robert Webbe & Joan his wife & the heirs between them legitimately procreated & in default of issue from them to the rightful heirs & assigns of the aforesaid Matilda in reversion. And the aforesaid Matilda confessed & examined before the steward says that she did this voluntarily by her will without coercion from her husband aforesaid. And thus all the same tenements remain in the hand of the lord until a fine has thence been made etc. Settled in the next year following in the court held on Wednesday the first day of the month of April namely the 12th year of the reign of King Henry IV

Tenement remains in the hand of the lord

William Webbe surrendered into the hands of the lord one cottage with curtilage adjacent in Roughtone so that he is able to retake to hold to himself & Margery his wife for the term of the lives of both of them from the lord etc. so that after their deaths the aforesaid cottage with curtilage remains with Stephen their son & Alice his wife & the heirs between them legitimately procreated. And in default of issue from them to the rightful heirs & assigns of the aforesaid William & Margery etc. And thus it remains in the hand of the lord until a fine has thence been made. Afterwards settled in the next year following in the court held on Wednesday the first day of the month of April namely the 12th year of the reign of King Henry IV

Fulling mill remains in the hand of the lord

By order of the council of the lord the fulling mill settled in the next year following namely on the first day of the month of April of Ryndelford is seized and taken into the hands of the lord. And thus it remains in the hand of the lord

Assessors for the 3 previous courts

Stephen Bradeney & Roger Waltone

Sum 26s 6d

In expenses of the steward 12d

Supervise

Inquiry concerning 4 oxen coming & delivered by Thomas Hugge

1410-1411 P314/W/1/1/239

Worfeld

Small court held there on Tuesday next after the feast of St Luke the Evangelist in the 12th year of the reign of King Henry IV after the conquest [21 October 1410]

Essoins

John Robyns & John Dalileie themselves from common [suit] by Thomas Tresele and William Newe

The 12

Roger Cattestre	William Gerbod	William Wermod	}
John Hethe	John Rowlowe	William Newe	} sworn
Roger Richardes	Roger Broke	John Janne	}
Roger Waltone	Thomas Merwelle	Stephen Bradeneie	}

amerced 4d

John atte Welle is in mercy because he did not come here to warrant his essoin

amerced 4d

distrain

Thomas Sonde plaintiff against John Henene in a plea of trespass who is distrained by 1 wheel did not come so the said John is in mercy. Furthermore it is ordered to the bailiff to better distrain John himself before the next [court] to respond to the aforesaid Thomas in the plea aforesaid

amerced 6d

William Yngemon put himself in mercy for a licence to agree with John Glover in a plea of debt by the pledge of Thomas Yngemon

amerced 6d

Thomas Jankys junior is in mercy because he is not prosecuting against Richard Parlour in a plea of broken agreement

the law

William Holigreve plaintiff against Thomas Yngemon & Edith his wife in a plea of trespass. And he says that the same Thomas and Edith broke and damaged one clasp/cloak of the same William which clasp/cloak they received from the same William on loan on Tuesday next before the feast of the Purification of the Blessed Virgin Mary last past to the grievous damage of the same William etc. And the aforesaid Thomas and Edith present here deny this. And thence the have a day for the law in the next [court] with 6 hands pledge for the law Mathew Bullok

amerced 12d

John Rogers put himself in mercy for a licence to agree with Henry Barker in a plea of trespass twice

amerced 4d

adjourned to the next

John Hokkombe plaintiff against Robert Taillour in a plea of debt pledge for the prosecution Thomas Jankys. The which John varied in his plea so the same John is in mercy. Furthermore they have a day to agree until the next [court] by the prayer of both parties

A day until the next

Still a day is given between William Bruggende plaintiff and Margaret Tresel defendant in a plea of trespass until the next.
And between Thomas Sonde plaintiff & William Huster defendant in a plea of debt

amerced 3d

tenement in the hand of the lord

The 12 jurors present that Roger Batemon who is bound to make suit at this court did not come so the said Roger (3d) is in mercy. And they say on their oath that Adam Robyns who died 20 years past held from the lord on the day he died two parcels of free land in Wynnescote rendering thence annually to the lord 6d as of fixed rent which parcels of land are being held in the hand of the lord for him and from because who thence is the heir they are wholly ignorant. On which the said two parcels of land are taken and seized into the hands of the lord saving the right of Matilda formerly the wife of the aforesaid Adam as of her dote and the aforesaid parcels of land are called

Lucerudynge and Stonyrudynge furthermore how much the said parcels of land are valued per annum beyond the deduction and who occupied the same parcels of land during the said time and thence received the profits they have a day to present until the next [court]

fine 12d

Andrew Fekkenham made a fine with the lord for suit of court to be commuted from the date of this court until the feast of St Michael the Archangel next in the future. And he gives to the lord for a fine 12d

Survey

John Harryes came here in court and claimed the aforesaid 2 parcels of land of which formerly Adam Robynes died seized as is clear above by the presentation of the 12 jurors as his inheritance as the closest heir of the aforesaid Adam who thence has to plead with the council of the lord etc.

Ordination of the reeve

William Webbe withdrew here from his office of reeve which office is approached by Thomas Tresele by the election of the 12 jurors aforesaid. And is sworn

tenement remains in the hand of the lord
survey

Still the fulling mill of Ryndelford all land and tenement, right, and claim remaining in the hand of the lord in the last court of the preceding year and also deposited in the last penultimate court of the preceding year remain until the coming of John Boerleie the steward for diverse matters in the same for the profit of the lord to be surveyed and determined

Affeerors: Roger Cattestre, John Hethe
Sum of this court 4s 3d
Expenses of Richard Bulveis the clerk of the court, the reeve and the beadle 12d

Worfeld

Small court held there on Tuesday next after the feast of St Lucy the Virgin in the 12th year of the reign of King Henry IV after the conquest [16 December 1410]

Essoins

Henry Barker & John Nicoles themselves from common [suit] by Richard Bulveis and Thomas Soonde

the 12

Roger Cattestre	William Gerbod	William Gerbod	}
John Hethe	John Walker	William Newe	} sworn
Roger Richardes	Roger Broke	John Janne	}
Roger Waltone	Thomas Merwelle	Stephen Bradeneie	}

amerced 6d

John Henene put himself in the mercy of the lord for a licence to agree with Thomas Sonde plaintiff in a plea of trespass

amerced 6d

John Hokkombe plaintiff & Robert Tailour defendant are for a licence to agree. And the same Robert put himself in mercy

amerced 6d

William Huster put himself in mercy for a licence to agree with Thomas Soonde plaintiff in a plea of debt

distrain

John atte Welle plaintiff against William Beore in a plea of debt the which William summoned did not come so to distrain before the next [court] to respond to the aforesaid John in the plea aforesaid

William Rowlowe plaintiff against William Wermod in a plea of debt pledge for the

the next	prosecution Thomas Sonde who is not summoned so let it be done
adjourned	Still a day is given between William Bruggend plaintiff and Margaret Tresel defendant in a plea of trespass until the next [court] And between William Holigreve plaintiff and Thomas Yngman & Edith his wife defendant in a plea of trespass
Fine 6d	Roger Batemon made a fine for suit of court to be commuted from the date of the last court aforesaid until the feast of the Annunciation of the Blessed Virgin Mary next in the future. And he gives to the lord for a fine 6d pledge for the fine Roger Smyth
amerced 3d remaining not assessed	The 12 jurors present that John Rowlowe (3d) & Thomas Forster remaining who are bound to make suit at this court did not come so each of them is in mercy
profit of free land remaining in the hand of the lord as is clear 2s survey	And they say on their oath that 2 parcels of free land in Wynnescote seized in the hand of the lord as is clear in the last court preceding annual value further reprised with a third part of the same land which Matilda former wife of Adam Robynes holds in the name of dote - 4d. And they say that John Robynes has occupied the said land for 9 years last past & received the profits thence. Which profits for the said 9 years by the oath of the aforesaid 12 jurors were further reprised *jumping back* (resaltant) to 2s concerning which the bailiff is charged to make a levy to the use of the lord. And concerning the profit of the same land for 11 years it is to be enquired etc. It is settled in the first court of the year next following
Remaining here not assessed	And they say that Roger Townessende felled 1 oak growing in the aforesaid 2 parcels of land after they were taken into the hands of the lord which remains until surveyed by the steward. It is being settled in the next small court following
tenement in the hand of the lord Survey	Still all the lands and tenements, right and claim of the fulling mill of Ryndelford remain in the hand of the lord from the last court of the year preceding and also deposited in the last penultimate court of the year preceding still remaining

Affeerors: Roger Cattestre, John Hethe
Sum of this court 4s 3d
Expenses of the steward and certain ministers of the lord 12d

Worfeld	Great court held there on Wednesday the first day of April in the twelfth year of the reign of King Henry IV after the conquest [April 1 1411]

	Roger Bulveis	Roger Richardes	John Barndeleie }	
	Roger Cattestre	Stephen Bradeneie	John Walker }	sworn
the 12	Robert Ewdenas	Roger Waltone	Thomas Merwelle }	
	John Tumpkys	John Hethe	William Wermod }	

Kyngeslowe & Stanlowe amerced 6s 10d in the hand of the lord until. To be surveyed	townships there present that John Stevens forestalled (6d) Nicholas the servant of Joan Regnald and drew blood (12d) from him so the said John is in mercy. And they say that William Brasiar (12d) & William Prestes (12d) fished in water in the severalty of the lord so each of them is in mercy. And they say that John Prestes (3s 4d) raised and made 2 stakings for fishing in the same water in the severalty of the lord without licences so the said John is in mercy. And they say that the Prioress of the black nunnery of Brewode holds a certain parcel of meadow within the township of Kyngeslowe without making any services & suits by what warrant they don't know. So it is ordered to the bailiff to seize into the hands of the lord the said parcel of meadow until etc.

Hultone amerced 2s strays 20d. 1 swarm of bees remains	township there presents that Hugh Baker made an assault (6d) on Lucy his servant & hit her (6d). And that the same Lucy justly drew blood (6d) from him & justly raised the hue and cry (6d) so the said Hugh is in mercy. And that there falls to the lord 1 swarm of bees being in a certain tree within the township there so the reeve is thence charged. Also they present 1 horse coming as a stray at the feast of St Michael last past delivered to the reeve to the use of the lord price 20d
Rowlowe, Bradene, Asturhull, Ewyk, Sonde strays 6d	townships there present 1 swarm of bees coming as strays & in the custody of John Bradeneie price of the bees 6d
Chesturtone amerced 2s 4d	township there presents that Roger Batemon (4d) who is bound to make appearance at this court did not appear so the said Roger is in mercy. And they say that William Prestes (6d) forestalled John Newe. And that the same John reforestalled (6d) the said William so each of them is in mercy. And that Margery Newe forestalled (6d) Simon the son of Alice Rugge and drew blood (6d) from him so the said Margery is in mercy
Roughtone, Barndeleie, Hoccombe, Swncote strays 6d amerced 4s 3d Waif 6d	townships there present 1 swarm of bees coming as strays price 6d & remaining in the custody of William Yate. And they say that William Webbe (6d) forestalled Alice the wife of Stephen Webbe & hit (6d) her. And they say that Joan the maid of William Hoccombe took one old handkerchief of muslin (cindone) price 6d of the goods of William Skynner. And the same Joan thence (3s 4d) at a fine with the lord
Burcote, Burcote, Ryndelford, Bromle amerced & fine 9s. 8d Waif 6d	townships there present that Margery Lawtone raised the hue and cry (12d) unjustly on William Prestes so the said Margery is in mercy. And they say that Joan the servant of John Bromleie unjustly took from the house of John Bromleie 3 pecks of barley price 6d and the said Joan thence (6s 8d) at a fine with the lord. And they say that Margery Lawtone harboured the said Joan herself knowing of the transgression aforesaid so the said Margery (2s) is in mercy
Alvescote, Wynscote, Cattestre, Newtone Starys 6d amerced 3d 4d Waif 2d	townships there present 1 swarm of bees coming as strays & being in the custody of Mathew Bullok price 6d. And they say that Agnes Nicoles unjustly took 1 hen of Robert Saundres price 2d. And the said Agnes (3s 4d) thence at a fine with the lord
Ewdenas, Oldyntone amerced 4d	townships there present that William Oldyntone (4d) who is bound to appear at this court did not appear so the said William is in mercy
Stapelford	township there presents nothing
Akeltone strays 6d waifs 6d	township there presents 1 swarm of bees coming as strays price 6d & it remains in the custody of Simon Broke. Also they present 1 strong-box of the goods and chattels of a certain unknown found by John Baret, Simon Broke, Thomas Tumpkys, John Wilot & Richard Underhull without a lock in their custody. So it is ordered that the same is handed over to the use of the lord to the reeve. Afterwards sold by the steward in full court for 6d. And they say that Simon Broke (6d) forestalled William the servant of Roger Hethe so the said Simon in mercy. And they say that Roger Dalileie (6d) forestalled Thomas Tumpkys so the said Roger in mercy. And they say that Stephen

	Draper (6d), John Cherletone (6d), John Corbyn of Brelaghtone (6d) made homesoken on Roger Dalileie so each of them in mercy. And they say that the same Stephen Draper (6d), John Cherletone (6d), John Corbyn (6d) forestalled and assaulted the aforesaid Roger Dalileie so each of them in mercy. And they say that Simon Broke made an encroachment (6d) on a certain lane unjustly to the nuisance of the people of the lord King within the township of Akeltone. And they say that
amerced 24s 6d	Richard Hethe of Hethe next to Baggesore led the malefactors aforesaid namely Stephen Draper, John Cherletone, & John Corbyn within the domain to kill Roger Dalileie aforesaid. So the said Richard (20s) is in mercy
Wyke amerced 13s 6d Waifs 10d 2 swarms of bees remaining until	township there presents that Matilda Smyth forestalled Joan the wife of William Yngemon & hit her so the said Matilda (6d) in mercy. And they say that the same Joan justly raised the hue and cry so the said Matilda (12d) in mercy. And they say that Thomas Cowper justly raised the hue and cry on the aforesaid Matilda so the said Matilda (12d) in mercy. And they say that there falls to the lord 1 swarm of bees being in a tree of William Rowlowe and thence the reeve is charged. And 1 other swarm of bees within the township aforesaid being in a tree of Thomas Heyne whereof the bailiff is charged. And they say that John Bokenhale unjustly took a cloth of Hamond Humele price 3d. So the said John (6s 8d) at a fine with the lord. And they say that Joan the wife of William Yngemon made a pound breach on Thomas Heyne so the said Joan (12d) in mercy. Also they present 1 fleece of wool abandoned price 4d in the hands of William Rowlowe. And they say that William Yngemon & Joan his wife unjustly and against the peace took 2 hens of John Smyth price 3d. And they say William & Joan thence (3s 4d) at a fine etc.
Haalen amerced 6d	township there presents that Robert Barker forestalled Roger Barker so the said Robert (6d) in mercy
Worfeld amerced 4d	township there presents that Elias Mustardmon who is bound to make appearance at this court did not appear so the said Elias (4d) in mercy
The tasters of ale amerced 24s	present that Thomas Sonde brewed 6 [times] (4s), John Smyth 6 (4s), Thomas Muychhale 2 (16d), William Bruggende 1 (8d), Hanund Humele 1 (8d), John Yate 2 (16d), William Nore 1 (8d), Robert Taillour 2 (16d), John Aleyn 1 (8d), Alice Goold 1 (8d), William Herdemon 1 (8d), Mathew Bullok 1 (8d), Richard Bulveis 1 (8d), Alice Taillour 1 (8d), Elena Taillour 3 (2s), Alice atte Soonde 2 (16d), John Smyth 2 (16d) & Matilda Stanlowe 1 (8d). And they say that all sold against the assize so each of them is in mercy & they say that Joan Smyth brewed 1 (8d) & sold against the assize so she is in mercy
Supervision	Still it is presented by the oath of the township of Wyke that John Smyth of Wyke has in his custody one goblet with silver binding of the goods of John Breghnok felon who is ordered to deliver the said goblet to the reeve to the use of the lord this side of the next court under pain and peril which will be incumbent
the 12 jurors	present that the townships aforesaid and the tasters of ale have well and faithfully presented and concealed nothing
amerced 4d	Roger Batemon is in mercy because he did not come here to warrant his essoin

1410-1411 P314/W/1/1/239

Small court held on the place, day and year aforesaid

The 12

Roger Cattestre	John Hethe	William Wermod }	
Roger Richardes	John Barndeleie	Thomas Hugge }	sworn say on
Stephen Bradeneie	John Walker	William Gerbod }	their path that
Roger Waltone	Thomas Merwelle	John Rowlowe }	

heriot 10s

John Ewdenas who held from the lord one messuage and one hide of land with appurtenances in the village of Ewdenas freely for the term of his life has died after whose death there falls to the lord one horse with saddle and bridle price 10s in the name of heriot. And afterwards Robert of Ewdenas & Alice his wife the daughter of the aforesaid John entered into the messuage and hide of land aforesaid as to remain to the aforesaid Alice because the aforesaid John enfeoffed in fee simple to Thomas Kyrkeby formerly the rector of the church of Stoktone concerning the messuage and hide aforesaid the which Thomas surrendered and regranted the messuage and hide of land aforesaid with its appurtenances aforesaid to John and Matilda his wife for the term of their lives. And after their decease to the aforesaid Alice the daughter of the aforesaid John and Matilda and to the male heirs of her body legitimately procreated. And in default of male issue of her body legitimately procreated to Elizabeth the sister of Alice and to the male heirs of her body legitimately & in default of male issue of her body legitimately procreated to Margery the sister of the aforesaid Elizabeth & the male heirs of her body legitimately procreated. And in default of male heirs to the rightful heirs and assigns of the aforesaid John for ever by virtue of which gift and enfeoffment aforesaid are entailed to the aforesaid Robert and Alice his wife. At present they hold the messuage and hide aforesaid as of the right and acquisition of the said Alice for which reasons they seek to be discharged against the lord from relief from the same plea. And because the allegation of them before the steward is proved to be true the same Robert and Alice his wife are discharged from the relief aforesaid and thence are quit and seisin from the hand of the lord is liberated concerning the messuage and hide of land aforesaid

heriot & escheat nothing for the reason evident

Ingress 10s

And they say that Lucy Mulwart who held from the lord by the custom of the manor one messuage and half a virgate of land with appurtenances in Newtone has died after whose death no heriots nor escheats fell to the lord because there was nothing. And they say that Nicholas Ellesmere her son is the closest heir. The which Nicholas came here in court and took from the lord the messuage and half a virgate of land aforesaid with its appurtenances to hold to himself, his heirs and assigns from the lord according to the custom of the manor. And he gives to the lord for ingress 10s to be paid half into the hands and the other half within the accounts. He made fealty to the lord. And he has seisin

Ingress 10s

And they say that Rose Knotte who held from the lord by the custom of the manor one messuage and half a virgate of land with appurtenances in Alvescote has died whereof concerning heriot and escheat the lord has nothing because there was nothing. And they say that Alice the wife of Roger Towneshende is her closest heir. And the aforesaid Roger and Alice came here in court and took from the lord the messuage and half a virgate of land aforesaid with its appurtenances to hold to themselves, their heirs and assigns from the lord according to the custom of the manor. And they give to the lord at ingress 10s paying half into the hands and the other half within the accounts. They made fealty to the lord. And they have seisin

William Gerbod & Roger his brother surrendered into the hands of the lord one messuage & one nook of land with appurtenances called Yngelbrondeslond in Haalen to the use of William Huster and Agnes Plummer his wife their heirs & assigns. The which William & Agnes came here in court & took from the lord the messuage and nook of land aforesaid with its appurtenances to hold to themselves, their heirs and assigns from the lord according to the custom of the manor by services thence due. And they give to the lord for a fine 5s paying half into the hands of the lord and the other half within the accounts. And they are seized

Fine 15s

Thomas Colier & Hawisia his wife came here in court and from the agreement of the lord released and for the said Hawisia and her heirs forever quitclaimed to Richard Bradeney and Joan his wife and the heirs of their bodies legitimately procreated. And for default of issue of them, the rightful heirs & assigns of the same Richard have the whole right and claim in one messuage and three nooks of land with appurtenances in Bradeneie as of the right of Hawisia herself to hold to them in the manner aforesaid from the lord according to the custom of the manor. And the said Hawisia thence confessed and examined by the steward acknowledged herself to have done this of her own free will, voluntarily without the coercion of her husband for the which relaxation and licence to have from the lord the same Richard and Joan give to the lord for a fine 15s to be paid thence to the lord half into the hands and the other half within the accounts etc.

Fine 20s

Robert Hogge surrendered into the hands of the lord two messuages & one virgate of land with appurtenances in Stapelford to the use of John Rowlowe. The which John came here in court & took from the lord the two messuages & one virgate of land aforesaid with appurtenances to hold to himself his heirs and assigns from the lord according to the customs of the manor by services thence due & accustomed. And he gives for a fine 20s paying half into the hands & the other half within the accounts, he made fealty to the lord. And is seised

Fine 20s

John Morfeld chaplain surrendered into the hands of the lord one toft and three nooks of land called Pirieplace with one messuage & one nook of land in Roughtone to the use of William Webbe & Margery his wife to hold for the term of their lives so that after their deaths all the toft, messuage and land aforesaid with its appurtenances remain with Robert the son of the said William and Margery and Joan the wife of the said Robert and the heirs of the bodies of the said Robert and Joan his wife legitimately procreated. And in default of the issue from them to the rightful heirs and assigns of the aforesaid William and Margery forever. The which William and Margery his wife came here in court and took from the lord all the toft, messuage and lands aforesaid with its appurtenances for the term of their lives to hold from the lord by services thence due and accustomed according to the custom of the manor. And for default of issue from them it remains with the rightful heirs of the aforesaid William and Margery his wife for ever to hold from the lord according to the custom of the manor. And thence they have seisin. And they give to the lord for a fine 20s to be paid half into the hands and the other half within the accounts. And they made fealty

Increase manifest

It is granted by the lord to Sir William Nore and Agnes his wife 1 toft with curtilage in Worfeld called the Smythes Place and 1 place of waste called the Mulnehelde in Haalen and 2 selions of land in the field of Haalen called the Overemes Wardyn for which they used render thence to the lord annually 2s to hold to themselves, their heirs and assigns from the lord according to the custom of the manor rendering thence annually to the lord 3s 4d at the usual terms. They made fealty to the lord and thence have seisin

At this court the fulling mill of Ryndelford is seized into the hand of the lord by the steward as a forfeit to the lord because Robert of Ryndelford who held from the lord the mill aforesaid from his lesser and base tenure sold the aforesaid mill in fee simple by his charter to John Walker against the form of his tenure aforesaid, a licence from the lord not obtained. And afterwards came the aforesaid John Walker and Thomas his son here in court and took the aforesaid mill to hold to themselves, their heirs and and assigns from the lord by the services and customs before the forfeit aforesaid owed and accustomed together with 1 staking for a fishery to be made at Ryndelford there that the water being from the pit (puteo) of the Floodgate to hold from the lord according to the custom of the manor under lesser and base tenure. And they give to the lord for the grant and gift aforesaid in the manner and form aforesaid to peacefully possess £10 for a fine to be paid to the lord, 100 shillings within the next account, 100 shillings within the year in accounts from then next following. And they made fealty to the lord. And thence they have seisin

Fine £10

John Rowlowe surrendered into the hands of the lord two messuages and one virgate of land with appurtenances in Stapelford which Robert Hogge formerly held so that he is able to take back the said messuage and land to himself and Joan his wife to hold to themselves & their heirs and the assigns of John himself. The which John and Joan came here in court and took from the lord the messuage and virgate of land aforesaid with its appurtenances to hold to themselves, their heirs and the assigns of John himself as above from the lord according to the custom of the manor by services thence due and accustomed. And they give to the lord for a fine 10s to pay within the account. They made fealty to the lord and they have seisin etc.

Fine 10s

It is granted by the lord to Thomas the son of John of Rowlowe and Benedicta his wife one messuage and one virgate of land with appurtenances in Hultone which the aforesaid John his father acquired from Stephen Heyne and on his death bed bequeathed to the aforesaid Thomas, his heirs and assigns as his younger son to hold the messuage and virgate of land aforesaid with its appurtenances to the aforesaid Thomas and Benedicta his wife, the heirs and assigns of Thomas himself from the lord according to the custom of the manor by services thence due and accustomed. And they give to the lord for a fine 20s to pay within the next account. They made fealty. And thence have seisin

Fine 20s

The bailiff is charged concerning 13 shillings and four pence to be raised for the herbage and profit of Sowdeleie for the enclosure for the time of three years last past whereof one year being of mast

Sowdeley 13s 4d

William the son and heir of Roger of Swancote came here in court and gives to the lord 12 pence for an inquiry of the 12 to be held to enquire if Thomas of Swancote his grandfather and the father of the aforesaid Roger demised and bequeathed to the aforesaid Roger his son one toft and one virgate of land with appurtenances in Bradeneie which the same Thomas previously acquired from Richard of Bradeneie to hold after the death of the said Thomas to the aforesaid Roger his son, his heirs and assigns according to the custom of the manor. And whether the aforesaid William has the better right in the toft and virgate of land aforesaid by virtue of the demise and bequest aforesaid in his claim than Margery formerly the wife of Thomas Swancote his uncle in her tenure. And on this the inquiry was held by the oath of Nicholas Rowlowe, Roger Richardes, William Gerbod, Roger Broke, Thomas Rowlowe of Burcote, Roger Gerbod, Mathew Bullok, Henry Barker, Thomas Rowlowe of Hultone, William Newe, John atte Welle & Robert Bruggende who thence charged and sworn say on their oath that the aforesaid William son and heir of Roger aforesaid by virtue of the demise and bequest aforesaid after the death of the aforesaid Roger his father has the better right in his claim in the toft and virgate of land aforesaid because the demise and bequest was as above than the aforesaid Margery in her

Fine 12d

tenure. So it is judged that the reeve has to make seisin in the aforesaid William. And thus he made a fine with the lord for the seisin aforesaid to be had. And he gives to the lord for a fine 20s to be paid within the accounts. And thence he has seisin

Fine 20s

William son and heir of Roger of Swancote surrendered into the hands of the lord one toft and one virgate of land with appurtenances which Thomas of Swancote his grandfather demised and bequeathed to Roger the father of the aforesaid William, his heirs and assigns in the village of Bradeneie so that he is able to re-hold to himself and Isabell his wife to hold to themselves, their heirs and assigns from the lord according to the custom of the manor. The which William & Isabell his wife came in court and took from the lord the toft and virgate of land aforesaid with appurtenances in the manner aforesaid to hold to themselves, their heirs and assigns from the lord according to the custom of the manor by services thence due and accustomed. And they give to the lord for a fine 10s to pay half into the hands and the other half within the accounts. They made fealty to the lord. And thence they have seisin

Fine 10s

Thomas Muychhale & Matilda his wife confessed and examined before the steward willingly and voluntarily surrendered into the hands of the lord two messuages, one virgate of land and half a nook of land with appurtenances in Stanlowe as of the right & heredity of Matilda herself to the use of Stephen the son of William Webbe and Alice his wife and the heirs of their bodies legitimately procreated. And in default of their issue that the messuages and land aforesaid with its appurtenances are to revert to the rightful heirs of the aforesaid Matilda. The which Stephen and Alice his wife came here in court and took from the lord the messuages and lands aforesaid with its appurtenances to hold to themselves & the heirs of their bodies legitimately procreated to hold from the lord by services thence due and accustomed according to the custom of the manor. And in default of their issue that the messuages and land aforesaid with its appurtenances remain with the rightful heirs of the aforesaid Matilda for ever to hold from the lord by services thence due and accustomed according to the custom of the manor. And thence they have seisin. And they made fealty to the lord. And they give to the lord for a fine 22s 6d

Fine 22s 6d

William Webbe surrendered into the hands of the lord one cottage with curtilage adjacent in Roughtone so that he is able to retake from the lord to himself and Margery his wife to hold for the term of their lives. And after their deaths that the cottage and curtilage aforesaid remain with Robert their son and Joan his wife and the heirs of their bodies legitimately procreated. And in default of their issue that the cottage and curtilage aforesaid with its appurtenances remain with the rightful heirs of the said William & Margery his wife. The which William & Margery came here in court and took from the lord the cottage and curtilage aforesaid with its appurtenances to hold to themselves for the term of their lives from the lord by services thence due and accustomed according to the custom of the manor. And after their deaths that the cottage and curtilage aforesaid with its appurtenances remain with the aforesaid Robert and Joan his wife & the heirs of their bodies legitimately procreated to hold from the lord by services thence due and accustomed according to the custom of the manor and for default of their issue that the cottage and curtilage aforesaid with its appurtenances remain with the rightful heirs of the aforesaid William and Margery for ever to hold from the lord by services thence due and accustomed according to the custom of the manor. And thence they have seisin. And they made fealty to the lord. And they give to the lord for a fine 2s

Fine 2s

Margery Hondesworth formerly the wife of William Hondesworth surrendered into the hands of the lord one cottage with curtilage adjacent in Sonde to the use of William Huster, his heirs and assigns. The which William came here in court and took from the lord the aforesaid messuage with curtilage to hold to himself, his heirs and assigns from the lord according to the custom of the manor. And he gives to the lord for a fine 12d. He made fealty to the lord. And thence has seisin

Fine 12d

Thomas Forster made a fine for suit of court to be commuted in the present year until the feast of St Michael next in the future. And he gives for a fine 6d. Thus granted by the steward because he is the forester & he behaved well towards the tenants of the lord etc.

Fine 6d

Thomas Richardes plaintiff against John Baret in a plea of trespass pledge for the prosecution the reeve. And he says that the same John unjustly and against the peace took & took away 1 sheep of Thomas himself here in the year last past to the damage of Thomas himself 2s 4d. And the aforesaid John present denied this & is thence to the law in the next with 6 [hands] pledge for the law John Rowlowe

The law

amerced 4d

Thomas Richardes aforesaid in mercy for his unjust plea against the said John Baret in a plea of debt

amerced 6d
distrain

Thomas Heyne plaintiff against John Fetherstone in a plea of trespass pledge for the prosecution the reeve who is attached and charged did not come. So John himself and his pledges namely Richard Bulveis and William Carter are in mercy. Furthermore it is ordered to better distrain before the next [court] to respond to the aforesaid Thomas in the plea aforesaid

amerced 6d

Robert Taillour put himself in mercy for a licence to agree with John Bokenhale in a plea of trespass

amerced 6d

The same Robert Taillour put himself in mercy for a licence to agree with the same John Bokenhale defendant in a plea of debt etc.

amerced 6d

John Bokenhale plaintiff & Robert Taillour defendant in a plea of debt are for a licence to agree. And the said John put himself in mercy

amerced 6d

William Holigreve is in mercy for an unjust plea against Thomas Yngeman & Edith his wife in a plea of trespass

the next

John the son of Thomas Jankys plaintiff against Thomas Heyne in a plea of trespass. Pledge for the prosecution Thomas Jankys. Who have a day to agree until the next [court]

amerced 6d

Margaret Tresele is in mercy for an unjust plea against John Ewyk in a plea of debt

Thomas Heyne plaintiff against Mathew Bullok in a plea of debt pledge for the prosecution William Rowlowe who seeks from the said Mathew 3s 4d which the same Mathew aforesaid promised to send to the aforesaid Thomas for diverse businesses. And the same Mathew present here denied this and is thence to the law in the next with 6 hands pledge for the law Richard Aldith

the law

Margaret Tresele put herself in mercy for a licence to agree with William Bruggende plaintiff in a plea of trespass

amerced 6d

amerced 6d	John atte Welle plaintiff & William Beore defendant in a plea of debt are for a licence to agree. And the said William put himself in mercy
amerced 6d	The bailiff is charged concerning 2d levy from Roger Townsehende for 1 small oak felled by him on the land of the lord etc.
the next to supervise	John Ewyk plaintiff against Roger Batemon & Isabell his wife in a plea of land pledge for the prosecution William Carter. And the aforesaid Roger Batemon & Isabell being charged the aforesaid Isabell appeared and Roger her husband made a default. So the suitors of the court are thence charged by the steward how and in what way it is to proceed in the suit aforesaid. Who say by their judgment that 1 messuage & 3 nooks of land in Chesturtone for the reason of the default aforesaid are taken into the hands of the lord until. Furthermore the parties aforesaid have a day to proceed in the plea until the next [court]
Attorney	John Ewyk put in his place his attorney William Carter of Wike to win or lose against Roger Batemon & Isabell his wife in the plea of land
the next Attorney	William Holigreve and Emmoter his wife plaintiff against Thomas Hugge of Hultone & Margery his wife & Richard Thorne of Hopstone in a plea of land pledge for the prosecution Richard Bulveis etc. William Holigreve and Emmoter his wife put in their place Richard Bulveis their attorney against Thomas Hugge aforesaid and Margery his wife & Richard Thorne of Hopstone to win or lose in the plea of land
Tenement remains in the hand of the lord	John Bokenhale surrendered into the hands of the lord one cottage with curtilage adjacent which was formerly John Huly's in Haalen to the use of John Smyth of Wyke. And thus it remains in the hand of the lord until
Increase Supervise	It is granted by the lord to Roger atte Townesende 2 parcels of land in Wynnescote which indeed Adam Robynes formerly held to hold from the feast of St Michael last past until the feast of St Michael next in the future. Rendering thence to the lord for the time 8d at the usual times. And he pays to rent for the year 8d
amerced 6d	William Wermod put himself in mercy for a licence to agree with William Rowlowe plaintiff in a plea of debt etc.
amerced 12d	Margery formerly the wife of Thomas Swancote is in mercy for withdrawing from the court at the suit of William the son and heir of Roger of Swancote plaintiff in a plea of land because it is judged by an inquiry of 12 as above shown
the next	Thomas Hugge plaintiff against Margaret Tresele and John her son in a plea of land pledge for the prosecution Richard Bulveis the which Margaret and John have a day until the next to respond in the plea aforesaid
	Affeerors: Nicholas Rowlowe, Stephen Bradeneie. Sum of this great court with the small following £24 14s 6d
	In the expenses of John Boerleie steward being there with 8 horses for 3 days and 4 nights for the holding of the court and for other diverse business of the lord and his tenants there to supervise and judge 59s 11d

1411-1412 P314/W/1/1/240

Worfeld	Small court held there on Thursday the first day of the month of October in the 13th year of the reign of King Henry IV after the conquest [1 October 1411]
Essoins	Thomas Richardes himself from common [suit] by Roger Richardes. John Walker from the same by the said Roger. Robert Bruggende from the same by William Bruggende. William Prestes from the same by William Newe. John Stevenes from the same by Richard Bulveis & John Robyns from the same by Richard Whitebrok
The 12	Roger Cattestre, John Hethe, Thomas Merwelle, Stephen Bradeneie, John Barndeleie, Roger atte Broke, Roger Richardes, John the son of Nicholas Rowlowe, William Newe, Roger Waltone, William Wermod, Mathew Bullok } sworn
amerced 6d amerced 6d	Thomas Richardes is in mercy for his unjust plea against John Baret in a plea of trespass Thomas Heyne is in for his unjust plea against Mathew Bullok in a plea of debt } whereof the law
	John the son of Thomas Jankys plaintiff against Thomas Heyne in a plea of trespass pledge for the prosecution Thomas Jankys who are for a licence to agree. And the said John put himself in mercy
amerced 6d	Thomas Jankys junior plaintiff against Thomas Heyne in a plea of broken agreement for a licence [to agree]. And the said Thomas put himself in mercy
amerced 6d	William Yngman plaintiff put himself in mercy for a licence to agree with Thomas Heyne defendant in a plea of trespass
amerced 6d	Thomas Heyne plaintiff put himself in mercy for a licence to agree with William Yngman in a plea of trespass
A day supervise	{ Still the plea between Thomas Heyne plaintiff & John Fetherston defendant in a plea of trespass adjourned to the next { Thomas Jankys plaintiff against Andrew Fekkenham in a plea of trespass { John Hethe plaintiff against William Poort clerk & Margaret Tresel in a plea of trespass {Thomas Hugge plaintiff against the aforesaid William the clerk & Margaret [Tresel] in a plea of trespass } who have a day
distrain	Thomas Jankys junior plaintiff against John Glover in a plea of debt who summoned did not come so distrain to the next [court]
amerced 9d remaining not assessed	the 12 jurors present that William Henene (3d), Roger Batemon (3d), John Nicoles (3d), & Thomas Forster remaining not assessed for his fine who are bound to make suit at this court did not come so each of them is in mercy
heriot 18d Escheat 12d Supervise	And they say that William Holigreve who held of the lord by custom of the manor one toft, one cottage & half a virgate of land in Haalen on the day he died from whose death the lady will have in the name of heriot 1 sheep with 1 lamb price 18d. And for escheat 1 piglet price 12d. Furthermore they seek an inspection of the old court rolls and also a day until the next [court] to present if he held more tenements on the day on which he died namely on the feast of Pentecost last past and if the lady should

have had more or better heriots or not. And who by the custom of the manor aforesaid will have for the aforesaid tenements after his death etc.

Heriot 11s
Escheat 19s 8d

And they say that John Dalilieie who held of the lady by the custom of the manor half of one messuage & one nook of land in Chesturtone has died from whose death the lady will have in the name of heriot 1 black ox price 11s. And for escheat the lady will have 2 draught animals (affri) price 6s 8d, 1 boar price 22d, 1 sow with 3 piglets price 20d, 3 pigs pice 5s, 4 small pigs price 4s and 1 piglet by itself price 6d. Concerning which heriots & escheats all and singular the bailiff is charged to respond to the greater profit of the lady. And they say that the tenement remains in the hands of Emmeline the widow of the same John, deceased.

Fine 10s

Nicholas Ellesemere surrendered into the hands of the lord one messuage and half a virgate of land with appurtenances in Newtone to the use of William Newtone , clerk, his heirs & assigns. The which William the clerk came here in court & took from the lady the aforesaid messuage and half a virgate of land with appurtenances to hold to himself & his heirs & assigns from the lady according to the custom of the manor by services & customs thence due. And he gives to the lady for a fine 10s. And he has seisin

Issue & profit being in arrears 2s 5d

Still the 12 jurors present that John Robyns has to respond to the lord concerning 2s 5d from the profit of 2 parcels of free land taken into the hands of the lord namely for 11 years previously not determined (terminatus) as is clear in the first and second courts this year preceding the last

Increase on sale with 2 swarms remaining as is clear 2s 2d

The bailiff is charged here concerning 6d for 1 swarm of bees remaining in the last great court preceding in the township of Hultone. And concerning 2d from the increased sale of one swarm appraised at 6d in the same great court in the township of Bradeneie because it was sold for a higher price by the said 2d. And concerning 4d from the increased sale of 1 swarm in the custody of Mathew Bullok appraised at 6d in the same great court because it was afterwards sold for 10d. And concerning 8d from the increased sale of 1 swarm in the custody of Symon Broke appraised at 6d in the same great court because it was sold for a higher price to the said Symon by the said 8d. Also he is charged concerning 6d for 1 swarm remaining in the same great court in a certain tree of Thomas Heyne in Wyke. And concerning another swarm remaining in the same township of Wike not charged here because they say that the bees are dead which is overseen etc.

Tenement in the hand of the lord

Andrew Fekkenham & Elianora his wife surrendered into the hands of the lord one toft & half a virgate of land called Kyngeslond in Haalen to the use of William Ewyk. And thus it remains in the hand of the lord until a fine thence made

Tenement remaining in the hand of the lord

Still remaining in the hand of the lord 1 cottage with curtilage adjacent in Haalen from a surrender by John Bokenhale to the use of John Smyth as is clear in the last court preceding

Adjourned until the next

{Still the plea between John Ewyk plaintiff & Roger Batemon & Isabell his wife defendants in a plea of land adjourned until the next

{And between William Holigreve & Emmoter his wife plaintiffs & Thomas Hugge of Hultone, Margery his wife, & Richard Thorne of Hopstone defendants in a plea of land

{And between Thomas Hugge plaintiff & Margaret Tresel & John her son defendants in a plea of land adjourned as above

1411-1412 P314/W/1/1/240

Election of reeve	John JonessonRowlowe & Roger Smyth are chosen by the 12 above-stated so that one of them will serve the lady this year next in the future in the office of reeve. On which by the agreement and will of the same inquiry as sworn the aforesaid John JonessonRowlowe is affirmed for the better. And he is sworn
Affeerors	Roger Cattestre, Stephen Bradeneie Sum of this court 51s 6d In expenses of the steward, Richard Bulveis, & others 12d
Supervise	Still it is to be enquired in the next [court] concerning 4 oxen received by Thomas Hugge in the time when he was reeve & by the same delivered outside the domain

Great Court of Joan Beauchamp, Lady of Bergavenny & Worfeld held at Worfeld on Tuesday the 27th day in the month of October in the thirteenth year of the reign of King Henry IV after the conquest

	Robert Ewdenas	Roger Waltone	John Walker }
	Roger Cattestre	John Barndeleie	Thomas Merwalle } sworn
The 12	Roger Richardes	John Tumpkys	John the son of Nicholas Rowlowe }
	Stephen Bradeneie	John Hethe	Roger Broke }

Kyngeslowe, Stanlowe	townships there present nothing
Chesturtone amerced 3s 6d strays 12d	township there presents that Margaret Tresele (12d) broke an arrest [confinement might be better] made by Thomas Tresele formerly the lady's reeve so the said Margaret is in mercy. And they say that Thomas the son of Richard Bradeneie forestalled (6d) Edward Crupel & drew blood (12d) from the said Edward so the said Thomas is in mercy. And they say that John Trafford (6d) forestalled Thomas Gorgan so the same John is in mercy. Also they say that William Bettone forestalled John Trafford so the said William (6d) is in mercy. Also they present 1 grey horse coming as a stray by the space of 1 year last past within the township there price of the horse 12d concerning which the reeve is charged to respond to the greater profit of the lady
Hultone amerced 12d	township there presents that Edith (12d) the daughter of Margaret Tresele broke the pound of Robert Bruggende so the same Edith is in mercy
Rowlowe, Bradene, Asturhul, Ewyk, Soonde amerced 9s 4d	townships there present that John Gille forestalled (6d) William Barewe & drew blood (12d) from him. So the said John both for the forestalling & for the bloodshed is in mercy. And they say that Henry Barker (6d) forestalled John Jankys so the said Henry is in mercy. Also they say that John Merwelle forestalled (6d) the said John Jankys so the same John Merwelle is in mercy. And they say that John Walker forestalled Henry Barker so the same John (6d) is in mercy. Also they say that Thomas the son of John Walker forestalled (6d) the said Henry Barker & drew blood (12d) from him so the said Thomas is in mercy. Also they say that Henry Barker forestalled the aforesaid John Walker so the same Henry (6d) is in mercy. Also they say that John Gille (6d) forestalled John Jankys so the same John Gille is in mercy. Furthermore they say that Henry Barker (3s 4d) lay in ambush and waited to beat John Jankys and made an assault on him so the said Henry is at a fine. And they say that John the son of Robert Smyth forestalled William Goold of Hultone so the same John (6d) is in mercy

Roughtone, Barndeleie, Hoccombe, Swancote amerced 6d	townships there present that John (6d) the son of Robert Smyth forestalled Hugh Baker so the said John is in mercy
Burcote, Burcote, Ryndelford, Bromle	townships there present nothing
Alvescote, Wynnescote, Cattestre, Newtone	townships there present nothing
Oldyntone, Ewdenas Waif 2d amerced 12d	townships there present that Agnes (12d) the wife of John atte Soonde unjustly took one goose price 2d from the goods and chattels of William Oldyntone junior so the said Agnes is in mercy
Stapelford	township there presents nothing
Akeltone Supervise because a stray	township there presents 1 ox coming as a stray at the feast of St Michael last past which is in the custody of the reeve
Haalen amerced 3s 6d	township there presents that John Jankys forestalled John Gille so the same John (6d) Jankys is in mercy. And they say that Edith Jones forestalled Isabell Englisch so the same Edith (6d) is in mercy. And that the same Isabell raised the hue and cry by mouth justly on the said Edith so the said Edith (12d) is in mercy. Also they say that John Gille forestalled (6d) John Jankys & drew blood (12d) from him so the said John Gille is in mercy
Wyke amerced 36s 4d	township there presents that Matilda (6d) the wife of John Smyth raised the hue and cry by mouth unjustly on William Barker so the said Matilda is in mercy. And they say that Joan the wife of William Yngeman broke the pound of Thomas Heyne twice so the said Joan (2s) is in mercy. Furthermore they present that John Fetherestone then bailiff of the Hundred of Brimestre unjustly & without a writ from the lord King against the peace & the custom of the manor of Worfeld entered the township of Wyke & from thence took one horse of Thomas Heyne & kept it until a fine was made to him of 2s 6d. So the said John (13s 4d) is in mercy. Also they say that Hugh Pors servant of Richard Laken with force & arms & against the peace of the lord King entered the township of Wyke & there made an assault on John Walker beat wounded and maimed on his hand so the said Hugh (20s) is at a fine
Worfeld amerced 20d	township there presents that Richard Parlour who is bound to make appearance at this court did not appear pardoned by the steward. Also they present the Kings road in Worfeld is deteriorated from the default of 1 tenement (8d) formerly Alice Rugge's so the occupiers of the said tenement are in mercy. And they say that John Hulle (6d) of Hultone forestalled James Leche of Coventry. And that the same James (6d) forestalled the said John so each of them is in mercy

The tasters amerced 13s	of ale present that William Newe (6d) brewed 1, Hugh Baker (6d) 1, William Goold (6d) 1, John Walle (6d) 1, John Smythe of Wyke (6d) 1, John Yate (6d) 1, Richard Bradeneye (6d) 1, John Rowlowe (12d) 2, Thomas Soonde (2s) 4, John Smyth of Sonde (12d) 2, William Rowlowe (6d) 1, John Cattestre (6d) 1, John Billyngesle (6d) 1, Richard Bulveis (2s 6d) 5, William Herdemon (6d) 1, Robert Taillour (6d) 1, John Walker (6d) 1, and all sold against the assize by illegal measures so each of them is in mercy
The 12 jurors Goods stolen 9s 11d Amerced 40s	present that the townships aforesaid & the tasters of ale have well & faithfully presented. Furthermore they say on their oath that William Prestes (20s), Alice his wife, Thomas Rugge (10s) & Margery (10s) Trafford entered the chamber of Edith Coliar in Chesturtone by one window & from thence unjustly took against the peace on Tuesday the 9th day of the month of June in the 12th year of the reign of King Henry IV from the conquest these goods and chattels namely 1 ?cover price 20d, 3 lynch-pins price 2s, 1 towel price 6d, 1 canopy price 4d, 1 long cloak price 2s 6d, 1 tunic price 2s, 2 pecks of oat flour price 6d, 7 white goblets price 3d & 1 adze price 2d of the goods of John Dalleleie. So the aforesaid William, Alice, Thomas & Margery are in mercy
	Affeerors: Robert Ewdenas, Roger Richardes Sum of this court £6 11d
Worfeld	Small court held there on Tuesday the 10th day of the month of November in the 13th year of the reign of King Henry IV after the conquest [10 November 1411]
Essoins	Thomas Toward & Thomas Merwalle themselves from common [suit] by John Rowlowe the reeve
amerced 4d	John Robyns is in mercy because he did not come to warrant his essoin
amerced 3d	The bailiff is charged concerning 3d to be raised from Thomas Forster for his default at the last suit of court preceding then not assessed

The 12				
	Roger Cattestre	John Walker	John Barndeleie }	
	Roger Richardes	John Hethe	Roger Broke }	sworn
	Stephen Bradeneye	William Wermod	John Bromleie }	
	Roger Waltone	William Newe	Mathew Bullok }	

Fine 12d	John Nicoles made a fine with the lady for suit of court to be commuted from the date of this court until the feast of St Michael the Archangel next in the future. And he gives for a fine 12d pledge for the fine Thomas Soonde
Fine 12d	Thomas Forster gives to the lady 12d for suit of court to be commuted from the date of this court until the feast of St Michael next in the future pledge for the fine William Gerbod
amerced 6d	John Glover put himself in mercy for a licence to agree with Thomas Jankys junior in a plea of debt etc.
The 12	jurors present that William Heneme (3d), Roger Batemon (3d), Andrew Fekkenham (3d) & John Robyns (3d) who were bound to make suit at this court did not come. So each of them is in mercy

1411-1412 P314/W/1/1/240

Ingress 15s	And they say that now there falls into the hands of the lady 1 messuage & three nooks of land in lesser tenure in Alvescote as after the death of William the son of Adam Robyns. And they say that Matilda the daughter of William Bullok & wife of Richard Whitebrok is the closest heir to take from the lady the aforesaid messuage & land & thence to make a fine with the lady etc. On which came here in court the aforesaid Richard Whitebrok & Matilda his wife & took from the lady the aforesaid messuage & three nooks of land with appurtenances to hold to themselves & their [heirs] from the lady as of the right and heredity of the aforesaid Matilda according to the custom of the manor by services & customs thence due. And they give to the lady for a fine for ingress thence to be had 15s. And they are seized in the manner aforesaid
Tenement in the hand of the lady	And they say that there remains in the hand of the lady 1 toft in Bromleie falling by the death of William Galian & it is charged annually at 1d fixed rent. And thus it remains in hand until
Tenement remains in the hand of the lady	Also still remaining in the hand of the lady one toft & half a virgate of land of lesser tenure in Haalen from the surrender by Andrew Fekkenham & Elianora his wife to the use of William Ewyk as is clear in the last court preceding
Tenement remains in the hand of the lady	Still remaining in the hand of the lady 1 cottage with curtilage adjacent in Haalen from a surrender by John Bokenhale to the use of John Smyth as is clear in the last & penultimate courts preceding
Adjourned until the next	{Still the plea between John Ewyk plaintiff & Roger Batemon & Isabell his wife {defendants in a plea of land {And between William Holigreve & Emmoter his wife plaintiff & Thomas Hugge {of Hultone, Margery his wife, & Richard Thorne of Hopstone defendants in a plea of land {And between Thomas Hugge plaintiff & Margaret Tresel & John her son defendants {in a plea of land adjourned etc.
Supervise the next	{ Still the plea between Thomas Heyne plaintiff & John Fethereston } defendant in a plea of trespass { And between Thomas Jankys plaintiff & Andrew Fekkenham } adjourned defendant in a plea of trespass } until { And between John Hethe plaintiff & William Port clerk & } the next Margaret Tresel defendants in a plea of trespass} {And between Thomas Hugge plaintiff & William Port clerk } & Margaret Tresel defendants in a plea of trespass
distrain	Thomas Heyne plaintiff against William Yngemon in a plea of trespass pledge for the prosecution William Yate who is not summoned nor attached so let it be done
Affeerors	Roger Cattestre, John Walker

Sum of this court 19s 1d
Expenses of the steward 12d

1411-1412 P314/W/1/1/240

Worfeld — Small court held there on Tuesday the 1st day of the month of December in the 13th year of the reign of King Henry IV after the conquest [1 December 1411]

Essoins — Thomas Richardes & John Stevenes themselves from common [suit] by John Rowlowe the reeve

the 12

Roger Cattestre	Roger Waltone	William Wermod }	
Roger Richardes	John Barndeleie	Roger Gerbod }	sworn
Stephen Bradeneie	Thomas Merwelle	Roger Broke }	
John Walker	William Newe	Mathew Bullok }	

Fine 12d — John Robyns made a fine for suit of court to be commuted from the date of this court until the feast of St Michael the Archangel next in the future. And he gives for a fine 12d pledge for the fine John Walker

distrain — Thomas Sonde agreed plaintiff against William Beore responded in a plea of trespass who is not distrained so let it be done

distrain — Thomas Sonde agreed plaintiff against Stephen Humeleie responded in a plea of trespass who is not attached so let it be done

distrain — Still Thomas Heyne plaintiff against William Yngmon in a plea of trespass who is still not attached because he has nothing whereof he can be distrained as is clear by the oath of the bailiff furthermore it is ordered the same William is distrained that he is at the next [court] to respond to the aforesaid Thomas in the plea aforesaid

Adjourned Supervise

{Still the plea between John Ewyk plaintiff & Roger Batemon & Isabell his wife defendants in a plea of land adjourned to the next
{And between William Holigreve & Emmoter his wife plaintiff & Thomas Hugge of Hultone, Margery his wife, & Richard Thorne of Hopstone defendants in a plea of land adjourned as above
{And between Thomas Hugge plaintiff & Margaret Tresel & John her son defendants
{in a plea of land adjourned as above

Adjourned Supervise

{ Still a day is given between Thomas Heyne plaintiff & John Fetherstone } defendant in a plea of trespass until the next
{ And between Thomas Jankys plaintiff & Andrew Fekkenham } adjourned
defendant in a plea of trespass as above } by the prayer
{ And between John Hethe plaintiff & William Port clerk & } of the parties
Margaret Tresel defendants in a plea of trespass }
{And between Thomas Hugge plaintiff & William Port clerk }
& Margaret Tresel defendants in a plea of trespass

the 12 — jurors present that Andrew Fekkenham (3d) who is bound to make suit at this court did not come so the said Andrew is in mercy. Also they seek an inspection of the court rolls before the next [court] to enquire whether Thomas Barbour, clerk, paid relief to the lord for 1 toft & 1 nook of free land which he holds in Wynnescote or not which tenement is charged at a fixed rent of 22½d

Fine 12d — Roger Batemon made a fine with the lady for suit of court to be commuted from the date of this court until the feast of St Michael the Archangel next in the future. And he gives for a fine 12d

1411-1412 P314/W/1/1/240

Affeerors	Roger Cattestre, John Walker Sum of this court 2s 3d Expenses of the steward 12d
Supervise	At the end of this court it is found by the evidence of Roger Gerbod that Thomas Barbor clerk, above-named, holds 2 assarts of free land in Hokkombe for which he gives annually to the lord a fixed rent of 4d over & above the toft and nook of land above
Worfeld	Small court held there on Tuesday next after the feast of St Thomas the Apostle in the 13th year of the reign of King Henry IV after the conquest [22 December 1411]
Essoins	Roger Richardes, William Prestes themselves from common [suit] by Richard Bulveis
the 12	Roger Cattestre, Nicholas Rowlowe, John Bromleie, Roger Waltone, Roger Broke, Mathew Bullok, John Walker, Thomas Hugge, Thomas Merwelle, John Barndeleie, Henry Barker, William Newe } sworn
Fine 12d	Andrew Fekkenham made a fine here for suit of court to be commuted from the date of this court until the feast of St Michael the Archangel next in the future. And he gives for a fine 12d pledge for the fine Nicholas Rowlowe
amerced 6d	William Beore put himself in mercy for a licence to agree with Thomas Sonde plaintiff in a plea of trespass
amerced 6d	Thomas Sonde plaintiff against Stephen Humele in a plea of trespass who are for a licence to agree. And the same Stephen put himself in mercy
amerced 3d	The 12 jurors present that William Heneme who is bound to make suit at this court did not come so the said William (3d) is in mercy
Relief 4s 5d Supervise	And they say that Thomas Barbour clerk holds 1 nook of free land in Wynnescote charged annually at 22½d fixed rent. And 2 assarts of free land in Hoccombe charged annually at 4d fixed rent for which tenements he is bound to pay the lord relief unless it will be possible to find what he first paid. On which it is ordered to the bailiff to make to raise 4s 5d from the aforesaid Thomas clerk for relief for the free tenements above-stated. Furthermore it is ordered to the bailiff to distrain the aforesaid Thomas that he is at the next court to make fealty to the lord and other services owed and to acknowledge how he holds the tenements aforesaid and also to show what title and how he is entered into the same
distrain	Still Thomas Heyne plaintiff against William Yngemon in a plea of trespass who still is not distrained so let it be done
adjourn	{ Still a day is given between Thomas Heyne plaintiff & John Fetherstone } defendant in a plea of trespass { And between Thomas Jankys plaintiff & Andrew Fekkenham }until defendant in a plea of trespass { And between John Hethe plaintiff & William Port clerk & }the next [court] Margaret Tresel defendants in a plea of trespass {And between Thomas Hugge plaintiff & the said William, clerk) & Margaret defendants

1411-1412 P314/W/1/1/240

adjourn	(The plea between John Ewyk plaintiff & Roger Batemon & Isabell his wife } defendants in a plea of land (And between William Holigreve & Emmoter his wife plaintiffs & Thomas Hugge of Hultone, Margery his wife, & Richard Thorne of Hopstone defendants in a plea of land (And between Thomas Hugge plaintiff & Margaret Tresel & John her son in a plea of land	) adjourned } until the next [court]

Tenement in the hand of the lady — Still remaining in the hand of the lady 1 toft & half a virgate of land in lesser tenure in Haalen from a surrender by Andrew Fekkenham & Elianora his wife to the use of William Ewyk as clear above in the court preceding

Tenement in the hand of the lady — Also remaining in the hand of the lady 1 cottage & curtilage adjacent in Haalen from a surrender by John Bokenhale to the use of John Smyth of Wyke as is clear in the court preceding

Affeerors — Roger Cattestre, John Walker

Sum of this court 6s 8d
In expenses of the steward 12d

Worfeld — Small court held there on Tuesday the 19th day of January in the 13th year of the reign of King Henry IV after the conquest [19 January 1412]

	Roger Richardes	John Walker	Mathew Bullok	}
	Roger Cattestre	William Newe	John Bromleie	} sworn
the 12	Stephen Bradeneie	John Barndeleie	John, son of Nicholas Rowlowe	}
	Roger Waltone	Roger Broke	Thomas Merwalle	}

distrain — Still Thomas Heyne plaintiff against William Yngemon in a plea of trespass who still is not yet distrained so let it be done

adjourned until the next — { Still a day is given between Thomas Heyne plaintiff & John Fetherstone defendant in a plea of trespass
{ And between Thomas Jankys senior plaintiff & Andrew Fekkenham defendant in a plea of trespass
{ And between John Hethe plaintiff & William Port clerk & Margaret Tresele } defendants in a plea of trespass } a day
{And between Thomas Hugge plaintiff & the said William, clerk & Margaret } defendants in a plea of trespass

adjourned until the next — The plea between John Ewyk plaintiff & Roger Batemon & Isabell his wife defendants in a plea of land adjourned until the next [court]
And between William Holigreve & Emmoter his wife plaintiffs &Thomas Hugge of Hultone, Margery his wife, & Richard Thorne of Hopstone defendants in a plea of land adjourned as above
And between Thomas Hugge plaintiff & Margaret Tresel & John her son in a plea of land adjourned as above

The 12 amerced 3d — jurors present that Thomas Tresele who is bound to make suit at this court did not come so the said Thomas (3d) is in mercy

And they say that Margery Bradeneie who held of the lady by the custom of the manor 1 messuage & three nooks of land in Bradeneie on the day she died from heriot 20d

Tenement in the hand of the lady Oversee

whose death there falls to the lady 1 mother sheep in the name of heriot price 20d. And for escheat nothing falls to the lord because there was nothing. Furthermore by the examination & overview of the old rolls it is found that the aforesaid Margery held from the lord on the day on which she died by the custom of the manor 1 nook of land more and 1 parcel of meadow at Torre in Bradenie aforesaid by what title & in what manner it is to be overseen and determined in the next [court]. And they say that John Bradeneie is the closest heir to take from the lady the aforesaid tenement. The which tenement remains in the hand of the lady until etc. beyond that remaining to the aforesaid John Bradeneie four parts of the messuage aforesaid & four parts of one nook of land by virtue of a fine previously made as is clear in the rolls of the court held in the 6th year of the reign of King Richard II. Which tenement is being settled and determined in the next court following

heriot 16d
Tenement in the hand of the lord

And they say that Emily the Hoore who held of the lord by the custom of the manor 2 cottages in Haalen has died from whose death there falls to the lord 1 sheep in the name of heriot price 16d. And for escheat nothing falls because there was nothing just as they say on their oath. And who is wholly her heir they don't know. And the tenement aforesaid remains in the hand of the lady. Being determined & settled in the court held on Tuesday the first day of the month of March next following

Tenement in the hand of the lord

Still remaining in the hand of the lord 1 toft in Bromleie by the death of William Galian

Also still remaining in the hand of the lord 1 toft & half a virgate of land in Haalen from a surrender by Andrew Fekkenham & Elianora his wife to the use of William Ewyk as clear above in the court preceding this year. It is being settled in the next court following

Tenement in the hand of the lord

Still remaining in the hand of the lord 1 cottage & curtilage adjacent in Haalen from a surrender by John Bokenhale to the use of John Smyth of Wyke as clear in the court preceding

distrain
the next

{Thomas Jankys a day junior plaintiff against John Bromleie in a plea of trespass
{Thomas Hugge plaintiff against Emily Hoore in a plea of debt
{John Holigreve plaintiff against the said Emily in a plea of debt

Supervise

Still the 12 jurors have a day until the next [court] to render the full verdict concerning the fine of William Holigreve deceased as is clear in the first court this year namely which tenements he held on the day on which he died & which cattle he had and what heriot the lady should have from the death of the same William

Affeerors

Roger Cattestre, Roger Broke

Sum of this court 3s 3d
In expenses of the steward 12d

Worfeld

Small court held there on Tuesday the 9th day of the month of February in the 13th year of the reign of King Henry IV after the conquest [9 February 1412]

the 12

Roger Cattestre	Roger Waltone	John Walker }	
Stephen Bradeneie	John Barndeleie	Thomas Merwelle	} sworn
Roger Richardes	John Hethe	John, son of Nicholas Rowlowe }	
John Janne	William Gerbode	Roger Broke }	

William Ewyk came here in court & took from the lady one toft & half a virgate of land in Haalen called Kyngeslond which Andrew Fekkenham & Elionora his wife surrendered into the hands of the lord to the use of the said William to have & to hold the said toft & half a virgate of land aforesaid with its appurtenances to the aforesaid William & his heirs from the lady by services thence due and accustomed according to the custom of the manor. And thence he has seisin. And he made fealty. And he gives to the lady for a fine 10s

Fine 10s

John Bradeneie son & heir of Richard Bradeneie came here in court & relieved the lady for three parts of one messuage, three nooks of land & for three parts of one nook of land the which was formerly Richard Bradeneie's his father, in Bradeneie. To hold to himself and his [heirs] from the lady by services thence due & accustomed according to the custom of the manor. And thence he has seisin. And he made fealty to the lady & gives to the lady for ingress 18s 9d

Ingress 18s 9d

It is granted to John Barndeleie that the same John is able to marry his daughter Isolda to Thomas the son of Thomas Merwelle for which licence to have he gives to the lady for a fine 6s 8d

Fine 6s 8d

Thomas Merwelle & Margery his wife surrendered into the hands of the lady one messuage with half a virgate of land adjacent in Stapelford to have back the said tenements themselves for the term of the lives of both of them from the lady according to the custom of the manor. So that after the deaths of them the aforesaid tenements should remain with Thomas their son & Isolda his wife & the heirs of their bodies legitimately issuing and in default of issue from them to the rightful heirs and assigns of the aforesaid Thomas junior. The which Thomas & Margery came here in court and took from the lady the messuage & land aforesaid with its appurtenances to hold to themselves for the term of their lives from the lady by services thence due according to the custom of the manor. And that after their decease the messuage & land aforesaid with its appurtenances remains with Thomas their son and Isolda his wife & the heirs of their bodies legitimately issued to hold from the lady by services thence due and accustomed according to the custom of the manor. And in default of their issue from them that the messuage and land aforesaid should remain with the rightful heirs of the same Thomas junior to hold from the lady by services thence due & accustomed according to the custom of the manor. And thence they have seisin. And they made fealty. And they give to the lady for a fine 10s

Fine 10s

It is granted by the lady to Thomas Cattestre & Alice his wife 2 parcels of land in Wynnescote called Stonyrudynge & Lucerudynge which Adam Robyns formerly held & which came into the hands of the lady in the name of escheat except a third part of the same which Matilda formerly the wife of the aforesaid Adam holds in dote. To have and to hold the parcels aforesaid except the pre-exempted to the aforesaid Thomas & Alice his wife for the term of the life of the lady only to render thence annually to the lady 8d at the usual terms. And they give to the lady for a fine 10s to be paid into the account. And thence they have seisin. And they made fealty to the lady. The reeve is charged annually to the lady 2d of new rent for the term of the life of Matilda formerly the wife of Adam Robyns for the third part of 2 parcels of free land in Wynnescote called Lucerudynge & Stonyrudynge which she holds in reversion in the name of dote by the death of the said Adam thence pertaining to the lady as escheat after the aforesaid Matilda because the said Adam died without heirs

Fine 10s
Increase 2d
Supervise

William Ewyke made a fine for suit of court to be commuted from the date of this court until the feast of St Michael the Archangel next in the future. And to the lady for a fine 12d

Fine 12d

amerced 6d distrain	The reeve is in mercy because he did not have John Fetherstone to respond to Thomas Heyne in a plea of trespass. Furthermore it is ordered the same reeve that he distrains the said John that he is at the next [court] to respond to the said Thomas in the plea aforesaid
amerced 6d	Thomas Jankys is in mercy for an unjust plea against Andre Fekkenham in a plea of trespass
Recover amerced 12d	Margaret Tresele plaintiff against Richard Aldith, William Cattestre, William Goold, Thomas Hugge & John Bromleie in a plea of trespass pledge for the prosecution John Stevenes. And she says that the said Richard, William, William, Thomas & John unjustly & against the peace took bread and ale and other victuals from the same Margaret at Chesturtone & destroyed the same victuals to the grave damage of teh same Margaret etc. And the aforesaid defendants present thence put themselves on the aforesaid 12 jurors that on their part they did no damage to the same Margaret etc. On the oath of the 12 jurors it is determined that Richard Aldith inflicted damage on the said Margaret's victuals to the damage of 12 pence which it is ordered to raise to the use of Margaret. And the said Richard is in mercy. And the other defendants above-stated on their part did no damage. So the said Margaret is in mercy for her unjust plea to the said
amerced nothing for the reason shown	William Holigreve & Emma his wife are in mercy because they are not prosecuting against Thomas Hugge, Margery his wife, & Richard Thorne in a plea of land remaining nevertheless not assessed because they are dead
the 12 jurors amerced 3d	present that William Kyngessone (3d) who is bound to make suit at this court did not come so the said William is in mercy
distrain	Still it is ordered to the bailiff that he distrain William Yngemon that he is at the next [court] to respond to Thomas Heyne in a plea of trespass
distrain	And that he distrains William Poort clerk & Margaret Tresel that they are at the next [court] to respond to John Hethe & Thomas Hugge in a plea of trespass
adjourned	Still the plea between John Ewyk & Roger Batemon & Isabell his wife in a plea of land adjourned until the next [court]
amerced nothing for the reason shown	The plea between Thomas Hugge & Margaret Tresele & John her son in a plea of land is determined as below by a fine
Adjourned	{ Still a day is give between Thomas Jankys junior plaintiff & John Bromleie defendant in a plea of trespass {Also a day is give between Thomas Hugge & Emily Hoore & her executors in a plea of debt {And between John Holigreve plaintiff & the said Emily & her executors in a plea of debt
distrain	William Prestes plaintiff against Edith Colier in a plea of trespass who is not attached so let it be done
distrain	Henry Barker plaintiff against Thomas Jankys senior in a plea of trespass who is not attached so let it be done

Tenement remains in the hand of the lady

Still remaining in the hand of the lady 1 toft in Bromley by the death of William Galian

Tenement remains in the hand of the lady

Still remaining in the hand of the lady 1 cottage & curtilage adjacent in Haalen from a surrender by John Bokenhale to the use of John Smyth of Wyke

Tenement remains in the hand of the lady

And still remaining in the hand of the lady 2 cottages of which Emily Hoore died seized in Haale etc. Which cottages are being settled in the next small court following

Supervise

Still the 12 jurors have a day until the next to render the verdict concerning the death of William Holigreve as is clear in the last court preceding namely who held the tenement on the day he died and what animals he had at that time and what heriots the lady should be having from the death of the same William. And who is his heir etc. Determined in the next court following

Fine 2s

Thomas the son of William Hugges of Hultone blood relative & heir of John Hugges of Chesturtone gives to the lady 2s for an inquiry by the 12 to be held to enquire whether the aforesaid John his grandfather died seized of 2 messuages & one virgate of land in Chesturtone in her domain as of fee & what by right of heredity they descended to a certain John the son & heir of the aforesaid John. The which John the son & heir of the aforesaid John after the death of his father aforesaid nevertheless thence had seisin from the hands of the lord as is clear by the rolls of the court but the messuage and virgate of land aforesaid were surrendered into the hands of the lord to the use of William his younger brother which acquisition being void & null because the aforesaid John the son of John did not have possession in the same messuage & virgate of land after the death of the aforesaid John his father freely from the hands of the lord. And thus the messuage and virgate of land aforesaid according to the custom of the manor belongs of right to the aforesaid Thomas as blood relative & heir of the aforesaid John his grandfather of which thence in the manner the aforesaid died seized. And thus he has the better right for the reasons aforesaid in his demand in the same than Margaret Tresele & John her son have in their tenure. On which specifically to enquire on the right condition by the court rolls of the lord by 12 to this chosen & appointed. On which the inquiry was held by the oath of John Hethe, William Newe, Roger Broke of Roughtone, William Yate, Thomas Rowlowe, Thomas Towart, Richard Aldith, William Prestes, Thomas Merwelle junior, John atte Welle, Robert Bruggende & Thomas Burcote of Burcote who are sworn and thence charged say on their oath that Margaret Tresele & John her son have a better right in their tenure than Thomas Hugges in his demand

No fine because she holds as by the right as widow

Agnes formerly the wife of Richard Bradeneie junior came here in court & took from the lady 1 parcel of meadow called the Torre whereof the aforesaid Richard formerly her husband died seised. To hold the parcel aforesaid for the term of her life according to the custom of the manor. And after her death to remain with John, son and heir of the aforesaid Richard. And concerning a fine the aforesaid Agnes gives nothing

Sum of this court 60s 8d

In expenses of John Boerleie the steward being there for 3 days & 3 nights with his horses both at this court & the great court & for other business of the lady to supervise 28s 6d

1411-1412 P314/W/1/1/240

Worfeld	Small court held there on Tuesday the first day of the month of March in the 13th year of the reign of King Henry IV after the conquest [1 March 1412]
Essoins	William Heneme & William Huster themselves from common [suit] by Richard Bulveis
The 12	Roger Cattestre, John Barndeleie, John Hethe, Roger Richardes, Roger Broke, William Newe, Stephen Bradeneie, John Walker, Thomas Merwelle, Roger Waltone, John Rowlowe, Mathew Bullok } sworn
Fine 12d Fine 4s	John Nelde gives to the lady 12d for an inquiry of 12 to be held to enquire if the same John according to the custom is the closest heir to take from the hand of the lady 2 cottages in Hale of which Emily the Hoore died seized as is clear in the penultimate court preceding etc. However on this the same John without further inquiry of his right on his behalf came here in court and took from the lady the aforesaid 2 cottages as if the closest heir of the aforesaid Emily to hold to himself and his [heirs] from the lady by services thence due and accustomed according to the custom of the manor saving the right of whoever is demanding the said cottages in the future. And in that manner he is seized. And he gives to the lady for a fine 4s. And he made fealty to the lady
the 12 amercements remain not assessed	jurors present that Thomas Tresele, Thomas Richardes & John Holigreve who are bound to make suit at this court did not come. So each of them is in mercy
Heriot 20d	And they say that concerning the death of William Holigreve as is clear in the first court of this year and in the penultimate court preceding that the lady will have for the lands and tenements of which he died seized now 1 sheep more in the name of heriot price 20d. And they say that at the time of his death he had no better animals and also that the lady now has from the death of the said deceased which of right and by custom she should have had. Further they say that all the land and tenements of which he died seized remain with John Holigreve his son by virtue of the fine first made as is clear by the record of the court rolls of the lord etc.
amercements remain not assessed Distrain	Still John Rowlowe the reeve is in mercy because he does not have John Fetherstone here to respond to Thomas Heyne in a plea of trespass. Furthermore it is ordered to the said reeve to distrain the aforesaid John Fetherstone that he is at the next to respond to the aforesaid Thomas in the plea aforesaid
amerced 6d	Thomas Jankys put himself in mercy for a licence to agree with Henry Barker in a plea of trespass
Increase on the sale of 1 stray horse 4d	The bailiff is charged here of 4d increase on the sale of one stray horse appraised at 12d by the township of Chesturtone as is clear in the great court preceding because it was sold by Richard Bulveis & the reeve for 16d
amerced 6d	Still it is ordered to the bailiff that he distrain William Yngmon that he is at the next [court] to respond to Thomas Heyne in a plea of trespass

Adjourned until the next [court]

{Still a day is given between John Hethe plaintiff & William Port clerk & Margaret Tresele defendants in a plea of trespass
{And between Thomas Hugge plaintiff & William Port clerk & Margaret Tresele defendants in a plea of trespass
{Also a day is given between Thomas Jankys junior plaintiff & John Bromleie defendant in a plea of trespass
{And between William Prestes plaintiff & Edith Colier defendant in a plea of trespass
{And between Thomas Hugge plaintiff & the executors of Emily Hoore defendants in {a plea of debt
{And between John Holigreve & the said executors defendants in a plea of debt

A day until the next — Still the plea between John Ewyk plaintiff & Roger Batemon & Isabell his wife defendants in a plea of land adjourned until the next [court]

Held in the hand of the lady — Still remaining in the hand of the lady 1 toft with curtilage in Bromleie by the death of William Galian

Held in the hand of the lady — Also remaining in the hand of the lady 1 cottage with curtilage and croft adjacent in Haalen from the surrender by John Bokenhale to the use of John Smyth of Wyke etc.

Sum of this court 7s 6d
Expenses of the steward 12d

Worfeld — Small court held there on Tuesday the 22nd day of the month of March in the 13th year of the reign of King Henry IV after the conquest [22 March 1412]

Essoins — Henry Barker himself from common [suit] by John Walker

The 12 jurors — Inquiry held for the lady by the oath of Roger Cattestre, Stephen Bradeneie, Roger Richardes, Roger Waltone, John Hethe, John Walker, Roger Broke, John Barndeleie, Nicholas Rowlowe, Thomas Merwelle, John Bromle & William Newe who at present presented nothing

amerced 6d — Thomas Heyne is in mercy for his unjust plea against William Yngemon in a plea of trespass

amerced 6d — Still Thomas Jankys junior plaintiff & John Bromleie defendant in a plea of trespass who is for a licence to agree. And the said John put himself in mercy

amerced 6d — Edith Colier put herself in mercy for a licence to agree with William Prestes in a plea of trespass

amerced 6d — John atte Welle put himself in mercy for a licence to agree with Thomas Heyne plaintiff in the name of William Yngman in a plea of broken agreement

Adjourned

{Still Thomas Heyne plaintiff against John Fetherestone in a plea of trespass who have a day adjourned until the next
{Also a day is given between John Hethe plaintiff & William Port clerk & Margaret Tresel defendants adjourned until the next in a plea of trespass
{And between Thomas Hugge plaintiff & the said William Port & Margaret defendants until the next in a plea of trespass
{And between John Holigreve & the executors of the will of Emily Hoore in a plea of debt until the next
{And between Thomas Hugge plaintiff & the said executors of Emily aforesaid in a plea of debt until the next

Adjourned {Also still a day is given between John Ewyk plaintiff & Roger Batemon & Isabell his wife in a plea of land

Also remaining in the hand of the lady 1 toft with curtilage in Bromleie by the death of William Galian

Also remaining in the hand of the lady 1 cottage with curtilage and croft adjacent in Haalen from the surrender by John Bokenhale to the use of John Smyth of Wyke until

Assessors: Roger Waltone, Roger Broke

Sum of this court 2s
Expenses of the steward 12d

Worfeld Small court held there on Tuesday the 12th day of the month of April in the 13th year of the reign of King Henry IV after the conquest [12 April 1412]

the 12

Roger Cattestre	John Barndeleie	John Walker }
Roger Richardes	William Newe	Thomas Merwelle } sworn
Stephen Bradeneie	John Hethe	John son of Nicholas Rowlowe}
Roger Waltone	Roger Broke	John Bromleie }

who say on there oath that they have nothing to present now

adjourned

{Still a day is given until the next [court] to Thomas Heyne plaintiff & John Fetherstone defendant in a plea of trespass
{And between John Hethe plaintiff & William Port chaplain & Margaret Tresel defendants in a plea of trespass
{And between Thomas Hugge plaintiff & the said William Port & Margaret defendants in a plea of trespass
{And between John Holigreve plaintiff & the executors of Emily Hoore in a plea of debt
{And between Thomas Hugge plaintiff & the said executors in a plea of debt
{And between John Ewyk plaintiff & Roger Batemon & Isabell his wife in a plea of land

Tenements remaining in the hand of the lady

{Still remaining in the hand of the lady 1 toft with curtilage in Bromleie as is clear in the court preceding

{Also remaining in the hand of the lady 1 cottage with curtilage and croft from the surrender of John Bokenhale to the use of John Smyth of Wyke

Fine 2s

Thomas Colier of Oldyntone & Hawisia his wife blood relative & heir of Agnes Adams namely the daughter of William Galian, son of William Bradeneie, brother of Roger Adams father of the aforesaid Agnes give to the lady 2s for an inquiry by 12 to be held to enquire if the aforesaid Agnes her ancestor whose heir is the same Hawisia died seized of 1 toft & 1 virgate of land in Hultone which descended to the said Hawisia by the right of heredity after the death of the said Agnes her ancestor. The which Agnes relieved the toft and land aforesaid and thence had seisin as is clear by the court rolls of the lady held at Worfeld on Wednesday next after the feast of St James in the 23rd year of the reign of King Edward III after the conquest. And afterwards indeed Richard le Hoore & Emily his wife in claiming the said Emily to be the blood relative and closest heir of the aforesaid Agnes, the said Agnes living they surrendered the toft & virgate of land aforesaid to the use of Roger Gold & Joan his wife the which surrender was void and null because the aforesaid Richard and Emily then had no property rights in the same o in their possession. And afterwards the aforesaid Richard Gold & Joan his wife surrendered into the hands of the lord to the use of Richard Thorne which surrender being void and null because the aforesaid Roger Gold and Joan his wife had no right in the same. And afterwards the said William Thorne married a certain Margery & died the which Margery held in possession the toft and virgate of land aforesaid married a certain Thomas Hugges which toft and virgate of land they now unjustly hold. And the said Agnes thus died seized of the toft and virgate of land aforesaid which of right and according to the custom of the manor ought to descend to the aforesaid Hawisia blood relative and heir of the said Agnes. And thus the aforesaid Thomas and Hawisia his wife have a better right as they say in their claim to the toft and virgate of land aforesaid than the aforesaid Thomas Hugges and Margery in their tenure. On which it should specifically be searched for so well by the court rolls of the lord by 12 to be elected and appointed for the purpose. And on this the inquiry was held by the oath of Nicholas Rowlowe, Nicholas Stanlowe, Roger Smyth, John Coletes, Roger Cattestre, Thomas Jankys, Roger Richardes, William Bromleie, Thomas Tresele, John Bromleie, Thomas Richardes & Thomas atte Sonde who thence charged before the steward present nothing. On which it is ordered to the reeve by the steward on behalf of the lady to seize into the hands of the lady 1 toft and 1 virgate of land in Hultone which Agnes Adams aforesaid formerly held there & thence died seized without heirs as it said which for which reason the toft and virgate of land aforesaid with its appurtenances should come into the hands of the lady as her escheat. So that none of them should be allowed to enter without a special licence from the lady or her council but in the next [court] better to enquire concerning the truth

Margin: It is ordered to seize as is clear in the next [court] Supervise

Sum of this court 2s
In expenses of the steward 12d

Worfeld — Small court held there on Tuesday the last day of the month of May in the 13th year of the reign of King Henry IV after the conquest [31 May 1412]

	Roger Cattestre	John Barndeleie	John Walker	}
the 12	Stephen Bradeneie	Roger Broke	Thomas Merwelle	} sworn
	Roger Richardes	William Newe	John Nelde	}
	Roger Waltone	John Rowlowe	Mathew Bullok	}

Margin: Heriot 27s Escheat 5s 8d Supervise

The which jurors say on their oath that William Barker who held of the lady by the custom of the manor 3 tenements in Haalen within the manor of Worfeld namely 1 messuage and 1 nook of land, one toft and half a virgate of land and half of one toft with 1 nook of land with appurtenances on the day he died from whose death the lady will have by the custom of the manor in the name of heriot 3 steers price 26s. And for escheat 1 draught animal (affram) price 4s and 2 colts price 20d. And concerning the land and tenement aforesaid with who or with whom they should remain they seek a day to render the full verdict until the next [court]

Margin: remaining not assessed Supervise

And they say that William Huster, Symon Dovy, John Blake & William Baker of Bruggenorth fished in water in the severalty of the lady within the manor of Worfeld so each of them is in mercy

Margin: Supervise

The aforesaid jurors on their oath say because that Robert Barker sold to William Barker his brother half of one toft called Veldeshous in Haalen two years last past and they say that the lord then ought thence to have a fine etc. Thence no more until it is supervised by the council of the lady because it is still not in the hands of the lady

amerced 6d	{John Holigreve executor of the will of Emily Hoore put himself in mercy for a licence to agree with Roger Swancote plaintiff in a plea of debt
amerced 6d	{The same John executor put himself in mercy for a licence to agree with Thomas Hugge in a plea of debt
amerced 6d	{The same John is in mercy because he is not prosecuting against the said Emily in a plea of debt
adjourned	{Still a day is given between Thomas Heyne plaintiff & John Fetherstone defendant in {a plea of trespass {And between John Hethe plaintiff & William Port chaplain & Margaret Tresel {defendants in a plea of trespass {And between Thomas Hugge plaintiff & the aforesaid William & Margaret {defendants in a plea of trespass {And between John Ewyk plaintiff & Roger Batemon & Isabell his wife in a plea of {land

Assessors: Stephen Bradeneie, William Webbe

Sum of this court 33s 2d

In expenses of the steward 12d

Worfeld	Small court held there on Tuesday the 21st day of the month of June in the 13th year of the reign of King Henry IV after the conquest [21 June 1412]
Essoins	John Hethe & John Barndeleie themselves from common [suit] by Richard Bulveis

	Roger Cattestre	Roger Broke	William Newe }	
the 12	Stephen Bradeneie	John Walker	John Rowlowe }	sworn
	Roger Richardes	Thomas Merwelle	Mathew Bullok }	
	Roger Waltone	Nicholas Stanlowe	John Nelde }	

Look on the back

[The dorse]

Still of the court

Tenement in the hand of the lady	And they say on their oath that concerning the lands and tenements of which William Barker died seized as is clear in the last court preceding that 1 messuage & 1 nook of land by their custom will remain with Margery the widow of William Barker for the term of her life and after her death to the rightful heirs of the aforesaid William Barker 1 toft & 1 nook of land will remain with Agnes the daughter of the same William Barker by virtue of a fine previously made. And they say that there remains in the hand of the lady 1 nook of land of the same toft. And that the same Agnes the daughter of the said William Barker is the closest heir to take the said nook of land from the hands of the lady. The aforesaid jurors also say that half of one toft and 1 nook of land remain with the aforesaid Margery the widow of the aforesaid William Barker for the term of the life of her life. And after her death to remain with the rightful heirs of the aforesaid William Barker.
Tenement remains in the hand of the lady	Robert Barker came here in court & surrendered into the hands of the lady half of one toft called Veldhous in Haalen to the use of Margery the widow of William Barker to hold from the lady for the term of the life of the same Margery. And after her death that the said half toft remains with the rightful heirs of the aforesaid William Barker. And thus it remains in the hand of the lord a fine will thence have been made

1411-1412 P314/W/1/1/240

Tenements remain in the hand of the lady	{Still remaining in the hand of the lady 1 toft & 1 curtilage in Bromleie as is clear in {the penultimate court preceding {Also there remains in the hand of the lady 1 cottage with curtilage and croft in {Haalen from a surrender of John Bokenhale as is clear in the penultimate court {preceding
Fine 5s	John Hulle & Agnes his wife the daughter of William Barker came here in court & took from the hands of the lady one nook of land in Haalen as of the right and heredity of the same Agnes as is clear above by the presentation of the 12 jurors to hold from the lady by services thence due according to the custom of the manor saving the right of whoever claims the said land in the future. And they give to the lady for a fine 5s. And in the form aforesaid they are seized. And they made fealty to the lady
Adjourned	{Still a day is given between Thomas Heyne plaintiff & John Fetherstone defendant in {a plea of trespass {And between John Hethe plaintiff & William Port clerk & Margaret Tresel {defendants in a plea of trespass {And between Thomas Hugge plaintiff & the said William & Margaret defendants in {a plea of trespass {And between John Ewyk plaintiff & Roger Batemon & Isabell his wife defendants in {a plea of land
Increase on the sale of heriots & escheats 3s 8d	(The reeve here is charged concerning 4d increase of the sale of 3 sheep falling to the {lady in the name of the heriot of William Holigreve & Emma his wife deceased {assessed by the 12 jurors at 4s 6d because they were sold for a higher price by they {say 4d (Also he is charged concerning 3s 4d concerning the increase of the sale of the heriot {and escheat of William Barker assessed at 31s 8d by an inquiry of 12 as is clear {above because they were sold for a higher price by the said 3s 4d

Sum of this court 8s 8d
Expenses of the steward 12d

Sum of the past 12 courts not assessed until
the coming of John Binley steward of the court £15 17s 8d
Also increase in rent 2d
Thence in expenses of the steward of the court 38s 6d

1412-1413 P314/W/1/1/241

Worfeld	Small court held there on Tuesday the fourth day of the month of October at the beginning of the 14th year of the reign of King Henry IV after the conquest [4 October 1412]
Essoins	Thomas Tresele, Thomas Richardes, John Janne, Stephen Webbe & William Huster themselves from common [suit] by John Rowlowe

The 12				
	Roger Cattestre	John Barndeleie	Thomas Merwelle	}
	Stephen Bradeneie	William Newe	John Billyngesleie	} sworn
	Roger Richardes	John Rowlowe	Mathew Bullok	}
	Roger Waltone	Roger Broke	John Bromleie	}

Fine 12d	Thomas Forster made a fine with the lady for suit of court to be commuted from the date of this court until the feast of St Michael the Archangel next in the future. And he gives for a fine 12d
Fine 12d	John Robyns gives to the lady 12d for suit of court to be commuted from the date of this court until the feast of St Michael the Archangel next in the future
Fine 12d	Roger Batemon gives to the lady 12d for suit of court to be commuted from the date of this court until the feast of St Michael the Archangel next in the future. Pledge for the fine Robert Hawkys
Fine 12d	William Ewyke made a fine with the lady for suit of court to be commuted from the date of this court until the feast of St Michael the Archangel next in the future.And for the fine he gives 12d. Pledge for the fine John Rowlowe
Fine 6s 8d	Andrew Fekkenham & Eleanor his wife confessed & examined according to the custom of the manor surrendered into the hands of the lady one messuage & one virgate of land with appurtenances called Ewyk which they hold for the term of the life of the same Eleanor by the custom of the manor within the manor of Worfeld to the use of John Rowlowe & Margery his wife to hold to the said John & Margery from the feast of St Michael the Archangel last past until the end of six years henceforth next following from the lady by services thence due according to the custom of the manor. So that after the term of the said six years the messuage and virgate of land aforesaid with its appurtenances will fully revert to the aforesaid Eleanor if then she should have lived without making a fine to hold from the lady by services thence due according to the custom of the manor. And on this William Ewyk son and heir of the same Eleanor to whom the reversion of the said tenement pertains after the death of the aforesaid Eleanor from a licence of the lady for himself and his heirs granted to the aforesaid John Rowlowe & Margery his wife peacefully to hold the tenement aforesaid during the whole term of the six years aforesaid without disturbance of the same William or his heirs etc. The which John Rowlowe & Margery came here in court & took from the lady the aforesaid tenement to hold to themselves during the aforesaid term of six years from the lady by services thence due according to the custom of the manor so that after the end of the same term the tenement aforesaid with its appurtenances to Eleanor should fully revert as it is said above, if she is at that time she should be living without making a fine to hold from the lady by services thence due according to the custom of the manor. And thus the aforesaid John & Margery have seisin. And they give for a fine 6s 8d to be paid within the account

Fine 3s 4d

Andrew Fekkenham & Eleanor his wife confessed & examined according to the custom of the manor surrendered into the hands of the lady one piece of pasture called Wolmoor within the manor of Worfeld to the use of John JonessoneRowlowe to hold to the same John for the term of the life of the same Eleanor from the lady by services thence due according to the custom of the manor etc. The which John came here in court & took from the lady the aforesaid piece of pasture to hold to himself for the term of the life of the aforesaid Eleanor from the lady by services thence due according to the custom of the manor. And he gives to the lady for a fine 3s 4d. And thus he is seized

Amerced 6d

The 12 jurors present that Roger Batemon (3d) & John Nicols (3d) agreed at the time of this court not to come so each of them is in mercy

Adjourned to the next

{Still a day is given between Thomas Heyne plaintiff & John Fetereston defendant in
{a plea of trespass
(And between Thomas Hugge plaintiff & William Port clerk & Margaret Tresel
{defendants in a plea of trespass
{And between John Hethe plaintiff & the aforesaid William Port & Margaret Tresele
{defendants in a plea of trespass
{And between John Ewyk plaintiff & Roger Batemon & Isabell his wife defendants in
{a plea of land

The law

Thomas Heyne plaintiff against Roger Cattestre of the Wode in a plea of trespass pledge for the prosecution William Noore. And he says that the same Roger unjustly & against the peace took into his possession (percepit) the revenue & profits of one nook of land of the same Thomas called Mercerslond in Haalen this year last past and more years before to the damage of the same Thomas 38s & thence he proffers suit. And the aforesaid Roger present in court denies this year. And thence he is at law in the next [court] pledge for the law Roger Richardes

Tenements remaining in the hand of the lady

{Still remaining in the hand of the lady one cottage with curtilage adjacent in Haalen
{formerly John Huly's
{Also remaining in the hand of the lady one toft with 1 curtilage in Bromleie
{Still remaining in the hand of the lady half of one toft in Haalen from the surrender
{by Roger Barker as is clear in the last court in the preceding year

Election of the reeve

John Rowlowe the reeve withdrew here from his office of reeve which office is entered by Roger Smyth by the election of the aforesaid 12 jurors. And he is sworn

Affeerors: Stephen Bradeneie, Roger Richardes

Sum of this court 14s 6d
Expenses of the steward 12d

Worfeld

Great court held there on Tuesday the 25th day of the month of October in the 14th year of the reign of King Henry IV after the conquest [25 October 1412]

Essoins

John Henene & William Noore themselves from appearance by Roger Smyth the reeve

the 12

Robert Ewdenas	Stephen Bradeneie	John Rowlowe	}
Roger Cattestre	Roger Waltone	John Walker	} sworn
Richard Bulveis	John Tumpkys	Roger Broke	}
John Hethe	Roger Richardes	Thomas Merwalle	}

amerced 4d	John Barndeleie is in mercy because he did not come here to affirm his oath for the inquiry aforesaid
Kyngeslowe & Stanlowe amerced 4d	townships there present nothing but that the township of Stanlowe (4d) did not appear in due time so the said township is in mercy
Chesturtone amerced 18d	township there presents that a certain chaplain from Schoffenhale whose name is not known forestalled John the son of Alice Rugge so the said chaplain (12d) is in mercy. And they say that a certain unknown miller forestalled the said John the son of Alice so the said miller (6d) is in mercy. Further they say that John Hethe has to respond to the lady for the aforesaid amercements because he became the pledge
Rowlowe, Asturhull, Ewyk, Soonde amerced 12d	townships there present that Richard Bradeney (6d) & John Glover (6d) present in court did not affirm their oath so each of them is in mercy
Hultone	township there presents nothing
Roughtone, Barndeleie, Hokkombe, Swancote amerced 2s 6d	townships there present that Lucy the maid of William Skynner hit (6d) David Walshe & drew blood (12d) from him so the said Lucy is in mercy both for the blow and for the bloodshed. And they say that the same Lucy broke (12d) the pound of William Knyght so the said Lucy is in mercy. And they say that William Skynner is bound to respond to the lady for the offence aforesaid because he is the pledge
Burcote, Burcote, Ryndelford, Bromleie	townships there present nothing
Alvescote, Wynnescote, Cattestre, Newtone	townships there present nothing
Ewdenas, Oldyntone amerced 6d	townships there present that William Oldyntone did not appear in time to swear with his neighbours nor take the oath so the said William is in mercy
Stapelford	township there presents nothing
Akeltone strays remaining amerced 3s 8d	township there presents 1 draught animal (affram) came as a stray in the week next before the feast of the Raising of the Holy Cross last past price of the draught animal 5s 6d and it remains in the custody of the bailiff. And they say that John Astwalle forestalled (6d) Symon Broke & from the said Symon drew blood (20d) so the said John is in mercy. And they say that Thomas Manlove forestalled (6d) Roger Dalileie so the said Thomas is in mercy. And they say that Joan the wife of the said Roger justly raised the hue and cry (12d) on the said Thomas so the said Thomas is in mercy
Haalen amerced 2s 8d	township there presents that William Noore forestalled (8d) Thomas Jankys junior and from him drew blood (12d) so the said William is in mercy. Also they say that the King's highway at Halfmedewe Stile is damaged from the want of cleaning the common ditch by John Huwessone to the nuisance of the neighbours so the said John (12d) is in mercy

Wyke amerced 2s 8d	township there presents that John Stevenes forestalled (6d) John Cattestre and from him drew blood (12d). And that the same John Cattestre re-forestalled (6d) the aforesaid John Stevenes and drew blood from him (12d) so each of them is in mercy. Also they present that John Cattestre forestalled (6d) John the son of Thomas Tresele and from him drew blood (12d) so the said John Cattestre is in mercy. Furthermore they say that certain unknown strangers on Tuesday next before the feast of the Nativity of St John the Baptist last past with force & arms & against the peace of the lord King entered the township of Wyke & from thence without a licence from the lady or her ministers took Henry Deikyn & John Deiken & they then took them outside the domain of Worfeld etc. And they say further that there remains one lined cape with a hood in the custody of Richard Bulveis forfeit to the lady price 3s 6d
Worfeld	township there presents nothing
The tasters of ale amerced 20s 6d	present that Robert Ewdenas (6d) brewed 1, John Walker of Ryndelford (16d) 2, John Billyngesle (8d) 1, in aid of the church 1 (pardoned), Richard Bulveis (2s) 3, Thomas Soonde 2 (16d), John Smyth of Soonde (16d) 2, Richard Smyth (8d) 1, William Noore (8d) 1, John Yate (3s 4d) 5, Hamo Humele (8d) 1, John Smyth (8d) 1, Robert Taillour (16d) 2, John the son of Nicholas (8d) 1, John Jonessone (16d) 2, Richard Bradene (8d) 1, John Kinvarton (8d) 1, William Prestes (8d) 1, William Newe (8d) 1, Thomas Hugges (8d) 1 & William Barwe (8d) 1. And all sold against the assize by illegal measures so each of them is in mercy
Plea Amerced 12d	John Hethe plaintiff against the township of Chesturtone in a plea of unjust presentation. And he says that the township aforesaid made an unjust presentation on him in this that they presented him to be the surety of a certain miller who forestalled John the son of Alice Rugge within the township aforesaid and thence he proffered his suit. The which township confirmed its presentation and thence the parties put [themselves] on the great inquiry which thence charged say that the township aforesaid faithfully presented so the said John (12d) is in mercy
Strays 8s	The bailiff is charged concerning 1 ox coming as a stray around the feast of St Luke the Evangelist in the 13th year of the reign of King Henry IV as is clear in the last great court of the preceding year presented by the township of Akeltone. The which ox is now appraised at 8s of which ox the reeve is charged to respond to the greater profit of the lord
The 12	jurors present that the townships aforesaid & the tasters of ale have well and faithfully presented
Fine for custody 4d	William Wodehouse of Albrightone gives to the lady 4d for the safety and custody of 1 cow
Constables	John Rowlowe & Thomas Richardes are elected constables. And they are sworn
Tasters of ale	Thomas Humelie & William Huster are elected tasters of ale. And they are sworn

Affeerors: Robert Ewdenas, John Tumpkys

Sum of this court 50s 4d

Expenses of the steward contained in the next court following

1412-1413 P314/W/1/1/241

Worfeld	Small court held there on Tuesday the 15th day of the month of November in the 14th year of the reign of King Henry IV after the conquest [15 November 1412]
Essoins	Roger Cattestre defendant himself from the law against Thomas Heyne in a plea of trespass by Roger Smyth
The 12	Roger Cattestre, Roger Richardes, John Walker, John Hethe, William Wermod, John Barndeleie, Stephen Bradeneie, John Janne, Roger Broke, Roger Waltone, John Rowlowe, Thomas Merwall } sworn
amerced 6d distrain	Thomas Heyne plaintiff against John Fetherestone in a plea of trespass the which John attached and charged did not come so he and his amercer (6d) are in mercy [ie the pledge]. And it is ordered to better distrain John before the next [court]
amerced 6d distrain	The bailiff is in mercy because he did not have here William Port clerk to respond to John Hethe in a plea of trespass. And it is ordered to better distrain the said William before the next [court]
amerced 6d	John Hethe is in mercy for his unjust plea against Margaret Tresel in a plea of trespass
amerced 6d distrain	Still the bailiff is in mercy because he did not distrain William Port clerk to respond to Thomas Hugge in a plea of trespass & on behalf of the lady it is ordered to the bailiff that he distrains the said William that he may be at the next [court] to respond to the aforesaid Thomas in the plea aforesaid
amerced 6d	Thomas Hugge plaintiff against Margaret Tresele in a plea of trespass. And he says that the same Margaret fraudulently & deceptively delivered (deliberavit) [freed, perhaps] livestock (averia) held by the same Thomas for certain causes to the damage of the same Thomas 2s. And the said Margaret present thence put herself on the judgment of the aforesaid 12 jurors & Thomas similarly. Who thence charged they say on their oath that the same Margaret thence is to blame so the said Margaret is in mercy
amerced 6d recovery	Thomas Hugge plaintiff against Hugh Baker in a plea of debt who seeks from the said Hugh 5s 4d which he owes to him & unjustly detains etc. the which Hugh recognises the said debt. And the said Hugh is in mercy
Stray appropriated	John Ordsleie appropriated here 1 horse from a stray as is related to the steward by the bailiff
the next distrain	Hugh Baker & Agnes his wife plaintiffs against John Bradeneie in a plea of accounts who is not attached so let it be done
Fine 12d the next	Robert Barker gives to the lady 12d for a fine for the judgment of the aforesaid inquiry of the 12 to be held namely to enquire whether the same Robert has the better right in half of one nook of land of Feldhouslond in Haalen in his claim or Margery Barker in her tenure who sworn and thence charged seek a day for the truth thence to render until the next [court] & by the wish of both parties they have a day

amerced 4s | The bailiff is charged here concerning 4s to be raised from William Huster, Symon Dovy, John Blake & William Barker of Bruggenorth for trespass made in the domain of Worfeld as was presented by the inquiry of the 12 in the court held on the last day of the month of May last past then not affeered

Tenement remains in hand | Margery Cowper surrendered into the hands of the lady one cottage with curtilage in Worfeld to the use of John Smyth & Richard his brother. And thus it remains in the hand of the lady until a fine will have been made

Fine 12d | Nicholas Stanlowe made a fine for suit of court to be commuted from the date of this court until the feast of St Michael the Archangel next in the future. And he gives for a fine 12d

Fine 2s | Robert Taillour & Alice his wife give to the lady for a fine 2s to have a licence to sell bread & ale within the township of Haalen from the feast of St Michael last past to the feast aforesaid hereafter next following providing always that they should use legal measures and should maintain the assize

Fine 5s | Thomas Heyne surrendered into the hands of the lady one nook of land with appurtenances in Haalen called the mercerslond to the use of Roger Cattestre. The which Roger came here in court and took from the lady the aforesaid nook of land with its appurtenances to hold to himself and his heirs from the lady by services thence due according to the custom of the manor. And he gives to the lady for a fine 5s to be paid within the account by the pledge of Thomas Heyne. And the same Roger Cattestre thence has seisin. And furthermore he releases & quitclaims for himself, his heirs & his executors to the aforesaid Thomas Heyne his heirs and executors for twenty shillings to the said Roger to paid into the hands six pounds in which the same Thomas is bound to the aforesaid Roger by acknowledgment as is clear in the court held at Worfeld on Wednesday in the second week of Easter in the 8th year of the reign of King Richard II

Relief … Fine 20s | Thomas Colier & Hawisia his wife blood relative & heir of Agnes the daughter of Roger Upinthetone namely from the daughter of William, son of Robert, brother of Roger, father of the aforesaid Agnes came here in court and paid relief for one toft and one virgate of land in Hultone of which the same Agnes, ancestor of the aforesaid Hawisia, whose heir she is as above was seized as is said. To hold from the lady by services and customs thence due according to the custom of the manor. And they give for relief 20s to be paid within the accounts. And thence they have seisin

Relief 20s | Thomas Hugges of Hultone blood relative and heir of John Hugynes namely the son of William son of the aforesaid John came here in court and paid relief for one messuage, one toft and one virgate of land with appurtenances in Chesturtone of which the aforesaid John died seized as it is said. To hold from the lady to himself and his [heirs] by services and customs thence due according to the custom of the manor. And he gives to the lady for relief 20s to be paid within the account. And thence he has seisin

Judgment concerning custom | The 12 jurors aforesaid namely Roger Cattestre, John Hethe, Stephen Bradeneie, Roger Waltone, Roger Richardes, William Wermode, John Janne, John Rowlowe, John Walker, John Barndeleie, Roger Broke & Thomas Merwelle sworn and charged by the steward on behalf of the lady to enquire if someone or anyone of the domain of Worfeld is able or are able to alienate the lands or tenements in lesser tenure descending to him or them after the death of their ancestors before he will have or they will have seisin or possession of the lands and tenements by the steward or in his place the tenants in the lord's court. The which jury say on their oath no-one is able or are able according to the custom of the manor to make alienation or demise of none of the lands or tenements aforesaid without this that they are freed and seized to him or theirs by the steward or in his place the tenants in full court from the same after the death of their ancestors was freed or were freed

Fine 10s

It is granted to Robert Taillour & Alice his wife one cottage with curtilage adjacent in Haalen which were formerly John Huly's to hold to the same Robert & Alice for the term of the life of the lady, from the lady by services & customs thence due according to the custom of the manor. And they give to the lady for a fine 10s to be paid within the account. And they are seized

Fine 12d

Margery the relict of William Barker came here in court and took from the hands of the lady half of one toft with its appurtenances in Haalen called the Veldhous to hold to the same Margery for the term of her life from the lady by services thence due according to the custom of the manor. And she gives for a fine 12d. And is seized

Profit of Sowdeleie for 2 years 10s

The bailiff is here charged concerning 10s to be raised for the enclosure at the time of pasture and of the wood of Sowdeleie for this present year and the last year preceding and no more because in the last year preceding there was no mast

amerced 6d

The bailiff is charged concerning 6d to be raised from John Rolowe because the same John did not have John Fetherestone to respond to Thomas Heyne in a plea of trespass as is clear in the small court held [blank] last past at that time not affeered

damages of the miller judged by the 12 jurors 53s 4d

The 12 jurors present and say on their oath that the lady's mills within the domain of Worfeld are deteriorated in default of William Skymor formerly its miller and William Newe, John Tumpkys, William Webbe, Hamond Humeleie, John Billyngesleie, Robert Hawkys, William Bruggende & Elie Mustardmon pledges of the same miller to the damage of the lady 53s 4d concerning which the aforesaid pledges are charged

goods forfeit 20d

John Smyth of Wyke is charged by the lady concerning 1 cup forfeit to the lady from the goods of John Breghnok a felon etc.

Fine 3s 4d

Thomas Hugges made a fine with the lady concerning 3s 4d because he liberated 4 oxen without a licence from the steward seized into the hands of the lady as of strays. And of the cattle aforesaid he should have discharged to the lady because the aforesaid oxen were of her own person which were to be delivered still not forfeit to the lady

Supervise

Subsequently at the amercement of Richard Hethe it is found by the oath of the 12 jurors that the same Richard can be distrained by his goods come upon within the domain of Worfeld if the ministers of the lady faithfully made an outlaw of them. And thus to respond to Thomas Tresele 20s the reeve in the 12th year of King Henry IV until etc. For which all other amercements of which the same Thomas seeks to be allowed it is found here in full court before the steward that well before this time they were able to be raised except 12d from Forsteres Weere. And by whom for the amercement of Hugh Pors namely of 20s from the charge of John Rowlowe it is found by the oath of the 12 jurors aforesaid that it is not possible to raise

1412-1413 P314/W/1/1/241

Remaining not affeered	Still the 12 jurors present & say on their oath that John Bruyn, Griffunus his servant, William Stapeleie & William Bowlewas of Brugge fished in water in the severalty of the lady within the domain of Worfeld
Affeerers of this court & the great court preceding	Robert Ewdenas, Stephen Bradeneie Sum of this court £6 15s 10d Expenses of John Boerleie & Richard Peper being there with 12 horses for 2 days and 3 nights for the holding of 2 courts 25s 6d ~~65s 10d~~
Worfeld	Small court held there on Monday next after the feast of St Valentine in the 14th year of the reign of King Henry IV after the conquest [20 February 1413]
Essoins	John Rowlowe himself from common suit by Richard Bulveis, Thomas Rowlowe himself from the same by Henry Barker, William Kyngessone himself from the same by William atte Yate and Thomas Richardes himself from the same by Roger Richardes
the 12	Roger Cattestre, John Walker, John Barndeleie, Roger Richardes, John Rowlowe, John Janne, Roger Waltone, William Wermod, Roger Broke, Stephen Bradeneie, John Hethe, Thomas Merwall } sworn
amerced 6d	Thomas Heyne is in mercy because he is not prosecuting against John Fetherstone in a plea of trespass
supervise	Where at the proceedings between Thomas Hugge plaintiff & William Port clerk defendant in a plea of trespass it is found by the oath of the bailiff that the said chaplain has nothing whereof to distrain. On which adjourned until etc.
distrain	Roger Haliday plaintiff against Thomas Heyne in a plea of trespass pledge for the prosecution Roger Cattestre who now attached by 52 sheep and 6 steers did not come so to better distrain to the next
distrain	The same Roger Haliday plaintiff against the said Thomas Heyne in a plea of debt, pledge for the prosecution Roger Cattestre who summoned did not come so distrain
distrain	Roger Cattestre plaintiff against Thomas Heyne in a plea of trespass who now is attached by sheep and steers above said did not come so to better distrain to the next
distrain	The same Roger Cattestre plaintiff against the said Thomas Heyne in a plea of debt who summoned did not come so distrain
adjourned	John Walker plaintiff against John Rowlowe in a plea of trespass who have a day to agree until the next by the prayer of the parties
amerced 6d	Thomas Jankys junior is in mercy for his unjust plea against William Carter in a plea of debt
amerced 6d	Thomas Heyne is in mercy because he is not prosecuting against Roger Cattestre in a plea of trespass whereof the law

amerced 6d	John Cattestre plaintiff & John Smyth defendant in a plea of debt for a licence to agree. And the said John Smyth put himself in mercy
fine 2s	Robert Smyth of Wyke surrendered into the hands of the lady one toft in Hyltone to the use of Robert Bruggende. The which Robert came here in court and took from the lady the aforesaid toft to hold to himself and his [heirs] from the lady by services thence due and accustomed according to the custom of the manor. And he gives to the lady for a fine 2s, made fealty to the lady and is seized
amerced 6d	Hugh Baker is in mercy for his unjust plea against John Bradeneie in a plea of accounts
strays remaining	Still remaining in the custody of the reeve 1 draught animal (affram) coming as a stray in the week before the feast of the Raising of the Holy Cross last past
tenement still remains in the hand of the lady	Still remaining in the hand of the lady one cottage with appurtenances in Worfeld from the surrender of Margery Cowper to the use of John Smyth & Richard his brother etc.
the 12 jurors amerced 4d	present that William Heneme (2d) & John Nicoles (2d) who are bound to make suit at this court did not come so each of them is in mercy
adjourned	Still the 12 jurors have a day until the next to present whether Robert Barker has the better right in half of one nook of land of Feldhouslond in Haalen in his claim or Margery Barker in her tenure for the sake of obtaining evidence from the old court rolls of this domain
supervise	John the son of Nicholas Rowlowe & William atte Yate of Roughtone came here in court & stood surety for Thomas Heyne and received from the goods of the same Thomas under their surety 52 sheep and 6 steers price £4 to respond to Roger Haliday and Roger Cattestre in pleas of debt and trespass in the next by the agreement of both of them
Affeerors	Roger Cattestre, John Walker

Sum of this court 4s 10d

Expenses of Richard Peper, the Receiver Richard, Richard Bulveis clerk & other ministers of the lady being there for 1 day and 1 night 3s 5d whereof of the expenses of Richard Bulveis the reeve and the beadle being there another day before the feast of the Nativity of the Lord to hold a certain court which is not written because all the actions which were done then are written in this court 12d by the view and agreement of Richard Peper

Worfeld	Small court held there on Tuesday next after the feast of the Annunciation of the Blessed Virgin Mary in the regnal year of [blank]
Essoins	John the son of Nicholas Rowlowe , John Janne, John Bromleie, Stephen Webbe & William Heneme themselves from common suit by Roger Smyth the reeve

the 12 jurors	Roger Cattestre	Stephen Bradeneie	John Barndeleie
	Roger Richardes	William Wermod	Thomas Merwalle
	John Walker	John Hethe	William Gerbode
	Roger Waltone	William Newe	John Rowlowe

Fine 7d	John Nicoles made a fine for suit of court to be commuted from the date of this court until the Feast of St Michael the Archangel next in the future. And he gives for a fine 7d
Fine 2d	John Billingesleie & Henry Barker give to the lady 2d for having permission to exchange two parcels of land lying in Hamondesmedewemoor to make a certain gate. And thus it is granted under condition if it pleases the lady and her council
amerced 12d	Thomas Heyne put himself in mercy for a licence to agree with Roger Haliday plaintiff in pleas of debt (6d) & trespass (6d)
amerced 12d	Roger Cattestre plaintiff against Thomas Heyne in pleas of debt (6d) & trespass (6d) who are for a licence to agree. And the said Thomas put himself in mercy
distraint	Thomas Jankys senior not prosecuting plaintiff against Robert Taillour in a plea of debt who summoned did not come so distrain to the next
distraint	Still on behalf of the lady it is ordered to the bailiff to distrain William Port chaplain that he is at the next to respond to Thomas Hugge in a plea of trespass
adjourned	Still a day is given between John Walker plaintiff & John the son of Nicholas Rowlowe defendant in a plea of trespass until the next
The 12 amerced nothing for the reason shown	jurors present nothing but that William Newtone chaplain who is bound to make suit at this court did not come but is not amerced because afterwards he came in their presentment
adjourned	Still the 12 jurors have a day until the next to present whether Robert Barker has a better right in half of one nook of land of Feldhouslond in Haalen or Margery Barker in her tenure for the reason to obtain evidence from the old court rolls
strays remaining	Still remaining in the hands of the bailiff 1 draught animal coming as a stray in the week next before the feast of the Raising of the Holy Cross last past
tenement remaining in the hand of the lady	Still remaining in the hands of the lady 1 cottage with appurtenances in Worfeld from the surrender of Margery Cowper to the use of John Smyth & Richard his brother Affeerors: Stephen Bradeneie, Roger Richardes Sum of this court 2s 9d In expenses of the steward 12d
Worfeld	Great court held there on Tuesday the 9th day of the month of the month of May in the first year of the reign of King Henry V after the conquest [9 May 1413]
Essoins	William Newton clerk & William Glover themselves from appearance by Roger Smyth the reeve
Amerced 6d	William Nore (6d) is in mercy because he did not come to warrant his essoin

The 12 jurors			
	Robert Ewdenas	Stephen Bradeneie	John Hethe
	Richard Bulveis	Roger Waltone	Thomas Merwell
	Roger Cattestre	John Walker	John Barndeleie
	Roger Richardes	John Jonnessone Rowlowe	Roger Broke

Kyngeslowe, Stanlowe	townships there present nothing
Chesturtone strays 12d	township there presents one horse coming as a stray for 1 full year and more past which was in the custody of William Preestes and is maintained (alongat*) by neglect by the same William, price of the horse 12d of which the reeve is charged by the steward to raise to the use of the lady
Hultone	township there presents nothing
Rowlowe, Asturhull, Ewyk, Soonde goods forfeit 2s 6d	townships there present that thieves of whose names they are ignorant took from out of the house of Richard Bradeneie 1 outer coat and 1 lynynge of a certain old cloak price 2s 6d. And thus they are sold by the steward in full court
Roughtone, Barndeleie, Hoccombe, Swancote	townships there present nothing
Burcote, Burcote, Ryndelford, Bromleie	townships there present nothing
Alvescote, Wynnescote, Cattestre, Newtone	townships there present nothing
Ewdenas, Oldyntone	townships there present nothing
Stapelford	township there presents nothing
Akeltone amerced 6d	township there presents that Thomas the son of Robert Olyntone forestalled John Gold of Akeltone. So the said Thomas (6d) is in mercy. And they say that John Hethe stands surety for the forestalling
Haalen amerced 2s	township there presents that John Hoccombe made homsoken (6d) on Robert Taillour and from the said Robert drew blood (12d). So the said John both for the homsoken and for the bloodshed is in mercy. And they say that Matilda Billyngsleie forestalled the aforesaid Robert Taillour. So the said Matilda (6d) is in mercy
Wyke	township there presents nothing
Worfeld Amerced 18d	township there presents that Joan Barndeleie forestalled (6d) Margery Jankys & drew blood (12d) from the said Margery. So the said Joan both for the forestalling & the bloodshed is in mercy
The tasters of ale	present that Thomas Soonde (2s) brewed 3, John Smyth of Soonde (16d) 2, John the son of Nicholas (8d) 1, John Hethe (8d) 1, Roger Dalleie (8d) 1, Robert Bruggende (8d) 1, John Yate (8d) 1, Henry Whitebrok (8d) 1, Robert Barker (8d) 1, Henry Barker (8d) 1, Robert Ewdenas (6d) 1, William Oldyntone junior (8d) 1, Thomas

amerced 13s 2d — Richardes (8d) 1, John the son of Mathew Bullok (8d) 1, John Bromleie (8d) 1, William Gerbod (8d) 1, Richard Bulveis (8d) 1. And all sold against the assize so each of them is in mercy

Stray 5s 6d — The bailiff is here charged by the steward concerning 1 draught animal (affram) from a stray presented by the township of Akeltone in the last great court preceding as is clear in the last and penultimate previous courts preceding price of the stray 5s 6d concerning which stray the bailiff is charged to respond to the greater profit of the lady

The 12 jurors say on their oath that the townships aforesaid and the ale tasters well and faithfully presented. Furthermore they say that the King's road at the cemetery from the east part of the church has deteriorated in default of Richard Parlour the which Richard ought to maintain and clean the said road for the reason of his tenure opposite the aforesaid road so the said Richard is in mercy. On which a day is given to the said Richard to properly repair before the next great court under a pain which will be incumbent

amerced 12d

Small court held on the place, day and year above said

The 12 — Inquiry held for the lady by the oath of Roger Cattestre, Roger Richardes, Stephen Bradeneie, Roger Waltone, John Walker, John the son of Nicholas Rowlowe, John Hethe, Thomas Merwelle, John Barndeleie, Roger Broke, John Janne & John Bromleie

amerced 6d — Thomas Jankys senior is in mercy because he is not prosecuting against Robert Taillour in a plea of debt

distrain — Henry Whitebrok & John Bromleie plaintiffs against Richard Underhull of Akeltone in a plea of debt pledge for the prosecution Henry Barker who summoned did not come so to distrain to the next [court] that he is etc.

adjourned to the next [court] — { A day is given between John Walker plaintiff & John the son of Nicholas Rowlow {defendant in a plea of trespass until the next [court]

(Also still the 12 jurors ex officio at the suit of Robert Barker as is clear in the last and {penultimate previous courts preceding have a day until the next to render their {verdict etc.

distrain — {Still on behalf of the lady it is ordered to the bailiff that he distrain William Port {clerk if he is able etc. that he should be at the next court to respond to Thomas Hugge in a {plea of trespass

The 12 jurors present that William Billyngesleie who held from the lady by custom of the manor 1 messuage & half a virgate of land in Haalen has died from whose death there falls to the lady one cow in the name of heriot with one suckling calf price 8s. And for escheat nothing because there was nothing. Also they say that the same William held from the lady half of one toft and one nook of land with appurtenances in Haalen aforesaid by custom of the manor on the day on which he died whence the lady will have in the name of heriot one black steer if it can be found but they say that the said steer has been taken back by whom they don't know so it is ordered to the bailiff to seize the said steer if it can be found into the hands of the lady. Furthermore they say that on the day William died he had many sheep from which the lady will have one in

heriot 9s 4d
escheat nothing for the reason shown

Supervise

Tenement in the hand of the lady

the name of heriot which is appraised at 16d if the aforesaid steer cannot be found concerning which sheep or its price the bailiff is charged to respond tin the form aforesaid. And for escheat nothing is due to the lady because there was nothing. Concerning which heriots the bailiff is ordered to respond to the greater profit of the lady. And the tenement remains in the hand of the lady. And they say that John Billyngesleie son of the said William is his closest heir. It is being settled immediately afterwards as is clear below

Fine 15s

John Billyngesleie the above-named son & heir of William Billyngseleie came here in court and took from the hands of the lady one messuage, half a virgate of land, half of one toft, and one nook of land with appurtenances in Haalen within the manor of Worfeld to have and to hold the aforesaid tenement with its appurtenances to the aforesaid John and his heirs from the lady by services thence due according to the custom of the manor. And he gives to the lady for a fine 15s half to be paid into the hands and the other half within the next account. He is seized. And he made fealty to the lady

Heriot 8s 6d

Also the aforesaid 12 jurors say on their oath that Roger Cattestre of Haalen who held of the lady by custom of the manor one messuage and one nook of land with appurtenances in Haalen has died whereof there falls to the lady from heriot 1 ox price 8s 6d concerning which the reeve is charged to respond to the greater profit of the lady. And for escheat nothing because there was nothing. And the tenement remains to Alice the widow of the said Roger for the term of her life according to the custom of the manor

Heriot & escheat nothing for the reason shown

And they say that Alice Bradeneie who held from the lady by the custom of the manor after the death of William Bradeneie formerly her husband one messuage and 3 nooks of land in Bradeneie has died from whose death the lady does not have a heriot nor escheat because there was nothing. And the tenement remains in the hand of the lady etc. And they say that Richard Bradeneie is the closest heir of the aforesaid William to take the aforesaid tenement. The which Richard Bradeneie the closest heir of the aforesaid William came here in court and took from the hands of the lady the aforesaid messuage and three nooks of land with appurtenances to hold to himself and his [heirs] from the lady by services thence due according to the custom of the manor. And he gives to the lady for a fine 14s half to be paid into the hands and the other half within the next account and no more because at another time he recently made a fine for the release of the tenement. He is seized and made fealty

Fine 14s

Stephen Bradeneie surrendered into the hands of the lady one messuage and one virgate of land with appurtenances in Bradeneie to the use of Roger his son, his heirs and assigns. The which Roger came here in court and took from the lady the aforesaid messuage and virgate of land with its appurtenances to hold to himself and his [heirs] from the lady by services thence due according to the custom of the manor. And he gives to the lady for a fine 20s half to be paid into the hands and the other half within the account. He is seized and made fealty

Fine 20s

Robert Ewdenas & Alice his wife confessed & examined according to the custom of the manor surrendered into the hands of the lady one toft, one nook of land and half a nook of land with appurtenances in Haalen to the use of Roger the son of Stephen Bradeneie & Matilda wife of the same Roger. The which Roger & Matilda came here in court and took from the lady the aforesaid tenement with its appurtenances to hold to themselves & their heirs from the lady by services thence due according to the

Fine 7s 6d — custom of the manor. And they give to the lady for a fine 7s 6d, are seized and they made fealty

Fine 20d — Thomas Hugge surrendered into the hands of the lady one parcel of meadow called Dikemedewe in Hultone to the use of John the son of Stephen Bradeneie & Christian his wife. The which John & Christian came here in court & took from the lady the aforesaid parcel of meadow to hold to themselves and their heirs from the lady by services thence due according to the custom of the manor. And they give to the lady for a fine 20d, are seized and they made fealty

Fine 16d — John Smyth & Richard his brother came here in court & took from the hands of the lady one cottage with appurtenances in Worfeld the which Margery Cowper surrendered into the hands of the lady to the use of the said John & Richard as is clear by the record of the rolls of the court of this year preceding. To hold to themselves & their [heirs] from the lady by services thence due according to the custom of the manor. And they give to the lady for a fine 16d. They made fealty. And they have seisin

Fine 20s — Richard Bradeneie above-named surrendered into the hands of the lady one messuage & one virgate of land with appurtenances in Bradeneie to re-hold the said tenement to himself and Joan his wife for the term of the life of both of them from the lady according to the custom of the manor. So that after their deaths the aforesaid tenement with its appurtenances should remain to Thomas the son of the same Richard and his heirs to hold from the lady according to the custom of the manor. And at the same time now the aforesaid tenement with its appurtenances are granted by the steward to the aforesaid Richard & Joan his wife to hold from the lady for the term of the life of each of them from the lady according to the custom of the manor. And after the deaths of them to the aforesaid Thomas the son of the said Richard and his heirs to hold from the lady according to the custom of the manor. And they give to the lady for a fine 20s half to be paid into the hands and the other half within the next account . And in the form aforesaid they are seized. And they made fealty to the lady

Fine 20s — Stephen Bradeneie surrendered into the hands of the lady one messuage & one virgate of land with appurtenances in Hultone to re-hold the said tenement for the term of his life to hold from the lady according to the custom of the manor. So that after his death the aforesaid tenement with its appurtenances should remain to John the son of the same Stephen & Christian the wife of the same John, the heirs and assigns of John himself to hold from the lady according to the custom of the manor. And in a similar way the aforesaid tenement with its appurtenances are granted by the steward to the aforesaid Stephen for the term of his life to hold from the lady according to the custom of the manor. And after his death to the aforesaid John & Christian his wife, the heirs and assigns of the same John to hold from the lady according to the custom of the manor. And they give to the lady for a fine 20s half to be paid in the hands and the other half within the next account. And in the form aforesaid they are seized. And they made fealty

Constable — For diverse reasons Roger Dalleie is appointed constable of the township of Akeltone. And he is sworn

Affeerors — Robert Ewdenas, Roger Cattestre

Sum of this great court with the small following £7 6s 6d
In expenses of the steward 10s 9d

1412-1413 P314/W/1/1/241

Worfeld	Small court held there on Monday next after the feast of St Mathew the Apostle in the first year of the reign of King Henry V after the conquest [25 September 1413]
Essoins	John Holigreve, Richard Bradeneie, William Newtone clerk & William Heneme themselves from common [suit] by Roger Smyth
The 12	Roger Cattestre, John Hethe, William Wermod, Stephen Bradeneie, John the son of Nicholas Rowlowe, Thomas Merwelle, Roger Richardes, Roger Broke, John Barndeleie, Roger Waltone, John Walker, William Newe
amerced 2d	The bailiff is in mercy because he did not distrain Richard Underhull to respond here to Henry Whitebrok & John Bromle in a plea of debt. Furthermore on the part of the lady to the same bailiff that he distrains the said Richard that he is at the next [court] to respond to the said plaintiffs in the plea aforesaid
Supervise	Still a day is given between John Walker plaintiff and John the son of Nicholas Rowlowe defendant in a plea of trespass until it is supervised by the council of the lady
Heriot 14d Tenement in the hand of the lady	The 12 jurors present that Thomas Colier who held from the lady by the custom of the manor one toft and one nook of land in Chesturtone on the day he died whereof there falls to the lady 1 sheep price 14d [in the name of heriot]. And for escheat nothing because there was nothing. And the tenement remains in the hands of the lady. And they say that Alice the daughter of Thomas Rugge is his closest heir to take the said tenement etc.
Heriot 8s 6d Tenement remains in the hand of the lady	And they say that John Ries who held from who held from the lady by the custom of the manor one toft and half a virgate of land in Worfeld has died whereof there falls to the lady 1 ox in the name of heriot price 8s which was sold at a higher price by 6d. And for escheat nothing because there was nothing within the manor. And the tenement remains in the hand of the lady. And they say that William the son of the same John is his closest heir.
Tenement in the hand of the lady	And they say that William Ewyk surrendered into the hands of the lady one toft and half a virgate of land with appurtenances in Haalen to the use to the use of John Cattestre and Rose his wife. And thus it remains in the hand of the lady until a fine thence will have been made
Tenement remains in the hand of the lady	And they say that John Huwessone & Isabell his wife confessed and examined according to the custom of the manor surrendered into the hands of the lady one toft with all the land adjacent called Horscroft in Roughtone with its appurtenances to the use of John Janne and Alice his wife. And thus it remains in the hand of the lady
Tenement remains in the hand of the lady	And they say that William Bruggende surrendered into the hands of the lady 1 acre of land with appurtenances in the field of Hultone at Dadymerche to the use of Robert his brother. And thus it remains etc

Look behind on the back

1412-1413 P314/W/1/1/241

[The Dorse]

Still concerning the court

Tenement remains in the hand of the lady	John atte Welle surrendered into the hands of the lady one messuage and half a virgate of land with appurtenances in Stapelford to the use of Thomas Undurhull. And thus it remains in the hand of the lady
Tenement remains in the hand of the lady	Thomas Jankys surrendered into the hands of the lady one toft & one nook of land with appurtenances in Kyngeslowe to the use of Nicholas Stanlowe etc. And thus it remains in the hand of the lady until etc.
Increase on sale 6d	The bailiff is charged here concerning 6d increase on the sale of 1 cow from the death of William Billingesle appraised at 8s as is clear within etc. because it was sold for a higher price by the said 6d
Election of reeve	William Gerbod & Thomas Rowlow of Burcote are elected by the 12 jurors as one of them is received to serve the lady this year next in the future in the office of reeve
Affeerors	Roger Cattestre, John Walker

Sum of this small court 10s 4d

In the expenses of Richard Bulveis the clerk of the court the reeve and the beadle 12d

Sum of 7 courts £18 ~~2s 10 … 4d 3s 1d~~ 5s 1d

And in the expenses of the steward ~~41s 8d~~ 42s 8d

1413-1414 P314/W/1/1/242

Worfeld	Great Court held there on Tuesday next after the feast of St Luke the Evangelist before William Boerleie steward there in the first year of the reign of King Henry V after the conquest [24 October 1413]
Essoins	William Noore himself from appearance by Richard Bulveis
The 12	Robert Ewdenas, Stephen Bradeneie, John Jonesone Rowlowe, Roger Richardes, Roger Broke, Roger Gerbod, Roger Cattestre, John Hethe, Thomas Merwelle, Roger Waltone, William Wermod, Roger Townessend } sworn
Kyngeslow, Stanlowe amerced 4d	townships there present that Matilda Stanlowe made an assault on John Hethe so the said Matilda (4d) is in mercy
Chesturtone amerced 20s 8d strays 10d	township there presents one swarm of bees coming as a stray in the custody of Alice Rugge . Price of the stray 4d and it was sold in full court by the steward at a higher price by 6d to William Newe. And they say that Margaret Tresele unjustly raised the hue and cry by mouth on whom they don't know so the same Margaret (8d) is in mercy. And they say that the doors of the houses of Margaret Tresele were sealed by the bailiff of the lady by virtue of a certain order by the steward directed to the same bailiff and that the same Margaret & John her son broke the seal and arrest thus made by the bailiff of the lady & diverse goods which were under the arrest aforesaid were carried away & taken from thence. So that the said Margaret & John are in mercy affeered by the affeeror at 20s
Hultone	township there presents nothing
Rowlowe, Bradeneie, Asturhull, Ewyk, Soonde	townships there present nothing
Roughtone, Barndeleie, Hoccombe, Swancote	townships there present nothing
Burcote, Burcote, Ryndelford, Bromleie Abandoned goods	townships there present nothing but that they have 1 small axe abandoned by whom they don't know price 3d and is in the custody of the reeve
Cattestre, Alvescote, Wynnescote, Newtone	townships there present nothing
Ewdenas, Oldyntone, amerced 6d	townships there present that John (6d) the son of Thomas Tresele forestalled Alice the wife of Robert Ewdenas so the said John is in mercy

Stapelford	township there presents nothing
Akeltone	township there presents nothing
Haalen amerced 3s 10d	township there presents that John (6d) the son of Thomas Tresele made a poundbreach on Robert Barker so the said John is in mercy. And that the same Robert Barker justly raised the hue and cry on the said John so the same John (8d) is in mercy. And they say that Thomas Gille forestalled (6d) Roger Barker and drew blood from him (12d) so the said Thomas both for the forestalling and for the bloodshed is in mercy. Also they say that Thomas Tresele (6d) made homsoken and forestalling on William Wermode so the said Thomas is in mercy. And that the same William Wermode raised the hue and cry by mouth justly on the said Thomas so the said Thomas is in mercy (8d)
Wyke	township there presents nothing
Worfeld amerced 20d	township there presents that John Stevenes forestalled Margery Jankys so the said John (6d) is in mercy. And they say that Margaret Tresele forestalled Margery Jankys so the said Margaret (4d) is in mercy. Also they say that the same John Stevenes forestalled Alice Goold so the said John (6d) is in mercy. And they say that Thomas Gille forestalled Roger Barker so the said Thomas (4d) is in mercy
The tasters of ale amerced 9s 8d	present that John Walker (6d) brewed 1, the lessees of the mill (6d) 1, John Billyngesleie (12d) 2, William Wermod (6d) 1, John Cattestre (6d) 1, William Womborne (6d) 1, Richard Bulveis (12d) 2, John Smyth of Sonde (18d) 3, Thomas Soonde (12d) 2, John Jonessone (6d) 1, John Yate (6d) 1, Richard Underhull (6d) 1, Robert Taillour 2d no more for fine, Hamund Humele (6d) 1, Stephen Humele (6d) 1, and all sold against the assize by illegal measures so each of them is in mercy
the 12	jurors say on their oath that the townships aforesaid and the ale tasters have well and faithfully presented
stray remaining	Richard Bulveis the bailiff of the liberty presents 1 boar coming as a stray around the feast of the Nativity of St John the Baptist last past. And it remains in the custody of the same Richard
Fine 2s	Robert Taillour made a fine here for having a licence to brew bread and ale to sell from the date of this court until the feast of St Michael the Archangel next in the future. And he gives for a fine 2s. Thus it is granted by the steward so that he should sell by legal measures and should hold to the assize
Pannage of Sowdeleie 6s	The reeve here is charged by the steward concerning 6s to raise from the issue and profit of the place and wood of Sowdeleie as for enclosure in the time of the present year namely for 6 weeks between the feast of St Michael last past and the feast of St Martin next in the future
Land granted for lesser rent than was formerly paid	To this court comes John Glover and took from the lady one parcel of land called Chilternegrene & lying next to Kyngeslowe & Stanlowe within the manor of Worfeld to hold from the lady the said parcel of land with its appurtenances to the said John and his [heirs] rendering thence annually to the lady two pence at the usual terms and other services according to the custom of the manor. And for a fine he gives nothing because of the increased rent. He made fealty. And thus he has seisin. And the said

parcel of land was formerly charged of 8d as of fixed rent

Adjourned — Still a day is given between John Walker plaintiff and John the son of Nicholas Rowlowe defendant in a plea of trespass until the coming of the council of the lady

next — Verdict of the 12 jurors ex officio at the suit of Robert Barker still adjourned until the next by order of the steward

Constables and tasters of ale — The constables and tasters of ale still stand elected and charged just as stood the preceding year etc. And William Gerbod is charged reeve as is clear in the next small court following

Affeerors: John Hethe, John Jonessone Sum of this court 45s 9d

Expenses of the steward nothing here because containein the third small the court next following

Worfeld — Small court held there on Thursday on the feast of St Clement the Pope in the first year of the reign of King Henry V after the conquest [23 November 1413]

The 12

John Janne	Roger Cattestre	Roger Broke	}
Thomas Hugges	Stephen Bradeneie	Roger Gerbode	} sworn
Roger Richardes	John Hethe	Thomas Toward	}
Roger Waltone	John Rowlowe	William Wermode	}

the 12 — jurors aforesaid presents that Thomas Rowlowe who held from the lady by the custom of the manor one messuage and one virgate of land with appurtenances in Hultone on the day he died whereof there falls to the lady in the name of heriot 1 steer price 7s. And for escheat the lady will have 4 young pigs [under 6 months of age] price 3s 4d, five piglets price 20d and 1 colt price 12d concerning which heriot and escheats the reeve is charged to respond to the greater profit of the lady. And they say that the tenement aforesaid remains with Benigna the widow of the aforesaid Thomas by their custom

heriot 7s, escheat 6s

heriot 7s 6d — And they say that John Bradeneie who held from the lady by the custom of the manor one messuage and one virgate of land with appurtenances in Bradeneie has died from which the lady will have in the name of heriot 1 cow price 6s. And for escheat nothing because as yet nothing was able to be found. And concerning the heriot the reeve is charged to respond to the greater profit of the lady. And the tenement aforesaid remains with Alice the widow of the said John deceased by their custom

heriot 12s, escheat 5s Supervise — And they say that Roger Bradeneie who held from the lady by the custom of the manor one messuage and one virgate of land in Bradeneie. And one messuage, one nook and half a nook of land in Haalen has died from whose death the lady will have 2 steers for heriot price 1 colour black 7s & the price of the other colour brown 5s. And for escheat the lady with have 4 young pigs [under 6 months of age] price 3s 4d & 3 piglets price 20d. And concerning 1 horse they seek a day to render the truth until the next [court]. Concerning which heriots & escheats the bailiff is charged to respond to the greater profit of the lady. And the tenement aforesaid remains with Matilda the widow of the said Roger deceased

And they say that Roger Wille who held from the lady by the custom of the manor one messuage, one toft and one virgate of land with appurtenances in Burcote has died from whose death the lady will have one ruby ox price 9s and one steer price 5s

heriot 14s, escheat 3s 8d Supervise	for heriot. And for escheat 1 draught animal price 3s & 1 piglet price 8d. And concerning bees they seek a day to present until the next [court]. Concerning which heriots & escheats the bailiff is charged to respond to the greater profit of the lady. And the tenement aforesaid remains with Agnes the widow of the same deceased
Supervise	{Still a day is given between John Walker plaintiff and John Rowlowe defendant in a {plea of trespass until it is supervised by the council of the lady
Adjourned	{And between Henry Whitebrook and John Bromleie plaintiffs and Richard Underhull {defendant in a plea of debt until the next [court]
Tenement remains in hand	There still remains in the hand of the lady 1 toft and 1 nook of land in Chestertone by the death of Thomas Colier as is clear in the last court of the preceding year. And who is the closest heir to take the said tenement from the hand of the lady is clear in the same last court of the said year preceding etc.
Tenement remains in hand	Also there still remains in the hand of the lady 1 toft and half a virgate of land in Worfeld by the death of John Ries as is clear in the last court of the preceding year. And who is the closest heir to take the said tenement from the hand of the lady is clear in the same last court of the said year preceding
Tenement remains in hand	Also there still remains in the hand of the lady 1 toft and half a virgate of land in Haalen from the surrender of William Ewyk to the use of John Cattestre & Rose his wife as is clear in the last court of the preceding year.
Tenement remains in hand	Also there still remains in the hand of the lady 1 toft with all the land adjacent called Horscroft in Roughtone from the surrender of John Huwessone & Isabell his wife as is clear in the said last court of the preceding year.
Tenement remains in hand	There still remains in the hand of the lady 1 acre of land in Hultone called Dadymersch from the surrender of William Bruggend to the use of Robert his brother as is clear in the last court of the preceding year etc.
Tenement remains in hand	Also there still remains in the hand of the lady 1 messuage with half a virgate of land adjacent in Stapelford from the surrender of John atte Welle to the use of Thomas Underhull as is clear in the said court of the preceding year
Tenement remains in hand	Also there remains in the hand of the lady 1 toft and one nook of land in Kyngeslowe from the surrender of Thomas Jankys to the use of Nicholas Stanlowe as is clear in the aforesaid last court of the preceding year etc.
Appointment of the reeve	Roger Smyth withdrew from his office of reeve to which office entered William Gerbod by the election of the named 12 jurors as is clear in the last court of the preceding year. And he is sworn
Fine 4s	Thomas Forster, Roger Batemon, John Robynes & John Nicoles made a fine for suit of court to be commuted from the date of this court until the feast of St Michael the Archangel next in the future. And each of them gives to the lady for a fine 12d just as granted by Richard Bulveis for the better use for the lady

Sum of this small court 58s 4d
In Expenses of the steward 12d

1413-1414 P314/W/1/1/242

Worfeld	Small court held there on Thursday on the 14th day of the month of December in the first year of the reign of King Henry V after the conquest [14 December 1413]
Essoins	Richard Bradeneie from common [suit] by Richard Bulveis
The 12	John Janne, Roger Cattestre, Roger Broke, Thomas Hugges, Stephen Bradeneie, Roger Gerbode, Roger Richardes, John Hethe, Thomas Toward, Roger Waltone, John Rowlowe, William Wermode } sworn
Adjourned	Still a day is given between John Walker plaintiff and John Rowlowe defendant in a plea of trespass until the coming of the council of the lady
Amerced 3d	Richard Underhull put himself in mercy for a licence to agree with Henry Whitebrok and John Bromleie plaintiffs in a plea of debt
the 12 Amerced 2d	jurors present that William Heneme who ought to have made suit at this court did not come so the said William is in mercy
Adjourned	And they say that Thomas Underhull ground his corn outside the manor in a mill outside against their custom but at present he is pardoned by the agreement of the lessees of the mills of the lady under condition if it will have pleased the council of the lady
Supervise	And they say that Margery Stevenes is dead and whether the same Margery was a tenant on the day on which she died or not & concerning other circumstances of the same Margery they seek a day to render the truth until the next [court]
Tenement remains in hand	And they say that Roger Bradeneie son of Stephen Bradeneie surrendered into the hand of the lady two parcels of meadow in Bradeneie of which one parcel is called Torre and the other parcel Mowynkhurste, one with 2 selions of land lying above the bridge of the Chirle in Bradeneie to the use of Stephen Bradeneie to hold for the term of the life of the same Stephen from the lady according to the custom of the manor
Escheat under condition 3s 3d	And they say that Roger Wille according to the knowledge of them had at the time of his death 1 horse not presented in the last court preceding which is escheat of the lady unless it can be proved that it was not from the goods of the same deceased on the day on which he died. Price of the horse 3s and that he had a portion of bees price 3d whereof the bailiff is charged
Tenement remains in the hand of the lady	Joan the daughter of John Smyth of Soonde surrendered into the hand of the lady 2 cottages with appurtenances in Soonde to the use of Edward Flode clerk and Agnes the daughter of the same Joan to hold for the term of the life of both of them from the lady according to the custom of the manor. And after the death of them that the said tenement is to be sold by the executors the last of them being dead and the profit thence will be put to the use of alms for the salvation of the souls of the aforesaid Edward, Joan and of the children of the aforesaid Joan. And it remains until a fine will thence be made with the lady
Increase of the sale of heriot and escheat 12d	The bailiff is here charged concerning 12d of increase of the sale of the heriot and escheat of Thomas Rowlowe appraised at 13s by the 12 jurors as is clear in the last court preceding because they were sold by the reeve for a higher price with the supervision of Richard Bulveis by the said 12d

Fine 12d	12d is given to the lady for a fine for an inquiry to be held by the 12 ex officio pledge for the fine John Walker to enquire if a lesser man lying on a sick bed at the point of death will be able to give and to sell his inheritance within the manor of Worfeld by the custom of the manor or not. On which the inquiry held by the oath of Roger Cattestre, Roger Richardes, John Walker, Roger Waltone, William Newe, Stephen Bradeneie, John Jonessone Rowlowe, John Rowlowe, Roger atte Broke, William Webbe, Roger Gerbode & Roger Smyth went out & came back and say on their oath that a man holding by the custom of the manor within the manor of Worfeld lying on a sick bed at the point of death is able to give and to sell his lands and tenements by the custom of the manor which he holds to himself and his [heirs] by the said custom
Tenements still remaining in the hands of the lady	Still all lands and tenements remaining in the hand of the lady in the last court of the preceding year so remain as is clear in the last court preceding namely 1 toft with 1 nook of land in Chesturtone, 1 toft with half a virgate of land in Worfeld, 1 toft with half a virgate of land in Haalen, 1 toft with all the land adjacent called Horscroft in Roughtone, 1 acre of land in Hultone, 1 messuage with half a virgate of land in Stapelford and 1 toft with 1 nook of land in Kyngeslowe. And in what form they fell into the hands of the lady and to whose use and who are the closest heirs to take the said tenements out of the hand of the lady is manifest in the last court of the preceding year and in the last court now preceding
Supervision of escheat	Still the 12 jurors present that Thomas Rowlowe had on the day of his death one pig and 3 piglets further to the escheats of the same Thomas presented in the last court preceding just as is now found by examination it is found between them and where they are they still don't know
Adjourned	Still the verdict of the 12 jurors ex officio at the suit of Robert Barker is adjourned until etc.
Supervise	The fishers in the waters of the lady whose names are contained in the rolls of the last court of the preceding year still remain etc.

Sum of this court 5s 8d whereof under condition 3s
In expenses of the steward and others 12d

Worfeld	Small court held there on Wednesday after the feast of St Hillary in the first year of the reign of King Henry V after the conquest [17 January 1414]
Essoins	John Walker plaintiff essoined himself against John Rowlowe in a plea of trespass

The 12	Roger Richardes	Roger Broke	Roger Gerbod	} sworn
	Roger Cattestre	John Hethe	Thomas Merwell	}
	Roger Waltone	William Wermode	Roger Towneshend	}
	Stephen Bradeneie	John Jonessone Rowlow	Roger Smyth	}

Fine 5s	Alice Rugge came here in court and took out of the hands of the lady one toft and one nook of land with appurtenances in Chesturtone as her right and inheritance after the death of Thomas Colier to hold the aforesaid tenement to the said Alice and her [heirs] from the lady by services thence due and accustomed according to the custom of the manor. And she gives to the lady for a fine 5s. She made fealty to the lady and thence has seisin

1413-1414 P314/W/1/1/242

To this court came William Ryes the son and heir of John Ryes and took from the hands of the lady one toft and half a virgate of land with appurtenances in Worfeld as his right and inheritance after the death of John Ryes above-said to hold the aforesaid tenement with appurtenances to the said William and his [heirs] from the lady by
Fine 10s services thence due and accustomed according to the custom of the manor. And he gives to the lady for a fine 10s, made fealty to the lady and has seisin

John Cattestre and Rose his wife came here in court and took out of the hands of the lady one toft with half a virgate of land with appurtenances in Haalen remaining in the hand of the lady from the surrender of William Ewyk to the use of the said John and Rose as is manifest in the last court of the year preceding and in the penultimate court now preceding To hold tenement with appurtenances to the aforesaid John and Rose
Fine 10s from the lady by services thence owed according to the custom of the manor And they give to the lady for fine 10s made fealty to the lady And are seised.

John Janne and Alice his wife came here in court and took out of the hands of the lady one toft with half a virgate of land adjacent called Horscroft in Roughtone which John Huwessone and Isabell his wife previously surrendered into the hands of the lady to the use of the said John Janne and Alice as clear in the last court of the year preceding and in the penultimate court now preceding to hold the aforesaid tenement with its
Fine 6s 8d appurtenances to the aforesaid John Janne & Alice and his heirs from the lady by services thence owed and accustomed according to the custom of the manor. And they give to the lady for a fine 6s 8d and no more because elsewhere they made a fine for the said tenement. They made fealty and they are seized

Robert the brother of William Bruggende took out of the hands of the lady one acre of land with appurtenances lying in the field of Hultone at Dadymerch which acre of land William Bruggende previously surrendered into the hands of the lady to the use of the said Robert as is clear in the last court of the preceding year to hold the aforesaid acre of land to the aforesaid Robert and his [heirs] from the lady by services
Fine 12d thence owed according to the custom of the manor. And he gives to the lady for a fine 12d, made fealty and he is seized

Thomas Underhull came here in court and took out of the hands of the lady one messuage and half a virgate of land with appurtenances in Stapelford which John atte Welle previously surrendered into the hands of the lady to the use of the same Thomas
Fine 10s as is clear in the last court of the preceding year to hold the aforesaid tenement with appurtenances from the lady by services thence owed according to the custom of the manor. And he gives to the lady for a fine 10s, made fealty and he is seized

Nicholas Stanlowe came here in court and took out of the hands of the lady one toft and one nook of land with appurtenances in Kyngeslowe which Thomas Jankys previously surrendered into the hands of the lady to the use of the same Nicholas as is clear in the last court of the preceding year to hold the aforesaid tenement with appurtenances to the aforesaid Nicholas and his [heirs] from the lady by services
Fine 5s thence owed & accustomed according to the custom of the manor. And he gives to the lady for a fine 5s, made fealty and is seized

Stephen Bradeneie came here in court and took out of the hands of the lady two parcels of meadow in Bradeneie of which one parcel is called Torre and the other parcel is called Mowynkhurst, one with two selions of land lying above the bridge of Chirle in Bradeneie which tenement Roger the son of the same Stephen previously

Fine 16d

surrendered into the hands of the lady to the use of the same Stephen as is clear in thelast court preceding to hold the aforesaid tenement from the lady to the aforesaid Stephen for the term of his life by services thence owed & accustomed according to the custom of the manor. And he gives to the lady for a fine 16d and has seisin

Fine 2s 8d

Edward Flode and Agnes the daughter of Joan the daughter of John Smyth of Soonde came here in court came here in court and took out of the hands of the lady two cottages with appurtenances in Soonde which cottages the aforesaid Joan the daughter of John Smyth previously surrendered into the hands of the lady to the use of the said Edward and Agnes as is clear in the last court preceding to have and to hold the aforesaid two cottages with appurtenances to the aforesaid Edward and Agnes for the term of the life of each of them from the lady by services thence owed and accustomed according to the custom of the manor. And after the death of them that the aforesaid 2 cottages are to be sold by the executors of the last of them dying and the profit thence should be put to the use of alms for the salvation of the souls of the aforesaid Edward & Joan and the children of the same Joan. And they give for a fine 2s 8d, made fealty to the lady and they are seized

Fine 8d

Roger the son of Stephen Bradeneie surrendered into the hands of the lady one acre of land lying in Hultone in the field called Stretfordefield to the use of John Bradeneie son of the said Stephen the which John took from the lady the aforesaid acre of land with appurtenances to hold to himself and his [heirs] from the lady by services thence owed according to the custom of the manor. And he gives to the lady for a fine 8d, made fealty and is seized

Fine 18s

The bailiff presents that Thomas Colier and Hawisia his wife confessed and examined according to the custom of the manor surrendered into the hands of the lady one toft and one virgate of land with appurtenances in Hultone which was formerly Roger Upynton's to the use of Margery formerly the wife of Thomas Hugge and Matilda the daughter of the same Margery the which Margery and Matilda came here in court and took from the lady the aforesaid toft and virgate of land with appurtenances to hold to themselves and their [heirs] from the lady by services thence owed and accustomed according to the custom of the manor. And they give to the lady for a fine 18s to be paid in the next account at the feast of St Michael now next in the future. They made fealty to the lady and they are seized

Heriot 4s
Escheat nothing

The 12 jurors present that Thomas Hugge who held from the lady by custom of the manor one messuage and one virgate of land with appurtenances in Hultone on the day he died whence there falls lady in the name of heriot 1 young brown steer price 4s concerning which the reeve is charged to respond to the greater profit of the lady. And for escheat nothing because they was nothing. And they say that the tenement aforesaid remains with Margery the relict of the said Thomas by the custom of the manor

Heriot 5s 6d
Escheat nothing as is clear

And they say that William Robynes who held from the lady by custom of the manor one messuage and half a virgate of land with appurtenances in Burcote has died by whose death there falls to the lady for heriot 1 black cow price 5s 6d. And for escheat nothing because they was nothing and concerning the heriot the reeve is charged to respond to the greater profit of the lady. And the tenement aforesaid remains with Margery the relict of the same deceased by the custom of the manor

Escheat 6d

And they say that the lady will have by their custom 2 hives of bees as for escheat of John Bradeneie price 6d concerning which escheat the bailiff is charged to respond to the greater profit of the lady.

+
Fine 10s

Alice Stevenes came here in court and took from the lady three nooks of land in Haalen which were recently called Steveneslond which were descending to her by the right of inheritance as the daughter and heir of Matilda Stevenes to hold the said tenement from the lady to the aforesaid Alice and her [heirs] by services thence owed according to the custom fo the manor. And she gives for a fine 10s and no more because recently a fine for the said tenement was made. And she is seized

The next. Supervise

A day is given to Robert Ewdenas concerning 1 horse seized into the hands of the ladyas for escheat from the death of Roger Bradeneie until the next to prove according to law and custom if the horse aforesaid at the time of the death of the same Roger was his or the aforesaid Robert's

The next

{John the son of Nicholas Rowlowe has a day to respond to John Walker in the next
{[court] in a plea of trespass because the same John Walker is now essoined as is clear
{above
{John Huwessone plaintiff against Margery formerly the wife of William Barker in a plea of trespass

Grant of the mills

At this court the lady granted Roger Cattestre, Roger Richardes, John Hethe, Stephen Bradeneie, William Gerbod, Roger Waltone, Thomas Rowlow of Burcote, John Bromleie, John Bullok, William Newe, Stephen Webbe, Robert Bruggende, Thomas Rowlowe of Hultone, John Bradeneie, John Rowlowe, John Rowlowe son of Nicholas, Robert Webbe, William Yate, John Walker, Roger Smyth, Thomas Soonde, Henry Barker and John Holigreve two water mills within the domain of Worfeld of which one is called Ryndelfordmylne and the other called Worfeldmylle to have and to hold the aforesaid mills with soken, ways, paths, weirs, fisheries, ponds, river banks, water courses and everything else pertaining to the aforesaid mills to the whole term of the life of the said lady. Rendering thence annually to the said lady and her assigns during the term aforesaid four pounds of sterling and two times of the year namely at the feast of the Annunciation of the Blessed Virgin Mary and St Michael by equal portions. And the aforesaid Roger Cattestre and his associates aforesaid will repair, sustain, and maintain well and competently at their own expense the aforesaid mills with the ponds, river banks, weirs and floodgates during the term aforesaid. And the aforesaid Roger Cattestre and his associates aforesaid for the maintenance and repair of the mills, ponds, river banks and floodgates aforesaid will have timber from the wood of the aforesaid lady there by the deliverance of the steward, attorney or bailiff of the said lady. So that if it should happen the said Roger Cattestre and his aforesaid associates bought, ordered or provided any wood in another place than in the wood of the lady for the repair and maintenance of the mills and other things aforesaid then the aforesaid Roger Cattestre and his aforesaid associates will have another tree in the wood of the lady in place of the same tree thus bought or provided by the deliverance as above. And in which case the same Roger & his aforesaid associates the said mills and floodgates in another place or places site or sites, than now being, wish to build or put that then clay, peat, rock and wood (trons) should be allowed to the aforesaid Roger Cattestre and his aforesaid associates for the repair of the mills and of the other things aforesaid to dig and fell in the waste and wood of the lady and carry away to make the repair aforesaid by the delivery as above, And they made fealty

1413-1414 P314/W/1/1/242

increase on sales 6d	The reeve is charged here for 6d of increase of sale of 1 cow for heriot of William Robyns appraised at 5s 6d as is manifest above because it sold for 6s by the reeve and Richard Bulveis
stray remains	There still remains in the custody of Richard Bulveis 1 boar a stray as is clear in the great court preceding until etc.
	Sum of this court £4 10s 10d Expenses of the steward being there at both this court held and the preceding great court for 2 days and 2 nights 13s 4d
Worfeld	Great Court held there on Tuesday next after the feast of St George in the second year of King Henry V after the conquest [24 April 1414]
Essoins	Nicholas Herdemon himself of appearance by Richard Bulveis
the 12	Roger Richardes, Roger Waltone, John Rowlowe, John Walker, John Rowlowe son of Nicholas, William Wermode, Stephen Bradeneie, Robert Ewdenas, Roger Broke, John Hethe, Roger Cattestre, Thomas Merwelle } sworn
Kyngeslowe, Stanlowe amerced 4d	townships there present nothing Chesturtone township there presents that Roger Batemon who is bound to make appearance at this court did not appear so the said Roger (4d) is in mercy
Hultone amerced 4d	township there presents that Hugh Baker who is bound to make appearance at this court did not appear so the said Hugh (4d) is in mercy
Rowlowe, Bradeney, Asturhull, Ewyk, Soonde	townships there present nothing
Roughtone, Barndeleie, Hoccombe, Swancote stray remains	townships there present 1 small pig coming as a stray at the feast of St Michael last past price 4d and is in the custody of the bailiff
Burcote, Burcote, Ryndelford & Bromleie	townships there present nothing
Cattestre, Alvescote, Wynnescote, Newtone amerced 3s 4d	townships there present that the town and community of Brugge blocked the water course of Worw at Yoremoor within the domain of Worfeld to the nuisance of the lady and her tenants there so the said community (3s 4d) is in mercy
Ewdenas, Oldyntone	townships there present nothing

Stapleford stray remains	township there presents one small pig coming as a stray at the feast of All Saints last past which is in the custody of the bailiff price 6d
Akeltone stray remains	township there presents one draught animal (affram) coming as a stray at the feast of the Purification of the Blessed Virgin Mary last past price 12d and it remains in the custody of John Wilot
Haalen amerced 4d	township there presents that Roger Gille who is bound to make appearance at this court did not appear so the said Roger (4d) is in mercy
Wyken	township there presents nothing
Worfeld amerced 4d	township there presents that John Elwalle who is bound to make appearance at this court did not appear so the said John (4d) is in mercy
The ale tasters amerced 5s	present that Alice Soonde brewed 1 (6d), John Smyth of Wyke 2 (12d), Katherine Bulveis 2 (6d pardoned 1), Henry Barker 1 (6d), William Noore 1 (6d), John Yate of Wyke 1 (6d), Margery Hugge 1 (6d), Benigna Rowlow 1 (6d), and that all sold against the assize so each of them is in mercy. And they say that John Smyth (6d) of Wyke from time to time regrated bread and ale so he is in mercy
6d	Hamund Humeleie (6d) one of the tasters is in mercy for his negligence in presentation
The 12 jurors	say on their oath that the townships aforesaid have well and faithfully presented
Fine 4s	Roger Dalleie (12d), John Glover (12d), William Webbe (12d) & Stephen Webbe (12d) are in mercy for an uproar and contempt made in full court so each of them is at a fine with the lady
Small Court	Small court held on the place, day and year aforesaid
The 12 jurors amerced 2d	Inquiry held for the lady by the oath of Roger Richardes, John Walker, Stephen Bradeneie, John Hethe, Roger Waltone, John Rowlowe son of Nicholas, Roger Cattestre, Thomas Richardes, William Newe, William Wermode, Roger Broke & Thomas Merwelle who say on their oath that Hugh Baker who owes suit at this court did not come so the said Hugh (2d) is in mercy
Fine 12d	William Huster surrendered into the the hands of the lady half of one cottage with appurtenances in Soonde which Thomas Soonde lately held to the use of Agnes Plummer the which Agnes came here in court and took from the lady the aforesaid half a cottage with appurtenances to hold to the said Agnes and her [heirs] from the lady by services thence owed and accustomed according to the custom of the manor. And she gives to the lady for a fine 12d, made fealty. And she has seisin
Adjourned	Still a day is given between John Walker plaintiff and John Rowlowe son of Nicholas defendant in a plea of trespass
amerced 6d	John Hulle is in mercy because he is not prosecuting against Margery Barker in a plea of trespass
the next	Thomas Jankys junior plaintiff against John Huwessone in a plea of trespass who has a day to respond until the next [court] etc

1413-1414 P314/W/1/1/242

distrain — Thomas Jankys junior plaintiff against John Smyth of Wyke in a plea of trespass who is not attached so let it be done

distrain — Henry Barker plaintiff against William Barewe to respond in a plea of trespass who is not attached so let it be done

distrain — Richard Bradeneie not prosecuting plaintiff against Thomas Jankys senior in a plea of debt who summoned did not come so distrain

distrain — Thomas Toward plaintiff against William Oldyntone junior in a plea of debt who summoned did not come so distrain

distrain — William Newtone clerk plaintiff against Thomas Jankys senior, Robert Ewdenas, & Roger Smyth in a plea of debt who summoned did not come so distrain

the next — John Baret plaintiff against Margery Barker in a plea of trespass pledge for the prosecution John Tumpkys

stray remains — Still remaining 1 boar from a stray as is clear in the preceding court in the custody of Richard Bulveis

supervise — Still on behalf of the lady an inquiry concerning 1 pig and 3 piglets from the escheat of Thomas Rowlowe etc.

Affeerors — Roger Richardes, John Walker

Sum of this great court with the small following 15s 10d

Expenses of the steward 10s 3d

Worfeld — Small court held there on Tuesday next after the feast of the Ascension of the Lord in the second year of the reign of King Henry V after the conquest [22 May 1414]

Essoins — William Heneme/Hemme, Thomas Richardes, Thomas Tresel & John Holigreve from common [suit] by Richard Bulveis

The 12

Stephen Bradeneie	Roger Cattestre	John Walker }
William Newe	John Hethe	Roger Waltone } sworn
Roger Broke	John Rowlowe	Thomas Merwelle }
Roger Gerbod	Roger Richardes	William Wermode}

+ taken
Fine 10s — Mathew Bullok surrendered into the hands of the lady one toft and half a virgate of land with appurtenances in Wynnescote within the manor of Worfeld to the use of John Bullok his son, his heirs and assigns the which John came here in court and took from the lady the aforesaid toft and half a virgate of land with appurtenances to hold to himself and his [heirs] from the lady by services thence owed and accustomed according to the customs of the manor. And he gives to the lady for a fine 10s, made fealty to the lady. And he is seised etc.

Adjourned — {A day is given until the next [court] between Thomas Jankys junior plaintiff and John Smyth of Wyke defendant in a plea of trespass
{And between the said Thomas Jankys plaintiff & John Huwessone defendant in a
{plea of trespass

Amerced 4d	William Barewe (4d) put himself in mercy for a licence to agree with Henry Barker in a plea of trespass
Amerced 4d	Richard Bradeneie (4d) is in mercy because he is not prosecuting against Thomas Jankys senior in a plea of debt
Amerced 4d Recover	Thomas Toward plaintiff against William Oldyntone junior in a plea of debt etc. who seeks from the said William 33s 4d of good money which he owes to him from a loan which the same William should have paid to him on a certain day and place at which day and place the said debt was not paid although it was frequently requested nor still but is unjustly detained to the damage of the same Thomas. And the said William present in court acknowledged the whole of the said debt which it is ordered to raise etc. And the same William is in mercy
Amerced 6d The law	William Newtone clerk plaintiff against Thomas Jankys senior, Robert Ewdenas & Roger Smyth in a plea of debt. And he says that the same Thomas, Robert and Roger owe him 13s 7d which they unjustly detain etc. And the aforesaid Thomas present as if in the name of the aforesaid defendants concerning the aforesaid debt acknowledged 2s 8d which it is ordered to raise. And the same Thomas (6d) is in mercy. And what remains of the aforesaid debt namely 10s 11d they totally deny and thence they have a day for the law in the next [court] pledge for the law Roger Cattestre
Adjourned	{Also a day is given between John Baret plaintiff and Margery Barker defendant in a {plea of trespass until the next {And between John Walker plaintiff and John Rowlowe defendant in a plea of trespass
The 12 Heriot 6s Escheat none as shown Supervise Tenement remains in the hand of the lady	jurors present and say on their oath that Petronilla Nelde who held from the lady one messuage, half a virgate of land and half a nook of land in lesser tenure in Haalen within the manor of Worfeld on the day she died after whose death there falls to the lady one black cow in the name of heriot price 6s concerning which cow the reeve is charged to respond to the greater profit of the lady. And concerning escheat nothing now is presented because at present they don't know whether she has escheat or not and whether she is bound by their custom to give escheat etc. but thence they have a day to enquire concerning the truth until the next [court]. And the tenement remains in the hands of the lady. And they say that Emmota the wife of John Aleyn & the daughter of Thomas Nelde is the closest heir to take the aforesaid tenement out of the hands of the lady
Verdict concerning Chilterne Grene	Still the 12 jurors present that whoever will have a certain parcel of land called Chilterne Grene a close within the manor of Worfeld ought to enclose the said close at his own expense on the soil and ground of the same place. And they say that in the same place is a common way for men and horses. And that the township of Stanlowe has in the same place a common way for horses and carts
Stray remains	Still remaining in the custody of Richard Bulveis 1 boar as a stray as is clear in the penultimate great court preceding
Strays remain	{Also remaining in the custody of the bailiff 1 stray piglet as is clear in the last {great court preceding {Also remaining in the custody of the bailiff 1 stray young pig as is clear in the {same last great court {Also remaining in the custody of John Wilot 1 stray draught animal (affram) as is {clear in the same last great court preceding

1413-1414 P314/W/1/1/242

Supervise	Still on behalf of the lady to be enquired concerning 1 pig and 3 piglets from the escheat of Thomas Rowlowe
Affeerors	John Walker, John Rowlowe Sum of this court 17s 6d Expenses of the steward 12d
Worfeld	Small court held there on Tuesday next after the feast of St Barnabus in the second year of the reign of King Henry V after the conquest [12 June 1414]
Essoins	Robert Bruggende, John Hulle & Hugh Baker themselves from common [suit] by Henry Barker
Amerced 4d	William Heneme (4d) is in mercy because he did not come here to warrant his essoin
the 12	Roger Cattestre, John Hethe, John Walker } Stephen Bradeneie, Roger Gerbod, Roger Waltone } sworn William Newe, Roger Richardes, Thomas Merwell } Roger Broke, John Rowlowe, William Wermode}
Adjourned	{Still a day is given between John Walker plaintiff & John Rowlowe son of Nicholas {defendant in a plea of trespass {And between Thomas Jankys junior plaintiff & John Smyth of Wyke defendant in a {plea of trespass
Amerced 4d	Thomas Jankys junior (4d) is in mercy because he is not prosecuting against John Huwessone in a plea of trespass
Amerced 4d	Margery Barker (4d) put herself in mercy for a licence to agree with John Baret in a plea of trespass
Amerced 6d	Thomas Jankys senior defendant who had a day for the law against William Newtone clerk in a plea of debt under the same law they are agreed. And the said Thomas (6d) put himself in mercy
the next	Roger Cattestre plaintiff against John Smyth of Wyke in a plea of debt who is not summoned so let it be done
the 12 jurors amerced 2d Heriot & escheat nothing for the reason shown Fine 10s	present that William Heneme who is bound to make suit at this court did not come so the said William (2d) is in mercy. And they said that John Saladyn who held from the lady by the custom of the manor one toft and half a virgate of land with appurtenances at Barndeleie within the manor of Worfeld has died whence concerning heriot and escheat nothing falls to the lady because there was nothing. And the tenement remains in the hands of the lady furthermore they said that Agnes the wife of John Smyth of Soonde is his closest heir. On which came here in court the aforesaid John Smyth of Soonde and Agnes his wife and took from the lady the aforesaid toft and half a virgate of land with appurtenances as the right and inheritance of the same Agnes to hold to the same John and Agnes, the heirs and assigns of the same Agnes from the lady by services thence owed and accustomed according to the customs of the manor. And they give to the lady for a fine 10s, made fealty and are seised
	Robert Barker of Haalen gives to the lady 12d as a fine for an inquiry of 12 ex officio to be held to enquire if a widow after the death of her husband is able to give or

Fine 12d

to alienate lands and tenements of lesser tenure within the manor of Worfeld which were her husband's concerning which she never had any title or not. On which the inquiry was held by the oath of Roger Richardes, John Walker, William Bromleie, Thomas Rowlowe of Burcote, Roger Broke, Roger Gerbod, Roger Smyth, John Coletes, William Newe, Richard Aldith, William Wermod & John Bronle who sworn thence charged say on their oath that a widow is able to make title by their custom of of lands and tenements of her deceased husband before completion made by a customary tenant between the lord and his tenants and after the said completion no title is able to be made except as for the term of her life unless she thence previously had title

Strays remain

{Still remaining in the custody of Richard Bulveis 1 stray boar as is clear in the court {preceding
{Also remaining in the custody of the reeve 1 piglet & 1 small pig from strays as is {clear in the court preceding
{Also remaining in the custody of John Wilot 1 stray draught animal (affram) as is {clear in the court preceding

Supervise

Also concerning 1 pig and 3 piglets from the escheat of Thomas Rowlowe concerning which nothing is charged. It is here presented by the oath of the 12 jurors that where the said pig and piglets are and have gone they are wholly ignorant but in the future thence to better enquire on behalf of the lady

Affeerors

Roger Cattestre, Roger Broke
Sum of this court 12s 8d Expenses of the steward 12d

Tenement remains in the hand of the lady

Still remaining in the hands of the lady 1 messuage, half a virgate and half a nook of land in lesser tenure in Haalen by the death of Petronilla Nelde as clear in the last court preceding. Furthermore it is presented here by the oath of the 12 jurors aforesaid that still they are not able to find between them that the aforesaid Petronilla had escheat at the time of her death etc.

1414-1415 P314/W/1/1/243

Worfeld	Great Court held there on Tuesday the 9th day of October in the second year of the reign of King Henry V after the conquest [9 October 1414]
The 12	Robert Ewdenas, Roger Waltone, John Jonesone Rowlow, Roger Cattestre, John Hethe, John Walker, Stephen Bradeneie, William Wermod, William Gerbod, Roger Richardes, Thomas Merwelle, William Newe } sworn
Kyngeslow, Stanlowe amerced 12d	townships there present that Thomas Colier is a common fisher in the waters of the lady so the said Thomas (12d) is in mercy
Chesturtone amerced 2s 10d	township there presents that William Dorset (8d) forestalled John Baret of Stoktone. And that Thomas Baret (8d) of Stokton miller forestalled William Dorset. And that William Kynnesleie (10d) made an assault on Richard Wilde. And that [blank] Lokier (8d) of Brugge forestalled William Kynnesleie so each of them for disturbing the peace are in mercy
Hultone amerced 4d	township there presents nothing. Rowlowe, Bradeneie, Asturhull, Ewyk, Soonde townships there present that John Glover did not appear at the due time so the said John is in mercy 4d
Roughtone, Barndeleie, Hoccombe, Swancote	townships there present nothing. Burcote, Burcote, Ryndelford, Bromleie townships there present nothing
Alvescote, Wynnescote, Cattestre, Newtone supervise	townships there present one pit made at Claymere near Newtone on the soil of the lady beside the King's road to the weakening of the same road & the nuisance of the tenants of the lady by who or by whom they have a day to present in the next [court]
Ewdenas, Oldyntone	townships there present nothing. Stapelford township there presents nothing. Akeltone township there presents nothing
Wyke amerced 4d	township there presents nothing. Haalen township there presents that John Holigreve who is bound to make appearance at this court did not appear so the said John (4d) is in mercy
Worfeld amerced 2s 2d	township there presents that John Elwalle (4d) and William Nore (4d) who are bound to make appearance at this court did not appear so each of them is in mercy. And they say that John Penford (8d) clerk forestalled Alice Goold and hit her (2d) so the said John both for the forestalling and for the blow is in mercy. Also they say that the same Alice raised the hue and cry justly on the said John, clerk, so the said John (8d) clerk is in mercy
The tasters of ale amerced 4s 2d	present that William Bakes (6d) brewed 1, John Cattestre (6d) 1, John Yate (6d) 1, Thomas Soonde (12d) 2, John Smyth of Soonde (6d) 1, Roger Coriour (6d) 1, Katherine Bulveis 2 (6d because 1 pardoned), Roger Broke 1 to the use of the repair of the chapel of St Martin so commuted. And that Alice Sonde (2d) and Katherine Bulveis (pardoned) were from time to time using itinerant vendors

the 12 jurors — present that the townships aforesaid and the tasters of ale have well and faithfully presented and concealed nothing

Constables — John Hethe & John Rowlowe son of Nicholas Rowlowe are elected constables. And they are sworn

Tasters of ale — William Carter & John Baret of Akelone are elected tasters of ale. And they are sworn

Small court held there at the place, day, and year above said

Essoins — Thomas Richardes, William Newe, William Wermod, William Newtone clerk, William Heneme, Richard Bradeney & William Stevenes from common [suit] by Richard Bulveis

	Stephen Bradeneie	Nicholas Rowlowe	John Janne }	
The 12	Roger Richardes	John Jonesone Rowlowe	Richard Aldith }	sworn
	William Webbe	Roger Smyth	John Hethe }	
	John Barndeleie	Roger Waltone	Thomas Toward }	

Fine 4s — Roger Batemon, Thomas Forster, John Nicols & John Robyns made a fine for suit of court to be commuted from the date of this court until the feast of St Michael the Archangel next following. And they give to the lady each of them for a fine 12d

The 12 jurors — present that Roger Broke of Roughtone surrendered into the hands of the lady one toft and half a virgate of land with appurtenances in Roughtone to rehold from the lady the said tenement to himself and Edith his wife for the term of the life of each of them from the lady according to the custom of the manor so that after their deaths the said tenement will remain with John their son and his [heirs] from the lady to hold according to the custom of the manor. And in a similar manner the aforesaid tenement is granted from the lady by the steward to the aforesaid Roger and Edith for the term of the lives of each of them to hold according to the custom of the manor and after their deaths to the aforesaid John to hold to himself and his [heirs] from the lady according to the custom of the manor. And they give to the lady for a fine 10s. And thus they are seised

Fine 10s

And they say that Roger Broke above-named who held from the lady by the custom of the manor one messuage with one virgate of land adjacent in Roughtone & one toft with half a virgate of land adjacent in Roughtone on the same day he died from whose death the lady will have by their custom 2 steers in the name of heriot price 17s whereof one is red in colour & the other falwe and they say that for escheat the lady will have 3 draught animals (affram) price 8s and 6 young pigs price 4s concerning which heriots and escheats the reeve is charged to respond to the greater profit of the lady. And they say that the tenements aforesaid remain with Edith the widow of the same Roger deceased for the term of her life by their custom

Heriot 17s.
Escheat 12s

And they say that Alice Rugge widow of the lady married herself to John Snel within the manor. And that Matilda Ewdenas married herself to Thomas Haselwode within the manor who thence made a fine. And they give to the lady each of them for a fine 20d so it is agreed by the steward

Fine 3s 4d

Fine 12d — John Barndeleie gives to the lady 12d for a fine for an inquiry of the 12 to be held to enquire what and how much of right and by their custom he ought to have from the issue and profit of that tenement which he held at fixed rent (ad firmam) from John Saladyn in Barndeleie for him and from him which the same John Saladyn died in the week of Pentecost last past after whose death the said tenement was falling to John Smyth of Soonde and Agnes his wife as the right and inheritance of the same Agnes. On which the inquiry held by the oath of Stephen Bradeneie, Roger Richardes, William Webbe, Nicholas Rowlowe, John Jonesonerowlow, Roger Smyth, John Janne, Thomas Tresele, Richard Aldith, Thomas Toward, John Bromleie & Roger Gerbod who sworn and thence charged went out, returned, and concerning their verdict they seek a day until the next [court] and adjourned by the agreement of each party

Fine 14s — To this court came John Aleyn of Humeleie and Emily his wife the daughter of Thomas Nelde and took from the hands of the lady one messuage, one toft, and half a nook and two butts of land in Haalen as the right & inheritance of the same Emily after the death of Petronilla Nelde to hold to the aforesaid John & Emily, the heirs and assigns of the same Emily from the lady by services and customs thence owed according to the custom of the manor. And they give to the lady for a fine 14s, made fealty to the lady and thus they are seised

Fine 2s — Roger Cattestre surrendered into the hands of the lady half a toft, a parcel of land called Lovestikkelond and two butts of land adjacent to the said half a toft in Haalen to the use of Henry Barker who came here in court and took from the lady the aforesaid tenement to hold to himself and his [heirs] from the lady according to the custom of the manor. And he gives to the lady for a fine 2s and thus is seised

Profit from Sowdeleie — The reeve is charged here by the steward concerning 5s to be raised from the herbage and wood of Sowdeleie as for the enclosure at the time of the present year

Amerced 12d — John Henene is in mercy for his unjust plea against John Penford clerk in a plea of trespass

Fine 6s — Roger Cattestre surrendered into the hands of the lady one messuage and one toft with half a virgate of land called Lovestikkeslond in Haalen to William the son of William Pirye of Billistone [Bilston] to hold to the same William the son of William and the heirs of his body issuing according to the custom of the manor. The which messuage, toft and half a virgate of land are granted to the aforesaid William the son of William by the steward in the form aforesaid to hold from the lady according to the custom of the manor. And he gives to the lady for a fine 6s and no more because elsewhere he made a fine for the same tenements as is clear by the rolls of the court held on Tuesday the ninth day of July in the tenth year of the reign of King Henry IV. And he made fealty

Fine 16d — Roger Taillour gives to the lady 2s for a fine for a licence to have to brew bread and ale to sell from the date of this court until the feast of St Michael the Archangel next following so that he keeps the assize and sells by legal measure

Amerced 6d — Thomas Jankys junior is in mercy because he is not prosecuting against John Smyth of Wyke in a plea of trespass

Distrain — Robert Smyth plaintiff against William Yngmon in a plea of a pledge not discharged who summoned did not come so distrain

Adjourned	Still a day is given between John Walker plaintiff and John the son of Nicholas Rowlow defendant in a plea of trespass
Supervise The next	Still the 12 jurors present one oak in the wood of the lady burned by whom they still don't know and thence they have a day until the next [court] better to enquire. And that the verdict of the inquiry of the 12 ex officio at the suit of John Barndeleie is adjourned until the next [court]
Supervise	Concerning a piglet coming as a stray at the feast of St Michael in the previous year of the reign of King Henry V as is clear in the last great court in the year preceding by the presentation of the townships of Roughtone, Barndeleie, Hoccombe & Swancote and appraised by the said townships at 4d and remains in the custody of William Gerbod then the reeve. And concerning another young pig coming as a stray at the feast of All Saints last past remaining in the custody of the said reeve as is clear in the said last court of the preceding year by the presentation of the township of Stapelford and appraised at 6d the which William says on his oath that the aforesaid stray piglet and the young pig are dead
Adjourned	Still the verdict of the 12 ex officio at the suit of John Barndeleie is adjourned until the next
Affeerors	Roger Richardes, John Jonessonerowlowe Sum of this great court with the small following £4 10s Expenses of the steward 10s 8d
Supervise	Stephen Bradeneie came here and claimed 1 draught animal (affram) presented as a stray by the township of Akeltone as is clear in the last great court in the year preceding. And thence they have a day to appraise the said draught animal at the coming of the steward
Worfeld	Small court held there on Monday the 19th day of the month of November in the second year of the reign of King Henry V after the conquest [19 November 1414]
Essoins	John Rowlow & William Bromleie themselves from common [suit] by Richard Bulveis

The 12			
Roger Richardes	John Jonessonerowlow	Thomas Rowlow	}
Roger Waltone	John Walker	William Webbe	} sworn
Stephen Bradeneie	William Gerbod	William Wermod	}
John Hethe	William Newe	Thomas Merwelle	}

Adjourned	John Waltone plaintiff against John Waas of Brugge in a plea of debt pledge for the prosecution William Carter. And he said that a dog of the said John Waas in default of custody on the Sunday before the beginning of Lent last past killed one steer of the same John Waltone in the forest of Morf in his pasture to his damage 6s 8d. And thence they have a day to agree until the next by the prayer of both parties fine however as before
Distrain	Nicholas Stanlow plaintiff against Thomas Jankys junior in a plea of debt who summoned did not come so distrain
	Robert Smyth who offered himself against William Yngmon just as the pledge of William Oldyntone as is clear in the last court preceding in a plea of debt etc. On

Amerced 6d Recover — which the said William Oldyntone appeared here as chief debtor from the which William Oldyntone the said Robert, plaintiff, seeks 20d of debt the which 20d the same William Oldyntone recognises so it is ordered to raise etc.. And the said William for his unjust detention is in mercy

Distrain — John Smyth of Soonde plaintiff against John Barndeleie in a plea of trespass who is not attached so let it be done

Distrain — Thomas Sonde plaintiff against Emmeline Colier in a plea of debt who summoned did not come so distrain

Adjourned — Still a day is given between John Walker plaintiff and John the son of Nicholas Rowlow defendant in a plea of trespass

The 12 Amerced 8d — jurors present that John Nelde (1d), John Hethe (1d), Alice Rugge (1d), William Newe (1d), Robert Hawkys (1d), Stephen [no surname given] (1d), John Walle (1d), & William Webbe (1d) who are bound to make suit to grind at the lady's mill ground outside the manor at mills elsewhere against the custom of the manor so each of them is in mercy. And concerning the oak burned in the wood of the lady still they are not able between them [determine] the truth of the matter and thence they have a day better to enquire until the next [court]

Adjourned — Still an inquiry by the 12 ex officio at the suit of John Barndeleie adjourned until the next [court]

Sum of this small court 14d — Expenses of the steward 12d

Supervise — But to appraise the 8 men who milled outside the manor it is taken under condition if it pleases the council of the lady

Worfeld — Small court held there on Monday next after the feast of the Conception of the Blessed Virgin Mary in the second year of the reign of King Henry V after the conquest [10 December 1414]

Essoins — Thomas Underhull, Hugh Baker, John Stevenes & John Nelde from common [suit] by Richard Bulveis

The 12			
	Roger Richardes	John Rowlow	William Gerbod }
	Roger Waltone	Thomas Merwelle	William Newe } sworn
	Stephen Bradeneie	John Walker	Roger Gerbod }
	John Hethe	William Wermod	William Webbe }

Amerced 4d Distrain — The reeve (… 4d) is in mercy because he did not distrain Thomas Jankys junior to respond here to Nicholas Stanlowe to respond in a plea of debt. And on behalf of the lady it is ordered to distrain the said Thomas that he be at that next [court] to respond to the said Nicholas in the plea aforesaid

Adjourned —
{Still a day is given between John Walker plaintiff and John the son of Nicholas
{Rowlow defendant in a plea of trespass
{Also a day is given between John Smyth of Soonde plaintiff and John Barndeleie
{defendant in a plea of trespass
{The verdict of an inquiry of the 12 ex officio at the suit of John Barndeleie adjourned
{until the next [court]

Amerced 4d Distrain	William Carter (2d) & William Yngemon (2d) pledges of John Waas are in mercy because they did not have the said John to respond to John Waltone in a plea of trespass. Furthermore it is ordered to better distrain the said John Waas that he be at that next [court] to respond to the said John Waltone in the plea aforesaid
The next	{Thomas Towart plaintiff against John Joukys in a plea of debt who is not summoned {so let it be done {The same Thomas Towart plaintiff against William Oldyntone junior in a plea of {debt so it is ordered to summon the said William before the next [court] to respond to {the said Thomas in the plea aforesaid
Amerced 6d	Emmeline Colier (6d) put herself in mercy for a licence to agree with Thomas Soonde plaintiff in a plea of debt
Fine 2s The next	Given to the lady 2s for a fine for an inquiry of 24 ex officio to be held to enquire who of right and by their custom has the better right to have and by the custom of the manor to hold 1 toft and one virgate of land called Upyntoneslond in Hultone. On which the inquiry was held by the oath of Roger Richardes, John Hethe, Roger Cattestre, Thomas Merwelle senior, Thomas Tresel, John Bromleie, Thomas Towart, Richard Aldith, Thomas Rowlow, Roger Gerbod, William Yate, William Bromleie, Richard Bradeneie, Thomas Soonde, William Newe, John Snel, Thomas Merwelle junior, Richard Whitebrok, John Coletes, Robert Barker, Nicholas Stanlow, Stephen Stanlowe, Henry Barker & William Stevenes who sworn and thence charged have a day for the verdict until the next [court] pledge for the fine Richard Bulveis
Affeerors	Stephen Bradeneie, John Hethe Sum of this small court 3s 2d Expenses of the steward 12d
Worfeld	Small court held there on Monday next after the feast of the Conversion of St Paul in the second year of the reign of King Henry V after the conquest [28 January 1415]
Essoins	William Heneme, John Rowlow & John Holigreve themselves from common [suit] by Richard Bulveis

	Stephen Bradeneie	William Gerbod	Roger Smyth	}
	Roger Waltone	William Wermod	John Janne	} sworn
The 12	Roger Richardes	Nicholas Rowlow	William Webbe	}
	John Barndeleie	John Jonessonerowlow	John Walker	}

Distrain	Roger Hethe plaintiff against Thomas Jankys junior in a plea of debt who summoned did not come so distrain
Recover Amerced 6d	{Thomas Towart plaintiff against John Jowkys in a plea of debt who seeks from the {said John 22shillings of silver which he owes to him from a loan and unjustly detains {etc. And the said John present recognises the whole of the said debt. So it is ordered {to raise etc. And the said John (6d) is in mercy
	{Thomas Towart plaintiff against William Oldyntone junior in a plea of debt and he {says that the same William owes to him 15s 6d from a loan he received which he {unjustly detains etc. And the said William present in court recognised the whole of

Recover Amerced 6d	{the said debt so it is ordered to raise to the use of the same Thomas. And the said {William is in mercy
Amerced 6d	Nicholas Stanlowe plaintiff & Thomas Jankys defendant in a plea of debt are for a licence to agree and the said Nicholas put himself in mercy
Recover Amerced 6d The law	John Cardmaker of Lichefeld plaintiff against Robert Galian taylor in a plea of debt pledge for the prosecution William Carter. And he says through William Carter his attorney that the same Robert owes to him 11s in silver for 15 pairs of cards bought and received from him and Robert cardmaker his servant. The which 11s ought to have been paid to the said John at Lichefeld within fifteen days after the feast of the Exaltation of the Holy Cross in the 11th year of the reign of King Henry IV at which day and place he did not pay nor yet but he detains to the damage of the same John 6s 8d. And the said Robert present in court recognises 8s of the said debt which it is ordered to raise. And the same Robert (6d) is in mercy. Concerning the damage adjourned until by the prayer of Richard Bulveis. And he denies 3s. And thence he has a day for the law in the next [court] pledge for the law Richard Bulveis
[Adjourned]	Still a day is given between John Waltone plaintiff and John Waas defendant in a plea of trespass by the prayer of the parties. And between John Walker plaintiff and John Rowlow defendant in a plea of trespass
Adjourned	{Also the inquiry of the 12 ex officio at the suit of John Barndeleie adjourned until the {next [court] together with the plea between himself and John Smyth plaintiff {Also the verdict of the inquiry of 24 ex officio adjourned until the coming of William {Boerleie the steward
The 12 jurors Amerced nothing as clear	present that Thomas Richardes not affeered ...... who is bound to make suit at this court did not come so the said Thomas is in mercy
Affeerors	Stephen Bradeneie, William Gerbod Sum of this small court 2s Expenses of the clerk of the court Richard Bulveis the reeve and the beadle 12d
Worfeld	Small court held there on Tuesday next after the feast of St Chad the Bishop in the second year of the reign of King Henry V after the conquest [5 March 1415]
Essoins	Hugh Baker himself from common [suit] by Richard Bulveis
Amerced 3d	John Holigreve is in mercy because he did not come to warrant his essoin
Fine 2s	It is given to the lady 2s for a fine for an inquiry of the 24 to be held ex officio to enquire of two articles from their custom namely first if a tenant of the manor of Worfeld to be expelled from his tenure which he holds by the custom of the same manor by the steward of the said manor or another servant of the lord without by the will of the same tenant or without the judgment of an inquiry of the 12 or 24 or not. Secondly if a woman holding lands and tenements to herself and her [heirs] within the manor of Worfeld by the custom of the same manor takes a husband who holds of the same woman, his wife should have alienated against the will of his wife the husband having died, whether the said woman his wife who will have outlived him the said tenement thus by her husband alienated as above it is said, will be able to recover by

their custom or not. Pledge for he fine Roger Cattestre. On which the inquiry was held by the oath of John Hethe, Roger Waltone, Roger Cattestre, John Walker, Roger Richardes, William Wermod, William Newe, Thomas Merwelle, Stephen Bradeneie, John Jonessonerowlow, Roger Gerbod, William Webbe, John Janne, William Gerbod, Thomas Towart, Henry Barker, John Barndeleie, Nicholas Stanlowe, John Bromleie, Thomas Tresele, Nicholas Rowlow, Roger Smyth, Robert Bruggende & Thomas

supervise Rowlowe who sworn and thence charged go out, return, and say on their oath concerning the first article that a tenant by the custom of the manor of Worfeld is not able by their custom to be driven out from his tenure which he holds by custom by the steward nor by any servant of the lady without the will of the tenant or without the judgment of an inquiry of the 1 or 24. Concerning the second article they have a day to present until the next [court]

Amerced 6d

Thomas Jankys junior put himself in mercy for a licence to agree with Roger Hethe plaintiff in a plea of debt etc.

{Still a day is given between John Waltone plaintiff and John Waas defendant in a
{plea of trespass by the prayer of the parties until the next [court]
{And between John Walker plaintiff and John the son of Nicholas Rowlow defendant
Adourned {in a plea of trespass as above
until the next {Also a day is given until the next [court] between John Cardmaker of Lichefeld
[court] {plaintiff and Robert Galian taylor in a plea of debt under the law etc.
{Still the plea between John Smyth of Soonde plaintiff & John Barndeleie defendant
{adjourned until the next by the prayer of each party in a plea of trespass
{Inquiry of the 12 ex officio at the suit of John Barndeleie adjourned until the next
{[court]
{Also the verdict of the inquiry of 24 adjourned until the coming of the steward

Affeerors

John Janne, John Jonessone Rowlow
Sum of this small court 2s 9d
Expenses of the clerk of the court being there at dinner with 1 horse together with the expenses of Richard Bulveis the reeve and the beadle 12d

Worfeld

Great Court held there with the small following on Monday the 8th day of April in the third year of the reign of King Henry V after the conquest [8 April 1415]

Essoins

William Noore himself from appearance by Richard Bulveis

The 12				
	Robert Ewdenas	Roger Richardes	William Wermod	}
	Roger Cattestre	Roger Waltone	Thomas Merwelle	} sworn
	John Hethe	John Rowlow	William Gerbod	}
	Stephen Bradeneie	John Walker	William Newe	}

Kyngeslow & Stanlowe townships there present nothing Chesturtone township there presents nothing

Hultone township there presents two sheep coming as strays at the feast of St Mathew the Apostle price 14d and remaining in the custody of the reeve until. And they say that

strays remain Hugh Baker entered the house of William Barewe in Hultone and from thence took

Amerced 20d unjustly one bowl in the name of distraint so that the said Hugh (8d) is in mercy. And they say that Margaret the wife of the same William Barewe justly raised the hue and cry on the said Hugh so the said Hugh (12d) is in mercy

Rowlowe, Bradeneie, Asturhull, Ewyk, Soonde strays remain	townships there present three sheep coming as strays at the feast of St Michael last past price 2s 6d. And they remain in the custody of John Rowlow & Thomas Soonde
Roughtone, Barndeleie, Hoccombe, Swancote Amerced 4s 6d Waifs 4d	townships there present that William Broke (6d) forestalled Robert Webbe. And they say that the same Robert Webbe reforestalled (8d) the said William Broke and from him drew blood (12d). So each of them is in mercy. And they say that the common way in Roughtone is deteriorated to the nuisance of the neighbours in default of Edith Broke (1d) and Joan Hulle (1d), widows, so each of them is in mercy. And they say that William Abbot unjustly and against the peace of the King took 2 hurdles of William Yate price 4d so the said William (20d) is in mercy for trespass
Burcote, Burcote, Ryndelford, Bromleie stray remains	townships there present nothing. Alvescote, Wynnescote, Cattestre, Newton townships there present 1 male sheep coming as a stray at the feast of St Michael last past price 6d. And it remains in the custody of the reeve until
Ewdenas, Oldyntone	townships there present nothing. Stapelford township there presents nothing
Akeltone Amerced 4s 8d	township there presents that John Clerk of Weston forestalled (12d) Thomas Tumpkys so the said John is in mercy. And they say that William Flode made a poundbreach (12d) on John Baret so the said William is in mercy. Also the say that Margaret (12d) the wife of William Flynt and Alice the wife (12d) of Richard Flynt raised the hue and cry unjustly. So each of them is in mercy. And they say that John Henene forestalled William Flynt so the said John (8d) is in mercy.
Haalen Amerced 6d	township there presents that Thomas Wermod forestalled (6d) John Cattestre and hit (6d) the same John so the said Thomas both for the forestalling and for the blow is in mercy
Wyke amerced 8d	township there presents that Roger Halidaie made an assault on Matilda Ody so the said Roger (8d) is in mercy
Worfeld amerced 5s 2d	township there presents that John Henene forestalled (6d) Thomas Gille and from the same Thomas drew blood (12d). And that the same Thomas reforestalled (8d) the said John Henene and from him drew blood (12d) so each of them both for the forestalling and for the flowing of blood is in mercy. And they say that John Henene aforesaid broke the arrest made by the constables so the same John (12d) is in mercy. Also they say that the same John Henene raised the hue and cry (12d) unjustly on the constables so the said John is in mercy
The tasters of ale amerced 9s 7d	present that Katherine Bulveis (18d) brewed 3, Alice Soonde (18d) 3, Agnes Smyth (18d) 3, John Yate (12d) 2, William Noore (6d) 1, John Billyngsleie (6d) 1, John the son of Nicholas Rowlow (6d) 1, William Bakes (6d) 1, Thomas Tresel (6d) 1, Richard Flynt (6d) 1, John Baret (6d) 1, Margery Hugges (6d) 1, Alice Soonde (1d) 1 of the 3 bushels brewed. And all sold against the assize so each of them is in mercy
Amerced 2s	The12 sworn present one pit was made at Claynere to the weakening of the common way there and the nuisance of the neighbours by Margery Barker so the said Margery (12d) is in mercy. And that this was concealed by the townships of Alvescote,

Wynnescote, Cattestre & Newtone so the said townships (12d) are in mercy. And concerning the others they say the townships aforesaid and the tasters of ale have well and faithfully presented

Amerced 12d

William Flynt plaintiff against the township of Akeltone in a plea of unjust presentation whereby it was presented that the same William made a poundbreach on John Baret as is clear above and thence he put himself on the judgment of the12 jurors & the township similarly who thence charged say on their oath that the township well and faithfully presented. So the said William is in mercy for his unjust (12d) plea

Appropriation of draught animal (affram)

Stephen Bradeneie appropriated here before the steward in full court 1 draught animal (affram) presented as a stray by the township of Akeltone as is clear in the last great court in the year preceding

Small court held there in the place at the place, day and year above said

The 12 jurors

Escheat 12d

of the inquiry held for the lady by the oath of Roger Cattestre, John Janne, John Hethe, Stephen Bradeneie, Roger Richardes, Roger Waltone, John Rowlow John Walker, William Wermod, Thomas Merwelle, William Gerbod , William Newe who say on their oath that the lady will have one male colt as from the escheat of Roger Broke previously not presented price 12d concerning which the reeve is charged to respond to the better profit of the lady

Fine 15s

Hugh Baker and Agnes his wife surrendered into the hands of the lady one messuage and three nooks of land with appurtenances in Hultone to the use of John Bradeneie, his heirs and assigns. And the aforesaid Agnes confessed and examined before the steward recognised she had done this voluntarily without coercion of her husband aforesaid. On which came the said John Bradeneie and took from the lady the aforesaid messuage and three nooks of land with appurtenances to hold to himself and his heirs from the lady according to the custom of the manor by services and customs thence due. And he gives to the lady for a fine 15s to pay half into the hands and the other half within the next account. He made fealty to the lady and is seised

Fine 12d

Thomas Richardes gives to the lady 12d for a fine for suit of court to be commuted from the feast of St Michael the Archangel last past until the said feast of St Michael next in the future

Fine 6d

Adjourned

Superinde

Affeerors

{John Waas put himself in mercy for a licence to agree with John Waltone plaintiff in
{a plea of trespass
{Still a day is given between John Walker plaintiff & John Rowlow defendant in a
{plea of trespass
{And between John Cardmaker of Lichfeld plaintiff & Robert Galian taylor in a plea
{of debt whence the law
{And between John Smyth of Soonde plaintiff and John Barndeleie defendant in a
{plea of trespass
{Also the verdict of the inquiry of 24 ex officio of the tenement called Upyntoneslond
{adjourned until the coming of the steward
{And the verdict of the 24 ex officio of certain customs as is clear in the last small
{court preceding adjourned etc

Still the fishers in the waters of the lady whose names are contained in the rolls of the penultimate court of the preceding year until by amercement to be imposed by the

Superinde council of the lady adjourned

Affeerors John Jonessonerowlowe, John Walker
Sum of this great court with the small court following 48s 2d. over and above strays
Expenses of the steward being there remaining for the reason of holding the aforesaid court 14s 10d

Worfeld Small court held there on Monday next after the feast of St James the Apostle in the third year of the reign of King Henry V after the conquest [29 July 1415]

Essoins John Swancote, William Bromlele, John Hollgreve, Thomas Toward, John Coletes & John Smyth themselves & each of them from common [suit] by Richard Bulveis

{Still a day is given between John Walker plaintiff & John Rowlow defendant in a
{plea of trespass until etc.
{And between John Cardmaker of Lichfeld plaintiff & Robert Galian taylor in a plea
{of debt under the law
{And between John Smyth of Soonde plaintiff and John Barndeleie defendant in a
{plea of trespass
Adjourned {Also the verdict of the inquiry of 12 ex officio at the suit of John Barndeleie
{adjourned until the next [court]
{Also the verdict of the inquiry of 24 ex officio of the tenement called Upyntoneslond
{adjourned until the coming of the steward
{And the verdict of the 24 ex officio of certain customs as is clear in the penultimate
{small court preceding adjourned as above

Distrain John White plaintiff against John Robynes in a plea of trespass pledge for the prosecution John Walker who is not attached so let it be

A day John the prior of Wombridge plaintiff against Richard Flynt in a plea of trespass pledge for the prosecution Richard Bulveis who have a day to agree until the next [court] by the prayer of the parties

Thomas Jankys senior plaintiff against William Newe in a plea of debt who seeks from the said William 3s 4d in silver which he owes and unjustly detains. And the said William present in court totally denies this. And thence they have a day for the law
The law until the next. Pledge for the law John Hethe

Roger Dalileie plaintiff against John Snel in a plea of debt pledge for the prosecution
The next Nicholas Stanlowe

John Aleyn and Emily his wife surrendered into the hands of the lady one messuage, half a virgate of land, one toft, half a nook of land, and 2 butts of land with appurtenances in Haalen of the right and inheritance of the same Emily to the use of Richard Aleyn their son and Agnes the wife of the same Richard. The which Richard and Agnes came here in court and took from the lady the aforesaid tenements to hold to themselves and the heirs of their bodies legitimately issuing from the lady by services and customs thence due according to the custom of the manor. And the aforesaid Emily before the steward confessed and examined acknowledged she did this voluntarily without coercion from her husband aforesaid. And if it should happen the aforesaid Richard and Agnes die without heirs of their bodies legitimately issuing then all the aforesaid tenements with their appurtenances are to revert & remain with

Fine 14s

the aforesaid John and Emily and their heirs to hold from the lady according to the custom of the manor. And they give to the lady for a fine 14s, made fealty to the lady and in the form aforesaid they are seised

Fine 2s

Verdict

John Hulle & Agnes his wife give to the lady 2s for a fine for an inquiry of the 24 to be held to enquire if William Barker by their custom was able to give to Agnes his daughter one toft and 1 nook of land of the tenement called Hoorelond in Haalen or not. And if the same Agnes after the death of her father aforesaid will have been able by their custom to draw to herself another nook of land of the same tenement or not. And whether the same John Hulle and Agnes his wife have a better right in that nook of land than William Stevenes & Margery his wife now tenants of the tenement aforesaid in their demand or the said William and Margery in their tenure. On which the inquiry was held by the oath of John Hethe, John Jonessonerowlowe, Robert Bruggende, William Webbe, Roger Gerbod, Thomas Rowlowe, Stephen Stanlow, John Snel, John Janne, John Bromleie, Nicholas Rowlow, Thomas Soonde, Richard Whitebrok, John Bullok, Thomas Tresel, William Yate, William Huster, Thomas Haslewode, Thomas Underhull, William Kyngessone, Richard Aldith, John Cattestre, William Heneme & John Stevenes who sworn and thence charged go out, return, and say on their oath that William Barker above-named is able to give theabove-named toft and nook of land aforesaid by their custom to Agnes his daughter. And that the same Agnes after the death of her father aforesaid is able by their custom to draw to herself another nook of land of the same tenement. They say also, the aforesaid jury, that the aforesaid John Hulle and Agnes his wife have a better right in that nook of land than the said William Stevenes and Margery his wife have in their demand than the said William and Margery have in their tenure by their custom. And they say that William Barker aforesaid on the day on which he died was not able to alienate by their custom the same nook of land from the said Agnes his daughter by their custom. Concerning the fine adjourned until better to be considered by the council of the lady

Supervise

Verdict

Supervise

Which at the judgment of the 12 at the suit of Robert Barker namely to enquire of the right of the same Robert in 1 toft and 1 nook of land called Feldhous in Haalen whether the same Robert has the better right in the same tenement in his demand or William Stevenes and Margery his wife in their tenure. On which the inquiry was held by the oath of John Rowlow, John Walker, John Hethe, Thomas Rowlow, John Bromleie, Stephen Stanlow, William Webbe, William Newe, Thomas Tresele, John Bullok, Richard Whitebrok & Richard Aldith who sworn and tried between the parties go out, return, and say on their oath that William Stevenes and Margery have a better right in the tenement aforesaid in their tenure than the said Robert Barker in his demand. On which it is judged that the same William and Margery should have the said tenement just as they formerly held. And concerning 12d for the fine to be paid to the lady adjourned until the next [court] because it is reported to the clerk of the court by Richard Bulveis that the said fine was previously paid as is clear by the record of the rolls here not obstructed on behalf of the lady to supervise if there is variance [or dispute perhaps?] between the petitioner the said Robert and the second

Strays remaining

All strays remaining in the last great court still remain

Tenement remains in the hand of the lady

Roger Richardes surrendered into the hands of the lady one messuage , half of one toft and three nooks of land with appurtenances in Newtone within the manor of Worfeld to rehold the said tenement with appurtenances to himself and Margery his wife, the heirs and assigns of the same Roger from the lady according to the custom of the manor. And thus it remains in the hand of the lady until a fine thence will be made with the lady

Increase on sale 2d

The bailiff is charged here concerning 2d or increase on the sale of one male colt bought at 12d in the last court preceding and coming as a stray of Roger Broke as is clear because it was sold for 14d

Sum of this court 16s 2d
Expenses of the steward 12d

1415-1416 P314/W/1/1/244

Worfeld	Great Court held there on Monday the 28th day of the month of October in the third year of the reign of King Henry V after the conquest [28 October 1415] with small court following [the roll is damaged in places so where … indicate a word is illegible it is lost]
Essoins	Nicholas Herdemon & Thomas Richardes themselves by Richard Bulveis & Roger Richardes
The 12	Robert Ewdenas, John Jonesone Rowlow, William Gerbod, Roger Cattestre, John Janne, John Rowlowe, Stephen Bradeneie, William Wermod, Roger Tounessend, Roger Richardes, Thomas Merwelle, William Newe } sworn
Kyngeslow, Stanlowe amerced 2s	townships there present that Thomas Tynker drew the blood (12d) of Alice Tynker. And that the same Alice raised the hue and cry justly (12d) on the said Thomas so the same Thomas both for the bloodshed and for the hue and cry is in mercy
Chesturtone	township there presents nothing
Hultone amerced 12d strays 4d	township there presents that Thomas the son of Richard Bradeneie made a poundbreach on Peter Hultone so the said Thomas is in mercy. And they say that there is there one swarm of bees in the custody of John the son of Stephen Bradeneie of a stray price 4d
Rowlow, Bradeneie, Asturhull, Ewyk, Soonde strays 4d waifs 3d amerced 4d	townships there present 1 stray swarm of bees in a tree of Thomas Haselwode in Bradeneie price 4d. And they say that Thomas the son of … Bradeneie unjustly took from the house called ….*hale Were* a certain instrument for fishing called …*Wile* price 3d so the said Thomas (4d) is in mercy
Roughtone, Barndeleie, Hoccombe, Swancote amerced 8d	townships there that William Skynner (8d) forestalled Roger Halidaie so the said William is in mercy
Burcote, Burcote, Ryndelford, Bromleie strays 8d	townships there present 2 stray swarms of bees price 8d and they remain in the custody of John Walker
Alvescote, Wynnescote, Cattestre, Newtone amerced 4d	townships there present that John Nicols (4d) who is bound to appear at this court did not appear so the said John is in mercy
Ewdenas, Oldyntone, amerced nothing as shown	townships there present nothing but that Richard Haselwode did not appear because he is infirm lying in bed

Stapelford amerced 18d — township there presents that Alice the wife of William Bakes made homsoken on on Thomas Underhull and made an assault on the said Thomas so the said Alice is in mercy both for the homesoken (8d) and for the assault (10d)

Akeltone waifs 6d amerced 16d — township there presents Florence the wife of Richard Boonde unjustly took from the house of William Baker 2 fleeces of wool price 6d so the said Florence (6d) is in mercy. And they say that John Astwelle made an assault on Roger Dalileie so the said John (10d) is in mercy

Wyke amerced 2s 4d — township there presents that Hamond Humeleie forestalled William Duddeleie and from the same William drew blood so the said Hamond both for the forestalling (8d) and for the bloodshed (12d) is in mercy. And they say that John Pomel (8d) forestalled Matilda Smyth so the said John is in mercy

Worfeld amerced 12d — township presents that Elcok (4d) Mustardmon, Richard Smyth (4d) and William Elwalle who are bound to make an appearance at this court did not appear so each of them in mercy

The tasters amerced 12s 9d — of ale present that John Hethe (6d) brewed 1, Hamund Humele (6d) 1, John Jonessone (6d) 1, Matilda Smyth (6d) 1, John Snel (6d) 1, Roger Dalleie (6d) 1, William Bakes (6d) 1, Matilda Stanlowe (6d) 1, William Noore (6d) 1, John Walle (6d) 1, Robert Bruggende (6d) 1, Richard Bulveis (pardoned by the steward 2, John Yate (12d) 2, Thomas Soonde (18d) 3, John Kynfartone (6d) 1, John Billyngesleie (6d) 1, John Smyth of Sonde (12d) 2, John Smyth of Wyke (6d) 1, William Newe (6d) 1, Alice Galian 2 not affeered as a fine was made, Alice Gerbod 1 of 8 bushels (3d), William Gold (6d) 1, Joan the daughter of William Noore (6d) 1, Stephen Humele (6d) 1, and all sold against the assize so each of them is in mercy

the 12 — jurors present and say on their oath that the townships aforesaid and the ale tasters faithfully presented. Also they say that the whole township of Roughtone is bound of right and custom to make a certain path near Reynesbrok at Roughtone. And they say that William Oldyntone who held from the lady one messuage and three half virgate of free land in Oldyntone within the manor of Worfeld on the day he died from whose death there falls to the lady one draught animal (affram) in the name of heriot price 12d and sold at the end of the court at a price higher by 6d. And they say that William Oldyntone son of the said William deceased, is the closest heir

heriot 18d

Fine 12d — William Oldyntone gives to the lord 12d for a fine for an inquiry of the 12 to be held to enquire if William his father would have been of full age at the time when he made title to Joan his sister of one messuage and three half virgates of free land in Oldyntone or not according to the manner of a charter made by John the Lord of Baggesore. On which the enquiry was held by the oath of the great inquiry above said which sworn and thence charged say on their oath that the said William at the time the alienation was made to Joan his sister by the same William was not except of age 18 years [18 years was added afterwards]

Haalen amerced 22d — township there presents that Margaret Tresel made an assault on Margery Jankys, forestalled and hit the said Margery so the said Margaret both for the assault (10d) and the forestalling (8d) and the blow (4d) is in mercy it is appraised by the oath of the great inquiry aforesaid

1415-1416 P314/W/1/1/244

strays 4s 2d	The bailiff here is charged of 4s 2d to be raised from 6 sheep coming as strays as is clear in the last great court of the year preceding just as in the same court appraised and no more in this court because it is found by the oath of the inquiry that 1 of the said sheep was dead from murrain before the feast of Easter
Fine 2s	Alice Galian gives to the lady 2s for a licence to be had to brew bread and ale to sell from the feast of St Michael last past until the said feast of St Michael next in the future just as agreed by the steward so that she should keep the assize
Fine 12d	Roger Warde came here in court and made a fine with the lady for a licence to be had to brew bread and ale to sell from the feast of St Michael last past until the said feast of St Michael next in the future namely for the term of one full year so that he should sell by legal measure and should keep the assize. And for a fine he gives 12d
The constables	John Walker of Ryndelford & Richard Underhull are elected constables and are sworn
Cattle nil 3s Waifs Supervise	Still the 12 jurors present 3 waif sheep in what manner and by whom is manifest by a bill in the custody of William Booreleie steward price 3s concerning which and other aforesaid waifs and strays the reeve is charged to respond to the better profit of the lady
Remains not affeered	William Noore is in mercy because he did not come to warrant his essoin at the last great court in the preceding year
[Worfeld]	Small court held there at the place, day, and year above-said
Amerced 14d	Inquiry held for the lady by the oath of Stephen Bradeneie, Roger Richardes, William Gerbod, John Janne, Roger Waltone, William Webbe, Roger Smyth, Thomas Towart, William Newe, John Jonesone Rowlow, Richard Aldith & John Hethe who sworn say on their oath that William Hemme (2d), John Stevenes (2d), Thomas Forster (2d), Thomas Broke (2d), Roger Batemon (2d), Thomas Richardes (2d) & John Nicols (2d), who are bound to make suit at this court did not come so each of them is in mercy
Adjourned	{A day is given here between John Walker plaintiff and John the son of Nicholas Rowlow {defendant in a plea of trespass {And between John Cardmaker of Lichfeld plaintiff & Robert Galian defendant in a {plea of debt whence the law {And between John Smyth of Soonde plaintiff and John Barndeleie defendant in a {plea of trespass {Also the verdict of the inquiry of the 12 ex officio at the suit of the said John {Barndeleie adjourned until the next [court] {Also the verdict of the inquiry of 24 ex officio concerning a certain custom just as {by the record of the rolls of the last year preceding adjourned as above {Still a day is given between John White plaintiff and John Robyns defendant in a {plea of trespass
Amerced 4d Distrain	John the Prior of Wombrugge plaintiff against Richard Flynt in a plea of debt pledge for the prosecution Richard Bulveis the which Richard Flynt attached and charged did not come so the same Richard is in mercy. And it is ordered to the bailiff to distrain the same Richard that he is at the next [court] to respond to the said Prior in the plea aforesaid

Amerced 6d — Thomas Jankys senior (6d) is in mercy because he is not prosecuting against William Newe in a plea of debt whence the law

Adjourned — Also a day is given between Roger Dalleie plaintiff and John Snel defendant in a plea of debt

The next — {John the Prior of Wombrugge plaintiff against William Flynt in a plea of debt who {is not summoned so let it be
{Thomas Tumpkys plaintiff against the said William Flynt & Margaret his wife in a {plea of debt
{Richard Underhull plaintiff against the said William Flynt & Margaret his wife in a {plea of trespass. Pledge for the prosecution Thomas Tumpkys
{Thomas Tumpkys plaintiff against the said William Flynt in a plea of trespass
{Thomas Soonde plaintiff against William Flynt and Margeret his wife in a plea of {trespass

The next — {Matilda Smyth plaintiff against John Ruyschcroft in a plea of debt }pledge for the
{The same Matilda plaintiff against John the son of Robert Smyth } prosecution
{in a plea of debt } John Hethe

Tenement remains in the hand of the lady — Still remaining in the hand of the lady 1 messuage, half of one croft and 3 nooks of land in Newtone from a surrender by Roger Richardes as clear in the last court in the preceding year

Election of the reeve — Roger Townesende withdrew from his office of reeve to which office came Thomas Underhull by the election of the aforesaid inquiry and is sworn

Fine 2s — Thomas Forster & Roger Batemon made this fine for suit of court to be commuted from the date of this court until the feast of St Michael the Archangel next in the future and each of them give to the lady for a fine 12d

Affeerors — John Hethe, Stephen Bradeneie

Sum of the great court with the small following 43s 10d

Expenses of the steward contained in the next small court following

Worfeld — Small court held there on Friday next after the feast of the Epiphany of the Lord in the third year of the reign of King Henry V after the conquest [11 January 1415]

Essoins — John Waltone & William Kyngessone of common suit by Roger Waltone & William Webbe

The 12

Roger Waltone	Roger Smyth	Henry Barker }	
John Hethe	Stephen Stanlow	John Bromleie }	sworn
John Walker	John Barndeleie	Roger Gerbod }	
William Newe	Thomas Toward	William Yate }	

Relief 6s 8d — William Oldyntone son and heir of William Oldyntone deceased made fealty to the lady and recognised himself to hold from the lady one messuage and three half virgates of free land in Oldyntone within the manor of Worfeld which tenement is charge annually of 3s 4d as of assized rent. And he gives to the lady for relief and ingress 6s 8d

Roger Richardes & Margaret his wife came here in court and took from the lady one messuage, half of one toft and three nooks of land with appurtenances in Newtone

Fine 14s	within the manor of Worfeld which tenements fell into the hands of the lady from a surrender of the same Roger as is clear in the last court in the preceding year to have and to hold the aforesaid tenement with its appurtenances to the aforesaid Roger and Margaret, the heirs and assigns of the same Roger from the lady by services thence due and accustomed according to the custom of the manor. And they give to the lady for a fine 14s, made fealty to the lady And in the form aforesaid are seised
Fine of Sowdeleie 5s	The reeve here is charged concerning 5s to be raised from the pasture and wood of Sowdeleie as for the enclosure from the time of this year
The 12 jurors Amerced 6d	present that John Stevenes (2d), Thomas Merwell junior (2d), and John Nicoles (2d) who are bound to make suit at this court did not come so each of them is in mercy
Amerced 6d	William Flynt (6d) put himself in mercy for a licence to agree with Thomas Tumpkys plaintiff in a plea of debt
Amerced 6d	The same William Flynt (6d) put himself in mercy for a licence to agree with the same Thomas plaintiff in a plea of trespass
Amerced 6d	The same William Flynt (6d) put himself in mercy for a licence to agree with Thomas Soonde plaintiff in a plea of trespass
Amerced 6d	John White plaintiff & John Robyns defendant in a plea of trespass are for a licence to agree. And the said John Robyns put himself in mercy
Amerced 6d Recover	John Janne plaintiff against Matilda Smyt in a plea of debt who seeks from the same 6s 6d which she owes to him and unjustly detains. And the same Matilda present in court recognised the said debt. And the said Matilda is in mercy
Amerced 6d Recover	William Newtone clerk plaintiff against Robert Ewdenas & Roger Smyt in a plea of debt. And he said that the same Robert & Roger owe to him 10s in silver which they promised to pay at a certain day & place at which they did not pay nor still but detain etc. And the said Robert & Roger present in court recognised the said debt so they are in mercy
Amerced 6d Recover Supervise to the next	Richard Underhull plaintiff against William Flynt & Margaret his wife in a plea of trespass. And he said that the same William & Margaret with their animals destroyed the meadow of the same Richard in Akeltone in the second year of the reign of King Henry V at the summer time to the damage of the same Richard of 12d. And the aforesaid William and Margaret recognised the trespass in part but not so much value and thence put themselves on the judgment of the 12 jurors and the aforesaid plaintiff similarly. And concerning the judgment it is adjourned until the next [court]. And the said William & M. are in mercy
Adjourned	{Still a day is given between John Walker plaintiff & John the son of Nicholas {Rowlow defendant in a plea of trespass until the next [court] {And between John Smyth of Soond plaintiff & John Barndele defendant in a plea of {trespass
Recover Remaining not affeered	Robert Galian who had a day for the law against John Cardmaker of Lichfeld in a plea of debt as is clear in the record of the rolls of the last year and the penultimate preceding defaulted of the same law so he and his pledge are in mercy. On which it is judged that the same John may have his debt with damages etc.

Adjourned

{Also a day is given between John the Prior of Wombrugge & Richard Flynt in a
{plea of debt
(And between the said John Prior plaintiff & William Flynt defendant in a plea of
{debt
(And between Roger Dalleie plaintiff & John Snel defendant in a plea of debt
{Also the verdict of the 24 ex officio of a certain custom adjourned until the next
{Also the inquiry of the 12 ex officio at the suit of John Barndel adjourned as above

Distrain

Still not prosecuting Matilda Smyth plaintiff against John Ruyscroft in a plea of debt who summoned did not come so distrain

Distrain

The same not prosecuting Matilda plaintiff against John Pomel in a plea of debt who summoned did not come so distrain

The next [court]

{Matilda Smyth not prosecuting plaintiff against Robert Smyth of Wyke in a plea of debt pledge for {the prosecution John Hethe
{The same Matilda not prosecuting plaintiff against William Yngemon in a plea of debt
{pledge for the prosecution John Hethe
{The same Matilda plaintiff against John Yate in a plea of debt pledge for the
{prosecution John Hethe

Fine 2s

At this court Richard Thorne & Margery Hugges came before the steward by their common agreement and for a fine of 2s to be paid by them to the lady they seek an inquiry by the 24 to be held to enquire by their oath whether the aforesaid Margery formerly the wife of Thomas Hugges has the better right in 1 messuage & 1 virgate of land with appurtenances in Hultone called Adameslond Upyntone in the manner and form which the aforesaid Margery claims to hold to herself, her heirs and assigns according to the custom of the manor and she demised not ever being examined of her will and confession or the aforesaid Richard because he claims the aforesaid lands and tenements after the death of the said Margery to himself, his heirs and assigns according to the custom of the manor from a surrender of Thomas Hugges and the aforesaid Margery formerly his wife into the hands of the lord to the use of the aforesaid Richard who is given a day Tuesday the 9th day of July in the 10th year of the reign of King Henry IV after the conquest to hold to himself, his heirs and assigns according to the custom of the manor after the which surrender the same Richard in the same year and day above-said surrendered the aforesaid lands and tenements into the hands of the lord to the use of the aforesaid Margery to have and to hold to the same Margery for the term of her life from the lord according to the custom of the manor and after her death the land and tenement aforesaid are to revert to the aforesaid Richard the heirs and assigns to hold from the lord according to the custom of the manor. On which the inquiry held by the oath of Roger Richardes, John Hethe, Roger Cattestre, Thomas Merwelle senior, Thomas Tresel, John Bromleie, Thomas Towart, Richard Aldith, Thomas Rowlow, Roger Gerbod, William Yate, William Bromleie, Thomas Soonde, William Newe, John Snel, Richard Whitebrok, John Coletes, Robert Barker, Nicholas Stanlow, Henry Barker , William Stevenes, William Gerbod, William Wermod & William Webbe who are sworn and to try between the parties aforesaid go out, return, and seek a day for the verdict thence to render until. And by the steward it is granted by the agreement of both parties

1415-1416 P314/W/1/1/244

Supervise Heriot & escheat nothing as shown	Still the 12 jurors present that William Rugge who held from the lady by the custom of the manor 3 cottages in Worfeld on the day he died whence concerning heriot and escheat at present nothing falls to the lady because nothing is yet able to be found but thence it should be better enquired into at the next [court]. And the tenement remains with Edith the widow of the said deceased by their custom
Supervise Fine 12d	Thomas atte Broke made a fine here for suit of court to be commuted from the date of this court until the feast of St Michael the Archangel next in the future. And he gives to the lady for a fine 12d
Affeerors	Stephen Bradeneie, John Hethe Sum of this court 32s 8d Expenses of William Boerleie steward accounted before him and to account as clear by the bill thence written in the custody of Richard Bulveis together with12d for the expenses of the clerk of the lady's court, of Richard Bulveis the reeve & the beadle being there at dinner for 1 day when 1 small court was held 28s 6d
Worfeld	View of Frankpledge held there with the small court following on Thursday the 14th day of May in the fourth year of the reign of King Henry V [14 May 1416]
Essoins	William Elwall himself from the view by John Byllyngesley
The 12	Robert Ewdenesse, John Walker, Roger Towneseynd, Roger Cattestre, John Hethe, Thomas Toward, Stephen Bradney, John Colynsone, William Warmod, Roger Waltone, William Gerbod, John Johnesone } sworn
Amerced 4d	Michael Hardman (4d) is in mercy because he did not come to warrant his essoin
Kyngeslow, Stanlow Strays 6d	townships there present one swarm of bees coming as a stray being in a certain tree of William Heme in Kyngeslowe
Chestertone stray remains	township there presents one black heifer coming as a stray at the feast of the Birth of our Lord last past price 14d and remaining in the custody of the reeve
Hyltone stray remains	township there presents one boar coming as a stray at the feast of St Andrew the Apostle last past price 14d and remaining in the custody of Peter Carpentier
Rowlow, Bradeney, Astyrhull, Ewyke, Sonde Amerced 3s 4d	townships there present that Thomas Sonde (8d) forestalled John Glover and from him drew blood (12d) so the same Thomas for the forestalling and the blood flow is in mercy. And that the same John Glover (8d) re-forestalled the said Thomas. And that the same Thomas justly raised the hue and cry on the said John (12d) so the same John both for the forestalling and the blood flow is in mercy
Roughtone, Barndeley, Hokkombe, Swancotes	townships there present nothing
Burcote, Burcote, Ryndelford, Bromleie	townships there present nothing

1415-1416 P314/W/1/1/244

Ewdenas, Oldyntone	townships there present nothing
Alvescote, Wynnescote, Cattestre, Newtone Pain	townships there present one pit made at Claymere whereby the king's road there is damaged to the nuisance of the neighbours by Margery Barker who has a day to properly repair the said defect before the next [court] under a pain of 3s 4d now not affeered because it is pardoned by the steward
Stapelford	township there presents nothing
Akeltone amerced 12d	township there presents that John Astwelle the bailiff of the hundred of Brimestre entered the house of William Flynt in Akeltone within the manor and liberty of Worfeld and took from thence without the presence of the bailiff of the same liberty 1 brass bowl in the name of distraint unjustly so the said John (12d) is in mercy
Haalen amerced 22d	township there presents Robert Taillour (2d) who is bound to make an appearance at this court did not appear so the said Robert in mercy. And they say that Thomas Underhull (8d) forestalled William Bates and from him drew blood (12d) so the said Thomas both for the forestalling and the bloodshed in mercy
Wyke	township there presents nothing
Worfeld amerced 2d	township there presents that Nicholas Herdemon (2d) who is bound to appear at this court did not appear so the same Nicholas is in mercy
The tasters of ale amerced 3s	present that Thomas Jankys junior (6d) brewed 1, Richard Bulveis (12d) 2, John Billyngesleie (6d) 1, Thomas Soonde (6d) 1, & John Smyth of Soonde (6d) 1. And that all sold against the assize so each of them is in mercy
The 12 jurors present Felony	& say on their oath that Richard Herdemon on Sunday after the feast of the Finding of the Holy Cross in the fourth year of the reign of King Henry V after the conquest came feloniously at Stapelford and there broke[into] the house of Thomas Underhull and there he feloniously took and carried away twenty shillings of silver of the same Thomas. And they say that the aforesaid Richard for the felony aforesaid withdrew himself and that he had no goods or chattels within the manor of Worfeld Also they say that the townships aforesaid and the tasters of ale have well and faithfully presented
Fine for trespass 6s 8d Waif cattle nothing here as shown	The reeve here is charged concerning 6s 8d to be raised from William Gerbod & Richard Gerbod for a fine of William Broke made for a trespass by the same William Broke namely because the same William Broke with force and arms and against the peace of the lord King took 3 sheep from Roger Waltone in Burcotefield within the manor of Worfeld concerning which sheep the bailiff was charged in the last great court aforesaid

The 12 for the small court	John Janne	Henry Barker	Roger Richardes }	
	Thomas Merwelle	William Webbe	Roger Gerbod }	sworn
	John Barndeleie	William Newe	Thomas Tresele }	
	John Bromleie	Robert Bruggende	Nicholas Rowlow }	

who say on their oath that Sibill Saundre who held from the lady by the custom of the manor one messuage, half of one virgate of land one toft with half a virgate of land with appurtenances in Newtone on the day she died whereof concerning heriot and escheat nothing falls to the lady because she had nothing on the day of her death of which tenements one messuage, half a virgate of land, half of one toft and one nook of land remain by their custom to Robert the son of the said Sibill by a fine thence previously made and half of one toft and one nook of land remain in the hand of the lady. And they say that the same Robert son of Sibill is the closest heir to take the said tenements. The which Robert came here in court and took from the hands of the lady the aforesaid half toft and nook of land with appurtenances to hold from the lady to himself and his [heirs] according to the custom of the manor. And he gives to the lady for a fine 5s. And he made fealty

Fine 5s

Heriot 16d Escheat nothing for the reason shown

And they say that Alice Janne who held from the lady by the custom of the manor one toft & half a virgate of land with appurtenances in Bromleie has died whereof there falls to the lady in the name of heriot one ram price 16d concerning which the bailiff is charged to respond to the greater profit of the lady. And concerning escheat nothing falls because they would have been nothing on the day of her death. And they say that the aforesaid remains with John the son of the same Alice by virtueof a fine thence previously made

And they say that Agnes Knyght who held from the lady by the custom of the manor one cottage with curtilage at Ryndelforde has died whereof concerning heriot and escheat nothing falls due because there was nothing on the day of her death. And the tenement remains in the hand of the lady. And they say that Roger Knyght is her closest heir. The which Roger came and took from the lady the aforesaid tenement to hold to himself and his [heirs] from the lady according to the custom of the manor. And he gives to the lady for a fine 8d. And he made fealty

Fine 8d

John Hethe & Alice his wife surrendered into the hands of the lady one toft and half of one virgate of land called Ammeplace with appurtenances in Kyngeslowe to the use of Roger their son and Isabell his wife to hold from the lady to the said Roger & Isabell and the heirs legitimately procreated between them according to the custom of the manor. And if it should happen that the said Roger & Isabell die without heirs of their bodies legitimately procreated then the aforesaid tenement with appurtenances should remain with the aforesaid Alice and her heirs to hold from the lady according to the custom of the manor. And they give to the lady for a fine 8s. They made fealty and are seized of the said tenement thus granted by the steward to hold from the lady in the form aforesaid according to the custom of the manor

Fine 8s

To this court comes Nicholas Rowlow & surrendered into the hands of the lady one one messuage & three nooks of land with appurtenances in Rowlowe within the manor of Worfeld to re-hold the said tenement with appurtenances to himself and Margery his wife for the term of the life each of them to hold from the lady according to the custom of the manor. And after their deaths that the said tenement with its appurtenances will remain with John their son and Margery his wife, the heirs & assigns of the same John. And in a similar way they are granted by the steward to the aforesaid Nicholas & Margery his wife for the term of the life of each of them to hold from the lady according to the custom of the manor. And after their deaths to the aforesaid John & Margery his wife,to the heirs & assigns of the same John to hold from the lady according to the custom of the manor. And they give to the lady for a fine 11s 8d. And they are seized

Fine 11s 8d

1415-1416 P314/W/1/1/244

Fine 12d

John Nicoles gives to the lady 12d for suit of court to be commuted from the feast of Easter last past until the said feast of Easter next in the future namely for 1 full year pledge for the fine William Newtone clerk

Fine 4d

John Glover surrendered into the hands of the lady one parcel of land called Chilternegrene in the townships of Kyngeslow & Stanlow within the manor of Worfeld to the use of Nicholas Stanlowe the which Nicholas came here in court and took from the lady the aforesaid parcel of land to hold to himself and his {heirs] from the lady by services & customs thence due according to the custom of the manor. And he gives to the lady for a fine 4d. And he made fealty

Adjourned until the next [court]

William Gerbod plaintiff against Henry Barker in a plea of accounts because in the time in which the aforesaid William Gerbod was reeve of the lady namely in the second year of the now King he had under him the said Henry Barker in the aforesaid year Beadle to raise and collect rents, fines, amercements & services as it pertained to the aforesaid Henry for the reason of his tenure at the time aforesaid on which the said William was charged by the lady of the raising aforesaid and whereof in such a way that the said William aforesaid often interrogated with him to account before this time the aforesaid Henry to do this he refused to do so and still refuses whence the aforesaid William brought a suit. And at this the aforesaid Henry comes here in court and defends himself and says that he is ready [paratus est] to account according as the court judged etc. And on this he is assigned by the chief steward William Aleyn & Henry Dunfowe auditors to hear the account aforesaid etc.

Fine 12d
Adjourned as is clear

John Hulle gives to the lady 12d for a fine to have an inquiry by the 12 ex officio to enquire to be shown and defined which and how much of one toft and half of one virgate of land called Horeplace in Haalen of right and custom pertains to himself and Agnes his wife. On which the inquiry was held by the oath of Roger Cattestre, William Wermod, Henry Barker, John Billyngesleie, Robert Barker, Robert Hawkys, Thomas Tresele, John Holigreve, Roger Townessende, John Bullok, John Cattestre & Richard Aleyn who sworn and thence charged went out returned and seek thence a day for the verdict until the next [court] on account of the shortness of time

Amerced 6d — John Flynt put himself in mercy for a licence to agree with John Priore of Wombrugge in a plea of debt

Amerced 6d — William Flynt put himself in mercy for a licence to agree with the said Priore in a plea of debt

Roger Dalleie plaintiff & John Snel defendant in a plea of debt are for a licence to agree. And the said John put himself in mercy

Amerced 6d — Matilda Smyth (6d) is in mercy because she did not }
prosecute against Joan Ruyschcroft in a plea of debt }

Amerced 6d — The same Matilda (6d) is in mercy because she did not
prosecute against John Pomel in a plea of debt }

The same Matilda (6d) is in mercy because she did not } pledge for the prosecution
prosecute against Robert Smyth of Wyke in a plea of debt } John Hethe

Amerced 12d — The same Matilda (6d) is in mercy because she did not }
prosecute against William Yngemon in a plea of debt }

Amerced 6d

The bailiff is charged here concerning 6d to raise from Robert Galian taylor (6d) & his amercement because of the default of his law against John Cardmaker of Lichfeld in a plea of debt

1415-1416 P314/W/1/1/244

Adjourned	{Still a day is given between John Walker plaintiff & John the son of Nicholas {Rowlow defendant in a plea of trespass {And between John Smyth of Soonde plaintiff & John Barndeleie defendant in a plea {of trespass {And between Matilda Smyth plaintiff & John Yate defendant in a plea of trespass
The next	Thomas Toward plaintiff against William Flynt and Margaret his wife in a plea of debt
Distrain	Margaret Tresel plaintiff against Margery Jankys in a plea of trespass who is not attached so let it be done
Adjourned	{Also the verdict of the 12 ex officio at the suit of John Barndeleie adjourned as {above {And the verdict of the inquiry of the 24 of the right between Richard Thorne and {Margery Hugges adjourned as above
Affeerors	John Walker, Roger Townesende Sum of this great court with the small 49s 10d Expenses of the steward 13s 5d
Remaining not affeered	Still amerce William Noore because he did not warrant his essoin as is clear in the last great court preceding remaining not affeered

1416-1417 P314/W/1/1/245

Worfeld

Great Court held there on Friday the 9th day of the month of October in the fourth year of the reign of King Henry V after the conquest [9 October 1416]

Essoins

Robert Taillour himself from appearance by John Billyngesle
Richard Bradeneie for the same by Nicholas Rowlow
William Hemme/Henene for the same by John Hethe
William Noore for the same by John Rowlow

The 12

Robert Ewdenas	Thomas Merwelle	John Jonesserowlowe	}
John Walker	Roger Richardes	William Wermod	} sworn
Roger Waltone	Thomas Tumpkys	John Hethe	}
Stephen Bradeneie	Roger Cattestre	William Newe	}

Kyngeslow, Stanlowe
Strays 4d

townships there present 1 swarm of bees being a stray in a tree of Roger Hethe price 4d whence the bailiff is charged to respond to the greater profit of the lady

Chesturtone
Amercements & Fines for trespass 26s 2d
Abandoned goods 12d

township there presents that John Stevenes who is bound to appear at this court did not appear so the said John (4d) is in mercy. And they say that the same John Stevenes forestalled John Hulle and drew blood from him so the same John Stevenes both for the forestalling (8d) and the bloodshed (12d) is in mercy. And they say that Nicholas Beck made an assault on Richard Underhull the constable and unjustly raised the hue and cry on the constable so the same Nicholas both for the assault (6d) and for the raising of the hue and cry (12d) is in mercy. And they say that William Buldewas forestalled Thomas Mansell and from him drew blood. And that a certain stranger woman whose name is not known raised the hue and cry justly on the said William so the said William both for the forestalling (8d) and for the bloodshed (12d) and for the raising of the hue and cry (12d) is in mercy. Also they say that Simon Rugge forestalled Edith Stevenes so the said Simon (8d) is in mercy. And they say that the same Edith reforestalled the said Simon and drew blood from him so the same Edith both for the forestalling (8d) and for the bloodshed (12d) is in mercy. Also they say that Thomas Rugge forestalled Margaret Stevenes and drew blood from her so the said Thomas both for the forestalling (8d) and the bloodshed (12d) is in mercy. And they say that Margaret Tresele unjustly and against the peace of the lord King entered the house of John Snel in Chesturtone and from him unjustly took salt and ale price 4d so the said Margaret (12d) is in mercy. Also they say that Agnes Stevenes broke an arrest made by the bailiff of the lady so the same Agnes is at a fine (6s). Also they say that Margaret Tresele unjustly unsealed and broke the doors sealed by the bailiff of the lady in Chesturtone for rent and services owed to the lady so the said Margaret thence at a fine (3s 4d). And they say that the same Margaret unjustly took 6 silver spoons put in a certain chest and arrested by the bailiff of the lady against the defence of the bailiff of the lady so the same Margaret thence at a fine (3s 4d). And they say that John Stevenes unjustly and against the peace of the lord King took one sheep of Stephen Bradeneie price of the sheep 8d. So the said John (3s 4d) is in mercy

Hultone
Strays 18d

township there presents 1 stray swarm of bees held in a certain tree in the same township on Hultonegrene which swarm was taken at night by whom they do not know but afterwards a fine was thence made for 18d to be raised to the use of the lady from the vicar of the church of Worfeld

Rowlow, Bradeney, Asturhull, Ewyk, Soonde Amerced 20d Strays 2d	townships there present that Roger Gille forestalled (8d) William Underwode and from the said William drew blood (12d). So the said Roger is in mercy. And they say that in a certain tree of Alice Bradeneie is 1 swarm of stray bees price 2d whence the bailiff is charged to respond to the better profit of the lady
Roughtone, Barndeley, Hoccombe, Swancote Amercements and fines 7s	townships there present that William Kyngessone (4d) who is bound to appear at this court did not appear so the said William is in mercy. Also they say that William Broke broke an arrest made by the bailiff of the lady so the said William thence at a fine (3s 4d). And they say that when the doors of the houses of Thomas Jankys were sealed by the bailiff of the lady in the name of distraint for rent and services being in arrears, Thomas Jankys junior unsealed and broke the said seals. So the same Thomas thence is at a fine (3s 4d)
Burcote, Burcote, Ryndelford, Bromley	townships there present nothing
Alvescote, Wynnescote, Cattestre, Newtone Amerced 18d	townships there present that Thomas Richardes (3d) & Thomas Cattestre (3d) did not appear so each of them is in mercy. Also they say that Sibill Soonde broke the pound of John Jowkys so the said Sibill (12d) is in mercy
Ewdenas, Oldyntone, Amerced 20d	townships there present that Sibill Soonde made a poundbreach on John Jowkys so the said Sibill (12d) is in mercy. And they say that Roger the servant of Robert Ewdenas forestalled Richard Okeleie so the same Roger (8d) is in mercy
Stapelford To enquire	township there presents one stray swarm of bees in a certain tree of Richard Aldith which stray is removed by whom they are still ignorant so the truth is being enquired into before the next [court]
Akeltone Goods abandoned 15½d amerced4s 10d Strays remain	township there presents 1 draught animal (affrum) coming as a stray at the Feast of the Nativity of St John the Baptist last past and is in the custody of the reeve price of the draught animal 10d. Also they say that Roger Hethe unjustly and against the peace of the lord King took 1 sheep from Margery the daughter of Thomas Tresele price of the sheep 6d. And they say that the same Margery (12d) & …took from the said Roger unjustly 1 pound of wool price 3d. And for the trespass on the said Roger (20d) is in mercy. Also they say that the same Roger (20d) unjustly and against the peace of the lord King took one sheep of Nicholas Rowlow price 6½d. So the said Roger is in mercy. And they say that Thomas Tresele with force and arms and against the peace of the lord King entered the house of the aforesaid Roger in Akeltone so the said Thomas (6d) is in mercy
Haalen Strays 4d	township there presents nothing but there is in a certain tree of Robert Barker 1 swarm of bees price 4d whence the bailiff is charged to respond to the greater profit of the lady
Wyke	township there presents nothing
Worfeld Fine for trespass 5s	township there presents that Margaret Tresele unjustly took Edith Stevenes from the custody of the bailiffs of the lady. So the said Margaret thence at a fine of 5s

1416-1417 P314/W/1/1/245

The tasters of ale Amerced 5s 8d	present that Stephen Bradeneie (6d) brewed 1, Julian atte Walle (6d) 1, Hamund Humeleie (6d) 1, John Gerbod (6d) 1, William Wermod (6d) 1, John Billyngesleie (12d) 2, Katherine Bulveis 2 (pardoned by the steward), Thomas Gille (6d) 1, Alice Soonde (12d) 2, Margery Smyth of Soonde (6d) 1. And the say that Joan Yngmon (2d) is a regrater of ale and that all sold against the assize so each of them is in mercy
The 12 jurors Amerced 3s Supervise	present and say on their oath that Thomas Jankys junior came at night to the house of Thomas Rowlowe in Burcote and there secretly stood beside the walls of the house hid himself from Thomas and his family to listen and see and he began to enter through one window of the house of Thomas Rowlowe. So the said Thomas Jankys (3s) is in mercy. Also they say that from the house of Roger Coriour in Worfeld was taken and stolen 2s in money by who or by whom & on which day they seek a day for the truth thence to render until the next great court. Further they say that the townships aforesaid and the tasters of ale have well and faithfully presented
Constables	Roger Townesende & John Jonkys are elected to the office of constable. And they are sworn
Fine for Sowdele 3s 4d	The bailiff here is charged concerning 3s 4d to be raised from the issue and profit of the wood and pasture of Sowdeleie as for the enclosure at this time of the year and no more because this year there was no mast
Appropriation	William Pype of Billestone came here before the steward and appropriated one black heifer presented fas a stray by the township of Chesturtone as clear in the last great court of the preceding year & of the same heifer he has handing over by the steward
Worfeld	Small court held there on the day and in the year above-said
The 12	Roger Richardes, William Webbe, Thomas Tresele, Roger Waltone, John Barndeleie, William Newe, Stephen Bradeneie, Thomas Towart, John Janne, William Gerbod, Richard Aldith, Nicholas Rowlow } sworn
Fine 3s	Richard Bradeneie, Thomas Broke & Roger Batemon made here a fine for suit of court to be commuted from the date of this court until the feast of St Michael next in the future. And each of them gives to the lady for a fine 12d
Fine 12d	John Robynes gives to the lady for a fine 12d for suit of court to be commuted from the date of this court until the feast of St Michael next in the future.
Fine 12d	Margery Huster surrendered into the hands of the lady one toft with curtilage in Soonde which William Hounesworth formerly held to the use of Thomas Foxhale & Agnes his wife. The which Thomas & Agnes came here in court & took from the lady the aforesaid toft and curtilage with appurtenances to hold to themselves and their heirs from the lady according to the custom of the manor by services and customs thence owed. And they give for a fine 12d, made fealty And they are seized
The 12 jurors Amerced 4d Heriot 8s 6d Escheat 2s 6d	present that John Stevenes (2d), Thomas Forster (pardoned by the steward) & Thomas Richardes (2d) who are bound to make suit at this court did not come so each of them is in mercy. And they say that John atte Welle who held from the lady by the custom of the manor one messuage and three nooks of land in Hultone on the day he died whence there falls to the lady in the name of heriot 1 black ox price 8s

6d. And for escheat 3 young pigs price 2s 6d concerning which heriot and escheat the bailiff is charged to respond to the better profit of the lady. And they say that the tenement aforesaid by their custom remains with Juliana the widow of the same deceased

Pain recovered 6s 8d — And they say that Thomas Jankys junior is prosecuted against John Bromleie by a writ of the lord King outside the manor against an ordinance thence ordained by agreement of the whole homage. So he incurs a pain of 6s 8d thence previously ordained in the seventeenth year of the reign of King Richard II as is clear by the rolls of the court of the same year

Election of the reeve — Thomas Underhull withdrew here from the office of reeve which office is approached by John Walker. And he is sworn by the election of the aforesaid inquiry

Fine 12d — To this court comes Richard Smyth & surrenders into the hands of the lady one cottage with curtilage adjacent in Worfeld which formerly John Gerbod held to the use of Elias Mustardmon. The which Elias came here in court and took from the lady the aforesaid cottage with curtilage to hold to himself and his [heirs] from the lady according to the custom of the manor. And he gives to the lady for a fine 12d And he is seized. And he made fealty

Fine 6d — Elias Mustardmon surrendered into the hands of the lady 2 selions of land lying separately in Hultonesfield whence 1 lies on the Merschforlong & the other lies on the Overeforlong to the use of Richard Smyth. The which Richard came here in court & takes from the lady the aforesaid selions of land with appurtenances to hold to himself and his [heirs] from the lady according to the custom of the manor. And he gives to the lady for a fine 6d And he made fealty And he is seized.

Fine 13s 4d — To this court comes Margery Hugges & surrenders into the hands of the lady one toft & one virgate of land called Upyntoneslond in Hultone to the use of Richard Thorne The which Richard came here in court and took from the lady the aforesaid toft and virgate of land with appurtenances to hold to himself and his [heirs] from the lady according to the custom of the manor. And he gives to the lady for a fine 13s 4d, made fealty And is seized

Fine 13s 4d — Richard Thorne above-named surrenders into the hands of the lady one toft & one virgate of land called Upyntoneslond in Hultone within the manor of Worfeld to the use of Margery Hugges. The which Margery came here in court and took from the lady the aforesaid toft and virgate of land with appurtenances to hold to herself, her heirs & assigns from the lady by services and customs thence owed according to the custom of the manor. And she gives to the lady for a fine 13s 4d , made fealty, and is seized

A day — {Still a day is given between John Walker plaintiff and John the son of Nicholas
{Rowlow defendant in a plea of trespass
{And between Thomas Toward & William Flynt & Margaret his wife defendants in a
{plea of debt

Amerced 6d — Matilda Smyth (6d) is in mercy because she is not prosecuting against John Pomel in a plea of debt

Amerced 6d — Margaret Tresele (6d) is in mercy because she is not prosecuting against Margery Jankys in a plea of trespass

1416-1417 P314/W/1/1/245

Amerced 4d	John Smyt of Soonde (4d) is in mercy because he is not prosecuting against John Barndeleie in a plea of trespass
The next	Thomas Merwalle plaintiff against Thomas Jankys junior in a plea of debt
Con.?	Agnes Mathew plaintiff against the said Thomas Jankys junior in a plea of debt pledge for the prosecution John Mathew
Distrain	John Rowlow plaintiff against John Pomel in a plea of debt who summoned did not come so distrain
Distrain	Thomas Soonde plaintiff against John Stevenes [essoined] in a plea of debt who summoned did not come so distrain
Summon Adjourned to the next	John Cook & Alice his wife plaintiffs against Margaret Tresele in a plea of detention of goods pledge for the prosecution John Billyngesleie who is not summoned so let it be done
Tried as clear	The verdict of the 12 between John Bardeleie & John Smyth of Soonde tried and settled by agreement of the parties
Verdict	Concerning the verdict of the inquiry of the 24 held on a certain day at this court for the full verdict to be rendered of the right of one toft and one virgate of land called Adames Upyntone in Hultone between Margery Hugges & Richard Thorne which of them has the better right in the aforesaid tenement. Appeared here before the steward the 24 namely Roger Richardes, John Hethe, Roger Cattestre, Thomas Merwell senior, Thomas Tresel, John Bromleie, Thomas Towart, Richard Aldith, Thomas Rowlow, Roger Gerbod, William Yate, William Bromleie, Thomas Soonde, William Newe, John Snel, Richard Whitebrok, John Coletes, Robert Barker, Nicholas Stanlowe, Henry Barker, William Stevenes, William Gerbod, William Wermod & William Webbe who say on their oath that concerning the right of the tenement aforesaid they have nothing now to present because the parties aforesaid thence fully and wholly are agreed as is clear above by a fine thence made with the lady etc. Furthermore the aforesaid 24 jurors are charged by the steward to enquire on this that is found in a certain old roll of the court of Worfeld held on Monday next after the feast of St John Before the Latin Gate in the 29th year of the reign of King Edward III after the conquest. Richard the Hoore and Emma his wife the closest heirs of Agnes Adames came in court and surrendered into the hands of the lord one messuage and one virgate of land with appurtenances in Hultone to the use of Roger Goolde and Joan his wife. To hold to themselves and their [heirs] according to the custom of the manor so that the aforesaid Roger and Joan will find for the aforesaid Agnes for the whole of her life sufficient food and clothing. And they give to the lord for a fine 13s 4d. If that surrender is just by their customs or not because the aforesaid Agnes at that time was living & no surrendered was thence made. On which the aforesaid 24 sworn and thence charged by the steward went out, returned, and say on their oath that that surrender thus by the aforesaid Richard & Emma was made well and justly by their custom here not withstanding that the aforesaid Agnes at that time was living and no surrender was thence made for it and from because the aforesaid Agnes then was mute and out of mind in which case they say on their oath that the aforesaid Richard & Emma as closest heirs of the aforesaid Agnes were able to surrender and to alienate well and legitimately according to the custom of the manor there and still in a similar case other closest heirs are well able
Adjourned	Still a day is given between William Gerbod plaintiff & Henry Barker defendant in a plea of account

The next	John Tresele plaintiff against Thomas Jankys junior in a plea of debt pledge for the prosecution Thomas Tresele who not summoned so let it be done
A day	Henry Barker plaintiff against Thomas Heyne in a plea of broken agreement who have a day to agree until the next
Affeerors	John Jonessonerowlowe, John Janne Sum of this great court with the small following £5 16s 11½d. Expenses of the steward 16s 6d
Worfeld	Small court held there on Thursday the 17th day of the month of November in the fourth year of the reign of King Henry V after the conquest [17 November 1416]
Essoins	William Newe, John Stevenes, John Coletes, John Bromleie, John Holigreve, Thomas Merwelle senior, Thomas Richardes & John Cattestre themselves from common suit by John Billynges
The 12 jurors Amerced 9d Pain	The inquiry held for the lady by the oath of Stephen Bradeneie, John Janne, John Hethe, William Gerbod, Roger Townessende, John Bromleie, William Webbe, William Wermode, Roger Richardes, Thomas Towart, John Jonessone & Nicholas Stanlowe who say on their oath that William Newtone (3d) clerk, Thomas Forster (3d), Robert Saundres (3d) who are bound to make suit at this court did not come so each of them is in mercy. Also they say that there are great defects in the mills of the lady namely in the roofs and the repair of the walls of the houses of the said mills. On which on behalf of the lady it is ordered to all and singular who are bound of right and custom to repair the said defects that they properly repair within the period of 15 days following ~~now~~ now in the future with the supervision of Richard Bulveis & John Walker of Ryndelford under a pain to pay 20s to the lady
Pain	Inquiry of the 12 ex officio at the suit of John Hulle have a day to show and to limit the diverse metes and bounds of the tenement of the same John before the feast of the Epiphany of the Lord now next in the future for a certain fine made in advance with the lady under a pain of each of the jurors to pay 12d to the lady
Adjourned	Still a day is given between John Walker plaintiff & John the son of Nicholas Rowlow defendant in a plea of trespass
Amerced 4d Distrain	{Thomas Towart plaintiff against Margaret Flynt in a plea of debt who attached and {charged did not come so the same Margaret (4d) is in mercy. And it is ordered she is {better attached before the next
Amerced 4d Distrain	{Thomas Merwelle junior plaintiff against Thomas Jankys junior in a plea of debt {who attached and charged did not come so he is in mercy. Furthermore it is ordered {to better distrain that he is at the next [court] to respond to the said Thomas Merwell {in the plea aforesaid
Amerced 6d	Thomas Jankys junior put himself in mercy for a licence to agree with Agnes Mathes in a plea of debt
Distrain	John Rowlow plaintiff against John Pomel in a plea of debt who is still not attached because it is not possible as is presented by the oath of the bailiff so let it be done

Adjourned	{Still a day is given between Thomas Sonde plaintiff & John Stevenes defendant in a {plea of debt {And between John Cook & Alice his wife plaintiffs and Margaret Tresel defendant {in a plea of detention of goods
Amerced 6d	Henry Barker put himself in mercy for a licence to agree with Thomas Heyne defendant in a plea of broken agreement
Amerced 4d Distrain	John Tresel plaintiff against Thomas Jankys junior in a plea of debt pledge for the prosecution Thomas Tresele the which Thomas Jankys attached and charged did not come so he is in mercy. And it is ordered to better distrain him before the next
Distrain	Alice the daughter of Roger Hattone plaintiff against Thomas Jankys junior in a plea of debt pledge for the prosecution Thomas Tresele who summoned did not come so to distrain. And the aforesaid Thomas becomes attorney for the aforesaid Alice
Fine 2d	John Walker of Ryndelford took here one parcel of land lying in Ryndelford between the land of John himself to hold the said parcel of land to himself and his[heirs] from the lady rendering thence annually to the lady at the time of St Michael a halfpenny and other services according to the custom of the manor. And so it is granted by Richard Bulveis in the name of the steward under condition if it pleases the lady and her council or until another will have come who thence will be able to render greater. And for a fine he gives to the lady 2d
Affeerors	Roger Richardes, William Webbe Sum of this small court 2s 11d Expenses of the steward 12d
Worfeld	Small court held there on Friday next after the Conversion of St Paul in the fourth year of the reign of King Henry V after the conquest [30 January 1417]
Essoins	Roger Kyngeslowe, Robert Saundres & Thomas Rowlowe themselves from common [suit] by John Walker
Amerced 6d	John Stevenes (6d) is in mercy because he did not come to warrant his essoin at the last court preceding
the 12	Roger Waltone, John Hethe, Thomas Towart } Stephen Bradeneie, John Jonessonerowlowe, Roger Gerbode } sworn John Rowlowe, William Wermode, William Newe } John Barndeleie, Roger Townessende, William Webbe }
Fine 12d The next	12d is given to the lady for a fine for an inquiry by the 12 ex officio to be held is Benedicta the wife of Thomas Rowlowe & John her son by the custom of the manor were able to make title of one messuage & one virgate of land in Hultone which were lately Thomas Rowlowe's or not. On which the inquiry was held by the oath of the 12 whose names are above named who thence seek a day for the full verdict to render until the next and it is granted. Pledge for the fine Richard Bulveis
Fine 20d	Thomas Tresele surrendered into the hands of the lady one cottage in Alvescote on the green to the use of John his son the which John came here in court and took from the lady the aforesaid cottage with appurtenances. To hold to himself and his from the lady by services & customs thence owed according to the custom of the manor. And he gives to the lady for a fine 20d just as agreed by Richard Bulveis in the name of the steward he made fealty And so he is seised

1416-1417 P314/W/1/1/245

John Stevenes son of William Stevenes of Chesturton surrendered into the hands of the lady one messuage and half a virgate of land called Huggelond in Chesturtone and one toft and half a virgate of land called Goselond in the same Chesturtone to the use of John the son of Roger Smyth of Hultone the which John the son of Roger came here in court and took from the lady the aforesaid tenements with appurtenances to hold to himself and his heirs from the lady by services & customs thence owed according to the custom of the manor. And he gives to the lady for a fine 20s. And he made fealty to the lady pledge for the fine Roger Smyth

Fine 20s

Roger Turnor came here & took from the lady one croft of land lying in Bromleiefield & for a long time lying in the hands of the lords of the manor of Worfeld for want of tenants. To hold the said croft land to the said Roger & his [heirs] from the lady by services thence from ancient times owed and accustomed according to the custom of the manor. And he gives for a fine 2d just as granted by Richard Bulveis made fealty And he is seized

Fine 2d

Richard Walker took from the lady two parcels of land lying by Haalenholeweye in the field of Haalen which were lying in the hand of the lady for want of tenants. To hold the aforesaid 2 parcels of land with appurtenances to himself and his [heirs] from the lady rendering thence annually to the lady at the usual times 3d and other services according to the custom of the manor & for a fine he gives 3d just as granted in the name of the steward as for better by Richard Bulveis until others will come who are able to render greater

Fine 3d

William Engliche surrendered into the hands of the lady 2 cottages with curtilages adjacent and their appurtenances in Haalen within the manor of Worfeld to the use of John Walker his heirs and assigns. And thus they remain in the hand of the lady until a fine was thence made provided that the same William will re-hold the said tenement for the term of his life from the lady according to the custom of the manor

Tenement remains in the hand of the lady

The 12 jurors present that Edith Broke widow of the lady married herself to Thomas atte Broke outside the manor who thence made a fine with the lady. And he gives for a fine as is clear

Fine half a mark

And that Edith the daughter of Henry Barker widow of the lady married herself outside the manor to John Elcok who thence made a fine with the lady. And he gives for a fine [blank]

Fine

And that Juliana atte Walle widow of the lady married herself to Thomas Baker within the manor who thence made a fine with the lady. And gives for a fine [blank]

Fine

And that Thomas Rowlowe married Margery his daughter outside the manor to Roger Cherlecote a licence from the lady not obtained who thence made a fine with the lady. And he gives for a fine 10s

Fine 10s

{Still a day is given between John Walker plaintiff & John the son of Nicholas
{Rowlow defendant in a plea of trespass until
{And between Thomas Soonde plaintiff & John Stevenes defendant in a plea of debt

Adjourned

{Still Thomas Towart plaintiff against Margaret Flynt in a plea of debt who is not
{attached because she had nothing whence they were able according as is presented
{by the oath of the bailiff further it is ordered to the bailiff on behalf of the lady that
{he distrain the said Margaret that she is at the next [court] to respond to the said
{Thomas in the plea aforesaid

Distrain

1416-1417 P314/W/1/1/245

Amerced 4d Distrain	Thomas Merwalle junior plaintiff against Thomas Jankys junior in a plea of debt who attached & charged did not come so the same Thomas is in mercy. And it is ordered the same Thomas be better distrained before the next [court]
Amerced 6d	John Pomel put himself in mercy for a licence to agree with John Rowlowe plaintiff in a plea of debt
Amerced 4d Distrain	Still John Tresel plaintiff against Thomas Jankys junior in a plea of debt the which Thomas attached & charged did not come so the same Thomas is in mercy. And it is ordered the same Thomas be better distrained before the next [court]
Amerced 4d Distrain	Alice the daughter of Roger Hattone plaintiff against the said Thomas Jankys junior in a plea of debt who attached & charged did not come so he is in mercy. And it is ordered to better distrain him before the next [court] to respond to the said Alice in the plea aforesaid
Amerced 6d	Richard Ewdenas put himself in mercy for a licence to agree with Thomas Haselwode plaintiff in a plea of debt
Distrain	Thomas Tresele plaintiff against Thomas Jankys junior in a plea of trespass who is not attached so let it be done
Distrain	John Pipar of Stottesdone & Alice his wife plaintiffs against Thomas Jankys junior in a plea of debt pledge for the prosecution John Walker who summoned did not come so distrain
Distrain	William Newe plaintiff against Thomas Jankys junior in a plea of debt who summoned did not come so distrain
Distrain	William Broke plaintiff against Thomas Jankys junior in a plea of debt pledge for the prosecution John Rowlowe who summoned did not come so distrain
Adjourned	{Still a day is given between William Gerbod plaintiff & Henry Barker defendant in {a plea of accounts {And between John Cook & Alice his wife plaintiffs and Margaret Tresele defendant {in a plea of detention of goods
Strays remaining	{Still remaining in the custody of Peter Carpenter 1 boar presented as a stray in the {last great court in the preceding year. Also remaining in the custody of the reeve 1 {draught animal presented as a stray in the last great court in the preceding {year by the township of Akeltone
Affeerors	John Hethe, John Janne Sum of this small court beyond the fines of Edith daughter of Henry Barker & Juliana atte Welle widows of the lady still not tried 62s 3d Expenses of Richard Bulveis clerk of the court the reeve & the beadle 12d

1416-1417 P314/W/1/1/245

Worfeld	Great court held there on Monday 20th day of the month of April in the fifth year of the reign of King Henry V [20 April 1417]
Essoins	Thomas Richardes & William Nore & Nicholas Herdemon from appearance by John Walker
The 12 jurors	Robert Eudenas, Stephen Bradeney, John Hethe, Roger Cattestre, Roger Waltone, John Barneley, John Jankys, John Jonessonrowlowe, Thomas Toward, Thomas Tomkys, William Wermod, Roger Gerbot } sworn
Kyngelowe, Stanlowe	townships there present nothing
Chesturtone	township there presents nothing
Hultone Amerced 20d	township there presents Stephen (8d) son of Juliana atte Wall forestalled Roger the son of Edith atte Broke and from him drew blood (12d). So the said Stephen for the forestalling and the bloodshed is in mercy
Rowlowe, Bradeney, Asturhull, Ewyk, Soonde Strays remaining 10d	townships there present 2 male sheep coming as strays around the feast of the Blessed Mary Magdalene last past price 10d and remaining in the custody of Thomas Haselwode
Roughtone, Barndeley, Hokkombe, Swancote	townships there present nothing
Burcote, Burcote, Ryndelford, Bromley Goods found and abandoned 9d Amerced 4d	townships there present one small sack found in the King's road price 2d. And they say that Roger Halyday took the said sack & without the supervision & licence of the bailiff unjustly sold it for 7d whence the said Roger Halyday is charged and for contempt (4d) is in mercy etc.
Alvescote, Wynnescote, Cattestre & Newtone Amerced 6s 10d	townships there present that John Nicoles (6d) who is bound to make appearance at this court did not appear so etc. And they say that Isabell (8d) the wife of William Palhoges forestalled Richard Walker. And that the same Richard (8d) re-forestalled the said Isabell & made homesoken (12d) on the same so each of them is in mercy. And they say that Agnes (40d) the wife of Richard Walker was accustomed to stand hidden day and night under the walls of the houses of neighbours acknowledged by their council unjust. So she is in mercy. Also they say that Isabell (8d) the wife of William Palhoges forestalled William the son of Richard Walker so she is in mercy
Ewdenas, Oldyntone,	townships there present nothing
Stapelford	township there presents nothing
Akeltone	township there presents nothing

1416-1417 P314/W/1/1/245

Haalen	township there presents nothing
Wyke Amerced 12d	township there presents that Thomas Heyne (12d) unjustly took one iron Bil William Carter found bu the servant of the same Thomas. So the said Thomas is in mercy
Worfeld Amerced 4d	township there presents that John Blewall (4d) who is bound to make appearance at this court & did not appear so he is in mercy
The tasters of ale Amerced 10s	present that Roger Jones (6d) brewed 1, John Yate of Wyke (12d) 2, Thomas Trysell of Alvescote (6d) 1, Thomas Yngmon (6d) 1, William Garbot (6d) 1, Joan the daughter of William Nore (6d) 1, Richard Smyth of Sonde (6d) 1, Thomas Sonde (12d) 2, Katherine Bolveyes (12d) 2, William Nore (6d) 1, William Baker (6d) 1, William Webbe (6d) 1, William Barowe (6d) 1, Thomas Undurhull (6d) 1, Henry Barker (6d) 1. And that all the said brewers sold against the assize by illegal measures so each of them is in mercy. Furthermore they say that Robert Taillour not affeered here on account of a fine made as is clear below affeered … … & Roger Warde were accustomed to continue to brew and sell how often and when they don't know so each of them is in mercy
Still the townships of Roughtone, Barnele, Hokkombe & Swancote Waif 3s Amerced 3s Waif 12d Amerced 20d	present 2 silver spoons abandoned goods price 3s. And that Edith atte Broke (3s unjustly took the said spoons and carried them away out of the Liberty of Worfeld. So the said Edith is in mercy. Also they say that William atte Broke (20d) unjustly & against the peace of the lord King took one cock and seven hens from Richard Bradeney price 12d. So the said William is in mercy
The 12 jurors	say on their oath that the townships aforesaid and the tasters of ale have well and faithfully presented

Small court held in the place, day & year above-said

The 12	Stephen Bradeney	John Hethe	John Janne }	
	Roger Waltone	John Barneley	John Colynsone }	sworn
	John the son of John Roulowe	Thomas Toward	John Bromley }	
	William Wermod	Roger Garbot	Roger Tounesende }	

Stray 14d	The bailiff is here charged concerning 14d to raise from the township of Hyltone for 1 boar coming as a stray as is clear by the record recorded in the last great court in the preceding year
the 12 jurors Amerced 6d Heriot & escheat nothing just as supervised	present that Thomas Richardes (3d) & John Nicoles (3d) who are bound to make suit at this court did not come so each of them is in mercy. And they say that William Hychyn who held from the lady by custom of the manor one messuage and one virgate of land in Hiltone on the day he died from whose death concerning heriot and escheat nothing falls to the lady because he had nothing at the time of his death. And the tenement aforesaid will remain with Alice the daughter of the said deceased by their custom by virtue of a fine thence previously made as they believe
Fine 5s	And they say that Agnes Wyllyn widow married herself within the manor to Roger Bromley who thence made a fine with the lady & for the fine gives [blank]

Distrain — Still it is ordered to the bailiff that he distrain Margaret Flynt that she is at the next [court] to respond to respond to Thomas Toward in a plea of debt

Amerced 2s — Thomas Jankys junior put himself in mercy for a licence to agree with Thomas Merewall, John Trysell, Alice the daughter of Roger Hattone & Thomas Trisell & each of them separately in pleas of debt & trespass

Amerced 6d — John Pyper & Alice his wife are in mercy because they are not prosecuting against Thomas Jankys junior in a plea of debt by the pledge of John Bromley

Amerced 6d — William Broke is in mercy because he is not prosecuting against Thomas Jankys junior in a plea of debt by the pledge of John Colynsone

Amerced 6d — William Newe is in mercy because he is not prosecuting against Thomas Jankys junior in a plea of debt

a day — {Roger Dallyley plaintiff against Thomas Trisell of Akeltone in a plea of debt pledge
{for the prosecution Richard Underhull who have a day to continue
{Thomas Trisell plaintiff against Roger Dallyley in a plea of trespass

Amerced 4d, Distrain — John Pertone plaintiff against John Cattestre & Alice his mother in a plea of trespass pledges for the prosecution John Bullok & Thomas Tomkys. The which John & Alice attached & charged did not come so they are in mercy. Furthermore it is ordered to the bailiff to better distrain them towards the next [court]

Distrain — Thomas Heyne plaintiff against Thomas Yngmone in a plea of debt pledge for the prosecution Roger Tounesende the which Thomas Yngmone attached and charged did not come so he is in mercy. Furthermore it is ordered to the bailiff to better distrain him towards to the next [court]

Void because he is dead — {Still a day is given between John Walker plaintiff & John the son of Nicholas
{defendant in a plea of trespass

Adjourned — {And between William Garbot plaintiff & Haney Barker defendant in a plea of
{accounts

Distrain — Still it is ordered to the bailiff on behalf of the lady that he distrain John Stevenes that he is at the next [court] to respond to Thomas Sonde in a plea of debt

Adjourned — Also still a day is given between John Cook and Alice his wife plaintiffs & Margaret Trysell defendant in a plea of detention of goods

Look on the back

[The Dorse] Still concerning the court

Fine 12d — 12d is given to the lady for a fine for an inquiry of the 12 ex officio to be held to enquire whether the sons of William Stevenes have a better right … in one tenement namely in half of one messuage and one nook of land of the tenement called Goslond in Chesturtone or Margery who was the wife of the same William pledge for the fine Richard Bulveyes on which the inquiry was held by the oath of John Hethe, Thomas Towart, John Bromley, Robert Bruggende, John Roulowe son of Nicholas,

1416-1417 P314/W/1/1/245

Adjourned	John Jonessone Roulowe, William Newe, Roger Cattestre, William Wermod, Roger Tounesende, John Janyn & William Webbe who sworn and thence charged have a day to continue from the aforesaid thence to render until the next [court] afterwards it was settled and determined as is clear below
Adjourned Inquest delayed because the petitioner did not come	Still the inquiry of the 12 ex officio to enquire if Benedicta lately the wife of Thomas Roulowe & John her son …[word lost] were able by their custom to make title of one messuage & one virgate of land which lately were Thomas Roulowe's in Hultone as is clear in the last small court adjourned until the next. Inquest delayed
Stray remains	Still remaining in the custody of the reeve one draught animal coming as a stray presented in the last great court preceding by the township of Akeltone
Verdict	Which at the inquiry of the 12 for the verdict of John Stevenes & Margaret Stevenes it is presented here by the oath of the 12 jurors whose names are written above who say on their oath that John Stevenes son of William Stevenes by agreement will hold to himself and his heirs the tenement in Chesturtone except a quarter part of one nook within the tenement which quarter part of the said tenement Margary Trysell will hold for the term of her life and after the death of Margary to remain to the aforesaid John Stevenes and his heirs
Fine 15s	William Kyngessone surrendered into the hands of the lady one messuage with 3 nooks of land called Haukys place in Roughtone to the use of William the son of Roger Waltone. The which William came here in court & took from the lady the aforesaid tenement with appurtenances to hold to himself and his [heirs] from the lady by services thence owed by the custom of the manor. And he gives to the lady for a fine 15s, made fealty & thus is seized
Fine 15s	William Kyngessone above-named surrendered into the hands of the lady one toft with 3 nooks of land called the Polehouse place in Roughtone to the use of Robert Webbe & Joan his wife. The which Robert & Joan came here in court & took from the lady the aforesaid tenement with appurtenances to hold to themselves & their [heirs] from the lady by services thence owed according to the custom of the manor. And they give to the lady for a fine 15s, made fealty & are seised
Fine 3s	Robert Taillour gives to the lady for a fine 3s for a licence to brew from the feast of St Michael last past until the said feast of St Michael next in the future
Fine 12d	Roger Warde gives to the lady for a fine 12d for a licence to brew from the feast of St Michael last past until the said feast of St Michael next in the future
Amerced 6d	Still the 12 jurors present that William Newtone (4d) clerk & William Hemme (2d) withdrew from court without licence before the end of the court so each of them is in mercy
Affeerors	John Hethe, Nicholas Rowlowe Sum of the last court fines of Edith the daughter of Henry Barker & Juliana atte Welle widow of the lady not tried £3 15s 9d Expenses of the steward & others coming for the sake of the court auditor and accountant as is clear by the schedule thence agreed 15s 6½d

1417 P314/W/1/1/246

Worfeld	Great Court with Leet held there on Monday next after the feast of the Nativity of St Francis in the fifth year of the reign of King Henry V [11 October 1417]
Essoins	Robert Taylour himself from suit of court by Roger Towneshende } John Smyth himself by Roger Towneshende } Roger Tornour of Ryndelforde himself from suit by the aforesaid Roger }affirmed Roger Knyght himself from suit of court by Henry Barkare } Thomas Richardes himself from suit of court by Roger Richardes }
Kyngeslowe, Stanlowe Amerced 18d Stray 6d	townships there present that John Devey (6d) forestalled John Kynvartone so the aforesaid John is in mercy. And that the aforesaid John Kynvartone (6d) forestalled the aforesaid John Devey and drew blood (6d) from him. Also they present 1 sheep (bidens) coming in the name of a stray price 6d & it remains in the custody of Stephen of Stanlowe for 3 quarters of the past year
Chesturtone	township there presents nothing
Hiltone	township there presents nothing
Rowlow, Bradeney, Asturhull, Ewyke, Soonde	townships there present nothing
Rowghtone, Barndeley, Hokkombe, Swankote Amerced 12d	townships there present that William Lowe (6d) drew the blood of Thomas Gyllen. And that the same Thomas Gyllen (6d) forestalled the aforesaid William Lowe
Burcote, Burcote, Ryndelforde, Bromley	townships there present nothing but all well
Alvescote, Wynnescote, Cattestre, Newtone Amerced 2d	townships there present that John Nicollus (2d) did not come
Ewdenas, Holdyntone	townships there present nothing but all well
Stapulforde	township there presents nothing but all well
Akyltone Amerced 2d	township there presents that Thomas Trecylle (2d) did not come
Halen	township there presents that John Henene (6d) forestalled Robert Taylour and drew blood (6d) from him. And that the same John Henene (6d) forestalled Alice the wife of Robert Taylour and drew blood (6d) from her. And that the same John Henene (6d) forestalled Alice Goold and drew blood (6d) from her. And that the same Alice Gold forestalled (3d) the aforesaid John Henene and drew blood (3d) from him. Also

Halen [contd.] Amerced 5s	they present that Margaret Barewe (6d) took and carried away one piglet of Richard Aleyn against the peace and against the will of the same Richard. Also they present that John Henene (12d) took and carried away one cock and one hen from Alice Galyan against the peace and against the will of the same Alice
Wyke	township there presents nothing but all well
Worfelde Amerced 2s 5d	township there presents that John Glovare (6d) forestalled John Henene. And that the same John Henene (6d) forestalled the aforesaid John Glovare. Also they present that the aforesaid John Henene (2d) took and carried away one hen of John Bloore Chaplain against the peace and against the will of the same John. And that the same John(3d) forestalled Alice Gold and drew blood (3d) from her. And that the same John Henene (4d) made an assault on Alice Herdemone and she raised the hue and cry justly on him so he (4d) is in mercy
The tasters of ale Amerced 2s 6d	present that John Billynggesley (2d) brewed 1, Katherine Bulveys (4d) brewed 2, John Jonesone of Rowlowe (4d) brewed 2, Stephen Hymley (2d) brewed 1, John Gerbode (2d) brewed 1, Thomas Jenkyns junior (2d) brewed 1, John Bulloke (2d) brewed 1, Hamo Hymley (4d) brewed 2, John Kynvarton (2d) brewed 1, Thomas Baker of Hultone (2d) brewed 1, William Noore (2d) brewed 1, John Glovare (2d) brewed 1, Roger Warde (2d) brewed 1

The jury of 12	Roger Cattestre	Thomas Tomkys	John Rowlowe	} sworn
	Stephen Bradeney	John Jowkys	Thomas Merewalle	}
	Robert Ewdenas	John Rowlowe Jonesone	John Jannen	}
	Roger Waltone	William Gerbode	& William Gerbode	}

Amerced 20d	These jurors affirm all the presentations aforesaid to be true in all things. And further they present that Thomas Gyllen (20d) took and carried away one swarm of bees out of a tree of the lady being in the wood of the lady without licence and there destroyed the swarm and took and carried away all the honey & honeycomb at the same time by theft whenever it was pleasing to him
Worfelde	Small court held there on Tuesday next before the feast of St Luke the Evangelist in the year aforesaid [12 October 1417]

Essoins	William Yate himself by Thomas Trecylle	} Affirmed
	John Bradeney himself from suit of court by Stephen Bradeney	}
	Richard Bradeney himself from suit of court by Roger Towneshende	}
	Thomas Haselwode himself from suit of court by John Rowlowe	}
	William Stevenes himself from suit of court by William Wormode	}
	John Smyth senior himself from suit of court by John Rowlowe	}
	Thomas Undurhul himself from suit of court by John Byllynggesley	}
	John Hulle himself from suit of court by John Colet	}

The 12 jurors	John Hethe	John Barndeley	John Jannen	} sworn
	William Wermode	John Byllynggesley	William Gerbode	}
	John Rowlowe	Stephen Bradeney	John Jonesone of Rowlow	}
	Roger Richardes	Roger Waltone	William Newe	}

To this court comes William Newe and makes a fine with the lady for trespass because he married............[lost in crease] [without] a licence namely for 40d

Margin	Entry
Fine 40d	pledge for the fine Roger Cattestre
Fine 40d	Thomas Merewalle made a fine with the lady because Joan his daughter married herself without a licence from the lady for 40d pledge for the fine John Hethe
Ordered to pardon profit	To this court comes Isolda the widow of John Walker and recognised herself to receive from the profits of the fulling mill at Ryndelforde without licence so it is ordered to the beadle that he answers concerning the profit namely 2s 8d. And afterwards she is pardoned by the steward and so nothing is to be put in the estreats of the court
Amerced 2s	Alice at Sonde (2s) brewed for the whole year last past and broke the assize so she is in mercy
Fine 12d	Roger Warde gives to the lady for a fine 12d for a licence to brew from the feast of St Michael last past until the same feast of St Michael next in the future
It is ordered £4 Letter	It is found by the aforesaid 12 jurors by their oath that Joan Reynold widow of John Regnold held and occupied without title a certain tenement in Kynggeslowe called Huggesplace which is a customary tenement during the 12 years last past and made ingress under the ...(colore) of John Regnolde her husband after the death of the same John when the same John nor the aforesaid Joan his wife never had ~~had~~ thence seisin during the life of them by the custom of the manor freed to them but they say further that Alice the daughter of the aforesaid John has more right by the custom of the manor to the same tenement than the aforesaid Joan. The which Joan thus occupied for 12 years last past whose annual value extended itself to 6s 8d amounting in total to £4 pro rata for the time. And so it is ordered to the reeve to take the tenement there into the hands of the lady and to respond for the profit and for the annual value aforesaid if John Hemme husband of the aforesaid Joan still wishes to acquire or otherwise let it be done by writ from the lady against the same John & Joan concerning the trespass for their intrusion and unjust occupation made in the time of the lady etc.
	Richard Whitebroke & Matilda his wife confessed & examined according to the custom of the manor surrendered into the hands of the lady the reversion of one messuage & half a virgate of land as of the right of the same Matilda which tenement John Robynnes holds for the term of his life in Alvescote & which formerly William Bulloke held to the use of William Underwode & Alice his wife & their heirs to hold from the lady according to the custom of the manor and they give to the lady for a fine 10s pledge for the fine Richard Whitebroke who stand in the charge of the reeve aforesaid whence he will respond
Amerced 2d	The jury aforesaid present that John Nicolles (2d) did not come to make suit of court so he is in mercy
Amerced 6d	Thomas Toward for his unjust plea against Margaret Flynt so he is in mercy
Order to distrain	Roger Daylley plaintiff appeared himself against Thomas Trecylle in a plea of debt and the aforesaid Thomas is attached by various corn price 2s and did not come so it is ordered to better distrain towards the next [court]
Amerced 6d	Thomas Trecille is not prosecuting his plea against Roger Dalley in a plea of trespass so he is in mercy

Amerced 6d — John Pertone plaintiff & John Cattestre & Alice his mother defendants are for a licence to agree & the aforesaid John Cattestre responds to the court so he is in mercy

Amerced 4d
Ordered to distrain — Thomas Heyne plaintiff appeared himself against Thomas Yngeman in a plea of debt. And the aforesaid Thomas Yngeman attached did not come and re-pledged by Robert Ewdenac & John Jay so they are in mercy because they do not have the aforesaid Thomas etc. so it is ordered to distrain the pledges

Amerced 6d — Thomas Sonde plaintiff & John Stevenes defendant in a plea of debt are for a licence to agree & the aforesaid John responded to the court so he is in mercy

Amerced 6d — John Cook & Alice his wife did not pesent their plea against Margaret Trecille in a plea of detention of goods so they are in mercy

It is ordered — Margaret Trecille plaintiff of Thomas Sonde & of Alice his wife in a plea of debt pledge for the prosecution Thomas Trecill & the aforesaid Thomas & Alice summoned did not come so it is ordered to attach to the next [court]

It is ordered — Margaret Trecille plaintiff of Thomas Underhull in a plea of trespass pledge for the prosecution Thomas Trecille & John Jay so it is ordered to attach to the next [court]

It is ordered — The same Margaret plaintiff of Robert Taylour & of Alice his wife in a plea of detention of goods pledge for the prosecution John Smyth summoned did not come so it is ordered to attach to the next

Adjourned — Richard Gerbode plaintiff of William Stevenes in a plea of trespass pledge for the prosecution Robert Barker & they have a day until the next [court] adjourned by the prayer of the parties

It is ordered — Thomas Heyne plaintiff of Thomas Jenkyns junior in a plea of debt pledge for the prosecution John Barndeley so it is ordered to summon to the next [court]

It is ordered — Thomas Heyne plaintiff of Nicholas Stanlowe in a plea of debt pledge for the prosecution John Barndeley so it is ordered to summon to the next [court]

Thomas Heyne plaintiff of Thomas Jenkyns junior in a plea of debt pledge for the prosecution John Barndeley so it is ordered to summon to the next [court]

Amerced 6d — Agnes Mathew plaintiff of John Mathew in a plea of debt pledge for the prosecution Thomas Trecille. And the aforesaid John ready in court responded. And the aforesaid Agnes pleads against him that he owes to her 8s 8d as it were pledged. And the same John here did not deny but well recognised the aforesaid debt so it is judged that the same Agnes recover the aforesaid debt & the aforesaid John is in mercy

It is ordered — John Trecille plaintiff of Richard Undurhull of Akyltone in a plea of debt pledge for the prosecution Thomas Trecylle & Thomas Jenkyns so it is ordered to summon to the next [court]

It is ordered — Thomas Jenkyns plaintiff of Agnes Mathewe in a plea of trespass pledge for the prosecution Roger Hulle and it is ordered to attach to the next [court]

William Mulleward of Kembertone plaintiff of Stephen Hymley in a plea of debt

It is ordered — pledge for the prosecution John Jowkys & the same Stephen summoned did not come so it is ordered to attach to the next [court]

It is ordered — Thomas Forster, Thomas Heyne & John Webbe plaintiffs of John Hulle of Hultone in a plea of debt pledge for the prosecution William Webbe so it is ordered to summon to the next [court]

It is ordered — Thomas Forster, Thomas Heyne & Robert Webbe plaintiffs of Thomas Merewall junior in a plea of debt pledge for the prosecution William Webbe & it is ordered to summon to the next [court]

It is ordered — Roger Dalley plaintiff of Thomas Trecille of Akyltone in a plea of trespass pledge for the prosecution Thomas Toward & John Jay so it is ordered to attach to the next [court]

It is ordered — Roger Dalley plaintiff of the same Thomas in a plea of trespass pledge for the prosecution Thomas Toward & John Jay so it is ordered to attach to the next [court]

It is ordered — Robert Webbe plaintiff of John Hethe in a plea of non-fulfilment of pledge pledge for the prosecution Roger Dalley & it is ordered to summon to the next [court]

Constables — John John Snel & John Jowkys are elected to the office of constable. And they are sworn

Affeerors — John Jonesone of Rowlowe & John Hethe

Fine 6s 8d — To this court came Thomas Jenkys junior & surrendered into the hands of the lady to the use of William Halghtone the reversion of one messuage & half a virgate of land with appurtenances in Hockombe after the death of Joan Malcherer widow of John Dawes which the same Joan holds for the term of her life the which reversion the aforesaid Thomas Jenkyns formerly acquired to himself and his [heirs] from Joan Hockombe in Hockombe to have and to hold to the aforesaid William Halghtone & his [heirs] the reversion aforesaid when it should happen after the death of the aforesaid according to the custom of the manor. And the aforesaid William gives [dat repeated] to the lady for a fine 40d for having the acquisition & made fealty. And afterwards the aforesaid William Halghtone surrendered into the hands of the lady the reversion of the tenements aforesaid with their appurtenances to the use of the aforesaid Thomas Jenkys and Elizabet his wife & the heirs of the same Thomas & for all according to the custom of the manor & he made a fine for having the acquisition 40d pledge for the fine William Wermode & made fealty

Fine 6s 8d — At this court it is found by the oath of the aforesaid jury that John Walker who held from the lady to himself and his heirs according to the custom of the manor two cottages and one moor and one parcel of meadow with their appurtenances in Ryndelforde and one toft with one nook of land to himself and his heirs by custom of the manor in Alvescote on the day he died on the morrow of St Bartholomew the apostle last past. And at the point of death, of sound mind according to the custom of the manor he surrendered through the hands of John Byllynggesley beadle into the hands of the lady all the land and tenement aforesaid with all their appurtenances to the use of Isolda wife of the same John Walker to have and to hold all and singular the lands and tenements aforesaid with all their appurtenances to the aforesaid Isolda

Fealty

& her heirs according to the custom of the manor just as the same John Walker formerly held & thus she is admitted & has seisin according to the custom of the manor & she made fealty. And she gives for a fine for the acquisition & ingress & to have seisin 6s 8d

The next

Also it is found by the oath of the same jury that the aforesaid John Walker who held of the lady one fulling mill with 1 stakyng for fishing to take from behind the floodgates at a pit of water flowing from the aforesaid Flodegates together with one piece of land called Teynturhull in Ryndelforde with all their appurtenances according to the custom of the manor in Ryndelforde aforesaid on the day he died on the morrow aforesaid. And before his death on the point of death, of sound mind according to the custom of the manor he surrendered through the hands of the aforesaid beadle into the hands of the lady the aforesaid mill with the stakyng and the piece of land on teynterhul aforesaid with all their appurtenances to the use of William Aleyn clerk to have to the same William and his heirs according to the custom of the manor the aforesaid mill & the stakyng and the piece of land aforesaid with all of their appurtenances by the same services and customs just as the aforesaid John Walker formerly held. And the aforesaid William Aleyn is not yet admitted but undecided until the next [court]

Heriot price 5s 6d
Escheat price 5s 6d

Also it is judged by the same jury that at the death of the aforesaid John Walker there falls to the lady one cow price 5s 6d in the name of heriot. Also there falls to the lady 1 draught animal price 2s. And 1 stall of bees and 3 swarms of bees price 3s 6d just as escheat by the custom of the manor. And that he had no other escheats

Distrain £4 16s

Also they present that Richard Bulveys who held of the lady one toft and one virgate of land in Asturhull with appurtenances who claimed himself to hold freely to himself and his heirs whence he should have paid the lady money if he should have been free of heriot and he had not but nevertheless it is found by the oath of the aforesaid jury that all that tenement in Asturhull with its appurtenances always was held from the lord and from the lady and their ancestors in lesser tenure according to the custom of the manor and not by common law according to many proofs and records of the rolls of the court now shown except in the time of Richard Bulveys leader of the lady [domain perhaps in this case] because the same Richard by collusion recovered that tenement there before the Justices at the assizes held at Bruggenorth against John Ewdenas by writ of mort d'ancestor to annul the lady of the manor aforesaid when the same lady never was party to this writ nor to the plea aforesaid nor thence had notice. They say also by their oath that the same Richard Bulveys seized thence the issue and profits by such collusion for nine years namely for each year 24s sum in total £10 16s. And so it is ordered to take and to seize that tenement into the hands of the lady and to respond for the profit. And to distrain the executors of the will of the aforesaid Richard to respond to the lady why not to give satisfaction nor owe from the profits or concerning the sum aforesaid £10 16s which and what the aforesaid Richard seized from the lands and tenements aforesaid in his time received thus by collusion

Sum of the great court with the small court aforesaid £17 8s
Expenses of the steward & others of the council of the lady being there for 3 nights 18s 7½d
Whence £3 concerning damages assessed on Joan Reynalds for the unjust occupation of a certain tenement as is clear above concerning £10 [indistinct] 16s of damages assessed on Richard Bolveys as above

1417 P314/W/1/1/246

Worfelde	Small court held there on the morrow of All Saints in the 5th year of the reign of King Henry V [2 November 1417]
Essoins	Thomas Jenkys junior himself against Thomas Heyne in a plea of debt essoined by William Gerbode Nicholas Stanlowe himself against Thomas Heyne in a plea of debt essoined by Roger Dalley
Fine 20s Fealty	To this court comes William Aleyn clerk and seeks to be admitted and to have seisin according to the custom of the manor to that fulling mill, stakyng & piece of land called Teynturhull which the same William lately acquired from John Walker on the point of his death as in the court preceding was found to himself and his [heirs] according to custom of the manor in Ryndelforde and is admitted to hold to himself and his [heirs] all the aforesaid mill with the stakyng and piece of land aforesaid with their appurtenances according to the custom of the manor. And by the same services and customs just as the aforesaid John Walkerer formerly held. And he made a fine for the acquisition and seisin thence to have 20s and he has seisin and made fealty
Fine 2s	To this court comes John Snel & Alice his wife and they give to the lady for a fine 2s to have an inquest who is the closest heir by the custom of the manor of Margery Rugge of all the lands and tenements which the same Margery held from the lady in lesser tenure in the manor of Worfelde
Sworn	And on this 24 jurors namely by the oath of Roger Waltone, John Jannen, William Gerbode, John Barndeley, William Webbe of Rowhtone, William Yate, Thomas Rowlowe of Burkote, Thomas at Sonede, Roger Richardes, William Bromley, John Hethe, John Rowlowe Jonesone, Roger Smyth of Hultone, John Colettes of Hultone, Thomas Merewalle junior, William Newe, Stephen Stanlowe, Richard Aldelf, William Stevenes, John Byllynggesley, Roger Kyngeslowe, Roger Hulle, Richard Aleyn & William Stevenes were charged to enquire & by the custom of the manor to do who is the closest heir of Margery Rugge deceased who held from the lady certain lands and tenements in lesser tenure in the manor of Worfeld. Who say and present on their oath that Alice the wife of John Snel, daughter of the aforesaid Margery is the closest heir of the same Margery to have and to hold according to the custom of the manor to the same Alice her heir in the same manor the which were conditional as of right of hereditary of the same Alice. And on this the aforesaid John Snel & Alice his wife claiming as of the right of heredity of the same Alice all the lands and tenements with appurtenances in Asturhull which the aforesaid Margery the mother of the same Alice held by the custom of the manor as is aforesaid as the next heir of the same Margery next and they are admitted etc.
Fine £4 Fealty	The same Alice confessed & for the purpose by agreement to have and to hold all the aforesaid lands and tenements with appurtenances in Asturhull in the manor aforesaid to the aforesaid John & Alice his wife & the heirs of the same Alice according to the custom of the manor. And they give to the lady for a fine £4 and made fealty
Amerced 4d	Also the aforesaid jury presents that John Nicolles (2d) who owed suit of court did not come. Also they present that William Sawndres (2d) did not come so they are in mercy
Fine 2s	To this court comes Thomas at Sonede & made a fine with the lady for 2s to brew for the following year namely from the feast of St Michael last past until to the same feast of St Michael next hereafter following for one full year

1417 P314/W/1/1/246

To the office of beadle

At this court it is found by the custom of the lady of the manor that there pertains to the township of Halen every year to the use and office of beadle whosoever was the beadle of the same township entitlement to one circuit around the boundary of the meadow of the lady called Kynggesmedowe at the time of mowing the meadow aforesaid together with 1 parcel of meadow in the same meadow called the Hurste each year at the same time of mowing which the aforesaid township and all its ancestors thence existed in possession from the time of which the memory of man does not exist to the use and office aforesaid. And so now the lady agreed to the aforesaid township and their successors to hold there the aforesaid Estate and hurste to hold to the use and office aforesaid according to the custom of the manor

John Mulleward plaintiff & Stephen Hymley defendant are for a licence to agree and the aforesaid Stephen responded in the court so the same is in mercy

Amerced 6d
Order to distrain

Roger Dalley plaintiff appeared himself against Thomas ~~Yngemon~~ Trecille in a plea of debt and the aforesaid Thomas attached did not come so it is ordered to distrain better to the next [court]

Amerced 6d

Thomas Heyne plaintiff appeared himself against Thomas Yngemon in a plea of debt and whence he complains that he owes him and unjustly detains 36s 8d for diverse corn bought from him. And the aforesaid Thomas Yngeman ready in court well recognised the debt aforesaid . So it is judged that the aforesaid Thomas Heyne should recover the debt aforesaid and the aforesaid defendant is in mercy

Plea
Amerced 6d

Margaret Trecille plaintiff appeared herself against Thomas Undurhull in a plea of trespass and whence she complains that the aforesaid Thomas took and carried away from the house of the same Margaret in Chesturtone 6 spoons of silver price 20s and hand towel cloths price 6s 8d & one maternal silver band price 10s. And diverse harness of one silver belt price 13s 4d. And 1 pair of rosaries price 18d. And 6 coverlets & sheets price 40s and other domestic utensils. And the aforesaid Thomas is ready in court to respond at law with 11 hands that he is not maliciously guilty and seeks that he make the law immediately & it is granted him. And afterwards he accomplished his law in this case that he is to blame in nothing namely with John Rowlowe, John Hethe, John Bromley, Roger Towneshende, Roger Galley, John Baret, John Bulloke, Stephen Webbe, William Bromley, John Byllynggesley & Thomas Sonde. So it is judged that the aforesaid Margaret is in mercy for the unjust plea

Plea
The law

Margaret Trecille plaintiff appeared herself against Thomas at Sonede in a plea of debt and whence she complains that the aforesaid Thomas owes her 5d and unjustly detains. And the aforesaid Thomas ready in court to respond is at law that he owes her nothing nor unjustly detains with six hands to the next [court] pledge for the law Henry Barker

Plea
Amerced 6d

Margaret Trecille plaintiff appeared herself against Roger Taylour and Alice his wife in a plea of detention of goods namely one brass bowl to the damage of the aforesaid Margaret 40d. And the aforesaid Robert ready in court to respond says that he is not bound to respond because she made an announcement and statement in the plea aforesaid namely on the day & year & place and here puts himself on the court and the same Margaret similarly. And afterwards the court thence was charged. And they said that the aforesaid Margaret ought not to maintain the plea aforesaid because she made an announcement on the day, year and place aforesaid so she is in mercy

1417 P314/W/1/1/246

Plea the next	The plea which is between Richard Gerbode plaintiff and William Stevenes defendant adjourned until the next [court] by the prayer of the petitioner
Plea the next	Thomas Heyne plaintiff appeared himself against Thomas Jenkyns junior in a plea of debt summoned did not come so it is ordered to attach to the next [court
Plea Amerced 6d	~~Thomas~~ John Trecylle plaintiff appeared himself against Richard Underhull in a plea of debt. And whence he complains that he owes him 6d and unjustly detains to the damage of the aforesaid plaintiff 12d. And the aforesaid Richard ready in court to respond denies this that he owes him nothing nor unjustly detains and he is at law with 6 hands and to make the law manifest. And afterwards the aforesaid Richard completed the law. So the aforesaid Thomas is in mercy for the unjust plea
Plea Amerced 6d	Thomas Forster, Thomas Heyne & Robert Webbe plaintiffs and John Hulle defendant are for a licence to agree and the same John responded to the court so in mercy
Plea The law	Thomas Heyne plaintiff appeared himself & Robert Webbe similarly against Thomas Merwalle in a plea of debt and whence they complain that he owes them 20d and unjustly detains. And the aforesaid Thomas ready in court to respond denies this that he owes them nothing nor unjustly detains. And he is to the law with six hands at the next [court] pledge for the law John Hethe
Amerced 6d	John Smyth chaplain plaintiff and John Sheyntone defendant in a plea of debt are for a licence to agree and the aforesaid John Sheyntone responded to the court so in mercy
Plea Ordered to distrain & summon	John Mathew plaintiff of Thomas Jenkys senior and of Roger Hulle in a plea of pledges not discharged pledge for the prosecution Robert Webbe and John Jay so it is ordered to attach to the next [court] Roger Hulle and to summon the aforesaid Thomas to respond
Amerced 2d Plea ordered to distrain	Roger Dalley plaintiff appeared himself against Thomas Trecille of Akeltone in a plea of trespass. And the aforesaid Thomas is attached by diverse corn price 6s 8d and did not come which it is ordered to retain and better distrain to the next [court]
Amerced 2d distrain	Roger Dalley plaintiff appeared himself against Thomas Trecille of Akeltone in a plea of trespass. And the aforesaid Thomas is attached by diverse corn price 6s 8d and did not come which it is ordered to retain and better distrain to the next [court]
Plea Amerced 6d	Robert Webbe plaintiff appeared himself against John Hethe in a plea of pledge not discharged. And whence he complains that he owes him 3s 3d & unjustly detains as the pledge of William Gold. And the aforesaid John ready in court responded whence he recognised the debt aforesaid. So it is judged that the aforesaid Robert recover and the same John is in mercy for unjust detention
the next	Thomas Haselwode plaintiff of Thomas Jenkyns junior in a plea of debt pledge for the prosecution John Bromley so it is ordered to summon to the next [court]
the next	Margaret Trecille plaintiff of Robert Galian in a plea of detention of goods pledge for the prosecution Roger Smyth so it is ordered to attach to the next [court]

1417 P314/W/1/1/246

the next Thomas Undurhull plaintiff of Margaret Trecille in a plea trespass pledge for the prosecution John Baret so it is ordered to attach to the next [court]

the next Thomas Jenkyns plaintiff appeared himself against Agnes Mathew in a plea of trespass so it is ordered to attach to the next [court]

the next Thomas Heyne plaintiff appeared himself against Thomas Jenkyns junior in a plea of debt above essoined

the next Thomas Heyne plaintiff appeared himself against Nicholas Stanlowe in a plea of debt above essoined

Sum of the court £5 8s 10d

Expenses of the steward and others more/ another five more 11s 2d

The Dorse

[the following is written on the dorse but we can make no sense of it]
5th, 5th & beginning of 6th Year 5 & 6

Sp*arrx
stafo ?stirrups of a horse
… …?domine

something father down… Angliae …

1418 P314/W/1/1/248

Worfeld	Small court held on Tuesday next before the feast of St Katherine the Virgin in the fifth year of the reign of King Henry V [23 November 1417]
Essoins	John Smyth of Sonede himself } John Hethe himself }by Roger Richardes John Cattestre himself } Thomas Richardes }
The 12	Stephen Bradeney, Roger Towneshende, Thomas Underhull } John Jonesone, John Rowlowe, William Wermode } sworn Roger Waltone, William Newe, John Bromley } William Gerbode, Stephen Bradeney, & William Webbe }
Amerced 4d	Roger Dalley plaintiff appeared himself against Thomas Trecylle in a plea of debt and the aforesaid Thomas attached did not come so it is ordered to distrain to the next [court]
Amerced 6d	Margaret Trecylle is not prosecuting her complaint against Thomas at Sonede so the same Margaret & Thomas Trecylle pledge of the same Margaret are in mercy
The next	The plea which is between Richard Gerbode plaintiff and William Stevenes defendant is adjourned by the prayer of the parties until the next [court]
Plea The law	Thomas Heyne plaintiff appeared himself against Thomas Jenkys junior in a plea of debt. And whence he complains that he owes him 34s 10d and unjustly detains. And the aforesaid Thomas Jenkys ready in court to respond denies this that he neither owes nothing to him nor unjustly detains. And he is at law with six hands to the next [court] pledge for the law Roger Smyth & John Baret. But he well recognised the debt to be his to pay on the feast of the Purification of the Blessed Mary the Virgin next following after the date of this court and not before
It is ordered The next	John Mathew plaintiff appeared himself against Thomas Jenkys senior & against Roger Hulle in a plea of pledge not discharged. Summoned they did not come so it is ordered to attach to the next [court]
Amerced 6d	Thomas Heyne & Robert Webbe plaintiffs and Thomas Merwall defendants are for a licence to agree and the same Thomas Merwall responded to the court so he is in mercy
Ordered to distrain Amerced 4d	Roger Dalley plaintiff appeared himself against Thomas Trecille of Akyltone in a plea of trespass and the aforesaid Thomas attached did not come so it is ordered to distrain to the next [court]
Ordered to distrain Amerced 4d	Roger Dalley plaintiff appeared himself against Thomas Trecille of Akyltone in a plea of trespass and the aforesaid Thomas attached did not come so it is ordered to distrain to the next [court]
Amerced 6d	Thomas Haselwode plaintiff appeared himself against Thomas Jenkys junior in a plea of debt. And whence he complains that he owes him 4s 10d and unjustly detains. And the aforesaid Thomas Jenkys ready in court to respond well recognised the debt aforesaid so it is judged that the aforesaid Thomas Haselwode recover the debt aforesaid and the aforesaid Thomas Jenkys is in mercy

1418 P314/W/1/1/248

Amerced 6d

Margaret Trecylle is not prosecuting her plea against Robert Galyan in a plea of detention of goods so she is in mercy by the pledge of Roger Smyth

Amerced 4d

Thomas Underhull plaintiff appeared himself against Margaret Trecylle in a plea of trespass. And the aforesaid Margaret is attached by one horse price 6s 8d & re-pledged by William Aleyn clerk and did not come so she is in mercy and the aforesaid William is in mercy because he did not have the aforesaid Margaret to respond

Amerced 6d

Thomas Jenkys junior plaintiff appeared himself against Agnes Mathew in a plea of trespass. And afterwards the same Thomas made an announcement in his plea so it is judged that the same Thomas is in mercy for the insufficient plea

Plea
The law

Thomas Heyne plaintiff appeared himself against Thomas Jenkys junior in a plea of debt. And whence he complains that he owes him 16d for strays he bought from him and unjustly detains to the damage of the aforesaid Thomas 2s. And the aforesaid Thomas Jenkys ready in court to respond denies this that he owes him nothing nor unjustly detains. And he is at law with six hands at the next [court]. Pledge for the law William Gerbode & John Jay

Amerced 2d
Ordered to distrain

Thomas Heyne plaintiff appeared himself against Nicholas Stanlowe in a plea of debt and the aforesaid Nicholas did not come to warrant his essoin so he is in mercy and it is ordered to distrain to the next [court]

Amerced 6d
Enquire by the rolls
Heriot 7s
In the hand of the lady

The aforesaid jurors present that Roger Kyngeslow (2d) who owed suit did not come. Also they present that John Bromley (2d) did not come, John Nicollus (2d) did not come. Also they present that Nicholas Rowlowe who held from the lady 1 messuage & 1 virgate of land with appurtenances in Rowlowe for the term of his life in reversion the same tenement should remain to John son of the same Nicholas and his heirs according to the custom of the manor by acquisition and fine made as it is said nevertheless it should be enquired by the rolls of the court concerning the title of the same John. Also they present that the same Nicholas held also the on day on which he died one toft with one nook of land in the Sonede for the term of his life the reversion should remain with the aforesaid John the son of the aforesaid Nicholas for the acquisition of the said John to the same John and his heirs according to the custom of the manor. Also they present that the same Nicholas held on the day on which he died one nook of land in the Sonede to himself and his heirs according to the custom of the manor whence there falls to the lady one ox in the name of heriot price 7s. And nothing is able to fall nor to have because he has no more. And the aforesaid nook of land remains in the hand of the lady until etc.

Fine 12d
It is ordered

William Hockombe gives to the lady for a fine 12d for having the judgment of the court by the 12 whether he has the better right in his demand who seeks the reversion of one messuage and half a virgate of land in Hockombe after the death of Joan Malecher his mother whose heir he is against Thomas Jenkys junior and Elizabeth his wife which the same Thomas and Elizabeth have in their tenure from that reversion when it should happen. And the court thence is charged to transcend the wrong. And it is ordered to take into the hands of the lady the aforesaid tenement with appurtenances until the aforesaid Joan Malecher will have come in court to show how she entered and holds the tenement aforesaid because it is said the same Joan holds and occupies the tenement there by intrusion & for a long time has so occupied

1418 P314/W/1/1/248

To this court came William Pallehog & Isabell his wife before the steward and the same Isabell duly confessed and examined who from the lady hold by the custom of the manor one messuage with half a virgate of land with appurtenances in Newtone in lesser tenure and surrender that tenement with all its appurtenances to Richard Haselwode and Edith his wife to hold to the same Richard and Edith and the heirs of the same Richard from the lady according to the custom of the manor by services and customs just as the aforesaid William and Isabell previously held. And the same Richard and Edith were thus admitted and thence have seisin etc. And they made fealty. And they give to the lady for a fine 10s for acquisition and ingress to have. However the aforesaid Richard and Edith wish for themselves and the heirs of the
Fine 10s same Richard that the aforesaid William Pallehog & Isabell his wife during their lives and of each other should have their easement, residence, occupation & profit with free ingress and egress in the aforesaid messuage and the site of the same messuage together with 12 acres of arable land from Newtones medew lying together with half of one croft of land lying below the messuage aforesaid similarly 2 bays in the barn built at the same messuage rendering thence annually to the aforesaid Richard and Edith and the heirs of the same Richard 6d at the feast of St Michael the Archangel quit from rendering all other services or any customs *as sometimes made or after their deaths may be granted or may* be had excepting the right of the holy church as by an indenture made between them made interchangeably fully completed [Note: please check the text in italics]

Sum of this court 22s 6d

Expenses of the steward on the day of the court 14d

In parchment bought 2d

1418 P314/W/1/1/248

Worfelde
Court held on Tuesday next after the feast of the Purification of the Blessed Virgin Mary in the fifth year of the reign of King Henry V [8 February 1418]

Essoins — Robert Newtone essoined himself by Thomas Richardes

The 12 sworn — {Stephen Bradeney, John of Rowlowe Jonesone, Roger Waltone, Roger Richardes, {John Rowlowe son of Nicholas Rowlowe, Stephen Stanlowe, Thomas Towart, John {Jannen, Roger Gerbode, William Wermode, William Gerbode & Roger {Towneshende

Recover 6d — Thomas Jenkys junior defaulted in his law against Thomas Heyne in a plea of debt so it is judged that the aforesaid Thomas may recover 16d and concerning damages 4d as is clear in the court preceding. And the aforesaid Thomas Jenkys is in mercy

Amerced 8d — Thomas Underhull plaintiff appeared himself against Margaret Trecille in a plea of trespass and the aforesaid Margaret elsewhere attached did not come so she is in mercy and the pledge of the same Margaret because he did not have the aforesaid Margaret is in mercy similarly

Recover Amerced 6d — Thomas Jenkys junior defaulted in his law against Thomas Heyne in a plea of debt so it is judged that the same Thomas Heyne may recover 39s 10d and the aforesaid Thomas Jenkys is in mercy

Amerced 6d — Richard Gerbode plaintiff & William Stevenes defendant are for a licence to agree and the same William to respond to the court

The next — Roger Hethe junior plaintiff of Thomas Merwall senior in a plea of debt pledge for the prosecution Stephen Stanlow so it is ordered to summon to the next

Amerced 6d — Thomas Heyne plaintiff & Nicholas Stanlowe defendant are for a licence to agree & the same Nicholas to respond to the court so he is in mercy

6d — Roger Dalley plaintiff & Thomas Trecille defendant are for a licence to agree & the same Thomas to respond to the court

12d — Roger Dalley plaintiff & Thomas Trecille defendant in 2 pleas are for a licence to agree & the same Thomas to respond to the court

The next — Thomas Trecille plaintiff of Thomas Gillen Taylour in a plea of detention of three and a half yards of woollen cloth namely medeley price 8s pledge for the prosecution John Smyth and so it is ordered to summon the aforesaid Thomas to the next [court]

The jury 4d — The aforesaid jury presents that John Barndeley (2d) did not come to make suit. Thomas Richardes (2d) did not come

Fine 6s 8d Fealty — To this court came Joan Malcher who recently was ingressed by intrusion into 1 messuage & half a virgate of land with appurtenances in Hockombe nevertheless the ingress was as the daughter and heir of Agnes Malcher now she comes and well recognised herself thus to have entered and to have held by intrusion in the messuage aforesaid with appurtenances which trespass the lady remitted to her by a fine made namely for 6s 8d and thus she is admitted now to the inheritance aforesaid to hold to herself and her heirs according to the custom of the manor and made fealty and has seisin. And afterwards the aforesaid Joan in the same court surrendered into the hands of the lady the tenement aforesaid with appurtenances to the use of William Bakus of Hockombe son and heir of the same Joan to have and to hold the aforesaid tenement with its appurtenances to the aforesaid William Bakus and his heirs according to the custom of the manor. And he gives to the lady for a fine 6s 8d for the acquisition and ingress to have and made fealty and thence has seisin

Fine 6s 8d

To this court comes John Rowlow son of Nicholas Rowlow & took from the lady one nook of land in the Sonede as of his inheritance happening to him after the death of the aforesaid Nicholas to hold to himself & his heirs according to the custom of the manor. And he gives to the lady for a fine 5s for ingress and to have seisin and made fealty and has seisin

Fine 5s

To this court comes the aforesaid John Rowlow & took from the lady as of the right of his inheritance happening to him after the death of the aforesaid Nicholas his father one fulling mill called Rowlow mulle with the water course and with all other of its appurtenances in Rowlow to hold to himself & his heirs according to the custom of the manor & thence has seisin. And he gives to the lady for a fine 5s and made fealty

Fine 5s

Fine 12d

To this court comes John Bromley and gives to the lady for a fine 12d to commute and exonerate him from suit of court for the following year after the present date

Fine 12d

John Kyngessone gives to the lady for a fine 12d to sell both bread and ale from the feast of the Nativity of the Lord until the feast of St Michael next following so that he is bound to the due assize

The next

A day is ordered to William Webbe of Rowghtone that he is at the next [court] to show how he is entered and holds one toft with a croft in Rowghtone which at some time was Roger Style's which he formerly acquired from John Holdyntone of the County of Staffordshire which he sold in the name of Margery his daughter etc.

The next

John Mathew plaintiff appeared himself against Thomas Jenkys senior and against Roger Hulle in a plea of pledge not fulfilled so it is ordered he is attached more to the next [court]

Sum of the court 29s 10d
Expenses of the steward 6s 4d. And for one bag for court money 4d

Worfelde

Court held there on Tuesday on the feast of the Conversion of St Paul in the fifth year of the reign of King Henry V [25 January 1418]

Essoins

Thomas Trecille }
Thomas Merwalle senior } [essoined] themselves by Thomas Richardes
William Newtone }
John Cattestre }
William Dudley }
William Hewstar }
William Newe }

1418 P314/W/1/1/248

The 12	John the son of John Rowlowe	Stephen Stanlowe	William Gerbode}	
	Roger Towneshende	Thomas Toward	John Barndeley }	
	Stephen Bradeney	William Wermode	John the son of Nicholas Rowlowe }	sworn
	Roger Waltone	John Bromley	William Webbe }	

Amerced 6d

Roger Richardes plaintiff of John Grene of Patyngham in a plea of debt pledge for the prosecution John Snell & John Jay
And afterwards in the same court they are for a licence to agree and the same Roger withdrew from the court so he is in mercy

Amerced 6d

Roger Richardes plaintiff of John Grene of Patyngham in a plea of trespass pledge for the prosecution John Snell & John Jay
And afterwards in the same court they are for a licence to agree and the same Roger responded to the court so he is in mercy

Amerced 12d

Thomas Undurhull plaintiff appeared against Margaret Trecylle in a plea of trespass and the aforesaid is attached etc. & she did not come so she is in mercy & the pledge because he did not have [her in court] etc.

The next

Roger Hethe junior plaintiff appeared against Thomas Merwalle senior in a plea of debt and the aforesaid Thomas summoned did not come so it is ordered to attach to the next [court]

Amerced 6d

Recover

John Mathew plaintiff appeared against Thomas Jenkys senior & Roger Hulle in a plea of pledge not discharged. And whence he complains that the same Thomas Jenkys & Roger were pledges of the aforesaid plaintiff to pay for him to Agnes Mathewe 9s 2d just as they promised and nothing thence was paid whence the aforesaid plaintiff at the suit of the same Agnes was charged to pay to the same Agnes aforesaid money which he paid in default to discharge to his damage 40d. The which Thomas & Roger well recognised themselves not to have discharged so it is judged that the aforesaid John Mathewe may recover the sum with damages aforesaid and the aforesaid Thomas & Roger are in mercy

The next

Thomas Trecille plaintiff appeared against Thomas Gyllen in a plea of detention of three and a half yards of woollen cloth. And the aforesaid Thomas summoned did not come so it is ordered to attach to the next

Fine 12d

To this court came Richard Bradeney setting out abroad made a fine for the year following from this court for 12d with the lady for suit of court to be commuted. Pledge for the fine John Waltone

Fine 16d

John at Sonede made a fine of 16d for his trespass because he married a widow of the lady namely Alice Bradeney without a licence pledge for the fine John the son of Nicholas Rowlowe

The next

The jury said for the lady that they doubt how John Hethe is entered into and holds 1 messuage & 3 nooks of land with appurtenances in Kynggeslowe for the term of his life by a grant of John Gylden or by intrusion so the rolls of the court are to be investigated from the time of King Richard or Henry the Fourth & adjourned to the next [court]

1418 P314/W/1/1/248

The next — The jury have a day at the next [court] to present how William Webbe is entered and holds one toft with a croft in Rowghtone which he formerly acquired from John Oldyntone as it is said

The next — Davy Walschemon plaintiff of William Englis in a plea of debt pledge for the prosecution Roger Waltone & John Jay so it is ordered to summon to the next [court]

The next — John Lye plaintiff of Thomas Merwalle and his wife in a plea of debt pledge for the prosecution Roger Rowlowe & William Ree so it is ordered to summon to the next [court]

The next — Stephen Stanlowe plaintiff of Thomas Heyne in a plea of broken agreement pledge for the prosecution William Webbe & John Naa so it is ordered to summon to the next [court]

Sum of the court 4s 10d
Expenses of the steward 13d

1418 P314/W/1/1/249

Worfeld	Great court with leet held there on Wednesday next before the feast of St George the Martyr in the sixth year of the reign of King Henry V [20 April 1418]

Robert Ewdenas	Stephen Bradeney	Roger Towneshende
Roger Cattestre	John the son of Nicholas Rowlowe	William Wermode
John Jowkys	Roger Waltone	William Gerbode
Thomas Thomkys	John son of John Rowlowe	Thomas Underhull

Kynggeslowe & Stanlow strays price 12d	townships there present that Joan the daughter of William Nore took and carried away one swarm (agmen) of bees beyond the townships aforesaid price 12d & took away as far as the township of Wyke which is forfeit to the lady & a stray & is in the custody of William Nore. It is ordered to the reeve sell for the same price or better
Chesterton strays price 6d	township there presents 1 sheep (bidens) coming as a stray price 6d & remaining in the custody of John Snell
Rowlow, Bradeney, Asturhull, Ewyke, Sonede Amerced 5s 4d Goods found price 4½d	townships there present that Roger Barker (6d) son of Henry Barker forestalled Thomas Bradeney and drew blood (12d) from him. And conversely (econverso) the same Thomas forestalled the aforesaid Roger and drew blood from him (12d). Also they present that Henry Barker (6d) forestalled the aforesaid Thomas Bradeney. Also they present that the aforesaid Henry Barker (6d) forestalled William Barewe. Also they present that William Bradeney (6d) forestalled the aforesaid Roger Barker and drew blood (12d) from him. Also they present 1 pair of shoes (soculare) as goods found price 4½d
Hultone strays price 14d	township there presents 1 small boar coming as a stray price 14d and remaining in the custody of Stephen Bradeney
Burkote & Burkote, Ryndelforde & Bromeley	townships there present nothing but all well
Akyltone	township there presents nothing but all well
Stapulforde Amerced 2s 8d	township there presents that William Lowe (6d) made homsoken on Thomas Merwall junior. And that the same William Lowe (6d) made homsoken on William Baker. Also they present that Joan (20d) the wife of the aforesaid William Lowe made a poundbreach
Halen	Halen township there presents nothing
Rowghtone, Barndeley, Hokombe & Swankote Amerced 12d	townships there present that Thomas Jenkys senior (4d) forestalled John Rogerus. Also they present that the same John (4d) made an assault on the aforesaid Thomas Jenkys. Also they present that Thomas Jenkys junior (4d) broke an arrest of the beadle
Wyke	township there presents nothing
Alveskote, Wynneskote, Cattestre, Newtone Amerced 11d	townships there present that Thomas Richardes (3d) did not come, John Nycolles (3d) did not come. Also they present that William (4d) the son of Richard Walker unjustly took one Newl etc. from the house of Richard Ewdenas

1418 P314/W/1/1/249

Worfelde	township there presents nothing
The ale tasters Amerced 5s 2d	present that John (4d) the son of John Byllynggesley brewed 1 & broke the assize, William Yate (4d) brewed 1, Katherine Bulveys (6d) brewed 2, Richard Aldith (4d) brewed 1, William Bakes (4d) brewed 1, Joan the daughter of William Nore (4d) brewed 1, John Bulloke (4d) brewed 1, William Gerbode (4d) brewed 1, John Ynggemon (4d) brewed 1, William Locke (4d) brewed 1, Roger Cattestre (4d) brewed 1, Roger Dalley (4d) brewed 1, John Gerbode (4d) brewed 1, John Byllynggesley (4d) brewed 1, John son of Nicholas Rowlow (4d) brewed 1, & broke the assize so they in mercy
Pain	It is ordered whosoever brews ale in the manor of Worfelde that they sell a gallon for 1 penny for better ale for this year following under pain for each & everyone failing 2s
	the aforesaid jurors ...[remainder missing in the stitching of two pages.]
Worfelde	Small court held there on the day and year above stated

John Rowlowe senior	Roger Towneshende	William Webbe}
John Rowlowe junior	William Wermode	John Bromley}
William Gerbode	Stephen Webbe	Thomas Merwall junior }
John Jannen	Thomas Undurhull	Stephen Bradeney }

Essoins	William Ellewalle, Thomas Toward themselves from common suit by Thomas Lee
Amerced 6d	John Lye plaintiff & Thomas Merwalle junior and Agnes his wife defendants are for a licence to agree and the same John withdrew the court so the same is in mercy
Inquiry by the rolls of the court	Still to enquire by the rolls of the court how John Hethe is ingressed and holds 1 messuage & 3 nooks of land with appurtenances in Kyngeslowe for the term of his life by a grant of John Gylden or not or by intrusion
Essoined	Thomas Heyne himself from his law against Stephen Bradeney in a plea of broken agreement
Fine 7s 6d	To this court comes Thomas Trecylle senior of Alveskote & surrendered into the hands of the lady one messuage and 1 toft and 3 nooks of land with appurtenances in Alveskote to the use of John Trecylle his son to have and to hold to the aforesaid John and his heirs according to the custom of the manor by services thence thence [repeated] owed and of right accustomed. And the same John gives to the lady for a fine to have ingress 7s 6s. And he thence has seisin and made fealty pledge for the fine John Bromley & Thomas Haselwode
Fine 7s 6d	At the same court comes John the son of Thomas Trecylle & surrendered into the hands of the lady one messuage and 1 toft and 3 nooks of land with appurtenances in Alveskote to the use of Thomas Trecylle senior, father of the same John to have and to hold to the same Thomas for the term of the life of the same Thomas according to the custom of the manor by services thence owed and of right accustomed with the reversion remaining to the aforesaid John and his heirs after the term aforesaid when it should happen. And he gives to the lady for a fine 7s 6d pledge for the fine John Rowlow son of Nicholas Rowlowe. And he thence has seisin

1418 P314/W/1/1/249

The law

Thomas Undurhull plaintiff against Margaret Trecylle in a plea of trespass. And whence he complains that on the feast of St Peter in Chains last past she with certaon of her draught animals and pigs depastured & consumed the corn and grass of the aforesaid plaintiff to the value and damage of 40d. And the aforesaid Margaret ready in court to respond denied this that she made no damage to him as against her above-related. And she is to the law with six hands at the next [court] pledge for the law Thomas Trecille & Roger Smyth

Amerced 6d
Recover

Roger ~~Undurhull~~ Hethe plaintiff appeared against Thomas Merwalle senior in a plea of debt. And whence he complains that on Thursday next after the feast of the Finding of the Holy Cross in the fourth year of the reign of King Henry V he lent the aforesaid Thomas 6s 8d and he unjustly detains. And the aforesaid Thomas ready in court to respond well recognised the debt aforesaid so it is judged that the aforesaid Roger may recover the debt aforesaid and the same Thomas is in mercy for the unjust detention

The law

Thomas Trecille plaintiff appeared himself in court against Thomas Gyllen Taylour in a plea of detention of 3½ yards of woollen cloth namely medeley price 8s because the wife of the aforesaid Thomas on the day and feast of St Anne in the fifth year of the now King handed over to the aforesaid Thomas Gyllen the aforesaid three yards of cloth and a half to make one pall (indumentum) and to make for the aforesaid, his wife. The which Thomas Gyllen did not then make nor hand back but forbad to hand back the aforesaid formed or not formed but unjustly detains to the damage of the aforesaid plaintiff 10s. And the aforesaid Thomas Gyllen ready in court to respond denies this that he received nor had no cloth from the wife of the aforesaid Thomas Trecille as the same Thomas stated and alleged against him and he is at law with six hands to the next [court] pledge for the law William Oldyntone and Roger Gyllen

Amerced 6d

David Walshemon plaintiff appeared himself against William Englys in a plea of debt and the same William responded to the court so he is in mercy

Fine 12d

To this court comes John Neeldone and surrendered into the hands of the lady by the hands of John Rowlowe son of Nicholas Rowlowe one cottage in Halen to the use of William Aleyn clerk to have and to hold to the same William and his heirs according to the custom of the manor. And he gives to the lady for a fine 6d. And he has seisin and made fealty

Heriots price 7s 6d
Escheat 3s
Escheat 3s
12d for the increase

To this court comes John Neeldone and surrendered into the hands of the lady one cottage in Halen to the use of Thomas Gyllen by the hand of Stephen Webbe to have and to hold to the same Thomas and his heirs according to the custom of the manor. And he gives to the lady for a fine 12d. And he has seisin and made fealty

The aforesaid jury presents that Thomas Rychards who owed suit at this court did not come. John Nycolles (2d) did not come. Also they present that John Neeldone who held from the lady one messuage with half a virgate of land with appurtenances and a quarter part of one nook of land with appurtenances in Stanlowe from the heredity of Alice his wife by the custom of the manor on the day he died at whose death there falls to the lady 1 ox in the name of heriot price 7s 6d. Also there falls to the lady for escheat namely one horse with a male foal and 1 hive of bees price 3s. Also falling to the lady Also falling to the lady 1 sow with 3 piglets price 3s so it is ordered to the reeve to sell more dearly if he is able. And afterwards he sold all the aforesaid heriots

To examine the rolls

and escheats to the increase to the lady of 12d. Also they present that Isolda Gerbode who held from the lady one message with half a virgate of land with appurtenances in Hokombe for the term of the life of the same Isolda on the day she died. Also the same Isolda held in Halen 1 toft with half a virgate of land on the day she died. And the toft aforesaid with 1 nook of land remains to Richard Gerbode and his heirs according to the custom of the manor. And for which he lately made a fine and is admitted. And the other nook of land is in the hands of the lady until another heriot comes etc. And of another nook it is doubted whether he had or not until the rolls of the court are examined. Also they present that the same Isolda who held from the lady 1 parcel of meadow in Halghmedewe for the term of the life of the same Isolda. And it remains with Richard Gerbode and his heirs according to the custom of the manor by a fine previously made it is ordered to seize for the lady heriots after the death of the aforesaid Isolda. And the parcel of meadow aforesaid remains in the hand of the lady until etc. Also they present that Edith Rugge who held from the lady 1 cottage with appurtenances in Worfelde on the day she died at whose death no heriot nor escheat fell to the lady on the day of her death because she had nothing because of poverty. And the cottage aforesaid remains in the hand of the lady until etc. And on this in the same court comes Thomas Rugge son and heir of the aforesaid Edith and took from the lady the aforesaid cottage with appurtenances to hold to himself and his heirs according to the custom of the manor by services thence owed and of right accustomed. And he gives to the lady for a fine 16d and thence has seisin and he made fealty

Ordered to seize 2 heriots

Fine 16d

Heriot price 5s

Also the aforesaid jury presents that Peter Hultone who held from the lady 1 messuage with half a virgate of land with appurtenances in Hultone of the right of heredity of Alice his wife on the day he died at whose death there falls to the lady 1 young steer price 5s. And no escheat fell to the lady because he had none on the day of his death

Fine 10s

To this court comes Thomas at Sonede and surrendered into the hands of the lady 1 messuage with half a virgate of land with appurtenances in Sonede to the use of John his younger son after the death of the aforesaid Thomas and Alice his wife when it should happen. And if it should happen that the aforesaid John dies, his aforesaid father and Alice at that time living, all the aforesaid lands and tenements with its appurtenances remain with the aforesaid Thomas & Alice & their heirs according to the custom of the manor to have and to hold all the aforesaid messuage with half a virgate of land aforesaid to the same John and his heirs after the death of the aforesaid when it should happen and according to the form aforesaid. And he gives to the lady for a fine 10s. And he thence has seisin

Fine 6d

To this court comes Thomas at Sonede and surrendered into the hands of the lady 1 parcel of land lying in the field called Sonedefeld to the use of Agnes the daughter of the aforesaid Thomas after the death of the aforesaid Thomas and Alice his wife when it should happen. And if it should happen that the aforesaid Agnes dies, her aforesaid father and Alice at that time living, all the aforesaid land remains with the aforesaid Thomas & Alice & their heirs according to the custom of the manor to have and to hold to the same Agnes and her heirs after the death aforesaid when it should happen and according to the form aforesaid. And she gives to the lady for a fine 6d And she thence has seisin

To this court comes John Dallyley and Alice Dallyley his wife and took from the lady as of the right of heredity of the same Alice the daughter and heir of John Regnold one messuage with half a virgate of land with appurtenances in

Kynggeslow formerly in the tenure of Roger Kynggeslowe to have and to hold to the aforesaid Alice and the heirs of the same Alice according to the custom of the manor by services thence owed and of right accustomed. And he gives to the lady for a fine 12s. And they have seisin thence and made fealty pledge for the fine Roger Dallyley

Fine 12s

To this court comes Thomas Gyllen and made a fine with the lady for trespass in the wood of the lady for 20d

20d

To this court comes Thomas Rugge son and heir of Edith Rugge and surrendered into the hands of the lady one cottage with appurtenances in Worfelde formerly in the hands of Walter Rugge to the use of Henry Barker to have and to hold to the same Henry and his heirs according to custom. And he gives to the lady for a fine 12d and made fealty

Fine 12d

Worfelde

Small court held there on Monday next after the feast of St Barnabus the Apostle in the sixth year of the reign of King Henry V [13 June 1418]

Essoins

John Cattestre }
William Hockombe }
John Jannen }
John Holigreve } by William Gappe
Thomas Merewall junior }
Roger Jones }
Richard Gerbod }

The 12 jurors

John son of Nicholas Rowlowe	Roger Towneshende	William Bromley
John son of Joan of Rowlowe	Thomas Undurhull	Stephen Stanlow
Roger Waltone	William Wermode	Robert Bruggehende
Roger Smyth	Roger Gerbode	William Gerbode

Amerced 6d

Thomas Trecylle plaintiff and Thomas Gyllen defendant are for a licence to agree and the same Thomas Gyllen withdrew from the court so he is in mercy

Pain

At this court a pain of 40d is imposed by the beadle that he make to raise all money recovered in diverse suits just as formerly he had in order let there be no more complaint of the parties

Amerced 4d

Amerced 7d

The aforesaid jury presents that Thomas Richardes (2d) who owed suit at this court did not come John Nicholles (2d) for similar. Also they present that Roger Towneshende (4d) made a trespass in the wood of the lady. Also they present that William Bromley (3d) fished in privately held [in severalty] waters there without licence so he is in mercy

Fine 5s

To this court comes Richard Gerbode son of William Gerbode of Hockombe and took from the hands of the lady one nook of land with appurtenances in Halon called Jorylond to have and to hold to the same Richard & his heirs according to the custom of the manor by services thence owed and of right accustomed. And he gives to the lady for a fine 5s and is admitted and he made fealty

Amerced 6d

Stephen Stanlowe plaintiff & Thomas Heyne defendant are for a licence to agree and both parties are in mercy by the pledge of John son of Nicholas Rowlowe

1418 P314/W/1/1/249

Heriots — At this court ~~comes~~ it is judged by the examination of the steward that the draught animals of Isolda Gerbode deceased price 5s which ought to have been seized as heriots of the aforesaid Isolda are taken away and removed by the default of Thomas Jenkys junior. And so the same Thomas is to respond for the price and because the same confesses to have so great a sum in his hands which sum is seized by the steward to the use of the lady until etc.

The next — A certain black horse seized as distraint by Roger Dallyley price 4s. And let it be proclaimed as intended etc. before the next [court] and it is in the custody of the same Roger

The next — Still the scrutiny of the rolls touching 1 nook of land which William Gerbode claims to hold is adjourned until the next [court] because there is doubt concerning the legal rights in the property which he had claims to have

Amerced 6d — Thomas Undurhull plaintiff appeared himself against Margaret Trecylle in a plea of trespass who elsewhere wagered the law and now she has defaulted in her law so it is judged that the aforesaid Thomas may recover 40d of damages as the same Thomas in the preceding court against her narrated so she is in mercy

Sum of this court 7s 5d
Expenses of the steward on the day of the court 6s 6d

It is granted to the bound men of Halen, Alvescote, Cattestre, Ryndelford that they may have mast for pannage for the whole time of pannage next following in the wood of Sowdley. And they give to the lady for a fine 2s

Affeerors: John Jannen, Roger Townshende

Sum of the courts with leet £4 4s 1½d
Thence in expenses of the steward 23s 8½d

1418 P314/W/1/1/250

Small court held there on Saturday next after the feast of St Peter in Chains in the sixth year of the reign of King Henry V [6 August1418]

	John Rowlow junior	Roger Gerbode	Roger Waltone
The 12	Stephen Bradeney	Thomas Undurhull	Roger Kyngeslow
	John Jannen	Roger Towneshende	Roger Smyth
	William Wermode	John Rowlow senior	Thomas Rowlow

Amerced 6d The aforesaid jury presents that William Nicholles (2d) did not come, Thomas Richardes (2d) did not come, William Newe (2d) did not come, Robert Sawndres did not come, John Cattestre (4d) did not come to warrant his essoin

Fine 10s fine 12d To this court comes Alice Neelden of Stanlow and granted to John Yate and Agnes his wife the reversion of one messuage with half a virgate of land in Stanlowe after the death of the same Alice to have and to hold the aforesaid tenement with appurtenances with their appurtenances to the aforesaid John and Agnes his wife, their heirs and assigns after the death aforesaid when it should happen according to the custom of the manor. And they give to the lady for a fine 10s and made fealty. Also the aforesaid Alice granted to the aforesaid John Yate and Agnes his wife the reversion of a quarter part of one nook of land with appurtenances in Stanlowe after the death of the same Alice to hold to the aforesaid John & Agnes his wife their heirs and assigns after the death aforesaid when it should happen according to the custom of the manor. And they give to the lady for a fine 12d and made fealty

The next Robert Webbe plaintiff of Roger Dallyley and of Nicholas Stanlow in a plea of debt pledge for the prosecution Stephen Stanlowe. It is ordered to summon to the next [court]

Fine 2s Edith Barker daughter of Henry Barker married herself to John Elkoc without a licence from the lady for which transgression she made a fine with the lady for for 2s pledge for the fine Henry Barker

The next John Gylden & Roger Hethe plaintiffs of Richard Bradeney in a plea of debt pledge for the prosecution Stephen Stanlowe so it is ordered to summon to the next [court]

Fine 5s To this court comes William Gerbode as the heir of William Gerbode his father deceased and seeks admittance as the next heir after the death of Isolda Gerbode and she is dead lately the wife of his father aforesaid who held for the term of her life to half a messuage and one whole nook of land with appurtenances in Hockombe. And the aforesaid William son of William is recognised as the heir and is admitted to hold to himself and his heirs according to the custom of the manor. And he gives to the lady for a fine 5s & is admitted and made fealty

Sum of this court 18s
Expenses of the steward 4s 7½d

1418 P314/W/1/1/251

Worfelde	Great court held there on Friday next after the feast of St Michael the Archangel in the sixth year of the reign of King Henry V [30 September 1418]
Essoins	William Skynner himself from appearance } by William Gappe John Trecille junior }
The 12	Roger Cattestre, John Jowkys, William Wermode } John Rowlowe junior, John Rowlowe senior, Roger Towneshende } sworn Robert Eudenas, Thomas Thomkys, Stephen Stanlowe } Stephen Bradeney, Roger Waltone, John Bromley }
Hultone Let it be proclaimed	township there presents one cow coming as a waif price 6s 8d previously seized in the feast of St John the Baptist last past and remaining in the custody of William Dudley so let it be proclaimed
Rowghtone, Barndeley, Hokombe	townships there present that John Corne (4d) from Clareley made a trespass with draught animals and his livestock in the field of Rowghtone so he is in mercy
Chesturton Let it be proclaimed	township there presents 1 red draught animal coming as a waif price 20d the which draught animal being a stray from the feast of Easter until at this court and remains in the custody of John Snell so let it be proclaimed
Alvescote, Wynnescote, Cattestre, Newtone Stray price 1d	townships there present that Thomas Richardes (3d) who owed suit did not come. John Nycolles (3d) did not come. Also they present that Richard (6d) the son of Robert Eudenas made a poundbreach. Also they present that Richard Walker (6d) made a poundbreach. Also they present 1 swarm of bees coming as a stray price 1d & remaining in the custody of Richard Whetebroke so it is ordered to the bailiff to sell dearer if he can. Also they present that the wife (2d) of Richard Walker is a common scold (contentrix). Also they present that the wife (8d) of the aforesaid Richard Walker came against the peace to the house of Roger Richardes on the feast of St Martin last past and there took and carried away 2 woollen fleeces of the aforesaid Roger price 6d. And oat flour price a halfpenny so she is in mercy
Rowlowe, Asturhull, Ewyke, Sonede Strays 10d	townships there present that John Henene (3d) did not come to make suit . Also they present 1 sheep (bidens) coming as a stray price 10d and remaining in the custody of John Snell senior so it is ordered to the beadle to sell dearer if he is able
Burkote & Burkote, Ryndelforde & Bromley	townships there present nothing but all well. Eudenas presents nothing. Oldyntone presents nothing.
Akyltone Let it be proclaimed	township there presents 1 male black draught animal previously seized for a stray at the feast of Pentecost last past price 3s and remains in the custody of Roger Dallyley so let it be proclaimed as intended (pu[te])
Wyke	township there presents that Matilda Ody (2d) forestalled Agnes Hymley. And that the aforesaid Agnes (4d) forestalled the aforesaid Matilda
Kyngeslowe & Stanlowe	townships there present nothing but all well. Stapulforde presents nothing. Worfeld presents nothing

Halen Amerced 6d	township there presents that William Barewe (4d) made an assault on Margery Stevenes. Also they present that the wife (2d) of the aforesaid William Barewe is a common scold (contentrix) against her neighbours (visinos)
The ale tasters Amerced 4s 4d	present that Roger Jones (2d) brewed 1 & broke the assize. Also they present that Margery Huggen (4d) brewed 1, Hamo Hymley (4d) brewed 1, John Jonesone of Rowlow (4d) brewed 1, William Barewe(4d) brewed 1, William Dudley (4d) brewed 1, William Yngemon (2d) brewed 1, Isolda Walker (4d) brewed 1, John Bromley (4d) brewed 1, Robert Bruggehende (4d) brewed 1, John Byllynggesley (4d) brewed 1, Margaret the servant of Isolda Walker (4d) brewed 1, Thomas Gyllen (4d) brewed 1, William Noore (4d) brewed 1 & broke the assize
	Small court held there on the day and year above stated
Essoin	John Bulloke himself by Roger Jones
The 12	John Rowlowe junior, William Wermode, William Newe, John Jannen, John Rowlowe senior, Roger Smyth, Stephen Bradeney, Roger Knotte, Thomas Trecille, Roger Waltone, Thomas Undurhull, Roger Richardes } sworn
The next	John Jowkys plaintiff of Richard Walker in a plea of trespass pledges for the prosecution William Holdyngtone & John Jay so it is ordered to summon to the next [court]
The next	John Jowkys plaintiff of Richard Walker in a plea of trespass pledges for the prosecution William Holdyntone & John Jay so it is ordered to summon to the next [court]
The next	Henry Barker plaintiff of John Stevenes in a plea of debt pledge for the prosecution William Stevenes so it is ordered to summon to the next [court]
Amerced 2d The next [court]	Robert Webbe plaintiff appeared himself against Roger Dalley & Nicholas Stanlowe in a plea of debt. And whence he pleads that they owe him 39s 11d & they unjustly detain. And the aforesaid Nicholas is ready in court to respond well recognises the debt aforesaid for himself & the aforesaid Roger and concerning damages adjourned until the next [court] so it is judged that the aforesaid Robert may recover the debt & the same Nicholas is in mercy for the unjust detention
The next [court]	John Gylden & Roger Hethe plaintiffs appeared themselves against Richard Bradeney in a plea of debt. And the aforesaid Richard summoned did not come so he is attached to the next [court]
Amerced 2d Heriot price 3s 4d Heriot price 12d	The aforesaid 12 jurors present that John Nicolles (2d) who owed suit at this court did not come. Also they present that William Webbe who held from the lady one messuage with 1 nook of land and 1 toft with 3 nooks of land with all their appurtenances in Rowghtone has died at whose death there falls to the lady 1 steer price 3s 4d and 1 two-tooth sheep (bidens) price 12d in the name of heriot and no escheat falls to the lady because she had nothing on the day of her death. And the tenements aforesaid remain with Margery the former wife of the aforesaid William for the term of her life.

1418 P314/W/1/1/251

Heriot price 4s 6d | In the hand of the lady — Also they present that Eleanor Ewyke who held from the lady 1 messuage with 1 virgate of land with appurtenances in Ewyke has died at whose death there falls to the lady 1 ruby heifer price 4s 6d and it remains in the custody of William Ewyke son and heir of the aforesaid Eleanor. And the tenement aforesaid remains in the hand of the lady until the heir comes to make a fine etc. Also they present that Margery Robyns who held from the lady 1 messuage with half a virgate of land with appurtenances in Burkote has died at whose death there falls to the lady 1 two-tooth sheep (bidens) price 12d and it remains in the custody of William Robyns. And the tenement aforesaid remains in the hand of the lady until etc. And on this in the same court comes William Robyns son and heir of the aforesaid Margery Robyns and took from the lady the tenement aforesaid with its appurtenances to have and to hold to the aforesaid William himself and his heirs according to the custom of the manor. And he gives to the lady for a fine 10s for ingress and seisin to have and he made fealty. Pledge for the fine Roger Waltone

Heriot 12d | fine 10s

Election of reeve — John Rowlowe son of Nicholas is elected to the office of reeve and took the oath

Fine 12d — To this court comes Thomas Richardes and made a fine with the lady to commute suit of court for the year following for 12d

Fine 2s 6d — To this court comes Margaret Stevenes and surrendered into the hands of the lady half a nook of land with appurtenances in Chesturtone to the use of John Smyth of Hultone to have and to hold to the same John, his heirs and assigns according to the custom of the manor. And he gives to the lady for a fine 2s 6d. And he made fealty and thence has seisin

Surety — Richard Walker found surety to keep the peace of the lord King towards William Palhog & Sibill his wife namely Robert Sawndres & Thomas Merwalle under a pain of £40

Surety — William Palhog & Sibill his wife found surety to keep the peace of the lord King towards Richard Walker namely Robert Ewdenas & Richard Whytebroke under a pain of £40

Affeerors: Stephen Bradeney, Thomas Undurhull
Sum of the courts 32s 7d
In expenses of the steward 16s 6d

1418 P314/W/1/1/252

Worfelde — Small court held there on Monday next after the feast of the Apostles Simon & Jude in the sixth year of the reign of King Henry V [31 October 1418]

Essoins — John Byllynggesley, John Holigreve, Roger Jones, John Hethe, [essoin] themselves from appearance by Richard Haselwode

The 12

Stephen Bradeney	Thomas Undurhull	John Barndeley }	
Roger Towneshende	John Bromley	Robert Webbe }	sworn
Roger Waltone	William Newe	John Jannen }	
John Rowlowe senior	Stephen Stanlowe	Roger Gerbode }	

The law — Henry Barker plaintiff appeared himself against John Stevenes in a plea of trespass. And whence he complains that he owes him 20s and unjustly detains to the damage of the aforesaid plaintiff 6s 8d. And the aforesaid John is ready in court to respond denies this that he owes him nothing nor unjustly detains and he is to the law with six hands at the next [court] pledge for the law Thomas Trecille & John Bulloke

The next — Roger Wheolar plaintiff of William Kynggessone in a plea of debt pledge for the prosecution John Rogers and John Jay so it is ordered to summon to the next [court]

The next — Roger Wheolar plaintiff of William Kynggessone in a plea of debt pledge for the prosecution John Rogers and John Jay so it is ordered to summon to the next [court]

The law — John Gylden & Roger Hethe plaintiffs appeared themselves against Richard Bradeney in a plea of debt. And whence they complain that he owes them 6s 8d and unjustly detains to the damage of the aforesaid plaintiffs 40s. And the aforesaid Richard ready in court denies this that he owes them nothing nor unjustly detains and he is to the law with six hands at the next [court] pledge for the law John Bradeney & John Smyth

The next — John Jowkys plaintiff appeared himself against Richard Walker in a plea of trespass and the aforesaid Richard is not attached so it is ordered to attach to the next [court]

The jury — The aforesaid jury presents that John Nicholles (2d) who owed suit at this court & did not come so the same in mercy

fine 20s — To this court comes Thomas Haselwode & Matilda his wife and the same Matilda confessed & was examined by the steward & surrendered into the hands of the lady 1 messuage with 1 virgate of land with appurtenances in Bradeney to the use of John Bradeney son of Stephen Bradeney to have & to hold to the same John & his heirs & assigns according to the custom of the manor. And he gives to the lady for a fine 20s. And he thence has seisin. And he made fealty

fine 10d — To this court comes Isolda Walker & surrendered into the hands of the lady 1 cottage with appurtenances in Ryndelforde lately in the tenure of John Walker to the use of John Bromley & Alice his wife to have and to hold to the same John & Alice their heirs and assigns from the chief lord of that fee by services which are pertaining to them. And they give for a fine 10d and made fealty

To this court comes Roger Tornour & surrenders into the hands of the lady 1 piece of waste of the lady in the fee of Bromley to the use of John Bromley & Alice his wife to have and to hold to the same John & Alice, their heirs and assigns from the chief lord of that fee by services which are pertaining to the same parcel. And they

Fine 2d	give to the lady for a fine 2d. And they make fealty and they thence have seisin

Sum of this court 21s
In expenses of the steward 8s 6½d

Worfelde	Small court held there on Tuesday next after the feast of St Martin the Bishop in the year above said [15 November 1418]
Essoins	John Yate, Henry Barker, William Newe, John Barndeley, Thomas Rowlow, Roger Bromley by John Rowlowe

John Rowlowe senior	Roger Towneshende	Roger Gerbode
John Jannen	Robert Webbe	Richard Aldyth
Stephen Bradeney	Stephen Stanlowe	Roger Richardes
Roger Waltone	John Bromley	John Byllynggesley

The next	Thomas Heyne plaintiff of Thomas Jenkys & of Roger Hulle & Roger Smyth in a plea of debt so it is ordered to summon to the next. Pledge for the prosecution Robert Bruggehende
The next	Thomas Heyne plaintiff of Thomas Jenkys in a plea of trespass so it is ordered to attach to the next. Pledge for the prosecution the aforesaid Robert
The next	Roger Wheolar plaintiff appeared himself against John Kynggessone in a plea of debt and the aforesaid John is not summoned so it is ordered to summon to the next [court]
The next	Roger Wheolar plaintiff appeared himself against John Kynggessone in a plea of debt and the aforesaid John is not summoned so it is ordered to summon to the next [court]
Amerced 6d	Henry Barker plaintiff & John Stevenes defendant are for a licence to agree & the same John Stevenes responds to the court so he is in mercy
The next	The plea which is between John Jowkys plaintiff & Richard Walker defendant in a plea of trespass by the prayer of the parties is adjourned to the next [court]
The next	John Cattestre plaintiff of John Glover in a plea of trespass pledge for the prosecution Robert Barker & John Jay so it is ordered to attach to the next [court]
12d	To this court comes John Hethe and gives to the lady for a fine 12d to commute suit of court from the date of this court until the feast of St Michael next in the future
12d	To this court comes John Nicholles and gives to the lady for a fine 12d to commute suit of court from the date of this court until the feast of St Michael next in the future
Amerced 6d	Richard Bradeney responded to the court against John Gylden & Roger Hethe in a plea of debt are for a licence to agree
The next	Elcok Mustardmon plaintiff of Margaret Huggen in a plea of debt pledge for the prosecution Henry Barker & John Jay so it is ordered to summon to the next [court]

1418 P314/W/1/1/252

Amerced 2d — The aforesaid 12 jurors present that William Hockombe (2d) did not come so he is in mercy

Sum of this court 3s 2d
Expenses of the steward 16d

Court held there on Tuesday on the feast of St Nicholas the bishop in the year aforesaid [6 December 1418]

Essoins — Roger Hethe, Richard Gerbode, William Hockombe, Thomas Jenkys essoined themselves against Thomas Heyne in a plea of debt

The 12					
	Stephen Bradeney	Stephen Stanlowe	Richard Gerbode	Thomas Undurhull }	
	Roger Waltone	William Newe	John Jannen	Roger Towneshende }	sworn
	John Rowlowe senior	John Barndeley	Henry Barker	Robert Webbe }	

Amerced 2d
The next — Thomas ~~Jenkys~~ Heyne plaintiff appeared himself against Thomas Jenkys junior & against Roger Smyth & Roger Hulle not essoined until the next [court]

The next — Thomas Heyne 6d for one cow plaintiff appeared himself against Thomas Jenkys in a plea of trespass. And the aforesaid Thomas is attached by one cow price 6s [above it looks like 6d] & did not come so it is ordered to distrain to the next [court]

Turn
[The dorse]

The next — The plea which is between Roger Wheolar plaintiff & John William Kyngessone defendant in a plea of debt the aforesaid seek an adjournment until the next [court]

The next — The plea which is between Roger Wheolar plaintiff & John William Kyngessone defendant in a plea of debt the aforesaid seek an adjournment until the next [court]

6d — John Jowkys plaintiff & Richard Walker defendant in a plea of trespass are for a licence to agree & the same Richard responded to the court so he is in mercy

6d — John Jowkys plaintiff & Richard Walker defendant in a plea of trespass are for a licence to agree & the same Richard responded to the court so he is in mercy

The next — Elkoc Mustardmon plaintiff appeared himself against Margaret Huggen in a plea of ~~trespass~~ debt summoned did not come so it is ordered to attach to the next [court]

The next — John the servant of Roger Swankote plaintiff of Stephen Hymley in a plea of debt pledge for the prosecution John Hulle & John Jay so it is ordered to attach to the next [court] because he is a stranger

Fine 16d — Thomas Gerbode made a fine for 16d with the lady to marry Emmota Colyar widow of the lady within the domain

Jury — Within the domain the jury presents nothing but all well

The next — John Cattestre plaintiff appeared himself against John Glover in a plea of trespass summoned did not come so it is ordered to attach to the next [court]

Sum of the court 2s 6d
Expenses of the steward 20d
In parchment 2d

1419 P314/W/1/1/253

Worfeld	Great court held there on Monday the 10th day of April in the seventh year of the reign of King Henry V [10 April 1419]
Essoins	John Catestre, John Elwalle & Richard Aleyn essoined themselves by John Est
The 12	Roger Eudenas Roger Waltone Thomas Tomkys Stephen Stanlowe } Stephen Bradeney John Jonkys Roger atte Tounende John Barneley } sworn Roger Cattestre John Roulowe Thomas Undirhull John Billyngesley}
Kyngeslowe & Stanlowe	townships there present nothing. Roulowe, Bradeney, Astone, Ewyke & Sonde present nothing. ~~Hiltone presents nothing~~. Chesturtone presents nothing
Akeltone Strays forfeited 2s	township there present nothing. Eudenas, Oldyngtone present nothing. Alvescote, Wynnescote, Catestre, Neutone present one ruby heifer price 2s coming as a stray on this side of the feast of St Peter in Chains last in the custody of Roger Tounesende
Stapulford Amerced 8d pain put 12d	township there presents nothing. Halen presents nothing. Burcote, Burcote, Ryndelford & Bromley present John Bromley (4d) of Adliscote owed appearance and did not come so etc. And they present Roger Knyght (4d) for the same. And it is agreed a certain road to be repaired at Ryndelford between the Roche & the Floodgates by the vicar of Worfeld before the 15th of Easter next under pain of 12d to be raised to the work of the lady
Hiltone Amerced 14d	township there presents that Richard Richardson (6d) son of Julian atte Walle made an assault on Henry the servant of Stephen Bradeney and drew blood (8d) from him
Wyken Strays 6d Amerced 16d	township there presents 1 plough share as a waif price 6d in the custody of William Roulowe. And they present Thomas Heyne (12d) unjustly raised the hue and cry on Thomas Bradeney. And they present that Richard Heuster (4d) broke the impoundment of 1 horse impounded by Thomas Heyne aforesaid for money owed to the Canons of Lychfield
Roughtone, Hokcombe, Swancote & Barnedley Goods forfeit 12d Amerced 16d	townships there present that the wife of Thomas Jenkyns junior found several goods in her barn price 12d in the custody of the aforesaid Thomas unjustly taken by Agnes Matheu (16d)
Worfeld Amerced 4d	township there presents that Roger Warde (2d) & Margaret Tresill (2d) blocked the King's way with dung at the Waturlade close to the house of St Mary so etc.
The tasters of ale Amerced 8s	present that William Newe (4d) 1 brew, William Bakes (4d) 1 brew, William Ingman (4d) 1 brew, Richard Bradeney (4d) 1 brew, Thomas Bradeney (4d) 1 brew, John Billyngesley (4d) senior 1 brew, Roger Warde (8d) 2 brews, William Bromley (4d) 1 brew, William Goolde (4d) 1 brew, William Kyngessone (8d)2 brews, Alice Taillour (4d) 1 brew, Stephen Hymley (4d) 1 brew, Joan the daughter of William Noore (4d) 1 brew, William Robyns (4d) 1 brew, Thomas Baker of Hiltone (4d) 1 brew, John Goolde (4d) 1 brew, William Noore (4d) 1 brew, John Baret (4d) 1 brew, Alice Sonde (12d) a common brewer & broke the assize so in mercy etc. & John (4d) Billyngesley junior 1 brew & similarly broke the assize etc.

1419 P314/W/1/1/253

Amerced 2s

The 12 jurors present that John Snell constable of the domain aforesaid arrested John Stevenes for the peace to be kept. Thomas Rigge & the aforesaid John Stevenes (2s) broke the arrest aforesaid so etc. And they say that the townships and ale tasters aforesaid presented well and concealed nothing

Affeerors: John Roulowe, Roger Tounesende

Sum of this court 16s 4d

Small court held there on the day and year above stated [10 April 1419]

Essoins

John Bromley of Adliscote, John Cattestre essoined themselves by John Hunt

The 12

John Janne	Robert Webbe	Robert Bruggeende	William Newe
Toward	Henry Baker	Roger Gerbot	Roger Smyth of Hiltone }sworn
John Bromley	William Gerbot	Thomas Tresill	John Waltone}

Fine 12d

William Ewyke made a fine for suit of court to be commuted from the date of this court until the same day of the year to come around. And he gives to the lady for a fine 12d

Amercements of pleas 4s 6d

Thomas Heyne (6d) in mercy for his unjust plea against Thomas Jenkyns junior, Roger Smyth & Roger Hull [in a plea] of debt

The same Thomas(6d) in mercy for his unjust plea against Thomas Jenkyns in a plea of trespass

Agnes Matheu (6d) in mercy because she withdrew the court against John Mittone in a plea of debt

William Kyngessone (12d) put himself in mercy for a licence to agree with Roger Wheler in 2 pleas of debt

Elcok Mustardman (6d) put himself in mercy for his unjust plea against Margery Huggyn in a plea of debt

Stephen Hymley (6d) put himself in mercy for a licence to agree with John the servant of Roger Swancote in a plea of debt

John Hethe (6d) put himself in mercy for a licence to agree with Roger Dalliley & Robert Bruggeende in a plea of trespass

John Glover (6d) put himself in mercy for a licence to agree with John Cattestre in a plea of trespass

Plea summon to the next [court]

Thomas Richardes not prosecuting plaintiff of Roger Richardes of Neutone in a plea of broken agreement pledge for the prosecution Roger Tounsende. And it is ordered to the bailiff to summon to the next [court]

Thomas Heyne plaintiff of Thomas Bradeney agreed put himself in a plea of debt pledge for the prosecution John Roulowe

Plea the law

The same Thomas Heyne plaintiff of Thomas Jenkyns junior made the law in a plea of debt etc. And he said that the aforesaid Thomas Jenkyns bought from the aforesaid Thomas Heyne on the feast of St Peter in Chains in the 5th year of the reign of King Henry V at Wykene diverse grain in sheaths from the tithes of Roughtone & Barnedley for 46s 8d to pay on the feast of the Purification of the Blessed Mary thereafter next following and on the feast of the Nativity of St John the Baptist thereafter next following equally which he owes and unjustly detains as he says to the damage of 15s. And the aforesaid Thomas Jenkyns came in his own person and defended the force and injury then etc. And he says that he owes him nothing further as he now alleges against him & thence to wager the law pledge for the law Robert Eudenas & Roger Hulle etc. And it is agreed by the steward that the aforesaid Thomas Jenkyns thus is at the next court with 5 hands and to make the law just as he above took up

Taking out of the hand of the lady. Fine 12d

Alice Swynney heir of John Walker of Ryndelford through John Bromley her attorney came and took from the hand of the lady 2 cottages with curtilage in Halene formerly in the tenure of William Inglissh to hold to the same Alice her heirs and assigns for ever according to the custom of the manor. And she gives to the lady for a fine 12d and has seisin

Surrender fine 12d

The same Alice through the aforesaid John Bromley came here in court and surrendered into the hands of the lady the 2 cottages aforesaid with curtilage to the use of William Inglissh to have and to hold to himself, his heirs and assigns according to the custom of the manor. And he gives to the lady for a fine 12d by the pledge of John Roulowe. And he made fealty and has seisin

Surrender Fine 5s

Roger Richardes came here in court and surrendered into the hands of the lady through John the son of John Rowlowe 1 toft & 1 nook of land with appurtenances in Neutone which the same Roger acquired from William Golde of Akeltone to the use of John the son of John Richardes after the death of the same Roger & Margery his wife to have and to hold to the aforesaid John the son of John Richardes his heirs and assigns for ever according to the custom of the manor. And he gives to the lady for a fine 5s by the pledge of John Jenkyns

Surrender Fine 12d

Alice the daughter of Walter Rigge came here in court and surrendered into the hands of the lady 1 cottage with appurtenances in Worfeld formerly in the tenure of William Palmer to the use of Henry Barker to have and to hold to himself, his heirs and assigns for ever according to the custom of the manor. And he gives to the lady for a fine 12d. And he made fealty and has seisin

Taking of land out of the hand of the lady Fine 20s

William Ewyk son & heir of William Ewyk came & took from the hands of the lady 1 message & 1 virgate of land with appurtenances in Ewyke which were in the hand of the lady after the death of Eleanor formerly the wife of William Ewyk to have and to hold to the same William his heirs and assigns according to the custom of the manor. And he gives to the lady for a fine 20s & made fealty and has seisin

Surrender & land remains in the hand of the lady

Roger Richardes & Margery his wife confessed & examined came here in court & surrendered into the hands of the lady 1 messuage & half a virgate of land with appurtenances in Neutone to the use of Roger Prestees after the death of the aforesaid Roger & Margery to have and to hold to the aforesaid Roger Prestees his heirs and assigns after the death of the aforesaid Roger Richardes and Margery for ever according to the custom of the manor. And the land remains in the hand of the lady etc.

Fine for inquiry to be held 2s

Thomas the son of the aforesaid Roger Richardes came here in court and gives to the lady for a fine 2s for an inquiry to be held of the 24 to enquire whether the aforesaid Roger Prestees has the greater right to make a fine with the lady for the aforesaid messuage and half virgate of land with appurtenances in Neutone or the aforesaid Thomas etc. And the inquiry aforesaid still elected to try and to judge have a day to enquire according to the custom of the manor until the next [court] whose names are contained on the dorse of the roll

Fine 12d

Alice Taillour made a fine with the steward for 12d to brew from the feast of the Annunciation of theBlessed Mary last until the same feast thereafter next following and she has a licence because she is poor

Heriot seized by the bailiff 5s 6d

John Snell the bailiff seized into the hands of the lady 1 steer price 5d 6d for the heriot of Richard Boulveys and it remains in the custody of the aforesaid John thence to answer

Fine 20d

The 12 jurors aforesaid say on their oath that Henry Halle took as his wife Alice formerly the wife of Peter Hiltone tenant of the manor without a licence from the lady etc. And he gives to the lady for a fine 20d

Surety to keep the peace with a pain of £60

Sureties of Thomas Richardes concerning keeping the peace to Roger Prestees. Roger Tounsende, John Bromley, John Jenkyns & Roger Waltone each of them under pain of £10. And the aforesaid Thomas under a pain of £20 forfeit to the lady

Affeerors: John Roulowe, Roger Tounsende

Sum of this court 43s 8d

Whence in expenses of the steward 8s 9d

Worfeld

Court held there on Wednesday in the week of Pentecost in the year above stated [7 June 1419]

Essoins

William Stevenes, John Bradeney, William Hockombe, Thomas Forster essoined themselves by John Est

The 12

Stephen Bradeney	Roger atte Tounesende	John Billyngesley	Robert Webbe}
Roger Waltone	Stephen Webbe	Roger Gerbot	John Barnedley}sworn
John Roulowe	Thomas Undirhull	John Janne	Robert Bruggeende}

Plea attach summon to the next [court] Amercements for pleas 18d

Roger Daliley plaintiff of Thomas Heyne in a plea of trespass pledge for the prosecution Thomas Merewalle. And it is ordered to the bailiff to attach him
Thomas Jankyns plaintiff of the same Thomas Heyne in a plea of debt pledge for the prosecution Roger Hulle. And it is ordered to the bailiff to summon him
Thomas Richardes (6d) is in mercy because he is not prosecuting his plea against Roger Richardes of Neutone in a plea of broken agreement etc.
Thomas Bradeney (6d) put himself in mercy for a licence to agree with Thomas Heyne in a plea of debt etc.
The same Thomas Heyne (6d) is in mercy for his unjust plea against Thomas Jankyns junior in a plea of debt

Surrender Fine 12d

Thomas Jankyns junior came here in court and surrendered into the hands of the lady 1 parcel of meadow lying in Hockombesmedu which he acquired from Joan Malecher after the death of the said Joan to the use of Fililode of Salop to hold from the lady to the heirs and assigns of the same William according to the custom of the manor for ever. And he gives to the lady for a fine 12d

For which concerning the inquiry held of the 24 at the last court held between Thomas Richardes & Roger Prestees to enquire which of them has the greater right to make a fine with the lady for 1 messuage and half a virgate of land with appurtenances in Neutone let there be no further execution by the 24 jurors aforesaid because the parties aforesaid are agreed concerning the fine aforesaid

Taking land out of the hand of the lady Fine 10s

Roger Prestees came here in court and made a fine with the lady to have from the hands of the lady one messuage and half a virgate of land with appurtenances in Neutone which Roger Richardes and Margery his wife surrendered into the hands of the lady at the last court preceding to the use of the same Roger Prestees after the death of the aforesaid Roger Richardes and Margery to hold from the lady to the aforesaid Roger Prestees his heirs and assigns after the death of the aforesaid Roger Richardes and Margery according to the custom of the manor for ever. And he gives to the lady for a fine 10s by the pledge of Thomas Richardes

Surrender Fine 10s

Roger Prestees came here in court and surrendered into the hands of the lady one messuage and half a virgate of land with appurtenances in Neutone to the use of Thomas Richardes after the death of the aforesaid Roger Richardes and Margery his wife to hold from the lady to the aforesaid Thomas his heirs and assigns for ever after the death of the aforesaid Roger Richardes and Margery his wife according to the custom of the manor. And he gives to the lady for a fine 10s

Fine for suit of court 12d

John Bromley of Adlescote came here in court and made a fine with the lady for suit of court from the feast of St Barnabus the Apostle until the feast of the Annunciation of the Blessed Mary next in the future. And he gives to the lady for a fine 12d by the pledge of T Jankyns

the 12 jurors amerced 2d

present that Henry Halle (2d) owed suit and did not come so in mercy

Affeerors: John Roulowe, Roger atte Tounesende

Sum of this court 23s 8d

In expenses of the steward and others for 2 days and 2 nights 3s 9d

More on the dorse

[The Dorse]

Court roll of Worfeld of the 7th year of the reign of King Henry V in the time of R. Bentley steward

[the rest of the first page is blank]

Names of the jurors for Thomas Richardes

Roger Waltone, Stephen Bradeney, John son of John Roulowe, Roger Tounesende, John Bromley, John Janyns of Swancote, Roger Garbot, Thomas Trisell of Aldescote, Thomas Merewalle of Hilton, Roger Smyth of Hiltone, John Colettes of Hiltone, Robert Bruggeende of Hiltone, William Newe of Chestertone, Henry Barker of Halone carpenter, Robert Webbe of Roughtone, Richard Aldeth of Stapulford, William Bromley of Bromley, Stephen Stanlowe, John Barneley of Barneley, William Gerbot of Hockombe, Thomas Burcote of Burcote, William atte Yate of Roughtone, John Waltone & Thomas Underhull

Court held there on Thursday on the the feast of St Bartholomew the Apostle in the year within written [24 August 1419]

Amerced 16d attach, distrain to the next [court]

John Baret (6d) of Basset Milne put himself in mercy for a licence to agree with John Hethe in a plea of trespass by the pledge of Stephen Webbe

Roger Daliley plaintiff of Thomas Heyne (2d) in a plea of trespass etc. And the aforesaid Thomas was attached and did not come so in mercy. And it is ordered to the bailiff to distrain him to the next court etc.

Thomas Jenkyns adjourned by the prayer of the parties plaintiff of the same Thomas Heyne 2d) in a plea of debt etc. And the aforesaid Thomas Heyne was summoned & did not come so etc. And it is ordered to the bailiff to attach him to the next [court] etc. Thomas Undirhull, Thomas Toward, Margery Swancote, William Bakes & Richard Aldith through Roger Daliley their attorney plaintiffs of John Colyns of Hugford (2d), Roger Baret (2d) of the same & Henry Pertone (2d) of the same in a plea of trespass. Pledge for the prosecution the aforesaid Roger Daliley. And they are attached by the bailiff and found a pledge for coming Roger Swancote and did not come so in mercy etc. And it is ordered to the bailiff to distrain them and the pledge for coming to the next [court] etc.

John Jannes & Roger Gerbot Wardens of the church of Worfeld plaintiffs of Thomas Toward executor of William Toward in a plea of debt pledge for the prosecution Stephen Bradeney And it is ordered to the bailiff to summon him etc. Richard Walker of Neutone plaintiff of Sibill Sonde agreed put herself of Neutone in a plea of trespass pledge for the prosecution the bailiff. And it is ordered to the bailiff to attach her to the next [court] etc.

Summon, attach to the next

The same Richard plaintiff of the same Sibill agreed put herself in a plea of debt pledge for the prosecution as before. And it is ordered to the bailiff to summon her etc. Thomas Jenkyns junior plaintiff of Roger Campione and Katherine his wife in a plea of debt pledge for the prosecution John Snell. And it is ordered to the bailiff to summon them to the next court etc.
The same Thomas plaintiff of the same Roger and Katherine his wife in a plea of broken agreement pledge for the prosecution as before. And it is ordered to the bailiff as above etc.
The same Thomas plaintiff of Thomas Roulowe of Burcote in a plea of debtpledge for the prosecution Roger Hill of Roughtone. And it is ordered to the bailiff to summon him etc.

The 12

Stephen Bradeney	Thomas Undirhull	John Billyngesley	}
Roger Waltone of Swancote	Stephen Stanlowe	John Bromley	}sworn
Roger Tounesende	Robert Webbe	John Janyn	}
John Roulowe	William Newe	Roger Gerbot	}

Fine 6d

John Osberne & Margary his wife made a fine with the lady to brew from the feast of the Nativity of St John the Baptist last past until the feast of St Michael the Archangel next in the future. And they give to the lady for a fine 6d

Surrender Fine 5s

Nicholas Stanlowe came here in court and surrendered into the hands of the lady 1 toft & 1 nook of land with appurtenances lying in Kyngeslowe formerly in the tenure of William Eddene to the use of Roger Daliley & Joan his wife to hold from the lady according to the custom of the manor to the aforesaid Roger and Joan, their heirs and assigns for ever. And they give to the lady for a fine 5s and have seisin

Surrender Fine 10s

The same Nicholas Stanlowe came here in court and surrendered into the hands of the lady 1 messuage & half a virgate of land with appurtenances in Stanlowe to the use of John Oldyngtone & Stephen Stanlowe to hold from the lady to the aforesaid John and Stephen, their heirs and assigns for ever according to the custom of the manor. And they give to the lady for a fine 10s by the pledge of Stephen Stanlowe. And made fealty and have seisin etc.

1419 P314/W/1/1/253

Surrender Fine 5s	The same Nicholas Stanlowe came here in court and surrendered into the hands of the lady 1 nook of land with appurtenances called the Oldefeld in Kyngeslowe to the use of the aforesaid John Oldyngtone & Stephen Stanlowe formerly in the tenure of William Huggyns to hold from the lady to the aforesaid John and Stephen, their heirs and assigns for ever according to the custom of the manor. And they give to the lady for a fine 5s by the pledge aforesaid. And have seisin etc.
Surrender Fine 4d	The same Nicholas Stanlowe came here in court & surrendered into the hands of the lady 1 parcel of pasture in Stanlowe called Chiltone Grene to the use of the aforesaid John Oldyngtone & Stephen Stanlowe to hold from the lady to the aforesaid John and Stephen, their heirs and assigns for ever according to the custom of the manor. And they give to the lady for a fine 4d and made fealty. And have seisin etc.
Increased rent 10d	William Bromley came here in court and took from the lady 1 weir of new build & situated in the waters of the Worf between the land of Roger Gerbot on the one side of the water aforesaid and a certain meadow called Alvescote medu on the other side of the water aforesaid rendering thence per annum 10d at the feast of the Annunciation of the Blessed Mary & St Michael to hold from the lady to himself for the whole of his life according to the custom of the manor. And he has seisin
Increased rent 2d	William Roulowe came here in court and took from the lady 1 stakyng on the waters of the Worf situated near to Bynsey furlong to hold from the lady to the aforesaid William for the whole of his life rendering thence per annum 2d at the feasts aforesaid. And he made fealty & has seisin
Presentation of the 12 jurors Amerced 2d Supervise	The 12 jurors present that Thomas Forster (2d) owed suit & did not come so in mercy etc. And they said that Nicholas Stanlowe surrendered into the hands of the lady a quarter part of 1 messuage in Stanlowe & a quarter part of 1 nook of land with appurtenances there to the use of John son of the same Nicholas, his heirs and assigns for ever. The which John died so the land and tenement aforesaid remain in the hand of the lady until the rolls of the court are surveyed because the aforesaid Nicholas said the land and tenement aforesaid were not surrendered in the form aforesaid. So to oversee

Affeerors: Stephen Bradeney, Roger Tounsende

Sum of this court 22s 4d
Thence in expenses of the steward & other officers 2s 4d
And for parchment 3d

Examined

1419-1420 P314/W/1/1/254

Worfeld	Great court held there on Wednesday next after the feast of St Michael the Archangel in the seventh year of the reign of King Henry V [4 October 1419]
Essoins	William Aleyn clerk, Roger Gille & John Walker and Roger Knyght essoined themselves by John
The 12	Roger Eudenas John Jenkyns Roger Waltone Thomas Undirhull } Roger Cattestre John Roulowe John atte Tounesende John Bromley } sworn Stephen Bradeney Thomas Tomkyns Stephen Stanlowe John Billyngesley}
Hultone stray price 16d fot forfieted, waifs price 8d	township there presents one male draught animal, brown, coming before the feast of the Conversion of St Paul price 16d. And they present 8d coming as abandoned goods in the custody of the wife of Roger Cattestre
Stapulford	township there presents nothing. Roulowe, Bradeney, Astone, Ewyk, & Sonde present nothing. Burcote, Burcote, Ryndleford & Bromley present nothing. Halen presents nothing.
Alvescote, Wynnescote, Cattestre, Neutone Stray price 4d not forfeited	townships there present 1 white piglet price 4d coming as a stray before the feast of the Purification last in the custody of Richard Whitbrook
Eudenas, Oldyntone. Amerced 6d	townships there present that William Oldyntone (6d) made a recovery of draught animals of John the servant of Thomas Haselwode
Akeltone Amerced 6s 6d	township there presents that John Kynmertone (8d) broke the impoundment of 1 horse impounded by Thomas Tomkyns. And they present that the same John (8d) made an assault on the same Thomas and drew blood from him (10d). And they present that John Astwalle (16d) broke the impoundment of 1 horse impounded by Roger Daliley. And they present that Thomas Gille (8d) made an assault on Margaret Hoggeman and hit her (4d). And they present that Thomas Tomkyns justly raised the hue and cry on John Kynnertone/Kynvertone (6d)
Chesturton Goods forfeited price 3s 4½d	township there presents that John Snell arrested an unknown man for suspected larceny & delivered him to seek his warrant & he did not return. And the aforesaid unknown had 4½d cash reckoned for 1 bow & 12 arrows price 12d, 1 cloak price 2s
Wyken	township there presents nothing. Roughtone, Hokcombe, Swancote & Barnedley present nothing
Kyngeslowe & Stanlowe Amerced 3s 2d Strays 4d	townships there present that John (8d) the servant of William Rugge broke the impoundment of draught animals by Roger Daliley impounded for trespass done by them to him. And they present that the same John (2s) broke the impoundment by Stephen Stanlowe and there took away 8 draught animals impounded by Roger Daliley for money owed to the lady. And they present 1 swarm of bees price 4d coming as strays for one year being in a certain ash tree of John Oldyntone & Stephen Stanlowe. And they present that John Oldyntone (6d) ought to swear with the townships aforesaid and stood in court and refused this

Worfeld Amerced 6d	township there presents that John Cattestre (6d) made an assault on William Dudley
The tasters of ale Amerced 6s	present that John Johnsone of Roulowe (4d) brewed once, Thomas Undirhull (4d) brewed once, Thomas Tomkyns (4d) brewed 1, John Smyth of Sonde (4d) brewed 1. Hamo Hymmuley (4d) brewed 1, Richard Bradeney (4d) brewed 1, Roger Warde (4d) brewed 1, John Bromley (4d) brewed 1, John Roulowe (4d) brewed 1, William Beer (4d) brewed 1, Richard Smyth (4d) brewed 1, Thomas Bradeney (4d) brewed 1, Thomas Tresill (4d) brewed 1, John Billyngesley (4d) senior brewed 1, William Kyngesone (4d) brewed 1 & Alice Sonde (12d) common brewer & broke the assize so in mercy
Pain put 12d Oversee at the next [court[	It is ordered by the steward from an agreement of all tenants that henceforth no baker within the domain to sell bread unless it was of the weight and edible (vultur) so far as good and white just as the bakers within the township of Bruggenorth bake under a pain of 12d forfeit to the lady
	The 12 jurors aforesaid present that the townships aforesaid have well and faithfully presented and concealed nothing
	Affeerors: Roger Tounesende, Robert Webbe Sum of this court 21s ½d
	Small court held there on Thursday next after the feast of St Michael above stated in the year above stated [5 October 1419]
Essoins	John Cattestre & John Billyngesley essoined themselves by John Est
The 12	Stephen Bradeney, Roger Tounesende, Henry Barker, Roger Smyth} John Roulowe, Thomas Richardes, Stephen Stanlowe, Roger Gerbot }sworn Roger Waltone, John Bromley, William Newe, William atte Yate}
Pleas summon and attach	William Aleyn clerk through John Blore his attorney plaintiff of John Stevenes in a plea of debt pledge for the prosecution the bailiff. And he was summoned by the bailiff and did not come so etc. And it is ordered to the bailiff to attach him to the next court etc. John Jannes & Roger Gerbot wardens of the church of Worfeld plaintiffs of Thomas Toward executor and administrators of the will of Agnes Toward in a plea of debt pledge for the prosecution Stephen Bradeney. And it is ordered to the bailiff to summon them
Pleas adjourned	Roger Daliley plaintiff of Thomas Heyne agreed put himself by the pledge of W. Roulowe in a plea of trespass etc. And from the agreement of the parties adjourned until the next etc. Thomas Jenkyns plaintiff of the same Thomas Heyne in a plea of debt etc. And from the agreement of the parties they have an adjournment etc. Thomas Undirhull, Thomas Toward, Margery Swancote, William Bakes & Richard Aldith through Roger Daliley their attorney plaintiffs of John Colyns of Huggeford, Roger Baret of the same & Henry Perton of the same in a plea of trespass etc. And from the agreement of the parties adjourned to the next etc.
	John Jannes, Roger Gerbot wardens of the church of Worfeld plaintiffs of Thomas Toward executor and administrator of the will of William Toward in a plea of debt And they have an adjournment from the agreement of the parties until the next [court] etc.

1419-1420 P314/W/1/1/254

Thomas Jenkyns junior plaintiff of Roger Campion pledges for the coming John Osbern & William Golde & Katherine his wife in a plea of debt. And they have an adjournment until the {next [court]

Pleas adjourned

The same Thomas plaintiff of the same Roger & Katherine in a plea of broken agreement etc. And they have an adjournment until the next [court] etc.

Sibilla Sonde (12d) of Neutone put herself in mercy for a licence to agree with Richard Walker of Neutone for s pleas of debt & trespass

Plea Amerced 14d Attached

Thomas Jenkyns adjourned plaintiff of Thomas Roulowe of Burcote in a plea of debt etc. And it was ordered to the bailiff to summon him And he did not come So in mercy And it is ordered to the bailiff to attach him to the next [court]

Surrender Fine 20d

William Inglissh came here in court & surrendered into the hands of the lady 2 cottages with curtilage & appurtenances in Halen formerly in the tenure of John Walker of Ryndleford to the use of Roger Barker to hold from the lady to the aforesaid Roger, his heirs & assigns for ever according to the custom of the manor. And he gives to the lady for a fine 20d. And made fealty and has seisin

Supervise

Henceforth it is approved to John Snell by the steward on the part of the lady that he takes into the hands of the lady 1 weir in the tenure of John Roulowe and 1 other weir called Perkyns Weir situated there in the tenure of the miller of Baggesovere because the water aforesaid is in severalty to the domain of Worfeld and it is not known to whom the warrant for the said weir there is held there because nothing thence was paid by them. And also that to distrain the lord of Baggesovere that he is at the next court to be held at Worfeld to show how he holds the manor of Baggesore and in what way he is ingressed because it is held from the manor of Worfeld for certain services etc.

Stray sworn on oath

Memorandum that John Hankyns/Haukyns of Nortone with five hands declared on oath 1 ruby heifer price 2s presented by the township of Alvescote as a stray at the great court held here on Monday 10th day of April in the year above said. And so he thence has delivery because it is not forfeited

Sureties to keep the peace with pains £40

Sureties of Roger Prestees for keeping the peace towards Thomas Richardes namely John Snell, Robert Webbe, Richard Haselwode & William Oldyntone each of them under a pain of £10. And the aforesaid Roger Prestee under a pain of £20 forfeit to the lady

Election of the reeve: John the son of Nicholas Roulowe withdrew from the office of reeve. And Stephen of Stanlowe is elected to the same office for the year about to be and sworn

The 12 jurors aforesaid present nothing

Affeerors: Roger Tounesende, Robert Webbe

Sum of this court 2s 10d
Thence in expenses of the steward, clerk, reeve , Beadle & others for 3 nights & 2 days 8s 10d

Small court held there on Friday next before the feast of the Nativity of the lord in the year above stated [22 December 1419]

Thomas Jenkyns junior plaintiff of William Aleyn formerly the vicar of the church of Worfeld in a plea of deception pledge for the prosecution Roger

1419-1420 P314/W/1/1/254

Pleas
Essoins

Roger Hull. And the aforesaid William Aleyn through John Fox essoined himself
The same Thomas plaintiff of the same William in a plea of debt pledge for the prosecution who [as] before. And essoined as above

Summon

Amerced 3d
Attach

Roger Dalliley plaintiff of Nicholas Stanlowe recognised 16d and 4s for a cloak in a plea of debt pledge for the prosecution John Goolde. And it is ordered to the bailiff to summon
The same Nicholas plaintiff of the same Roger (3d) granted from the agreement of the parties in a plea of debt pledge for the prosecution Robert Webbe. And it was ordered to the bailiff to summon him. And the bailiff responded that he is summoned. And he did not come so is in mercy. And it is ordered to the bailiff to attach him to the next [court] etc.

Amerced 4d
Distrain

William Aleyn clerk through John Blore his attorney plaintiff of John Stevenes (2d) in a plea of debt pledge for the prosecution the bailiff. And it was ordered to the bailiff to attach him. And the bailiff responded that he is attached and he found a pledge for the coming namely John the son of Nicholas Roulowe. And because he did not have so in mercy. And it is ordered to the bailiff to distrain him etc.

Adjourned

The law
The next

John Jannes & Roger Gerbot still adjourned wardens of the church of Worfeld plaintiffs of Thomas Toward & Richard Aldith executors and administrators of the will of Agnes Toward in a plea of debt etc. And it was ordered to the bailiff to summon them. And the bailiff responded that they are summoned. And on this came the aforesaid Thomas & Richard etc. And the aforesaid John & Roger & said that the aforesaid Agnes bequeathed one roof price 6s 8d to the building of the church of Worfeld which still is unjustly detained to the damage of 2s 6d. And the aforesaid Thomas denied this. And thence is ready to prove (verificare) in any way whatsoever. And the aforesaid Richard recognised the debt aforesaid. So it is adjourned until etc.

Summon

The same John & Roger plaintiffs of Thomas Toward executor and administrator of the will of William Toward in a plea of debt etc. And it is ordered to the bailiff to summon him. And the bailiff responded that he is summoned. And he came etc. And the aforesaid John & Roger said that the aforesaid William Toward in the time when he was guardian of the light of All Saints in the church aforesaid owed and still owes 6s 8d for the light aforesaid to the damages of 2s 6d etc. And the aforesaid Thomas denied all this & thence to wager the law pledge for the law Roger Dalliley

Roger Dalliley plaintiff of Thomas Jenkyns senior in a plea of debt pledge for the prosecution John Hethe. And it is ordered to the bailiff to summon to the next [court] etc.

Amerced 15d
attach,
distrain

Thomas Heyne (6d) put himself in mercy for a licence to agree with Roger Dalliley in a plea of trespass
Thomas Jenkyns junior plaintiff of the same Thomas Heyne 3d put himself in a plea of debt And it was ordered to the bailiff to summon him. And the bailiff responded that he is summoned And did not come So in mercy And it is ordered to the bailiff to attach him

The same Thomas Jenkyns plaintiff of Roger Campyone (3d) & Katherine his wife in a plea of debt. And it was ordered to the bailiff to attach them etc. And the bailiff responded that they are attached. And they found pledges for their coming namely John Osberne & William Goolde. And because they do not have them [in court] so in mercy. And it is ordered to the bailiff to distrain them and the pledges aforesaid to the next [court] etc.

The same Thomas plaintiff of the same Roger (3d) and Katherine in a plea of broken agreement etc. And it was ordered to the bailiff as above etc. And the bailiff responded as above etc. And it is ordered as above

Adjourned

The same Thomas Jenkyns plaintiff of Thomas Roulowe agreed put himself of Burcote in a plea of deb etc. And they have an adjournment

Thomas Undirhull adjourned defendants to respond, Thomas Toward, Margery Swancote, William Bakes & Richard Aldith through Roger Dalliley their attorney plaintiffs of John Colyns of Huggeford, Roger Baret of the same & Henry Pertone of the same in a plea of trespass etc. And they have an adjournment etc.

The 12				
	John Johnsone of Roulowe	Thomas Toward	William Newe	}
	Stephen Bradeney	William Wermot	Roger Gerbot	} sworn
	John Nichollson of Roulowe	John Janne	John Barnedley	}
	Roger Tounesende	Robert Webbe	John Bromley	}

Fines 7s 4d

William Ingman & Joan his wife came here in court and made a fine for 2s with the steward to brew from the feast of St Michael last until the same feast thereafter next following

Thomas Sonde & Alice his wife came here in court and made a fine for 2s with the steward to brew & sell ale from the feast above said last until the same feast thereafter next following

The townships of Halene, Ryndelford, Cattestre & Alvescote made a fine with the steward for mast in the wood of Soudeley for this year for 40d

Surrender
Fine 20s

William Aleyn clerk through Stephen Webbe reeve there came here in court & surrendered into the hands of the lady to the use of Richard Parlour & Margery his wife one fulling mill of Ryndleford, 1 staking to do fishing & thence to take fish at Ryndleford there from the water issuing from the floodgate pit & a piece of land called the Teynturs hull with all their appurtenances which the same William formerly acquired from John Walker to hold from the lady to the aforesaid Richard & Margery, the heirs and assigns of the same Richard for ever by services and customs before forfeited for the aforesaid mill together with the aforesaid staking & Teyntursshull owed and accustomed just as the aforesaid John Walker previously held. And the aforesaid Richard & Margery gave to the lady for a fine 20s. And they made fealty and have seisin

Surrender
Fine 4d

The same William Aleyn through the aforesaid reeve came here in court & surrendered into the hands of the lady one cottage with curtilage in Halen next to the Castell to the use of Joan the daughter of John Barnedley to hold from the lady to herself, the heirs & assigns of the same Joan according to the custom of the manor forever. And she gives to the lady for a fine 4d. And she made fealty & has seisin

Heriot 20s 6d
Escheat 4s 2d

The homage presents that Margery Swancote who held from the lady 2 messuages and 1 virgate of land in Stapulford & 1 messuage & 1 virgate of land with appurtenances in Swancote has died after whose death there falls to the lady 1 red ox price 7s 6d for heriot in the custody of Roger Swancote. And 1 black ox price 6s 8d for heriot in the custody aforesaid and also 1 black ox tagget price 6s 4d for heriot in the custody aforesaid. And they present that there falls to the lady after the death of the same Margery 1 black, male, draught animal price 12d for escheat. And they present 1 sow with 4 piglets price 3s. And 1 hive of bees price 1d

Taking of land Fine 40s	And on this comes Roger Swancote son and heir of Thomas Swancote & the aforesaid Margery & seeks to have delivery of all the lands and tenements aforesaid with all their appurtenances out of the hand of the lady & seisin. And on this by the judgment of the steward he is admitted to hold from the lady, the heirs and assigns of the same Roger according to the custom of the manor forever. And he gives to the lady for a fine 40s. And he made fealty & has seisin. And he has seisin of all the land & tenements aforesaid with all their appurtenances. And he has a day to pay 20s of the fine aforesaid before the first view of the accounts
Fine 2s	John Knotte of Claverley came here in court & made a fine for 2s with the steward to marry Margery Webbe widow of the lady
Taking of a weir into the hands of the lady for the reason shown within to supervise	It is ordered to the bailiff by the steward to take into the hands of the lady 1 weir of new build by William Bromley situated in the water of the Worf between the meadow of Swancote on the one side and the moor called Cherlesmore on the other side permission from the lady on this not obtained. And concerning the true annual value it remains to enquire until the next great court. Still it is ordered to the bailiff to seize into the hands of the lady 2 weirs called HoggemansWere at Eleshale in the water of the Worf & Perkyns Were situated in the same water held by the lord of Baggesovere by what right the homage of Worfeld don't know until the lord aforesaid will show in what way he holds them. And concerning the annual value of the same the homage have an adjournment to enquire until the great court aforesaid

Affeerors: John Roulowe, Robert Webbe

Sum of this court £4 16s

Thence in expenses of the steward, clerk, reeve, Beadle & others for 2 nights & 1 day 4s 1d

Small court held there on Friday next before the feast of St Gregory the Pope in the year above said [8 March 1420]

Pleas Amerced 9d Distrain to the next	Thomas Jenkyns junior plaintiff of William Aleyn (3d) formerly vicar of the church of Worfeld in a plea of deception etc. And the aforesaid William Aleyn at the last court was essoined & now did not come so in mercy. And it was ordered to the bailiff to distrain him and Robert Webbe pledge of the same William concerning coming to the next etc. The same Thomas plaintiff of the same William (3d) in a plea of debt etc. And the aforesaid William was essoined as above and now does not come so etc. And it is ordered to the bailiff to distrain the same William & the pledge aforesaid as above William Aleyn clerk through John Blore his attorney plaintiff of John Stevenes {(3d) in a plea of debt etc. And it was ordered to the bailiff to distrain him and John the son of Nicholas Roulowe pledge of the same John. And because he did not come so in mercy etc. And to distrain etc.
Adjourned	John Jannes & Roger Gerbot wardens of the church of Worfeld plaintiffs of Thomas Toward & Richard Aldith executors of the will of Agnes Toward in a plea of debt etc. And they said that the aforesaid Agnes bequeathed one roof price 6s 8d as is clear in the last court preceding etc. And it is adjourned etc.

1419-1420 P314/W/1/1/254

Amerced 6d — Nicholas Stanlowe (6d) is in mercy for the unjust detention of 16d & 4s which he recognised to owe to Roger Dalliley of a debt. And concerning 18d of damages it is adjourned to be assessed until the next court

The same Nicholas plaintiff of the same Roger adjourned by the agreement of the parties in a plea of debt etc. And they have an adjournment by the agreement of the parties etc.

Adjourned — John Jannes (6d) & Roger Gerbot in mercy for their unjust plea against Thomas Toward in a plea of debt

Thomas Heyne (6d) put himself in mercy for a licence to agree with Thomas Jenkyns junior in a plea of debt

Thomas Roulowe of Burcote (6d) put himself in mercy for a licence to agree with the same Thomas Jenkyns in a plea of debt

Amerced 2s — Roger Coryour otherwise the said Roger Warde (6d) in mercy for the unjust detention of 40d debt which he recognises to owe to Thomas Sonde etc.

Thomas Jenkyns plaintiff of Roger Campyone (3d) & Katherine his wife in a plea of debt etc. And it was ordered to the bailiff to distrain etc. And they found a pledge as is clear in the last court preceding. And because the same does not have so in mercy etc.

Amerced 6d Distrain — The same Thomas plaintiff of the same Roger & Katherine (3d) in a plea of broken agreement etc. And it was ordered to the bailiff as above etc. And the bailiff responded as above.And it is ordered to the bailiff to distrain John Osbern & William Golde pledges aforesaid to have the bodies of the said Roger & Katherine at the next court

Adjourned — Thomas Undurhull, Thomas Toward, William Bakes & Richard Aldith through Roger Dalley their attorney plaintiffs of John Colyns of Huggeford, Roger Baret of the same & Henry Pertone of the same in a plea of trespass etc. And they have an adjournment by the prayer of the parties to defend

Amerced 3d Attach — Alice Cattestre plaintiff of Hamond Hymley (3d) ... 12d for unjust detention .....in a plea of unjust detention of goods pledge for the prosecution John Cattestre. And it was ordered to the bailiff to summon him. And he is summoned and did not come etc. So it is ordered to the bailiff to attach him

The law the next — Roger Cattestre plaintiff of Thomas Jenkyns senior essoined adjourned in a plea of debt pledge for the prosecution Robert Webbe. And he said that he owes him and unjustly detains 13s 4d which he lent to him on Saturday next before the feast of St Peter in Chains in the 4th year of the reign of King Henry IV at Cattey medu etc. And the aforesaid Thomas denies this emtirely. And thence to wager the law pledge for the law Henry Barker

The Dorse

Summon — Thomas Nicholes of Bruggenorth plaintiff of Thomas Jenkyns senior in a plea of debt pledge for the prosecution Robert Baret. And it is ordered to the bailiff to summon him.

Adjourned — Thomas Sonde plaintiff of Thomas Jenkyns junior in a plea of debt pledge for the prosecution William Golde. And it is adjourned

Richard Thorne not prosecuting by the pledge of Rob Bruggende plaintiff of William Goolde in a plea of trespass pledge for the prosecution Robert Bruggeende. And it is ordered to the bailiff to attach him.

1419-1420 P314/W/1/1/254

Attach Amerced 6d	The same Richard not prosecuting by the pledge aforesaid plaintiff of the same William (6d) in a plea of debt 16d for 1 pair of wheels. And concerning damages for unjust detention 6d. And the aforesaid William recognised the debt aforesaid. And concerning the damages put himself on assessment by the court so in mercy
The law The next	The same William Goolde not prosecuting plaintiff of the same Richard in a plea of debt pledge for the prosecution Roger Smyth of Hultone. And he says that on the feast of the Finding of the Holy Cross in the 8th year of the reign of King Henry IV at Worfeld sold to the same Richard Thorne his right in 1 nook of land with appurtenances in Hultone for which nook of land aforesaid Richard Thorne should have given the same William Goolde 33s 4d which he owes and unjustly detains to the damage of 20s etc. And the aforesaid Richard Thorne came in his own person and denied this entirely & thence to wager the law pledges for the law Robert Bruggeende & Richard Gerbot
To assess Supervise	The same William Goolde not prosecuting plaintiff of the same Richard in a plea of trespass pledge for the prosecution who previously. And he says that on the day of Good Friday in the 11th year of the reign of King Henry IV in the field at Hultone with his pigs he destroyed and trampled 3 acres sown with peas and thus he continued until the feast of the Nativity of St John the Baptist thereafter next following to the damage of 5s 4d. And the aforesaid Richard Thorne came in his own person and said that no such damage was continued just as the same William above alleged against him. And he put himself on the township of Hultone to be assessed etc.
The 12	Stephen Bradeney, John Jannyn, Roger Gerbot, Roger Waltone, William Wermot, Robert Webbe, John Roulowe, John Roulowe, John Bromley, Roger Swancote, Roger Tounesende, William Newe } sworn
Essoins	John Barnedley & Thomas Richardes essoined themselves through John Hunt
Fine 12d	John Knot made a fine with the steward for 12d for suit of court to be commuted from the date of this court for one full year next following
Amerced 12	The homage present that John Bromley (4d) of Ryndleford, John (4d) the son of Roger Tournour & William (4d) the son of Henry Barker cut green wood in the wood of Soudeley without licence so in mercy etc.
Sureties to keep the peace	Sureties of Roger Warde otherwise called Roger Coryour to keep the peace to Roger Smyth & all the people of the lord King Roger Tounesende & Thomas Undirhull of Stapulford each mainpernors of the aforesaid under pain of 100s. And the aforesaid Roger Warde under pain of £10 forfeit to the lady
	Affeerors: John Roulowe, John Janyn

Sum of this court 6s 6d

Thence in expenses of the steward, clerk, reeve, beadle & others for 2 nights & 2 days 3s 9½d

1420 P314/W/1/1/255

Worfeld	Great court held there on Monday next before the feast of St George in the eighth year of the reign of King Henry V [22 April 1420]
Essoins	John Roulowe, John Roulowe & Thomas Merewalle essoined themselves by John Hunt
The 12	Robert Eudenas Roger Tounesende Thomas Undirhull Roger Swancote } Roger Cattestre Robert Webbe Thomas Tomkyns Robert Bruggende } sworn John Jonkyns Roger Waltone John Janyn William Wermot}
Akeltone Amerced 8d	township there presents that John Baret (8d) forestalled Richard Undirhull
Alvescote, Wynscote, Cattestre, Neutone Amerced 2s 2d	townships there present that John Tresill junior (6d) & Thomas Richardes (6d) owed suit and did not come so in mercy etc. And they present that Richard Walker (12d) of Neutone unjustly took 1 leather bag price 2d
Roulowe, Bradeney, Asturhull, Ewyke, Sonde Strays not forfeited Supervise	townships there present 1 brown horse coming as a stray before the feast of St Michael last past price 14d in the custody of John Johnsone. Also they present 1 grey horse price 18d coming as a stray before the feast aforesaid in the custody of the aforesaid John
Stapulford Amerced 18d	township there presents that William Lowe (8d) made an assault on Thomas Merewalle senior and drew blood (10d) from him
Burcote, Burcote, Ryndleford & Bromley Amerced 14d	townships there present that John Elcok (8d) made an assault on William Gregge (6d) and hit him
Wykene Amerced 7s 6d Kyngeslowe & Stanlowe	township there presents that William Ingman (8d) made an assault on Agnes the wife of John Smyth of Sonde & hit her (6d). And they present that Richard Smyth (12d) son of the aforesaid John, Thomas the son of Simon Taillour, & William his brother made an assault on William Ingman. And they present that Joan the wife of the said William justly raised the hue and cry (8d) on the same Richard, Thomas & William. And they present that John Ingman (6d) unjustly took 1 russet tunic price 2d of the goods of Thomas Heyne so etc. And they present 1 linen cloth (linthiamen) unjustly taken by Thomas Bradney (40d) price 8d in the custody of John Snell so etc.
Worfeld Amerced 2s 10d Money forfeit 2s	township there presents that Sibill Coryour (6d) made an assault on Margery Tresill. And the aforesaid Margery justly raised the hue and cry (8d) on the said Sibill. And they present 2s in money found coming as a waif unjustly taken by Edith Stevenes (20d) from the goods and chattels of Roger Warde
Hultone	township there presents nothing. Roughtone, Hokcombe, Swancote & Barnedley present nothing. Kyngeslowe, Stanlowe present nothing
Halene	township there presents nothing. Eudenas, Oldyngtone present nothing. Chesturtone presents nothing

The tasters of ale Amerced 2s 6d

present that John Billyngesley (6d) 1 brew, John Cattestre (6d) 1 brew, Stephen Bradeney (6d) 1 brew, Thomas Baker (6d) 1 brew, Roger Warde (6d) 1 brew & they broke the assize so in mercy

The 12 jurors say on their oath that all the townships aforesaid have well and faithfully presented and concealed nothing

Pain for keeping the peace £20

Surety of Thomas Bradeney of himself commanded to behave well towards all the people of the lord king namely John Bradeney of Hulton, William son ……… [blank] each going bail for the above said under pain of £20 forfeit to the lady

Attachment of Thomas Gylle on a charge of felony

Thomas Gille of Halene within the domain of Worfeld in the County of Salop taillour on Saturday next before the feast of St George the Martyr in the year above-said with stolen goods namely 1 piece of wax comprising 6lbs price 3s was attached to respond to John Oldyngtone because he with many others unknown on Friday next after the feast of St Valentine in the seventh year of the reign of the above-said King feloniously broke into the house of the aforesaid John at Oldyngtone at night. And at Worfeld the same day there was feloniously stolen 1 belt with silver adornment, 1 dagger with silver adornment price 30s, one leather garment price 3s & the aforesaid piece of wax of the goods and chattels of the aforesaid John whereof he is accused pledge for the prosecution William Noure, John Kynnertone, Thomas Tomkyns & Thomas Undirhull

Inquiry held on the charge aforesaid as is clear within when the aforesaid Thomas Gille is convicted and to hang

And on this at this court before the steward namely on Monday next before the feast of St George in the above said eighth year came the aforesaid John Oldyngtone and indicated (pretendit) himself to assert as true against the aforesaid Thomas Gille the accused aforesaid. And the aforesaid Thomas Gille came in the custody of John Snell & John Jonkyns constables of the lord King there. And he said that he is not thence to blame. And here put himself on the 12 whose names follow here namely Robert Eudenas , Roger Cattestre, John Jonkyns, Robert Webbe, Thomas Undirhull, Robert Bruggende, William Wermot Roger atte Tounesende, Thomas Ingman, Richard Haslewood, John Collettes of Hultone, William atte Yate of Roughtone still both on the part of the lord King & the aforesaid John Oldyngtone and on the part of the aforesaid Thomas Gille chosen to try and judge said on their oath that the aforesaid Thomas Gille is to blame for the felony aforesaid. So it is judged by the steward that the aforesaid John Oldyngtone has delivery of the stolen goods aforesaid. And the said Thomas Gille be hanged for the felony aforesaid

Land forfeit. No value this year

The which Thomas Gille has in the village of Halene 1 cottage with curtilage holding to himself and his heirs forever. And on this day on which he was convicted for the felony aforesaid thence was seized without any title to anyone thence made. The which cottage with curtilage is forfeit to the lady. And no value this year beyond retribution

Goods and chattels forfeit

And the aforesaid Thomas Gille had diverse goods and chattels on the said day on which he was convicted namely 5 swarms of bees price 8s. Also 1 cover (coopertoram) price 2s 6d. Also 1 lined outer garment (togam) price 40d. Also Thomas Hicokes has half a hive of bees price 2d. Also 3 linen cloths. Also salted meat price 3s 10d. Also 6 bushels of rye price 2s 6d. Also 1 saddle price 2s. Also 1 bolt (sera) price 4d. Also wool and hemp price 5d. Also 1 bird trap with a coloured cloth to take partridge price 12d. Also Richard Aleyn of Halene has 2 mattresses price 5s. Also the same Richard has 2 iron spits price 18d. Also the same Richard

Goods and chattels forfeit [contd.]

has 1 iron Gridiron price 3d. Also the same Richard has 1 piece of linen cloth price 1d. Also the same Richard Aleyn owes to the aforesaid Thomas 2s. Also Thomas Hicokes owes to the aforesaid Thomas for 4 bushels of rye 20d. Also the same Thomas owes to the same Thomas Gille for 1 pair of stockings 7d. Also the same owes to the same Thomas Gille 4d. Also John Walker of Ryndleford owes to the same Thomas Gille 8d. Also William Yate owes to the same Thomas Gille 12d. Also William the son of John Roulowe owes the same Thomas Gille 41s 6d. Also 1 white male sheep price 18d in the custody of Thomas Hikokes. The which goods and chattels are forfeited to the lady on account of the reason aforesaid

Affeerors: Thomas Undirhull, Robert Webbe

Sum of this court 20s 4d
And of the chattels forfeited £4 2s 2d

Small court held there on Tuesday in the feast of St George in the year above-said [23 April 1420

Essoins — Roger Swancote & John Oldyngtone essoined themselves by Richard Hunt

the 12 — Roger Waltone John Roulowe William Wermot Robert Webbe}
John Roulowe Roger Tounesende John Bernedley Richard Haselwode} sworn
Stephen Bradeney Thomas Undirhull John Janyn John Bromley}

Plea summon — William Huggyns of Claverley Home plaintiff of Thomas Jenkyns senior in a plea of debt pledge for the prosecution Richard Gerbot

Plea amerced 3d attach — Thomas Jenkyns junior plaintiff of Thomas Heyne (3d) of Wykene in a plea of debt pledge for the prosecution John Smyth. And he was summoned and did not come so in mercy. And it is ordered to the bailiff to attach him to the next [court]

Plea summon — Hamo Hymley plaintiff of Alice Cattsetre agreed put herself in a plea of debt pledge for the prosecution John Hunt

Plea amerced 9d distrain — Thomas Jenkyns junior plaintiff of William Aleyn (6d) formerly the vicar of the church of Worfeld in a plea of deception etc. And he was attached & he found a pledge for the coming namely Robert Webbe and he did not come so in mercy. And it is ordered to the bailiff to distrain the same William and his pledge above said
The same Thomas plaintiff of the same William (3d) in a plea of debt. And it was ordered to the bailiff as above. And he did not come so etc.
The same William Aleyn, through John Blore his attorney, plaintiff of John Stephens concerning a plea of debt etc. and he was attached and he found a pledge for coming namely John Roulowe and because he did not have the same [in court] so in mercy

John Jannes & Roger Gerbot Wardens of the Church of Worfeld plaintiffs of Thomas Toward agreed put himself & Richard Aldith executors of the will of Agnes Toward in a plea of debt etc. And they have an adjournment

Adjourned — Nicholas Stanlowe plaintiff of Roger Daliley in a plea of debt. And they have an adjournment
Thomas Jenkyns junior plaintiff of Roger Campyon & Katherine his wife in a plea of debt. And they have an adjournment
The same Thomas plaintiff of the same Roger & Katherine his wife in a plea of broken agreement. And they have an adjournment

1420 P314/W/1/1/255

Adjourned	Thomas Undirhull, Thomas Toward, William Bakes & Richard Aldith through Roger Daliley their attorney plaintiffs of John Colyns of Huggeford, Roger Baret of the same & Henry Pertone of the same in a plea of trespass. And they have an adjournment etc.
Amerced 6d	Hamo Hymley (6d) is in mercy for the unjust detention of one piece of cloth price 12d which he recognises to hold from Alice Cattestre
Plea essoin	Roger Cattestre plaintiff of Thomas Jenkyns senior in a plea of debt etc. And the aforesaid Thomas Jenkyns essoined himself from the law by Thomas Jenkyns junior
Adjourned	Thomas Nicoles of Bruggenorth plaintiff of Thomas Jenkyns senior in a plea of debt. And they have an adjournment etc. Thomas Sonde plaintiff of Thomas Jenkyns junior in a plea of debt. And they have an adjournment etc.
Amerced 18d	Richard Thorne (6d) is in mercy because he did not prosecute his plea against William Goolde in a plea of trespass The same William Goolde (12d) is in mercy because he did not prosecute his plea against the said Richard in 2 pleas of trespass & debt
Fine 12d	John Bromley of Adlescote made a fine for suit of court to be commuted from the date of this court for 1 full year for 12d
Fine 12d but the aforesaid is pardoned by the steward 6d for the reason shown within	Thomas Forster made a fine in the same way for 12d but the steward pardoned the same Thomas 6d for acting in favour of the tenants of the lady in his office of Morff
Surrender Fine 8d	Richard Smyth came here in court through Stephen Stanlowe his attorney and surrendered into the hands of the lady 2 butts of land whereof one lies on the Merssh Furlong extending on the merssh in the field of Hultone and the other lying at Eden Crosse on the road extending between Hultone & Wykene to the use of Johnthe son of Thomas Roulowe of Hultone to hold from the lady to himself and his heirs for ever according to the custom of the manor. And he gives to the lady for a fine 8d. And he made fealty and has seisin
Amerced 2d	The homage presents that Thomas Richardes (2d) owed suit and did not come so in mercy
	Affeerors: Thomas Undirhull, Robert Webbe Sum of this court 5s 4d [Dorse]
Worfeld	Court held there on Friday next before the feast of St Margaret the Virgin in the eighth year within written [19 July 1420]
Essoined	Henry Halle, Robert Webbe, Thomas Roulowe of Burcote, Thomas Merewalle senior essoined themselves by John Estone
The 12	Roger Swancote John Johnesone William Wermot William Newe } Stephen Bradeney John Nycolsone Roger Gerbot John Bromley } sworn Roger Waltone Roger atte Tounesende William Gerbot Roger Daliley}

Plea Summon — John Nycholsone plaintiff of Thomas Jenkyns junior agreed put himself in a plea of debt. Pledge for the prosecution Henry Halle. And it is ordered to the bailiff to summon him to the next [court]

Amerced 3d Attach — Thomas Heyne plaintiff of Richard Walker (3d) in a plea of trespass pledge for the prosecution Stephen Webbe. And it was ordered to the bailiff to summon him. And the bailiff responded that he is summoned. And he did not come so in mercy. And it is ordered to the bailiff to attach him to the next [court]

The Law — William Huggyns of Claverley Home plaintiff of Thomas Jenkyns senior essoined in a plea of debt pledge etc. And he said that he owes him 40s which he ought to have paid him on Tuesday in Easter Week in the 13th year of the reign of King Henry IV. And he has sot yet paid to him to the damage of half a mark etc. And the aforesaid Thomas came in his own person and denies all this. And thence to wager the law pledge for the law Thomas Jenkyns junior & John Bullok

Plea amerced 21d Distrain to the next [court] — Alice Cattestre (6d) put herself in mercy for a licence to agree with Hamond Hymley in a plea of debt
Thomas Jenkyns junior plaintiff of William Aleyn (3d) formerly the vicar of Worfeld in a plea of deception etc. And he was attached & found a pledge for the coming as is clear in the last court preceding and he did not come so in mercy. And it is ordered to the bailiff to distrain the pledge aforesaid to have the body of the said William here at the next [court]
The same Thomas plaintiff of the same William (3d) in a plea of debt. And he was attached & found a pledge as above. And he did not come so he [is] in mercy. And it is ordered to the bailiff aforesaid to distrain as above etc.
The same William Aleyn not prosecuting by John Blore his attorney plaintiff of John Stephens (3d) in a plea of debt. And he was attached and found a pledge John Roulowe for the coming. And he did not come so he is in mercy. And it is ordered to the bailiff to distrain them
Thomas Toward (6d) & Richard Aldith executors of the will of Agnes Toward put themselves in mercy for a licence to agree with John Jannes & Roger Gerbot Wardens of the Church of Worfeld in a plea of debt

Plea Adjourned — Nicholas Stanlowe not prosecuting plaintiff of Roger Daliley in a plea of debt. And they have an {adjournment until the next [court]
Thomas Undirhull, Thomas Toward, William Bakes & Richard Aldith through Roger Dalley their attorney plaintiffs of John Colyns of Huggeford, Roger Baret of the same & Henry Pertone of the same in a plea of trespass. And it is adjourned

The law — Thomas Jenkyns junior plaintiff of Roger Campyon & Katherine essoined his wife in a plea of debt. And he says that they owe him 26s which he ought to have paid on Tuesday next before the feast of Easter last etc. And the aforesaid Roger & Katherine came here in court and deny all this. And thence to wager at law pledge for the law John Jannes & William Golde
The same Thomas plaintiff of the same Roger & Katherine essoined in a plea of broken agreement. And he said that Katherine sold to him 1 outer garment (togam) for half a mark, 1 saddle with a bridle for 6s on the Sunday next before the feast of Easter aforesaid. And the aforesaid Roger & Katherine deny all this. And thence to wager at law pledge for the law as above

The law
Adjourned

Roger Cattestre plaintiff of Thomas Jenkyns senior [agreed put himself] in a plea of debt etc. And the aforesaid Thomas Jenkyns wagered at law as is clear at the court held on Friday next before the last feast of St Gregory the Pope. And here adjourned

Plea
Adjourned

Thomas Nicoles of Bruggenorth plaintiff of Thomas Jenkyns senior in a plea of debt. And it is adjourned etc.
Thomas Sonde plaintiff of Thomas Jenkyns junior [agreed put himself] in a plea of debt. And it is adjourned etc.

Plea
Attached
Amerced 3d

Thomas Jenkyns junior plaintiff of Thomas Heyne (3d) of Wykene in a plea of debt etc. And it was ordered to the bailiff to attach him and he did not come so in mercy etc. And it is ordered to distrain him to the next [court]

Amerced 14d

The 12 jurors said that Robert Saundres (2d), William Bromley (2d) & Thomas Richardes (2d) owed suit at this court and did not come so in mercy etc. And they present that Richard Walker (4d) & Roger Richardes absent themselves from grinding at the mills of the lady so etc.

Still goods
and chattels
forfeit 8s 10d
Supervise

And they present that Thomas Gille who was hanged for diverse felonies which he made still had diverse goods and chattels namely 1 pair of scales with weights 1lb and a half price 4d in the custody of Stephen Webbe. Also they said that William Kyngessone owed the same Thomas for 1 green and red outer garment 2s. Also they said that John Snell has 1 pair of shears price 8d. Also they said that John Jenkys has 1 green cloak with a hood (hoec) price 16d. Also they say that Stephen Webbe 1 pair of leather gloves (manutheca) price 6d. Also they present that the said Stephen has one broad arrow with 2 arrows and 4 bolts price 4d. Also they said that John Gerbot has 1 sword price 2s. And they present that the aforesaid Thomas Gille has 1 small meadow for the term of 5 years not yet completed which he took from Robert Baker called Badrychparrok and valued to reprise further 20d per annum. Concerning which the reeve is to respond

Affeerors: John Nycolsone, John Johnsone

Sum of this court 12s 3d
Thence in expenses of the steward 2s 3d

Worfeld

Court held there on Wednesday next after the feast of St Bartholomew the Apostle in the eighth year of the above said King [28 August 1420]

Essoins

John Bullok, John Bradeney, John Colettes, Thomas Jenkyns senior, John Jannes of Swancote, Roger Swancote, JohnWaltone, Thomas Gerbot. William Hokcombe, William Wermot, John Bromley of Bromley, William Newe, William Bromley, essoined themselves by Hugh Halle

The 12

John Nycolsone	Roger Tounesende	Robert Webbe	Richard Haselwode }
Roger Waltone	William Gerbot	Robert Bruggeende	John Hethe } sworn
Stephen Bradeney	Thomas Undirhull	Thomas Roulowe	John Byllyngesley}

1420 P314/W/1/1/255

Roger Daliley plaintiff of Thomas Jenkyns senior agreed put himself in his own person in a plea of debt pledge for the prosecution the bailiff etc. And they have an adjournment

Plea adjourned Attach

Margaret Tresill by J. Nicolsone her attorney plaintiff of Alice Galyan not summoned in a plea of unjust detention of 1 pot and 1 brass pan price 10s detained from Friday next before the feast of All Saints in the fifth year of the reign of King Henry IV until this to the damage of the same Margaret 6s 8d. And it is ordered to the bailiff to summon her etc.

Thomas Jenkyns junior (6d) put himself in mercy for a licence to agree with John Nycholsone in a plea of debt

Pleas Amerced 9d Attach

Thomas Heyne plaintiff of Richard Walker (3d) made the law in a plea of trespass etc. And it was ordered to the bailiff to attach him. And he did not come so in mercy. And it is ordered to the bailiff to distrain him to the next [court]

William Huggyns of Claverley Home plaintiff of Thomas Jenkyns senior default of law in a plea of debt etc. 40s etc. And the same Thomas wagered the law against the said William concerning the debt above alleged by the same William against the him as is clear in the preceding rolls etc. And at this court the same Thomas is essoined by John Reede

Plea The law essoined

Thomas Jenkyns junior plaintiff of William Aleyn (3d) agreed put himself by the pledge of J. Snell formerly the vicar of Worfeld in a plea of deception etc. And it was ordered to the bailiff to attach him and he was attached as is clear in the rolls of the preceding court. And he did not come so he and his pledge specified in the said roll are in mercy. And it is ordered to the bailiff to distrain him and the pledge aforesaid to the next [court]

Pleas Amerced 18d Distrain

The same Thomas plaintiff of the same William (3d) in a plea of debt as above. And he was attached etc. and he found a pledge as above etc. And he did not come so he is in mercy. And it is ordered to the bailiff aforesaid to distrain them to the next [court]

The same William Aleyn (6d) & his pledge are in mercy because he is not prosecuting his plea against John Stevenes in a plea of debt

Nicholas Stanlowe (6d) is in mercy because he is not prosecuting his plea against Roger Daliley in a plea of debt

Plea Amerced 3d Distrain

Thomas Undirhull, Thomas Toward, William Bakes & Richard Aldith through Roger Daliley their attorney plaintiffs of John Colyns of Huggeford (3d), Roger Baret of the same & Henry Pertone of the same in a plea of trespass. And it was ordered to the bailiff to attach them. And they were attached. And they found a pledge for their coming namely Roger Swancote. And they did not come. So he & the pledge are in mercy. And to distrain to the next [court]

Thomas Jenkyns junior not prosecuting plaintiff of Roger Campyon & Katherine his wife in a plea of debt etc. And at the last court the said Roger and Katherine wagered the law against the said Thomas as is clear in the said court. And now they essoined themselves from the law aforesaid by William Golde

Pleas The law Essoins

The same Thomas not prosecuting plaintiff of the same Roger & Katherine in a plea of broken agreement etc. And thence that Roger & Katherine wagered the law as above. And they essoined themselves as above

1420 P314/W/1/1/255

Thomas Jenkyns senior (6d) put himself in mercy for a licence to agree with Roger Cattestre in a plea of debt

Pleas — Thomas Nicoles of Bruggenorth plaintiff of Thomas Jenkyns senior agreed put himself in
Amerced 15d — mercy by his own person in a plea of debt. And adjourned until the next
Adjourn — Thomas Jenkyns junior (6d) put himself in mercy for a licence to agree with
Distrain — Thomas Sonde in a plea of debt

The same Thomas Jenkyns essoined plaintiff of Thomas Heyne (3d) of Wykene in a plea of debt etc. And it was ordered to the bailiff to distrain him and he did not come so in mercy etc. And it is ordered to the bailiff still to distrain him etc.

The 12 jurors say that Richard Gerbot (2d) owes suit and did not come so etc. And they said that William Waltone who held from the lady 1 messuage and 3 nooks of land in Roughtone has died after whose death there falls to the lady in the name of heriot 1 black cow price 4s. And they say that 1 weir newly built by William
Amerced 2d — Bromley situated in the waters of the Worff as is fully clear at the court held there
Heriot 4s — on Friday next before the feast of the Nativity of the Lord last has no value this year because it lies in decay

Decayed

The goods of Thomas Gille forfeited sold by the reeve & approved namely 1 lined outer garment 20d. Also for 5 swarms of bees 2d. Also 1d for 1 gridiron

Affeerors: John Roulowe, Thomas Jenkyns

Sum of this court 9s 10d
Thence in expenses of the steward 2s 2d
And for parchment …s 6d

… Webbe, William Roulowe, Stephen …
for their costs and expenses

…..[1 line illegible at the bottom of the page]

1420 P314/W/1/1/256

Worfeld	Great court held there on Monday next before the feast of St Luke the Evangelist in the eighth year of the reign of King Henry V [14 October 1420]
Essoins	William Bear, John Tresill, Roger Knyght, Richard Parlour & John Rogeres essoined themselves by Simon Hunt
The 12	Robert Eudenas John Nicolsone of Roulowe Thomas Tomkys Thomas Undirhull} Roger Waltone of Swancote Stephen Bradeney William Wermot John Johnsone } sworn Roger Cattestre John Jonkyns Roger atte Tounesende Robert Webbe}
Hultone	township there presents nothing. Akeltone presents nothing. Stapulford presents nothing. Burcote, Burcote, Ryndleford & Bromley present nothing. Chesturtone presents nothing. Kyngeslowe, Stanlowe present nothing. Worfeld presents nothing.
Roughtone, Hockombe, Swancote & Barnedley amerced 8d	townships there present that Thomas Bradeney (8d) broke the impoundment of 2 oxen impounded by William atte Yate so etc.
Alvescote, Wynnescote, Cattestre, Neutone Amerced 4d Strays 8d	townships there present that Thomas Richardes (4d) owed suit of court & did not come. And they present that 1 male white sheep price 6d pronounced as a stray for one full year in the custody of Roger Tounsende. And they present 1 swarm of bees coming as a stray price 2d in the custody of John Robyns
Roulowe, Bradeney, Asturhull, Ewyke, Sonde Amerced 8d	townships there present that Joan (8d) the wife of Richard Bradeney broke the impoundment of 1 draught animal impounded by John Bradeney
Eudenas, Oldyntone Strays 12d	townships there present 1 white female sheep coming as a stray beforethe feast of the Nativity of St John the Baptist last in the custody of John Jonkyns price 6d. And they present 1 white male sheep coming as a stray for a year past price 6d in the custody of William Oldyngtone
Halene Goods forfeited 11s Amerced 16d	township there presents 1 belt with silver decoration price 10s taken by Roger Gille (12d) from the custody of John Cattestre formerly Thomas Gille's deceased the which Thomas forfeited all his goods and chattels for the reason of felony done by him. And they present one pair of gloves with Otter fur price 6d taken by the said Roger (4d) from the custody of Roger Barker from the goods of the aforesaid Thomas. And they present 1 malt sieve of the goods of the same Thomas price 4d in the custody of John Cattestre. And also they present 1 mele sieve price 2d in the custody of Alice Cattestre from the goods of the aforesaid Thomas
Wyken Amerced 20d. Goods forfeit 2s 11d	township there presents that Thomas Bradeney (8d) took 1 securima called a scythe price 11d from the goods of John Smyth. And they present one linen cloth called Wynnocloth [winnowing sheet] price 2s unjustly taken by the said Thomas (12d) from the goods of William Rys of Claverley Home
The tasters of ale present that amerced 9s 6d	Thomas Tresill (6d) brewed once, John Billyngsley senior (6d) brewed 1, John Gerbot (6d) brewed 1, Thomas Jenkens junior (6d) brewed 1, Hamo Hymley (6d) brewed 1, Stephen Hymley (6d) brewed 1, William Bear (6d) brewed 1, John Johnsone (6d) of Roulowe brewed 1, William Gold (6d) brewed 1,

The tasters of ale Amerced 2s 6d	Robert Bruggeende (6d) brewed 1, Thomas Baker (6d) brewed 1, William son of John Roulowe (6d) brewed 1, John Smyth (6d) brewed 1, Sibill Newe (6d) brewed 1, Thomas Gerbot (6d) brewed 1 & broke the assize. And they present that Alice (6d) the wife of Thomas Sonde who is a common brewer was forbidden to sell ale outside the lord's domain has within & sold by false measure. And they present that Alice (6d) Galyan brewed from the feast of the Annunciation of the Blessed Mary last etc.
	The 12 jurors say that all the townships aforesaid have well and faithfully presented and concealed nothing
	Election of constables. Robert Webbe & Thomas Undirhull are elected to the office of constable and sworn
	Affeerors: Thomas Undirhull, Robert Webbe Sum of this court 28s 9d
Worfeld	Small court held there on Tuesday next before the feast of St Luke the Evangelist in the eighth year of the reign of King Henry V [15 October 1420]
Essoins	John Cattestre, John Johnsone, John Oldyngtone, Thomas Jenkyns junior & Richard Parlour essoined themselves by Thomas Hunt
The 12	John Nicolsone of Roulowe, Roger Waltone, William Wermot, Thomas Undirhull} Roger Swancote, John Janyn, Roger Dalliley, William Gerbot} sworn Stephen Bradeney, Roger Tounesende, Robert Webbe, William Newe}
Plea Attach	Richard Walker plaintiff of Thomas Heyne in a plea of trespass pledge for the prosecution Roger Cattestre. And it was ordered to the bailiff to attach him.
Plea Summon	Thomas Jenkyns senior plaintiff of William Higges of Hopstane in a plea of broken agreement pledge for the prosecution Roger Gerbot pledge for the coming Roger Gerbot of Halen
Amerced 4s	John Kynnertone (6d) is in mercy because he is not prosecuting his plea against Stephen Webbe in a plea of taking and unjust detention Thomas Jenkyns senior (6d) put himself in mercy for a licence to agree with Roger Dalliley in a plea of debt Thomas Heyne (6d) is in mercy for his unjust plea against Richard Walker in a plea of trespass Thomas Jenkyns senior (6d) is in mercy because he defaulted at law against William Huggyns of Claverleyhome in a plea of debt William Aleyn (6d) formerly vicar of Worfeld put himself in mercy for a licence to agree with Thomas Jenkyns junior in a plea of deception by the pledge of J. Snell Thomas Jenkyns junior (12d) is in mercy because he is not prosecuting 2 pleas against Roger Campyone & Katherine his wife in 2 pleas of debt and broken agreement Thomas Jenkyns senior (6d) put himself in mercy for a licence to agree with Thomas Nycoles of Bruggenorth in a plea of debt
Essoin	Thomas Jenkys junior plaintiff of Thomas Heyne of Wyken in a plea of debt. And it was ordered to the bailiff to still distrain him. And on this to the same court came the same Thomas Jenkys by John Sumpter & essoined himself

1420 P314/W/1/1/256

Plea still to summon	Margaret Tresill through John Nicholsone her attorney plaintiff of Alice Galyan in a plea of unjust detention of one brass pot & one brass pan price 10s as is clear in the preceding roll. And it is ordered to the bailiff still to summon her
Amerced 3d Distrain	Thomas Toward, Thomas Undirhull, William Bakes & Richard Aldith through Roger Daliley their attorney plaintiffs of John Colyns of Huggeford, adjourned, Roger Baret (3d), of the same & Henry Pertone of the same in a plea of trespass. And it was ordered to the bailiff to distrain them. And they did not come. So they and Roger Swancote their pledge are in mercy. And it is ordered to the bailiff to distrain the same defendants & the pledge aforesaid etc. to have the bodies etc. [at the next court]
Taking a weir	John Nicholsone of Roulowe came here in court & took from the lady 1 weir called Eleshales Weir rendering thence per annum 12d at the feast of the Annunciation of the Blessed [Virgin Mary] & St Michael equally etc.
Surrender Fine 10s	Alice the daughter of John Reynald through Stephen Webbe the reeve there came here in court & surrenders into the hands of the lady 1 messuage and half a virgate of land with appurtenances in Kyngeslowe to the use of Joan the wife of William Hemme to hold from the lady to the aforesaid Joan and her heirs for ever according to the custom of the manor. And she gives to the lady for a fine 10s. And made fealty and has ingress etc. Pledge for the fine Roger Cattestre & Roger Dalliley
Goods forfeit 2s	John Snell approver of the lady presents that John Clerk servant of John Roulowe owed the felon Thomas Gille 2s
Amerced 2d Heriot 3s 4d Relief 22½d	The 12 jurors present that Thomas Richardes (2d) owed suit of court & did not come so in mercy etc. And they present that Richard Aleyn who held from the lady 1 messuage & half a virgate of land & half a nook of land with appurtenances in Halene has died after whose death there falls to the lady in the name of heriot 1 red heifer price 2s 6d in the custody of Agnes wife of the aforesaid Richard. And they say the messuage with land aforesaid remains to the aforesaid Agnes etc. And they present that Alice the daughter of John Reynald a tenant of the lady has died after whose death there falls to the lady in the name of heriot 1 sheep price 10d in the custody of Roger Dalliley. And they present that Thomas Ingman junior who held from the lady 1 messuage & half a virgate of land with appurtenances in Oldyngton freely by charter etc. And he had no goods nor chattels etc. And they say that Richard Ingman is the brother of the same Thomas and his closest heir etc. And he gives for relief 22½d etc. And he made fealty and thence has seisin etc.
Sureties Supervise	The sureties of Roger Gille namely Thomas Merewall junior & Robert Bruggende to have the body of the aforesaid Roger at the next court to respond to the lady who will charge him then there under pain of 40s forfeit to the lady etc.
Election of the reeve	John Bromley of Adlescote & Robert Webbe are elected by the 12 jurors aforesaid to the office of reeve for the future year according to the custom etc. concerning which the steward elected John Bromley & not the sworn for the reason of absence etc.

Affeerors: Robert Webbe, Thomas Undirhill }Sworn

Sum of this court 221s 6½d
Thence in expenses of the steward for 2 days and 2 nights 7s 8d
And in parchment 4d

1421 P314/W/1/1/257

Worfeld	Great court held there on Monday on the last day of March in the ninth year of the reign of King Henry V after the conquest [31 March 1421]
Essoins	Thomas Richardes, Robert Eudenas, John Oldyngtone, John Heven, John Rogeres, John Walker of Ryndleford & Thomas Forster essoined themselves by John Wymond
The 12	Roger Cattestre, John Jonkyns, Roger Swancote, Roger atte Tounesende, John Roulowe, Stephen Bradeney, John Johnsone, Stephen Stanlowe, Richard Parlour, Roger Waltone, Thomas Tomkyns, Thomas Underhull } sworn
Kyngeslowe, Stanlowe	townships there present nothing. Hultone presents nothing. Eudenas, Oldyngtone present nothing. Chesturtone presents nothing. Burcote, Burcote, Ryndleford, Bromley present nothing. Roughtone, Barnedley Hockombe, Swancote present nothing. Halene presents nothing. Alvescote, Wynnescote, Catestre & Neutone present nothing.
Roulowe, Bradeney, Asterhull, Ewyk, Sonde Strays 8d	townships there present 1 white lamb price 8d coming as a stray around the feast of the Nativity of St John the Baptist last past in the custody of John Johnsone
Akeltone Goods forfeited 2s 4d	townships there present 1 deplommis called a Dowblet [doublet] price 18d forfeited by John Gregge who for a felony which he made withdrew himself in the custody of Roger Dalliley. And they present one hood (capicium) of green and red price 10d forfeited as above in the custody of the aforesaid Roger
Worfeld Amerced 2s 11d	township there presents that John (6d) the son of John Roulowe chaplain forestalled Roger Barker and drew blood from him (8d). And that the same Roger (6d) forfeited the said John and drew blood from him (9d). And that Stephen Smyth of Hultone (6d) forestalled the said Roger
Wyken Amerced 20d. Goods forfeited 3s 2d	township there presents that Joan (10d) the wife of Richard Bradeney made homesoken on Joan the wife of Thomas Bradeney & drew blood from her (8d). And that the same Joan justly raised the hue and cry (10d) on the said Joan the wife of the aforesaid Richard. And the same Joan the wife of the said Thomas drew blood (10d) on the said Joan the wife of the said Richard
Stapulford Goods forfeited 8s 1d	township there presents that John Gregge who for a felony he made withdrew himself had diverse goods and chattels which goods and chattels are forfeit to the lady by reason of the felony aforesaid namely one Sythe price 2s in the custody of Roger Swancote. Also one old cover called a blanket (chalo) price 8d in the custody of the aforesaid Roger. Also one pair of linen sheets price 14d in the custody of the aforesaid Roger. Also one piece of linen cloth price 4d in the custody of the aforesaid Roger. And one iron box (cista) price 4d. Also one old pair of leggings (ocrearum) price 3d in the custody of the aforesaid Roger
The tasters of ale Amerced 5s 10d	present that Roger Hulle (4d) brewed once, John Billyngsley senior (4d) brewed 1, Alice Sonde (18d) brewed 3, Katherine Campyon (6d) brewed 1, William Bakes (4d) brewed 1, Stephen Hymley (4d) brewed 1, Matilda Stanlowe (4d) brewed 1, John Sonde (4d) of Bradeney brewed 1, Agnes Hyne (4d) brewed 1, Thomas Merewalle junior (4d) brewed 1, John Baret (4d) brewed 1 & Margaret Osbern(10d) brewed 2 and broke the assize so in mercy etc.

1421 P314/W/1/1/257

The 12 jurors say that all the townships & the tasters of ale aforesaid have well and faithfully presented and concealed nothing

Affeerors: John Johnsone of Roulowe, Stephen Stanlowe
Sum of this court 23s

Worfeld — Small court held there on the first day of April in the year above said

Essoin — Thomas Undirhull essoined himself by Simon Gomond

The 12 —

John Roulowe	Stephen Stanlowe	Roger atte Tounesende	William Wermot	}
Roger Waltone	Roger Swancote	Robert Webbe	John Johnsone	} sworn
Stephen Bradeney	John Janne	Roger Gerbot	John Bromley	}

Summon — Richard Aldith plaintiff of John Glover wager at law millward of Sonde in a plea of debt 8s 6d pledge for the prosecution John Snell. And it is ordered to the bailiff to summon him to the next court etc.

The law — John Hethe not prosecuting plaintiff of Thomas Heyne in a plea of debt pledge for the prosecution Stephen Stanlowe. And the said John says that he owes him & unjustly detains [blank]. The which Thomas came in his own person and denied the aforesaid debt in the manner & form which is claimed against him above. And he says that he owes him nothing. And thence to wager at law pledge for the law Roger atte Tounesende & Thomas Ingman

Adjourned — John Hull of Hultone plaintiff of William Stevenes adjourned put himself of Halene in a plea of trespass pledge for the prosecution John Snell. And they have an adjournment
The same John plaintiff of the same William adjourned put himself in a plea of trespass pledge for the prosecution who before. And they have an adjournment as above etc.
Thomas Walker through Roger Dalliley his attorney plaintiff of Isolda Walker in a plea of trespass pledge for the prosecution John Snell. And at this court adjourned from agreement etc. And she found pledges for the coming to the next court etc. John Bullok, John Whitbrook & John Bromley
The same Thomas essoined plaintiff of the same Isolda in a plea of debt etc. pledge for the prosecution as above. And it is ordered to the bailiff to attach her etc.
John Henen plaintiff of Robert Barker adjourned put himself of Halene in a plea of trespass pledge for the prosecution John Snell. And it is ordered to the bailiff to attach him
The same John plaintiff of Thomas Bradeney of Wykene in a plea of trespass pledge for the prosecution who before. And it is ordered to the bailiff to attach him as above
William the son of the aforesaid John Henen plaintiff of John Hethe agreed in a plea of debt etc. pledge for the prosecution John Snell. And it is ordered to the bailiff to summon him
William Noure plaintiff of John Rogeres of Roughtone recognised 6d for the remainder wager at law in a plea of trespass pledges for the prosecution Stephen Bradeney & John Snell

Summon Attach Distrain — Thomas Ingman plaintiff of Robert Eudenas adjourned in a plea of trespass pledges for the prosecution William Stevenes & John Snell. And it is ordered to the bailiff first to attach him
The same Thomas plaintiff of the same Robert adjourned in a plea of trespass pledges or the prosecution who before. And to be attached as above etc.
Thomas Jenkyns senior plaintiff of William Huggyns adjourned in a plea of broken agreement. And he was attached. And he came. And at the request of the parties they have an adjournment until the next court to be held

1421 P314/W/1/1/257

Margaret Tresill through John Nicolsone her attorney plaintiff of Alice Galyan denied & thence wager at law in a plea of unjust detention as is clear in the preceding roll. And it is ordered to the bailiff to attach her to the next court etc.

Attach
Distrain

Thomas Toward, Thomas Undirhull, William Bakes & Richard Aldith through Roger Dalliley their attorney plaintiffs of John Colyns of Huggeford, Richard Baret & Henry Pertone of the same in a plea of trespass etc. pledge for coming Roger Swancote. And it is ordered to the bailiff to distrain them and the pledge aforesaid to the next court etc.

Robert Herkedale put himself in mercy for a licence to agree with John Blake of Bruggenorth in a plea of debt for to respond to Robert Barker
Richard Walker is in mercy for his insufficient plea against Thomas Heyne in a plea of trespass etc.
Thomas Heyne of Wykene is in mercy because he recognises against Thomas Jenkyns junior in a plea of unjust detention of 1 bushel of rye & 1 bushel of barley ~~price 2s~~ with 4d of damages

Amerced 18d

The 12 jurors present that John Oldyngtone (2d), Thomas Baker of Hultone (2d) & Thomas Richardes (2d) owe suit and did not come so etc.

Amerced 6d
Heriot 3s 4d

And they present that Thomas Sonde who held from the lady one messuage & half a virgate of land with appurtenances in Sonde has died after whose death there falls to the lady 1 black heifer price 40d in the name of heriot in the custody of Alice formerly the wife of the aforesaid Thomas. And the land remains to the aforesaid Alice etc.

Recognition of free tenant
Relief 3s 9d

And the aforesaid 12 jurors say that Thomas Barbour chaplain who held from the lady freely by charter one toft and one nook of land with appurtenances in Wynnescote has died after whose death nothing falls to the lady because the death was outside which tenement should be charged annually of 22½d as of assized rent. And they say that William Barbour is his closest heir. The which William came here in court & made fealty to the lady and recognised himself to hold from the lady the aforesaid toft and nook of land with appurtenances. And he gives to the lady for relief 3s 9d at ingress. And he has ingress

Heriot 10d
Land remains in the hand of the lady

And they say that Agnes Aleyn who held from the lady one messuage, half a virgate of land, half a nook of land with a toft and 2 butts of land with appurtenances in Halene has died after whose death there falls to the lady one white sheep price 10d as from heriot. And the land remains in the hand of the lady

Land remains in the hand of the lady
Fine to have land out of the hand of the lady 5s

And they say that Edith the wife of John Elcok who held from the lady one nook of land with appurtenances in Halene after whose death nothing falls to the lady because the death was outside etc. And the land remains in the hand of the lady. And on this came Roger son and heir of the aforesaid Edith through Roger Cattestre his attorney here in court & took from the hands of the lady the aforesaid nook of land with appurtenances to hold to himself, his heirs and assigns according to the custom of the manor. And he gives for a fine 5s pledge for the fine Roger Cattestre. And has seisin

John Aleyn & Emma his wife came here in court & took from the hands of the lady one messuage, half a virgate of land, half a nook of land with a toft and 2 butts of land which came to the hand of the lady by the death of Agnes Aleyn as is clear in this court fully appears to hold from the lady all the aforesaid land and tenements

Taking of land
Fine 14s

as is above said to the aforesaid John & Emma & his heirs and assigns for ever according to the custom of the manor. And they give to the lady for a fine 14s pledge for the fine John Colynsone. And they made fealty and have seisin

Surrender
Fine 6s 8d

Isolda Walker came here in court through John Snell her attorney & surrendered into the hands of the lady one toft and 1 nook of land with appurtenances in Alvescote called putelond & one cottage with an adjacent garden in Rindleford with one meadow called Hethe Medu lying between Bromley Medu & The More there with one moor lying between the said meadow & the village of Ryndelford & one toft called Laghten in Ryndelford next to the more there with one parcel of land lying between the said Toft & the More there to the use of John Whytbrook of Alvescote to hold from the lady all the aforesaid land and tenements with its appurtenances as is aforesaid to John Whytbrook of Alvescote, his heirs and assigns for ever according to the custom of the manor. And he gives to the lady for a fine 6s 8d. And he made fealty and has seisin

Swearing of the reeve
Fine 18d

John Bromley of Adlescote is sworn to the office of reeve. And he placed himself in the grace of the lady because he kept himself from the office aforesaid as he was elected at the last court preceding namely from Tuesday next before the feast of St Luke the Evangelist in the eighth year of King Henry V until the first day of April henceforth next following in the ninth year of the above said King. And the aforesaid John Bromley found Roger Tounsende & John Bromley of Bromley pledges to do his office aforesaid well and faithfully & also for the contempt aforesaid

Henry Jones came here in court & made a fine with the steward for 18d to marry Margery Smyth widow of the lady by the pledge of Robert Webbe & William Noure

Affeerors: John Roulowe, Stephen Bradeney

Sum of this court 37s 1d
Thence in expenses of the steward, clerk, reeve & others at the same court aforesaid 10s 10d. And for parchment 4d

Worfeld

Court held there on Tuesday next before the feast of St George the Martyr in the 9th year of the reign of King Henry V [22 April 1421]

Essoins

Thomas Walker, Roger Johnes, John Johnsone of Roulowe, Thomas Richardes, Henry Barker, William ~~William~~ Hokcombe & John Oldyngtone essoined themselves through John Hunt

The law with 6 hands

Richard Aldith in mercy for an unjust plea plaintiff of John Glover made the law millward of Sonde in a plea of debt 8s 6d pledge for the prosecution John Snell. And he was summoned etc. to respond to the aforesaid Richard in the plea aforesaid. And he appeared. And the same Richard said that he owes him the aforesaid debt for because the same Richard being the lessee of the mill of Worfeld delivered to the aforesaid John floodgates there for the money aforesaid the which money the aforesaid John still owes to Richard and has detained for thirteen years past. And the aforesaid John came in his own person and said that he owes him nothing. And thence wager at law pledge for the law Elias Mustardman & William Heuster

John Hethe (6d) plaintiff of Thomas Heyne is in mercy because he is not prosecuting his plea against Thomas Heyne in a plea of debt pledge Roger Tounesende

Amerced 18d William Stevenes (6d) of Halene put himself in mercy for a licence to agree with John Hulle of Hultone in a plea of trespass
The same William (6d) put himself in mercy for a licence to agree with the same John in a plea of trespass

Essoin Thomas Walker not prosecuting plaintiff of Isolda Walker in a plea of trespass pledge for the prosecution John Snell. And she was attached. And she came pledges for the coming John Bullok, John Whitbrook & John Bromley at the last court. And at that court the aforesaid Thomas was essoined. ~~And he has a day until the next court by essoin~~
The same Thomas not prosecuting plaintiff of the same Isolda in a plea of debt pledge for the prosecution who before. And she found pledge for the coming as above. And the same Thomas is essoined as above. ~~And he has a day until the next~~ etc.

Amerced 6d Robert Barker (6d) of Halene put himself in mercy for a licence to agree with John Henen in a plea of trespass

Amerced 3d Distrain Adjourned The same John essoined plaintiff of Thomas Bradeney (3d) of Wykene in a plea of trespass . And it was ordered to the bailiff to attach the same Thomas and he is attached by to respond to Robert Barker. And he did not come so etc. And distrained until the next [court]
William the son of John Henen plaintiff of John Heth recognised in a plea of debt. And they have an adjournment until the next [court]

Amerced 6d The law William Noure through ~~John Hethe~~ Snell his attorney plaintiff of John Rogeres (6d) of Roughtone adjourned in a plea of trespass. And he says that John Rogeres destroyed the corn of the same William at Gravenore to the damage of the same William 20s. And the said John Rogeres opposed etc. And thence wager at law pledge for the law John Waltone & Roger Smyth. Nevertheless he recognised 6d of the damage aforesaid

Adjourned Thomas Ingman plaintiff of Robert Eudenas wager at law in 1 plea & of another plea in mercy for because an unjust plea in 2 pleas of trespass. And they are adjourned until the next [court]
Thomas Jenkyns senior plaintiff of William Huggyns of Hopstane recognised Richard Gerbot pledge in a plea of broken agreement. And it is adjourned

The law Margaret Tresill through John Nicholsone her attorney plaintiff of Alice Galyan recognised in a plea of unjust detention as is clear in the roll in the preceding [court]. And it was ordered to the bailiff to attach her and she was attached. And she came and defended the damages alleged against her above. And thence to wager the law pledges for the law John Hethe & John Glover

Amerced 3d Distrain Thomas Toward, Thomas Undirhull, William Bakes & Richard Aldith through Roger Dalliley their attorney plaintiffs of John Colyns of Huggeford, Roger Baret & Henry Pertone of the same in a plea of trespass etc. pledge for the coming Roger Swancote (3d). And it was ordered to the bailiff still to distrain them. And they did not come so etc. And to distrain until the next court etc.

The 12

Roger Waltone	Thomas Undirhull	Roger Swancote	Stephen Bradeney	}
John Rowley	William Gerbot	John Bromley	Roger Dalley	} sworn
Robert Webbe	Roger atte Tounesend	William Wermot	Richard Haselwode	}

Amerced 2d They present that William Hemme (2d) owes suit & did not come so in mercy

1421 P314/W/1/1/257

Affeerors: John Roulowe, William Gerbot

Sum of this court aforesaid 3s 2d
Thence in expenses of the clerk 12d

Worfeld	Court held there on Saturday next after the feast of the Assumption of the Blessed Mary in the 9th year of the reign of King Henry V [16 August 1421]
Essoins	Richard Parloure, William Hemme, JRobert Saundres & Thomas Forster essoined themselves through John Hunt
The 12	Stephen Bradeney Stephen Stanlowe Robert Webbe Robert Brugeende } John Colynsone William Wermot John Bromley Roger Gerbot } sworn Roger atte Tounesende John Johnsone William Gerbod William Newe}
Amerced 2s 6d	Richard Aldith (6d) is in mercy for his unjust plea against John Glover millward of Sonde in a plea of debt Thomas Walker (6d) is in mercy because he is not prosecuting his plea against Isolda Walker in a plea of trespass The same Thomas Walker (6d) is in mercy because he is not prosecuting his plea against the said Isolda in a plea of debt John Hethe (6d) is in mercy because he recognised against William the son of John Henen in a plea of debt Thomas Ingman (6d) is in mercy for his unjust plea against Robert Eudenas in a plea of trespass
The Law The next	The aforesaid Thomas Ingman plaintiff of the same Robert Eudenas adjourned in a plea of trespass . And he says that the same Robert at Durwall with his animals destroyed corn in the barn of the same Thomas to the value of 16d. And the aforesaid Robert came her in his own person and defended the force and injury etc. where etc. when etc. And thence to wager at law pledge for the law Robert Bruggeende & Roger Dalley
The Law Adjourned	William Noure through ~~John Hethe~~ Snell his attorney plaintiff of John Rogeres (6d) of Roughtone adjourned in a plea of trespass. And at the last court preceding the aforesaid John Rogeres to wager the law against the said William in the plea aforesaid. And at this court he has an adjournment of the law aforesaid until the next court at the request of the tenant etc. For the reason the same plea as is clear in the aforesaid court next preceding
Amerced 6d	William Huggyns of Hopstane (6d) is in mercy because he recognised against Thomas Jenkyns senior in a plea of broken agreement pledge Richard Gerbot
Amerced 6d	Alice Galyan (6d) is in mercy because she recognised against Margaret Tresill in a plea of unjust detention
Amerced 3d Distrain	{Thomas Toward, Thomas Undirhull, William Bakes & Richard Aldith through {Roger Dalliley their attorney plaintiffs adjourned of John Colyns (3d) of Huggeford, {Roger Baret & Henry Pertone of the same in a plea of trespass etc. And the {defendants found Roger Swancote pledge for coming. And they did not come so {they and the pledge are in mercy. And to distrain them and the pledge to the next {[court] etc.

More in full of this court

1421 P314/W/1/1/257

[The Dorse]

William Dudley plaintiff of Thomas Bradeney of Wykene is distrained by rye in sheaves price 6d
Plea in a plea of trespass pledge for the prosecution Robert Smyth & William Ingman.
Adjourned And they have an adjournment from the prayer of the parties

{William Gerbot (6d) is in mercy because he is not prosecuting his plea against
Amerced 6d {Richard Gerbot in a plea of trespass
{Richard Herkedale plaintiff adjourned of William Stevenes in a plea of trespass pledge
{for the prosecution the reeve
{John Glover millward of Sonde plaintiff of Richard Aldith in a plea of trespass
{pledge for the prosecution William Heuster. And it is ordered to the beadle to
{attach him
Summon {Elias Mustardman plaintiff of Margery Osberne still distrain in a plea of debt pledge
{for the prosecution William Dudley. And summon to the next [court]
Adjourned (Thomas Manlove Vicar of Worfeld plaintiff of adjourned Thomas Jenkyns junior in a
{plea of debt. And they have an adjournment to the next court etc.

Amerced 10d The 12 jurors present that Thomas Halle (2d) owes suit & did not come so in mercy, Henry Jones (2d), Roger Swancote (2d), Thomas Richardes (2d) & Thomas Walker (2d) similarly. So in mercy etc.

Affeerors: Stephen Bradeney, Stephen Webbe } sworn

Sum of this court 5s 1d
Thence in expenses of the steward, clerk & others 2s 3d

1421-1422 P314/W/1/1/258 &/259 & /260

Worfeld	Great court held there on Thursday on the feast of St Denis the martyr in the ninth year of the reign of King Henry V after the conquest [9 October 1421]
Essoins	William Oldyngtone, Nicholas Stanlowe, Roger Campion, & John Tresill essoined themselves by Edmund Comptone
The 12	Robert Eudenas, Roger Cattestre, Thomas Tomkys, William Wermot, Stephen Bradeney, Richard Parlour, John Janyn, Stephen Stanlowe, John Colynsone, John Jonkys, Roger Swancote, Robert Webbe } sworn
Kyngeslowe, Stanlowe strays 1d	townships there present one Wele [fish trap probably of wicker] for taking fish coming as a stray price 1d in the custody of John Hethe
Roulowe, Bradeney, Asturhull, Ewywyk, Sonde Amerced 8d Strays 10d	townships there present that Margaret Tresill (8d) unjustly raised the hue and cry on William Goolde & his kinsmen. And they present 1 white female sheep price 10d coming as a stray before the feast of the Nativity of St John the Baptist in the custody of John Colynsone
Alvescote, Wynnescote, Cattestre, Neutone Amerced 8d	townships there present that Thomas Richardes (4d) owes appearance and did not come so etc. And they say that Richard Walker (4d) turned the water from the rightful course at yerthyngestone so etc.
Akeltone Strays not Forfeited 4s 8d	township there present one black male draught animal price 20d coming as a stray before the feast of Pentecost last past in the custody of the bailiff. Also they present one other black male draught animal price 3s coming as a stray before the feast of the Nativity of St John the Baptist last in the custody of Roger Dalley
Hultone Amerced 14d	township there present that John Henen (6d) forestalled Roger Barker son of Robert Barker. And that the same John (8d) unjustly raised the hue and cry on the aforesaid Roger
Worfeld Amerced 20d	township there present that John Couper (4d) owes suit and did not come. And they present that Thomas Jenkyns (8d) junior forestalled Robert Herkedale. And the same Robert (8d) forestalled the said Thomas etc.
Roughtone, Barnedley. Hokcombe & Swancote Amerced 4d	townships there present that William Skynner (4d) owes suit and did not come so in mercy
Eudenas, Oldyngtone Amerced 6d	townships there present that Thomas Ingman (6d) broke the impoundment of animals impounded by Alice Eudenas so in mercy etc.
Halene Amerced 6d	township there present that Robert Herdale (6d) made a recovery on one cow arrested by John Rogeres
Wykene Amerced 7d	township there present one branch of one apple tree hanging over the high way there to the grave nuisance of the tenants of the lady in default of William Ingman (3d). And they present that the same William Ingman (4d) broke the impoundment of one cow impounded by William Noure. And they have an adjournment of a certain trespass made by the said William to William Roulowe namely concerning wool stolen as it is said etc.

1421-1422 P314/W/1/1/258 &/259 & /260

Nothing	Burcote, Burcote, Rynelford & Bromley present nothing, Stapulford present nothing, Chestertone present nothing
The tasters of ale present. Amerced 7s 10d	Thomas Baker (4d) brewed 1, William Ingman (8d) brewed 2, Thomas Walker (4d) brewed 1, John Billyngesley senior (4d) brewed 1, Hamond Hymley (4d) brewed 1, John Johnsone of Roulowe (4d) brewed 1, John Gerbot (4d) brewed 1, William Dudley (4d) brewed 1, John Bromley (4d) brewed 1, Stephen Bradeney (4d) brewed 1, Sibill Newe (4d) brewed 1, Richard Botiller (4d) brewed 1, William Robyns (4d) brewed 1, Margaret Kyngesone (4d) brewed 1, Alice Sonde (10d) common brewer for a certain time, John Snell (4d) brewed 1, John Cattestre (4d) brewed 1, John Mason (4d) brewed 1, under the name of the name of the light of the Blessed Mary(4d) 1 brew, Alice Galyan (8d) brewed 2 and broke the assize
The 12 jurors present Amerced 4d	The 12 jurors present that Roger Gille (4d) removed two doors from the house of the lady in Halene. And they say that all the townships & the tasters of ale aforesaid have presented well and faithfully and concealed nothing
Fine 6d	Alice Sonde made a fine with the steward to brew from the date of this court until the feast of the Nativity of the Lord next in the future for 6d
Fine 16d	Joan Ingman made a fine with the steward to brew from the date of this court until the end of one year next in the future paying at the feast of the Annunciation of the Blessed Mary & St Michael in equal portions 16d
Fine 12d	Alice Galyan made a fine with the steward to brew from the date of this court for one full year following for 12d to pay at the feast of the Annunciation of the Blessed Mary & St Michael equally
Election of ale tasters	Roger Kyngeslowe & William Bromley are elected to the office of ale taster and sworn
	Affeerors: John Roulowe, Roger Swancote } Sworn Sum of this court 22s 8d with 5s 6d concerning strays not yet forfeited
Worfeld	Small court held there on the Friday next after the feast of St Denis the martyr in the ninth year of the reign of King Henry V after the conquest [10 October 1421]
Essoins	William Heuster, John Colettes of Hultone, William atte Yate of Roughtone, John Oldyngtone & John Whitebrok essoined themselves by John Huntyngtone

The 12	John Colynsone	Stephen Stanlowe	John Roulowe	Robert Webbe	}
	Stephen Bradeney	Roger atte Tounesende	William Gerbot	William Newe	} sworn
	John Jannes	Thomas Undirhull	John Bromley	Thomas Tresill	}

The law adjourned	Thomas Ingman not prosecuting plaintiff of Robert Eudenas in a plea of trespass. And thence the same Robert wagered the law against the aforesaid Thomas as clear in the last court preceding. And they have an adjournment on the law aforesaid at this court until the next [court]

William Noure not prosecuting by John Snell his attorney plaintiff of John Rogeres of Roughtone in a plea of trespass. And they have an adjournment on the law
Thomas Toward, Thomas Undirhull, William Bakes & Richard Aldith by Roger Dalley their attorney plaintiffs of John Colyns of Huggeford, Roger Baret & Henry
Adjourned — Pertone of the same in a plea of trespass. And they have an adjournment until the next [court]

William Dudley plaintiff of Thomas Bradeney of Wykene (4d) in a plea of trespass
Amerced 4d — etc. And at the last court preceding they had an adjournment until now. And because he did not come to this court he is in mercy etc. And to distrain etc.

Robert Herkedale ~~not prosecuting~~ plaintiff of William Stevenes in a plea of trespass etc.
Adjourned — And they have an adjournment until the next [court] etc.
Richard Aldith (6d) is in mercy because he withdrew from court against John
Amerced 6d — Glover Mulward in a plea of trespass etc.
Elias Mustardman plaintiff of Margaret Osbern to respond to the court against Elie Mustardman in a plea of debt. And it is ordered to the bailiff to distrain her to the next court etc.
Distrain — Thomas Manlove vicar of the church of Worfeld plaintiff of adjourned Thomas Jenkyns junior (4d) in a plea of trespass etc. And they have an adjournment until the next
Adjourn — [court] etc.
Thomas Jenkyns junior plaintiff of Thomas Manlove vicar of the church of Worfeld adjourned in 2 pleas of trespass pledge for the prosecution Robert Barker
John Heven plaintiff of Thomas Bradeney adjourned in a plea of trespass etc. And they have an adjournment until the next court etc.

Hugh Fremon elsewhere it is said Hugh Lendemore came here in court and took from the lady one toft in Halene formerly in the tenure of Thomas Nedle to hold to
Increased Rent 6d — the same Hugh & his heirs for the term of ten years next following etc.. Rendering thence per annum 6d at the usual times. And suit of court twice per annum for all things etc.

John Aleyn of Hymley & Emma his wife correctly & alone was examined and came here in court & surrendered into the hands of the lady one messuage, one toft, half a virgate of land, half a nook of land & two butts of land of the inheritance of the aforesaid Emma which lands and tenements were formerly Thomas Nedle's, father of the aforesaid Emma in Halene within the domain of Worfeld to the use of John
Surrender Fine 15s — Elcok to hold to the same John Elcock his heirs and assigns according to the custom of the manor for ever. And he gives to the lady for a fine 15s. And made fealty. And has seisin. Under this condition namely that thus the aforesaid John Elcok or any other in his name should pay or make a payment to the aforesaid John Aleyn & Emma his wife or one of their heirs or their executors on the feast of St Michael the Archangel next in the future after the date of this court twenty shillings of good money & on the feast of St Michael the Archangel thereafter next in the future twenty shillings of good money & on the feast of St Michael the Archangel thereafter next in the future twenty shillings of good money & on the feast of St Michael the Archangel thereafter next in the future twenty shillings of good money & on the feast of St Michael the Archangel thereafter next following twenty shillings of good money. And if the aforesaid John Elcok defaults of any payment of the said payments at any feast or feasts aforesaid in part or in the whole beyond one fifteen days after any feast of the said feast that thereafter it is well permitted to the aforesaid John Aleyn & Emma his wife or one of their heirs or assigns to revert and retake the aforesaid Messuage, toft, half a virgate of land, half a nook of land & two butts of land in its former title, peacefully in the future by a surrender this not obstructed

1421-1422 P314/W/1/1/258 &/259 & /260

Increased rent 8d

Robert Herkedale & Margery his wife came here in court & took from the lady one Cottage situated in Halene within the domain of Worfeld which was formerly Thomas Gille's to hold to the aforesaid Robert & Margery his wife, their heirs and assigns for the term of twenty-four years by rendering thence annually per annum 8d at the usual times. And suit of court according to the custom of the manor with other services and customs according to the custom & use of the manor aforesaid accustomed

Amerced 2d

The 12 jurors present that Thomas Richardes (2d) owes suit and did not come so the same is in mercy etc.

Heriot 4s 2d
Taking land out of the hands of the lady
Fine 5s

The aforesaid 12 jurors present that Joan Hull tenant of the lady of one messuage with three nooks of land & one virgate with appurtenances in Roughtone after whose death there falls to the lady one black steer price 3s 4d in the name of heriot, one sheep in the name of heriot 10d. And the aforesaid nook of land remains in the hands of the lady. And they say that Roger Hull son of the aforesaid Joan is her closest heir. The which Roger came here in court & made a fine to have from the hands of the lady the aforesaid nook of land with its appurtenances to himself, his heirs & assigns according to the custom of the manor. And he gives to the lady for a fine 5s and made fealty. And thence has seisin

Heriot 4s

And they say that Edith formerly the wife of John Elcok tenant of the lady of one nook of land in Halene has died after whose death there falls to the lady one black cow price 4s in the name of heriot. And they say that the aforesaid nook of land remains to Roger the son of the aforesaid Edith

Amerced 2s 2d

And they say that Matilda daughter of John Huggyn married John Taillour of Seisdone without a licence from the lady so etc
And they present that Thomas Manlove vicar of the church of Worfeld was fishing in water in the severalty of the lady without a licence

Heriot 10d

And they present that John Smyth tenant of the lady of one messuage and half a virgate of land with appurtenances in Barnedley has died after whose death there falls to the lady one sheep price 10d in the name of heriot. And the land remains to Agnes the wife of the aforesaid John

Fine for Soudeley 3s 4d

The township of Halene made a fine with the steward for to have easement within the wood of Soudeley with its cattle for two years past for 3s 4d

Fine 2s

William Batemon & Agnes his wife made a fine with the steward for 2s for an inquiry to be held of the 24 to enquire whether the aforesaid William and Agnes have the greater right in one messuage & half a virgate of land with its appurtenances in Kyngeslowe or William Hemme & Joan his wife formerly the wife of John Reynald to hold the said messuage and tenement aforesaid. And on this it is ordered to the bailiff to summon the aforesaid William Hemme & Joan to show here at the next court to show their right of the messuage and tenement aforesaid and to do what the court here agrees in this part. And also that he makes to come here 24 tenants to this court to judge the right of the messuage and tenement aforesaid between the parties aforesaid

Election of reeve

John Bromley of Adlescote at this court withdrew from the office of reeve. And Roger Swancote is elected and sworn to the same office for the future year

1421-1422 P314/W/1/1/258 &/259 & /260

Affeerors: John Roulowe, Roger Swancote } sworn

Sum of this court 38s 7d with 14d from increased rent

Thence in expenses of the steward, clerk, reeve and others around this court with the great court aforesaid for two days and three nights 9s

And for parchment 4d

Worfeld	Small court held there on Tuesday on the feast of St Hillary in the ninth year of the reign of King Henry V [13 January 1422]
Essoins	John Hethe, Roger Hulle, & Henry Jones & John Bromley of Adlescote essoined themselves by Thomas Hunt
The 12	John Roulowe, Roger Tounesende, Stephen Stanlowe, John Johnesone} Roger Waltone, Robert Webbe, John Bromley, William Gerbot } sworn Stephen Bradeney, William Wermot, Thomas Undirhull, Robert Bruggende}
Amerced 12d	Thomas Ingman (6d) is in mercy because he is not prosecuting his plea against Robert Eudenas in a plea of trespass William Noure (6d) is in mercy because he is not prosecuting his plea against John Rogeres of Roughtone in a plea of trespass
Amerced 3d Distrain	Thomas Toward, Thomas Undirhull, William Bakes & Richard Aldith through Roger Dalliley their attorney plaintiffs of John Colyns of Huggeford (3d), Roger Baret & Henry Pertone of the same in a plea of trespass etc. And at the last court they had an adjournment. And because now now they did not come so in mercy. And it is ordered to the bailiff to distrain the same to the next court etc.
Amerced 3d Distrain	William Dudley plaintiff of Thomas Bradeney of Wykene in a plea of trespass And it is ordered to the bailiff to distrain him to the next court. And he did not come So in mercy etc. And it is ordered to the bailiff to distrain the same to the next court etc.
Amerced 6d	Margaret Osberne is in mercy because to respond in court against Elias Mustardman in a plea of debt by the pledge of the aforesaid Elias
Pleas adjourned	Thomas Manlove vicar of the church of Worfeld plaintiff of Thomas Jenkyns junior adjourned in a plea of debt etc. And they have an adjournment The same Thomas Jenkyns not prosecuting plaintiff of the same Thomas Manlove in 2 pleas of trespass etc. And they have an adjournment John Heven plaintiff of Thomas Bradeney to respond to the court in a plea of trespass. And they have an adjournment as above
Plea Attach	John Hull of Hultone not prosecuting pledges Roger Dalley & John Colettes plaintiff of William Dudley of Halene in a plea of trespass pledge for the prosecution the bailiff. And it is ordered to the bailiff to attach him to the next court.
Amerced 3d Distrain	Thomas Jenkyns junior plaintiff of Margaret Osberne (3d) in a plea of trespass pledge for the prosecution the bailiff. And it was ordered to the bailiff to attach her. And the bailiff responds that she is attached by one piglet for to respond to John Snell. And she did not come so in mercy. And it is ordered to the bailiff to distrain etc.
Amerced 2d	The 12 jurors present that William Hockombe (2d) mynstrell owes suit and did not come so in mercy etc.

1421-1422 P314/W/1/1/258 &/259 & /260

Declaration stray

John Adames of Rytone came here in court with five hands and declared on oath for himself and appropriated one black male draught animal price 3s presented by the township of Akeltone as a stray at the great court held here on Thursday on the feast of St Denis the Martyr in the year as above. And thence he has delivery because not forfeited

Heriot 2s 4d

Taking of land from the hands of the lady

Fine 5s

The aforesaid 12 jurors present that Edith Colyer tenant of the lady of one nook of land in Chestertone has died after whose death there falls to the lady one red heifer in the name of heriot price 2s 4d. And the land remains in the hands of the lady. And they say that Thomas Colyer is her closest heir. The which Thomas comes here in court and made a fine with the steward to have from the hands of the aforesaid lady the aforesaid nook of land with appurtenances to hold to himself, his heirs and assigns for ever according to the custom of the manor. And he gives to the lady for a fine 5s to be paid at the feast of St Michael the Archangel next etc. And he has seisin

Plea of land Adjourned until the next

It was ordered to the reeve at the last court that he summon William Hemme & Joan his wife adjourned formerly the wife of John Reynald that they are here at this court to show their right in one messuage and half a virgate of land with appurtenances in Kyngeslowe which William Batemon & Agnes his wife claimed to be the right of the aforesaid Agnes. And also that he summon 24 upright & legal men tenants of the domain according to the custom of the manor that they are here at the next court to judge the right between the parties aforesaid concerning the land and tenement aforesaid. And the parties aforesaid appeared here. And the 24 were examined as is clear in the schedule stitched to this roll whose names are contained in the same schedule. And on this it is adjourned with the agreement of the parties until the next court. And it is ordered to the reeve to have the bodies of the aforesaid 24 to judge the right between the parties aforesaid concerning the land and tenement above said at the next court

Affeerors: John Janne, Thomas Undirhull } sworn

Sum of this court 9s 9d

Thence in expenses of the steward, clerk, reeve and others 3s 5d

P314/W/1/1/259 [Attached]

By the venerable & discreet man the Steward of Worfeld & the whole homage there showing William Batemon & Agnes his wife that Alice the daughter of John Reynald died seized in its domain as of fee [feudal tenure] in one messuage and half a virgate with appurtenances in Kyngeslowe concerning which land and tenement aforesaid the aforesaid Agnes the wife of the aforesaid William is the closest heir of the aforesaid Alice namely a paternal aunt of the aforesaid Alice and sister ~~& sister~~ of the aforesaid John Reynald. So to enquire according to the custom of the manor whether the aforesaid Agnes has the better right in the aforesaid messuage and half a virgate of land with appurtenances just as the aforesaid William and Agnes his wife as of the right of the same Agnes claim or that William Hemme & Joan his wife formerly the wife of the aforesaid John Reynald which messuage and half virgate of land with appurtenances they hold have the better right in its tenure aforesaid

1421-1422 P314/W/1/1/258 &/259 & /260

P314/W/1/1/260[Attached]

Robert Webbe }
Stephen Stanlowe } sworn

Thomas Undirhull }
Roger Tounesende } sworn

Roger Smyth of Hultone }
Roger Gerbot } sworn

John Bromley }
William Bromley } sworn

John Bullok }
Thomas Tresill } sworn

William Wermot }
Henry Barker }sworn

Thomas Toward }
John Billyngesley } sworn

Roger Hull of Roughtone }
William Yate of Roughtone }sworn

Thomas Roulowe of Burcote }
Richard Haselwode }sworn

John Colynsone }
John Collettes } sworn

Richard Gerbot }
John Bradeney of Hultone } sworn

William Robyns }
Roger Jones } sworn

1422 P314/W/1/1/261 & /262

Worfeld	Great court held there on Thursday on the feast of St Denis the martyr in the ninth year of the reign of King Henry V after the conquest [9 October 1421]
Essoins	William Oldyngtone, Nicholas Stanlowe, Roger Campion, & John Tresill essoined themselves by Edmund Comptone
The 12	Robert Eudenas, Roger Cattestre, Thomas Tomkys, William Wermot, Stephen Bradeney, Richard Parlour, John Janyn, Stephen Stanlowe, John Colynsone, John Jonkys, Roger Swancote, Robert Webbe } sworn
Kyngeslowe, Stanlowe strays 1d	townships there present one Wele [fish trap probably of wicker] for to take fish coming as a stray price 1d in the custody of John Hethe
Roulowe, Bradeney, Asturhull, Ewywyk, Sonde Amerced 8d Strays 10d	townships there present that Margaret Tresill (8d) unjustly raised the hue and cry on William Goolde & his kinsmen. And they present 1 white female sheep price 10d coming as a stray before the feast of the Nativity of St John the Baptist in the custody of John Colynsone
Alvescote, Wynnescote, Cattestre, Neutone Amerced 8d	townships there present that Thomas Richardes (4d) owes appearance and did not come so etc. And they say that Richard Walker (4d) turned the water from the rightful course at yerthyngestone so etc.
Akeltone Strays not forfeited 4s 8d	township there present one black male draught animal price 20d coming as a stray before the feast of Pentecost last past in the custody of the bailiff. Also they present one other black male draught animal price 3s coming as a stray before the feast of the Nativity of St John the Baptist last in the custody of Roger Dalley
Hultone Amerced 14d	township there present that John Henen (6d) forestalled Roger Barker son of Robert Barker. And that the same John (8d) unjustly raised the hue and cry on the aforesaid Roger
Worfeld Amerced 20d	township there present that John Couper (4d) owes suit and did not come. And they present that Thomas Jenkyns (8d) junior forestalled Robert Herkedale. And the same Robert (8d) forestalled the said Thomas etc.
Roughtone, Barnedley. Hokcombe & Swancote Amerced 4d	townships there present that William Skynner (4d) owes suit and did not come so in mercy
Eudenas, Oldyngtone Amerced 6d	townships there present that Thomas Ingman (6d) broke the impoundment of animals impounded by Alice Eudenas so in mercy etc.
Halene Amerced 6d	township there present that Robert Herdale (6d) made a recovery on one cow arrested by John Rogeres
Wykene Amerced 7d	township there present one branch of one apple tree hanging over the high way there to the grave nuisance of the tenants of the lady in default of William Ingman (3d). And they present that the same William Ingman (4d) broke the impoundment of one cow impounded by William Noure. And they have an adjournment of a certain trespass made by the said William to William Roulowe namely concerning wool stolen as it is said etc.

1422 P314/W/1/1/261 & /262

Nothing	Burcote, Burcote, Rynelford & Bromley present nothing, Stapulford present nothing, Chestertone present nothing
The tasters of ale present. Amerced 7s 10d	Thomas Baker (4d) brewed 1, William Ingman (8d) brewed 2, Thomas Walker (4d) brewed 1, John Billyngesley senior (4d) brewed 1, Hamond Hymley (4d) brewed 1, John Johnsone of Roulowe (4d) brewed 1, John Gerbot (4d) brewed 1, William Dudley (4d) brewed 1, John Bromley (4d) brewed 1, Stephen Bradeney (4d) brewed 1, Sibill Newe (4d) brewed 1, Richard Botiller (4d) brewed 1, William Robyns (4d) brewed 1, Margaret Kyngesone (4d) brewed 1, Alice Sonde (10d) common brewer for a certain time, John Snell (4d) brewed 1, John Cattestre (4d) brewed 1, John Mason (4d) brewed 1, under the name of the name of the light of the Blessed Mary(4d) 1 brew, Alice Galyan (8d) brewed 2 and broke the assize
The 12 jurors present Amerced 4d	The 12 jurors present that Roger Gille (4d) removed two doors from the house of the lady in Halene. And they say that all the townships & the tasters of ale aforesaid have presented well and faithfully and concealed nothing
Fine 6d	Alice Sonde made a fine with the steward to brew from the date of this court until the feast of the Nativity of the lord next in the future for 6d
Fine 16d	Joan Ingman made a fine with the steward to brew from the date of this court until the end of one year next in the future paying at the feast of the Annunciation of the Blessed Mary & St Michael in equal portions 16d
Fine 12d	Alice Galyan made a fine with the steward to brew from the date of this court for one full year following for 12d to pay at the feast of the Annunciation of the Blessed Mary & St Michael equally
Election of ale tasters	Roger Kyngeslowe & William Bromley are elected to the office of ale taster and sworn
	Affeerors: John Roulowe, Roger Swancote } Sworn Sum of this court 22s 8d with 5s 6d concerning strays not yet forfeited
Worfeld	Small court held there on the Friday next after the feast of St Denis the martyr in the ninth year of the reign of King Henry V after the conquest [10 October 1421]
Essoins	William Heuster, John Colettes of Hultone, William atte Yate of Roughtone, John Oldyngtone & John Whitebrok essoined themselves by John Huntyngtone

The 12				
	John Colynsone	Stephen Stanlowe	John Roulowe	Robert Webbe }
	Stephen Bradeney	Roger atte Tounesende	William Gerbot	William Newe } sworn
	John Jannes	Thomas Undirhull	John Bromley	Thomas Tresill }

The law Adjourned	Thomas Ingman not prosecuting plaintiff of Robert Eudenas in a plea of trespass. And thence the same Robert wagered the law against the aforesaid Thomas as clear in the last court preceding. And they have an adjournment on the law aforesaid at this court until the next [court]
Adjourned	William Noure not prosecuting by John Snell his attorney plaintiff of John Rogeres of Roughtone in a plea of trespass. And they have an adjournment on the law

1422 P314/W/1/1/261 & /262

Adjourned

Thomas Toward, Thomas Undirhull, William Bakes & Richard Aldith by Roger Dalley their attorney plaintiffs of John Colyns of Huggeford, Roger Baret & Henry Pertone of the same in a plea of trespass. And they have an adjournment until the next [court]

Amerced 4d

William Dudley plaintiff of Thomas Bradeney of Wykene (4d) in a plea of trespass etc. And at the last court preceding they had an adjournment until now. And because he did not come to this court he is in mercy etc. And to distrain etc.

Adjourned

Robert Herkedale ~~not prosecuting~~ plaintiff of William Stevenes in a plea of trespass etc. And they have an adjournment until the next [court] etc.

Amerced 6d

Richard Aldith (6d) is in mercy because he withdrew from court against John Glover Mulward in a plea of trespass etc.

Distrain

Elias Mustardman plaintiff of Margaret Osbern to respond to the court against Elie Mustardman in a plea of debt. And it is ordered to the bailiff to distrain her to the next court etc.

Adjourn

Thomas Manlove vicar of the church of Worfeld plaintiff of adjourned Thomas Jenkyns junior (4d) in a plea of trespass etc. And they have an adjournment until the next [court] etc.

Thomas Jenkyns junior plaintiff of Thomas Manlove vicar of the church of Worfeld adjourned in 2 pleas of trespass pledge for the prosecution Robert Barker

John Heven plaintiff of Thomas Bradeney adjourned in a plea of trespass etc. And they have an adjournment until the next court etc.

Increased Rent 6d

Hugh Fremon elsewhere it is said Hugh Lendemore came here in court and took from the lady one toft in Halene formerly in the tenure of Thomas Nedle to hold to the same Hugh & his heirs for the term of ten years next following etc.. Rendering thence per annum 6d at the usual times. And suit of court twice per annum for all things etc.

Surrender Fine 15s

John Aleyn of Hymley & Emma his wife correctly & alone was examined and came here in court & surrendered into the hands of the lady one messuage, one toft, half a virgate of land, half a nook of land & two butts of land of the inheritance of the aforesaid Emma which lands and tenements were formerly Thomas Nedle's, father of the aforesaid Emma in Halene within the domain of Worfeld to the use of John Elcok to hold to the same John Elcock his heirs and assigns according to the custom of the manor for ever. And he gives to the lady for a fine 15s. And made fealty. And has seisin. Under this condition namely that thus the aforesaid John Elcok or any other in his name should pay or make a payment to the aforesaid John Aleyn & Emma his wife or one of their heirs or their executors on the feast of St Michael the Archangel next in the future after the date of this court twenty shillings of good money & on the feast of St Michael the Archangel thereafter next in the future twenty shillings of good money & on the feast of St Michael the Archangel thereafter next in the future twenty shillings of good money & on the feast of St Michael the Archangel thereafter next in the future twenty shillings of good money & on the feast of St Michael the Archangel thereafter next following twenty shillings of good money. And if the aforesaid John Elcok defaults of any payment of the said payments at any feast or feasts aforesaid in part or in the whole beyond one fifteen days after any feast of the said feast that thereafter it is well permitted to the aforesaid John Aleyn & Emma his wife or one of their heirs or assigns to revert and retake the aforesaid Messuage, toft, half a virgate of land, half a nook of land & two butts of land in its former title, peacefully in the future by a surrender this not obstructed

1422 P314/W/1/1/261 & /262

Increased rent 8d

Robert Herkedale & Margery his wife came here in court & took from the lady one Cottage situated in Halene within the domain of Worfeld which was formerly Thomas Gille's to hold to the aforesaid Robert & Margery his wife, their heirs and assigns for the term of twenty-four years by rendering thence annually per annum 8d at the usual times. And suit of court according to the custom of the manor with other services and customs according to the custom & use of the manor aforesaid accustomed

Amerced 2d

The 12 jurors present that Thomas Richardes (2d) owes suit and did not come so the same is in mercy etc.

Heriot 4s 2d
Taking land out of the hands of the lady
Fine 5s

The aforesaid 12 jurors present that Joan Hull tenant of the lady of one messuage with three nooks of land & one virgate with appurtenances in Roughtone after whose death there falls to the lady one black steer price 3s 4d in the name of heriot, one sheep in the name of heriot 10d. And the aforesaid nook of land remains in the hands of the lady. And they say that Roger Hull son of the aforesaid Joan is her closest heir. The which Roger came here in court & made a fine to have from the hands of the lady the aforesaid nook of land with its appurtenances to himself, his heirs & assigns according to the custom of the manor. And he gives to the lady for a fine 5s and made fealty. And thence has seisin

Heriot 4s

And they say that Edith formerly the wife of John Elcok tenant of the lady of one nook of land in Halene has died after whose death there falls to the lady one black cow price 4s in the name of heriot. And they say that the aforesaid nook of land remains to Roger the son of the aforesaid Edith

Amerced 2s
2d

And they say that Matilda daughter of John Huggyn married John Taillour of Seisdone without a licence from the lady so etc
And they present that Thomas Manlove vicar of the church of Worfeld was fishing in water in the severalty of the lady without a licence

Heriot 10d

And they present that John Smyth tenant of the lady of one messuage and half a virgate of land with appurtenances in Barnedley has died after whose death there falls to the lady one sheep price 10d in the name of heriot. And the land remains to Agnes the wife of the aforesaid John

Fine for Soudeley 3s 4d

The township of Halene made a fine with the steward for to have easement within the wood of Soudeley with its cattle for two years past for 3s 4d

Fine 2s

William Batemon & Agnes his wife made a fine with the steward for 2s for an inquiry to be held of the 24 to enquire whether the aforesaid William and Agnes have the greater right in one messuage & half a virgate of land with its appurtenances in Kyngeslowe or William Hemme & Joan his wife formerly the wife of John Reynald to hold the said messuage and tenement aforesaid. And on this it is ordered to the bailiff to summon the aforesaid William Hemme & Joan to show here at the next court to show their right of the messuage and tenement aforesaid and to do what the court here agrees in this part. And also that he makes to come here 24 tenants to this court to judge the right of the messuage and tenement aforesaid between the parties aforesaid

Election of reeve

John Bromley of Adlescote at this court withdrew from the office of reeve. And Roger Swancote is elected and sworn to the same office for the future year

1422 P314/W/1/1/261 & /262

Affeerors: John Roulowe, Roger Swancote } sworn

Sum of this court 38s 7d with 14d from increased rent

Thence in expenses of the steward, clerk, reeve and others around this court with the great court aforesaid for two days and three nights 9s

And for parchment 4d

Worfeld	Small court held there on Tuesday on the feast of St Hillary in the ninth year of the reign of King Henry V [13 January 1422]
Essoins	John Hethe, Roger Hulle, & Henry Jones & John Bromley of Adlescote essoined themselves by Thomas Hunt
The 12	John Roulowe Roger Tounesende Stephen Stanlowe John Johnesone} Roger Waltone Robert Webbe John Bromley William Gerbot } sworn Stephen Bradeney William Wermot Thomas Undirhull Robert Bruggende}
Amerced 12d	Thomas Ingman (6d) is in mercy because he is not prosecuting his plea against Robert Eudenas in a plea of trespass William Noure (6d) is in mercy because he is not prosecuting his plea against John Rogeres of Roughtone in a plea of trespass
Amerced 3d Distrain	Thomas Toward, Thomas Undirhull, William Bakes & Richard Aldith through Roger Dalliley their attorney plaintiffs of John Colyns of Huggeford (3d), Roger Baret & Henry Pertone of the same in a plea of trespass etc. And at the last court they had an adjournment. And because now now they did not come so in mercy. And it is ordered to the bailiff to distrain the same to the next court etc.
Amerced 3d Distrain	William Dudley plaintiff of Thomas Bradeney of Wykene in a plea of trespass And it is ordered to the bailiff to distrain him to the next court. And he did not come So in mercy etc. And it is ordered to the bailiff to distrain the same to the next court etc.
Amerced 6d	Margaret Osberne is in mercy because to respond in court against Elias Mustardman in a plea of debt by the pledge of the aforesaid Elias
Pleas adjourned	Thomas Manlove vicar of the church of Worfeld plaintiff of Thomas Jenkyns junior adjourned in a plea of debt etc. And they have an adjournment The same Thomas Jenkyns not prosecuting plaintiff of the same Thomas Manlove in 2 pleas of trespass etc. And they have an adjournment John Heven plaintiff of Thomas Bradeney to respond to the court in a plea of trespass. And they have an adjournment as above
Plea Attach	John Hull of Hultone not prosecuting pledges Roger Dalley & John Colettes plaintiff of William Dudley of Halene in a plea of trespass pledge for the prosecution the bailiff. And it is ordered to the bailiff to attach him to the next court.
Amerced 3d Distrain	Thomas Jenkyns junior plaintiff of Margaret Osberne (3d) in a plea of trespass pledge for the prosecution the bailiff. And it was ordered to the bailiff to attach her. And the bailiff responds that she is attached by one piglet for to respond to John Snell. And she did not come so in mercy. And it is ordered to the bailiff to distrain etc.
Amerced 2d	The 12 jurors present that William Hockombe (2d) mynstrell owes suit and did not come so in mercy etc.

1422 P314/W/1/1/261 & /262

Declaration stray

John Adames of Rytone came here in court with five hands and declared on oath for himself and appropriated one black male draught animal price 3s presented by the township of Akeltone as a stray at the great court held here on Thursday on the feast of St Denis the Martyr in the year as above. And thence he has delivery because not forfeited

Heriot 2s 4d

Taking of land from the hands of the lady

Fine 5s

The aforesaid 12 jurors present that Edith Colyer tenant of the lady of one nook of land in Chestertone has died after whose death there falls to the lady one red heifer in the name of heriot price 2s 4d. And the land remains in the hands of the lady. And they say that Thomas Colyer is her closest heir. The which Thomas comes here in court and made a fine with the steward to have from the hands of the aforesaid lady the aforesaid nook of land with appurtenances to hold to himself, his heirs and assigns for ever according to the custom of the manor. And he gives to the lady for a fine 5s to be paid at the feast of St Michael the Archangel next etc. And he has seisin

Plea of land Adjourned until the next

It was ordered to the reeve at the last court that he summon William Hemme & Joan his wife [adjourned] formerly the wife of John Reynald that they are here at this court to show their right in one messuage and half a virgate of land with appurtenances in Kyngeslowe which William Batemon & Agnes his wife claimed to be the right of the aforesaid Agnes. And also that he summon 24 upright & legal men tenants of the domain according to the custom of the manor that they are here at the next court to judge the right between the parties aforesaid concerning the land and tenement aforesaid. And the parties aforesaid appeared here. And the 24 were examined as is clear in the schedule stitched to this roll whose names are contained in the same schedule. And on this it is adjourned with the agreement of the parties until the next court. And it is ordered to the reeve to have the bodies of the aforesaid 24 to judge the right between the parties aforesaid concerning the land and tenement above said at the next court

Affeerors: John Janne, Thomas Undirhull } sworn

Sum of this court 9s 9d

Thence in expenses of the steward, clerk, reeve and others 3s 5d

P314/W/1/1/259 [Attached]

By the venerable & discreet man the Steward of Worfeld & the whole homage there showing William Batemon & Agnes his wife that Alice the daughter of John Reynald died seized in its domain as of fee [feudal tenure] in one messuage and half a virgate with appurtenances in Kyngeslowe concerning which land and tenement aforesaid the aforesaid Agnes the wife of the aforesaid William is the closest heir of the aforesaid Alice namely a paternal aunt of the aforesaid Alice and sister ~~& sister~~ of the aforesaid John Reynald. So to enquire according to the custom of the manor whether the aforesaid Agnes has the better right in the aforesaid messuage and half a virgate of land with appurtenances just as the aforesaid William and Agnes his wife as of the right of the same Agnes claim or that William Hemme & Joan his wife formerly the wife of the aforesaid John Reynald which messuage and half virgate of land with appurtenances they hold have the better right in its tenure aforesaid

1422 P314/W/1/1/261 & /262

P314/W/1/1/260[Attached]

Robert Webbe }
Stephen Stanlowe } sworn

Thomas Undirhull }
Roger Tounesende } sworn

Roger Smyth of Hultone }
Roger Gerbot } sworn

John Bromley }
William Bromley } sworn

John Bullok }
Thomas Tresill } sworn

William Wermot }
Henry Barker }sworn

Thomas Toward }
John Billyngesley } sworn

Roger Hull of Roughtone }
William Yate of Roughtone }sworn

Thomas Roulowe of Burcote }
Richard Haselwode }sworn

John Colynsone }
John Collettes } sworn

Richard Gerbot }
John Bradeney of Hultone } sworn

William Robyns }
Roger Jones } sworn

1422 P314/W/1/1/261 & /262

Worfeld	Great court held there on Tuesday the 14 April in the 10th year of the reign of King Henry V after the conquest [14 April 1422]
Essoins	Thomas Richardes essoined by John Hunt
the 12	Roger Cattestre John Jonkys Roger Touneshende William Wermot } John Roulowe John Janne Robert Webbe John Jonsone }sworn Stephen Bradeney Thomas Tomkys Stephen Stanlowe John Undurhull }
Chestertone Strays 6d	The township there presents 1 sheep price 6d coming as a stray on this side of the last feast of St Peter in Chains last in the custody of John Snell
Akeltone Strays 4d	The township there presents 1 sheep price 4d coming as a stray on this side of the last feast of St Michael in the custody of John Kynertone
Roughtone, Barnedley, Hokombe, Swancote amerced 4d, strays 6d	The townships there present that William Skynner (4d) owed suit and did not come. And they present one black sheep price 6d coming as a stray on this side of the feast of the Nativity of John the Baptist in the custody of William Gerbot
Alvescote, Wynnescote, Cattestre, Neutone strays 4d	The townships there present one sheep coming as a stray on this side of the last feast of Saint Michael price 4d in the custody of John Bullok
Hultone amerced 16d	The township there presents Stephen (8d) the son of Julian atte Walle forestalled John the son of Thomas Roulowe and drew blood from him (8d)
Roulowe, Roulowe, Bradeney, Asterhull, Ewyk, Sonde. Strays 8d amerced 4d pain	The townships there present a swarm of bees price 8d as a stray in the custody of John Roulowe. And they present one way broken down at Lampittes to the grave nuisance of the tenants in default of William Bromley (4d). And he has a day to repair the aforesaid road before the feast of St Michael next in the future under a pain of 6s 8d forfeit to the lady
Burcote, Burcote, Ryndleford, Bromley strays 6d	The townships there present 1 sheep price 6d coming as a stray on this side of the feast of St Michael in the custody of John Bromley
Eudenas & Oldyngton Strays 3s amerced 6d	The townships there present 1 sheep with fleece price 6d coming as a stray for the whole year in the custody of Thomas Haselwode. And they present 5 sheep price 2s 6d coming as strays on this side of the feast of St Michael last past in the custody of Thomas Haselwode. And they present that John Snell (6d) broke the impoundment of one draught animal impounded by Robert Eudenas. The aforesaid 5 sheep were pledged and appropriated by Henry Buffrey Chaplain and John Baret of Stoktone according to the custom of the manor
Wyken amerced 6d pain	The township there presents one bridge called Wyken bridge decayed and ruined in default of the Canons (6d) of Lichfield. And they have a day to repair until the next great court under pain of 6s 8d forfeit to the lady

1422 P314/W/1/1/261 & /262

Worfeld	The township there presents nothing, Stapleford presents nothing, Kyngeslowe, Stanlowe present nothing, Halone presents nothing,
Presentation of the ale tasters amercements 4s 4d	John Bullok (4d) 1 brew, John Billyngesley (4d) 1 brew, Henry Barker (4d) 1 brew, William Stevenes (4d) 1 brew, Matilda Stanlowe (4d) 1 brew, Richard Smyth (4d) 1 brew, William Golde (4d) 1 brew, Joan Merewall (4d) 1 brew, Roger Dalley (4d) 1 brew, John Baret (4d) 1 brew, Alice Sonde (6d) for brewing for a certain time and they broke the assize. And they present that William Ingman (4d) and Alice Taillour (2d) sold ale without inspection of the ale taster
Fealty to the lord King	Simon Rugge servant of John Snell, age 20 years, John Gerbot age 30 years, Roger Feltone age 24 years, Richard Nethirtone age 20 years, Roger Prestees age 20 years, John Willen age 26 years, John the son of John Jonsone age 20 years, John Brook age 22 years, John Gerbot age 23 years, John Matheu age 30 years, William Barker age 16 years, Roger Roulowe age 20 years, William Golde age 24 years, William the son of John Jonsone age 18 years, Thomas Janne age 20 years, Roger Jenkyns age17 17 years, John Nedell age 19 years, Roger Gerbot the son of William Gerbot age 12 years and more, Roger Gerbot the son of Roger Gerbot age 13 years, Hugh Valance age 15 years, Thomas Huggecockes age 26 years, William Dalley age 14 years, William Haukys age 18 years, Richard othe Walle age 14 years and Thomas the son of John Roulowe age 18 years residing within the domain of Worfeld for a year & more came to this court and made fealty to the lord King etc.
Presentment	The 12 jurors say that all the townships and ale tasters aforesaid have presented well and faithfully and concealed nothing etc.

Affeerers: John Colynsone and Thomas Underhull sworn
Sum of this court 13s 2d

Worfeld	Small court held there on the day and year above-stated
Essoins	Thomas Richardes essoined himself by John Hunt

The 12

John Roulowe	Stephen Stanlowe	Roger Waltone	John Bromley	}
Stephen Bradeney	Roger Gerbot	John Barnedley	Thomas Underhull	} sworn
John Janne	Robert Webbe	Henry Barker	Robert Bruggeende	}

Amerced 3d	Thomas Toward, Thomas Undirhull, William Bakes and Richard Aldith by Roger Dalley their attorney adjourned plaintiffs of John Colyns (3d) of Huggeford, Roger Baret and Henry Perton of the same in a plea of trespass. And it was ordered to the bailiff at the last court to distrain towards this court. And because now they did not come so in mercy etc. And it is ordered that the bailiff distrain thus further.
Amerced 6d	Thomas Bradeney (6d) is in mercy for withdrawing from the court against William Dudley in a plea of trespass etc.
Adjourned	Thomas Manlove not prosecuting Vicar of the Church of Worfeld plaintiff of Thomas Jenkyns junior in a plea of debt. And they have not appeared in court when ordered
Amerced 12d	Thomas Jenkyns junior (12d) is in mercy because he did not prosecute twice against Thomas Manlove, Vicar of Worfeld, in a plea of trespass

1422 P314/W/1/1/261 & /262

Thomas Bradeney (6d) is in mercy because he withdrew from court against John Heven in a plea of trespass etc.

Amerced 18d

John Hulle of Hultone (6d) is in mercy because he did not pursue his plea against William Dudley in a plea of trespass etc. by the pledge of Roger Dalley and John Collettes
Margaret Osberne (6d) is in mercy because she withdrew from the court against Thomas Jenkyns junior in a plea of trespass and the said Thomas recovered from the aforesaid Margaret 2s for damages by pigs by the aforesaid Margaret done to the said Thomas by the survey of the Steward and the Recorder there

Summon

William Baker plaintiff of Giles Hide of Dalley responded to the court in a plea of debt pledge for the prosecution Thomas Undirhull. And it is ordered to the bailiff he summon him to the next court
Thomas Jenkyns junior plaintiff of Edith Stevenes wager at law pledge for the law J.Hethe, T. Merewalle in a plea of broken agreement pledge for the prosecution the bailiff and the bailiff is ordered to summon the same as above

Land taken for a term of years
Fine 16d

Richard Bradeney came here in court and surrendered into the hands of the lady one parcel of meadow lying in Waltford in the township of Hultone between the meadow of William Dudley on the one side and the water called Chirle on the other side to the use of Thomas Bradeney, son of the aforesaid Richard to hold to the same Thomas and his assigns for a term of twelve years next following and fully completed. And he gives to the lady for a fine 16d pledge for the fine Thomas Merwalle junior to be paid on the Feast of Saint Michael next

Surrender in reversion.
Fine 20s

Robert Barker and Isabelle his wife she examined alone according to custom came here in court and surrendered into the hands of the lady the reversion of one messuage and half a virgate of land with appurtenances called Barkerslond and one toft and half a virgate of land with appurtenances called Wynterplace in Halene to the use of Roger Barker, son of the aforesaid Robert and Isabella, and Alice his wife, the heirs and assigns of the aforesaid Roger, after the death of the aforesaid Robert and Isabelle to hold from the lady all the aforesaid land and tenements with their appurtenances, as is above said, to the aforesaid Roger and Alice his wife and the heirs of the same Roger for ever after the death of Robert and Isabelle his wife, with the reversion whence it should happen according to the custom of the manor. And they give to the lady for a fine 20s.

amerced 2d
view of metes and bounds

The 12 jurors previously charged at this court by the steward on behalf of the lady to inspect the metes and bounds of a certain parcel of meadow of John Hull of Hultone called Hamondmedewe lying next to Roulowe Mill which they said on their oath that William Stevenes (2d) broke and removed the boundaries and boundary marks put there from ancient times so in mercy etc. And the boundaries and boundary marks (metes and bounds) aforesaid at this court by the inspection of the jury aforesaid are newly lawfully restored

Died having nothing

And they say that Joan Malcher tenant of the lady of one messuage and half a virgate of land with appurtenances in Hokombe has died thence seized and she had no goods or chattels whereof something falls to the lady

And they say that 3 shops near the Churchyard of the Church of Worfeld are situated and built on the waste of the lady by Richard Bulvas formerly approved by the lady are now disused. And they say that the Deacon and Chaplain of Lichfield have ~~& received~~ occupied the aforesaid shops and received profit thence and it is ordered to the reeve to seize the shops into the hand of the lady as well as the issue & profit of the same until etc.

plea of land adjourned

It was ordered to the reeve at the last court that he summon 24 upright adjourned and legal men to this court to try the right between William Batemon and Agnes his wife plaintiffs and William Hemne and Joan his wife defendants of land and tenements in Kyngeslowe as is clear in the last court preceding. And from the agreement of the aforesaid parties they have an adjournment until the next court following ~~to this court~~. And it is ordered to the reeve still that he makes the 24 aforesaid to come ~~as is aforesaid~~ etc.

fine for inquiry of 24 2s

Richard Goldesmyth of Worcester and Joan his wife came here in court and made a fine with the Steward for 2s for an inquiry to be held of 24 to enquire whether the aforesaid Richard and Joan his wife have a greater right in one messuage and its appurtenances in Bromley within the domain of Worfeld as of the right of the aforesaid Joan or Joan Swynney, otherwise the said Joan Bromley tenant of the messuage & appurtenances aforesaid. And on this it is ordered to the bailiff that he summon the aforesaid Joan Swynney to be here at the next court following to show her right of the messuage & aforesaid and to do that which the court in this matter will have given judgment. And also that he makes to come here 24 tenants of the domain there to the same court to try the right of the messuage and appurtenances aforesaid between the same parties etc.

Affeerors: John Colynson and Thomas Undirhull } sworn
Sum of this court 26s 9d
Thence in the expenses of the steward, recorder & others 6s 6½d
And for parchment 4d

Worfeld

Court held on the 3rd day of July in the 10th year of the reign of Henry V [3 July 1422]

Essoins

Henry Barker, William Hemme, William Golde, John Whitbrook, John Holygreve, Henry Halle, John Waltone, Roger Hulle of Roughtone, Nicholas Stanlowe, Roger Jones, John Bromley of Bromley, William Bromley, Thomas Undirhull, essoined themselves by John Hunt

the 12

John Roulowe	Roger Tounesende	Stephen Stanlowe	Roger Garbot	}
Stephen Bradeney	William Wermot	William Newe	John Johnesone	}sworn
John Janne	Robert Webbe	John Barnedley	Richard Haselwode	}

amerced 2s 2d

The 12 jurors present that John Bromley (2d) of Adlescote owed suit at this court and did not come so in mercy etc. And they present that William Bakes (2s) took as his wife Agnes Willene, widow of the lady without a licence so in mercy etc.

summon

John Cattestre, plaintiff of William Ingman responded to the court in a plea of debt pledge for the prosecution John Roulowe & it is ordered to the bailiff to summon him etc.

attach

William Newe plaintiff of John Bradeney responded to the court in a plea of trespass pledge for the prosecution William Gold & it is ordered to the bailiff to attach him etc.

1422 P314/W/1/1/261 & /262

Thomas Jenkyns junior, plaintiff of Edith Stevens essoined in a plea of broken agreement & it was ordered to the bailiff to summon her to this court and she came and to wager the law at the next court against the aforesaid Thomas at the next court pledge for the law John Hethe and Thomas Merewall

More on the dorse

amerced 12d Giles Hide of Dalley (6d) is in mercy because he withdrew from the court against William Baker in a plea of debt etc.

Thomas Manlove (6d) vicar of the church of Worfeld is in mercy because he did not prosecute his plea against Thomas Jenkyns junior in a plea of debt

to the next Thomas Toward, Thomas Undirhull, adjourned William Baker and Richard Aldith by Roger Dalley, their attorney plaintiffs of John Colyes of Huggeford, Rogert Baret and Henry Perton of the same in a plea of trespass. And they have an adjournment until the next court etc.

plea of land adjourned It was ordered to the reeve at the last court that he adjourned until the next summon 24 upright and legal men to try the right between William Batemon and Agnes his wife, plaintiffs and William Hemme and Joan his wife defendants concerning land and tenement in Kyngeslowe as is clear in several preceding courts and they have an adjournment until the next court etc. And a day is given to the aforesaid 24 until the same court next in the future etc.

plea of land adjourned It was ordered to the reeve at the last court adjourned that he summon 24 upright and legal men to this court to try the right between Richard Goldesmyth of Worcester and Joan his wife plaintiffs and Joan Swynney otherwise it is said Bromley defendant of land and tenement in Bromley within the domain of Worfeld as is clear in the last court preceding and at this court they have an adjournment until the next. And a day is given for the aforesaid 24 to be here at the next court to try the right between the aforesaid parties

Affeerors: John Colynsone and Stephen Stanlowe sworn
Sum of this court 3s 2d.In expenses of the clerk, reeve, beadle & others 14d

Attached: In this roll *written* evidence concerning three shops …the churchyard of the church of Worfeld

1422-1424 P314/W/1/1/263

Worfeld	Great court held on Wednesday on the morrow of St. Michael the Archangel in the first year of the reign of King Henry VI after the conquest [30 September 1422]
Essoins	John Tresill, Roger Jones, John Barnedley, Roger Gille, Thomas Webbe of Ryndelford, William Hockombe, John Heth, Henry Jones, Richard Ingman and Roger Knyght essoined by John Welles
The 12	John Colynsone John Janyns John Johnsone of Roulowe John Bromley } John Jonkys Stephen Bradeney Robert Webbe William Wermot} sworn Thomas Tomkys Roger Tounesende Stephen Stanlowe Thomas Underhull }
Roulowe, Bradeney, Asterhull, Ewyk & Sonde Amerced 16d	townships there present that Henry Bufferey (6d) chaplain made an assault on Thomas Prestees and from him drew blood (10d) so in mercy
Alvescote, Wynscote, Cattestre, Neuton Amerced 4d	townships there present that Thomas Richards (4d) owes suit and did not come so in mercy etc.
Chestertone strays 3s	township there presents one brown steer price 3s coming as a stray before the Feast of the Annunciation of the Blessed Virgin Mary last past in the custody of John Snell
Halene Amerced 14d	township there presents that John Elcok (6d) made an assault on Roger Barker and the same Roger (8d) made an assault on the said John
Wykene Amerced 2s 10d Forfeit 1d	township there presents that Thomas Bradeney (6d) on Saturday next before the Feast of the Nativity of Saint John the Baptist in the tenth year of the reign of King Henry V at Wykene entered the house of John Gerbot by night against the will of the same John and the peace of the lord King. And that the same Thomas (6d) made homesoken on the same John. And the same John (6d) made an assault on the aforesaid Thomas. And they present that Joan (4d) wife of the aforesaid Thomas Bradeney unjustly took 1 hen price 1d of the goods of William Cartere. And they present that Thomas Bradeney (6d) made an assault on William Ingman with a drawn bow. And that Joan the wife of the same William justly raised the hue and cry (6d) on the aforesaid Thomas so the same Thomas is in mercy
Roughtone, Barnedley, Hockombe, Swancote amerced 4d	townships there present that William Skynner (4d) owes suit and did not come so etc.
Worfeld amerced 2s 8d	township there presents that John Elcok (14d) came to the mill of the lady intending to to fish and plunder the mill banks by night with force and arms against the peace of the lord King and there made an assault (6d) on Roger Mulward the servant of the lady. And that Roger Coriour (6d) made an affray on Thomas Jenkys junior. And that William Cartere (6d) made an affray on the said Thomas Jenkys
Eudenas, Oldyngtone	townships there present nothing. Akeltone presents nothing, Hultone presents nothing, Kyngeslowe, Stanlowe present nothing, Stapulford presents nothing, Burcote, Burcote, Ryndleford & Bromley present nothing

The tasters of ale present

Amercements 8s 8d

John Jenkys (4d) 1 brew, Giles Hide (4d) 1 brew, William Kyngesone (4d) 1 brew, Margaret Osberne (8d) 2 brews, John Elcok (4d) 1 brew, Agnes Derre (4d) 1 brew, Thomas Jenkys junior (4d) 1 brew, Richard Cotiller (4d) 1 brew, John Gerbot (4d) 1 brew, Hamond Hymley (4d) 1 brew, William Dudley (4d) 1 brew, John Colynsone (4d) 1 brew, John Johnsone (4d) 1 brew, William Bear (4d) 1 brew, Roger Warde (4d) 1 brew, Roger Swancote (4d) 1 brew, John Walker of Ryndelford (4d) 1 brew, William Stevenes (4d) 1 brew, Agnes Heuster (4d) 1 brew, Alice Sonde (8d) a common brewer for a certain time, Joan Ingman, Alice Taillour (8d) for a fine to brew and they broke the assize.

Amerced 12d

The 12 jurors present that the township of Halene(12d) unjustly presented ~~that~~ on William Rys because the same William had held in separate enclosures a certain croft called Alison Croft Harres at the common time so the township aforesaid is in mercy for the unjust presentation

Pain supervise

A pain is put on all that the bridge called Bradbrugge at Stapulford ought to be maintained that before the Feast of the Nativity of Saint John the Baptist next they have sufficiently maintained under a pain of 6s 8d forfeit to the lady

Fine 12d

David Rogeres Smyth made a fine with the steward to brew from the date of this court until the end of one year next in the future for 12d to be paid at the Feast of the Annunciation & Saint Michael the Archangel equally

Fine 10d

Alice Taillour made a fine with the steward to brew from the date of this court until the end of one year next in the future for 10d to be paid at the Feast of the Annunciation & Saint Michael the Archangel equally

Fine 12d

Agnes Derre made a fine with the steward to brew from the date of this court until the end of one year next in the future for 12d to be paid at the Feasts aforesaid equally

Fine 12d

Margaret Osberne made a fine with the steward to brew from the date of this court until the end of one year next in the future for 12d to be paid at the Feasts aforesaid equally

Presentment under oath

The 12 jurors say that all the townships and the ale tasters except the township of Halene as shown above have presented well and truthfully and concealed nothing

Election of the tasters of ale

John Cattestre and William Golde are elected to hold the office of ale taster & sworn

Affeerors: John Colynsone & Thomas Underhull }sworn

Sum of this court: 22s 4d. over & above 3s from strays presented above still not forfeited

Worfeld

Small court held on Thursday next after the Feast of Saint Michael the Archangel in the first year of the reign of King Henry VI after the conquest [1 October 1422]

Essoins

John Jannes, John Barnedley, John Cattestre, Henry Jones, Robert Bruggende, John Bromley of Adlescote, Thomas Merewall junior, Roger Waltone, John Heth, essoined themselves by Thomas Wode

the 12

Stephen Bradeney	Roger Gerbot	John Colynsone	Roger Tounsende	}
William Wermot	Stephen Stanlowe	Thomas Underhull	John Billyngsley	}sworn
Robert Webbe	Richard Haselwode	John Bromley	Roger Hull	}

Thomas Jenkys junior plaintiff of William Hokcombe in a plea of trespass pledge for the prosecution the bailiff. And he says that the same William mowed the meadow of the same Thomas at Hokcumbe with force and arms etc. against the will of the

Adjourned — aforesaid plaintiff to the damage of the aforesaid plaintiff 2s. And they have an adjournment to the next [court] etc.

Thomas Bradeney and Joan his wife, plaintiffs of William Ingman in a plea of trespass, pledge for the prosecution the bailiff because the same William came to the house of the same Thomas aforesaid, Joan lying in bed there and made an assault on her and beat her to the grave damage of 20s etc. and against the peace of the King etc.

The same Thomas and Joan his wife plaintiffs of the aforesaid William adjourned in a plea of trespass pledge for the prosecution as before because the same William came with force and arms & against the peace of the King to the house of the aforesaid Thomas and made an assault on the aforesaid Joan intending to rape her etc.

Summon Attach — The aforesaid Thomas plaintiff of the same William and Joan his wife in a plea of trespass pledges for the prosecution as before. And he says that when the geese of the same William and Joan destroyed the corn of the same plaintiff to the damage of 12d Joan the wife of the aforesaid Thomas came & sought to impound the same geese for the damage aforesaid & Joan the wife of the aforesaid William came and did not wish the aforesaid geese to be impounded for the same damages by which the same plaintiff has grave damage

The same Thomas and Joan his wife plaintiffs of the same William and Joan his wife in a plea of trespass pledge for the prosecution as before. And they say that Joan the wife of the aforesaid William with force and arms and against the King's peace took one brandiron price 6d from the house of the aforesaid Thomas to his damage 2s

The aforesaid Thomas plaintiff not prosecuting of John Gerbot in a plea of trespass pledge for the prosecution as before because he took with force and arms etc. one horse of the same Thomas and put the same horse to work in his cart without permission of the same plaintiff to the damage of 2s etc.

The same Thomas plaintiff not prosecuting of the same John in a plea of trespass pledge for the prosecution as before. And he says that he took from the enclosure of the same Thomas one barrow of the same Thomas with force and arms and against the peace of the King to the damage of the aforesaid plaintiff 6d

Thomas Undirhull plaintiff of John Sonde of Bradeney responded to the court in a plea of trespass pledge for the prosecution John Clerk etc.

Amercements 12d — William Ingman (6d) is in mercy because he responded to the court against John Cattestre in a plea of debt
John Bradeney (6d) is in mercy because he responded to the court against William Newe in a plea of trespass etc.

Essoin — Thomas Jenkyns junior plaintiff of Edith Stevenes adjourned in a plea of broken agreement and she has a day to be at this court by essoin granted on the law above as is clear in the last court preceding

Adjourned — Thomas Toward, Thomas Undirhill, William Bakes and Richard Aldith by Roger Dalley their attorney plaintiffs of John Colyns of Huggeford, Roger Baret and Henry Pertone of the same of the same in a plea of trespass. And they have adjournment to the next court etc.

Plea of land Adjourned — By which at the plea pending in the last court between William Batemon and Agnes his wife plaintiffs and William Hemme and Joan his wife defendants in a plea of land & tenements in Kyngeslowe as is clear in several courts preceding a day is given to the parties aforesaid & also to the 24 to judge the right between the same parties named in the aforesaid court until the next court etc.

Plea of land adjourned

Which at the plea pending in the last court between Richard Goldesmyth of Worcester and Joan his wife plaintiffs and Joan Swynney elsewhere it is said Bromley, defendant concerning land and tenements in Bromley as is clear in diverse courts aforesaid a day is given to the parties aforesaid by the judgment of the court until the next [court]. And also to choose 24 jurors & to try between the same parties to try the right of the aforesaid land and tenements they have a day

Fine for having the reversion 10s

John the son of Roger Willene came here in court saying that William Bakes and Agnes his wife tenants for the term of the life of the aforesaid Agnes according to the custom of the manor of one messuage and half a virgate of land, one toft and half a virgate of land with appurtenances in Burcote in reversion thence after the death of the aforesaid Agnes will pertain to the aforesaid John her son. The which John comes here in court and seeks admittance to the reversion aforesaid when it should happen and seeks admittance to the reversion aforesaid when it should happen & he is admitted by agreement of the court. And he gives to the lady 10s for a fine pledge for the fine Roger Swancote

Fine to have an inquiry by the 12 12d

Thomas Jenkys junior came here in court and made a fine with the steward for 12d for an inquiry to be held of 12 men to enquire whether the aforesaid Thomas has the greater right in one messuage and half a virgate of land with appurtenances in Hokcombe or William Hokcombe tenant of the messuage and half a virgate of land aforesaid with appurtenances. And on this 12 are chosen to judge the same matter namely John Barnedley, Roger Gerbot, William Robyns, John Janne, Robert Webbe William atte Yate, Robert Bruggeende, Stephen Stanlowe, John Colynsone, Thomas Undirhull, John Colettes of Hultone, and John Matheu of Roughtone sworn & tried. And with the agreement of the parties aforesaid a day is give from the agreement of the court for the aforesaid 12 until the next court etc.

Amerced 2d

heriot 4s land in the hands of the lady

The 12 jurors say that Thomas Richardes (2d) owes suit and did not come. And they present that Robert Saundres tenant of the lady of one toft and half a virgate of land with appurtenances and one toft and half a virgate of land with appurtenances in Neutone died seised after whose death there falls to the lady in the name of heriot 1 black heifer price 3s and 1 sheep price 12d in the name of heriot similarly and no more because he died outside the domain. And the land remains in the hand of the lady. And they say that William Neutone clerk is his closest heir

Election of reeve

Roger Swancote withdrew at this court from the office of reeve. And Thomas Merewall junior for the forthcoming year for the same office is chosen and sworn

Affeerors: Roger Dalley, Stephen Webbe }sworn
Sum of these 2 courts above-stated 38s 5d
Thence in expenses of the steward 6s 4d and for parchment 4d

Worfeld

Court held there on Monday next before the Feast of St Hillary in the first year of the reign of King Henry VI after the conquest [11 January 1423]

Essoins

William Hokcombe, Thomas Tresill of Alvescote, Thomas Richardes, John Oldyngtone & William Dudley essoined themselves by John Light

the 12

John Roulowe	John Bromley	Stephen Stanlowe	William Newe	}
Stephen Bradeney	John Johnesone	William Wermot	John Billyngesley	}sworn
Robert Bruggende	Roger Tounsende	Roger Gerbot	Thomas Undirhull	}

Amerced 2d — Thomas Jenkyns junior is essoined by John Snell plaintiff of William Hokcombe (2d) in a plea of trespass. And because now he did not come he is in mercy etc. And to distrain him to the next court etc.

Adjourned — Thomas Bradeney and Joan his wife plaintiffs of William Ingman in a plea of trespass as is clear in the preceding court and they have an adjournment etc.

The same Thomas and Joan his wife plaintiffs of the aforesaid William in a plea of trespass etc. as is clear in the preceding court and it is adjourned as above

The aforesaid Thomas Bradeney plaintiff of the aforesaid William and Joan wife of the same William in a plea of trespass as is clear in the same court preceding and adjourned

The aforesaid Thomas and Joan his wife plaintiffs of the same William & Joan his wife in a plea of trespass as is clear in the preceding court and adjourned

Amerced 18d — The aforesaid Thomas Bradeney (12d) is in mercy for not prosecuting 2 pleas against John Gerbot in pleas of trespass etc.

John Sonde of Bradeney (6d) is in mercy because to respond to the court against Thomas Undirhull in a plea of trespass etc.

Adjourned — Thomas Jenkyns not prosecuting junior plaintiff of Edith Stevens in a plea of broken agreement etc. And adjourned on the law as is clear in the preceding court etc.

Thomas Toward, Thomas Undirhill, William Bakes and Richard Aldith by Roger Dalley their attorney plaintiffs of John Colyns of Huggeford, Roger Baret and Henry Pertone of the same in a plea of trespass. And they have an adjournment until the next court

Robert Webbe, Roger Hull & John Mathewe, plaintiffs of John Janne in a plea of trespass pledge for the prosecution the bailiff. And it is ordered to attach him until the next [court]

Attach — Henry Barker plaintiff of Thomas Toward in a plea of trespass pledge for the prosecution the bailiff. And it is ordered to attach the same Thomas ~~until until~~ to the next court to be held etc.

Plea of land — Which at the plea pending in the last court between William Batemon and Agnes his wife, plaintiffs and William Hemme and Joan his wife defendants concerning land and tenements in Kyngeslowe as is clear in diverse courts preceding and a day is given to the parties aforesaid and also to the 24 named in the aforesaid court to try thence the right between the same parties until the next [court] to be held

Plea of land — Which at the plea pending in the last court between Richard Goldsmyth of Worcester and Joan his wife, plaintiffs and Joan Swynney elsewhere it is said Bromley defendant concerning land & tenements in Bromley as is clear in diverse courts preceding a day is given to the parties aforesaid & also the 24 named in the previous court concerning the judging of the right between the same parties until the next court to be held

Plea of land — Which at the plea pending in the last court preceding between Thomas Jenkyns junior, plaintiff & William Hockcombe defendant concerning land and tenements in Hockombe as is clear in the preceding court and a day is given between the parties aforesaid & also the 24 named in the same court to judge concerning the right between the same parties until the next court to be held from the agreement of the parties aforesaid

1422-1424 P314/W/1/1/263

Fine 12d

John Janne made a fine with the steward for 12d for an inquiry to have the 12 above in this court sworn to enquire whether a certain parcel of land called Horscroft in Roughtone [of] the aforesaid John Janne ought to be in common for the tenants of Roughtone from the Feast of St Martin the Bishop in winter until the Feast of the Purification of the Blessed Virgin Mary which matter indeed the aforesaid 12 jurors have in effect that right to try according to the custom of the manor. And it is adjourned until the next court to be held etc.

Fine 12d

Plea of land until the next

John Colynsone of Roulowe came here in court and made a fine with the steward for 12d for an inquiry of 12 to enquire according to the custom of the manor concerning a certain annual rent of 2s derived from the fulling mill of Ryndelford whether the aforesaid John Colynsone and his predecessors and the Guardians of the light of the Blessed Mary in the Church of Worfeld were possessed of and seised of the aforesaid annual rent from the time of which the memory of man does not exist and also if the aforesaid John Colynsone lawfully and of right is able to distrain in the mill aforesaid for the default of not paying the whole rent aforesaid or not. And on this 12 are chosen according to the custom of the manor for to try the same matter namely Stephen Bradney, Roger Waltone, John Jonsone, Stephen Webbe, Robert Bruggeende, Roger Smyth of Hultone, Thomas Undirhull, Thomas Toward, William Newe, John Billyngesley, William Wermot and Thomas Merewall senior the which 12 it is ordered to the bailiff that he makes them come to the next court and also the tenant and occupier of the mill aforesaid

Fine for Soudley 2s

The township of Halon made a fine with the steward for easement within the wood at Soudley for one whole year for 2s

Amerced 4d

Henry Jones (4d) is in mercy for not coming to warrant his essoin at the last court granted until this court

Affeerors Johnesone & William Wermot } sworn
Sum of this court 6s thence in expenses of the steward 4s 4d

1422-1424 P314/W/1/1/263

Worfeld	Great Court held there on Saturday before the Feast of St George the martyr in the first year of the reign of King Henry VI after the conquest [17 April 1423]
essoins	Hamond Hymley, William Rys, William Kyngesone, William Skynner, Thomas Jenkys, John Jannes, John Gyldene, Robert Herkedale essoined themselves by John Estmon
The 12	John Colynsone, Stephen Bradeney, William Wermot, Stephen Stanlowe} Thomas Thomkys, Roger Swancote, Roger Tounsende, Roger Gerbot }sworn Roger Cattestre, Robert Webbe, John Waltone, John Bromley}
Chestertone Amerced 4d	township there presents that Sibill Newe (4d) broke the impoundment of a two-tooth sheep impounded by Thomas Colyer for trespass in the corn there
Roulowe, Bradeney, Asterhull, Ewyke, Sonde Strays 6d Amerced 12d	townships there present one white sheep price 6d coming as a stray before the Feast of St Peter in Chains last and in the custody of John Johnesone. And they present Roger Prestees (12d) and Richard his brother made homesoken on John Jonsone, pledge the township
Roughtone Barndley, Hokcombe, Swancote Waif 12d	townships there present an abandoned *flammeck* price 12d because it was stolen by unknowns & *drovers/exiles*
Ewdenas, Oldyngton Amerced 4s	townships there present that Roger Prestees (12d) made homesoken on John Jewkes. And that Agnes the wife of the same John justly raised the hue and cry (6d) on the aforesaid Roger. And they present that Richard Prestees (12d) made homesoken on the house of John and drew blood from him (12d) pledge the township. And they present that Roger Prestees (6d) forestalled the said Joan Jewkes. Pledge aforesaid.
Stapleford Amerced 4d	township there presents that David (4d) servant of Roger Swancote broke the impoundment of animals impounded by John Johnesone pledge the township
Amerced 2s 8d	William Golde and John Cattestre ale tasters present John Snell (4d) for 1 brewing, John Golde (4d) 1 brewing, William Barowe (4d) 1 brewing, William Gregg (4d) 1 brewing, William Kyngeson (4d) 1 brewing, Hamon Hymley (4d) 1 brewing, John Johnson (8d) 2 brewings, & they broke the assize so in mercy
Nothing	Hultone presents nothing, Kyngeslowe and Stanlowe present nothing, Burcote, Burcote, Ryndleford, Bromley present nothing, Halene presents nothing, Wykene presents nothing, Alvescote, Wynnescote, Cattestre and Neuton present nothing, Worfeld presents nothing, Acultone presents nothing
Presentment	the 12 jurors aforesaid say that all the townships & the ale tasters above said have presented well and faithfully and concealed nothing

Affeerors: Roger Swancote & Robert Bruggeende } sworn
Sum of this court 9s 10d

Worfeld	Small court held there on the day and year above said
The 12	John Johnsone John Colynsone John Bromley John Waltone } Roger Tounesende Thomas Undirhull Stephen Webbe Roger Gerbot}sworn Stephen Bradeney John Jannes Robert Webbe Henry Barker}
Essoin	Thomas Jenkys junior plaintiff of William Hokcombe defendant in a plea of trespass. And the same plaintiff is essoined at this court by John Snell.
	Thomas Bradeney and Joan his wife, plaintiffs of William Ingman adjourned in a plea of trespass. And they have an adjournment by the prayer of the parties until the next court.
Adjourned	The same Thomas & Joan his wife plaintiffs of the same William adjourned in a plea of trespass. And from an agreement of the parties they have an adjournment until the next [court]
	The aforesaid Thomas Bradeney plaintiff of the same William and Joan adjourned wife of the same William in a plea of trespass. And they have an adjournment until the next [court]
	The aforesaid Thomas Bradeney and Joan his wife, plaintiffs of the same William & Joan adjourned his wife in a plea of trespass. And they have an adjournment as above
Amerced 6d	Thomas Jenkys (6d) is in mercy for not prosecuting his plea against Edith Stevenes in a plea of broken agreement
Adjourned	Thomas Toward, Thomas Undirhill, William Bakes and Richard Aldith through Roger Dalley their attorney, plaintiffs of John Colyns of Huggeford, Roger Baret and Henry Perton of the same in a plea of trespass & they have an adjournment until the next [court]
Attached	Robert Webbe & not prosecuting and Roger Hull and John Mathewe, plaintiffs of John Janne in a plea of trespass. And it is ordered to the bailiff to attach them until the next [court]
Amerced 6d	Thomas Toward (6d) defendant is in mercy because he withdrew from the court against Henry Barker in a plea of trespass
Plea of land Adjourned	By which at the plea pending in the preceding court between Richard Goldsmyth of Worcester and Joan his wife plaintiffs and Joan Swynney elsewhere it is said, Bromley, defendant in a plea of land and tenements in Bromley as is clear in the court preceding a day is given until the next court for the parties aforesaid and also the 24 named in the aforesaid court to be held concerning the right between the same parties of the land and tenements above stated
Plea of land Adjourned	A day is given until the next court to Thomas Jenkys junior, plaintiff and William Hokcombe defendant in a plea of land and tenements in Hokcombe & also the 12 tenants thence to judge the right of those whose names are specified in the court preceding
Plea of land Adjourned	A day is given until the next court for John Janne, plaintiff and the tenants of Roughtone defendants in a plea of common to judge as shown at the last court preceding more fully presented
plea of land summon	It is ordered by the bailiff that he summon the tenants and occupiers of the fulling mill at Ryndelford that they are at the next court to respond to John Colynsone in a plea of land according to the custom of the manor as in the last court preceding fully shown

Plea of land Complete

Bu which at the inquiry held of the 24 at the court held at Worfeld on Wednesday on the Feast of St Hillary in the ninth year of the reign of King Henry V between William Batemon and Agnes his wife petitioners and William Hemme and Joan his wife deforciants to enquire of the right of one messuage and half a virgate of land with appurtenances in Kyngeslowe as fully specified in the preceding court. Let there be no further action against the 24 jurors aforesaid because the parties aforesaid are agreed as shown below

Fine 10s

William Hemme & Joan his wife confessed & alone examined separately came here in court in their own persons and remised, released and quitclaimed to William Batemon and Agnes his wife their heirs and assigns the whole right and claim which they have or in any way are able to have in one messuage and half a virgate of land with appurtenances in Kyngeslowe formerly John Reynald's so that neither the same William & Joan his wife nor their heirs nor anyone else in their names has any right or claim in law in the aforesaid land and tenements with its appurtenances nor in any parcel of the same henceforth to be able to enforce or to sell but thence totally forever are excluded by this withdrawal. And on this came the aforesaid William and Agnes and sought delivery of the aforesaid land and tenements with its appurtenances. And they are admitted. And they give to the lady for a fine 10s and thence have seisin

Surrender Fine 12d

John Glover through Thomas Merewall the reeve there came here in court and surrendered into the hands of the lady one cottage lying in the Sonde formerly Isolda Walker's to the use of Margery the wife of the aforesaid John to hold to the said Margery and her heirs according to the custom of the manor and she gives to the lady for a fine 12d and has ingress

Land in the hands of the lady

The 12 jurors say that Joan Hitchcockes tenant of the lady of one messuage, three nooks and a third part of one nook of land and one toft called the Howyerd in Bromley has died after whose death there falls to the lady nothing because she had nothing except from alms. And the land remains in the hands of the lady etc. And they say that Thomas Hitchekokes is the closest heir.

Affeerors: Roger Swancote & Robert Bruggende } sworn
Sum of this court 12s Thence in expenses of the steward, the clerk, reeve, beadle, affeerors, and others for holding this court and the great preceding- 7s 6d
And for parchment 4d

Worfeld

Great Court held there on Monday next after the Feast of St Michael the Archangel in the second year of the reign of King Henry VI after the conquest [4 October 1423]

Essoins

Hamond Hymley, Thomas Richards, William Oldyngtone, William Hokcombe, John Tresill, Richard Ingman, Nicholas Stanlowe, John Barnedley, William Dudley, Thomas Merewall, essoined themselves by John Rounde

The 12

John Colynsone	Roger Cattestry	John Jonkys	William Wermot	}
Thomas Tomkys	Stephen Bradeney	Roger Tounesende	Stephen Stanlowe	} sworn
Richard Parlour	Roger Swancote	John Janyn	Robert Webbe	}

Kyngeslowe & Stanlowe Strays 3d

townships there present one black sheep price 3d coming as a stray for one whole year past in the custody of John Yate

Akeltone Strays 8d

township there presents one ruby horse with one star price 8d coming as a stray before the Feast of St John the Baptist last in the custody of the township there

Alvescote, Wynnescote, Catstre, Neutone Strays 16d	townships there present one female calf colour brown price 16d coming as a stray before the Feast of St Luke the Evangelist last in the custody of Roger Tounesende
Roulowe, Bradeney, Asterhull, Ewyk and Sonde Amerced 4s 8d	townships there present that Edith Stevenes (20d) made homesoken on Margaret formerly the servant of Hugh Burley and forestalled the same Margaret (6d) & drew blood (10d) from her. And that the same Margaret (6d) justly raised the hue and cry on the aforesaid Margaret [This is what is written] And that the same Margaret (6d) forestalled the aforesaid Edith in her defence and drew blood (6d) from her in her defence. And they present that Edith (2d) forestalled Hugh Burley son of the aforesaid Hugh Burley
Halene Amerced 16d	township there presents that Hugh Lendemore (4d) owes suit and did not come and they present that John Walker (8d) forestalled John Cattestry and hit him. And they present that John Walker (4d) owes suit and did not come so he is in mercy
Burcote, Burcote, Ryndleford, Bromley Strays 10d	townships present one mother sheep with a lamb price 10d came as a stray before the Feast of St Katherine the Virgin last in the custody of Thomas Roulowe not yet forfeited
Stapleford Amerced 12d Strays 12d	township there presents that John (6d) the servant of Thomas Toward forestalled David the servant of Roger Swancote and hit him. And they present one swarm of bees price 12d coming as a stray in the custody of Thomas Toward. And they present that David (6d) the servant of Roger Swancote broke the pound of Thomas Toward so he is in mercy
Amerced 4s	The tasters of ale present John Billyngsley (4d) for 1 brew, Richard Bradeney (4d) 1 brew, William Dudley (4d) 1 brew, Robert Bruggeende (4d) 1 brew, William Yate (4d) 1 brew, William, Kyngesone (4d) 1 brew and broke the assize so they are in mercy. And they present Alice (2s) formerly wife of Thomas Sonde for common brewing and selling bread and she holds the common inn/lodging house (hospit*) thus for the whole year past so she herself is in mercy etc.
Nothing	The townships of Chesterton, present nothing, Hultone present nothing, Eudenas, Oldyngtone present nothing, Wyke present nothing, Worfield present nothing Roughtone, Barnedley, Hokcombe, Swanncote present nothing
Presentment	The 12 jurors & the ale tasters aforesaid have presented faithfully & concealed nothing
Constables	John Bromley & Stephen Stanlowe were chosen for the office of constable to keep for the following year & sworn
The tasters of ale	John Gerbot & John Sonde are chosen for the office of taster of ale to keep for the following year
	Affeerors: Roger Tounesende, Thomas Underhull }sworn
Worfeld	Small Court held on the day and year above
Essoins	John Barnedley, William Dudley, Thomas Gerbot, Nocholas Stanlowe, William Hockombe, Thomas Merewall senior and Thomas Richardes essoined themselves by Edmund Hempton
The 12	John Roulowe Roger Swancote Stephen Bradeney John Hethe } Robert Webbe Roger Gerbot William Wermot Roger Smythe } sworn Roger Tounesende Stephen Stanlowe Thomas Underhull John Janne }

Amerced 2d Distrain — Thomas Jenkyns junior plaintiff of William Hokcombe adjourned in a plea of trespass. And the same William was essoined at the last court and because now he did not come so he is in mercy and to distrain

Thomas Bradeney and Joan his wife plaintiffs of William Ingman in a plea of trespass etc. & they have an adjournment until the next court by the prayer of the parties

Adjourned — The same Thomas and Joan his wife plaintiffs of the same William in a plea of trespass and they have an adjournment as above

The aforesaid Thomas Bradeney plaintiff of the same William & Joan the wife of the same William in a plea of trespass. And they have an adjournment to the next court as above

The aforesaid Thomas Bradeney and Joan his wife plaintiffs of the same William and Joan his wife in a plea of trespass. And they have an adjournment as above

Thomas Toward, Thomas Undirhull, William Bakes and Richard Aldith through Roger Dalley their attorney, plaintiffs of John Colyns of Huggeford, Roger Baret and Henry Pertone of the same in a plea of trespass. And they have an adjournment to the next court from the prayer of the parties

Amerced 18d — Robert Webbe, Roger Hull and John Mathewe are in mercy because they did not present their plea against John Janne in a plea of trespass

William Stevenes (12d) and Margery his wife are in mercy because they responded to the court against Elias Mustardman in 2 pleas of trespass & debt

John Elcokes plaintiff of John Billyngsley and Matilda his wife in a plea of debt pledge for the prosecution the reeve and the defendants are essoined at this court etc.

Thomas of Sonde plaintiff of Edith Stevenes in a plea of trespass and it is ordered to the bailiff to distrain her

Amerced 2s — The township of Hallon (2s) is in mercy for having made a trespass with their cattle in the woods of Soudeley without a licence

Fine 13s 4d — Thomas Huchecokes, son and closest heir of Richard Huchecokes came here in court and made a fine with the steward to have from the hands of the lady one messuage, three nooks of land and a third part of one nook of land and one toft called the Howyerd with their appurtenances in Bromley which are in the hand of the lady after the death of Joan Huchecokes as is clear in the last court preceding to hold to the same Thomas and his heirs forever according to the custom of the manor. And he gives to the lady for a fine 13s 4d to be paid at the Feast of the Annunciation of the Blessed Mary and the Feast of St Michael the Archangel equally

Void — By which at the plea pending between Richard Goldsmyth of Worcester and Joan his wife and John Swynney otherwise it is said Bromley of land and tenements in Bromley ceases because of the death of the defendant aforesaid

Plea of land — A day is given for Thomas Jenkyns junior plaintiff & William Hokcombe defendant in a plea of land and tenements in Hokcombe and also the 12 tenants thence to try the right whose names have been specified in the preceding court. And at this court the aforesaid Thomas appeared and the aforesaid William did not appear. And the aforesaid 12 tenants were charged and did not appear. So it is granted by the custom of the court 6 other such tenants for to judge this matter at the next court. And thus it is ordered to the bailiff that he summon the aforesaid 12, and the other six and also the parties aforesaid that they are here at the next court that is to do in this matter

Verdict — An inquiry held of the 12 jurors according to the custom of the manor for John Janne for which inquiry to have the same John Janne gave to the lady for a fine 12d as is clear in the penultimate court preceding to verify whether a certain parcel of land called Horscroft in Roughtone of the aforesaid John Janne ought to be common to the tenants of Roughtone each year from the Feast of St Martin the Bishop in winter until the Feast of the Purification of the Blessed Mary next following or not. The which jury aforesaid namely John Roulowe, Stephen Bradeney, Robert Bruggeende, John Bromley, John Jonsone, Roger Tounesende, Stephen Stanlowe, William Wermot, Roger Gerbot, William Newe, John Billyngesley and Thomas Undirhull sworn say on their oath that the same parcel of land is a separate enclosure of the aforesaid John Janne and at no time of the year held in common tenure according as Robert Webbe, Roger Hull and John Mathewe, tenants of Roughtone aforesaid supposed and affirmed by another trespass taken against the right of the aforesaid John Janne in the last court preceding. So it is granted by the court the aforesaid John Janne to have and to hold the parcel of land separately in future according as he formerly held

Plea of land — It is ordered to the bailiff that he does give notice to the tenants and occupiers of the fulling mill at Ryndleford that they are at the next court to respond to John Colynsone in a plea of land according to the custom of the manor as is clear in diverse preceding courts. And also to summon the 12 jurors for the same matter whose names are specified in the penultimate court preceding that they are here at the next court to try the right of the matter prescribed

Election of reeve — Thomas Merewall junior at this court withdrew from the office of reeve and Richard Parlour is chosen and sworn to the same office for the future year

Affeerors: Roger Townesende, Thomas Undirhull } sworn
Sum of this court with the great court preceding - 27s 7d
Thence in expenses of steward, clerk, reeve, beadle. affeerors & others coming with 4d for parchment- 7s 9d

Worfeld — Great court held there on Tuesday next after the Feast of St George the martyr in the second year of the reign of King Henry VI after the conquest [25 April 1424]

Essoins — William Batemon, William Kynges, William Skynner, Henry Halle, John Bullok, & William Heuster essoined themselves by John Fox

The 12 —

Roger Cattestre	John Janne	Roger Swancote	John Barnedley	}
Stephen Bradeney	John Roulowe	Roger Tounesende	Thomas Undirhull	} sworn
Thomas Tomkys	Robert Webbe	Stephen Stanlowe	Roger Gerbot	}

Roughtone, Barnedley, Hokcombe, Swancote Stray 10d — townships there present one mother sheep with a lamb price 10d coming as a stray before the Feast of St Mary Magdalene last in the custody of Edith atte Brook still not yet forfeited

Burcote, Burcote, Ryndleford, Bromley Strays 2d — townships there present one infirm sheep price 2d coming as a stray at the Feast of the Nativity of John the Baptist last past in the custody of John Bromley still not yet forfeited

Hultone Stray 2d — township there presents one two-tooth sheep price 2d coming as a stray one full year past now in the custody of Stephen Bradeney

Alvescote, Wynnescote, Cattestry, Neutone Strays 14d	townships there present two mother sheep price of the same 8d coming as strays before the Feast of St Peter in Chains last past in the custody of Roger Tounesende and John Bullok. And they present one two-tooth sheep price 6d coming as a stray at the Feast of St Michael the Archangel last in the custody of Roger Cattestre which strays still not been forfeited
Kyngeslowe, Stanlowe Strays 20d Amerced 12d	townships there present 4 two-tooth sheep price of them 20d coming as strays at the Feast of St Michael the Archangel last in the custody of John atte Yate. And they present that William Castell (12d) unjustly enclosed from the common pasture one parcel of land of the mill croft to the great damage of the tenants there
Wykene Amerced 20d Strays 6d	township there presents that Margaret Stevenes (10d) raised the hue and cry unjustly on John Billyngesley. And they present that Robert Barker justly raised the hue and cry on William Ingman (10d) . And they present one swarm of bees price 6d coming as a stray in the custody of Richard Botiller
Halene Amerced 4d Strays 9s 6d	township there presents that Hugh Lendemore (4d) owes suit and did not come so he is in mercy. And they present one swarm of bees price 6d coming a stray in the custody of Robert Barker. And they present 2 bullocks and one heifer price 9s coming as strays at the feast of St Michael last in the custody of the bailiff
Roulowe, Bradney, Asterhull, Ewyk, Sonde. Strays 3s 3d	townships there present one black female calf price 2s 6d coming as a stray before the Feast of St Luke the Evangelist last in the custody of John Roulowe. And they present one two-tooth sheep price 8d coming as a stray before the Feast of St John before the Latin gate in the custody of the aforesaid John. And they present one white sheep price 1d coming as a stray at the feast of St Michael the Archangel last in the custody of Thomas Prestees of Sonde
Akeltone strays 10s	township there presents delivered to John Snell the appraiser of the lady one black ox price 10s coming as a stray at the penultimate feast of All Saints
Ewdenas & Oldyngtone	Townships there present nothing. Chesterton presents nothing, Worfeld presents nothing, Stapleford presents nothing
Presentation of brewers amerced 6s	The tasters of ale present William Goolde of Hultone (4d) for 1 brew, Stephen Bradeney (4d) 1 brew, William Ingman (4d) 1 brew, James Harpur (12d) 4 brews, Marjorie Osberne (4d) 1 brew, Giles Hide (4d) 1 brew, John Taillour (4d) 1 brew, Agnes Derre (8d) 2 brews, Thomas Jenkys (4d) 1 brew, Alice Taillour (8d) 2 brews, William Gerbot (4d) 1 brew, John Bromley (4d) 1 brew, John Bulker (4d) 1 brew, and John Cattestre (4d) 1 brew, and they broke the assize so they are in mercy
Goods forfeit	The 12 jurors say on their oath that John atte Yate junior who was taken for suspected felony by Stephen Stanlowe and John Bromley the constables there on Sunday next before the Feast of St Matthew the Apostle in the second year of the reign of King Henry VI and remained in the custody of the same constables for 3 days and three nights consecutively and afterwards they delivered him to the sheriff of the County of Shropshire at Shrewsbury into the gaol there the same John Yate to be held in safe custody. And the aforesaid jury say that the same John had diverse household utensils price of them 16s. And they say that he had one cloak with a hood price 4s which domestic utensils & the cloak with a hood taken are forfeits for diverse trespasses made by the same John atte Yate etc. which goods aforesaid remain in the hands of the bailiff

1422-1424 P314/W/1/1/263

Frith and grith	John Bradeney junior, Roger Brook, Thomas son of Roger Hull, William Gerbot junior, William son of Thomas Roulowe, Thomas Willot, John Baret junior, Thomas Bradeney, William Colyer, David ap Geffrey and James Cresset came here in court and were separately sworn to be true to the lord King and his successors.
Presentment	The 12 jurors aforesaid say that all the townships and the tasters of ale have presented well and faithfully and concealed nothing
	Affeerors: John Janne, John Roulowe} sworn Sum of this court 39s 2d
Worteld	Small court held there on Wednesday next after St George the Martyr in the second year of the reign of King Henry VI after the conquest [26 April 1424]
Essoins	William Batemon and John Bullok excused by John Rollertone
the 12	John Roulowe, John Barnedley, Stephen Stanlowe, William Newe } Stephen Bradeney, Robert Webbe, Thomas Undirhull, John Bromley } sworn John Janne, Roger Tounesende, Roger Gerbot, Henry Barker }
Distrain	Thomas Jenkys junior plaintiff of William Hokcombe in a plea of trespass etc. And they have an adjournment until the next court from the agreement of the parties
Amerced 2s	William Ingman is in mercy because he withdrew from the court against Thomas Bradeney and Joan his wife in a plea of trespass etc.
Adjourned	Thomas Toward, Thomas Undirhull, William Bakes and Richard Aldith by Roger Dalley their attorney, plaintiffs of John Colyns of Huggeford, Roger Baret and Henry Pertone of the same in a plea of trespass. And they have an adjournment until the next court to be held from the prayer of the parties etc.
Amerced 6d	John Elcockes is in mercy for not prosecuting his plea against John Billyngesley and Matilda his wife in a plea of debt etc.
The law	Thomas of Sonde plaintiff of Edith Stevenes in a plea of trespass etc. And whereof the same Thomas says that the same Edith came to the house of Thomas himself at Sonde with force & arms etc. and there made an assault on Margaret the servant of Hugh Burley and wounded her and treated her badly whereby the aforesaid Thomas etc. And the aforesaid Edith came in her own person and defended herself and said she was not to blame and thence to wager the law. Pledges of law J. Hethe and W. Hokcombe
Amerced 6d	Thomas Jenkyns junior is in mercy for not prosecuting his plea against John atte Yate junior in a plea of debt by the pledge of William Wermot
Adjourn	A day is given for Thomas Jenkys junior plaintiff and William Hokcombe defendant in a plea of land and tenements in Hokcombe and also 12 tenants thence to try the right whose names are specified in the preceding court from the agreement of the parties until the next court to be held
Summon	Still it is ordered to the bailiff to make the tenants and occupiers of the fulling mill at Ryndleford that they are at the next court to respond to John Colynson in a plea of land according to the custom of the manor as is clear in the preceding courts and also to summon the 12 jurors for the same matter whose names are specified in the preceding court that they are at the next court to try etc.

The 12 jurors aforesaid say that William Dudley (2d) and Henry Hall (2d) owe suit at this court and did not come. So the same are in mercy etc. And they say that Roger
Heriot 11s Waltone of Swancote who held from the lady one messuage and half a virgate of land with appurtenances in Swancote & one messuage and half a virgate of land with appurtenances in Burcote has died after whose death there falls to the lady one ruby steer price 6s and one black cow price 5s in the name of heriot. And the aforesaid messuage and half a virgate of land with appurtenances in Swancote are to remain to John Waltone son of the aforesaid Roger by a surrender previously made for which land and tenements the same John made a fine before this time. And the aforesaid messuage and half a virgate of land with appurtenances in Burcote remain in the hand of the lady. And they say that the aforesaid John Waltone is the closest heir of the aforesaid Roger. And on this came the same John as the closest heir of the aforesaid Roger his father and made a fine to have from the hand of the lady the aforesaid messuage and half a virgate of land with appurtenances in Burcote to hold to the
Fine 10s aforesaid John and Agnes his wife, their heirs and assigns for ever according to the custom of the manor. And they give to the lady for a fine 10s pledge for the fine Richard Parlour. And they have ingress

John Elcock came to court and surrendered into the hand of the lady one messuage,
Surrender half a virgate of land and one nook of land with appurtenances in Halene of demesne land there to retake to himself and Joan his wife their heirs and assigns for ever
Fine 6s 8d according to the custom of the manor. And they give to the lady for a fine 6s 8d pledge for the fine Henry Barker. And they have ingress.

Thomas Jenkyns senior came here in court and surrendered into the hands of the lady
Surrender two small parcels of meadow of which one lies in the Home Medewes of Roughtone between Robert Webbe's meadow on the one side and the meadow of the aforesaid Thomas on the other side and another parcel of meadow lies in Foulesiche Medewe there at a certain meadow of the aforesaid Robert with enclosures of the same parcels
Fine 12d to the use of the of the aforesaid Robert with an enclosure to the same parcel to the use of the same Robert to hold to the same Robert and Joan his wife their heirs and assigns for ever according to the custom of the manor and they give to the lady for a fine 12d pledge for the fine John Janne. And they have seisin.

Thomas Haselwode and Matilda his wife confessed & examined came here in court
Surrender and surrendered into the hands of the lady one toft, one and half nooks of land lying in
fine 7s Halene called Rowne halles londe with appurtenances, demesne land there from the inheritance of the aforesaid Matilda to the use of Roger son of Henry Barker to hold to himself, his heirs and assigns for ever according to the custom of the manor. And he gives to the lady for a fine 7s pledge for the fine John Roulowe. And he has seisin.

The reeve of the preceding year charges himself concerning 3s for the hay coming
Approved 3s from the meadow formerly Robert Saunders in Neutone being in the hand of the lady for diverse reasons further 6s 6d charged in the last small court from the issue and profit of the land and tenements of the aforesaid Robert there

Thomas Preestes of Sonde came here in court and made a fine with the steward to
Fine 2s brew from the date of this court until at the end of the whole year next in the future for 2s paying at the feast of St Michael the Archangel next in the future thence 12d and at the feast of Easter thereafter next in the future 12d

1422-1424 P314/W/1/1/263

fine 5s 4d

The 12 jurors aforesaid present that Henry Barker (3s 4d) married Alice his daughter to John Preestes outside the domain without a licence from the lady. Also they present that William Gerbot (2s) married Isolda his daughter to William Golde without a licence from the lady so they are in mercy

John Waltone came here in court and made a fine with the steward for 2s to have an inquiry of the 24 they are reconciled by their neighbours out of court according to the custom of the manor to enquire if Henry Jones and Margery his wife made waste selling and destroying in the land, houses and gardens in Roughtone which Margery holds for the term of her life to remain thence after the death of the aforesaid Margery to John Waltone. And on this 24 are elected for to judge the same matter namely Stephen Bradeney, William Gerbot, Thomas Roulowe, Roger Gerbot, Richard Tounesende, Henry Barker, Robert Barker, Thomas Toward, Thomas Undirhull, William Newe, Robert Bruggeende, John Colettes, Thomas Merewall junior, John Johnsone, John Colynsone, William Robyns, Roger Smyth, Roger Swancote, John Smyth, Richard Gerbot, William atte Yate, William Bromley, Roger Kyngeslowe and John Hull who it is ordered to the reeve to summon to the next [court] etc.

Affeerors: John Janne, John Rowlowe }sworn

Sum of this court 41s 4d. Thence in expenses of the steward, Richard Horde for 2 days and 2 nights and for the clerk, reeve, beadle, affeerors and others coming 14s 4d. And for parchment 4d

1422-1424 P314/W/1/1/263

Worfeld	Great court held there on Saturday on the morrow of Saint Michael the Archangel in the 3rd year of the reign of King Henry VI after the conquest [30 September 1424]
Essoins	John Holygreve, Roger Hull, Roger Knyght, William Kyngesone and John Walker essoined themselves by Thomas Willes
The 12	Roger Cattestre, Roger Swancote, Roger Heth, John Roulowe, Roger Tounesende, Robert Webbe, Stephen Bradeney, John Janyn, Thomas Undirhull, Thomas Tomkyns, John Rowelowe senior, Roger Gerbot } sworn
Roulowe, Bradeney, Asturhull, Ewyk, Sonde. Strays 2d	townships there present one swarm of bees price 2d coming as a stray in the custody of John Roulowe of Roulowe etc.
Hultone stray 6d	township there presents 1 white sheep price 6d coming as a stray before the Feast of the Nativity of the Lord last past. And it remains in the custody of Stephen Bradeney until etc.
Alvescote, Wynnescote, Cattestre, Newton strays forfeit 18d amerced 4d	townships there present 1 red heifer price 18d coming as a stray for one full year past in the custody of Roger Tounsend. And they present that Roger Catstre (4d) owed appearance at this court and did not come so he is in mercy
Eudenas & Oldyngton amerced 3s 6d	townships there present that Thomas Bradeney (6d) forestalled John Cattestre and from him drew blood (10d) and that the same John (6d) forestalled the aforesaid Thomas and from him drew blood (10d). And that Joan the wife of the aforesaid Thomas justly raised the hue and cry on the aforesaid John (10d)
Roughtone, Barnedley, Hokcombe, Swancote Strays forfeit 4d Strays remaining until	townships there present one swarm of bees price 4d coming as a stray in the custody of John Waltone. And they present one black heifer price 4s coming as a stray from before the Feast of the Finding of the Holy Cross last past and remaining in the custody of the villages until
Stapleford Amerced 14d Strays 4d	township there presents that Roger the servant (6d) of Roger Swancote forestalled David the servant of Giles Hyde and from him drew blood (8d). And they present one swarm of bees price 4d coming as a stray in the custody of Richard Aldith etc.
Wyken Amerced 3s 4d	The township there presents that the bridge called Wyken Brugge is ruined and not adequately maintained and repaired in default of the Dean and Chapter (3s 4d) of Lichfield to the grave damage of the tenants & the people of the lord King so the Dean and Chapter are in mercy
Halene Amerced 2s 6d	township there presents that Sibill (6d) Turnour unjustly raised the hue and cry on Thomas Prestees and William Barwe and that the wife (6d) of William Barwe made a recovery of a goose to be impounded by Rose the wife of John Cattestre for trespass in the corn there And that the same Rose justly raised the hue and cry on the wife of William Barowe (6d) And that William Barwe (6d) forestalled the same Rose and the same Rose justly raised the hue and cry on the aforesaid William Barwe (6d)
Chesturtone	Township there presents that John Jowkys (8d) forestalled John Jones and they present one ruby draft animal appraised at 2s coming as a stray & seized at the

1422-1424 P314/W/1/1/263

Chestertone Amerced 14d Strays remain until the next to enquire	Feast of St Peter in Chains last remaining in the custody of John Snell remaining until. And they present that Roger Barker (6d) forestalled William the servant of John Massy. And for other diverse offences made there against the peace of the lord King and the liberty of the manor they have a day to present the truth of the matter at the next great court so to enquire
Burcote, Burcote, Ryndeleford, Bromley	present nothing, Kyngslowe & Stanlowe present nothing, Akeltoun presents nothing, Worfeld presents nothing
The ale tasters Amerced 6s	present that John Gerbot (4d) brewed 1, John Kyngesone (4d) 1, Hamo Hymley (4d) 1, John Johnesone (4d) 1, John Willot (4d) 1, William Golde senior (4d) 1, Thomas Baker (4d) 1, John Walker (8d) brewed 2, Thomas Jenkys (4d) 1, John Elcok (12d) 3, Alice Taillour (8d) is a common brewer, Alice Sonde (12d) brewed by fine
Amerced 12d	Roger Barker (12d) is in mercy because he insulted the village of Chestertoun in court and said before the steward that an unjust presentation had been made of the same Roger's forestalling on William the servant of John Massy. So he is in mercy etc.
Profits of the woods of Soudeley 2s strays 2s 11d	The reeve is charged concerning 2s from the township of Halene for easement here within the wood of Soudeley with the beasts of the same village And concerning 6d for the price of a certain two-tooth sheep thus appraised at the last great court as a stray within that court not forfeit. And concerning 20d for the price of 4 two-tooth sheep appraised as above as strays and then not forfeited. And concerning 8d the price of one two-tooth sheep appraised as above as a stray and then not forfeited. And concerning 1d the price of one sheep appraised as above as a stray and then not forfeited. etc. Of which all the aforesaid strays are now forfeit
Presentment on oath	The aforesaid 12 jurors present that all the townships and ale tasters have presented well and faithfully and with nothing concealed
Election of constables	Thomas Tomkys and John Waltone are elected as Constables to hold for the forthcoming year and sworn
Election of ale tasters	John Kynnerton and William Ingman are elected to the office of ale taster and sworn

Affeerors: John Johnesone and John Waltone }sworn
Sum of this court 26s 1d

Worfeld	Small court held there on Monday next after the Feast of St Michael the Archangel in the third year of the reign of King Henry VI after the conquest of England [2 October 1424]
Essoins	John Barnedley, John Billyngesley, Henry Hall, William atte Yate, William Hokcombe, John Bromley, Roger Jones and Roger Hull essoined themselves by John Tymme

The 12				
	John Colynsone	Roger Smyth	Thomas Toward	John Johnsone }
	John Jannes	William Newe	Roger Tounesende	Roger Swancote } sworn
	Stephen Bradeney	Thomas Merewall junior	Roger Gerbot	William Gerbot }

Amerced 3d	Thomas Jenkys junior plaintiff of William Hokcombe 3d wager at law in a plea of trespass. And at the last court they had an adjournment to the next. And because now he did not come so the same William is in mercy. And it is ordered to distrain him to the next court etc.

1422-1424 P314/W/1/1/263

Still distrain

Thomas Toward, Thomas Undirhull, William Bakes and Richard Aldith by Roger Dalley their attorney plaintiffs of John Colyns, Roger Baret, and Henry Pertone of Huggeford in a plea of trespass etc. And adjourned at this court by the prayer of the parties until the next court etc. by the pledge of R. Swancote

Amerced 6d

Edith Stevenes (6d) is in mercy because of a recovery against Thomas atte Sonde in a plea of trespass

Plea of land
Adjourned

A day is given for Thomas Jenkys junior plaintiff [adjourned] and William Hokcombe defendant in a plea of land and tenements in Hokcombe and also 12 tenants thence elected to judge the right from the agreement of the parties until the next court to be held whose names are clear in the preceding court

Plea of land

Still it is ordered to the bailiff that he make a summons of the tenants and occupiers of the fulling mill of Ryndelford that they are here at the next court to respond to John Colynsone in a plea of land according to the custom of the manor as is more clear in diverse preceding courts. And also it is ordered to the bailiff that he summon 12 tenants thence chosen to try for the same matter that they are here at the next court whose names are clear in the court preceding

Plea of land
Adjourned

Henry Jones and Margery his wife were to respond to John Waltone in a plea whereof the same Henry and Margery made waste, felled wood & distressed the land of the houses and gardens in Roughton which the aforesaid Margery holds for the term of her life to remain thence after the death of the aforesaid Margery to the aforesaid John Waltone as it is said. Whereof an enquiry of the 24 according to the custom of the manor was held at the last court thence to swear those whose names in the same court were specified. And thus at this court the aforesaid Henry and Margery were examined and appeared. And the aforesaid plaintiff came in his own person and said that the aforesaid Henry & Margery unjustly took & carried away one part of a certain chamber called a bey, one fymerell [vent on the roof for extracting smoke] in the hall one door, one lock with a key and another door there found to the damage of the plaintiff of 30s. And the aforesaid defendants said that they are thence not to blame which they above stated. And about this they put themselves on the 24 to prove and the plaintiff similarly. And on this the 24 were charged to judge and try etc. And at the request of the parties aforesaid the aforesaid 24 have a day to present on oath until the next court

Heriot 14s 6d
Escheat 17s 4d

The 12 jurors aforesaid present that Stephen Stanlowe tenant of the lady of two messuages and one virgate of land with appurtenances in Stanlowe and a quarter part of a nook of land there has died after whose death there falls to the lord one ruby ox, tagget, price 7s 6d, one ruby ox price 7s in the name of heriot. And they present three horses after the death of Stephen of which one is grenowe, another dun and a third black. Price of them 9s 4d as escheat. And they present 8 piglets from the escheat of the said Stephen price of them 3s. And present 6 swarms of bees as escheat after the death of Stephen price of them 5s. And the land remains to Alice wife of the aforesaid Stephen

Amerced 3s 4d

The same jury presents that Roger (4d) son of Robert Barker fished in the severalty water of the lady of the Worfe without licence so he is in mercy. And they present that Alice (20d) lately the wife of Stephen Stanlowe widow married herself to Thomas Jenkys junior without a licence from the lady & against the custom of the manor so she etc. And they present that William Golde (16d) married Alice his daughter without a licence from the lady & against the custom etc.

Fine 12d

John Elcok made a fine to brew from the date of this court until the Feast of St Michael the Archangel next in the future 12d and no more in great recompense for his rent of a certain messuage which he holds in Worfeld from the lady paying at the Feast of the Annunciation of the Blessed Mary and on the eve of the Feast of St Michael the Archangel in equal portions

Surrender in exchange Fine 8d

Margery Huggyn in her pure widowhood came here in court and surrendered into the hands of the lady one parcel of land called the Chittey lying in the field of Hultone between the land of Roger Smyth on the one side and the land of John Tournour on the other side with one selion of land pertaining to the said parcel there to the use of the aforesaid John Turnour in exchange for one parcel of land lying in the field of Hultone on a certain strip (stadium) called Dadymerssh between the land of Stephen Bradeney on the one side and the land of Roger Smyth on the other side to hold to the same John his heirs and assigns in exchange as is aforesaid according to the custom of the manor and he gives to the lord 6d for a fine and made fealty and has seisin. And on this comes here in court the aforesaid John and surrendered into the hands of the lady the said parcel of land lying on the same strip called Dadymersh to the use of the aforesaid Margery in exchange for the aforesaid parcel of land surrendered by the aforesaid Margery. To hold to the same Margery, her heirs and assigns in exchange as is above said according to the custom of the manor and she gives to the lady for a fine 2d and made fealty and is seized

Surrender Fine 6d

Margery Huggyn in her pure widowhood comes here in court and surrendered into the hands of the lady one parcel of pasture called Adamesmerssh lying in the field of Hulton between the land of Stephen Bradeney on the one side and the land of Robert Bruggeende on the other side to the use of John the son of Stephen Bradeney. To hold to the same John and his heirs according to the custom of the manor. And he gives to the lady for a fine 6d and made fealty and is seized according to the custom etc.

Surrender Fine 10s

William Batemon and Agnes his wife, alone confessed and properly examined, came here in court and surrendered into the hands of the lady one messuage and half a virgate of land with appurtenances in Kyngeslowe formally John Reynald's to the use of Roger Dalley and Joan his wife. To hold to the same Roger and Joan and the heirs of Roger himself according to the custom of the manor and they give to the lord for a fine 10s and made fealty and are seized

Surrender Fine 20s

William Dudley and Benedicta his wife, she confessed and properly examined separately, came here in court and surrendered into the hands of the lady through William Wermot, beadle, one messuage and one virgate of land in Hultone formerly Thomas Roulowe's to the use of John Roulowe son of Thomas Roulowe of Hultone. To hold to himself and his heirs according to the custom of the manor and he gives to the lady for a fine 20s and made fealty and has seisin

John Roulowe son of Nicholas Roulowe deceased and Margery his wife, she separately confessed & properly examined came here in court and surrendered into the hands of the lady one toft and half a virgate of land with appurtenances in Chestertoun formerly William Ewyk's to the use of John Smyth of Hultone and Margery his wife. To hold to the aforesaid John Smyth and Margery his wife and the heirs of their bodies legitimately procreated according to the custom of the manor by services thence due and accustomed. And they give to the lady 10s for a fine and made fealty and are seized. And on this the aforesaid John Roulowe at this present court remises, releases and entirely for ever by him and his heirs quit claims to the aforesaid John Smyth and Margery his wife and the heirs of their bodies legitimately

Surrender Fine 10s Release on seisin	procreated all their right and claim which they have or in any way their heirs may be able to have in the lands and tenements aforesaid with its appurtenances. So that neither the same John Roulowe and his heirs nor anyone else in their name have any right or rightful claim in the aforesaid land and tenements with its appurtenances nor in any part of the same henceforth will be able to drive out or sell but thence entirely forever are excluded by this surrender and release etc.
To release at the end of the term Fine 10s	John Bullok came here in court and surrendered into the hand of the lady one messuage and one virgate of land with appurtenances in Alvescote and one toft and half a virgate of land with appurtenances in Wynnescote to the use of Roger Tounesende and John Whitbrook to hold to the same Roger and John Whitbrook and their assigns according to the custom of the manor from the date of this court until the end of ten years next following and fully completed. And they give to the lady for a fine 10s and have ingress
Election of reeve	Richard Parlour at this court withdrew from the office of reeve and Robert Webbe is chosen to the same office for the following year in the future & sworn
	Affeerors: John Johnesone, John Waltone }sworn
	Sum of this court £4 8s 1d. Thence in expenses of the steward, clerks, reeve, beadle, affeerors, approvers and others with the expenses from the previous last great court 8s 11d. And for parchment 4d
Worfeld	Great Court held at Worfeld on Tuesday the 10th day of April in the 3rd year of the reign of King Henry VI after the conquest [10 April 1425]
Essoins	Henry Hall is essoined by Robert Bruggeende
The 12	John Johnsone Stephen Bradeney Thomas Tomkys John Bromley } John Colynsone Roger Tounesende William Wermot Thomas Undirhull }sworn John Janne Roger Swancote Roger Gerbot Roger Kyngeslowe }
Kyngeslowe Stanlowe nil	townships there present nothing. Roulowe, Bradeney, Asterhull, Ewyke and Sonde, present nothing. Eudenas & Oldyngton, Akelton presents nothing Alvescote, Wynscote, Cattestre and Neutone present nothing
Chestertone Strays remaining until	township there presents 1 mother sheep and 2 two-tooth sheep coming as strays at the feast of St Katherine the Virgin last past appraised at 17d remaining in the custody of John Snell until
Wyken Amerced 2s	township there presents that James Harpour (6d) forestalled Richard Botiller and from him drew blood (12d) and they present that the same James (6d) forestalled Henry Webbe by the pledge of the township aforesaid
Hultone Strays remaining	township there presents one ewe a stray from the Feast of the Lord's Nativity last past appraised at 3d remains in the custody of Roger Smyth until
Halene Amerced 4d	township there presents that Richard Walker (4d) owes appearance and did not come so in mercy
Stapleford Amerced 5d	township there presents that Joan (2d) the wife of Roger Swancote forestalled John the servant of Thomas Toward & from him drew blood (3d) etc. to the impairment of the same John

Worfeld Amerced 18d	township there presents that Edmund Harley (6d) made an assault on Roger Jenkyns son of Thomas Jenkyns. And they present that the same Edmund (6d) made an assault on William Kyngesone. And they present that the aforesaid Edmund (6d) made an assault on Roger the son of Henry Barker pledge the township
Roughtone, Barnedley, Hokcombe, Swancote Strays remaining Amerced 6d	townships there present that William atte Yate (6d) forestalled Roger Brook. And they present one lamb coming as a stray at the Feast of St Andrew the Apostle last past appraised at 4d remaining in the custody of William atte Yate until etc.
Burcote, Burcote, Ryndleford & Bromley Amerced 18d	townships there present that Thomas Cok (6d) forestalled John Newe and from him drew blood (12d) pledge the townships aforesaid
Amerced 5s Pain imposed	The 12 jurors present that the bridge called Wyken Brugge is ruinous & not properly repaired in default of the Dean (3s 4d) and Chapter of Lichfield to the grave damage of the tenants etc. and the King's people. So the same the Dean and Chapter are in mercy etc. And it is ordered that the same Dean and Chapter sufficiently amend and repair the said bridge before the Feast of Pentecost next in the future under pain of 3s 4d forfeit to the lady as aforesaid. The 12 jurors present that the township (20d) of Wyken concealed the presentation of the ruinousness of the aforesaid bridge so the same township is in mercy etc
Presentation of the tasters of ale Amerced 6s 10d	The tasters of ale present that Thomas Hichecokes (4d) brewed once, William Bromley (4d) 1 brew, John Billyngesley (4d) 1 brew, Roger Barker (4d) 1 brew, Robert Herkedale (4d) 1 brew, Giles Hyde (4d) 1 brew, John Billyngesley junior (4d) 1 brew, James Harpur (4d) 1 brew, Stephen Hymley (4d) 1 brew, William Bear (4d) 1 brew, Richard Smyth (4d) 1 brew, Thomas Baker (4d) 1 brew, Matilda Stanlowe (4d) 1 brew, John Yate (4d) 1 brew, John Kynnertone (4d) 1 brew, John Baret (4d) 1 brew, Alice Taillour (6d) a common brewer for a short time & Alice Sonde (12d) a common brewer by fine and they broke the assize so they are all are in mercy etc.
Presentment	The 12 jurors say that all the townships and the ale tasters aforesaid except the township of Wyken have presented well and faithfully and concealed nothing

Affeerors: Roger Tounesende, John Janne
Sum of this court 18s 1d

Worfeld	Small court held on Wednesday the 11th April in the third year of the reign of King Henry VI [11 April 1425]

The 12	John Roulowe	Stephen Bradeney	Thomas Undirhull	Thomas Toward }	
	John Jannes	William Wermot	Roger Kyngslowe	John Bromley }	sworn
	Richard Parlour	Roger Tounesende	Roger Gerbot	Richard Haslewode }	

Summons	Roger Jenkyns plaintiff of Thomas Bradeney in a plea of debt pledge for the prosecution Robert Bruggeende. And it is ordered to the bailiff to summon him to the next court etc.
Amerced 6d	Thomas Jenkyns junior is in mercy for an unjust plea against William Hokombe in a plea of trespass

1422-1424 P314/W/1/1/263

Plea amerced 3d Distrain to the next

Thomas Toward, Thomas Undirhull, William Bakes and Richard Aldith through Roger Dalley their attorney plaintiffs of John Colyns (3d) attached by the pledge of Roger Swancote and did not come Roger Baret & Henry Perton of Huggeford in a plea of trespass etc.. And at the last court they had an adjournment. And because now they did not come to this court so they are in mercy etc.. And it is ordered to the beadle to distrain them to the next court

Amerced 3d Heriot 7s 6d

The 12 jurors aforesaid present that John Oldyngton (3d) owes suit and did not come therefore in mercy etc.. And they present that William Stevenes tenant of the lady of 2 messuages & 5 nooks of land with appurtenances in Halene has died after whose death there falls to the lady one black ox price 7s 6d in the name of heriot and he had no other chattels on the day of his death. And the aforesaid 12 say that the aforesaid two messuages and 5 nooks of land with appurtenances remain with Margery formerly the wife of the aforesaid William.

Amerced 2s

They present that the aforesaid Margery (2s) married John Been without a licence from the lady or her steward so she is in mercy etc. pledge the same John Been

Surrender Fine 12d

John Heth came here in court & surrendered into the hands of the lady one pasture called Whicheford parrok with its enclosure lying in the township of Kyngeslowe at Whichford between the meadow of Roger Dalley on the one side & the pasture called Kingslowe Heth on the other side to the use of John Gyldene & Matilda his wife the which John and Matilda came here in court and took from the lady the aforesaid pasture with its enclosure to hold to the same John & Matilda their heirs and assigns by services thence due and of right accustomed according to the custom of the manor. And they give to the lord a fine of 12d and thence have seisin of the same

Profit of the land being in the hand of the lady 5s

The reeve is charged concerning 5s the revenue and profit of the land and tenements formerly Richard Bulvas's in Worfeld being in the hand of the lady for diverse causes of the lady and her council etc. concerning the year past etc.

Stray appraised 5d

The same reeve is charged concerning 5d approved from the price of one sheep coming as a stray at the last great court forfeited, appraised & charged in the same court at 1d because then it was almost dead now sold to Thomas Prestees as is clear above etc.

Taking of land for a term of years. Increase in rent supervise

John Elcok came here in court and took from the lady one message with garden adjoining and enclosed and one barn attached to the same message as well as with 4 selions pertaining to the same message situated and lying in the township of Worfeld and the field all of which were formerly Richard Bulvas's to hold to the same John from the date of this court until the end of a term of 2 years next following and fully completed rendering thence annually to the lady and her assigns five shillings of good money at the two usual terms of the year there. And to make thence annually to its chief and all others all rent, services and charges thence due and accustomed. And the same John will well and sufficiently repair the message and barn with the enclosed garden aforesaid and maintain them for the term aforesaid and he has ingress

Fine for brewing supervise

Thomas Prestees of Sonde came here in court and made a fine with the steward to brew from the date of this court until the end of one whole year next in the future for 2s to pay at the Feast of St Michael the Archangel and the Annunciation of the Blessed Mary next in the future by equal portions

Plea of land adjourned until the next

A day is given for Thomas Jenkyns junior plaintiff and William Hokcombe defendant in a plea of land and tenements in Hokcombe between them pending as is clear in several courts preceding until the next court. And also the 12 jurors in the same matter to judge between the parties aforesaid according to the custom of the manor thence the chosen were sworn and examined whose names are given in a schedule attached to this roll.

Plea of land adjourned

A day is given for John Colynsone plaintiff and the occupiers of the fulling mill of Ryndelford defendants in a plea of land for the fulling mill of Ryndelford between them pending as is clear in several preceding courts until the next court. And also a day is given for the 12 tenants elected to try the same matter between the parties aforesaid according to the custom of the manor whose names are given in a schedule attached to this roll.

Plea of land adjourned

A day is given for John Waltone plaintiff and Henry Jones still a day and Margery his wife defendants in a plea of waste, sale and destruction of land, houses and gardens in Roughtone between them pending as is clear in the preceding court until the next court to be held. And also a day is given for 24 tenants elected to the same matter to judge between the parties aforesaid according to the custom of the manor until the next court whose names are specified in the penultimate court aforesaid

Affeerors: Roger Tounesende, John Jannes
Sum of this court 16s 11d. Thence in expenses of the steward and others 10s 4½d.
And for parchment 4d with the expenses of the great court next preceding

[More on the back]

Worfeld

Small court held there on the Saturday after the Feast of St Peter in Chains in the third year of the reign of King Henry VI after the conquest [4 Aug. 1425]

Essoins

John Bradeney, Roger Hull, Roger Jones, William Bakes, Thomas Merewall senior essoined themselves by Simon Wyldemortone
John Whitbrook is essoined by Thomas Estmon, Thomas Richardes is essoined by John Hunt

The 12

Stephen Bradeney	William Wermot	John Barnedley	Thomas Toward }	
Roger Tounesende	Thomas Undirhull	John Johnesone	William Newe }	sworn
John Colynsone	John Bromley	Roger Gerbot	John Colettes }	

Attach

Roger Jenkys plaintiff of Thomas Bradeney (3d) withdrew from court in a plea of debt etc. and he was summoned and did not come so in mercy etc . And it is ordered that he is attached to the next

Distrain
Amerced 6d

Thomas Toward, Thomas Underhull, William Bakes and Richard Aldith through Roger Dalley their attorney, plaintiffs of John Colyns (3d), Roger Baret and Henry Perton of Huggeford in a plea of trespass etc. And they are attached by the pledge of Roger Swancote and did not come so they are in mercy and it is ordered to distrain

1422-1424 P314/W/1/1/263

Plea of land

A day is given to Thomas Jenkys junior plaintiff and William Hokcombe defendant in a plea of land and tenements in Hokcombe from the agreement of the same parties until the next court. And also the 12 jurors to try the same matter between the parties aforesaid according to the custom of the manor thence elected etc. and whose names are specified in one schedule stitched to the last court preceding

Plea of land

A day is given between John Colynsone void by agreement of the parties plaintiff and the occupiers of the fulling mill at Ryndleford defendants in a plea of land for the mill aforesaid until the next court by agreement of the parties. And also the 12 jurors to try the same matter thence elected whose names are specified in one schedule stitched to the last court until the next court to be held etc.

Plea of land

A day is given between John Waltone plaintiff and Henry Jones and Margery his wife defendants in a plea of waste, sale and destruction of land, houses and gardens in Roughtone until the next court etc. And the bailiff is ordered to distrain the 24 tenants for trying the same matter that they are at the next court whose names are specified in the third court next preceding etc.

Amerced 8d

The 12 jurors aforesaid say that Richard Haselwode (2d), William Ewyk (2d), John Bromley (2d), John Nicoles (2d) owes suit at this court and did not come so in mercy

Land taken out of the hand of the lady
Fine 20s

William Neuton clerk elsewhere it is said William Saundres clerk came and took from the lady one messuage, one toft and one virgate of land with appurtenances in Neuton within the manor of Worfeld being in the hand of the lady by the death of Robert Saundres brother of the aforesaid William to hold from the lady to the same William and his heirs the aforesaid messuage, toft and virgate of land with appurtenances according to the custom of the manor by services and customs thence due and he gives to the lady for a fine 20s and made fealty and is seized

Affeerors: Roger Tounesende, John Bromley }sworn
Sum of this court: 21s 2d
Thence in the expenses of the steward, clerk, reeve, beadle and others coming 3s 9½d

Sum of 5 courts this year £8 10s

1422-1424 P314/W/1/1/263

P314/W/1/1/265

Jury between Thomas Jenkyns junior & William Hokcombe in a plea of land

John Barnedley }sworn
Roger Gerbot }

William Robyns }sworn
John Janne }

William atte Yate }sworn
Robert Bruggeende }

John Colynsone } sworn
Thomas Undirhull }

John Colettes } sworn
Thomas Merewall junior }

Henry Barker } sworn
Thomas Roulowe }

P314/W/1/1/266

Jury between John Colynsone & the occupier of the fulling mill of Ryndleford

Stephen Bradeney
John Johnesone
Robert Bruggeende
Roger Smyth
Thomas Undirhull
Thomas Toward
William Newe
John Billyngesley
William Wermot
Thomas Merewall senior
John Colettes
Thomas Merewall junior
Roger Gerbot

1425 P314/W/1/1/267

Worfeld	Great court held there on Monday next after the feast of Saint Michael the Archangel in the fourth year of the reign of King Henry VI after the conquest [1 October 1425]
Essoins	John Colynsone, Roger Gille, Hamo Hymley, Roger Knyght, William Barbour, John Smyth of Hultone, John Johnesone, William Rys, Roger Jones, John Nicoles, Henry Jones, Thomas Richardes, Thomas Cattestre, John Bromley of Adlescote and William Ewyk essoined themselves by Richard Gape
The 12	Roger Cattestre Thomas Tomkyns William Wermot John Bromley } John Jannes Roger Tounesende Roger Kyngeslowe Robert Bruggeende } Stephen Bradeney Thomas Undirhull Roger Gerbot Richard Haselwode } sworn
Chestertone Strays remain	township there presents one two-tooth sheep coming as a stray at the feast of Easter last past price 6d remaining in the custody of John Snell until etc.
Wykene Amerced 2s	township there presents that Henry Heuster (2s) broke the harvest of hay arrested by Thomas Bradeney for rent of the Dean and Chapter of Lichfield. So etc.
Roulowe, Bradeney, Asterhull, Ewyk, Sonde. Strays 5d	townships there present one swarm of bees price 3d coming as a stray in the custody of John Roulowe. And they present one other swarm of bees price 2d coming as a stray in the custody of the same John
Kyngeslowe, Stanlowe Strays 4d Amerced 2s	townships there present one swarm of bees price 4d coming as a stray in the custody of Roger Dalley. And they present that Thomas Rugge (2s) broke the impoundment of one cow with a calf impounded for trespass in the corn of Thomas Jenkyns impounded by the same Thomas
Hultone Amerced 4d	township there presents that Thomas Merewall junior (4d) forestalled a certain stranger so he is in mercy etc.
Stapulford Strays 4d	township there presents one swarm of bees price 4d coming as a stray in the custody of Thomas Toward
Roughtone, Barnedley, Hokcombe, Swancote Strays 4d	townships there present one swarm of bees price 4d coming as a stray in the custody of William Hokcombe
Halene Amerced 4d	township there presents that Richard Walker owes suit and did not come so he is in mercy
Nothing	Alvescote, Wynnescote, Cattestre & Neuton present nothing. Worfeld presents nothing. Akeltone presents nothing. Eudenas, Oldyngtone present nothing. Burcote, Burcote, Ryndleford, Bromley present nothing
Presentation of the tasters of ale Amerced 5s 4d	John Kynnertone & William Ingman tasters of ale present that John Bromley (4d) brewed once, John Billyngesley (4d) brewed 1, William Bear (4d) brewed 1, John Johnesone (4d) brewed 1, John Cattestre (4d) brewed 1, John Gerbot (4d) brewed 1, Hamo Hymley (4d) brewed 1, Robert Bruggeende (4d) brewed 1, John Roulowe of Hultone (4d) brewed 1, John Yate (4d) brewed 1, Thomas Tomkys (4d) brewed 1, Thomas Roulowe of Burcote (4d) brewed 1, Alice Sonde (12d) for brewing by fine

& Alice Taillour (4d) for brewing for a certain time etc. & broke the assize

Presentation of the 12 jurors
Amerced 14s 4d
Cattle forfeit 10d
Presentment

The 12 jurors aforesaid present that John Billyngesley (6d) dug and made an encroachment on the land of the lady on the highway. Also they present that William Heuster (6d) enclosed one parcel of highway to his tenure so he is in mercy. Also they present that the township of Worfeld (20d) concealed a certain presentation of the same encroachment of the highway in Worfeld by John Billyngesley made as is clear above. Also they present that the same township (20d) concealed a certain presentation for a trespass made by William Heuster unjustly enclosing one parcel of highway in Worfeld at Ingbrondwalle etc. And they present that Joan wife of Richard Bradeney unjustly took two ewes price 10d of the goods of John Colynsone of Roulowe etc. And they present that all the townships and tasters of ale have well and faithfully presented & concealed nothing except the township of Worfeld as is clear above

Election of the tasters of ale

Thomas Jenkyns junior & William Bakes are elected to the office of ale taster & sworn keeping for the year in the future

Affeerors: John Bromley, William Bakes } sworn

Sum of this court 26s 6d

Worfeld

Small court held there on Tuesday next after the feast of St Michael the Archangel in the fourth year of the reign of King Henry VI after the conquest [2 October 1425]

Essoins

John Nicoles, John Bromley of Adlescote, William Ewyk, Thomas Richardes, Thomas Cattestre, Thomas Tresill & William Neutone essoined themselves by John Est

The 12

John Roulowe	Roger Tounesende	Roger Swancote	Roger Smyth of Hulton }
Stephen Bradeney	Thomas Undirhull	John Johnsone	John Hethe} sworn
John Jannes	William Wermot	John Waltone	Thomas Toward }

Amerced 6d

Thomas Bradeney (6d) is in mercy because he withdrew from court against Roger Jenkyns in a plea of debt

Amerced 12d
Distrain

Thomas Toward, Thomas Underhull, William Bakes and Richard Aldith through Roger Dalley their attorney, plaintiffs of John Colyns (12d), Roger Baret and Henry Pertone of Huggeford in a plea of trespass etc. And it was ordered to the bailiff to distrain etc. And they did not come so the same in mercy. And it is ordered still to distrain etc.

Plea of land

Still a day is given to Thomas Jenkys junior plaintiff and William Hokcombe still distrain defendant in a plea of land and tenements in Hokcombe from the agreement of the same parties until the next court. And also a day is given to the 12 jurors to try the right of the said land and tenements between the parties aforesaid according to the custom of the manor thence elected judge & jury whose names are specified in one schedule stitched to the last court preceding etc.

Plea of land

Still day is given to John Waltone plaintiff and Henry Jones and Margery his wife defendants in a plea of waste, sale of wood and destruction of land, houses and gardens in Roughtone until the next court etc. And the bailiff is ordered to distrain the 24 tenants whose names are specified in the fourth court next preceding that they are here at the next court to be held to the right of the waste, sale and destruction aforesaid to judge between the parties aforesaid according to the custom of the manor

1425 P314/W/1/1/267

Inquiry of the 12
Fine 12d

Roger Dalley came here in court & made a fine with the steward for 12d adjourned for an inquiry to be held of the 12 to enquire according to the custom of the manor if the said Roger ought to have of right one common footway for himself and his servants for the whole time of the year within the croft of John Hethe called Churle Croft lying within the township of Kyngeslowe leading from Kyngeslowe towards the church of Worfeld and from the said church until the same village. And on this the 12 are elected thence to try the right and to present on oath namely John Jannes, Stephen Bradeney, John Colynsone, Thomas Undirhull, Roger Tounesende, Roger Gerbot, John Bromley, Roger Swancote, Robert Bruggeende, William atte Yate, John Johnsone & Richard Haselwode who it is ordered to the bailiff to summon to the next court to be held that they are here etc.

Surrender
Fine 15s

Richard Whutbrrok & Matilda his wife came here in court through Robert Webbe the reeve surrendered into the hands of the lady the reversion of one messuage and three nooks of land with appurtenances in Alvescote which the same Richard holds for the term of his life from the concession of the same Matilda & surrendered the reversion thence after the death of the same Richard to the same Matilda when it should happen to the use of Alice the wife of Thomas the son of Roger Cattestre daughter of the aforesaid Richard and Matilda to hold to the same Alice and her heirs according to the custom of the manor after the deaths of the aforesaid Richard & Matilda when the reversion thence will have fallen. And he gives for a fine 15s to be paid at the feast of the Annunciation of the Blessed Mary and St Michael the Archangel equally

Surrender
Fine 15d

Walter Plate of Dudley otherwise it is said Walter Highman of Dudley & Margery his wife formerly of John Glovere alone confessed & rightfully examined by Robert Webbe the reeve at this court surrendered into the hands of the lady one cottage lying in the Sonde which the aforesaid Margery formerly held from the surrender of the aforesaid John Glovere to the use of John Elcok & Joan his wife who came here in court and took from the lady the aforesaid cottage to hold to the same John Elcok & Joan his wife their heirs and assigns according to the custom of the manor. And they give to the lady for a fine 12d. And made fealty and they are seised etc.

Profit of the wood of Soudeley

The reeve is charged concerning 2s from the township of Halene for easement with its cattle within here

When Thomas atte Sonde at the court held at Worfeld on Wednesday next before the feast of St George the Martyr in the sixth year of the reign of King Henry V surrendered into the hands of the lady one messuage and half a virgate of land with appurtenances in Sonde to the use of John his younger son after the death of the aforesaid Thomas & Alice his wife in joint tenure following in these words. To this court comes Thomas Sonde & surrenders into the hands of the lady one messuage and half a virgate of land with appurtenances in Sonde to the use of John his younger son after the death of the aforesaid Thomas & Alice his wife when it will have happened And if it should happen that the aforesaid John dies, while his aforesaid father & Alice are living then all the aforesaid land and tenements with its appurtenances remain to the aforesaid Thomas & Alice and their heirs according to the custom of the manor to have and to hold all the aforesaid messuage with half a virgate of land aforesaid to the same John and his heirs after the death of the aforesaid when it should happen and according to the form aforesaid. And he gives for a fine 10s. And has seisin. And now it is found by the tenants at this court that the aforesaid Thomas and John the younger son are dead. And on this came Thomas Prestees and Alice his wife formerly the wife of the aforesaid Thomas atte Sonde and made a fine to have the aforesaid messuage

Fine 10s — & half virgate of land with appurtenances to hold to the same Thomas Prestees & Alice his wife the heirs and assigns of the same Alice according to the custom of the manor by services thence due and accustomed and they are admitted by virtue of the surrender aforesaid. And they give to the lady for a fine 10s and are seised etc.

Election of the reeve — At this court Robert Webbe withdrew from the office of reeve and William Ewyk is elected to the same office for the future year and sworn

Affeerors: John Bromley, William atte Yate & sworn

Sum of this court 30s 6d
Thence in expenses of the steward, clerk, reeve, beadle, affeerors & others with 4d for parchment 9s 3d

1426 P314/W/1/1/268

Worfeld	Great court held there on Monday on the morrow of the feast of Saint Michael the Archangel in the fifth year of the reign of King Henry VI after the conquest [30 September 1426]
Essoins	John Holygreve of Halene, William Kyngesone, Thomas Cattestre, William Oldyngtone, Roger Gylle, John Billyngesley, Roger Hulle, Roger Jones, William Hokcombe & William Barwe essoined themselves by Thomas Wallertone
The 12	Roger Cattestre, Robert Webbe, John Janne, John Bromley, John Colynsone, Thomas Tomkys, Roger Kyngeslowe, Henry Barker, Stephen Bradeney, Roger Roulowe, Thomas Undirhull, Richard Haselwode } sworn
Roughtone, Barnedley, Hokcombe, Swancote Strays 4d	townships there present one swarm of bees price 4d coming as a stray being in the custody of William atte Yate.
Roulowe, Bradeney, Asterhull, Ewyk, Sonde. Amerced 6s goods forfeit 4d	townships there present that Joan the wife of Thomas Bradeney (6d) forestalled Joan the wife of Richard Bradeney & from her drew blood (12d). William Bradeney chaplain (6d) forestalled Thomas Bradeney & Joan the wife of the aforesaid Thomas justly raised the hue and cry (8d) on the aforesaid William. And they present that Joan (3s 4d) the wife of John Elcok unjustly took one smock from the goods of Richard Smyth price 4d
Halene Amerced 18d	township there presents that John Roulowe (6d) forestalled John Been. And they present that the same John Been (6d) forestalled the same John Roulowe. And they present that John Whyte (6d) forestalled Roger Barker
Hultone Strays 3d	township there presents one infirm swarm of bees price 3d in the custody of Thomas Baker of Hultone
Amerced 7s 8d	The tasters of ale present that John Bromley (4d) brewed 1, Thomas Hichecokes (4d) brewed 1, John Johnesone (4d) brewed 1, John Walker (4d) brewed 1, William atte Yate (4d) brewed 1, Hamond Hymley (4d) brewed 1, John Gerbot (4d) brewed 1,Thomas Baker of Hultone (4d) brewed 1, John Roulowe of Hultone (4d) brewed 1, Thomas Tomkys (4d) brewed 1, John son of John Kynnertone (4d) brewed 1,William Kyngesone (8d) brewed 2, William Barwe (4d) brewed 1, Roger Dalley (4d) brewed 1, Henry Heuster (4d) brewed 1, John Elcok (4d) brewed 1, Agnes Derre (4d) brewed 1, William Bear (4d) brewed 1 & William Barker (4d) brewed 1 and broke the assize so they [are] in mercy etc. And they present that Alice (12d) the wife of Thomas Prestees is a common brewer and broke the assize so she [is] in mercy. And they present Alice (4d) Galyan for 1 brew & broke the assize
Alvescote, Wynnescote, Cattestre, Neutone	townships there present nothing. Burcote, Burcote, Ryndleford, Bromley present nothing. Kyngeslowe, Stanlowe present nothing. Akeltone presents nothing. Eudenas, Oldyngtone present nothing. Chesturtone presents nothing. Wykene presents nothing. Stapulford presents nothing. Worfeld presents nothing.
Amerced 5s 6d Goods forfeit 1d Presentment	The 12 jurors present that Joan Elcok (6d) unjustly sold one yoke of the goods of William Bakes price 1d so she [is] in mercy etc. And they present that the township (6s) of Worfeld concealed the same presentation so the township aforesaid is in mercy. And further they say that all the townships aforesaid except this township of Worfeld

have well and faithfully presented & concealed nothing

Election of constables	John Snell & John Walker of Ryndleford are elected constables to hold the office of constable for the future year & sworn etc.
Election of the tasters of ale	William atte Yate & John Willot of Akeltone were elected to the office of ale taster to keep for the future year & sworn etc. Affeerors: John Johnesone, Roger Swancote } sworn
	Sum of this court 21s 8d
Worfeld	Small court held there next after the feast of St Michael the Archangel in the fifth year of the reign of King Henry VI after the conquest [30 September 1426]
Essoins	John Holygreve essoined himself by William Wermot, William Bailly of Walle is essoined by John Jowkys against Thomas Cokkes of Wolverhamptone in a plea of trespass. John Oldyngtone is essoined by Roger Dalley, Thomas Richardes is essoined for his suit at this court by John Clerk
The 12	John Janne John Roulowe Roger Swancote Roger Smyth of Hulton } Robert Webbe Roger Tounesende Thomas Merewall junior John Waltone } sworn Stephen Bradeney Thomas Undirhull John Barnedley William Newe }
Pleas attach	Richard Smyth & Margery his wife plaintiffs of John Elcok to respond to the court by John Been Elcok & Joan his wife in a plea of trespass pledge for the prosecution the bailiff. And it is ordered to the bailiff to attach the said John and Joan his wife to the next court to be held Thomas Cokkes of Wolverhamptone etc. plaintiff of Richard Bailly of Walle recover/withdrew in a plea of trespass pledge for the prosecution John Colynsone and he is attached by the pledge of John Jowkys Richard Bailly of Walle plaintiff of Morice the son of Hugh Purs in a plea of broken agreement pledge for the prosecution the bailiff. And it is ordered he attach John Been plaintiff of John Hull of Hultone in a plea of trespass pledge for the prosecution William Wermot. And it is ordered to attach him to the next [court] etc. Roger the son of Henry Barker plaintiff of John Been & Margery his wife in a plea of trespass pledge for the prosecution John Johnsone. And it is ordered to summon them The same Roger plaintiff of the same John & Margery in a plea of trespass pledge for the prosecution as before. And it is ordered to summon them etc. The same Roger plaintiff of the same John in a plea of trespass pledge for the prosecution as before. And it is ordered to attach him to the next [court] etc. John Johnsone plaintiff of Henry Heuster of Worfeld in a plea of pledge pledge for the prosecution the reeve. And it is ordered to the beadle to attach him to the next [court]
Plea Amerced 12d Distrain	Thomas Toward, Thomas Undyrhull, William Bakes & Richard Aldith by Roger Dalley their attorney plaintiffs of John Colyns (12d), Roger Baret & Henry Pertone of Huggeford in a plea of trespass etc. And it was ordered to the bailiff at the last court to distrain them to this court. And because now they did not come so they are in mercy etc. And it is ordered to the bailiff still to distrain them to the next court to be held etc.
Plea Adjourn	Thomas Jenkyns junior plaintiff of John Gybbons adjourned in a plea of trespass etc. And they have an adjournment at this court until the next court to be held etc.

Thomas Bradeney (6d) of Wykene in mercy because to respond to the court against Roger Jenkyns in a plea of debt

Amerced 12d John Oldyngtone (6d) is in mercy because he is not prosecuting his plea against Roger Dalley in a plea of debt

Void Thomas Jenkyns junior is not prosecuting his plea against William Hokcombe in a plea of land & tenements in Hokcombe taken against the same William by the aforesaid Thomas as shown in full in diverse courts preceding thence no amercement because previously it was done etc.

Void By which at the plea between John Waltone plaintiff and Henry Jones and Margery his wife deforciants pending in a plea of waste the said parties are agreed to an agreement on behalf of the parties. Thence no amercement because the plaintiff previously thence made a fine as fully shown in a certain court preceding

Void By which at the inquiry held to enquire if Roger Dalley ought to have of right one common footway for himself and his servants within the croft of John Hethe or not the same Roger as fully shown in diverse courts preceding. The same Roger & John are agreed from their knowledge at this court thence no amercement because the aforesaid Roger for the inquiry aforesaid made a fine previously

Verdict The 12 jurors sworn, charged and examined according to the custom of the manor whose names are specified below here namely Roger Rowley of Alvescote, Roger Swancote, John Jannes, Robert Webbe, John Colynsone, Thomas Undirhull, Thomas Toward, Roger Kyngeslowe, William Newe, Roger Garbot, John Colettes of Hultone, Roger Smyth, Roger Hull of Roughtone, William atte Yate of the same, William Garbot, John Waltone of Swancote, John Billyngesley senior, Thomas Roulowe of Burcote, William Bromley, John Hethe, John Hull of Hultone, John Smyth, John Roulowe of Hultone & John Bromley who say on their oath that Thomas Prestees & Alice his wife as of the right of the same Alice have been able and are able to justly make an alienation of one messuage & half a virgate of land with its appurtenances in Sonde for which lands and tenements with their appurtenances the aforesaid Thomas Prestees & Alice his wife at the penultimate court next preceding made a fine as is fully clear in the same court. And also they say that no-one other has or had at the same last court or so far has or have a better right to make a fine for the same lands and tenements than the aforesaid Thomas Prestees & Alice his wife as of the right of the same Alice

Heriot 6s The 12 jurors present that Robert Eudenas free tenant of the lady of one messuage with its appurtenances in Eudenas as of the right of Alice his wife has died after whose death there falls to the lady one grey horse and one saddle with a bridle price 6s in the name of heriot

The aforesaid 12 jurors for the lady sworn say that Emma Mathewe held from the lady one messuage & three nooks of land with its appurtenances in Roughtone and also one toft & half a virgate of land with appurtenances there called Pirylonde has died after whose death nothing falls to the lady because she had no goods or chattels on the day she died within the domain etc. And they say that all the land there remains in the hands of the lady in reversion from the same death. And also they say that John Mathewe son of the same Emma is her closest heir the which John comes here in court and took from the lady all the lands and tenement above said with their appurtenances to hold to himself and his heirs according to the custom of the manor

Fine 25s

by services thence due and accustomed. And he gives to the lady for a fine 25s to be paid at the feast of the Annunciation of the Blessed Mary & Saint Michael the Archangel next in the future by equal portions. And he made fealty and is seised

Amerced 4d

John Oldyngtone (4d) is in mercy because he did not come to warrant his essoin granted at the last court

Surrender
Fine 5s

Hugh Whyte and Margery his wife, daughter of Richard Colyer deceased came here in court through John Snell improver of the lady and surrendered into the hands of the lady one toft and one nook of land with appurtenances in Chestirtone called Waltone londe to the use of Thomas Gerbot & Emma his wife. The which Thomas & Emma came here in court & took from the lady the aforesaid toft and one nook of land with appurtenances to hold to the same Thomas & Emma his wife, their heirs and assigns according to the custom of the manor by services thence due and accustomed. And they give to the lady for a fine 5s to be paid at the feast of the Annunciation of the Blessed Mary & Saint Michael the Archangel next in the future etc. And they made fealty. And thence they have seisin etc.

Surrender
Fine 8d

John Snell & Alice his wife, Thomas Huchecokes, John Smyth of Hultone, Thomas Gerbot & Emma his wife, William Newe, Isabel Reynald & Agnes her daughter and Thomas Colyer by William Ewyk the reeve of the lady surrendered into the hands of the lady one small parcel of meadow lying in the field of Chestirtone called the Small Doles next to Wyldmore to the use of John Hull of Hultone who came here in court & took from the lady the aforesaid parcel of meadow to hold to himself and his heirs according to the custom of the manor by services thence due & accustomed and also by rendering thence annually to the lady & her heirs one silver halfpenny at the feast of Saint Michael the Archangel. And he gives to the lady for a fine 8d. And he made fealty and thence has seisin

Surrender
Fine 5s

Alice Cattestre came here in court by William Wermot the beadle of the lady and surrendered into the hands of the lady one nook of land with appurtenances in Halen which aforesaid Alice holds for the term of her life according to the custom of the manor after the death of Roger Cattestre formerly husband of the same Alice to the use of John Cattestre son of the aforesaid Roger and Alice to hold to the same John, his heirs and assigns according to the custom of manor by services thence due & accustomed. And he gives to the lady for a fine 5s. And he made fealty and has seisin

Inquiry of the 12
Fine 12d

Thomas Jenkyns junior came here in court and made a fine with the steward for12d for an inquiry to be held of the 12 according to the custom of manor to enquire if Philip Dawe deceased sought to make of right the alienation of one messuage and half a virgate of land with appurtenances in Hokcombe which were Joan Malcher's formerly the wife of the aforesaid Philip whose names for the inquest aforesaid are shown below. John Janne, John Barnedley, Roger Hull fo Roughtone, John Waltone, William Yate of Roughtone, William Wermot, John Hethe, John Colettes, William Newe, William Bromley, Stephen Bradeney & John Roulowe of Hultone the which 12 it is ordered to the reeve and beadle to summon to the next court etc.

Election of the reeve

At this court William Ewyk withdrew from the office of reeve to which office Richard Haselwode is elected for the future year & sworn etc.

1426 P314/W/1/1/268

Election of reeve

Affeerors: John Johnesone, Roger Swancote } sworn

Sum of this court 45s. Thence in expenses of the steward, clerk, reeve, beadle, affeerors & others coming to the great and small court next preceding with 4d for parchment 9s 2d

Worfeld

Small court held there on Tuesday on the morrow of St Katherine the Virgin in the fifth year of the reign of King Henry VI after the conquest [26 November 1426]

Essoins

Stephen Bradeney, William Hokcombe, Roger Hulle, William Newe, John Johnesone, John Hethe & Henry Jones essoined themselves by Richard Hunt

The 12

Roger Swancote   Roger Garbot   Robert Bruggeende   Roger Hethe }
John Janne   Robert Webbe   William Wermot   John Colynsone } sworn
Roger Tounesende   John Waltone   John Bromley   Thomas Undirhull }

Amerced 18d

John Elcok (6d) & Joan his wife in mercy for a licence to agree with Richard Smyth & Margery his wife in a plea of trespass
Richard Bailley (6d) of Walle in mercy for a licence to agree with Thomas Cokkes of Wolverhamptone in a plea of trespass by the pledge of John Jowkys
The same Richard (6d) is in mercy because he is not prosecuting his plea against Morice the son of Hugh Purs in a plea of broken agreement

Pleas adjourned

John Been plaintiff [not prosecuting] of John Hull of Hultone in a plea of trespass etc. And they have an adjournment from the agreement of the parties until the next court etc.
Roger the son of Henry Barker plaintiff of John Been [adjourned] & Margery his wife in a plea of trespass. And they have an adjournment from the prayer of the parties until etc.
The same Roger plaintiff of the same John & Margery [adjourned] in a plea of trespass etc. And they have an adjournment as above etc.
The same Roger plaintiff of the same John [adjourned] in a plea of trespass etc. And they have an adjournment as above etc.
John Johnsone plaintiff of Henry Heuster [adjourned] in a plea of pledge etc. And they have an adjournment etc.
Thomas Toward, Thomas Undyrhull, William Bakes & Richard Aldith by Roger Dalley their attorney plaintiffs of John Colyns (12d), [adjourned] Roger Baret & Henry Pertone of Huggeford in a plea of trespass etc. And it was ordered to the bailiff at the last court to distrain them to this court. And they have an adjournment to the next court from the prayer of the parties etc.
Thomas Jenkyns junior plaintiff of John Gybbons [adjourned] in a plea of trespass etc. And they have an adjournment until the next court to be held etc.

A day is given for an inquiry of the 12 for Thomas Jenkyns junior elected according to the custom of the manor as clear in the last court preceding until the next court to be held

Profit in the wood of Soudeley 2s

The township of Halene concerning a fine for easement with their beasts and draught animals here within the wood of Soudeley for the year past before the feast of Michael the Archangel last past 2s

The 12 jurors aforesaid present that Thomas Richardes (2d) owes suit and did not come so he is in mercy. And they present one black colt price 16d and 4 piglets price 2s 8d of escheat after the death of Thomas Tresill coming forth beyond other heriots

& escheats after the death of the same Thomas Tresill presented at the court held on Monday the second day of the month of September in the year above said. And they present that Thomas Roulowe tenant of the lady of one messuage and half a virgate of land with appurtenances in Burcote of one toft & half a virgate of land with appurtenances in Burcote has died after whose death there falls to the lady one brindle steer price 7s and one black cow price 5s in the name of heriot and one infirm white draught animal price 12d & one small sow with three small piglets price 2s 8d and five small pigs price of the same 16d from escheat. And the land remains to Alice wife of the aforesaid Thomas Roulowe according to the custom of the manor etc.

Affeerors: Roger Swancote, Thomas Merewall junior } sworn

Sum of this court 24s 8d. Thence in expenses of the clerk, reeve, beadle, affeerors & others 2s 1d

Worfeld — Court held there on Tuesday next before the feast of St Thomas the Apostle in the fifth year of the reign of King Henry VI after the conquest [17 December 1426]

Essoins — John Whitbrook, Henry Barker, William Heuster, John Barnedley is dead, William Yate, John Bromley of Adlescote, John Oldyngtone & Henry Halle essoined themselves from suit at this court by John Hunt etc.

The 12 —

Stephen Bradeney	John Colynsone	John Bromley	William Wermot }
Roger Swancote	John Janne	Roger Garbot	William Newe } sworn
Robert Webbe	Roger Tounesende	John Johnesone	Roger Hethe }

Amerced 6d — John Been (6d) is in mercy because he is not prosecuting his plea against John Hull of Hultone in a plea of trespass etc.

Pleas adjourned

Roger the son of Henry Barker plaintiff of John Been & Margery his wife in a plea of trespass. And they have an adjournment from the prayer of the parties until the next [court] etc.
The same Roger plaintiff of the same John & Margery in a plea of trespass etc. And they have an adjournment as above etc.
The same Roger plaintiff of the same John in a plea of trespass etc. And they have an adjournment as above etc.
John Johnsone plaintiff of Henry Heuster in a plea of pledge etc. And they have an adjournment as above etc.
Thomas Toward, Thomas Undyrhull, William Bakes & Richard Aldith by Roger Dalley their attorney plaintiffs of John Colyns (12d), Roger Baret & Henry Pertone of Huggeford in a plea of trespass etc. And they have an adjournment to the next court to be held by the prayer of the parties etc.
Thomas Jenkyns junior plaintiff of John Gybbons adjourned in a plea of trespass etc. And they have an adjournment until the next court to be held by the prayer of the parties etc.

Attach — Henry Heuster & Henry his son plaintiffs of William Ingman in a plea of trespass pledge for the prosecution William Barwe. And it is ordered to the bailiff to attach him etc.

Summon — The same Henry & Henry plaintiffs of the same William in a plea of debt pledge for the prosecution as before. And it is ordered to the bailiff to summon him to the next court

1426 P314/W/1/1/268

Thomas Aldith by William Noure his attorney plaintiff of Thomas Undirhull in a plea of trespass pledge for the prosecution Thomas Jenkyns junior. And whence he complains that the same Thomas Undirhull with force and arms etc on Tuesday in the second week next after the feast of All Saints in the fifth year of the aforesaid King at Stapulford took and carried away grain of diverse kinds from the same plaintiff etc. to the damage of 6s 8d. And on this came the aforesaid defendant and denied this and said that he is not thence tguilty. And thence to wager at law pledge for the law John Colynson & Stephen Bradeney. And thus he has a day to make the law at the next court with 4 hands etc.

Plea the law

Amerced 2d

Still a day is given for the inquiry of the 12 for Thomas Jenkyns junior chosen according to the custom of the manor until the next court to be held etc.

The 12 jurors say that Agnes Derre (2d) broke time and again around the enclosure called Smythes Place so she is in mercy etc.

Surrender in reversion. Fine 10s

Richard Aldith of Stapulford by John Snell improver came here in court & surrendered into the hands of the lady the reversion of one message and half a virgate of land with appurtenances in Stapulford to the use of Thomas Aldith son of the aforesaid Richard & to Joan the wife of the same Thomas. To hold to the same Thomas & Joan his wife, their heirs & assigns according to the custom of the manor after the death of the aforesaid Richard when the reversion thence will have happened by services thence due and accustomed. And they give to the lady for a fine 10s

Fine 8d

William Ewyk comes here in court & gives to the lady for a fine 8d for suit of court to be commuted from the date of this court until the feast of St Michael the Archangel next in the future etc. To pay at the feast of the Annunciation of the Blessed Mary & St Michael next equally

Increased price of heriots & escheat 16d

The reeve is charged here concerning 4d from the increased price of four sheep for heriot after the death of Richard Whitbrook & Matilda his wife beyond the price of the same four sheep charged as is clear in the court held on Wednesday on the third day of the month of April last past. And concerning 12d from the increased price of the heriot & escheat appraised at the last court past after the death of Thomas Rowlowe as is clear in the same last court

More on the back

1426 P314/W/1/1/268

[The dorse]

The reeve is charged here concerning 5s from the price of 2 steers coming as strays presented by the townships of Alvescote, Wynnescote, Cattestre & Neutone at the great court held next after the feast of Easter in the 4th year of the now King remaining in the custody of Roger Tounesende. And concerning 4d from the price of one mother sheep coming as a stray presented at the same court by the townships of Eudenas & Oldyngtone in the custody of Thomas Ingman. And concerning 14d from the price of two mother sheep presented as strays by the same townships at the same court in the custody of Richard Haselwode. And concerning 4d from the price of one white sheep presented as a stray by the same townships at the same court in the custody of John Jowkys. And concerning 4s from the price of one black steer presented as a stray at the same court by the townships of Roulowe, Bradeney, Asterhull, Ewyke & Sonde in the custody of John Colynsone. And concerning 8d from the price of one mother sheep at the same court presented as a stray by the same townships in the custody of John Johnesone. And concerning 3s 4d from the price of one heifer presented at the same court as a stray by the townships of Roughtone, Barnedley, Hokcombe & Swancote in the custody of Robert Webbe. And concerning 6d from the price of one mother sheep presented as a stray at the same court by the township of Stapulford in the custody of Roger Swancote. And concerning 20d from the price of one black male calf presented as a stray at the same court by the township of Halene sold to William Barker by William Ewyk formerly the reeve

Strays forfeit as clear in the rolls preceding 17s

Affeerors: William Newe, Thomas Colyer } sworn

Sum of this court 29s 8d. Thence in expenses of the clerk and others coming 2s 3d

1427 P314/W/1/1/269 & /270

Worfeld	Great court held there on Tuesday in the week of Easter in the fifth year of the reign of King Henry VI after the conquest [15 April 1427]
Essoins	William Barbour, Henry Halle, William Rys, Robert Barker, Roger Swannecote, John Waltone, John the son of John Roulow, Henry Jones & Thomas Richars these essoined themselves for suit of court
The great inquiry	Thomas Tomkys, John Janne, John Bromley, William Wermot, Stephen Bradeney, Robert Webbe, John Jonkys, Thomas Undurhull, John Roulow, Roger Tounesinde, Roger Kyngeslowe, Roger Garbot } sworn
Sworn in tithing	William the son of John Willot, Roger the son of William Cattestre, John the son of Roger Tounesende & William the son of John Kynnertone of twelve years and more are sworn in the tithing and made fealty
	Eudenas, Oldyngtone townships there present nothing. Burcote, Burcote, Ryndelford & Bromley townships there present nothing. Wycone township there presents nothing.
Akyltone	township there presents that John Roulowe (4d) enclosed one parcel of land called the Cowsale which of right ought to be common so he is in mercy
Roulow, Bradeney, Asterhull, Euwyk, Sonde Stray 18d	townships there present one heifer aged one year coming as a stray price 18d & it remains in the custody of John Colynsone
Amerced 2d	Roughtone, Barndeley. Hoccombe & Swannecote townships there present that John Waltone (2d) keeps Roger his son aged 12 years & more not sworn in the tithing so in mercy
Chestertone Strays 6s	township there presents one red steer coming as a stray price 12d on the feast of the Nativity of the Lord last past and remaining in the custody of John Snell. And they present one horse price 2s & 2 foals price 3s at the feast of St Katherine last past and remaining in the custody of John Snell
Hultone	township there presents nothing. Kyngeslowe & Stanlowe present nothing
Alvescote, Wynnescote, Newtone & Cattestre Strays 10d	townships there present 2 sheep, 1 male price 6d & the other female price 4d coming as strays at the feast of St Andrew the apostle last past & remaining in the custody of Richard Minsterley
Worfeld Amerced 20d	township there presents that Roger (6d) son of Henry Barker forestalled Stephen Garbot so he is in mercy. And that the aforesaid Stephen (6d) forestalled the aforesaid Roger so he is in mercy. And that Margaret (4d) the wife of William Barw made the hue and cry unjustly on Henry Wefer so she is in mercy. And that the aforesaid Henry (4d) did not wish to permit William Yngman to take one distraint in his house. So he is in mercy
Halene Amerced 6d	township there presents that Richard Boteler (6d) forestalled Rose the wife of John Cattestre so he is in mercy etc.

Stapulford — township there presents one horse price 8d coming as a stray & remains in the custody of John Beene. And that the aforesaid horse came as a stray in the feast of the Nativity of the Lord last past etc.

Amercements ale tasters 13s — William atte Yate & John Wylot of Akeltone the tasters of ale there present Agnes Dorre (4d) brewed 1, William Warde (4d) brewed 1, William Yngman (4d) brewed 1, John Colyns (4d) brewed 1, John atte Yate (4d) brewed 1, Richard Boteler (4d) brewed 1, Agnes Hattone (4d) brewed 1, Richard Smyth (4d) brewed 1, John Mathew (4d) brewed 1, John Bylyngeley(4d) brewed 1, Roger Pristes (4d) brewed 1, William Gold (4d) brewed 1, William Robyns (4d) brewed 1, William Kyngsone (4d) brewed 1, Henry Webbe (4d) brewed 1, John Bromley (4d) brewed 1, Thomas Jenkys (4d) brewed 1, Roger Barker (4d) brewed 1, John Baret (4d) brewed 1, John Cattestre (4d) brewed 1, Thomas Garbot (4d) brewed 1,John Beene (4d) brewed 1, Roger Smyth (4d) brewed 1, Alice Eudenas (4d) brewed 1, Alice Galian (8d), brewed 2, Alice Sonde (2s) brewed 6, John Smyth (4d) brewed 1 & John Byllyngesley brewed 1, they all brewed and broke the assize so they are in mercy

The 12 jurors say on their oath that the aforesaid townships and tasters of ale have well and faithfully presented & in nothing concealed or omitted

Affeerors: Roger Dalley, Thomas Merewall } sworn

Sum of this court 15s 4d

Worfeld — Small court held there on Wednesday in Easter Week in the fifth year of the reign of King Henry VI after the conquest [16 April 1427]

Essoins — Henry Jones, Robert Barker, Thomas Richardes, Roger Swannecote, John Waltone essoined themselves for suit of court

Stephen Bradeney	Robert Webbe	William Wermot	Thomas Merewall junior	}
John Janne	Thomas Undurhull	John Bromley	William attYate	} sworn
Roger Tounesende	Roger Kyngeslow	Roger Garbot	Thomas Toward	}

Heriot 8s 10d — The 12 jurors there present that John Barndeley on the day he died held from the lady one messuage & one virgate of land in Barndeley & Joan his daughter is the closest heir of descent after whose death there falls to the lady one heifer price 3s 10d in the name of heriot and one black horse price 2s and one swarm of bees price 12d and 2 small pigs price 2s. And on this came the aforesaid Joan the daughter & heir of the aforesaid John and has seisin of the land aforesaid with its appurtenances

Fine 20s — to hold at the will of the lady to herself & her [heirs] according to the custom of the manor & she gives to the lady for a fine 20s and made fealty. Ans she thence has seisin pledge Robert Webbe etc.

Also they present that John Robyns on the day he died before the ~~next~~ last court who held from the lady for the term of his life one messuage & half a virgate of land with appurtenances in Alvescote & one nook of land with appurtenances in Wynnescote to remain of the aforesaid holdings with appurtenances after the death of John Robyns to Alice the wife of William Undurwode. And nothing falls to the lady after the death of the aforesaid John Robyns because he did not have goods nor chattels etc. And on this came the aforesaid William Undurwode & Alice his wife & the aforesaid Alice had seisin of the tenements aforesaid to hold at the will of the lady to herself and her [heirs] according to the custom of the manor gives nothing for a fine at this court because elsewhere made a fine for the reversion of the tenements aforesaid with appurtenances after the death of John Robyns according to

the custom of the manor & they made fealty etc. Also they present that Roger Richars on the day he died before the last court who held from the lady one messuage & half a virgate of land in Newtone & one toft & one nook of land in the same township of Newtone & Margery his wife holds the messuage, toft & land
Heriot 9s aforesaid with appurtenances for the term of her life after whose death there falls to the lady one ox price 9s in the name of heriot

Also they present that Richard Aldyth on the day he died before the last court who
Heriot 3s held from the lady one messuage & half a virgate of land in Stapulford after whose death there falls to the lady one heifer price 3s 4d in the name of heriot and it remains in the custody of Thomas Undurhull. The reversion thence to Thomas Aldyth & Joan his wife, their heirs and assigns according to the custom of the manor & they give to the lady for a fine as is clear in the small court of Tuesday next before the feast of St Thomas the Apostle in the fifth year of the reign of King Henry VI after the conquest etc.

To this court came Richard Hasulwodde beadle of the lady saying that John Robyns on the Sunday next before the feast of the Annunciation of the Blessed Mary in his own person came before the aforesaid bailiff & surrendered to the aforesaid bailiff into the hands of the lady one toft and one nook of land to the use of Roger Roulowe & Alice his wife, their heirs and assigns for ever to hold according to the custom of the manor. And now the aforesaid Roger & Alice come and thence have
Fine 5s seisin & they give to the lady for a fine 5s pledge for the fine Richard Hasulwod bailiff of the lady etc.

To this court came John Roulow Colynsone and it is agreed with the steward for
Fine 12d suit of court for one whole year and he gave to the lady for a fine 12d

To this court came William Kyngsone & Edith his wife and made an agreement
Fine 12d with the steward to brew for one whole year and he gave to the lady for a fine 12d

To this court came William Hokcombe & gives to the lady for a fine 2s for an
Fine 2s inquiry to be held by 24 jurors to enquire if the aforesaid William and Edith his wife have such title in one messuage and half a virgate of land with appurtenances which the aforesaid William and Alice his wife hold in Hokcombe that they are able to give or to alienate or not. And on this it is ordered the bailiff that he should make the 24 jurors come to the next court etc.

To this court came William Undirwode & Alice his wife & they give to the lady for
Fine 2s a fine 2s for an inquiry to be held by 24 jurors to enquire if the aforesaid William and Edith his wife have such title in one messuage and half a virgate of land with appurtenances which the aforesaid William and Alice his wife hold in Alvescote that they are able to give or to alienate or not. And on this it is ordered the bailiff make the 24 jurors to come to the next court etc.

Roger the son of Henry Barker plaintiff of John Bene and Margery his wife in a
Amerced 2d plea of trespass and they have an adjournment until at the next court etc. The same Roger plaintiff of the same John in a plea of trespass etc. And they have an adjournment etc.And it is ordered to the bailiff to attach him etc. Also John Jonsone (2d) is in mercy because he is not prosecuting his plea against John Heuster in a plea of trespass etc. Also Thomas Toward, Thomas Undurhull & William Bakes by Roger Dalley their attorney plaintiffs of John Colyns together with Roger Baret & Henry Pertone of Hugford in a plea of trespass etc. And they have an adjournment

to the next court etc. Also Thomas Jenkys junior plaintiff of John Gylone (2d) in a plea of trespass etc. And the aforesaid John was not present to respond to the aforesaid Thomas in his plea. So he is in mercy etc. And it is ordered to the bailiff to attach him etc. Also Henry Heuster & Henry his son plaintiffs of William Ingman in a plea of trespass etc. And they have a day an adjournment etc. Also the same Henry & Henry plaintiffs of the same William in a plea of debt etc. And they have a day an adjournment until at the next court etc. Still a day is given for the inquiry by 12 jurors for Thomas Jenkys chosen according to the custom of the manor until the next court etc.

Sum of this court 52s 4d
Thence is expenses of the steward 8s 8d & in parchment 4d
Affeerors: Roger Dalley, Thomas Merewall } sworn

P314/W/1/1/270

John Janne }
Robert Webbe} sworn

John Jonsone }
Thomas Merewall junior } sworn

Stephen Bradeney }
Robert Bruggeend } sworn

Thomas Toward }
Roger Jones } sworn

Roger Gerbot }
John Bromley } sworn

William Bromley }
~~William Roulowe~~
Roger Dalley } sworn

William Yate }
John Colettes } sworn

William Wermot }
Henry Barker }sworn

Richard Hasulwod }
~~John Broke~~
John Mathewes }

Roger Kyngeslowe }
Thomas Hitchekokes }

Roger Smyth }
William Newe} sworn

Thomas Prestes }
John Hulle } sworn
~~John Byllyngesley~~

1427 P314/W/1/1/272

[Worfeld]	Small court held there on Tuesday on the feast of Saint Bartholomew the Apostle in the sixth year of the reign of King Henry VI after the conquest [24 August 1428]
Essoins	Roger Hulle, William Hockombe, John Mathewe, John Byllyngeseley, these essoined themselves for suit of court by John Roo
The 12	John Jannen, Thomas Undurhull, John Jonesone of Roulowe, Robert Webbe, William Wermod, Thomas Merwalle, Stephen Bradeney, Roger Gerbod, Thomas Preestes, Roger Townesende, Roger Kyngeslowe, Richard Haselwode } sworn
Amerced 6d	The 12 jurors say on their oath that William Undurwode (2d), Thomas Richardes (2d), John Bromley of Aldescote (2d) who owe suit at this court & did not come. Also they say that John Gyldone who held from the lady one pasture called Wicheford Parrok with its enclosure lying within the township of Kyngeslowe near to Wicheford between the meadow of Roger Dalley on the one side and the pasture called Kyngeslowe Hethe on the other side together with Matilda his wife joint feoffees on the day of his death after whose death there falls to the lady certain heriots and escheats but of what value the aforesaid jury are wholly ignorant and on this they seek a view until at the next court. And on this a day is given to the jury at the next court concerning the view aforesaid etc.
Amerced 6d	Richard Beere (6d) is not prosecuting his plea against Henry Wevar in a plea of debt so he is in mercy
Fine 4d	To this court comes Stephen Bradeney and surrendered into the hands of the lady one small parcel of land lying within the township of Hultone between the barn of Robert Bruggeende on the one side and the land called Lynotlond on the other side to the use of the aforesaid Robert Bruggeende to hold to the same Robert and his heirs for ever by services thence owed and of right accustomed & according to the custom of the manor. And he gives to the lady for a fine for to have ingress 4d. And he thence has seisin
Fine 4d	To this court comes Robert Bruggeende and surrendered into the hands of the lady one parcel of land called fethur lying within the township of Hultone in a certain field called Hultone feld on smale Heth between the land of Thomas Merwalle junior on the one side and the land of Stephen Bradeney on the other to the use of the aforesaid Stephen Bradeney to hold to the same Stephen and his heirs by services thence owed and of right accustomed & according to the custom of the manor. And he gives to the lady for a fine 4d. And he thence has seisin. And he made fealty
Fine 4d	To this court comes William Bromley and surrendered into the hands of the lady one parcel of meadow lying within the township of Bradeney in a certain meadow called Oldecroft between the meadow of Richard Bradeney on the one side and the river called Churle on the other side to the use of John Bradeney to hold to the same John and his heirs by services thence owed and of right accustomed & according to the custom of the manor. And he gives to the lady for a fine 4d. And he thence has seisin. And he made fealty

1427 P314/W/1/1/272

Fine 6s 8d

To this court comes Joan Aldith formerly the wife of Thomas Aldyth of Stapulford by John Snell bailiff of the lady and surrendered into the hands of the lady one messuage with half a virgate of land with appurtenances in Stapulforde to the use of Roger Swancote & Joan his wife, their heirs & assigns. And on this in the same court comes the aforesaid Roger & Joan and took from the hands of the lady the aforesaid messuage with the half virgate of land aforesaid with its appurtenances to hold to the same Roger & Joan their heirs & assigns for ever by services thence owed and of right accustomed & according to the custom of the manor. And they give to the lady for a fine for to have ingress and seisin 6s 8d. And they thence have seisin & made fealty

The law

John Waltone plaintiff of Joan Barndeley in a plea of broken agreement pledges for the prosecution John Snell & John Ro. And whence he pleads that on Sunday next after the feast of Easter last past after the present date he sold to the aforesaid Joan one messuage & three nooks of land with appurtenances in Rowghtone for £4 19s 8d & the same Joan agreed to pay thence to the aforesaid John Waltone namely on Sunday next thereafter following 20s which she did not pay to the damage of the aforesaid John Waltone of 40d. And the aforesaid Joan present in court responding says that no such agreement was made with themselves as he stated against her and alleged & on this to wager the law with eleven hands at the next [court] pledge for the law Thomas Merwall & Thomas Undurhull

It is ordered to distrain to the next [court]

Thomas Jenkys plaintiff appeared himself against Matilda Jenkys in a plea of trespass & the aforesaid Matilda is summoned & did not come so she is in mercy & it is ordered to distrain to the next [court]

It is ordered to distrain to the next [court]

The same Thomas plaintiff appeared himself against Roger Jenkys in a plea of debt & the same Roger is summoned & did not come so he is in mercy & it is ordered to distrain to the next [court]

Amerced 2d

Thomas Toward, Thomas Undurull & William Bakus plaintiffs appeared themselves against John Colyns in a plea of trespass. And the aforesaid John (2d) is attached as clear in the preceding court and did not come so he is in mercy. And it is ordered to retain & better distrain to the next [court]

Affeerors: John Jannen, John Waltone} sworn

Sum of this court 8s 10d. Thence in expenses of the steward 2s

1427 P314/W/1/1/272

Worfeld	Great court held there on Thursday next after the feast of St Michael the Archangel in the sixth year of the reign of King Henry VI after the conquest [2 October 1427]
Essoins	Roger Ygman, John Smyth of Hultone, John Sonde, William Undurwod & John Bromley these essoined themselves for suit of court
	Roger Swannecote, Stephen Bradeney, Roger Tounesende, Roger Kyngeslowe, Thomas Tomkys, John Jannes, Thomas Undurhull, Roger Garbot, Robert Webbe, John Jonsone, William Wermot, John Bromley } sworn
Amerced 2d Alvescote, Wynnescote, Newtone & Cattestre Strays	townships there present that William Barbour (2d) owes suit of court and did not come so he is in mercy. Also they present that one swarm of bees came as a stray at the feast of St John the Baptist price 4d & it remains in the custody of Richard Haselwodde the bailiff of the lady
Hultone	township there presents that one male black sheep came as a stray at the feast of the Nativity of the Lord price 8d & it remains in the custody of Stephen Bradeney
Chestertone Amerced 12d	township there presents nothing. Wykene township there presents Joan Hockeley servant of Henry Hockeley made a hue and cry on Simon Bernard (6d) in default of the same Simon so he is in mercy. Also they present that Joan Yngman (6d) made a hue and cry on John Beene unjustly so she is in mercy etc.
Roulowe, Bradeney, Asturhull, Euwyk & Sonde Amerced 12d	townships there present that John Henene (2d) owes suit of court and did not come so he is in mercy. And that one steer colour black came as a stray at the feast of Pentecost price six shillings & remaining in the custody of John Colynsone. And that two cows came as a stray at the feast aforesaid one brocked and the other black tagged price of both of them 5s & remaining in the custody of the aforesaid John Roulowe Colynsone. And that John Beene (4d) forestalled John Willen so etc. And that Roger Barker (6d) made an assault on the aforesaid Willen so he is in mercy.
	Burcote, Burcote, Ryndelford & Bromley townships there present nothing
Worfeld Amerced 12d	township there presents that Roger Deykyn (6d) forestalled Thomas Smyth & hit him with his fist so he is in mercy etc.
Roughtone, Barndeley	Hoccombe & Swannecote townships there present that Matilda Stanlowe (6d) made an assault on Joan Barndeley so she is in mercy. And that Joan Barndeley (6d) forestalled Joan Webbe so she is in mercy etc. Eudenas, Oldyngtone townships there present nothing. Akyltone township there presents nothing
Halene Amerced 3s	township there presents that Roger Deykyn (6d) forestalled Joan the wife of Thomas Bradeney & the aforesaid Joan (6d) made a hue and cry on the aforesaid Roger on his own by default so she is in mercy. And the aforesaid Joan drew the blood of the aforesaid Roger so etc. And that Roger (6d) the son of Henry Barker forestalled Matilda Byllyngesley so etc. And that the aforesaid Roger (12d) the son of Henry Barker broke the fold of the lady & took away his beasts without a licence of any official or minister of the lady so etc. And that Robert Barker (6d) made a hue and cry on Henry Barker in default of the aforesaid Henry so he is in mercy

Kyngeslowe, Stanlowe Amerced 2s 6d — townships there presents that John the servant of Thomas Jenkys (6d) junior broke the fold of Roger Dalley and took away his beasts without licence of the aforesaid Roger or any of his ministers or by the order of the aforesaid Thomas. So he is in mercy. And that John the servant of the aforesaid Thomas (6d) elsewhere broke the fold of the aforesaid Roger so he is in mercy. And that Matilda Stanlowe (6d) made an assault on John Yate and hit him with a stick so etc. And that the aforesaid John (6d) made an assault on the aforesaid Matilda so etc. And the aforesaid Matilda (6d) made a hue and cry on the aforesaid John unjustly so she is in mercy etc.

Stapulford Amerced 6d — township there presents that William Rugge (6d) broke the arrest of the bailiff of the lady for the grain of Richard Aldyth of Stapulford so he is in mercy

For keeping the peace — To this court came William Barowe & he found sufficient sureties to keep the peace towards Edith the wife of William Kyng namely Roger Roulowe, John Elcok, John Colynsone & Henry Wever namely the aforesaid William Barowe under pain of £10 and each of the sureties aforesaid under pain of 100s the which sums they wish and by the presents grant and each of them agreed that all the aforesaid be raised from the goods and chattels of their land and tenements

Amerced 2s 8d — William atte Yate & John Wilot of Akeltone the tasters of ale there present that John Gerbot (4d) for 1 brew, Hamond Hymley (4d) for 1 brew, John White (4d) for 1 brew, William Golde (4d) for 1 brew, John Jonsone of Roulowe (4d) for 1 brew, Richard Smyth (4d) for 1 brew, John Walker (4d) for 1 brew, William Barowe (4d) for 1 brew, these brewed and broke the assize of ale so they [are] in mercy

John Mathewe of Roughtone & Thomas Gerbot of Chestertone are elected tasters of ale and are sworn

The 12 jurors say on their oath that the aforesaid townships have well and faithfully presented & concealed nothing

Sum of this View 12s 8d

Affeerors: Roger Swannecote, Robert Webbe } sworn

Worfeld — Small court held there on Friday next after the feast of St Michael the Archangel in the sixth year of the reign of King Henry VI after the conquest [3 October 1427]

Essoins — William Undurwod, John Roulowe of Hultone, Henry Halle, John Whitbrok, John Smyth of Hultone, William Newtone Rector of Stoctone, John Bromley of Adelescote these essoined themselves for suit of court

Roger Swannecote Stephen Bradeney John Waltone Roger Kyngeslowe }
Roger Tounesende John Jonsone William Wermot Thomas Toward } sworn
John Janne Thomas Undurhulle Thomas Merewall junior Robert Webbe}

Heriot 5s — The 12 say on their oath that Thomas Aldyth on the day he died held from the lord one messuage & half a virgate of land with appurtenances in Stapulford together with Joan his wife jointly enfeoffed after whose death there falls to the lady one black cow price 5s in the name of heriot etc.

1427 P314/W/1/1/272

Fine 15s 4d

To this court came Richard Hasulwode bailiff of the lady saying that John Oldyngtone on Friday next before the feast of Pentecost last past in his own person came before the aforesaid bailiff & surrendered into the hands of the lady one messuage & half a virgate of land with appurtenances in Stanlowe & 1 nook of land adjacent in Oldefeld in Kyngeslowe & one parcel of land called Cliltrum/Cliltrum Grene to the use of Nicholas Stanlowe his heirs and assigns for ever to hold to himself and his [heirs] according to the custom of the manor & he gives to the lady for a fine for his ingress to be had 15s 4d pledge for the fine Roger Dalley & Roger Kyngeslowe etc. And thence he has seisin etc. And he made fealty etc.

Fine 15s

To this court came Henry Jones & Margery his wife alone confessed & rightly examined & surrendered into the hands of the lady through Richard Hasulwodd bailiff of the lady one messuage and three nooks of land called Hawkeslond with appurtenances in Roughtone to the use of John Waltone his heirs and assigns for ever to hold to himself and his [heirs] according to the custom of the manor & he gives to the lady for a fine 15s etc. And thence he has seisin etc. And he made fealty etc. pledge for the fine Roger Swannecote

Fine 6d

To this court came Hamo Hymley & surrendered into the hands of the lady through Richard Hasulwode bailiff of the lady one acre of land lying on Mersheforlong in Hultone feld to the use of Robert Bruggeende & Margery his wife the heirs and assigns of the said Robert for ever to hold to themselves and his [heirs] according to the custom of the manor & he gives to the lady for a fine for his ingress to be had 6d etc. And thence he has seisin etc. And he made fealty etc. pledge for the fine Stephen Bradeney

Fine 15s

To this court came Richard Hasulwode bailiff of the lady saying that William Undurwod & Alice his wife alone confessed & rightly examined surrendered as into the hands of the lady one messuage and half a virgate of land with appurtenances in Alvescote to the use of John Walker & Alice his wife their heirs and assigns for ever to hold to themselves & their [heirs] according to the custom of the manor & he gives to the lady for a fine for his ingress to be had 15s. And thence he has seisin etc. And he made fealty etc.

Fine 12d

To this court came John Beene beadle of the lady saying that John Elcok & Joan his wife surrendered into the hands of the lady through the aforesaid beadle one cottage in Sonde to the use of Richard Bere & Margery his wife their heirs and assigns for ever to hold to themselves & their [heirs] according to the custom of the manor & he gives to the lady for a fine for ingress to be had 12d pledge for the fine William Barwe. And they thence have seisin etc. & made fealty etc.

The 24 sworn and tried according to the custom of the manor say on their oath that all whose names are specified below namely Roger Tounesende, John Jannes, Robert Webbe, Stephen Bradeney, Roger Heth, Thomas Undurhull, William Wermot, Henry Barker, John Roulowe Jonsone, Thomas Merewall junior, Robert Brugend, Robert Gerbot, William Gerbot, Thomas Toward, William atte Yate, John Trisull, Roger Hull, Roger Smyth, Roger Jones, John Holigreve, John Bromley, William Bromley, William Newe & John Colettes who say on their oath that William Hoccombe & Edith his wife have such title in one messuage & half a virgate of land with appurtenances which the aforesaid William & Edith his wife hold in Hockombe that they are able to give or to make alienation of the aforesaid messuage & half virgate of land with appurtenances to whosoever they wish

1427 P314/W/1/1/272

Rent 6d

To this court came John Busshetone & took from the lady one parcel of water to put one weir in the river between Blacke Wallemore & Sidemore rendering thence annually at the usual times during his life 6d

Thomas Jenkys junior plaintiff of John Gybons in a plea of trespass whence he complains how with force and arms the aforesaid John on Monday next before the feast of St Michael the Archangel in the third year of the reign of King Henry VI after the conquest within the domain of Worfeld the aforesaid John took and carried away one bay horse price 6s 8d of the same Thomas Jenkys whence he says that it is deteriorated & has damage to the value of 10s. And thence the aforesaid suit etc. And the aforesaid John Gybons comes and defends the force and injury etc. and he says that he is in nothing thence guilty and for this to wager his law with twelve hands at the next court pledge for the law Thomas Richardes etc.

Turn

[The Dorse]

Amerced 12d

Henry Heuster (6d) & Henry his son (6d) are not prosecuting their plea of debt towards William Yngman so in mercy
Roger the son of Henry Barker plaintiff of John Beene in a plea of trespass & they have an adjournment to the next court etc.
The same Roger plaintiff of the same John in a plea of trespass & they have an adjournment to the next court. Pledge for the prosecution John Walker etc.
William Underwod plaintiff of Roger Hordeman in a plea of trespass etc.
Thomas Toward, Thomas Undurhull & William Bakes by Roger Dalley their attorney plaintiffs of John Colyns together with Roger Baret of Hugeford & they have an adjournment to the next court etc.
Henry Wever plaintiff of William Yngman in a plea of trespass & they have an adjournment to the next court etc.

Election of the reeve

Richard Hasulwodde is removed from the office of reeve and in his place are elected John Bradeney & John Sonde of Bradeney from which the steward elected John Bradeney & is sworn

Sum of this court 8s 4d

Affeerors: Roger Swannecote, Robert Webbe } sworn

Thence in expenses of the steward and other supervisors remaining there for three days & three nights with four horses in all money accounted and to be accounted 9s 4d
And in parchment with paper 4d

[Note the reference to the purchase of paper]

1428 P314/W/1/1/273

Worfeld	Great court held there on Tuesday in the week of Easter in the sixth year of the reign of King Henry VI after the conquest [30 March 1428]
Essoins	John Bromley, Thomas Richardes, Roger Knyght, Thomas Cattestre, William Barewe, William Barbour, John Waltone, Richard Haselwode & Henry Wevar these essoined themselves by John Roo for suit of court
The 12	Stephen Bradeney, John Janne, Roger Kyngeslowe, Thomas Tomkys, William Wermode, William Bromley, Robert Webbe, John Jonesone, Roger Swankote, Roger Tounesende, Thomas Undurhull, Roger Gerbode } sworn
Alvescote, Wyneskote, Newtone & Cattestre Strays	townships there present nothing. Chesturtone township there presents nothing. Burkote, Burkote, Ryndelford & Bromley nothing presented
Hultone Strays	township there presents that three ewes came as a stray at the feast of St Michael the Archangel last past price for each of them by itself 6d & they remain in the custody of Thomas Merewalle junior
Rowlowe, Bradeney, Asturhull, Ewyk & Sonde Amerced 12d Strays 22s	townships there present that William Rowlowe (12d) forestalled William Golde of Bradeley & from him drew blood so the aforesaid William Rowlowe is in mercy. Also they present that two steers & two heifers price 22s came as strays & they remain in the custody of John Rowlowe Colynssone.
Wyke Amerced 4d	township there presents nothing. Roughtone, Bardeley, Hockombe Barndeley townships there present that Joan Barndeley (4d) forestalled Isota the wife [blank] so she is in mercy
Stapulford Stray 4d	township there presents that one black heifer price 3s came as a stray at the feast of the Raising of the Holy Cross last past. Also they present that 3 mature sheep price 18d came as strays at the feast of St Martin of which one ewe remains in the custody of Thomas Toward and the other 2 males remain in the custody of Roger Swankote. Also they present 1 swarm of bees price 4d came as a stray & remains in the custody of William Rowlowe
Kyngeslowe, Stanlowe Strays 5d	townships there present that 1 swarm of bees came as a stray price 2d & remains in the custody of Thomas Tomkys. And that another swarm of bees price 3d came as a stray & remains in the custody of Roger Hethe
Eudenas & Oldyntone	townships there present nothing. Halen township there presents nothing
Akyltone Strays 2d	township there presents that one swarm of bees came as a stray price 2d & remains in the custody of Thomas Tomkys
Worfeld Amerced 8d	township there presents that Henry Wevar (4d) forestalled Roger Deken and hit him and the same Roger (4d) forestalled the aforesaid Henry and hit him so they are in mercy

1428 P314/W/1/1/273

The tasters of ale Amerced 3s

Thomas Mathewe & John Gerbod the tasters of ale present that Richard Preestes (4d) brewed 1, John Cattestre (4d) brewed 1, John Preestes(4d) brewed 1, Roger Barkar (4d) brewed 1, John Bromley (4d) brewed 1, William Gold (4d) brewed 1, Thomas Jenkys (4d) brewed 1, Matilda Jenkys (4d) brewed 1, William Barkar (4d) brewed 1, these brewed and broke the assize so they are in mercy

Sworn in tithing

Stephen the son of John Coletes aged 12 years and more is sworn in the tithing and made fealty. William the son of John Henene aged 12 years, William the son of William Rowlowe aged 12 years, Roger the son of William atte Yate aged 12 years & more all of them are sworn in the tithing and made fealty

A pain is put by the custom of Wyke Brugge that the aforesaid bridge is made before the feast of St John the Baptist next following under pain of 3s & the roads around the same bridge under the same pain because they are ruinous

The 12 jurors say & that the aforesaid townships & tasters of ale have well and faithfully presented & concealed nothing

Sum of this Court 27s 11d

Worfeld

Small court held there on Wednesday in the week of Easter in the year above said [31 March 1428]

Essoins

Roger Townesende, John Rowlowe of Hultone, John Bromley of Adelescote, Thomas Cattestre, Thomas Richardes, these essoined themselves for suit of court

The 12

Robert Webbe	John Jonesone	Thomas Toward }	
Stephen Bradeney	Roger Kyngeslowe	Roger Gerbode }	sworn
John Janne	William Wermode	Robert Bruggende }	
Thomas Undurhull	John Bromley	Roger Hulle)	

Heriot 3s
Escheat 2s

The aforesaid 12 jurors present that Thomas Jenkys senior who long before his death held from the lady one messuage & one toft & one cottage & five nooks of land with their appurtenances in Roughtone the which lands and tenements long before his death he demised according to the custom of the manor to a certain Roger his son & Matilda his daughter their heirs and assigns after the death of the same Thomas & Matilda his wife after whose death there falls to the lady one calf price 2s, one ewe price 12d in the name of heriot & three pigs price 2s in the name of escheat. And on this to the same court comes John Holigreve beadle of the lady saying that Thomas Jenkys senior before the last court before the death of the same Thomas surrendered into the hands of the same beadle just as into the hands of the lady according to the custom of the manor five nooks of land with its appurtenances within the fee of Roughtone after the death of the aforesaid Thomas Jenkys & Matilda his wife to the use of Roger the son of the aforesaid Thomas & Matilda the daughter of the same Thomas to hold to the aforesaid Roger & Matilda heirs of the aforesaid Thomas Jenkys and Matilda his wife theirs heirs and assigns for ever according to the custom of the manor . And on this came the aforesaid Roger & Matilda heirs of the aforesaid Thomas Jenkys and Matilda his wife & made a fine for the aforesaid five nooks of land for to have ingress 25s. And thence they have seisin & made fealty pledges for the fine Roger Dalley & John Mathewe etc.

Fine 25s

The same jury presents that Roger Barker on the day he died before the last court held from the lady for the term of his life one messuage and half a virgate of land with its appurtenances in Halen and one toft and half a virgate of land with its appurtenances in the same township the which land and tenement ought to remain after the death of the same Robert to Roger his son and Alice his wife the heirs & assigns of the same Roger after whose death there falls to the lady one calf price 2s 10d and one male sheep price 12d in the name of heriot and one small pig in the name of escheat price 8d

Taking of land fine 15s

To this court comes John Elkoc & Joan his wife the aforesaid Joan examined alone and surrendered into the hands of the lady one messuage and half a virgate of land and half a nook of land and one toft and one acre of land with appurtenances in Halen to the use of John Preestes & Alice his wife, the heirs and assigns of the same John Preestes to hold according to the custom of the manor by services owed and accustomed. And on this came the aforesaid John Preestes & Alice his wife & took from the lady the tenements aforesaid by services previously owed in the form aforesaid. And they give to the lady for a fine for ingress to be had 15s & made fealty pledges for the fine John Rowlowe Colynssone & William Barker

Taking of land fine 6s 8d [sic]

To this court comes William Newe and surrenders into the hands of the lady one messuage and half a virgate of land with its appurtenances in Chesturtone the which messuage and land was formerly held by William Newe to the use of Sibill the wife of John Newe son of the aforesaid William, his heirs and assigns forever to hold according to the custom of the manor by services owed and accustomed. And on this came the aforesaid Sibill & took from the lady the aforesaid messuage and half virgate of land with their appurtenances to hold from the lady & by services & customs owed & accustomed. And she gives to the lady for a fine for her ingress to be had 6s [sic] & made fealty pledges for the fine John Snell & Thomas Merwalle

To this court came Edith the wife of William Kyngessone & made a fine with the steward to sell ale for the year next in the future from this court

Presentment on oath

The 24 jurors charged and tried according to the custom of the manor of Worfeld whose names [are] in the roll of the court held at Worfeld above said on Tuesday in the week of Easter in the fifth year of the reign of King Henry VI after the conquest Who say on their oath that William Underwode and Alice his wife have such title in one messuage and half a virgate of land with appurtenances which the aforesaid William and Alice hold in Alvescote that they are able to give or to alienate to whosoever they wish

The next — Thomas Jenkys plaintiff of Matilda Jenkys in a plea of trespass pledge for the prosecution John Holigreve it is ordered to distrain to the next

The next — The same Thomas plaintiff of Roger Jenkys in a plea of debt pledge for the prosecution John Holigreve it is ordered to distrain to the next

The next — William Beore plaintiff of Henry Wevar in a plea of debt pledge for the prosecution John Cattestre it is ordered to distrain to the next

The next — Roger the son of Henry Barker plaintiff of William Barewe in a plea of trespass pledge for the prosecution John Holigreve it is ordered to distrain to the next

Sum of this Court 47s 2d
Thence in expenses of the steward 9s 4d
And in parchment 4d

Affeerors: Thomas Merwall junior, John Colettes

1428-1429 P314/W/1/1/274

Worfeld	Great court held there on Thursday next after the feast of St Michael the Archangel in the seventh year of the reign of King Henry VI after the conquest [30 September 1428]
Essoins	Roger Kyngeslowe, William Hockombe, Richard Ingeman, John Bradeney, John Smyth, Thomas Merwall junior, Thomas Undurhull, Roger Hulle, John Whitebrok, John Jowkys, William Oldyntone, Roger Jones, William Rys, John Trecille, John Walker, William Bromley, William Newe, William Hewstar, John Hultone, Thomas Merwall senior, Roger Townesende, John Elkoc & Roger Barker these were essoined for suit of court through John Roo

The 12	Roger Swankote	Roger Gerbode	Robert Webbe }	sworn
	Thomas Tomkys	William Wermode	John Colettes }	
	Stephen Bradeney	John Jonesone of Rowlowe	Thomas Prestes }	
	John Jannen	John Bromley	Richard Haselwode }	

Rowlowe, Bradeney, Asturhull, Ewike & Sonede Amerced 10d	townships there present that John Henene (2d) who owes suit of this court & did not come so he [is] in mercy. Also they present that Richard Beore (4d) son of William Beore took unjustly & against the peace one sheaf of barley of the goods of John Rowlowe son of Nicholas Rowlowe price 1d in the field called Sonede feld namely on Thursday next after the feast of St Laurence the Martyr in the sixth year of the aforesaid King so he [is] in mercy. Also they present that Katherine (4d) daughter of William Beore took unjustly from a money box of Margery Smyth one penny so she is in mercy
Ewdenas, Oldyntone	townships there present nothing but all well. Burkote & Burkote, Ryndelford, Bromley present nothing. Hultone present nothing.
Alvescote, Wynskote, Cattestre, Newtone 4d	townships there present that William Undurwode (4d) who owes suit of this court & did not come so he [is] in mercy.
Worfeld The next Amerced 2s 4d	township there presents that the way is blocked next to the tenement of William Kyng for default of cleaning by Henry Webbe (2d) so he [is] mercy & it is ordered that he repairs before the next [court]. Also they present that the same Henry Webbe (6d) forestalled William Barewe against the peace of the King so he [is] in mercy. Also they present that the aforesaid William Barewe (12d) forestalled the aforesaid Henry Webbe & from him drew blood against the peace of the King so he [is] in mercy. Also they present that Henry Hewstar (4d) & Henry his son (4d) made an assault on the aforesaid William Barewe & against the peace of the King so he [is] in mercy
Wyken	township there presents nothing but all well
Stapulford Amerced 4s 6d	township there presents that John Colyns (6d) forestalled John Taylour against the peace of the King so he [is] mercy. Also they present that Thomas Toward (12d), John Colyns (12d), John Taylour (12d), & William Rowlowe (12d) broke the arrest of one bundle of hay which was arrested by the bailiff of the lady in Stapulford so they are in mercy
Chesturtone Stray price 2s	township there presents that one brown calf came as a stray price 2s first seized in the feast of Easter last past & it remains in the custody of John Snell

Akyltone Amerced 4d	township there presents that the high way at Clerkesyate is obstructed for default of cleaning of one ditch there by Thomas Haselwode (4d) so the same Thomas is in mercy
Halen Amerced 8d	township there presents that Roger (4d) the son of Henry Barker broke the pound of Henry Barker and from there took his own animals so he [is] in mercy. that Henry Weaver (4d) unjustly enclosed one held [*heldam*] of land of William Hewster within the township aforesaid & took the aforesaid held separatelywhich should have been situate in common this year so he [is] in mercy
Rowghtone, Barndeley, Hockombe, Swancote Amerced 4d	townships there present that William Skynnar (4d) who owes suit of this court & did not come so he [is] in mercy.
Kyngeslowe, Stanlowe Amerced 4s 2d	townships there present that Richard Syngar (4d) blocked the severalty water of the lady called the Churle with peat turves & fished in the same without a licence from the lady so he [is] in mercy. Also they present that Thomas Jenkys (8d) forestalled Matilda Gyldone & from her unjustly took 14 sheaves of oats price 6d of the goods and chattels of the aforesaid Matilda & against the peace of the King so he [is] in mercy. Also they present that the aforesaid Matilda (6d) made an assault on the aforesaid Thomas & hit him & against the peace of the King. Also they present that the same Thomas Jenkys (4d) made an assault on the aforesaid Matilda & hit her & against the peace of the King. Also they present that the aforesaid Matilda raised the hue and cry justly on the aforesaid Thomas (4d) so he [is] in mercy. Also they present that Roger Dalley (12d) made an assault on the aforesaid Thomas Jenkys & from him drew blood & against the peace of the King. Also they present that the aforesaid Thomas says that the aforesaid townships concealed one default and furthermore he says that Roger Dalley, John Hether, Roger Hethe should clean a certain ditch in Kyngeslowe so that in default of cleaning the ditch whence it flooded the King's way there to the nuisance of the people of the lord King. And on this the aforesaid townships say that nothing was concealed but well & faithfully presented & on this put themselves on the 12 jurors. And the aforesaid Thomas similarly. And on this the aforesaid jury went out & returned who say on their oath that the aforesaid townships well & faithfully presented & concealed nothing so the same Thomas (6d) [is] in mercy for his unjust plea. Also they present that John Gerbode (6d) sold meat at an excessive [price] so he [is] in mercy
The tasters of ale Amerced 4s	present that John Walker (4d) brewed 1, John Byllyngesley senior (4d) brewed 1, William Barewe (4d) brewed 1, Richard Smyth (4d) brewed 1, John Jonesone of Rowlowe (4d) brewed 1, Petronella Gold (4d) brewed 1, Roger Dalley (4d) brewed 1, Robert Bruggeende (4d) brewed 1, Thomas Bakar (4d) brewed 1, Hamo Hymley (4d) brewed 1, Roger Hulle (4d) brewed 1, & they broke the assize so they [are] in mercy. Aldo they present that John Elkoc (4d) brewed 1 & broke the assize
Fine 12d	Richard Smyth made a fine with the steward to brew ale from the date of this court until the end of one year next in the future to be paid at the next account 12d
Fine 2s	Alice at Sonede made a fine with the steward to brew ale from the date of this court until the end of one year next in the future to be paid as above 2s
Fine 8d	Alice Galian made a fine with the steward to brew ale from the date of this court until the end of one year next in the future to be paid as above 8d

1428-1429 P314/W/1/1/274

Fine 12d

John Rowlowe son of Nicholas gives to the lady for a fine 12d for suit of court to be commuted until the feast of St Michael next in the future

Sum of this Court 23s 2d

Worfeld

Small court held there on Friday next after the feast of St Michael the Archangel in the eighth year of the reign of King Henry VI after the conquest [10 October 1428]

Essoins

John Whitebrok, Roger Bruggeende, William Newtone, Thomas Richardes, Roger Jones, John Trecille, Thomas Cattestre, John Smyth of Hultone, John Bene, HenryHalle, Willliam Yate, William Bromley, Roger Townesende & William Gerbode these essoined themselves through Richard Willes from common suit

The 12

Stephen Bradeney	Roger Swankote	John Bromley }	
Robert Webbe	William Wermode	Thomas Preestes }	sworn
Thomas Undurhull	John Jannen	Richard Haselwode }	
Roger Gerbode	Roger Kyngeslowe	John Colettes }	

Heriot 5s & Escheat price 6s

To this court came the 12 jurors at the last court next preceding sworn on the view of the value both of the heriots and escheats which should have fallen to the lady after the death of ~~John~~ John Gyldon lately deceased who say on their oath that there falls to the lady in the name of heriot one steer price 5s & they say also that there falls to the lady in the name of escheat one draught animal price 3s and six small pigs price of each of them 6d

Heriot nothing

Amerced 2d

Also the aforesaid jury presents that John Bromley (2d) of Adlescote who owes suit at this court & did not come so he [is] in mercy. Also they present that Alice Needone who held from the lady one messuage with half a virgate of land with their appurtenances in Stanlowe on the day he died after whose death nothing falls to the lady because thc aforesaid Alice was living outside the domain as if by alms & having no goods nor chattels etc. And John Yate & Agnes his wife are tenants of the aforesaid messuage with half a virgate of land aforesaid by the grant of the aforesaid Alice after the death of the same Alice as is clear in the court held there on Saturday next after the feast of St Peter in Chains in the sixth year of the reign of King Henry V after the conquest. And on this the aforesaid Yate & Agnes his wife came & took from the lady the aforesaid messuage with half a virgate of land with their appurtenances by services thence formerly due and of right accustomed & according to the custom of the manor. And they have seisin & made fealty

Fine 10s

To this court came William Pyrie son of William Pyrie of Bylstone & Roger Cattestre and surrendered into the hands of the lady one toft with half a virgate of land with its appurtenances in Halen called lovestikeslond to the use of William Barker & Anne his wife their heirs & assigns for ever to hold at the will of the lady according to the custom of the manor by services thence formerly owed & accustomed. And the aforesaid Roger Cattestre for himself and his heirs & executors quitclaimed, released & guaranteed all the aforesaid toft with half a virgate of land with its appurtenances . And the aforesaid William & Anna have seisin thence. And they give to the lady for a fine for ingress to have 10s. And they made fealty pledge for the fine John Rowlowe

Amerced 6d

John Elkoc miller of Worfeld presents that Thomas ~~that Thomas~~ Jenkys (4d) & Thomas Colyar (2d) did not grind corn at the mill of the lady just as the custom is to grind there so they are in mercy

Amerced 12d — John Walker miller of Ryndeford presents that John Colyns (4d), John Taylour (4d) & William Rowlowe (4d) did not mill at the mill of the lady there just as the custom is to mill so they are in mercy

Whence the law — The plea which is between Thomas Jenkys plaintiff & John Gybones defendant in a plea of trespass by the prayer of the parties is adjourned until the next [court] whence the law

Amerced 4d — Thomas Toward, Thomas Undurhull & William Bakus plaintiffs appeared themselves against John Colyns in a plea of trespass & the same John is attached as is clear at the court held etc. and did not come so he [is] in mercy & the pledge because he does not have [him there]so it is ordered to better distrain until the next [court]

Amerced 6d — John Waltone plaintiff & Joan Barndeley defendant in a plea of broken agreement are for a licence to agree & the same John withdrew from the court

Amerced 6d — Roger Barker plaintiff & William Barewe defendant in a plea of trespass are for a licence to agree & the same William withdrew from the court

Adjourned — The plea which is between Thomas Jenkys plaintiff & Roger Jenkys defendant in a plea of trespass by the prayer of the parties is adjourned until the next [court]

The next [court] — The plea which is between Thomas Jenkys plaintiff & Matilda Jenkys defendant by the prayer of the parties is adjourned until the next [court]

A day — Roger Dalley plaintiff appeared himself against Thomas Jenkys in a plea of trespass & whereof he complains that the aforesaid Thomas on a certain day and year destroyed and depastured the corn of the aforesaid plaintiff with his ox and with one pig to the damage of the aforesaid plaintiff of 6d. And on this in the same court a day is given for the parties aforesaid until the next [court]

It is ordered — Stephen Bradeney plaintiff of Thomas Jenkys in a plea of trespass pledge for the prosecution John Snell & John Roo so it is ordered to summon the aforesaid Thomas to the next [court]

Fine 6s 8d — To this court came John Jannen & Alice his wife through John Snell the bailiff of the lady & the same Alice duly confessed & examined according to the custom of the manor before the steward & surrendered into the hands of the lady the reversion of one messuage with half a virgate of land with its appurtenances in Swankote which the same John & Alice hold for the term of their lives & of the longer living of them to the use of Thomas Jannen their son & Agnes his wife & the heirs of their bodies legitimately procreated. And on this in the same court came the aforesaid Thomas & Agnes & took from the lady the reversion of the aforesaid messuage with half a virgate of land aforesaid with its appurtenances when it will have happened to hold to themselves & the heirs of their bodies legitimately procreated at the will of the lady by services thence owed & of right accustomed & according to the custom of the manor. And if it should happen the aforesaid Thomas & Agnes die without heirs of their bodies legitimately procreated that thenceforth the whole of the aforesaid messuage with half a virgate of land aforesaid with its appurtenances should remain forever to the direct heirs of the aforesaid John Jannen. And they give to the lady for a fine for ingress & seisin to have 6s 8d. And they made fealty

1428-1429 P314/W/1/1/274

Affeerors: Thomas Merwalle, John Colettes

Sum of the Court 30s 8d
Thence in expenses of the steward, clerk, improver, reeve, beadle & other ministers of the lady for 2 days & 2 nights being there to hold the aforesaid 2 courts & the court of Kemburtone 9s 1d

Worfeld	Small court held there on Wednesday next after the feast of the Conversion of St Paul in the seventh year of the reign of King Henry VI after the conquest [26 January 1429]
Essoins	Stephen Bradeney, Henry Barker, John Holigreve, William Hockombe, these essoined themselves from common suit
The 12	Robert Webbe, Richard Haselwode, John Jonesone of Rowlowe, John Jannen, John Bromley, John Colettes, Thomas Undurhull, William Wermode, William Newe, Robert Bruggeende, Thomas Preestes, John Bradeney } sworn
It is ordered to distrain	John Jonesone of Rowlowe plaintiff of John Bene in a plea of trespass pledges for the prosecution John Snell & John Roo so it is ordered to distrain to the next [court]
The law	Richard Undurhull plaintiff of Henry Wevar in a plea of debt pledges for the prosecution John Baret & John Ro. And the same Henry was distrained by one cart & four horses price 10s 2d. And whereof he complains that he owes him 10s & unjustly detains to the damage of the aforesaid plaintiff of 20d. And the aforesaid Henry present in court to respond says that he owes him nothing nor unjustly detains and he is to the law with 6 hands at the next [court] pledges for the law John Baret & John Roo & William Gold
Amerced 4d	Thomas Toward, Thomas Undurhull & William Bakus plaintiffs appeared themselves against John Colyns in a plea of trespass. And the same John is attached & did not come & is repledged by Roger Swankote so the aforesaid John Colyns is in mercy & the pledge because he did not have the aforesaid John [in court]
Adjourned	The plea which is between Roger Dalley plaintiff & Thomas Jenkys defendant in a plea of trespass of 2 pleas adjourned by the prayer of the parties to the next [court]
Adjourned	Thomas Jenkys plaintiff & Roger Jenkys defendant in a plea of debt is still adjourned by the prayer of the parties until the next [court]
It is ordered	Thomas Jenkys plaintiff appeared himself against Matilda Jenkys in a plea of trespass. And the aforesaid Matilda is still not attached so it is ordered to the beadle to attach to the next [court]
Whence the law	The plea which is between Thomas Jenkys plaintiff & John Gybones defendant in a plea of trespass is adjourned by the prayer of the parties to the next [court] whence the law
Amerced 6d	The jury aforesaid came and presented that John Trecille (2d) did not come to make suit of court, John Bene (2d) did not come, John Hethe (2d) did not come so they [are] in mercy

Fine 2s
The next

To this court came Thomas Bradeney son of John Bradeney & gives to the lady for a fine 2s for an inquiry to be held of the 24 to enquire & present on oath whether the same Thomas should have the better right in one parcel of meadow lying in a certain meadow called Torremedewe in Bradeney as of the right of the same Thomas after the death of Margery Bradeney in his claim than Hugh Baker & Agnes his wife have in their tenure. On which the 24 jurors thence charged went out & returned seek a day to render the verdict until the next [court]. And thus they have a day

Fine 10s

To this court came Richard Gerbode through John Baret the beadle of the lady & surrendered into the hands of the lady the reversion of one toft with half a virgate of land with its appurtenances in Halene called Jorylond to the use of Roger Gerbode his son after the death of the same Richard & Agnes his wife and whichever of them is the longer living. And on this in the same court came the aforesaid Roger & tookfrom the hands of the lady the reversion of the aforesaid toft with the half a virgate aforesaid with its appurtenances when it will have happened to hold to the same Roger his heirs and assigns at the will of the lady by services thence owed & of right accustomed & according to the custom of the manor. And he gives to the lady for a fine thence to have ingress & seisin 10s

Fine 12d

To this court came John Jonesone of Rowlowe & gives to the lady for a fine 12d for an inquiry of the 12 to be held to enquire & present on oath whether the same John has the better right in one seilion of land lying in a certain field called Cronemerefeld at the gate called Cattestre Gate within the township of Halen in his claim than John Bene & Margery his wife have in their tenure. On which the 12 jurors thence charged went out & returned seek a day to render the verdict until the next [court]. And thus they have a day

Fine 20s

To this court came William Gold of Hultone through John Baret the beadle of the lady & surrendered into the hands of the lady the reversion of one messuage with one virgate of land with its appurtenances in Hultone to the use of Henry Wevar after the death of the same William. And on this in the same court came the aforesaid Roger & took from the hands of the lady the reversion of the aforesaid messuage with the virgate of land aforesaid with its appurtenances when it will have happened to hold to the same Henry his heirs and assigns at the will of the lady by services thence owed & of right accustomed & according to the custom of the manor. And he gives to the lady for a fine thence to have ingress & seisin 20s. Pledge for the fine Robert Webbe & William Barker

It is ordered to attach

Thomas Preestes plaintiff of William Beore in a plea of trespass pledge for the prosecution the beadle so it is ordered to attach to the next [court]

Plea adjourned

Stephen Bradeney plaintiff &Thomas Thomkys defendant in a plea of trespass adjourned by the prayer of the parties to the next [court]

It is ordered to distrain

Thomas Preestes plaintiff of Agnes Smyth in a plea of unjust detention of goods & chattels pledge for the prosecution William Hewster so it is ordered to attach to the next [court]

It is ordered to attach

William Kyngessone plaintiff of Henry Wevar in a plea of trespass pledge for the prosecution John Baret so it is ordered to attach to the next [court]

It is ordered to distrain

William Kyngessone plaintiff of the aforesaid Henry in a plea of unjust detention of goods & chattels pledge for the prosecution William Hewstar so it is ordered to distrain to the next [court]

1428-1429 P314/W/1/1/274

The next [court]	William Hewstar plaintiff of Henry Wevar in a plea of debt pledge for the prosecution William Kyngessone so it is ordered to summon to the next [court]

Affeerors: Robert Bruggeende, William Wermode

Sum of the Court 30s 8d
Thence in expenses of the steward & other officials of the lady 20d In parchment 4d for writing the rolls aforesaid

Worfeld	Small court held there on Thursday on the feast of St Mathew the Apostle in the seventh year of the reign of King Henry VI after the conquest [24 February 1429]
Essoins	Robert Bruggeende, John Jannen, John Bromley of Adlescote, essoined themselves from common suit
Whence the law	Henry Wevar defendant essoined himself against Richard Undurhull in a plea of debt whence the law

Roger Swancote	John Bromley	Roger Gerbode }	
John Jonesone	Thomas Undurhull	Thomas Toward	} sworn
Robert Webbe	John Colettes	Thomas Prestes }	
William Wermode	Roger Kyngeslowe	William Bromley }	

Plea adjourned	The plea which is between Roger Dalley plaintiff & Thomas Jenkys defendant in a plea of trespass of 2 pleas is adjourned by the prayer of the parties to the next [court]
The law	Thomas Jenkys plaintiff against Roger Jenkys his brother in a plea of debt & whence he complains that he owes him 16s and unjustly detains to the damage of the aforesaid Thomas of 40d. And the aforesaid Roger present in court responded saying that he owes him nothing nor unjustly detains and he is to the law with 12 hands at the next [court] pledges for the law Roger Dalley & John Bene
Judged Amerced 6d	John Jonesone of Rowlowe plaintiff appeared himself against John Bene in a plea of trespass and whence he complains that the same John unjustly made one hedge on the land of the aforesaid John Rowlowe at Haukesplace by which the same John had damages to the value of 20d And the aforesaid John Bene preent in court to respond well acknowledged that he made damages to the value of twenty pence just as the aforesaid John Jonesone alleged and stated against him & on this he put himself on the assessment of the 12 jurors & the aforesaid John Jonesone similarly. And on this the aforesaid jury charged & thence sworn went out & returned & judged the aforesaid damages at 4d so it is judged that the same John Bene [is] thus in the mercy of the lady
Amerced 6d	Thomas Prestes plaintiff of William Beore in a plea of trespass are for a licence to agree & the same William withdrew from the court
Amerced 6d	Stephen Bradeney plaintiff &Thomas Thomkys defendant in a plea of trespass are for a licence to agree & Robert Webbe & Thomas Undurhull withdrew from the court
Amerced 6d	Thomas Preestes plaintiff & Agnes Smyth in a plea of trespass are for a licence to agree & the same Agnes withdrew from the court
Amerced 4d	William Kyngessone plaintiff appeared himself against Henry Wevar in a plea of unjust detention of goods & chattels of 2 pleas & the aforesaid Henry is summoned and did not come so it is ordered to attach to the next [court]

Amerced 2d
The next

William Hewstar plaintiff appeared himself against Henry Wevar in a plea of debt & the same Henry is summoned and did not come so it is ordered to distrain to the next [court]

Amerced 8d
The next

Thomas Toward, Thomas Undurhull & William Bakus plaintiffs appeared themselves against ~~William~~ John Colyns in a plea of trespass. & the same William is attached & did not come so he & his pledge are in mercy & it is ordered to better distrain to the next [court]

Adjourned whence the law

The plea which is between Thomas Jenkys plaintiff & John Gybones defendant in a plea of debt still is adjourned to the next [court] whence the law

Plea adjourned

The plea which is between Thomas Jenkys plaintiff & Matilda Jenkys defendant in a plea of trespass is adjourned to the next [court] by the prayer of the parties

Plea
Distrain to the next

Thomas Jenkys plaintiff of William Ingemon in a plea of broken agreement pledge for the prosecution John Baret & John Bene so it is ordered to distrain to the next [court]

Plea
Distrain to the next

Edmund Burnell through John Snell his attorney plaintiff of William Ingemon in a plea of debt so it is ordered to distrain to the next

The next
Adjourned

Still the 24 jurors have a day to enquire & to present on oath whether Thomas Bradeney son of John Bradeney has the better right in one parcel of meadow lying in one parcel of meadow lying in a certain meadow called Torremedewe in Bradeney in his claim by a fine made in the next court preceding as is clear in the same [court] than Hugh Baker & Agnes his wife have in their tenure for the sake of proof between the parties to prove and view at the next [court]

Adjourned

Still the 24 jurors have a day until the next [court] to enquire & to present on oath whether John Jonesone of Rowlowe has the better right in one seilion of land lying in a certain field called Cronemerefeld at the gate called Cattestre Gate within the township of Halen in his claim by a fine made in the next court preceding than John Bene & Margery his wife have in their tenure.

Amerced 2d

The aforesaid jury present that Richard Bradeney (2d) who owes suit at this court & did not come so he [is] in mercy

Sum of this court 3s 4d.
In expenses of the steward 20d

Affeerors: John Bromley, Robert Webbe

Worfeld

Great court held there on Thursday next after the feast of the annunciation of the Blessed Virgin Mary in the seventh year of the reign of King Henry VI after the conquest [31 March 1429]

Essoins

John Waltone, Roger Swankote, William Bakus, John Bromley of Adlescote, William Barbour of Wynscote, these essoined themselves for suit of court through John Roo

1428-1429 P314/W/1/1/274

The 12	Robert Webbe	Robert Bruggende	John Jonesone }	
	Thomas Tomkys	Richard Haselwode	Roger Kyngeslowe }	sworn
	William Wermode	Thomas Toward	John Colettes }	
	Thomas Undurhull	Roger Gerbode	John Bromley }	

Alvescote, Wynscote, Cattestre, Newton Stray 1d	townships there present 1 skin of a sheep dead in murrain coming as a stray price 1d & it is ordered to the beadle to sell dearer if he can
Kyngeslowe, Stanlowe	townships there present nothing but all [is] well
Ewdenas, Oldyngton	townships there present nothing but all [is] well Hultone township there presents nothing as all [is] well
Chesturtone Stray price 4d	township there presents two-toothed sheep coming as a stray formerly seized in the feast of Easter last past after the present date price 4d & it remains in the custody of William Newe & it is ordered to the beadle to sell dearer if he can
Wyke Amerced 20d	township there presents that William Ingemon (20d) broke the arrest of the bailiff of the lady so he [is] in mercy
Rowlowe, Bradeney, Ewyke ,Asturhull, Sonede Amerced 12d	townships there present that John Hultone (4d) owes suit at this court and did not come. Also they present that John Rowlowe (8d) so of Nicholas enclosed one parcel of land & holds it separately which from ancient times should lie in common called Hethhull in Ewyke so he is ordered to amend before the next court & he is in mercy
Fine 4d	William Barewe made a fine with the lady to brew ale from the date of this court until the feast of St Michael next in the future 4d
Burkote & Burkote, Ryndelford, Bromley	townships there present nothing but all [is] well. Roughton, Barndeley, Hockombe, Swankote townships there present nothing but all [is] well
Stapulforde Amerced 12d	township there presents that Joan (6d) the wife of Roger Swankote made an assault on John Colyns & hit him. Also they present that the same John Colyns (6d) made an assault on the aforesaid Joan & hit her so they [are] in mercy
Halen	township there presents nothing but all [is] well. Akyltone township there presents nothing but all [is] well.
Worfeld Amerced 3s 4d	township there presents that William Barewe (14d) forestalled Roger Jenkys & from him drew blood against the peace of the King. Also they present that Henry Kyng (14d) forestalled John Broke & from him drew blood against the peace of the King so they [are] in mercy. Also they present that Agnes (6d) daughter of William Kyng on a certain day and year unjustly took one flannolum [loosely woven cloth] of the goods and chattels of Marion Broke price 4d & against the peace of the King so she [is] in mercy. Also they present that John Elkoc (6d) made an assault on Richard Beore against the peace so he [is] in mercy.
The tasters of ale Amerced 2s 2d	present that John Preestes (4d) brewed 1, Matilda Byllyngesley (4d) brewed 1, Henry Wevar (4d) brewed 1, Richard Preestes (4d) brewed 1, John White (4d) brewed 1, John Mathewe (4d) brewed 1, William Barewe (4d) brewed 1

Sum of this court 9s 11d

1428-1429 P314/W/1/1/274

Worfeld	Small court held there on Friday on the feast of the Annunciation of the Blessed Mary in the seventh year of the reign of King Henry VI [1 April 1429]
Essoins	John Hulle, Roger Hulle, Thomas Richardes, John Mathewe, John Bradeney, William Yate, Roger Kyngeslowe, John Trecyll, & John Bromley of Adlescote, these essoined themselves from common suit though John Nicolls
The 12	John Jonesone, Thomas Prestes, Thomas Toward, Robert Bruggende, Stephen Bradeney, Roger Smyth, William Wermode, John Colettes, Thomas Jenkys, Roger Gerbode, Roger Dalley, Henry Barker } sworn
Amerced 6d	Richard Undurhull plaintiff & Henry Wevar defendant in a plea of debt [are] for a licence to agree & the same Henry withdrew from the court so he [is] in mercy
Damages adjudged amerced 6d	Roger Dalley plaintiff appeared himself against Thomas Jenkys in a plea of trespass & whence he complains that three oxen & one pig of the aforesaid Thomas depastured & trampled the barley, peas & corn of the aforesaid Roger in a certain field called Stanlowefeld during the time of harvest to the damage of the aforesaid Roger of 16d. And the aforesaid Thomas present in court to respond says that he made the damage to him & not to the value of the sum aforesaid. And on this they put themselves on the 12 jurors aforesaid. And the aforesaid Roger similarly. And on this the aforesaid jury thence charged & sworn went out & returned & adjudged the damages at 4d so the same Thomas [is] in mercy
The law	Roger Dalley plaintiff appeared himself against Thomas Jenkys in a plea of trespass. And whence he complains that on a certain day and year the aforesaid Thomas came into a certain field called Crowallefeld & one parcel of one acre of land being sown with barley of the goods of the aforesaid Roger there with force & arms & against the peace of the King mowed & from thence carried away to the damage of the aforesaid plaintiff of 40d. And the aforesaid Thomas present in court to respond says that he mowed no barley nor carried it away as the same Roger against him alleged & stated and on this to wager the law with six hands at the next [court] pledge for the law John Snell & John Doo
Amerced 12d	William Kyngessone plaintiff & Henry Wevar in 2 pleas of unjust detention of goods & chattels [are] for a licence to agree & the same Henry withdrew from the court so he [is] in mercy
It is ordered to distrain. Amerced 2d	William Hewstar plaintiff appeared himself against Henry Wevar in a plea of debt & the same Henry is attached by one brass pot price 4s and did not come so it is ordered to retain & better distrain to the next [court]
Completed the law 6d	To this court came Roger Jenkys & completed his law in a plea of debt against Thomas Jenkys at the preceding court waging with six hands so it is judged that the same Thomas is in mercy for his unjust plea & the same Thomas withdrew quit
Adjourned until the next	The plea which is between Thomas Toward, Thomas Undurhull & William Bakus plaintiffs & John Colyns defendant concerning a plea of trespass is still adjourned by the prayer of the parties
	Thomas Jenkys plaintiff appeared himself against Matilda Jenkys in a plea of trespass. And whence he complains that the aforesaid Matilda at the feast of St Michael the Archangel in the fifth year of the aforesaid King came to the house of the aforesaid Thomas in Roughton with force & arms & against the peace of the King & broke into & entered the house of the same & carried away and burnt timber to the damage of the aforesaid plaintiff of 30s. And the aforesaid Matilda present in court

The law

to respond says that in nothing is she to blame & thence to wager the law with six hands at the next [court] pledge for the law Thomas Undurhull & John Davy

Fine 2s

The aforesaid 12 jurors present that Matilda Gyldone widow of the lady married herself to John Blakemere without a licence from the lady so she made a fine with the lady for the trespass aforesaid 2s

Fine 20s

To this court came Alice Rowlowe formerly the wife of Thomas Rowlowe & surrendered into the hands of the lady through John Baret the beadle of the lady the reversion of one messuage & one virgate of land with their appurtenances in Burkote & the reversion of 1 toft with half a virgate of land with its appurtenances in the other Burkote to the use of Roger the son of the aforesaid Alice & Agnes his wife his wife after the death of the aforesaid Alice to have & to hold the reversion of the aforesaid lands & tenements with their appurtenances when they will have happened to the same aforesaid Roger & Agnes the heirs and assigns of the same Roger to hold from the lady in fee there by services thence owed and of right accustomed & according to the custom of the manor. And they give to the lady for a fine 20s. And they thence have seisin & made fealty

Fine 8d

To this court came John Hethe & surrendered into the hands of the lady through John Baret the beadle of the lady three parts of one toft of land with its appurtenances in Kyngeslowe to the use of Matilda the daughter of the same John & on this in the same court came the aforesaid Matilda & took from the lady the aforesaid three parts of the aforesaid toft with its appurtenances to hold to herself, her heirs & assigns to hold for ever from the lady by services thence owed and of right accustomed & according to the custom of the manor. And she gives to the lady for a fine 8d. And thence has & seisin & made fealty

Amerced 4d
The next [court]

Thomas Jenkys plaintiff appeared himself against William Yngemon in a plea of broken agreement & the same William is attached by 1 pitchfork (pykevell) & 1 kneading trough & one bundle of hay price 8d & did not come so it is ordered to retain & better distrain to the next

Amerced 2d
Heriot 10s
Relief 8s
It is ordered to seize into the hands of the lady

The aforesaid jury present that Roger Swankote (2d) who owes suit at this court & did not come. Also they present that Roger Cattestre junior who held freely from the lord by charter one messuage with one virgate of land with its appurtenances in Cattestre has died after whose death there falls to the lady one ox in the name of heriot price 10s. And they say also that the aforesaid land & tenements remain to Roger the son of William the son of the aforesaid Roger blood relative & heir of the aforesaid Roger whence there falls to the lady for relief 8s. And he thence has seisin & made fealty. Also they present that William Ewyke handed over and demised at a fixed payment to John Rowlowe son of Nicholas Rowlowe all his lands & tenements in Ewyke for a term of seven years, a licence from the lady thence not obtained & against the custom of the manor of the manor of Worfeld so it is ordered to the beadle to seize all the aforesaid lands & tenements into the hands of the lady until the aforesaid William Ewyke makes a fine with the lady for the trespass aforesaid

Pain

Also they present that the ponds of the mill of Worfeld are deteriorated & broken in default of the lessee there because the waters overflowed the king's road there to the grave nuisance of all the tenants & residents there so a pain of 40d is put on the aforesaid lessee that he repairs before the feast of Pentecost next in the future after the present date And so to be paid to the lady on the fifteenth [day] if not amended

Default of law Amerced 6d	At this court John Gybones defaulted from his wager at law against Thomas Jenkys in a plea of debt so it is considered that the same Thomas recover from the aforesaid John Gybones 6s 8d of debt and from damages 20d which it is ordered to raise to the use of the aforesaid Thomas Jenkys so the same John is in mercy
The next [court]	William Gerbode plaintiff of William Yate in a plea of trespass pledge for the prosecution John Snell so it is ordered to attach to the next [court]
The next [court]	William Gerbode plaintiff of John Broke in a plea of trespass pledge for the prosecution the beadle so it is ordered to attach to the next [court]
The next [court]	William Hockombe plaintiff of William Yate in a plea of trespass pledge for the prosecution the beadle so it is ordered to attach to the next [court]
The next [court]	William Hockombe plaintiff of John Broke in a plea of trespass pledge for the prosecution the beadle so it is ordered to attach to the next [court]
Inquiry pending	To this court came John Neeldone son of Stephen Neeldone & gives to the lady for a fine 2s pledge for the fine John Baret for an inquiry to be held of the 24 to enquire & present on oath whether he has the better right in his claim to hold one messuage with half a virgate of land with their appurtenances in Stanlowe as of the right of heredity after the death of Alice Neeldone [as] blood relative of the same Alice than John Yate has in his tenure. And on this the 24 thence charged & sworn went out & returned seek an adjournment to say the verdict until the next [court]. And they have a day until the next [court]
Fine 20d	At this court came William Skynner through John Baret, the beadle of the lady and surrendered into the hands of the lady one cottage with one selion of land with appurtenances in Roughtone called the Forgecroft to the use of Joan Barndeley her heirs and assigns And on this in the same court came Joan & took from the lady the aforesaid Cottage with selion of land aforesaid with their appurtenances to hold to herself her heirs & assigns by services thence owed & of right accustomed & according to the custom of the manor And she gave to the lady for fine 20d and thence has seisin & made fealty
Inquiry pending to the next by the prayer of the parties	At this court the inquiry pending between John Rowlowe Joneson plaintiff & John Bene & Margery his wife defendants concerning a plea of land is adjourned by the prayer of the parties until the next [court]
Fine 6s 8d	To this court came William Rys through John Baret the beadle of the lady & surrendered into the hands of the lady one toft of land one together with 2 crofts of land with their appurtenances in Worfeld which Alice Harries formerly held there to the use of William Wermode & Joan his wife, their heirs & assigns. And on this in the same court came the aforesaid William & Joan & took from the lady the aforesaid toft with the aforesaid 2 crofts of land with their appurtenances to hold to the same William & Joan his wife, their heirs & assigns by services thence owed and of right accustomed & according to the custom of the manor. And they give to the lady for a fine 6s 8d
Fine for suit of court to be commuted 12d	To this court came John Hultone & made a fine with the lady for suit of court to be commuted from the feast of the Annunciation of the Blessed Mary the Virgin in the year aforesaid until the same feast henceforth next in the future for one whole year 12d

1428-1429 P314/W/1/1/274

Inquiry adjourned by the prayer of the parties until the next [court]	Still the inquiry of the 24 jurors adjourned between Thomas Bradeney plaintiff & Hugh Baker & Agnes his wife defendants in a plea of a certain meadow called Torremedewe is adjourned by the prayer of the parties until the next [court]
	Sum of this Court 53s 8d Thence in expenses of the steward & other officials of the lady being there for 2 days & 2 nights with four horses 10s
Worfeld	Small court held there on Thursday next after the feast of the Invention of the Sacre Cross in the seventh year of the reign of King Henry VI [5 May 1429]
Essoins	John Walker, Roger Dalley, John Jannen, John Colyns, Thomas Colyar, John Bene, John Bromley of Adlescote
Essoin	Matilda Jenkyns defendant essoined herself from her wager at law at the last court against Thomas Jenkys in a plea of trespass
The 12	John Jonesone, Thomas Underhull, John Bromley, Roger Swankote, Richard Haselwode, Robert Brugende, William Wermode, Robert Webbe, Thomas Preestes, JohnWaltone, Roger Gerbode, Roger Kyngeslowe } sworn
The law	Roger Jenkys plaintiff of Thomas Jenkys in a plea of debt pledge for the prosecution John Cattestre. And whence he complains that the aforesaid Thomas owes him 15s & unjustly detains because the same Roger worked with the aforesaid Thomas for sixty days at harvest time during a time of seven years now past & nothing was paid to him. And the aforesaid Thomas present in court to answer says that he owes him nothing nor unjustly detains nor no agreement was made with him. And he is to the law with six hands at the next [court] pledge for the law John Snell & John Dawe
To recover Amerced 6d	Thomas Undurhull plaintiff of John Taylour in a plea of debt pledge for the prosecution John Baret. And whence he complains that he owes him 20d & unjustly detains which he agreed to pay on the feast of St Andrew last past. And the aforesaid John present in court to respond well recognised the debt aforesaid so it is judged that the same Thomas recovers the debt aforesaid and the same John is in mercy
Amerced 4d	The aforesaid jury presents that Thomas Richardes (4d) did not come to warrant his essoin so he is in mercy
Amerced 6d	Roger Dalley plaintiff & Thomas Jenkys defendant in a plea of trespass are for a licence to agree so the same Thomas (6d) withdrew from court so in mercy
Amerced 6d	William Hewstar plaintiff & Henry Wevar defendant in a plea of debt are for a licence to agree so the same Henry (6d) withdrew from court so in mercy
It is ordered to attach Amerced 6d	Thomas Jenkys plaintiff appeared himself against William Ingemon in a plea of broken agreement & the same William is attached & did not come so he is in mercy & it is ordered to better attach to the next [court]

Amerced 12d
It is ordered to distrain to the next [court]

Thomas Undurhull, Thomas Toward, & William Bakus plaintiffs appeared themselves against John Colyns in a plea of trespass & the same John is attached & did not come & has made five more defaults so in mercy & it is ordered to better distrain until the next

It is ordered to distrain to the next [court]
Amerced 4d

Edmund Burnell through John Snell his attorney plaintiff of William Ingemon in a plea of debt & the same William is attached & did not come so he is in mercy & it is ordered to better distrain to the next [court] it is void [vacat seems to have been added later]

Adjourned to the next

Also the aforesaid 12 jurors present that Agnes Trecyll widow married herself to John Crochurste without a licence from the lady so a fine thence adjourned until the next

Fine 5s

To this court came William Hewstar & Agnes his wife & the same Agnes duly confessed & examined before the steward surrendered into the hands of the lady through John Baret the beadle of the lady one toft with one nook of land with its appurtenances in Halen called Ingebrondeslond to the use of Roger the son of Henry Barker his heirs & assigns. And on this in the same court came the aforesaid Roger & took from the lady the aforesaid toft with the nook of land aforesaid with its appurtenances to hold from the lady to himself, his heirs & assigns for ever by services thence owed & of right accustomed & according to the custom of the manor. And he gives to the lady for a fine 5s. And thence he has seisin. And he made fealty

Fine 15s

To this court came William Goold & Margery his wife & the same Margery duly confessed & examined before the steward according to the custom of the manor through John Baret the beadle of the lady & Henry Webbe & Alice his wife in their own persons & the same Alice duly confessed & examined before the steward according to the custom of the manor surrendered into the hands of the lady one messuage with three nooks of land with its appurtenances in Hultone called Goldesplace to the use of John Hulle & Agnes the heirs & assigns of the same John. And on this in the same court came the aforesaid John & Agnes his wife & took from the lady the aforesaid messuage with the three nooks of land aforesaid with its appurtenances to hold to the same John & Agnes the heirs & assigns of the same John from the lady under a rent of 6s 8d & by other services owed & of right accustomed & according to the custom of the manor. And they give to the lady for a fine 15s. And thence have seisin. And made fealty

It is ordered The next [court]

William Gerbode plaintiff appeared himself against William Yate in a plea of trespass & the same William still just as at the last court is not attached so it is ordered to attach to the next [court]

The next [court]

William Gerbode plaintiff of John Broke in a plea of trespass & the same John still is not attached just as was ordered to the beadle so it is ordered to attach to the next [court]

The next [court]

William Gerbode plaintiff of John Broke in a plea of trespass & the same John still is not attached so it is ordered to attach to the next [court]

1428-1429 P314/W/1/1/274

The next [court] — William Hockombe plaintiff appeared himself against William Yate in a plea of trespass & the same William just as was ordered to the beadle still is not attached so it is ordered to attach to the next [court]

The next [court] — William Hockombe plaintiff appeared himself against John Broke in a plea of trespass & the same John still is not attached so it is ordered to attach to the next [court]

Inquiry pending until the next — Still the inquiry of the 24 pending between Thomas Bradeney plaintiff & Hugh Baker & Agnes his wife defendants in a plea of a certain meadow called Torremedewe adjourned by the prayer of the parties to the next [court]

Inquiry pending until the next — Still the inquiry pending between John Rowlowe Jonesone plaintiff & John Bene & Margery his wife defendants in a plea of land by the prayer of the parties adjourned to the next [court]

Inquiry pending until the next — Still the inquiry pending between John Neeldone petitioner & John Yate defendant in a plea of land by the prayer of the parties adjourned to the next [court]

Sum of this Court 23s 6d
Thence in expenses of the steward 16d

1429-1430 P314/W/1/1/275

Worfeld	Great court held there on Monday next after the feast of St Michael the Archangel in the eighth year of the reign of King Henry VI after the conquest [3 October 1429]
Essoins	Thomas Prestes, John Billyngesley senior, Roger Gyllone, Thomas Cattestre, John Holigreve, William Oldyntone, William Hockombe, John Smyth, John Colettes, John Rogerus, William Wermode, Roger Knyght, Roger Jones, William Barewe, Roger Swancote these essoined themselves by John Roo
The 12	Robert Webbe, John Janne, John Jowkys, Stephen Bradeney, Thomas Toward, William Barker, John Colynssone, Roger Gerbode, John Jonesone, Thomas Undurhull, Roger Kyngeslowe, John Waltone } sworn
The tasters of ale Amerced 12d	present that Stephen Hymley (4d) brewed 1, John Byllyngesley junior (4d) brewed 1, John Clerke (4d) brewed 1 and broke the assize so they [are] in mercy
Hultone	township there presents nothing but all well. Chesturtone township there presents nothing but all well.
Burkote, Burkote, Ryndelford, Bromley Stray 40d	townships there present 1 male foal coming as a stray price 40d first seized in the feast of the Finding of the Holy Cross last past and it remains in the custody of Thomas Hichekocus and it is ordered to the beadle to sell dearer if he can
Rowghtone, Barndeley, Hockombe, Swankote	townships there present nothing but all well. Oldyntone, Ewdenas townships there present nothing but all well.
Worfeld Amerced 2s 4d	township there presents that William Kyng (4d) forestalled Margery Herkedale against the peace of the lord King. Also they present that the aforesaid Margery (4d) forestalled the aforesaid William Kyng against the peace of the lord King so they [are] in mercy. Also they present that Roger Barker (4d) ought to enclose and keep safe one well called Ingerbrondwell & it lies open which is to the grave nuisance of all the tenants there so he [is] in mercy. Also they present that John Rowlowe (8d) made an assault on the aforesaid Roger Barker against the peace of the lord King. Also they present that John Jonesone (8d) made an assault on the aforesaid Roger Barker against the peace of the lord King so they [are] in mercy.
Rowlowe, Bradeney, Asturhull, Ewyk & Sonede Strays price 12d still not forfeited	townships there present that 1 brown male foal came as a stray price 12d first seized at the feast of St Peter in Chains last past and it remains in the custody of John Colynssone
Kyngeslowe, Stanlowe Stray 10d	townships there present that one two-tooth sheep came as a stray price 10d first seized at the feast of St Chad the Biship last past and it remains in the custody of John Blakemere
Wyken Goods forfeited 4d Amerced 10d	township there presents that John Gerbode (6d) broke the pound of John Wylkys and thereafter unjustly took his own two horses so he [is] in mercy. Also they present one unknown woman came to the house of John Wylkys on a certain day & in the year aforesaid and entered the aforesaid house with force and arms and 1 linen cloth being in the aforesaid house unjustly took it and carried it away and

Wyken Goods forfeited 4d Amerced 10d	against the peace of the lord King. Also they present that Joan Mathewe (4d) wife of John Mathewe made an assault on Isabelle the daughter of Robert Taylour against the peace of the lord King.
Akyltone Amerced 6d	township there presents that the wife of John Taylour broke the pound of Thomas Tomkys & from there took her own 2 cows without a licence so she is in mercy
Stapulford	township there presents nothing but all well.
Amerced 6s 8d	The aforesaid jury present that William Ingemone disobeyed the arrest by the steward and fled from the domain
Fine 4d	To this court came William Barewe & made a fine with the steward to brew ale from the date of this court until the feast of the Annunciation of the Blessed Virgin Mary next in the future 4d
Fine 12d	To this court came Alice at Sonede & made a fine with the steward to brew ale from the date of this court until the feast of St Michael the Archangel next in the future 12d
Fine 8d	To this court came Alice Galian & made a fine with the steward to brew ale from the date of this court until the feast of St Michael the Archangel next in the future
Put in the tithing	Thomas the son of Roger Townesende is put in a tithing and is sworn
	The aforesaid jurors present that the aforesaid townships have well and faithfully presented & concealed nothing
Election of the tasters of ale	At this court John Beene & Robert Taylour are elected into the office of tasters of ale and are sworn

Sum of this Court 18s 10d
Thence in expenses of the steward and other ministers of the lady 11s

Worfeld	Small court held there on Tuesday next after the feast of St Michael the Archangel in the eighth year of the reign of King Henry VI after the conquest [4 October 1429]
Essoins	Henry Halle, John Smyth, Thomas Richardes, Roger Jones, John Holygreve, John Cattestre, Roger Barker son of Robert Barker these essoined themselves for common suit by John Snell
Whence the law	Roger Jenkys himself against Thomas Jenkys wagered his law at the preceding court whence the law

The 12	Robert Webbe	John Janne	John Jowkys }	
	Stephen Bradeney	Thomas Toward	William Barker }	sworn
	John Colynssone	Roger Gerbode	John Jonesone }	
	Thomas Undurhull	Roger Kyngeslowe	John Waltone }	

The jurors present	The aforesaid jurors present that Elys Mustardmon who from the lady held one cottage with curtilage adjoining and one other curtilage with their appurtenances in Worfield died concerning which many years have elapsed & no heriot has fallen due because she had none on the day of her death. And they say also that John

Elkoc son of the aforesaid Elys has entered the aforesaid cottage with curtilage with their aforesaid appurtenances not obtaining a licence of the lady so it is ordered to seize the aforesaid cottage with curtilage into the hands of the lady until etc. Also they present that Alice Gerbode who of the lady held one cottage with curtilage with their appurtenances in Worfeld died after the last court and no heriot has fallen to the lady because she had none on the day she died. And the cottage remains in the hands of the lady until etc.

Elected reeve — At this court John Bradeney of Bradeney is elected to the office of reeve & is sworn

Fine 10s — To this court came William Gerbode and surrendered into the hands of the lady one toft with half a virgate of land with its appurtenances in Barndeley to the use of Roger Gerbode son of the aforesaid William & Agnes his wife their heirs and assigns. And on this in the same court came the aforesaid Roger & Agnes his wife & took from the lady the aforesaid toft with half a virgate of land with its appurtenances to hold to the same Roger & Agnes their heirs and assigns for ever to hold from the lady of that fee by services thence owed & of right accustomed & according to the custom of the manor. And they give to the lady for a fine for ingress & seisin thence to have 10s pledge for the fine John Snell. And made fealty

Fine 2s — To this court came Agnes Trecyll & made a fine with the lady to marry herself to John Crochurste outside the domain wheresoever it will have pleased her 2s pledge for the fine John Snell

for copy; Fine 5s — To this court came John Crochurste & Agnes his wife and surrendered into the hands of the lady one messuage with one nook of land with its appurtenances in Halen as of the right of the same Agnes and thus the aforesaid messuage with the nook of land with its appurtenances remains in the hands of the lady until etc. And on this in the same court came the aforesaid John & Agnes his wife & took from the lady the aforesaid messuage with the nook of land aforesaid with its appurtenances to hold to the same John & Agnes the heirs and assigns of the same Agnes to hold from the lady of that fee by services thence owed & of right accustomed & according to the custom of the manor. And they give to the lady for a fine for ingress & seisin thence to have 5s pledge for the fine John Snell. And made fealty

Fine 6d — To this court came Agnes Tetenhale formerly the servant of William Trecill clerk through William Wermode tenant of the lady and surrendered into the hands of the lady one meadow called Stokyng medewe with its appurtenances in Sonede which Nicholas Rowlowe formerly held there to the use of John Rowlowe son of the aforesaid Nicholas Rowlowe his heirs and assigns. And on this in the same court came the aforesaid John & took from the lady the aforesaid meadow with its appurtenances to hold to the same John his heirs and assigns for ever by services thence owed & of right accustomed & according to the custom of the manor. And he gives to the lady for a fine for ingress & seisin thence to have 6d. And he made fealty. And that in the same court came Richard Parlour of Bruggenorth & John son of the same Richard & remised and released to the aforesaid John Rowlowe his heirs and assigns all their rights & claims they have in the aforesaid meadow with its appurtenances for ever

Plea adjourned — The plea which is between William Gerbode plaintiff & William Yate defendant in a plea of trespass is adjourned by the prayer of the parties until the next [court]

Plea adjourned — The plea which is between William Gerbode plaintiff & John Broke defendant in a plea of trespass adjourned by the prayer of the parties until the next [court]

1429-1430 P314/W/1/1/275

Assessment pending until the next [court]

John Preestes plaintiff of Roger the son of Henry Barker in a plea of trespass. And whence he complains that the aforesaid Roger unjustly cut the crop & lop of one oak of the aforesaid John price 8d growing in a certain field in Halen called Chelmechilfeld & from thence took and carried away to the damage of the aforesaid John of 6d. And the aforesaid Roger present in court responded saying that he took nor carried away unjustly as stated & alleged against him no crop & lop of no oak. And on this he put himself on the assessment of the township of Halen & the aforesaid John similarly until the next [court]. And on this the township aforesaid are thence charged and sworn

The law

John Preestes plaintiff of the aforesaid Roger Barker in a plea of trespass. And whence he complains that the aforesaid Roger unjustly ploughed one parcel of land of the same John being at the end of a croft of the aforesaid John in Halen aforesaid. And the aforesaid Roger present in court to respond says that in nothing is he thence to blame. And he is to the law with six hands at the next [court] pledge for the law Hamo Hymley & Richard Roo

Plea adjourned

The plea which is between William Hockombe plaintiff & William Yate defendant in a plea of trespass is adjourned by the prayer of the parties until the next [court]

It is ordered to distrain to the next [court]

William Hockombe plaintiff appeared himself against John Broke in a plea of trespass & the same John is summoned & does not come so it is ordered to attach to the next [court]

Inquiry pending

The inquiry pending between Thomas Bradeney plaintiff & Hugh Baker & Agnes his wife defendants in a plea of one meadow in Torremedewe. And thence the 24 have a day thence to say the verdict until the next [court] under pain of 6s 8d for each of them not coming

Amerced 6d

Thomas Undurhull, Thomas Toward & William Bakus plaintiffs in a plea of trespass & William Colyns defendant are for a licence to agree & the same William Colyns withdrew from the court so he [is] in mercy

Fine 14d

To this court came John Elkoc & took from the lady one cottage with curtilage adjacent with its appurtenances in Worfeld & one other curtilage in the same township which Elys mustardmaker father of the aforesaid John formerly held there. To have and to hold to the same John, his heirs and assigns by services thence owed and of right accustomed & according to the custom of the manor. And he gives to the lady for a fine for ingress & seisin thence to have 14d & made fealty

Fine 40d

To this court came William Ewyke & made a fine with the lady for to have a licence to demise & grant to John Rowlowe son of Nicholas one messuage with 1 virgate of land with its appurtenances in Ewyke for the term of seven years next following after the present date 40d

Fine 40d

To this court came Thomas Yonge through Roger Townesende tenant of the lady & surrendered into the hands of the lady two cottages with three crofts of land with their appurtenances in Ryndelford to the use of John Walker of Ryndelford his heirs and assigns. And on this in the same court came the aforesaid John the son of John & took from the lady the aforesaid two cottages with the aforesaid three crofts with their appurtenances to hold to the same John the son of John his heirs and assigns by services thence owed and of right accustomed & according to the custom of the manor. And he gives to the lady for a fine for ingress & seisin thence to have 40d, pledge for the fine Roger Townesende & he made fealty

1429-1430 P314/W/1/1/275

Fine 4d

To this court came John Bradeney & surrendered into the hands of the lady one parrock of land lying at le Wyldemore & formerly was part of Turbervile lond to the use of John Hulle his heirs & assigns by services thence owed and of right accustomed & according to the custom of the manor. And he gives to the lady for a fine for ingress & seisin thence to have 4d & he made fealty

Fine 8d

To this court came John Elkoc & surrendered into the hands of the lady one cottage with curtilage adjacent with its appurtenances in Worfeld to the use of William Barewe & Margaret his wife the heirs and assigns of the same William. And on this in the same court came the aforesaid William & Margaret & took from the lady the aforesaid cottage with curtilage with its appurtenances to hold to the same William & Margaret the heirs and assigns of the same William by services thence owed and of right accustomed & according to the custom of the manor. And they give to the lady for a fine for ingress & seisin thence to have 8d & made fealty

Fine 6d

To this court came Thomas Bradeney & gives to the lady for a fine 6d for to have a licence to demise & hand over to John Rowlowe of Hultone one parrock called the mersche lying in Hultone for the term of six years next following after the date of this court

Fine 4d

To this court came John Jonesone & surrendered into the hands of the lady one parrock of land with its appurtenances in Chesturtone in a certain place called Streford to the use of John Rowlowe of Hultone his heirs and assigns. And in the same court came the aforesaid John Rowlowe of Hultone & took from the lady the aforesaid parrock of land with its appurtenances to hold to himself, his heirs and assigns by services thence owed and of right accustomed & according to the custom of the manor. And thence he has seisin and made fealty.And he gives to the lady for a fine 4d.

Fine 5s

To this court came Thomas Jenkys junior & took from the lady one messuage with one toft & one cottage with their appurtenances in Rowghtone as of the right of the same Thomas after the death of Thomas Jenkys father of the aforesaid Thomas Jenkys junior to hold to the same Thomas Jenkys junior his heirs and assigns for ever by services thence owed and of right accustomed & according to the custom of the manor. And he gives to the lady for a fine for ingress & seisin thence to have 5s & made fealty

Inquiry pending

Still the inquiry pending between John Jonesone & John Bene & Margery his wife defendants in a plea of land by the prayer of the parties is adjourned until the next [court]

Election of beadle

At this court William Wermode is elected to the office of beadle and is sworn

Amerced 4d the next

Edward Burnell plaintiff appeared against William Ingeman in a plea of debt & the same William is attached and did not come so it is ordered to retain and better distrain to the next and the same William thus [is] in mercy

Amerced 4d the next

Thomas Jenkys plaintiff appeared against William Ingemon in a plea of debt & the same William is attached and did not come so he [is] in mercy & it is ordered to better distrain to the next [court]

Sum of this Court 33s 4d
Expenses nothing because in the court preceding

1429-1430 P314/W/1/1/275

	Small court held there on Wednesday on the feast of the Conversion of St Paul in the eighth year of the reign of King Henry VI after the conquest [25 January 1430]
Essoins	John Bradeney of Hultone, Roger Hulle, John Yate, Roger Jenkys, John Bromley of Adlescote, John Walker, John Whitebrok, Roger Kyngeslowe these essoined themselves through John Snell the bailiff
The 12	Stephen Bradeney, Roger Townesende, Robert Bruggende, Robert Webbe, Roger Gerbode, Thomas Preestes, Richard Haselwode, William Wermode, William Yate, Thomas Undurhull, John Bromley, John Colettes } sworn
The law	Roger Barker essoined himself from his wager of law at the preceding court against John Preestes in a plea of trespass one law
Adjourned	Still the assessment pending between John Preestes plaintiff & Roger Barker defendant in a plea of trespass by the prayer of the parties is adjourned until the next [court]
It is ordered	William Hockombe plaintiff appeared against John Broke in a plea of trespass and the same John still is not attached so it is ordered to attach to the next [court]
Amerced 4d It is ordered to better distrain	Thomas Jenkys plaintiff of William Ingemon in a plea of trespass pledge for the prosecution John Snell. And the same William is attached by one sow price 2s and did not come so he [is] in mercy & it is ordered to retain & better distrain to the next [court]
It is ordered	William Gerbode plaintiff appeared against John Broke in a plea of trespass & the same John still is not attached so it is ordered to attach to the next [court]
Fine 12d	William Byllyngesley came here in court & made a fine with the steward to brew ale from the feast of St Michael the Archangel last past until at the aforesaid feast of St Michael the Archangel now next following
Amerced 6d	Roger Jenkys is not prosecuting his plea in a plea of debt against Thomas Jenkys so he [is] in mercy
Fine 8d	William Kyng made a fine with the steward to brew ale from the feast of St Michael the Archangel last past until the same feast of St Michael the Archangel now next following
Amerced 6d	Richard Smyth plaintiff & Henry Webbe defendant in a plea of trespass are for a licence to agree & the same Henry withdrew from the court so he [is] in mercy
It is ordered	Thomas Undurhull plaintiff of John Taylour in a plea of trespass & the same John is summoned and did not come so it is ordered to attach to the next [court]
Heriot 4s Heriot 14d Escheat 16d	The aforesaid 12 jurors charged & sworn went out & returned. Who say on their oath that Matilda formerly the wife of Thomas Jenkys who held from the lady for the term of her life one toft & one virgate of land with its appurtenances in Rowghtone & one messuage with one nook of land with their appurtenances in the same township & one cottage with its appurtenances in the same township has died

after the last court whence there falls to the lady one black heifer in the name of heriot as for the toft & virgate of land aforesaid price 4s. Also there fell to the lady one white sheep in the name of heriot as for the messuage & nook of land aforesaid price 14d which land & tenements she held for the term of the life of the aforesaid Matilda. Also there falls to the lady one pig for escheat price 16d. And one one other pig price 16d killed on the day of the death of the aforesaid Matilda whether they ought to do legitimately by their custom or not is to be enquired at the next. Also they present one black draught animal coming from escheat formerly of Thomas Jenkys senior price 12d & it remains in the custody of Thomas Jenkys junior and it is ordered to the beadle to sell the aforesaid draught animal at a greater profit to the lady by which he can

To enquire at the next

It is ordered

Also they present that Thomas the son of John Walker burned one oak growing in the wood of Sowdeley so he is to make a fine with the steward at the next court. Also the aforesaid jury seek an adjournment until the next to enquire ———& present on oath whether Stephen the son of John Rowlow burned gorse in Sowdeley or William the servant of John Byllyngesley of Wyke so it is being enquired

The next

Inquiry

A pain of 40d is put on Richard Parlour that he well & competently repairs & improves the bridge being between the fulling mill of Ryndelford & the mill of the lady there on this side of the feast of the Purification of the Blessed Virgin Mary next in the future

Pain

Still the plea which is between William Gerbode plaintiff & John Yate defendant in a plea of trespass in 2 pleas by the prayer of the parties is adjourned to the next [court]

Adjourned

Henry Barker plaintiff of John Rowlowe of Hultone in a plea of detention of goods & chattels pledge for the prosecution Roger Barker so it is ordered to attach to the next [court]

To the next [court]

Still the inquiry pending between Thomas Bradeney plaintiff & Hugh Baker & Agnes his wife defendants in a plea of one meadow in Torremedewe. And thence the 24 have a day for the verdict thence to say until the next [court] under a pain of 6s 8d on each of them not coming

Inquiry pending

Still the inquiry pending between John Jonesone plaintiff & John Bene & Margery his wife defendants in a plea of land by the prayer of the parties is adjourned until the next [court]

Inquiry pending

Sum of the Court 9s 6d And of the price of one draught animal
Thence in expenses of the steward 17d And for parchment 4d

1430 P314/W/1/1/276

Worfeld	Great court held there on the sixth of April in the eighth year of the reign of King Henry VI [6 April 1430]
Essoins	John Waltone, John Jowkys, John Crochurst, Roger Townesende, William Barker, Henry Wevar, William Gerbode all of them essoined themselves from common suit through John Was
The 12	Richard Parlour, Thomas Thomkys, John Colynssone, Robert Webbe, William Wermod, Thomas Undurhull, Richard Haselwode, Roger Kyngeslowe, John Bromley, Robert Bruggende, Roger Gerbode, Thomas Toward } sworn
The tasters of ale Amerced 16d	The tasters of ale present that Richard Smyth (4d) brewed 1 & broke the assize. Also they present that William Byllyngesley(4d), William Barewe (4d), Alice Sonede (4d), sold ale from before it was tasted by the tasters so they [are] in mercy
Hultone Stray price 4s 6d so let it be proclaimed	township there presents that one brown cow came as a stray price 4s 6d first seized on the feast of All Saints last past and it remains in the custody of Thomas Baker so it is ordered to make a proclamation
Kyngeslowe & Stanlowe Stray price 2s so let it be proclaimed	townships there present one grey (grisen) draught animal coming as a stray price 2s and it remains in the custody of John Blakemere first seized on the feast of St Luke the Evangelist last past so let it be proclaimed
Wyken	township there presents nothing but all well. Chesturtone township there presents nothing but all well. Cattestre, Alvescote, Wynskote, Newtone townships there present nothing but all well.
Burkote, Burkote, Ryndelford, Bromley Strays 6d & 8d	townships there present one grey (grisen) draught animal coming as a stray price 6d and it remains in the custody of John John Bromley first seized before the feast of St Luke the Evangelist last past. Also they present one two tooth sheep of white colour coming as a stray price 8d and it remains in the custody of William Bromley first seized at the feast of St Peter in Chains last past
Rowlowe, Bradeney, Asturhull, Ewyke, Sonede Strays 2s Amerced 6d	townships there present that 2 two tooth sheep came as strays price of each of them 12d & they remain in the custody of John Colynsone & one of them was seized at the feast of St St Michael the Archangel & the other at the feast of St Peter in Chains last past. Also they present that William Byllyngesley (6d) son of John Byllyngesley forestalled Thomas Smyth against the peace of the King so he [is] in mercy
Worfeld Amerced 8d	township there presents that Joan Walsche (8d) forestalled Alice Herkedale & against the peace of the lord King so she [is] in mercy
Akyltone Strays 16d Let it be proclaimed	township there present that 2 two tooth sheep came as strays price 16d & they remain in the custody of John Baret seized at the feast of St St Michael last past so let it be proclaimed
Chesturtone	township there presents nothing but all well.
Roughtone, Barndeley, Hockombe, Swankote	townships there present nothing but all well.

Stapulforde Stray 9d	township there presents one two tooth sheep came as a stray price 9d seized at the feast of All Saints last past and it remains in the custody of Roger Swankote
Halen Amerced 2s 1d	township there presents that John Preestes (4d) forestalled William Barker against the peace of the King. Also they present that Joan Walsche (4d) unjustly on a certain day & year took one linen cloth price 4d from the goods & chattels of Matilda Byllyngesley & against the peace of the lord King. Also they present that John Cattestre found in his barn one sheaf of corn price 1d by whom it was abandoned he doesn't know. Also they present that Roger (12d) the son of Henry Barker unjustly ploughed one common path leading from the village of Halen to the field of maswardyn which is to the grave nuisance of the tenants there so he [is] in mercy
Oldyntone, Ewdenas Amerced 10d	townships there present that Richard Mynsturley (6d) & Sibill his mother made a pound breach so they [are] in mercy. Also they present that William Newtone (4d) chaplain did not come to make suit
	Sum of this Court 5s 5d strays excepted
	Small court held there on the seventh day of April in the year above said [7 April 1430]
Essoins	John Yate, John Smyth, William Bromley, John Janne, John Bromley, John Waltone, essoined themselves from suit of court through John Baret
The 12	Robert Webbe, Robert Bruggende, Thomas Preestes, Stephen Bradeney, Richard Haselwode, John Colettes, John Jonesone, John Bromley, Roger Townessende, Thomas Undurhull, William Wermode, Thomas Toward } sworn
Escheat 12d	Thomas Jenkys junior has to respond to the lady concerning the price of one draught animal for the escheat formerly of Thomas Jenkys junior 12d
Amerced 6d	Thomas Jenkys junior plaintiff appeared himself against William Ingemon (6d) in a plea of trespass. And the same William is attached by one sow price 20d and did not come so he [is] in mercy & it is ordered to retain & better distrain to the next [court]
Amerced 6d	William Gerbode plaintiff & John Broke defendant in a plea of trespass are for a licence to agree & the same William withdrew from the court
Amerced 6d	Roger Barker defaulted from his law against John Preestes so the same Roger is in mercy
Amerced 6d	Roger Barker plaintiff & John Preestes defendant are for a licence to agree & the same Roger withdrew from the court
Amerced 6d	William Hockombe plaintiff & William Yate defendant are for a licence to agree & the same William Yate withdrew from the court
Amerced 6d	William Hockombe plaintiff & John Broke defendant in a plea of trespass are for a licence to agree & the same William withdrew from the court
Amerced 6d	Henry Barker plaintiff & John Rowlowe of Hulton defendant in a plea of unjust detention of goods & chattels are for a licence to agree & William Barker & John Elkoc through their agreement withdrew from the court

1430 P314/W/1/1/276

The aforesaid 12 jurors present that William Byllyngesley junior (4d), John Barker (4d), Roger (4d) the servant of Henry Barker (4d), the son (4d) of Roger Townessende the son of Agnes Heyne of Wyke (4d), the servant of John Bradeney, Henry Wevar (4d), John (4d) the servant of Thomas Toward (4d), Henry Kyng (4d), John Bradeney of Hultone (4d), Stephen Rowlowe (4d), Richard Undurhull (4d), of Akyltone, John Clerk, the son of William Yate (4d), fished in the severalty waters of the lady without a licence so they are in mercy

Amerced 5s 4d

To this court came William Barewe & took from the lady one toft with one held and 2 headlands of land with their appurtenances in Worfeld which Henry Wevar formerly held there to hold to the same William for the term of his life under a rent of 2s to be paid at the usual times there & other services according to the custom of the manor. And he gives to the lady nothing for a fine because it is exceedingly barren. And thence he has seisin & made fealty

Taking of land

Amerced 4d

To this court came John Walker (4d) & made a fine with the lady for a trespass made on the heath of the lady there just as was presented at the last small court so he [is] in mercy

Also the aforesaid jury of the court present that William (4d) the servant of John Byllyngesley burned heath in the wood of the lady so he is in mercy

To this court came Margery Richardes and surrendered into the hands of the lady one messuage with half a virgate of land with its appurtenances in Newtone to the use of Thomas Richardes & Agnes his wife. And on this in the same court came the aforesaid Thomas & Agnes & took from the lady the aforesaid messuage with half a virgate of land with its appurtenances to hold to the same Thomas & Agnes their heirs and assigns for ever by services thence owed & of right accustomed for ever & according to the custom of the manor. And they give to the lady for a fine 10s & are seized & made fealty. Pledges for the fine John Baret & William Neutone clerk

Fine 10s

To this court came Margery Richardes who holds from the lady one toft with one nook of land with its appurtenances in Newtone for the term of her life the reversion pertaining, after the death of the same Margery Thomas Richardes son and heir of Roger Richardes surrendered into the hands of the lady the aforesaid toft with one the nook of land aforesaid with its appurtenances to the use of the aforesaid Thomas Richardes to hold to the same Thomas, his heirs & assigns by services thence owed & of right accustomed & according to the custom of the manor. And he gives to the lady for a fine 12d And made fealty

Fine 12d

Also the aforesaid jury present that Roger Cattestre (4d) who owed suit & did not come. Also they present that John Taylour (4d), William Byllyngesley of Wyke (4d), John White (4d), William Hewstar of Brugge (4d), Roger Gerbode of Wyke (4d), fished in the severalty water of the lady without a licence so they are in mercy

Amerced 2s

The plea which is between Thomas Undurhull plaintiff & John Taylour defendant by the prayer of the parties adjourned until the next

The next

Goods forfeit 12d

And that the beadle has to respond to the lady concerning 12d of certain goods forfeited by Joan Skydmore because she made a trespass within the domain

1430 P314/W/1/1/276

Pain	A pain is put on the lessees of the mills Worfeld & Ryndelford that they will well and adequately repair & maintain the aforesaid mills & that they will well and adequately repair the aforesaid mills in everything before the feast of St Michael the Archangel next in the future under a pain of each of the mills of 6s 8d
Pain	A pain of 40d is put on all the tenants & residents of Worfeldehome that none of them receive nor harbour Joan Skydmore by day or by night at any time in the future
Amerced 6d	John Preestes & Laurence the servant of Richard Archer plaintiff of Richard Mynsturley defendant in a plea of debt are for a licence to agree
The next	Henry Parsones plaintiff of Henry Wevar in a plea of detention of goods & chattels pledge for the prosecution John White & John Roo so it is ordered to attach to the next
Increase 2d	And that the beadle has to respond to the lady concerning 2d of increase of one two tooth sheep sold to John Blakemere

Sum of the Court 25s 10d
Thence in expenses of the steward 12s

Small court held there on Tuesday next after the feast of St Dunstan the Bishop in the eighth year of the reign of King Henry VI [23 May 1430]

Essoins	Thomas at Sonede, John Walker, John Whitebrok, Henry Barker, John Smyth, Roger Jones, John Mathewe, Thomas Richarde, William Yate, John Crochurste these essoined themselves from suit through the beadle

	Stephen Bradeney	John Janne	John Bromley }	
	Roger Townessende	William Wermode	William Gerbode }	sworn
	Thomas Undurhull	Thomas Toward	John Byllyngesley }	
The 12	Roger Gerbode	Robert Bruggende	John Colettes }	

The next The law	John Trecyll plaintiff of John Rogeres in a plea of trespass. And whence he complains that the same John Rogeres cut down a certain crop of oak growing in one hedge being between the metes & bounds of Alveskote & Ryndelford to the damage of the aforesaid plaintiff of 12d. And the same John Rogeres thence wagered the law that in nothing is he thence guilty pledge for the law John Rowlowe & John at Stile with six hands at the next [court]
6d	Thomas Undurhull plaintiff & John Taylour defendant in a plea of trespass are for a licence to agree and the same John withdrew from the court
Fine 10s	John Hulle & Agnes his wife came here in court before the steward & the same Agnes duly confessed & examined according to the custom of the manor by John Baret the beadle of the lady & and surrendered into the hands of the lady one toft with half a virgate of land with its appurtenances in Halen to the use of Henry Wevar & Alice his wife his wife. And on this in the same court came the aforesaid Henry & Alice & took from the lady the aforesaid toft with half a virgate of land with its appurtenances to hold to the same Henry & Alice their heirs and assigns for ever to hold from the lady by services thence owed & of right accustomed & according to the custom of the manor. And they give to the lady for a fine 10s & thence have seisin & made fealty. Pledges for the fine William Gold & Richard Smyth

20d	And that the beadle has to respond to the lady concerning 20d for the last year past for on pasture called Sowdeley
Taking of one stakyng & increased rent 4d	To this court came Richard Gerbode & gives to the lady for a fine 4d for a licence to have to make one stakyng in a certain place called Bettemore being beside the meadow of John Colettes called Waturlademedewe to hold to the same Richard for the term of seven years next following after the present date under a rent of 4d
	Affeerors: Robert Webbe, Roger Kyngeslowe } sworn

Sum of the Court 12s 6d
Expenses of the steward 18d

Small court held there on Wednesday on the feast of St Anne the mother of Mary in the eighth year of the reign of King Henry VI after the conquest [26 July 1430]

Essoins	John Walker, John Mathewe, Thomas Richardes, essoined themselves from common suit			
	Robert Webbe	Thomas Toward	Roger Kyngeslowe }	
The 12 jurors	John Jonesone	John Jannen	John Bromley	} sworn
	William Wermode	Roger Gerbode	Roger Townessende }	
	Thomas Undurhull	Stephen Bradeney	Richard Haselwode }	

Completed the law 6d	To this court came John Rogers & completed his law towards John Trecyll in a plea of trespass so it is judged that the same John Rogers retired quit and the same John Trecyll should go without a day & is in mercy for his unjust plea
Amerced 6d	John Cattestre plaintiff of Richard Smyth in a plea of debt And he complains that he owes him 4s 8d and unjustly detains. And the aforesaid Richard Smyth present in court to respond well recognised the debt aforesaid so it is judged that the same John should recover the aforesaid debt. And the same Richard is in mercy.
Amerced 8d	The aforesaid jury present that Henry Halle (2d), John Coletes (2d), John Smyth (2d), John Bradeney of Hultone (2d), who owe suit & did not come so they [are] in mercy
Amerced 6d	Richard Wylde plaintiff of Richard Smyth in a plea of debt. And whence he complains that he owes him 12d and unjustly detains. And the same Richard present in court to respond well recognised the debt aforesaid so it is judged that the same Richard Wylde should recover from the aforesaid the aforesaid debt. And the same Richard Smyth is in mercy
	Below the said jury present that William Hockombe (2d) & John Walton (2d) who owed suit of court & did not come so they are in mercy. Also they present that John Taylour (4d) & Richard Smyth (4d) fished in the severalty water of the lady there so they [are] in mercy

Sum of the Court 3s 2d
Thence in expenses of the steward 14d

1430-1431 P314/W/1/1/277

Worfeld	Great court held there on Wednesday next after the feast of St Michael the Archangel in the ninth year of the reign of King Henry VI after the conquest [4 October 1430]
Essoins	John Whitebrok, William Beore, John Holigreve, John Byllyngesley, Roger Jones, Richard Ingemon, John Smyth, John Trecyll, Thomas Cattestre, Roger Gyllen, Roger Swankote, Roger Kyngeslowe, William Bowlas, Henry Hulle these essoined themselves from common suit through John Jacke
The 12	Robert Webbe, Thomas Tomkys, William Wermode, John Waltone, Stephen Bradeney, Thomas Undurhull, Roger Gerbode, Thomas Toward, Thomas Preestes, John Blakemere, John Jonesone, Roger Townesende } sworn
Hultone	township there presents nothing but all [is] well. Rowlowe, Bradeney, Asturhull, Ewyk, Sonde townships there present nothing but all [is] well
Burkote, Burkote, Ryndelford, Bromley Stray 4d	township there presents one two-tooth ewe came as a stray price 4d and it remains in the custody of Thomas Hichekocus forfeit
Ewdenas, Oldyngton	townships there present nothing but all [is] well
Chesturtone Amerced 8d	township there presents that John Hawkewode (6d) made an assault & homsoken on Sibill the wife of Thomas Colyar & hit her & from her drew blood against the peace of the King. Also they present that the aforesaid Sibill (2d) made an assault on the aforesaid John
The tasters of ale Amerced 2s	John Bene & Robert Mathewe the tasters of ale present that John Gerbode (4d) brewed 1, John Walker (4d) brewed 1, John Byllynggesley senior (4d) brewed 1, John Broke (4d) brewed 1 & broke the assize so they [are] in mercy. Also they present that Thomas at Sonede (4d) & Henry Webbe (4d) brewed ale and sold before it was tasted by the tasters so they are in mercy
Wyke Amerced 3s	township there presents that William Ingemon (12d) broke the arrest of the constables so he [is] in mercy. Also they present that the wife (10d) of Thomas Bradeney made an assault on the wife of John Gerbode & hit her & drew blood from her. Also they present that the wife of the aforesaid John Gerbode raised the hue & cry justly on the wife (4d) of the aforesaid Thomas Bradeney so she [is] in mercy. Also they present that the wife (4d) of the aforesaid John Gerbode made an assault on the wife of the aforesaid Thomas Bradeney so she [is] in mercy. Also they present that the wife (6d) of the aforesaid William Ingemon raised the hue & cry unjustly on the aforesaid constable so she [is] in mercy.
Rowghtone, Barndeley, Hockombe, Swankote	townships there present nothing but all [is] well. Stapulford township there presents nothing but all [is] well
Worfeld Amerced 16d	township there presents that William Gold (4d) forestalled Henry Wevar against the peace of the lord King. Also they present that Henry Wevar (4d) made an assault on Richard Beore again. Also they present that Margery Herdemon raised the hue & cry justly on William Kyng (4d). Also they present that Richard Beore (4d) made an assault on Henry Wevar against the peace of the lord King so he [is] in mercy

Halen
Strays 7d
Amerced 8d

township there presents one swarm of bees came as a stray price 4d and it remains in the custody of Roger Barker. Also they present that one other swarm of bees came as a stray price 3d and it remains in the custody of Roger Cattestre. Also they present that Roger (4d) the son of Henry Barker made an assault on William Barker. Also they present that the same William (4d) made an assault on the aforesaid Roger and drew blood from the same in defence so he is in mercy

Akyltone
Stray 4d

township there presents one swarm of bees came as a stray price 4d and it remains in the custody of Thomas Undurhull

Put in a tithing

At this court John Stevenes aged 16 years & more is put in a tithing & sworn

Strays 4s 6d
Dead in murrain
Stray 6d
Stray 8d
Strays 2s
Strays 16d
Stray 9d

At this court it is presented that at a court held at Worfeld on the sixth day of April in the eighth year of the reign of King Henry VI at which court the township of Hultone came & presented one brown cow came as a stray price 4s 6d now is forfeited & it remains in the custody of Roger Swankote. Also the townships of Kyngeslowe & Stanlowe presented at the same court one grey (grisen) draught animal came as a stray price 2s & was then in the custody of John Blakemere & is dead in murrain so nothing falls to the lady. Also Burkote, Burkote, Ryndelford & Bromley presented at the same court one grey (grisen) draught animal came as a stray price 6d & it remains in the custody of John Bromley is now forfeited. Also they presented one two-tooth sheep came as a stray price 8d & it remains in the custody of William Bromley is now forfeited. Rowlowe, Bradeney, Asturhull, Ewyk, Sonede townships there present that at the same court it was presented 2 two-tooth sheep came as strays price 2s & they remain in the custody of John Colynssone are forfeited. The township of Akyltone presented 2 two-tooth sheep came as strays now in the custody of John Baret price 16d are forfeited. Stapulford township there presents one two-tooth sheep came as a stray price 9d & it is in the custody of Roger Swankote

Abandoned goods

John Snell supervisor for the lady has to respond for 18d of abandoned goods one stranger namely of the price of one silver spoon

Fine 40d

And that to this court came Henry Wevar and made a fine with the lady because he unjustly and against the custom of the manor surrendered into the hands of the beadle under certain conditions one messuage with half a virgate of land so he is put at a fine of 40d

Fine 12d

Also it is ordered the beadle to raise from Edith Kyng namely for a fine to brew for the last year 12d

Amerced 18d
Goods forfeit 12d

Also the aforesaid 12 jurors present and say on their oath that Margery (6d) the servant of Roger Dalley unjustly took one bushel of barley and delivered it to the wife of Thomas Jenkys to the use of the aforesaid Margery price 6d . Also they present that Margery (6d) servant of the aforesaid Roger unjustly purloined and carried away a bushel of malt of dredge and delivered it to the aforesaid wife of Thomas Jenkys to the use of the same Margery price 6d. Also they present that Roger Dalley (4d) unjustly and without permission from Thomas Jenkys came to the house of the aforesaid Thomas & one two-tooth sheep and a lamb he being out of the aforesaid house he took but at that time the aforesaid two-tooth sheep and the lamb being in his fold he released them. Also they present that Roger Dalley (2d) came to the sheep-house of the aforesaid Thomas Jenkys unjustly and against the will of the same Thomas and on the lamb aforesaid put his own mark whether the aforesaid lamb belongs to the aforesaid Thomas or to the aforesaid Roger the 12 jurors don't know and seek an adjournment before the next [court] to enquire better

Sum of this Court 27s

Worfeld — Small Court held there on Thursday next after the Feast of St Michael the Archangel in the 9th year of the reign of King Henry VI [5 October 1430]

Essoins — Roger Jones, John Smyth, John Holigreve, John Bromley of Adlescote, Roger Hulle, William Yate, Thomas Undurhull, John Crokhurst these essoined thmselves from common suit through Roger Barker

the 12

John Colynssone	Roger Townsende	Thomas Thoward	}
Robert Webbe	Thomas Merwall	Richard Haselwode	} sworn
John Janne	William Wermode	Roger Gerbode	}
John Bromley	Roger Kyngeslowe	John Jonesone	}

amerced 12d — The aforesaid 12 jurors present that John Devey of Rugge (4d) and Roger his son (4d) and Henry Kyng (4d) fished in the severalty water of the lady without a licence from the lady so they are in mercy

amerced 2s — At this court Roger Barker withdrew from court against John Preestes in a plea of trespass in 4 pleas so he is in mercy

amerced 12d — At this court John Preestes withdrew his 2 pleas in a plea of trespass against the aforesaid Roger so he is in mercy

fine 2s — To this court came William Ryndelford and gives to the lady for a fine 2s for an enquiry to be held of the 24 to enquire & present under oath whether he has the better right in his claim to the fulling mill at Ryndelford as his right and inheritance after the death of Robert of Ryndelford his father than Richard Parlour has in his tenure. On this in the same court came the aforesaid Richard Parlour and he says that at a court held at Worfeld on Wednesday the first day of the month of April in the 12th year of the reign of King Henry IV after the conquest the fulling mill at Ryndelford was seized into the lord's hands by the steward as forfeit to the lord because Robert of Ryndelford who held the mill aforesaid from the lord in lesser and base tenure sold the aforesaid mill in fee simple by his charter to John Walker against the form of his aforesaid tenure not obtaining thence a licence from the lord. And afterwards came the aforesaid John Walker and Thomas his son here in court and took the mill aforesaid to hold to themselves, their heirs and assigns from the lord by services and customs before the forfeit aforesaid owed and accustomed etc. To hold from the lord according to the custom of the manor under lesser and base tenure. And he gives to the lord for the grant and gift aforesaid in the manner and form aforesaid to be possessed peaceably £10 for a fine whose title the aforesaid Richard Parlour now has. And on this he seeks aid from the lady and it is granted to him

seeks aid from the lady

To this court came Isabell Batemon formerly wife of Richard Regnold through John Bradeney the beadle of the lady seized for the term of her life of one messuage with one virgate of land with its appurtenances in Chesturton with the reversion thence after the death of the aforesaid Isabella to Agnes, daughter and heir of Isabell, the wife of William Batemon pertaining to the use of the aforesaid Agnes except for one parcel of meadow called Small Dole in Chesturton aforesaid and surrendered the aforesaid messuage with the virgate of land aforesaid with appurtenances into the hands of the lady except for the exception to the use of the aforesaid Agnes to hold to herself, her heirs and assigns by services thence owed and of right fine 20s — accustomed and according to the custom of the manor. And she gives to the lady for a fine 20s and thence has seisin and made fealty. Pledge for the fine John Rowlowe of Hultone

To this court came William Batemon and Agnes his wife and the same Agnes duly confessed & examined before the steward according to the custom of the manor and surrendered into the hands of the lady the aforesaid messuage with the virgate of land aforesaid with its appurtenances except for a small parcel of land called Wyldemore in Smaledole and the aforesaid messuage called Regnoldes Place to the use of John Rowlowe of Hulton and Sibill his wife. And on this in the same court came the aforesaid John Rowlowe and Sibill his wife and took from the lady the aforesaid messuage with the virgate of land with its appurtenances except for the exceptions to hold to the same John and Sibill, the heirs and assigns of the same John by services thence owed and of right accustomed and according to the custom of the manor. And thence they have seisin and made fealty. And they give to the lady for a fine 20s — fine 20s

election of reeve — At this court Thomas atte Sonede is elected in the office of reeve & is sworn

To this court came William Batemon and Agnes his wife & the same Agnes duly confessed & examined according to the custom of the manor before the steward granted and confirmed to John Hulle of Hulton all title and possession which they have in one parcel of meadow with its appurtenances in Chesturton called Smale Dole to hold to the aforesaid John, his heirs and assigns by services thence owed and of right accustomed & according to the custom of the manor. And he gives to the lady 4d for a fine. And made fealty — fine 4d

Affeerors: Robert Webbe, Thomas Merewall }sworn
Sum of this court 46s 4d. In expenses of the steward 12s 8d

Small court held there on Thursday next after the Feast of St Martin the Bishop in the ninth year of the reign of Henry VI [16 November 1430]

essoins — William Newton, John Crokehurste, John Mathewe, John Whitebrok, John Trecyll and John Yate these essoined themselves from suit through John Newe.

Robert Webbe	Roger Townesende	Roger Gerbode
John Jonesone	William Wermode	John Walton
John Colynssone	William Gerbode	Robert Bruggende
Thomas Underhull	Roger Kyngeslow	Thomas Toward

The aforesaid 12 jurors present that William Hockombe who held from the lady one messuage with half a virgate of land with its appurtenances in Hockombe has died and there falls to the lady one ox price 8s 4d in the name of heriot and one sow with three piglets from escheat price 2s. And the messuage with the land aforesaid remain with Edith wife of the aforesaid William for the term of her life according to the custom of the manor etc. Also they present that Roger Barker 2d cut down one parcel of underwood without a licence under Steynesowere so he is in mercy — heriot 8s 4d; escheat 2s; 2d

pain — A pain of 8d is put on whoever is the lessee of the mill of Worfeld that he well and properly repair and mend the aforesaid mill in everything before the Feast of St Nicholas the Bishop next in the future

Amerced 40d — To this court came Roger Dalley (40d) in full court before the steward sitting in the court of the lady and John himself the aforesaid steward then hearing the whole court, he [Roger] unjustly and maliciously condemned by speaking against him shameful words & disturbed the aforesaid court and made contempt so he is in mercy And concerning that the bailiff has to answer concerning 12d from the fine of William Kyng for the year last past

Sum of this court 13s 10d. Expenses of the steward 16d

Worfeld	Great court held here on the 12th day of April in the 9th year of Henry VI after the conquest [12 April 1431]
Essoins	Thomas Tomkys, John Holygreve, John Waltone, John Jowkys, John Sonede, Thomas Undurhull, John Bromley of Adlescote these essoined themselves from suit of court through Henry Barker
the 12	Richard Parlour, John Colynsone, John Bromley, Thomas Merewall, Roger Gerbode, Richard Haselwode, Robert Webbe, Thomas Toward, William Bromley, William Gerbode, William Wermode, John Colettes } sworn
Burkote, Burkote, Ryndelford, Bromley, Stray 4d	townships present one swarm of bees coming as a stray price 4d and remains in the custody of John Walker and it is ordered to the beadle to sell dearer if he is able
Roughton, Barndeley, Hockombe, Swankote	townships there present nothing but all [is]well. Hulton township there presents nothing but all [is]well
Ewdenas, Oldynton	townships there present nothing but all [is]well
Rowlowe, Bradeney Asturhull, Ewyke, Sonede Amerced 20d	townships there present that Thomas Preestes (4d) forestalled Henry Kyng against the peace of the lord King. Also they present that Richard Beore (6d) make homesoken on Agnes Smyth and forestalled (4d) her against the peace of the lord King. Also they present that the same Agnes justly raised the hue and cry on the aforesaid Richard (6d)
Akylton	township there presents nothing but all [is] well. Chesturton township there presents nothing but all [is] well
Worfeld amerced 13d	township there presents that John Elkoc (4d) who owed suit of court and did not come. Also they present that William Kyng (4d) unjustly raised the hue and cry on William Barewe against the King's peace. Also they present that Edith Kyng (3d) purloined 6 bushels of malt from John Hulle (2d) son of Roger Hulle from the goods and chattels of Roger himself and against the wishes of the same Roger price 3d
Alvescote, Wynscote, Cattestre, Newtone strays 4d	townships there present 1 swarm of bees coming as a stray & it remains in the custody of Richard Mynsturley
Wyken amerced 10d	township there presents that Henry Wevar (6d) forestalled David Borewardesley against the peace of the lord King. Also they present that the wife (4d) of Thomas Bradeney unjustly raised the hue and cry on John Gerbode so she is in mercy
Kyngslowe & Stanlowe	townships there present that John Agot (12d) made one breach of the pound because he took two steers of Thomas Jenkys. Also they present that the same Thomas justly raised the hue and cry on the aforesaid John (12d). Also they present that the same

Kyngslowe & Stanlowe strays not forfeit

John (6d) made an assault on the aforesaid Thomas. Also they present one brended ox came as a stray price 4s And one brended heifer coming as a stray price 2s first seized on the morrow of the Feast of the Beheading of John the Baptist last past and they remain in the custody of John Snell.

Halen

township there presents that Alice (6d), the wife of Robert Taylor made an assault on Joan Barndeley against the King's peace. Also they present that Roger Gyllen (4d) owed suit and did not come so he is in mercy

Stapulforde

townships there present nothing but that all [is] well

The tasters of ale amerced 9s 4d

present that Roger Hulle (4d) brewed once, John Rowlowe (4d) brewed once, Thomas Prestes (2s) brewed 6, Edith Kyng (2s) brewed 6, Alice Galian (16d) brewed 4, John Elkoc (4d) brewed 1, John Mathewe (4d) brewed 1, Richard Netherton (4d) brewed 1, Roger Gerbode (4d) brewed 1, Sibill Newe (4d) brewed 1, John Bromley (4d) brewed 1, Richard Smyth (4d) brewed 1, John Byllynggesley (4d) brewed 1, William Barker (4d) brewed 1, William Barewe (4d) brewed 1 and broke the assize so they are in mercy

fine 12d

To this court came Alice at Sonede and gives to the lord for a fine to brew ale from the date of this court until the Feast of the Annunciation of the Blessed Virgin Mary next following 12d

fine 16d

To this court came Edith Kyng & gives to the lord for a fine 16d to brew ale from the date of this court until the Feast of the Annunciation of the Blessed Virgin Mary next following 16d

fine 12d

To this court came Alice Galian & gives to the lord for a fine 12d to brew ale from the date of this court until the Feast of the Annunciation of the Blessed Virgin Mary next following 12d

Sum of this court 16s

Worfeld

Small court held there on the 13th day of April in the ninth year of the reign of King Henry V1 after the conquest [13 April 1431]

Essoins

John Walton, John Smyth, Thomas Richardes, John Holigreve, Thomas Undurhull these essoined themselves from common suit by Thomas Walle

Richard Parlour	Richard Haselwode	Robert Bruggende	}
Robert Webbe	John Bromley	Thomas Toward	} sworn
John Colynssone	Roger Townessende	Roger Swankote	}
William Wermode	Roger Kyngeslowe	Roger Gerbode	}

heriot 7s
Escheat 5s 4d

The aforesaid 12 jurors present that Roger the son of William Gerbode who held of the lady according to the custom of the manor one toft of land and half a virgate of land with its appurtenances in Barndeley has died since the last court whence there falls to the lady in the name of heriot one brown ox price 7s Also there falls to the lord one brown draught animal price 3s in the name of escheat and 1 other brown draught animal in the name of escheat price 2s and 1 small pig price 4d in the name of escheat and they remain in the custody of Hamond Hymley. And the tenement aforesaid ought to remain with Agnes the wife of the same Roger to herself and her heirs by a fine thence previously made

To this court came Agnes Smyth, widow through Thomas at Sonede, reeve of the lady & surrendered into the hands of the lady one messuage and half a virgate of land with its appurtenances in Barnedeley to the use of Robert Webbe of Roughton.

And on this in the same court came the aforesaid Robert and took from the lady the aforesaid messuage with the half a virgate of land aforesaid with its appurtenances to hold to the same Robert, his heirs and assigns from the lady by services thence owed and of right accustomed & according to the custom of the manor. And he gives to the lady for a fine 10s and thence has seisin and made fealty

fine 10s

To this court came Agnes Hewstar, widow through Thomas at Sonede reeve of the lady and surrendered into the hands of the lady the reversion of one cottage with curtilage adjacent with its appurtenances in Sonede to the use of Richard Whetheges Rector of the Church of Styrcheley. And on this in the same court came the aforesaid Richard and took from the lady the reversion aforesaid when it will have happened to hold to the same Richard his heirs and assigns from the lady according to the custom of the manor by services thence owed and of right accustomed. And he gives to the lady for a fine 2s. And he made fealty. And thence has seisin.

fine 2s

To this court came John Jannyn & surrendered into the hand of the lady the reversion of one toft and half a virgate of land with its appurtenances in Bromley through John Walton tenant of the lady after the decease of the same John and Alice his wife to the use of Thomas Jannyn. And on this in the same court came the aforesaid Thomas came and took from the lady the reversion of the aforesaid toft & half a virgate of land aforesaid with its appurtenances to hold to the aforesaid Thomas, his heirs and assigns from the lady by services thence owed and of right accustomed & according to the custom of the manor. And he gives to the lady for a fine 10s. And thence has seisin and made fealty

fine 10s

To this court comes Roger Jenkys and Matilda sister of the aforesaid Roger and they give to the lady for a fine 2s for an inquiry of 24 to be held and to present on oath to enquire if the aforesaid Roger and Matilda have the right and title to one messuage and in one toft with its appurtenances in Roughton formerly from a gift and surrender of Thomas Jenkys their father or not

fine 2s
Inquiry
pending

To this court came Richard Parlour and gives to the lady for a fine 2s for an inquiry to be held of 24 upright & legal men & to present on oath whether Richard Parlour has the right and title of his possession in the fulling mill at Ryndelford to himself and his heirs according to the custom of the manor or anyone else or not. And on this the aforesaid 24 men charged and sworn by the oath of Robert Webbe, Robert Bruggende, Thomas Merewalle junior, John Colettes, John Colynssone, William Wermode, John Jonesone, Roger at Townessende, Thomas Toward, Roger Gerbode, William Gerbode, Roger Hethe, John Bromley, William Yate of Newton, Roger Smyth of Hulton, Roger of Newton, John Mathewe, John Rowlowe of Hulton, John Blakemere, John Bradeney of Hulton, William Barker, John Byllyngesley senior, John Bradeney of Bradeney and Roger Dalley who say on their oath that the aforesaid Richard has the right and title in the mill aforesaid and in the possession of the same to hold to himself and his [heirs] in the manner aforesaid from the Lady of Bergevenny as of her Manor of Worfeld

fine 2s

And that the reeve has to respond to the lady concerning 45s 8d of the goods and chattels of Edith Stevenes and Margaret Stevenes which fell to the lady in the name of forfeit for diverse felonies made by them in the domain of Worfeld etc. as is clear by one schedule sewn to this Roll

forfeit 45s 8d

1430-1431 P314/W/1/1/277

Sum of this court 36s 4d together with 45s 8d of the goods and chattels of Edith Stevenes and Margaret Stevenes falling to the lady in the name of forfeit. Thence in expenses of the steward and John Massy the supervisor and receiver there and others of the council of the lady being there for 2 days and 2 nights to hold 2 courts & to do other business there together with expenses made around the arrest of the bodies of Edith Stevenes and Margaret Stevenes held there for diverse felonies made by them 19s 6d. In parchment 4d

[Schedule sewn to roll]

Goods of Edith Stevens and Margery Stevens forfeit for diverse felonies made by them. First, one piece of Russet cloth 18d, 12 woollen cloths (flannola) price 2s, 1 other woollen cloth (flannolum) price 4d. Also 1 towel price 4d. And 4 shirts (camisias) called smocks price 2s. Also 3 aprons price 8d. Also1 other hand towel price 6d. And 2 linen cloths (linthia) price 16d. Also 1 foot of linen price 2d. Also 6 hurden sheets price 18d. Also 1 old towel price 1d. Also2 grateres price 2d. Also 1 cloak price 2s. Also 1 tester price 4d. Also 1 old coverlet (keverlet) price 4d. Also 1 other coverlet (keverlet) price 8d. Also 2 old pillows (pelewes) price 4d Also 1 small chest price 6d, a strong box (forcet) price 4d. Also a parcel of wool and yarn (yoren) price 8d, 1 old bench cover (banker) price 1d. Also 1 old hood price 1d. And 1 canvas (canubum) price 10d. Also 2 brass pots 6s, Also 1 brass dish price 4s And 1 other brass dish price 12d. Also 2 brass skillets price 6d. Also 1 small cooking pot (posnet) price 8d, Also 1 iron hook (drag) 1d. Also 1 brass skimmer price 2d. Also 2 frying pans (frixona) price 10d. Also 1 tripod and 1 hachet price 3d. Also1 pair of combs 2d. Also 1 old pair of cards price 1d. Also1 bushel measure for grain price 6d. Also 2 pails price 4d. Also 2 bags (meoles) price 2d. Also 1 parcel of tallow price 1d. And 1 barrel for verjuice price 3d. Also a wooden bucket price 4d. Also1 ring price 4d. Also 1 small parcel of flax price 1d. Also 2 bags (sackus) of leather price 4d. Also 1 parcel of salt price 1d. Also 1 cheese vat (chesevat), stool (skabell) and dish (discer) price 6d. Also 1 turner for wool price 5d. Also 1 chest price 12d. Also 1 other chest price 8d. Which goods and chattels were sold to Thomas Preestes for 5s of increase on the valuation by the steward by proclamation proclaimed in full court and thus the sum total together is 40s 8d for which the reeve is charged on the account

Printed in Great Britain
by Amazon

45179191R00225